Win32 System Services

The Heart of Windows® 95 and Windows NT

Second Edition

Marshall Brain

Prentice Hall P T R
Upper Saddle River, New Jersey 07458

For book and bookstore information

http://www.prenhall.com

Library of Congress Cataloging-in-Publication Data

Editorial/production supervision: *Lisa Iarkowski*
Cover design: *Design Source*
Cover Illustrations: *Ship design by Rick McCollum, courtesy of the Image Bank; Compass design by Isabella Bannerman, courtesy of The Stock Illustration Source, Inc.*
Manufacturing Manager: *Alexis Heydt*
Acquisitions editor: *Mike Meehan*

Prentice-Hall, Inc.
A Simon & Schuster Company
Upper Saddle River, New Jersey 07458

The publisher offers discounts on this book when ordered in bulk quantities.
For more information, contact:

Corporate Sales Department
Prentice Hall PTR
1 Lake Street
Upper Saddle River, NJ 07458

Phone: 800-382-3419
Fax: 201-236-7141
E-mail: corpsales@prenhall.com

Printed in the United States of America
10 9 8 7 6 5 4 3 2

ISBN 0-13-324732-5

Prentice-Hall International (UK) Limited, *London*
Prentice-Hall of Australia Pty. Limited, *Sydney*
Prentice-Hall Canada Inc., *Toronto*
Prentice-Hall Hispanoamericana, S.A., *Mexico*
Prentice-Hall of India Private Limited, *New Delhi*
Prentice-Hall of Japan, Inc., *Tokyo*
Simon & Schuster Asia Pte. Ltd., *Singapore*
Editora Prentice-Hall do Brasil, Ltda., *Rio de Janeiro*

Contents

Preface ix

1 Introduction 1

1.1 One Hundred and Ten Questions About Windows NT and 95 1
1.2 Compiling Code 9
1.3 Terminology 9
1.4 Error Handling 11
1.5 Handles and Objects 13
1.6 Using the Microsoft Documentation 17
1.7 Bugs in the 32-Bit API 18
1.8 Differences Between Windows 95 and Windows NT 20

2 Files 24

2.1 The Possibilities 25
2.2 Overview 25
2.3 Opening and Reading from a File 27
2.4 Getting and Setting File Information 33
2.5 File Operations 45
2.6 Temporary Files 49
2.7 File Reading and Writing 52
2.8 Asynchronous File Operations 59

2.9 File Locking 59
2.10 Compressed Files 68
2.11 File Mapping 76
2.12 Conclusion 83

3 Drives 84

3.1 The Possibilities 86
3.2 Getting Volume Information 86
3.3 Getting Drive Types 89
3.4 Getting Free Space 91
3.5 Getting Logical Drives and Drive Strings 94
3.6 Setting the Volume Label 96
3.7 WNet Functions 98
3.8 Conclusion 114

4 Directories 115

4.1 The Possibilities 116
4.2 Creating and Deleting Directories 116
4.3 Getting and Setting the Current Directory 119
4.4 Searching for a File 121
4.5 Traversing Directory Trees 124
4.6 Combining Capabilities 132
4.7 Detecting Changes to Directories and Files 137
4.8 Conclusion 138

5 Processes and Threads 139

5.1 The Possibilities 139
5.2 Introduction 141
5.3 Simple Examples 143
5.4 Using Threads in GUI Applications 158
5.5 Matching the Number of Threads to the Number of CPUs 171
5.6 Using Thread Local Storage 181
5.7 Thread Priorities 186
5.8 Other Thread Functions 191
5.9 Processes 193

5.10 Inheriting Handles 198
5.11 Interprocess Communication 202
5.12 Conclusion 203

6 Synchronization 204

6.1 Understanding the Problem 204
6.2 Four Different Synchronization Methods 211
6.3 Deadlocks, Starvation, and Other Synchronization Bugs 241
6.4 Wait Functions 255
6.5 Overlapped I/O 258
6.6 Change Functions 272
6.7 Integrating Synchronization into MFC Programs 276
6.8 Conclusion 281

7 Network Communications 282

7.1 The Possibilities 282
7.2 Understanding Your Options 285
7.3 Mailslots 288
7.4 Named Pipes 307
7.5 Named Pipe Client/Server Systems 317
7.6 Connecting with UNIX and Other TCP/IP Machines 336
7.7 UDP Connections 340
7.8 TCP Connections 354
7.9 Conclusion 372

8 Remote Procedure Calls 373

8.1 The Possibilities 373
8.2 The Basic Idea 375
8.3 Design Issues 376
8.4 Creating RPCs 380
8.5 Understanding RPCs at a High Level 389
8.6 Parameter Passing 394
8.7 Understanding the Code 396
8.8 Setting up a Name Server in the Registry 401

8.9 Manual Binding with Implicit Handles 402
8.10 An RPC Server for Mandelbrot Sets 419
8.11 Improving the Mandelbrot RPC Server 435
8.12 Explicit Handles 445
8.13 Context Handles 451
8.14 Common Questions 461
8.15 Conclusion 464

9 Services **465**

9.1 The Possibilities 466
9.2 Understanding Services 467
9.3 Service Choreography 468
9.4 The Simplest Service 470
9.5 Installing and Removing a Service 488
9.6 Displaying Dialogs from within a Service 498
9.7 Multiple Services in an Executable 503
9.8 Getting and Setting Configuration Information 510
9.9 Controlling Services 518
9.10 Enumerating Services 521
9.11 Placing an RPC Server in a Service 525
9.12 Conclusion 539

10 Security **540**

10.1 The Possibilities 540
10.2 Understanding the Terminology and Concepts of the NT Security System 541
10.3 NT Security Vocabulary 544
10.4 Simple Examples 549
10.5 Securable Objects and Access Rights 561
10.6 Examining Existing Access Tokens and Security Descriptors 573
10.7 Privileges 601
10.8 Adding and Deleting ACEs 610
10.9 Impersonation 633
10.10 Conclusion 639

11 Consoles 640

11.1 The Possibilities 640
11.2 Raw versus Cooked Input 641
11.3 Simple Examples 642
11.4 Raw Input 651
11.5 Other Input Events 665
11.6 Other Capabilities 673
11.7 Conclusion 681

12 Communications 682

12.1 The Possibilities 682
12.2 Understanding Serial Communications 683
12.3 A Simple Communications Application 685
12.4 Getting Communications Events 695
12.5 A Simple Bulletin Board System 699
12.6 Flow Control 703
12.7 A Simple TTY Terminal Program 706
12.8 Other Communications Functions 716
12.9 Conclusion 718

13 System Information 719

13.1 The GetSystemInfo Function 719
13.2 Other System Information Functions 721
13.3 Getting and Setting Environment Strings 730
13.4 Shutting Down the System 732

14 Dynamic Link Libraries 741

14.1 The Possibilities 741
14.2 Overview 742
14.3 Creating a Simple DLL 744
14.4 Understanding a Simple DLL 749
14.5 Load-time versus Run-time Linking 752
14.6 DLL Entry Points 758
14.7 Memory Models 763
14.8 Conclusion 768

15 Miscellaneous **769**
15.1 Registry 769
15.2 The Event Log 786
15.3 Time 799
15.4 Memory 810
15.5 Structured Exception Handling 819
15.6 Error Handling 832

A Compiling the Code in This Book **837**

B Contacting the Author **846**

C Error Codes **849**

Index **851**

PREFACE

The Win32 system services are the innovative, cutting-edge capabilities that make Windows NT and Windows 95 interesting and exciting. Amid all of the media attention surrounding Windows NT or 95, you have probably heard and read about many of the modern capabilities that these operating systems contain:

- Processes and threads
- Synchronization
- Remote Procedure Calls (RPCs)
- Event logging
- Network communications
- TCP/IP networking with UNIX and OS/2 machines
- File mapping
- Interprocess communication
- Compressed file access
- Network drive and printer sharing
- Serial communications
- Services (background processing like UNIX daemons)
- Object and file security

The goal of this book is to show you how to use all of these different services in your own applications. This book contains hundreds of concise, clear, and easy-to-understand example programs and explanations. The examples show you how to access the system services listed above, as well as many others.

You can use these examples directly to understand the concepts. You can also drop the sample code into your own programs and then extend it to give your applications new and useful features.

By learning about the many and varied system services available inside of Windows, you can make your programs much more interesting to the user. For example, if you learn about threads and then add multiple threads to your applications, the user gets a much smoother interface (see Chapter 5). Your program will also take advantage of multiple processors on machines that have them. If you add network support to your applications, then the user is able to access network resources that are unavailable on a single machine (see Chapter 7). If you add modem support, then you can use it to let the user dial into a remote system (see Chapter 12). Or you might use a modem to let the user dial a support line or registration system for a product that your company sells.

The goal of this book is to give you a thorough and clear understanding of the system services so that you can take advantage of all of the capabilities that Windows has to offer.

Audience

This book is designed for two types of people. If you are a devoted connoisseur or student of programming, the study of the system functions is interesting in its own right. It's fun to see what is available, and to try to think of ways to exploit those capabilities. One way to use this book is to simply browse through it and see what is possible. You can work with the examples and extend them in ways that you find enjoyable.

If, on the other hand, you are a programmer with a deadline, enjoyable entertainment is probably not your goal. You may have looked at the huge number of functions in the Windows API and found it discouraging. Where do you start? What you want is a set of useful examples and clear explanations that quickly solve your specific problems. You will find this book useful because it organizes concepts logically and provides the material that you need to master a specific topic very quickly.

If you are migrating from another operating system to Windows, this book will help you to quickly map your existing knowledge into the Windows framework. See Chapter 1 for a list of the 110 most common programming questions in Windows as well as the sections that contain the answers.

Organization

This book is organized by functional categories. For example, Chapter 2 talks about all of the functions that pertain to File I/O and file handling. Chapter 3 deals with disk drives. Chapter 4 discusses directories. Chapter 5 talks about processes and threads. And so on. You will find that each chapter starts with a general overview of the topic, followed by sections that describe and give examples for subsets of functions.

In many chapters you will find integrating examples that combine different capabilities from several chapters to create larger applications. Many of these larger examples form complete applications that you can use as starting points for new projects of your own.

Philosophy

Several principles guide the design of this book. The first principle is the most important and is therefore woven throughout: it is *simplicity.* There is nothing worse than trying to look up a function, only to find that its example is embedded within sample code that takes three days to comprehend because it is 28 pages long. In all cases functions are first demonstrated in code that is as simple as possible so that you can extract the essence of each one very quickly. Then they may also be integrated into larger examples. In many cases you will look at the example code and say to yourself, "This is easy!" That is exactly the intent. If the book makes everything look simple and easy for you, then it has accomplished its goal.

The second principle found in this book revolves around the idea of functional *families.* Functions in the 32-bit API very rarely exist on their own--it is far more common to find small collections of functions that relate very closely to one another. For example, the **ReadFile** function reads from a file, but you must open the file with **CreateFile** before you can read from it and then remember to close it with **CloseHandle** afterwards (see Chapter 2). These functions belong to a family. In this book you will generally find small groupings of functions described as logical units.

The third principle in this book is that of *currency.* The Windows API has been around for some time, and when you look at it you will find that there is a certain layering. The documentation will often say things like, "this function is retained for compatibility with version 1.8, but has been superseded by function xyz." This book deals only with the current functions, and leaves the superseded ones to die in peace.

The last principle guiding this book is *independence*. Each chapter in this book is as stand-alone as possible, so that you can jump around in the book as you please. In cases where material from other chapters is important, you will find references to the related sections.

Prerequisites and Languages

This book makes no assumptions about former knowledge of systems programming in Windows or in any other system. Its only real assumption is that you know C and/or C++. You will find that the example code divides into two categories:

1. Text examples that run in "console mode." These programs run from the MS-DOS prompt, accept keyboard input, and produce text output. They form the vast majority of the code in this book because they are simple. These programs are C++ compatible, but the only elements really being used from C++ are the I/O stream libraries.
2. "Windows" programs that use the Windows GUI. These programs use C++ and the Microsoft Foundation Class library (MFC). The book *Visual C++: Developing Professional Applications in Windows 95 and NT using MFC* by Marshall Brain and Lance Lovette (ISBN 0-13-305145-5) describes how to create programs with MFC, and will be helpful to you in understanding these examples if you are not already familiar with MFC.

If you are a C programmer with no C++ experience, you will have no trouble understanding the console programs. The only unusual thing you will see is code that looks like this:

```
char s[100];
// Prompt the user
cout << "Enter a line of text: ";
// Read a line of text from the user
cin.getline(s,100);
// Echo the user's input to stdout
cout << s << endl;
```

This code declares a character string **s**, and then uses "cout <<" to output a prompt to the user. The "cin.getline" statement reads a line of text from the user. The final "cout" statement echoes the line. The book *Visual C++: Developing Professional Applications in Windows 95 and NT using MFC* by Marshall Brain and Lance Lovette (ISBN 0-13-305145-5) contains an extensive C++ appendix to help you get started with the language if you are interested. It will also help you to understand the MFC code.

The Diskette and the On-line Index

The diskette included with this book contains the source code for all of the examples in the book, as well as the source and data for an on-line indexing program. The index is broken down by sections and includes every word found in the manuscript.

To use the index, follow the directions in the README file on the disk to compile the program. When you run the index, you will see a display that contains an edit area, three buttons (Help, Search and Quit), and a list area. Any words that you type in the edit area are used to search for appropriate sections. For example, if you want to find out how to create a DLL entry point, you would type "DLL entry point" in the edit area. Press the "Search" button to begin the search. The index program will list all sections that contain all three of those words. Enter as many words as you like to hone the search. Word matching is exact and case-insensitive. If a word does not appear in the book the program will tell you.

There are many cases where an exact match does not work well. For example, there may be a section that contains "thread" and "create" but not "creating" and "threads," so if you enter the line "creating threads" on the edit line you get no matches. You can use the "*" wild card character at the end of a word to solve this problem. For example, by entering "creat*" the system will OR together all words with the root "creat" ("create," "creates," "creation," etc.). You may want to get in the habit of using the wild card character at the end of all words: "creat* thread*," for example. This often yields more accurate results.

If an obvious word seems to be missing from the index, try to find it in the book to make sure you are spelling it correctly. For example, "resize" is spelled "re-size" in the book, and you need to spell it the same way.

Contents of the Book

Each chapter in this book talks about a different service in the 32-bit API. Chapter 1 contains a list of the 110 most common questions about the system services, and it will help you to very quickly find material that interests you. The list below summarizes the different chapters in the book to help you with browsing.

- Chapter 1 is an introduction. It contains a list of the 110 most common programming questions about the Windows system services. This list will serve as a good road map for you. The chapter also contains general information that is useful throughout the book.
- Chapter 2 discusses files. It shows you how to open, read, and write files, how to read from compressed files, how to map files into memory, and so on. The 32-bit API contains quite a few very interesting file capabilities.
- Chapter 3 talks about the directory structure. It shows you how to create and traverse directory trees.
- Chapter 4 introduces the drive structure of Windows. You will learn how to query the drives on your local machine, and also how to query and connect to drives on the network.
- Chapter 5 offers a complete introduction to processes and threads in the Windows environment. You will see how to multi-thread your own applications, and the chapter shows you how to multi-thread MFC applications as well. There is also a discussion of processes, interprocess communication, and inheritance.
- Chapter 6 discusses Windows synchronization mechanisms. Critical sections, mutexes, semaphores and events help you to write multi-threaded code that does not step on itself. The chapter introduces you to general synchronization principles and bugs, and shows solutions to a number of standard problems. It also shows you how to incorporate synchronization mechanisms into an MFC program without stalling its event loop.
- Chapter 7 talks about network communications. Windows contains two different native technologies for communicating over the network: mailslots and named pipes. Windows also supports UPD and TCP packets on TCP/IP networks. The latter capabilities let you intercom-

municate with UNIX and other TCP/IP machines. The chapter includes a complete introduction to network principles and terminology.

- Chapter 8 talks about Remote Procedure Calls, or RPCs. An RPC lets you make a function call that is transmitted over the network and executed on another machine. This chapter contains a complete introduction to the hows and whys of RPCs, as well as design principles to keep in mind when creating client/server systems with RPCs. It contains examples of auto, implicit, explicit, and context binding, and also shows how to incorporate RPCs into MFC programs.
- Chapter 9 discusses NT services. These are background processes that start at boot time and run regardless of who is logged in, just like daemons in UNIX. This chapter shows you how to create your own services and install them in NT's service manager. It also shows you how to place RPC servers into services so they run continuously.
- Chapter 10 offers a complete introduction to the NT security system. This system is uniform across all NT objects, so you learn how to secure files, registry keys, pipes, semaphores, and so on. It teaches you everything you need to know to create and modify access control lists and security descriptors.
- Chapter 11 discusses consoles, which you will use when you want to create text-based programs in Windows. For example, if you want to create a terminal emulator, consoles offer an easy way to handle the keyboard input and character output for the emulator.
- Chapter 12 talks about communications ports in Windows systems. It shows you how to access both the serial and parallel ports, and demonstrates a simple terminal emulator and bulletin board system.
- Chapter 13 shows you how to access system information, and how to log users off and shutdown or reboot the system. For example, this chapter shows you how to determine how many CPUs a system contains, or how many buttons there are on the mouse.
- Chapter 14 shows you how to modularize your programs using dynamic link libraries (DLLs). Windows can be thought of as an extensible operating system because of DLLs. A programmer can easily add capabilities that others can use by creating a DLL and publishing its interface. Windows itself places much of its functionality in DLLs.

- Chapter 15 contains short discussions and examples on six miscellaneous topics: the registry, the event log, the Windows time model, error handling, structured exception handling, and the memory model.
- Appendix A shows you how to compile the different types of code found in the book.
- Appendix B contains information on contacting the author via Email to ask questions and retrieve free supplements and updates to this book.

Contacting the Author: Questions, Comments, and Version Changes

One thing about Microsoft is that it never stands still for very long. Its compilers change versions and the libraries are upgraded constantly. One of the goals in creating this book is to make its code as compatible as possible with existing and future releases of Microsoft compiler products. Another goal is to give you "investment-grade" knowledge—knowledge that does not lose its value over time, and that is transferable between as many different platforms as possible.

As things change however, you need a way to get updates and corrections. You may also have questions, comments or suggestions for improving this book. If so, we would like to hear from you. You can use our free Email information server to get updates and supplements to this book. You can also send questions and comments via Email or U.S. mail. Please see Appendix B for instructions.

Acknowledgments

I would like to sincerely thank Shay Woodard for his effort on this book. Shay developed quite a few of the example programs that you will find here, including most of the code in Chapters 5, 7, 8, 10, and 15.

This book would not exist were it not for Mike Meehan.

A group of very high-intensity systems programmers helped this book by providing technical proofing skills. I would like to thank Michael S. Yoder, Lida Chen, T. Ramjee, Richard P. Basch, Kevin Hanrahan, Tony Morris, Vladimir Svirsky, Jasmine Ved, Ben Rosenbaum and Paul Horan for their help.

I also thank Leigh Ann Brain for being my wife, and for her tremendous support, patience, and back rubs.

1 INTRODUCTION

The advanced system services in the 32-bit API are the heart of Windows NT and Windows 95. You may have heard or read about many of them while learning about and experimenting with Windows NT and 95: function calls that execute over the network, multi-threading, standardized and heterogeneous network communications, the advanced C2 security system of Windows NT, and so on. These are the cutting-edge capabilities that make both Windows NT and Windows 95 unique and interesting. The goal of this book is to show you how to use all of the Windows system services in your own applications.

The purpose of this chapter is to act as a road map and introduction. It also discusses several concepts that are of general interest because they are used constantly throughout the book. You may want to scan through this chapter briefly now to see what is available, and then come back to specific sections as you need them.

1.1 One Hundred and Ten Questions About Windows NT and 95

Many programmers coming to Windows NT and Windows 95 have many questions about it. This section contains 110 of the most common system programming questions, and where to look in the book to find the answers. Use this list as a road map for the rest of the book. These questions start with the most common and move toward the exotic.

1.1.1 General

1. How do I compile code on an Windows system? See Section 1.2 and Appendix A.
2. What is an object and a handle? Why do they exist? See Section 1.5.
3. Why do there seem to be so many bugs in the 32-bit API? See Section 1.7.

1.1.2 File Operations

4. How do I read from and write to a file? See Sections 2.3 and 2.7.
5. How do I read and write a large quantity of data in a way that does not stall out my user interface? See Section 6.5 (overlapped I/O) or Chapter 5 (threads).
6. How do I move, copy, and delete files from within a program? See Section 2.5.
7. How do I move a file, but postpone the actual move operation until the next time the system reboots because the file is currently in use? See Section 2.5.
8. How do I create a temporary file? See Section 2.6.
9. How do I create a temporary file that automatically deletes itself when the program is done with it? See Section 2.7.
10. How do I map a file into memory to drastically improve read/write performance? See Section 2.11.
11. How do I read compressed files without decompressing them? See Section 2.10.
12. How do I uncompress a compressed file from within an application? See Section 2.10.
13. How do I tune system performance while reading certain files? For example, I have to read a large file from beginning to end, and it is flushing out the disk cache. How do I prevent that? See Section 2.7.
14. How do I access file information such as the size of the file, the last change date, and the attribute bits? See Section 2.4.
15. How do I lock whole files or individual records for exclusive or read-only access? See Section 2.9.

1.1.3 Drive Operations

16. How do I find out if a certain disk drive is mounted locally or over the network? See Section 3.3.
17. How do I find out which file system (FAT, HPFS, NTFS, etc.) a volume was formatted with? See Section 3.2.
18. How do I find out how much free space is available on a drive? See Section 3.4.
19. How do I determine which of the 26 drive letters currently are attached to a drive? See Section 3.5.
20. How do I change the volume label of a drive from within an application? See Section 3.6.
21. How can I create a list of all of the machines on the network? See Section 3.7.
22. How do I loop through all of the machines on the network and list all of the printers and drives they are currently sharing? See Section 3.7.
23. How do I form or cancel a connection to a remote drive or printer? See Section 3.7.

1.1.4 Directory Operations

24. How do I create and delete directories? See Section 4.2.
25. How do I set the current directory or find out the current directory? See Section 4.3.
26. How do I search the PATH and system directories for a file? See Section 4.4.
27. How do I search a directory for a file? See Section 4.5.
28. How do I recursively traverse all of the directories on a drive? See Section 4.5.
29. How do I detect changes to files and directories? For example, if a new file is added to a directory, is there an easy way to detect that immediately? See Section 4.7.

1.1.5 Processes and Threads

30. How do I multi-thread an application? What does that mean? What is a thread? See Chapter 5.

31. How do I design an application so that it runs lengthy operations in the background rather than making the user wait? For example, my application has to recalculate an aerodynamic model and I do not want the user interface to hang for half an hour during the computation. See Chapter 5.
32. How can I take advantage of multiple threads to simplify the design of simulations that contain many separate and interacting entities? See Chapter 5.
33. How do I create separate threads that can handle high-priority events successfully without monopolizing the CPU? See Section 5.7.
34. How does the scheduling and priority system work? See Section 5.7.
35. How do I multi-thread an application so that it takes maximum advantage of multiple-CPU architectures in Windows NT? See Section 5.5.
36. How do I launch a new separate and independent process from within an application? See Section 5.9.
37. How can I let two separate processes share data between one another? For example, I want to be able to run an application that controls a service, so the application needs to be able to talk to the service. See Section 5.11.
38. How can I create a new process that inherits handles from its parent? See Section 5.10.
39. How do I assign local storage to each thread in a multi-threaded application? See Section 5.6.
40. How do I add multiple threads to an MFC program? See Section 5.4.

1.1.6 Synchronization

41. Why does Windows contain so many different synchronization mechanisms? Semaphores, Critical section, Mutexes—what good are they? See Chapter 6.
42. How do I guarantee that two threads do not access the same resource at the same time? See Chapter 6.
43. I have a multi-threaded program that occasionally locks up for no apparent reason. What is causing this problem? See Section 6.3.

44. How do I integrate synchronization mechanisms into an MFC program without shutting down the event loop? See Section 6.7?

1.1.7 Network Communications

45. How can I create an application that can talk with other copies of the same application, or other different applications, on the network? See Chapter 7.
46. How do I broadcast information on the network so that all of the machines on the network see it? See Section 7.3.
47. How do I create point-to-point network connections between two Windows machines? See Section 7.4.
48. How do I create client/server architectures? What code and techniques are necessary to create the server and the client? See Section 7.5.
49. How do I communicate with UNIX and other TCP/IP machines using UDP and TCP packets? See Section 7.6.
50. How do I read and write to the same pipe in a multi-threaded application? See Section 7.5.

1.1.8 Remote Procedure Calls

51. How do I use Remote Procedure Calls? What is a Remote Procedure Call? See Chapter 8.
52. How do I appropriately design a program so that it effectively uses Remote Procedure Calls? How do I know when and when not to use RPCs? See Section 8.3.
53. How do I create client/server architectures using RPCs? See Chapter 8.
54. How do I create an IDL file and use the MIDL compiler? See Chapter 8.
55. How do I create an RPC server in Windows? See Section 8.5.
56. What is the RPC name server? How do I register an RPC server that I create with the name server? See Sections 8.6 and 8.8.
57. How do I create an RPC server that runs on its host machine all of the time, starting when the host boots? See Section 9.11 and Chapter 9.
58. How do I call an RPC from an RPC client program? See Chapter 8.

59. Can an RPC client on a Windows machine access an RPC server on a UNIX machine? What about the reverse? See Section 8.8.
60. What is the difference between automatic and manual binding in RPCs? See Chapter 8.

1.1.9 Services

61. How do I run an application in the background under Windows NT, starting when the machine boots and regardless of who is logged on? For example, I need to run a background data logging program in my lab, but I don't want to tie up the entire machine. See Chapter 9.
62. How do I integrate a service into the Services applet of the Windows NT Control Panel? See Section 9.5.
63. How do I create multiple service threads that share global variables? See Section 9.7.
64. How can a service communicate with the user? See Section 9.5.

1.1.10 Security

65. How does NT's security system work? See Chapter 10.
66. How do I change the security attributes on a file from within one of my applications? See Sections 10.4 and 10.8.
67. How do I secure a named pipe so that only certain users on the network can access it? See Sections 10.4 and 10.9.
68. How do I unsecure a named pipe so that any user can access it? See Section 10.9.
69. How do I create a named pipe server than any user on the network can access, but at the same time preserve security? Is there a way for a named pipe server to impersonate a connected user? See Section 10.9.
70. How do I access the auditing features of the security system so that accesses to certain objects get logged in the event viewer? See Section 10.2.
71. What is an ACL, DACL, SACL, SID, and ACE? See Section 10.3.
72. How do I modify existing security descriptors? See Section 10.8.

73. How do I set the system time or shut down the system? Even though I'm the NT administrator, the system functions for these operations fail when I run the code. See Section 10.7.
74. What is a privilege? How do I enable and disable privileges? See Section 10.7.

1.1.11 Consoles

75. How do I port a text program (for example, a program based on the curses library in UNIX or a vt-100 terminal emulator) over to Windows? See Chapter 11.
76. How do I access keystrokes from the keyboard one character at a time (raw input) in a console program? See Section 11.4.
77. How do I add streaming text output to a normal Windows or MFC program to help with debugging? See Section 11.3.

1.1.12 Communication Ports

78. How do I use communications ports in Windows? I want to create a BBS or a terminal emulator. See Chapter 11.
79. How do I send and receive characters from a communications port? See Section 12.4.
80. How do I set communications parameters like baud rate and parity on a communications port? See Section 12.4.
81. How do I manage different flow control policies on a communications port? See Section 12.6.
82. How do I easily communicate with other telnet servers on the network? See Section 12.7.

1.1.13 System Functions

83. How do I find out the number of buttons on the mouse? See Section 13.2.
84. How do I find out the screen width and height? See Section 13.2.
85. How do I get and set system colors? See Section 13.2.
86. How do I find out the number of processors in the machine? See Section 13.1.

87. How do I find out the machine's name on the network? See Section 13.2.
88. How do I find out what version of Windows is currently running? See Section 13.2.
89. How do I get and set environment variable information? See Section 13.3.
90. How do I shut down the system or log off the current user? How do I shut down remote machines on the network? See Section 13.4.

1.1.14 Dynamic Linking

91. What is a Dynamic Link Library? What are the advantages of DLLs? See Chapter 14.
92. How do I create, compile, and load a DLL? See Sections 14.3 and 14.4.
93. What is the difference between run-time and load-time linking? What are the advantages of each approach? See Section 14.5.
94. How do I distribute a DLL so that other programmers can use it? See Chapter 14.
95. What is a DLL entry point? How can I use one to improve memory management? See Section 14.6.
96. How do I create global and dynamic variables that are shared or private inside a DLL? See Section 14.7.

1.1.15 Miscellaneous

97. What is the registry? See Section 15.1.
98. Where is the best place to store configuration information for my application? See Section 15.1.
99. How do I add a new key to the registry? See Section 15.1.
100. How do I read and write registry values? See Section 15.1.
101. How do I store events from my own applications in the event log? See Section 15.2.
102. How do I determine which events belong in the event log? See Section 15.2.
103. How do I create strings for my event log messages? See Section 15.2.

104. How do I get and set the current system time? See Section 15.3.
105. How do I find out what time zone the current machine is in? See Section 15.3.
106. How do I allocate and free memory at the system level? See Section 15.4.
107. How can I play sounds other than a simple beep during errors? See Section 15.6.
108. When creating my own libraries, how can I make their functions conform to Windows' **GetLastError** format? See Section 15.6.
109. What is structured exception handling? How can I use it in my programs? See Section 15.5.
110. How do I contact the author? See Appendix B.

1.2 Compiling Code

This book contains hundreds of listings. You will find that these listings break down into four different categories:

1. Pure console programs that read and write text data
2. GUI programs using the 32-bit API
3. GUI programs using MFC
4. Other programs: DLL code, RPC code, and so on.

Appendix A contains information on compiling the first three types of code. The fourth type is covered when the code appears. For example, Chapter 8 on RPCs contains makefiles for using the MIDL compiler and compiling RPC programs.

1.3 Terminology

Windows, like UNIX or VMS, is a complete operating system. When you use this operating system you refer to it as "Windows NT," or "Windows 95," or generically as "Windows" and leave it at that. When you program for the system, you are programming for Windows as well. More specifically however, you are using the "Win32 API" (Application Programmer Interface), also known as "the 32-bit API." In this book, programming for "Windows," "Win32," and "the 32-bit API" are equivalent, and you will find them used interchangeably.

The 32-bit API is huge. It contains thousands of functions broken up into hundreds of categories. It is a comprehensive, all-encompassing programmer interface to the many capabilities provided by the Windows operating system. The API is the same whether you are using Windows NT or Windows 95. However, a number of functions will report "not implemented" errors in Windows 95 because they are not supported. See Section 1.8 for a description of the differences between Windows 95 and Windows NT.

The 32-bit API is so called to distinguish it from the older 16-bit API used by standard Windows 3.1 running on top of MS-DOS. The 16-bit API contains all of the Windows and Graphics functions found in the 32-bit API (that is why most older Windows programs port to NT and 95 so easily), but the 16-bit API does not have any of the system services found in the 32-bit API. The 32-bit API also includes a number of operations normally found in the standard C libraries in an attempt to centralize things. For example, the 32-bit API includes functions to move, zero, and copy blocks of memory (see Section 15.4).

Win32s is a subset of the 32-bit API. It runs on DOS machines, and provides a way to execute Win32 applications in the older Windows environment. Win32s is missing about half of the system services. For example, it does not support threads, services, event logging, RPCs, and so on. You can call these functions in Win32s, but they will return error codes.

This book deals with the *system services* of the 32-bit API. The system services are the core of the operating system. They give you access to the modern capabilities that make the 32-bit versions of Windows interesting:

- Processes and threads
- Synchronization
- Remote Procedure Calls (RPCs)
- Event logging
- Network communications
- TCP/IP networking with UNIX and OS/2 machines
- File mapping
- Interprocess communication
- Compressed file access
- Network drive and printer sharing
- Serial communications

- Services (background processing like UNIX daemons)
- Object and file security

The two other major sections of the API are the Graphics Device Interface (GDI) for drawing and printing, and the Window Management functions for creating GUIs. Both of these sections are encapsulated by MFC, which is described below. Because of MFC, you generally do not access either of these sections directly when creating Windows applications in C++.

You will generally write and compile your Win32 programs using either "the Microsoft Win32 SDK" or Visual C++. The SDK is a command-line environment, while Visual C++ is a graphical environment.

Visual C++ (but not the SDK) ships with a C++ class library called the Microsoft Foundation Class library, or MFC. MFC makes the creation of GUI programs much easier. It encapsulates all of the window management and GDI functions available in the 32-bit API. Another book in this series is called "Visual C++: Developing Professional Applications in Windows 95 and NT using MFC" and it covers MFC programming in detail. Many of the system services examples in this book show you how to apply the concepts to MFC code. For example, Chapter 5 contains examples that show you how to multi-thread MFC programs, Chapter 6 shows you how to handle semaphores, mutexes, and events in MFC code, and Chapter 8 applies RPCs to an MFC program.

1.4 Error Handling

Most functions in the 32-bit API return error status in two different ways. Many functions return the first indication of an error in the return value for the function. For example, the **RemoveDirectory** function in Chapter 4 is typical:

RemoveDirectory
`BOOL RemoveDirectory(`
`   LPTSTR dirName)`
	Removes an empty directory

dirName	Name/path of the directory to remove
Returns TRUE on success	

The **RemoveDirectory** function returns a boolean value that is TRUE if the function was successful and FALSE otherwise. Other functions return a specific value to indicate an error:

OpenService	*Opens a connection to the specified service*
`SC_HANDLE OpenService( SC_HANDLE scm, LPCTSTR name, DWORD access)`	
scm	A handle to the SCM from **OpenSCManager**
name	The name of the service used internally
access	The desired access
Returns a handle to the service or NULL on error	

The **OpenService** function returns 0 when something goes wrong. A typical use of the **GetLastError** function is shown below:

```
success = RemoveDirectory(s);
if (!success)
   cout << "Error code = " << GetLastError()
      << endl;
```

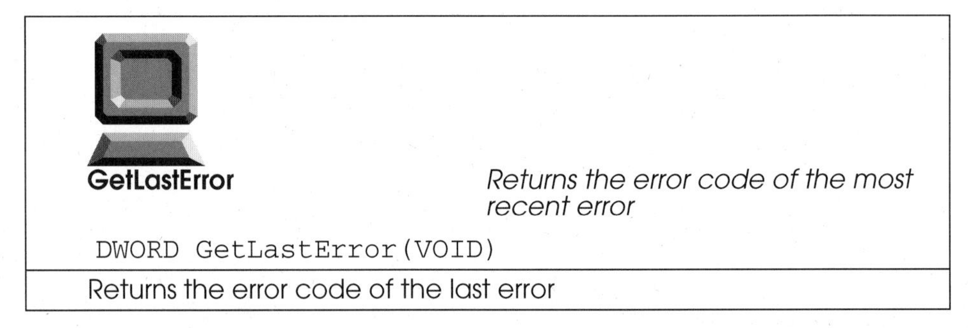

GetLastError	*Returns the error code of the most recent error*
`DWORD GetLastError(VOID)`	
Returns the error code of the last error	

When the return value indicates an error, you can obtain a numeric error code identifying the exact problem by calling the **GetLastError** function. **Get-**

LastError returns an integer that you can look up in the "Error Codes" section of the API help file (see Section 1.6). For example, in the example above the error value might be 5. When you look up that value in the Error Codes section, you will find that it translates to "Access Denied," which means that the file system's security features will not allow you to delete the specified directory.

1.5 Handles and Objects

Windows uses the concepts of a *handle* and an *object* throughout the system services. An object is owned by the operating system and represents a system resource. For example, a thread is represented as an object. The operating system stores all information about the thread in the thread's object. The object is opaque to the programmer.

A handle points to an object. It is possible to create a single object and refer to it with several different handles. You can think of the handles as pointers that let you access the object.

The 32-bit API defines the following "kernel objects." All of them return a handle when they are created or opened:

Object	Function	Chapter
Access tokens	OpenProcessToken	Chapter 10
	CloseHandle	
Console	CreateConsoleScreenBuffer	Chapter 11
	CloseHandle	
Console device	GetStdHandle	Chapter 11
	CloseHandle	
Communication port	CreateFile	Chapter 12
	CloseHandle	
Event	CreateEvent	Chapter 6
	CloseHandle	
Event log	OpenEventLog	Chapter 15
	CloseEventLog	
File	CreateFile	Chapter 2

Object	Function	Chapter
	CloseHandle	
File change	FindFirstChangeNotification	Chapter 6
	FindCloseChangeNotification	
File mapping	CreateFile	Chapter 2
	CloseHandle	
Find file	FindFirstFile	Chapter 4
	FindClose	
Mailslot	CreateMailslot	Chapter 7
	CloseHandle	
Mutex	CreateMutex	Chapter 6
	CloseHandle	
Named pipe	CreateNamedPipe	Chapter 7
	CloseHandle	
Pipe	CreatePipe	
	CloseHandle	
Process	CreateProcess	Chapter 5
	CloseHandle	
Semaphore	CreateSemaphore	Chapter 6
	CloseHandle	
Thread	CreateThread	Chapter 5
	CloseHandle	

Of these objects, some are global. For example, there is one instance of the event log and any process can open a handle to it. Some are private. For example, a Find File handle is private to the process that opens it. Others can be shared among processes:

- Process
- Thread
- File
- File mapping

- Event
- Semaphore
- Mutex
- Named pipe
- Mailslot
- Communication device

For example, one thread or process might create a semaphore, and other processes and threads can open handles to it so that they can all use it for synchronization. The single semaphore object is shared by the all of the processes and threads. It is also possible to duplicate and inherit (Chapter 5) handles to these objects.

Most objects that return a handle can be secured using the NT security system. See Chapter 10 for a complete list and details. Security is a primary reasons for this "object" model. The other reason for it is that it adds a level of abstraction to the operating system that keeps programmers from knowing too much. A HANDLE is a generic 32-bit pointer. It tells you, as a programmer, nothing about the object it points to, so you are unable to get into the low-level structures and code directly to them. This allows the operating system to change over time without its designers having to worry about code that breaks the rules.

If you want to open a file and access it through the 32-bit API, you use the **CreateFile** function (see Chapter 2) as shown below:

```
// file3.cpp

#include <windows.h>
#include <iostream.h>

void main()
```

Listing 1.1
An API-level program that reads from a file and writes to it (Page 1 of 2)

```
{
   HANDLE fileHandle;
   BOOL success;
   char s[10];
   DWORD numRead;
   char filename[MAX_PATH];

   // get the file name
   cout << "Enter filename: ";
   cin >> filename;

   // Open the file
   fileHandle = CreateFile(filename, GENERIC_READ,
      0, 0, OPEN_EXISTING, 0, 0);
   if (fileHandle == INVALID_HANDLE_VALUE)
   {
      cout << "Error number " << GetLastError()
         << " occured on file open." << endl;
      return;
   }

   // Read from file until eof, writing to stdout
   do
   {
      success = ReadFile(fileHandle, s, 1,
         &numRead, 0);
      s[numRead] = 0;
      cout << s;
   }
   while (numRead>0 && success);

   // Close the file
   CloseHandle(fileHandle);
}
```

Listing 1.1
An API-level program that reads from a file and writes to it (Page 2 of 2)

Note that the call to **CreateFile** returns a HANDLE to the variable **fileHandle**. This variable points to a *file object* that talks to the actual file on the disk. The file object in this case remembers the state of the file. For example, it remembers where the file pointer is in the file. The code in Listing 1.1 uses the **fileHandle** in the call to **ReadFile** to read from the file, and then again in the call to **CloseHandle** to close the file.

As another example, let's say that you want to use a mutex object (see Chapter 6) to control access to a global resource. The program calls **CreateMutex** to create a mutex object, and the function returns a handle to the object. The object is owned by the operating system and remembers the state of the mutex, while the handle lets your program reference the object to query and change the state using functions like **WaitForSingleObject** and **ReleaseMutex** (see Chapter 6). When you create the mutex you can give it a name.

Now another program can call **OpenMutex** with that same name. The process will receive a handle that refers to the same operating system object. It can query the mutex and change its state, so now the two programs can synchronize their behavior using the single mutex object managed by the operating system. Once *both* processes close their handles to the object, the operating system deletes the object.

For more information on objects and handles, see Chapters 6 and 10, and the "Handles and Objects" section in the documentation. See the following section for a discussion on the documentation.

1.6 Using the Microsoft Documentation

The 32-bit API comes with quite a bit of good documentation. It is available both on-line and on paper. On paper it is referred to as the Win32 Programmer's Reference books (five volumes). On-line it is in a help file named `api32.hlp`. The on-line version is generally much easier to use both because of the hypertext links and because of the **Search** button (especially the NEAR capability) that lets you find any word in the entire file instantly.

The goal of this book is not to duplicate the information already available in these references. That would be impossible. Here the goal is to help you see how to use the functions available in the API to solve problems. Therefore, this book is full of concise, easy-to-understand example code and explanations that help you to understand how to use the capabilities of the 32-bit API in your own programs.

You should use Microsoft's 32-bit API documentation as a supplement to this book. When you are working through an example, look up each function or structure in the API documentation so that you can see what all the parameters and members actually do. See Section 1.7 for an explanation of why this can be important. The explanations in the on-line help file are generally quite clear, and will make sense in the context of the example. Also click over to some of the related structures and functions to read about them as well. You can master the API quite rapidly this way.

1.7 Bugs in the 32-Bit API

Occasionally you will write a new Windows program, and it simply will not work the way you expect it to work. You will write the program, run it, and it will crash. You will look at the code, diddle with it a little bit, and the problem will remain. After 15 minutes, your response to this improbability is going to be, "Wow, I found a bug in the 32-bit API. I can't believe that they don't test this stuff more carefully." At dinner that night you will rail at your spouse about the inept programmers at Microsoft.

That is the natural human reaction. However, I'd say that in 99.9% of the cases, the problem lies in your code rather than in the API. In many cases, the problem lies in your perception of how you *think* the code should work, even though the documentation clearly states otherwise and you skipped over or missed that part.

To let you see just how easy it is to create problems when working with the API, let me show you five of my own bugs. These bugs all arose while developing the sample code for this book. You, of course, won't make mistakes this stupid, but they demonstrate some of the possibilities. In each one of the five cases, it seemed at first that there was a mysterious and unknown bug somewhere deep in the bowels of the API, but it later turned out to be a stupid mistake on my part.

1. In Listing 5.2, the original code did not contain the **volatile** keyword. The program worked fine as long as there was a call to **Sleep** or some other API function inside the thread function, but as soon as I removed

the call to **Sleep**, **count** remained resolutely at zero. However, if I turned on debugging, the code worked just fine. Obviously there was a bug in the thread handling portion of the API causing **count**'s faulty behavior. However, it turned out to be compiler optimizations that caused the **count** variable to get placed in a register. Adding the **volatile** keyword turns off those optimizations, so the code works fine.

2. When developing the inheritance example in Listings 5.13 and 5.14, it seemed to be impossible to get the child process to inherit anything. I would run the code, and the child would display an "invalid handle" error every time. In some cases, the behavior was even more bizarre: The child process would get created over and over again, even though there are no loops anywhere in the code. Obviously there was a bug in the handle inheriting portion of the API. However, it turned out that I was passing the **sa** parameter to **CreateProcess** as the last parameter rather than as the fourth. Changing the erroneous parameter list eliminated the problem. The **sa** parameter *is* last in the call to **CreateNamedPipe**, but not to **CreateProcess**.
3. In the multi-threaded client program shown in Listing 7.11, the code simply refused to handle the incoming pipe data correctly. Either the incoming data was ignored completely, or the program would read one piece of data and then stop, or, if the overlapped structures were made global, the program would work with one client but then mysteriously and continuously loop in the server whenever a second client connected. Obviously it was a serious bug in the way overlapped I/O works with named pipes. However, it turned out that I was not creating the events and placing them in the overlapped structures to properly initialize them. I was thinking that because I didn't use the events anywhere in the code, I did not need to create them. Once I created the events correctly, the code worked just fine.
4. In the bounded buffer example using semaphores in Listing 6.8, the first version I created just would not work at all. It would terminate immediately, or run a little and die, without any hint of an error message. Nothing seemed to be wrong—it just would up and die for no apparent reason. Obviously the semaphore portion of the API was seriously flawed, or the mixing of two different synchronization mechanisms led

to internal interactions that rendered the entire API inoperable. However, it turned out that I was placing the two thread handles into `handles[1]` and `handles[2]` rather than into `handles[0]` and `handles[1]`. Fixing that minor problem had a wonderful effect on the code.

5. I worked on the simple **push** and **pop** functions in Chapter 6 very early in my Windows career. I happen to like synchronization problems and I wanted to try out critical sections. The test code would run a tiny bit and then hang. I'd run it again and it would hang again. Every now and then it worked fine, but then it would hang again in the next test. Nothing seemed to fix the problem. I tried everything, but adding in the critical sections just destroyed the ability of the program to execute. Obviously the critical section portion of the API was totally flawed. Apparently Microsoft had added it at the last minute and never bothered to test it. However, it turned out that I had forgotten to place a call to **LeaveCriticalSection** before the first return in the **pop** function, so the code could not proceed if that branch got executed. Adding the function call solved the problem.

As you can see, I make my fair share of mistakes, just like everybody else. For the record, let me state that I have written and helped test thousands and thousands and thousands of lines of Windows code, and I have seen many hundreds of "mysterious API bugs." However, I have *never* seen one that did not go away once the programmer wrote the code correctly. It's something to keep in mind when one of your programs is misbehaving. Read the manual, and look carefully at your code. The bug is in there somewhere, staring back at you.

1.8 Differences Between Windows 95 and Windows NT

Windows NT and Windows 95 are very similar at the API level. In fact, a good way to think about Windows 95 is to think of it as "Windows NT Lite." Windows 95 does most of the things that Windows NT can do, but there are several capabilities that NT has that Windows 95 lacks. In particular, Windows 95 is missing parts of NT's security system (Chapter 10), NT services (Chapter 9), and some NT network functionality (Chapter 7). A good way to understand these differences is to compare Windows NT, Windows 95 and Windows 3.1 and see how they evolved from one another.

Windows 3.1 and Windows for Workgroups 3.1were built on top of MS-DOS, the Microsoft operating system for PC-class machines. This layering is a liability because MS-DOS is primitive by today's standards. MS-DOS has a very simple file system with limited features and no security. MS-DOS offers none of the capabilities the user would expect to find in a "real" operating system—features such as virtual memory, multiple processes, interprocess communication, and so on. Windows 3.1 takes care of some of these problems itself as best it can. For example, it offers a good memory management system and cooperative multi-tasking. But because it is built on DOS the system is fragile, and the file management facilities are poor. The system is also permanently attached to PC-compatible hardware. There is really no easy way to move it to other platforms.

Windows NT is Microsoft's answer to these problems. It is a complete and modern operating system built from the ground up as a total solution to workstation computing. NT offers everything you would expect to find in a modern operating system:

- 32-bit instructions and memory addressing: Like any other modern workstation operating system, NT uses a 32-bit numeric and address format. Unlike older DOS and Windows machine, memory addressing is "flat," so you can create arrays as large as you like in memory.
- Preemptive multi-tasking (processes and threads): Microsoft Windows 3.1 uses *cooperative multi-tasking*, in which applications yield the processor to one another at each application's discretion. Windows NT, like UNIX, instead uses *preemptive multi-tasking*. Under this system the OS automatically allocates CPU time to each application (called a *process*). Because the OS, rather than the individual applications, is in control of CPU time slices, the system is extremely stable and robust. In addition, NT applications can divide themselves up into separate *threads* of execution. An application might do this in order to perform a lengthy calculation in the background without affecting the user interface. The OS can schedule threads independently.
- Symmetric Multi-processing: An NT machine can contain more than one CPU. In a multi-processor machine, NT will allocate different threads to different CPUs to take full advantage of all CPU power available. In addition, NT is itself multi-threaded, and its different threads can run on separate processors.

- Multiple platforms (Intel, MIPS, Alpha, etc.): NT is designed to run on a variety of processor architectures. At the time of publication, NT had been ported to Intel 80x86 machines, MIPS platforms, DEC's Alpha chips, and the Power PC. Unlike UNIX, which looks different depending on whose hardware it is running on, NT looks exactly the same to both the user and the programmer no matter which sort of architecture is running it.
- Remote procedure calls: NT supports OSF-style Remote Procedures Calls (RPCs), which can be used to easily build client/server applications that run efficiently on a network.
- Total network support (TCP/IP, NetBEUI, etc.): Windows NT is designed to run on a network, and supports a native format for communication with other NT machines as well as Windows for Workgroups systems and machines running TCP/IP protocols.
- C2 certified security: When using the NT File System (NTFS), Windows NT creates a secure system. All users must log in with an account name and password. Files and directories on the disk are protected by access control lists (ACLs). Applications are isolated from one another in memory so that the crash of one does not affect any of the others.
- DOS and POSIX support: Windows NT, regardless of the platform, can run DOS applications using the MS-DOS prompt, a command-based interface to NT's capabilities. The MS-DOS prompt looks like MS-DOS, using the same commands as DOS does on a PC. However, the MS-DOS prompt is completely simulated, so it looks exactly the same on any CPU architecture. You can also execute POSIX and character-mode OS/2 applications in this environment.

As you can see, NT's capabilities are patterned along the lines of an operating system like UNIX, and in several cases features such as RPCs were borrowed directly and completely from the UNIX world.

Microsoft has covered all of the power in Windows NT with the familiar Windows interface found in the other Windows products. This decision means that anyone familiar with previous versions of Windows can use NT right out of the box—everything looks identical. The only real additions that the user sees when comparing NT to the Windows for Workgroups interface are the security features in the File Manager and the logon screen that ensures that those security features work.

From an administrative standpoint, NT contains a wealth of new features. NT attempts to completely separate *use* of the system from *administration* of the system so that users do not have to waste their time on administrative tasks. A user may "own" the machine on his or her desktop, but that does not mean that the user wants to spend time backing up the hard disks, installing software, or configuring the network. Those administrative tasks are better left to a trained administrator. NT therefore provides separate administrative tools that allow remote access. For example, if a machine is sitting on a network in a large company, an administrator can attach to the machine over the network to update software, change accounts, and so on. Windows 95 contains very little in the way of administrative features.

From a programmer's standpoint, NT uses the Win32 API, which contains a wealth of advanced operating system services. These services are the subject of this book.

Windows 95 contains most of the API features of Windows NT. The Win32 API in Windows NT and Windows 95 are identical, and Windows 95 therefore uses the same process and thread model, the same file access functions, the same network access functions, and so on. Most of the differences between Windows NT and Windows 95 are omissions. Features were removed from Windows 95 to improve its performance on low-end hardware. The list below summarizes these differences:

- Symmetric Multi-processing: Windows 95 works only on single-CPU hardware architectures.
- Multiple platforms: Windows 95 currently runs only on Intel hardware.
- C2 certified security: Windows 95 contains only part of NT's advanced security features.

You will learn about other more subtle differences in the process of reading this book.

In general, you can think of Windows NT as a complete workstation operating system intended for use in corporate, university and engineering environments. Windows 95 is a lower-end product intended more for home and small business applications.

2 FILES

File access is one of the most basic services provided by any operating system. For example, the word *DOS*, which has become something of a generic synonym for an operating system in many circles, stands for Disk Operating System. The "Disk" portion of the name demonstrates how important files are in the grand scheme of things.

This chapter discusses file access. It shows you how to open and close files, how to read and write from them, and how to gather information about files in Windows NT and Windows 95. Many of the functions discussed here are duplicated or combined in higher-level libraries. For example, when you use **fprintf** in C or **ofstream** in C++ you access many of these functions indirectly. The **CFile** class in MFC also uses these functions extensively to provide a high-level interface. Because of these high-level libraries, you may have little or no need to work at the API level when you begin programming in Windows and want to open a file or two.

In many cases, however, it is beneficial to drop down to the API level to access files. Generally, you do this because you want to take advantage of a feature not exposed in the high-level implementation. A good example is NT's security options, discussed in Chapter 10. The only way to access security features in one of your programs is to work at the API level when opening the file.

Compatibility Note: All of the code in this chapter works identically in both Windows NT and Windows 95, with only one minor exception noted for the ***MoveFileEx*** *function in Section 2.5.*

2.1 The Possibilities

Files are important in Windows because you access many different objects using the file routines. Certain techniques are used in the 32-bit API to open a file, read from it and write to it, and close the file. The API uses identical techniques to work with communications ports (Chapter 12), Named pipes, and mailslots on the network (Chapter 7). Therefore, understanding how to work with files is central to understanding any communications task in Windows.

Files are quite interesting in Windows because of all the different capabilities built into the 32-bit API for working with them. For example:

- As you would expect, you can open, read, and write files. (See Sections 2.3 and 2.7.)
- You can also open and read compressed files *without decompressing them.* (See Section 2.10). If you happen to have a file type that is very large and that compresses very well, you can work with it in its compressed form and save quite a bit of disk space.
- You can open files and read and write them asynchronously. (See Section 6.5.) This *overlapping* technique makes it possible to perform background I/O tasks without necessarily multi-threading your application. Overlapped I/O is also the basis for multi-threaded access to a named pipe, as discussed in Section 7.5.
- You can access a great deal of status information about files through the 32-bit API. (See Section 2.4.)
- You can map files into the virtual memory system to significantly improve their performance. (See Section 2.10.) This technique is also used for high-speed interprocess communication (See file mapping in Section 5.11.)
- You can lock files or individual records of a file. (See Section 2.9.)

A topic like file access that would be mundane in many other operating systems has a good bit of variety and interest in the 32-bit API.

Directories and disk drives are closely related to files, and are discussed in detail in the following two chapters. File security is covered in Chapter 10

2.2 Overview

A file, in the strictest sense of the word, is a set of sectors on a disk identified under a unique file name. In many systems and languages, at least at a low level, you treat a file just that way—you can actually read off buffered or unbuffered sectors of information in sector-sized chunks. Most programming languages and operating systems also offer a character-based (as well as a structure-based) abstraction that allows you to deal with information at a more natural level.

In the 32-bit API, you think of a file as a collection of bytes. This is identical to the low-level access paradigm provided by UNIX. You can seek to any byte offset and read a block of bytes of any size. If you want to work at a higher level of abstraction, for example thinking of the file as a set of text lines, you use the libraries in a language like C or C++ to handle the abstraction for you. One of the nice things about the low-level file access functions in the API is that they are fairly easy to understand and use.

Figure 2.1 shows two ways that you will access files in Windows. Files typically contain either text, or binary data in the form of structures stored directly onto the disk. You can use the **ReadFile** and **WriteFile** functions to access these characters or structures. If you have ever used the **fread** and **fwrite** functions in <stdio.h> you will find the use of these API functions very similar.

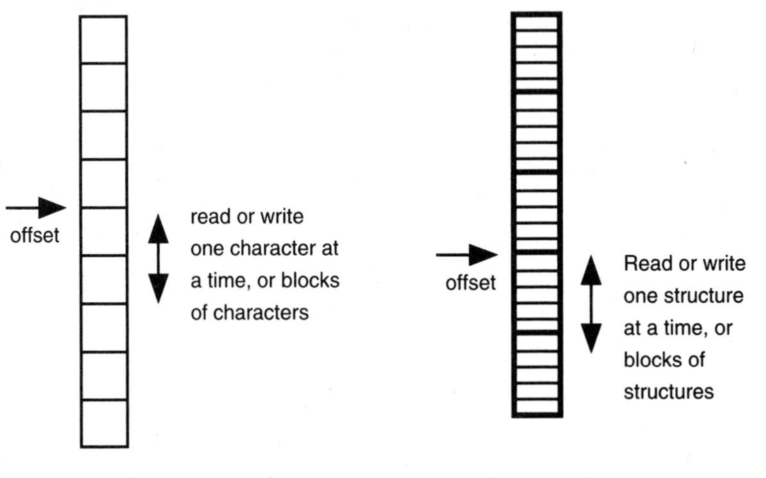

Figure 2.1
Text files and files of structures.

These same **ReadFile** and **WriteFile** functions appear throughout the API in a variety of roles. You will use them, for example, to read from and write to communication ports and the network. In these applications you will also be able to think of the data in terms of single characters or structures.

A number of functions in the API allow you to gather information about a file once you open it. For example, given an open file you can determine its size, type, creation times, and so on. You can also use the API functions to move, copy and delete files.

2.3 Opening and Reading from a File

Let's say that you want to write a program that performs the simplest possible file operation: you want to open a file, read from it, and write its contents to the screen. The easiest way to do this is to use the I/O library that ships with C or C++. Listings 2.1 and 2.2 demonstrate a simple file reading program in straight C, and then in C++. To learn how to compile this code, see Appendix A.

```
// file1.cpp

#include <windows.h>
#include <stdio.h>

void main()
{
   char filename[MAX_PATH];
   char c;
   FILE *f;

   // get file name
   printf("Enter filename: ");
   gets(filename);
```

Listing 2.1
A C program that reads from a file and writes its contents to the screen (Page 1 of 2)

```
    // open the file
    f = fopen(filename, "r");
    if (f)
        // read until eof
        while ((c = fgetc(f)) != EOF)
            printf("%c",c);

    // close the file
    fclose(f);
}
```

Listing 2.1
A C program that reads from a file and writes its contents to the screen (Page 2 of 2)

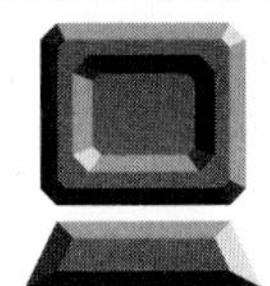

```
// file2.cpp

#include <windows.h>
#include <iostream.h>
#include <fstream.h>

void main()
{
    char filename[MAX_PATH];
    char c;

    // get the file name
    cout << "Enter filename: ";
    cin >> filename;

    // open the file
    ifstream infile(filename);
```

Listing 2.2
A C++ program that reads from a file and writes its contents to the screen (Page 1 of 2)

```
        if (infile)
            // read until eof
            while (infile.get(c))
                cout << c;

        // close the file
        infile.close();
    }
```

Listing 2.2
A C++ program that reads from a file and writes its contents to the screen (Page 2 of 2)

In both of these simple programs, the code requests a file name from the user, opens the file, and reads characters from the file until it reaches the end of the file. Each character appears on the screen.

If you want to perform this same task at the level of the API, then you need to learn about three different functions: **CreateFile**, **ReadFile**, and **Close-Handle**. Accessing the file at the API level follows the same general pattern seen in Listings 2.1 and 2.2, as shown in Listing 2.3. The program gets a file name, opens the file, reads until EOF, and then closes the file.

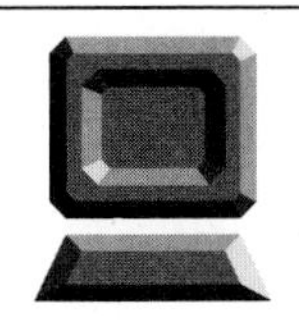

```
// file3.cpp

#include <windows.h>
#include <iostream.h>

void main()
{
    HANDLE fileHandle;
    BOOL success;
    char s[10];
    DWORD numRead;
```

Listing 2.3
An API-level program that reads from a file and writes to it (Page 1 of 2)

```
        char filename[1000];

        // get the file name
        cout << "Enter filename: ";
        cin >> filename;

        // Open the file
        fileHandle = CreateFile(filename, GENERIC_READ,
           0, 0, OPEN_EXISTING, 0, 0);
        if (fileHandle == INVALID_HANDLE_VALUE)
        {
           cout << "Error number " << GetLastError()
              << " occured on file open." << endl;
           return;
        }

        // Read from file until eof, writing to stdout
        do
        {
           success = ReadFile(fileHandle, s, 1,
              &numRead, 0);
           s[numRead] = 0;
           cout << s;
        }
        while (numRead>0 && success);

        // Close the file
        CloseHandle(fileHandle);
    }
```

Listing 2.3
An API-level program that reads from a file and writes to it (Page 2 of 2)

The **CreateFile** function opens a file for read and/or write access. We will see in later chapters that this same function also opens mail slots, named pipes, communication ports, and so on. It is also dealt with in more detail in Section 2.7.

CreateFile *Opens a file, named pipe, mailslot, or communications port*

```
HANDLE CreateFile(
    LPCTSTR name,
    DWORD accessMode,
    DWORD shareMode,
    LPSECURITY_ATTRIBUTES securityAttributes,
    DWORD create,
    DWORD attributes,
    HANDLE templateFile)
```

name	Name of the file to open
accessMode	Read/Write mode
shareMode	The way the file should be shared
securityAttributes	Address of a security structure. See Chapter 10
create	The way the file should be created
attributes	Settings for file attribute bits and flags
templateFile	File containing extended attributes

Returns a handle on success, or INVALID_HANDLE_VALUE

In Listing 2.3, the **CreateFile** function accepts the name of the file, a GENERIC_READ access mode that stipulates that the file will be used in a read-only mode, a share mode that prevents any other process from opening the file, and an OPEN_EXISTING creation mode that specifies that the file already exists. The call uses no security information, no attributes, and no template. The function returns either a handle to the file object that it opened, or an error value to indicate an error. If an error occurs, you can use the **GetLastError** function to retrieve an error code (see Section 1.3).

Once the file is open, the **ReadFile** function reads data from it one character at a time. **ReadFile** is a generic block-reading function. You pass it a buffer and the number of bytes for it to read, and the function retrieves the specified number of bytes from the file starting at the current offset. Listing 2.3 requests blocks of size one byte.

ReadFile *Reads bytes from the specified file*

```
BOOL ReadFile(
   HANDLE file,
   LPVOID buffer,
   DWORD requestedBytes,
   LPDWORD actualBytes,
   LPOVERLAPPED overlapped)
```

file	File handle created with **CreateFile**
buffer	Buffer to hold the read bytes
requestedBytes	The number of bytes desired
actualBytes	The number of bytes actually placed in the buffer
overlapped	Pointer to overlapped structure. See Section 6.5

Returns TRUE on success

In Listing 2.3 the code reads the file one character at a time until **ReadFile** indicates end-of-file. The **CloseHandle** function closes the file once the operations on it are complete.

CloseHandle *Closes an open handle*

```
BOOL CloseHandle(
   HANDLE object)
```

object	The handle to close

Returns TRUE on success

Section 2.7 deals with the topic of file access in much more detail. In this section the goal has been to show that file access at the API level is not much different from normal file access techniques that you already understand.

2.4 Getting and Setting File Information

The API contains several functions that are useful for retrieving file information. For example, you can find out when a file was last modified, how its attribute bits are currently set, and the size of the file. The following sections detail the different capabilities that are available. Several of these functions require an open file handle rather than the file's name. See the previous section or Section 2.7 for details on the **CreateFile** function.

2.4.1 Getting the File Times

The **GetFileTime** function retrieves three different pieces of time information from an open file: the Creation time, the Last Access time, and the Last Write time. The FAT file system supports only the last write time, but NTFS and HPFS support all three.

GetFileTime — *Get file time information*

```
BOOL GetFileTime(
    HANDLE file,
    LPFILETIME creationTime,
    LPFILETIME lastAccessTime,
    LPFILETIME lastWriteTime)
```

file	Handle to a file from **CreateFile**
creationTime	Time of file creation
lastAccessTime	Time of last file access
lastWriteTime	Time of last file write

Returns TRUE on success

In Listing 2.4, the **CreateFile** function opens the requested file name. **GetFileTime** uses the handle that it returns to access the file times, and then passes the last write time up to the **ShowTime** function to dump the time to stdout.

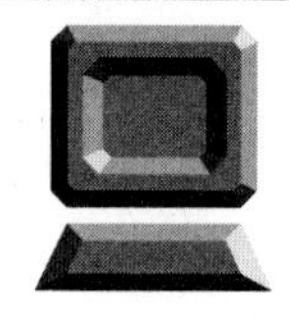

```
// filetime.cpp

#include <windows.h>
#include <iostream.h>

void ShowTime(FILETIME t)
// Dumps the t to stdout
{
   FILETIME ft;
   SYSTEMTIME st;

   FileTimeToLocalFileTime(&t, &ft);
   FileTimeToSystemTime(&ft, &st);
   cout << st.wMonth << "/" << st.wDay
      << "/" << st.wYear << "   " << st.wHour
      << ":" << st.wMinute << endl;
}

void main()
{
   HANDLE fileHandle;
   char filename[MAX_PATH];
   FILETIME create, lastWrite, lastAccess;
   BOOL success;
   FILETIME ft;
   SYSTEMTIME st;

   // get the file name
```

Listing 2.4
Retrieving the file time (Page 1 of 2)

```
        cout << "Enter filename: ";
        cin >> filename;

        // open the file
        fileHandle = CreateFile(filename, GENERIC_READ,
           FILE_SHARE_WRITE,
           0, OPEN_EXISTING, 0, 0);
        if (fileHandle == INVALID_HANDLE_VALUE)
        {
           cout << "Error number " << GetLastError()
              << endl;
           return;
        }
        else
        {
           // get the file times
           success = GetFileTime( fileHandle, &create,
              &lastAccess, &lastWrite);
           cout << "Last write time: ";
           ShowTime(lastWrite);
           // the other two won't work in FAT systems
        }
        CloseHandle(fileHandle);
     }
```

Listing 2.4
Retrieving the file time (Page 2 of 2)

FILETIME is a structure that contains two 32-bit values. The 64 bits together represent the number of 100-nanosecond time increments that have passed since January 1, 1601. The **FileTimeToLocalTime** and **FileTimeToSystemTime** functions convert the 64-bit value to local time and then to a form suitable for output—see Chapter 15 for details.

2.4.2 Getting File Size

The **GetFileSize** function returns the size of the file in bytes, or 0xFFFFFFFF on error. In the FAT file system the largest file size possible can be represented in less than 32 bits, but NTFS is a 64-bit file system and **Get-**

FileSize therefore returns 64 bits of size information if you request it. Since the NT File System can accommodate single volumes that span multiple drives, it is not unreasonable to expect to find occasional files larger than 4 gigabytes, although they are quite rare now. There is currently no easy way to deal with integers larger than 32 bits, but Microsoft provides a library called "largeint" (see `\mstools\h\largeint.h`) that does help.

GetFileSize	*Returns a 64-bit size value for the file*

`DWORD GetFileSize(`
`HANDLE file,`
`LPDWORD fileSizeHigh)`	

file	Handle to an open file from **CreateFile**
fileSizeHigh	High order 32-bits of size (pass address)
Returns the low-order 32 bits of the file size, or 0xFFFFFFFF	

The low-order 32 bits of size information come from the return value, while the high-order 32 bits come from the **fileSizeHigh** parameter when you pass in a pointer to a DWORD. You can also pass in NULL for this parameter if you are not interested in receiving the high-order 32-bits of information. Listing 2.5 shows how to access the information.

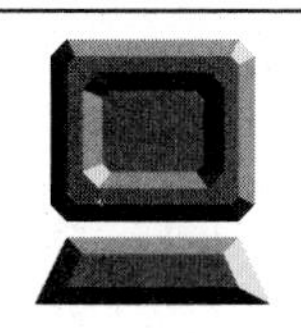

```
// filesize.cpp

#include <windows.h>
#include <iostream.h>
```

Listing 2.5
Obtaining the size of a file (Page 1 of 2)

```
void main()
{
   HANDLE fileHandle;
   char filename[1000];
   DWORD sizeLo, sizeHi;

   // get file name
   cout << "Enter filename: ";
   cin >> filename;

   // open the file
   fileHandle = CreateFile(filename, GENERIC_READ,
      FILE_SHARE_WRITE, 0, OPEN_EXISTING, 0, 0);
   if (fileHandle == INVALID_HANDLE_VALUE)
   {
      cout << "Error number " << GetLastError()
         << endl;
      return;
   }

   // report file size
   else
   {
      sizeLo = GetFileSize(fileHandle, &sizeHi);
      cout << "Size (low 32 bits)  = " << sizeLo
         << endl;
      cout << "Size (high 32 bits) = " << sizeHi
         << endl;
   }
   CloseHandle(fileHandle);
}
```

Listing 2.5
Obtaining the size of a file (Page 2 of 2)

2.4.3 Getting File Attributes

Files have associated with them attribute bits that hold special information about the file. You can view the attributes from the File Manager by selecting a file and then choosing the **Properties** option in the **File** menu. Inside a program you can examine attribute bits with the **GetFileAttributes** function.

GetFileAttributes	*Gets the attribute bits for a file*
`DWORD GetFileAttributes( LPTSTR fileName)`	
fileName	The name of the file
Returns the attribute bits in a DWORD, or 0xFFFFFFFF on error.	

Listing 2.6 demonstrates how to acquire and examine the attribute bits. The system returns not only the four standard bits seen in the File Manager (archive, read only, system, and hidden), but also bits indicating that the file name is actually a directory, as well as a temporary status bit to mark temporary files.

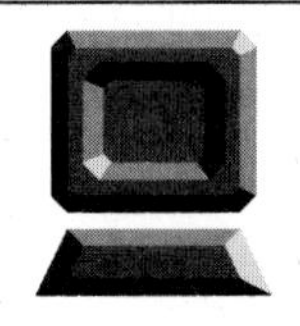

```
// fileattr.cpp

#include <windows.h>
#include <iostream.h>

void ShowAttributes(DWORD attributes)
// Shows the file attributes on stdout
{
   if (attributes & FILE_ATTRIBUTE_ARCHIVE)
      cout << "   archive\n";
```

Listing 2.6
Retrieving the file attributes (Page 1 of 2)

```
        if (attributes & FILE_ATTRIBUTE_DIRECTORY)
           cout << "   directory\n";
        if (attributes & FILE_ATTRIBUTE_HIDDEN)
           cout << "   hidden\n";
        if (attributes & FILE_ATTRIBUTE_NORMAL)
           cout << "   normal\n";
        if (attributes & FILE_ATTRIBUTE_READONLY)
           cout << "   read only\n";
        if (attributes & FILE_ATTRIBUTE_SYSTEM)
           cout << "   system\n";
        if (attributes & FILE_ATTRIBUTE_TEMPORARY)
           cout << "   temporary\n";
     }

     void main()
     {
        char filename[MAX_PATH];
        DWORD attributes;

        cout << "Enter filename: ";
        cin >> filename;
        attributes = GetFileAttributes(filename);
        ShowAttributes(attributes);
     }
```

Listing 2.6
Retrieving the file attributes (Page 2 of 2)

It is also possible to set file attributes using the **SetFileAttributes** function. This function accepts a file name and one or more attribute constants, and returns a Boolean value indicating success or failure.

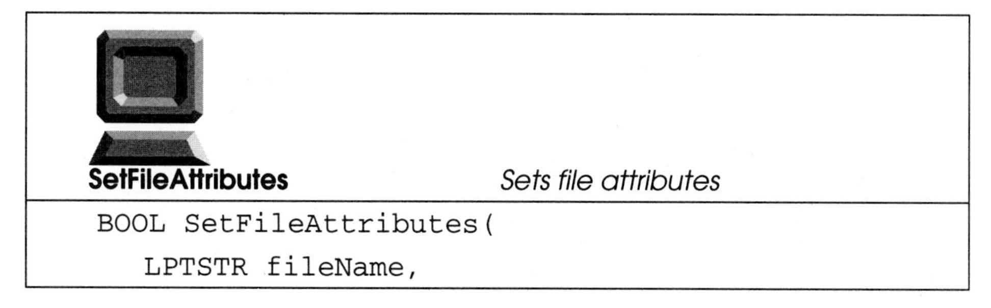

SetFileAttributes *Sets file attributes*

```
BOOL SetFileAttributes(
   LPTSTR fileName,
```

```
    DWORD attributes)
```

fileName	The name of the file
attributes	One or more attributes
Returns TRUE on success	

The same attribute constants seen in the **ShowAttributes** function of Listing 2.6 are available. For example, you might set a file as hidden and read only with the following statement:

```
success = SetFileAttributes("xxx",
    FILE_ATTRIBUTE_HIDDEN |
    FILE_ATTRIBUTE_READONLY);
```

Generally those are the only two attributes you will want to set. The other bits, for example the directory bit, are set automatically by system calls when they are appropriate and should not be altered.

Another way to set attribute bits is during file creation. See Section 2.7.

2.4.4 Getting All File Information

The API contains a function named **GetFileInformationByHandle** that returns all of the information described in the previous three sections in one call. It is useful when you want to access or display all information about a file in one call.

GetFileInformationByHandle	*Retrieves all file information*

```
BOOL GetFileInformationByHandle(
    HANDLE file,
    LPBY_HANDLE_FILE_INFORMATION fileInformation)
```

file	Handle to an open file from **CreateFile**
fileInformation	Information about the file
Returns TRUE on success	

The information comes back in a structure that contains the attributes, size, and time data discussed in the previous sections, along with volume, index, and link information not available anywhere else. The volume serial number is a unique number assigned to the volume when it was formatted. The file index is a unique identifier attached to the file while it is open. Listing 2.7 demonstrates the process.

```
// fileinfo.cpp

#include <windows.h>
#include <iostream.h>

void ShowAttributes(DWORD attributes)
{
   if (attributes & FILE_ATTRIBUTE_ARCHIVE)
      cout << "   archive\n";
   if (attributes & FILE_ATTRIBUTE_DIRECTORY)
      cout << "   directory\n";
   if (attributes & FILE_ATTRIBUTE_HIDDEN)
      cout << "   hidden\n";
   if (attributes & FILE_ATTRIBUTE_NORMAL)
      cout << "   normal\n";
   if (attributes & FILE_ATTRIBUTE_READONLY)
      cout << "   read only\n";
   if (attributes & FILE_ATTRIBUTE_SYSTEM)
      cout << "   system\n";
   if (attributes & FILE_ATTRIBUTE_TEMPORARY)
      cout << "   temporary\n";
}

void ShowTime(FILETIME t)
{
   FILETIME ft;
```

Listing 2.7
Retrieving file information (Page 1 of 3)

```
   SYSTEMTIME st;

   FileTimeToLocalFileTime(&t, &ft);
   FileTimeToSystemTime(&ft, &st);
   cout << st.wMonth << "/" << st.wDay
      << "/" << st.wYear << "   " << st.wHour
      << ":" << st.wMinute << endl;
}

void main()
{
   char filename[MAX_PATH];
   HANDLE fileHandle;
   BOOL success;
   BY_HANDLE_FILE_INFORMATION info;

   cout << "Enter filename: ";
   cin >> filename;
   fileHandle = CreateFile(filename, GENERIC_READ,
      FILE_SHARE_WRITE, 0, OPEN_EXISTING, 0, 0);
   if (fileHandle == INVALID_HANDLE_VALUE)
   {
      cout << "Error number " << GetLastError()
         << endl;
      return;
   }
   else
   {
      success =
         GetFileInformationByHandle(fileHandle,
         &info);
      if (success)
      {
         ShowAttributes(info.dwFileAttributes);
         cout << "Last write time: ";
```

Listing 2.7
Retrieving file information (Page 2 of 3)

```
                ShowTime(info.ftLastWriteTime);
                cout << "Volume serial number: "
                   << info.dwVolumeSerialNumber << endl;
                cout << "File size: " << info.nFileSizeLow
                   << endl;
                cout << "Number of links: "
                   << info.nNumberOfLinks << endl;

                cout << "High index: "
                   << info.nFileIndexHigh << endl;
                cout << "Low index = "
                   << info.nFileIndexLow << endl;
            }
        }
    }
```

Listing 2.7
Retrieving file information (Page 3 of 3)

The index information, combined with the volume serial number for the drive, forms a unique identifier for the file. The number of links is useful only on file systems that support symbolic links.

2.4.5 Getting the File Path

The **GetFullPathName** function is simply a convenience. It appends the requested file name to the current path to form a complete path name. However, it does no checking on the resulting path name to ensure that it is valid.

GetFullPathName — *Concatenates a file name to the current path*

```
DWORD GetFullPathName(
   LPCTSTR fileName,
   DWORD bufferSize,
   LPTSTR buffer,
```

LPTSTR filePart)	
fileName	The name of the file
bufferSize	Size of buffer for resulting path name
buffer	Buffer for the resulting path name
filePart	Pointer to the file name in the buffer
Returns the length of the full path name, or 0 on error	

Listing 2.8 shows how to use the **GetFullPathName** function and then display its output to stdout.

```
// filepath.cpp

#include <windows.h>
#include <iostream.h>

const int BUFFSIZE = 1000;

void main()
{
   char filename[1000];
   DWORD pathSize;
   char pathBuffer[BUFFSIZE];
   char *address;

   cout << "Enter filename: ";
   cin >> filename;
   pathSize = GetFullPathName(filename, BUFFSIZE,
      pathBuffer, &address);
   if (pathSize < BUFFSIZE)
      pathBuffer[pathSize] = 0;
   else
```

Listing 2.8
Creating a complete path name for a file (Page 1 of 2)

```
            pathBuffer[0] = 0;
        cout << pathBuffer << endl;
        cout << address << endl;
    }
```

Listing 2.8
Creating a complete path name for a file (Page 2 of 2)

2.5 File Operations

The API provides three functions for the common file operations of moving, copying, and deleting files. You can use these functions inside of your programs to duplicate the functionality of the command-line equivalents.

The **CopyFile** function copies the source file to the destination file name. If an error occurs during the copy, **GetLastError** contains the error code (see Sections 1.4 and 15.6).

CopyFile	*Copies a file*

```
BOOL CopyFile(
   LPTSTR sourceFile,
   LPTSTR destFile,
   BOOL existFail)
```

sourceFile	File name for the source file
destFile	File name for the destination
existFail	Determines if an existing destination file should be preserved

Returns TRUE on success

The **existFail** parameter controls the behavior of the function when the destination file name already exists. If you set it to TRUE, then the function fails when the destination file name already exists. When set to FALSE, the function overwrites an existing file. Listing 2.9 demonstrates the use of this function.

```
// copyfile.cpp

#include <windows.h>
#include <iostream.h>

void main()
{
   char sourceFilename[MAX_PATH];
   char destFilename[MAX_PATH];
   BOOL success;

   cout << "Enter source filename: ";
   cin >> sourceFilename;
   cout << "Enter destination filename: ";
   cin >> destFilename;
   success = CopyFile(sourceFilename, destFilename,
      TRUE);
   if (!success)
      cout << "Error code = " << GetLastError();
   else
      cout << "success\n";
}
```

Listing 2.9
Copying files

The API supports both a simple and an enhanced move function. The simple version moves a file from one name to another on a single volume. It simply changes the pointers in the directory structure, so it is fast. However, it does not allow movement across volumes or between different drive letters. The enhanced version allows files to move across volumes by copying and then deleting the original file, and it can also protect existing files or delay movement. Listing 2.10 demonstrates the **MoveFileEx** function.

MoveFileEx — *Moves files on or between volumes*

```
BOOL MoveFileEx(
    LPTSTR sourceFile,
    LPTSTR destFile,
    DWORD flags)
```

sourceFile	Source file name
destFile	Destination file name
flags	Flags that control how the move is performed

Returns TRUE on success

The flags can be set to either MOVEFILE_REPLACE_EXISTING, MOVEFILE_COPY_ALLOWED, or MOVEFILE_DELAY_UNTIL_REBOOT. The first option lets you control whether or not the function deletes an existing destination file during the move. The second determines whether cross-volume moves are allowed. The third works only in Windows NT. It sets up for the move but does not actually perform it until the very beginning of the next reboot. This is handy for moving operating system files and other files that are open (and therefore immobile) when the move request is made.

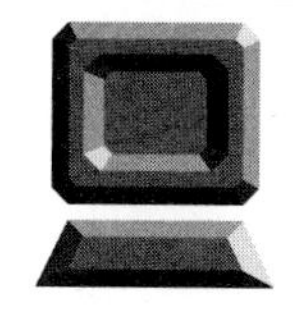

```
// movxfile.cpp

#include <windows.h>
#include <iostream.h>

void main()
```

Listing 2.10
Moving a file (Page 1 of 2)

```
    {
       char sourceFilename[MAX_PATH];
       char destFilename[MAX_PATH];
       BOOL success;

       cout << "Enter source filename: ";
       cin >> sourceFilename;
       cout << "Enter destination filename: ";
       cin >> destFilename;
       success = MoveFileEx(sourceFilename,
          destFilename, 0);
       if (!success)
          cout << "Error code = " << GetLastError();
       else
          cout << "success\n";
    }
```

Listing 2.10
Moving a file (Page 2 of 2)

The **DeleteFile** function deletes an existing file provided that it is not open. It accepts the name of the file and deletes it immediately.

DeleteFile	*Deletes a file*
`BOOL DeleteFile(` `   LPTSTR fileName)`	
fileName	Name of the file to delete
Returns TRUE on success	

If the return value is FALSE, use the **GetLastError** function to retrieve the error code, as shown in Listing 2.11.

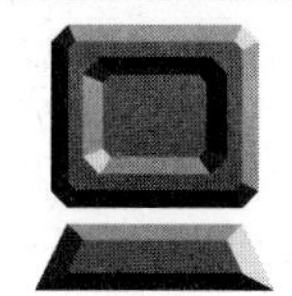

```
// delfile.cpp

#include <windows.h>
#include <iostream.h>

void main()
{
   char filename[MAX_PATH];
   BOOL success;

   cout << "Enter filename: ";
   cin >> filename;
   success = DeleteFile(filename);
   if (success)
      cout << "success\n";
   else
      cout << "Error number: " << GetLastError();
}
```

Listing 2.11
Deleting a file

2.6 Temporary Files

The API contains two functions that make it easy to create temporary files. The first function retrieves the path to the Windows temporary directory, while the second creates a unique temporary file in that directory.

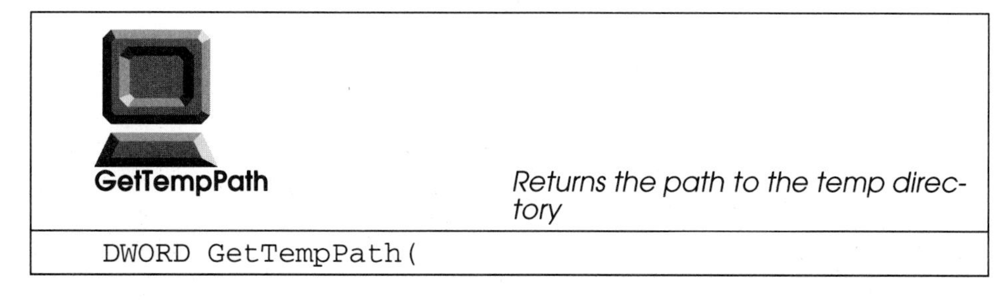

GetTempPath *Returns the path to the temp directory*

```
DWORD GetTempPath(
```

```
    DWORD bufferSize,
    LPTSTR buffer)
```

bufferSize	Maximum size of the buffer
buffer	The buffer that holds the path

Returns the number of characters placed in the buffer or, if greater than **bufferSize**, the required size of the buffer

GetTempFileName *Returns the name and path of a unique temp file*

```
UINT GetTempFileName(
    LPCTSTR path,
    LPCTSTR prefix,
    UINT unique,
    LPTSTR tempFile)
```

path	The path for the new temporary file
prefix	The prefix used on the new file name
unique	A number, either zero or unique
tempFile	Buffer to hold the new name, at least MAX_PATH long

Returns the unique number used in the name, or 0 on error

You can specify a prefix of up to three characters that the function places at the beginning of the new file name. An application might use the same prefix on all temporary files so that it can easily clean them up later. The **unique** number can be either zero or a number of your choosing. If it is zero the system will pick a number that generates a unique file name. When **unique** is zero, the system automatically creates the new file in the temporary directory and closes it. When you supply a non-zero value for **unique** you should create the new temporary file with **CreateFile**.

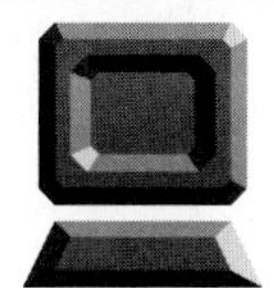

```
// tempfile.cpp

#include <windows.h>
#include <iostream.h>

const int BUFFSIZE = 1000;

void main()
{
   DWORD pathSize;
   char pathBuffer[BUFFSIZE];
   char tempFilename[MAX_PATH];
   UINT uniqueNum;

   pathSize = GetTempPath( BUFFSIZE, pathBuffer);
   if (pathSize < BUFFSIZE)
      pathBuffer[pathSize] = 0;
   else
      pathBuffer[0] = 0;
   cout << pathBuffer << endl;

   uniqueNum = GetTempFileName(pathBuffer, "smp",
      0, tempFilename);
   cout << tempFilename << endl;
   cout << hex << uniqueNum << endl;
}
```

Listing 2.12
Creating a temp file

In Listing 2.12, the system requests the name of the temp directory, and then uses it to create a new temporary file. The program outputs the new file name. Since **unique** is zero in this code, you can also look in the temp directory and see that the new file exists.

See also the FILE_FLAG_DELETE_ON_CLOSE option in Section 2.7.

2.7 File Reading and Writing

Section 2.3 briefly introduced simple file reading using **CreateFile**, **ReadFile**, and **CloseHandle**. In this section we will examine file seeking, reading, and writing in more detail, and look at the **CreateFile** function more carefully. The operations here are all synchronous, so they block until complete. Section 2.8 discusses asynchronous file operations.

Listing 2.3 contains a program that performs a simple file read designed for a text file or a file of bytes. Listing 2.13 demonstrates a file write operation that writes structures to a new file.

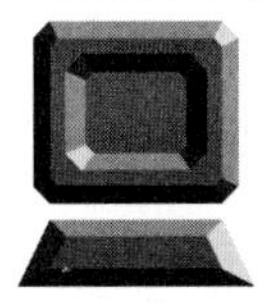

```
// filewrit.cpp

#include <windows.h>
#include <iostream.h>

typedef struct
{
   int a, b, c;
} data;

void main()
{
   HANDLE fileHandle;
   BOOL success;
   DWORD numWrite;
   char filename[MAX_PATH];
   int x;
   data dataRec;
```

Listing 2.13
Writing structures to a file (Page 1 of 2)

```
    // get the file name
    cout << "Enter filename: ";
    cin >> filename;

    // Open the file
    fileHandle = CreateFile(filename, GENERIC_WRITE,
       0, 0, CREATE_NEW, 0, 0);
    if (fileHandle == INVALID_HANDLE_VALUE)
    {
       cout << "Error number " <<
          GetLastError() << endl;
       return;
    }

    // write 10 structures to the file
    x = 0;
    do
    {
       dataRec.a = dataRec.b = dataRec.c = x;
       success = WriteFile(fileHandle, &dataRec,
          sizeof(data), &numWrite, 0);
    }
    while ((x++ < 10) && success);

    // Close the file
    CloseHandle(fileHandle);
}
```

Listing 2.13
Writing structures to a file (Page 2 of 2)

The **WriteFile** function is similar to the **ReadFile** function, writing the specified number of bytes to disk. The function does not care what the bytes represent, so you can use it to write text or structures. In Listing 2.13, the program writes one structure's set of bytes in a single operation, and repeats the operation ten times.

WriteFile	*Writes a block of bytes to a file*

```
BOOL WriteFile(
    HANDLE fileHandle,
    CONST VOID *buffer,
    DWORD bytesToWrite,
    LPDWORD bytesWritten,
    LPOVERLAPPED overlapped)
```

fileHandle	Handle to a file created by **CreateFile**
buffer	Data to write
bytesToWrite	The number of bytes to write
bytesWritten	The number of bytes actually written
overlapped	Overlapped structure. See Section 6.5.

Returns TRUE on success

Both Listings 2.3 and 2.13 use the **CreateFile** function in its simplest configuration. For example, in Listing 2.13 the GENERIC_WRITE constant signals that we need write access to the file, and the CREATE_NEW constant indicates that the system should create a new file rather than overwriting an existing one (if the file name already exists, the function fails). However, **CreateFile** has many other capabilities.

CreateFile	*Opens a file*

```
HANDLE CreateFile(
    LPCTSTR name,
    DWORD accessMode,
    DWORD shareMode,
```

```
    LPSECURITY_ATTRIBUTES securityAttributes,
    DWORD create,
    DWORD attributes,
    HANDLE templateFile)
```

name	Name of the file to open
accessMode	Read/Write mode
shareMode	The way the file should be shared
securityAttributes	Address of a security structure. See Chapter 10
create	The way the file should be created
attributes	Settings for normal file attribute bits
templateFile	File containing extended attributes

Returns a handle to the file, or INVALID_HANDLE_VALUE on failure

When using the **CreateFile** function, you have control over several different things:

1. The read and write mode
2. The way the file will be shared
3. A variety of attributes and performance hints

You can also send the function security attributes, as discussed in detail in Chapter 10.

The second parameter passed to **CreateFile** controls read and write access. You can pass in any of the following three combinations:

GENERIC_READ	Read only
GENERIC_WRITE	Write only
GENERIC_READ | GENERIC_WRITE	Read/write

Generally you use the third option when you plan to open a file of structures that you will read and modify simultaneously. You use GENERIC_READ when you want read-only access, and GENERIC_WRITE when you need write-only access.

The third parameter passed to **CreateFile** controls the share mode of the file. You control access to the entire file using this parameter. The following four variations are possible:

0	exclusive use of the file
FILE_SHARE_READ	read-share from the file
FILE_SHARE_WRITE	write-share the file
FILE_SHARE_READ | FILE_SHARE_WRITE	open access

If you pass 0 to the **shareMode** parameter, then the entire file is locked while you have it open. Any other process attempting to open the file will receive a share violation. The remaining options grant increasing levels of access to other processes. Alternatively, you can lock individual byte ranges as discussed in Section 2.9.

The **security** parameter is discussed in Chapter 10.

The **create** parameter controls the failure behavior of **CreateFile** during creation. Any of the following options are possible:

CREATE_NEW	Create a new file. Fails if file name exists
CREATE_ALWAYS	Create a new file. Destroys any existing file
OPEN_EXISTING	Opens an existing file. Fails if file not found
OPEN_ALWAYS	Creates a file if one does not exist, or opens the existing file
TRUNCATE_EXISTING	Deletes the contents of the file if it exists. Fails if it does not exist

The **attributes** parameter lets you set the file attributes, and it also lets you tell the system your intended use of the file so that you can improve overall system performance. You can OR together non-conflicting combinations of the following constants as needed in an application:

FILE_ATTRIBUTE_ARCHIVE	Mark file for backup
FILE_ATTRIBUTE_NORMAL	Default
FILE_ATTRIBUTE_HIDDEN	Mark file as hidden
FILE_ATTRIBUTE_READONLY	Mark file as read only
FILE_ATTRIBUTE_SYSTEM	Mark file for OS use only
FILE_ATTRIBUTE_TEMPORARY	Mark file as temporary

FILE_FLAG_WRITE_THROUGH	Write through cache to disk
FILE_FLAG_OVERLAPPED	See Section 6.5
FILE_FLAG_NO_BUFFERING	Use no cache on this file
FILE_FLAG_RANDOM_ACCESS	File will be accessed randomly
FILE_FLAG_SEQUENTIAL_SCAN	File will be accessed sequentially
FILE_FLAG_DELETE_ON_CLOSE	Delete file when closed
FILE_FLAG_BACKUP_SEMANTICS	Create as backup file
FILE_FLAG_POSIX_SEMANTICS	Follow POSIX naming rules

Many of the flag options are hints that you give to help the operating system improve its overall performance. For example, if you know you are opening a 10 meg file that you will read from beginning to end and never use again, then it is a waste for the operating system to cache any of it. You should therefore use the FILE_FLAG_NO_BUFFERING and FILE_FLAG_SEQUENTIAL_SCAN options. If you are creating a temporary file that you want to delete when you close it, you can let the OS do it automatically using the FILE_FLAG_DELETE_ON_CLOSE and FILE_ATTRIBUTE_TEMPORARY flags. See the API documentation for details on all of these different options. You can set file attributes at creation or change them later as shown in Section 2.4.3.

It is possible to read from or write to a file either sequentially or at random byte offsets in the file. You typically use random offsets when the file contains a set of structures. The **SetFilePointer** function moves the file pointer to the indicated position.

SetFilePointer *Moves the file pointer*

```
DWORD SetFilePointer(
    HANDLE fileHandle,
    LONG distance,
    PLONG distanceHigh,
    DWORD method)
```

fileHandle	Handle created by **CreateFile**
distance	Distance to move pointer (low 32 bits)
distanceHigh	Pointer to distance to move pointer (high 32 bits), or NULL
method	FILE_BEGIN, FILE_CURRENT, or FILE_END
Returns the new location of the file pointer, or 0xFFFFFFFF on error	

The new file position can move a distance that is relative to the beginning of the file, the end of the file, or the current position. Positive values move forward, and negative values move backward. The program fragment in Listing 2.14 demonstrates a program that seeks through a file in 1,000 byte hops and extracts 10 bytes at a time.

```
do
{
   success = ReadFile(fileHandle, s, 10,
      &numRead, 0);
   s[numRead] = 0;
   cout << s << endl;
   SetFilePointer(fileHandle, 1000, 0,
      FILE_CURRENT);
}
while (numRead>0 && success);
```

Listing 2.14
Code fragment demonstrating the use of the **SetFilePointer** function

It is also common to store fixed-size structures in a file and to seek randomly to a specific structure. In many cases you will lock the structure while you are accessing it. See Section 2.9 for an example.

2.8 Asynchronous File Operations

The API supports an asynchronous form of file access that allows you to start an I/O operation and then proceed with other activities while the operation completes in the background. The technique is referred to as *overlapped I/O*. It exists in Windows for two reasons:

1. Overlapped I/O lets you create the impression of multi-threading without actually implementing a separate thread. In certain situations this makes the code more compact, or it lets you handle asynchronous file I/O more easily than a second thread would.
2. Overlapped I/O makes it possible for separate threads in a single program to manipulate the same file object simultaneously. With overlapped I/O, each thread can keep track of its file position independently of other threads, and this lets threads simultaneously access the same pipe, file, etc.

Asynchronous operations can be extremely useful when you want to perform multiple file operations on the same file handle simultaneously. For example, in Section 7.5.2 a single named pipe is read in one thread and written in another. Overlapped I/O is the only way to handle this situation.

See Chapter 6 for a complete description of events and overlapped I/O.

2.9 File Locking

When we discussed the **CreateFile** function in Section 2.7, you saw that its third parameter controls the accessibility of an open file to other processes. For example, if you specify FILE_SHARE_READ when you open a file with **CreateFile**, then other processes can open the file for read access but not for write access. You can also open a file so that no other process can access it at all by passing a zero in for the share mode.

While this file-wide access control scheme is appropriate in many cases, there are many others where it is simply too general. For example, you may have a file of structures available on a server. It might contain employee records, and there may be many users on the network who need to simultaneously access the file to retrieve or modify employee information. The file-wide access control system implemented by **CreateFile** has a granularity that is too coarse for this sort of activity. What you want is the ability to lock individual records while they are in use, and to then free them up when the user has finished with them. See Figure 2.2.

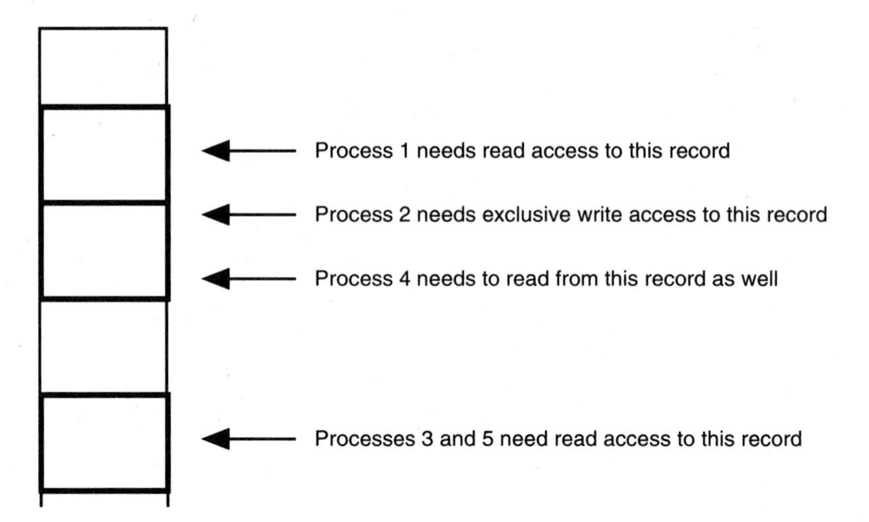

Figure 2.2
Many users may need access to different parts of the same file. File locking lets each user lock just the part they need.

The API offers two different functions, **LockFile** and **LockFileEx**, to implement this functionality.

LockFile	*Locks a range of bytes*

```
BOOL LockFile(
   HANDLE fileHandle,
   DWORD fileOffsetLow,
   DWORD fileOffsetHigh,
   DWORD lockLow,
   DWORD lockHigh)
```

fileHandle	Handle to the file to lock

fileOffsetLow	Offset to start of locked section (low-order 32 bits)
fileOffsetHigh	Offset to start of locked section (high-order 32 bits)
lockLow	Number of bytes to lock (low-order 32 bits)
lockHigh	Number of bytes to lock (high-order 32 bits)
Returns TRUE on success	

UnlockFile *Unlocks a locked range of bytes*

```
BOOL UnlockFile(
    HANDLE fileHandle,
    DWORD fileOffsetLow,
    DWORD fileOffsetHigh,
    DWORD unlockLow,
    DWORD unlockHigh)
```

fileHandle	Handle to the file to lock
fileOffsetLow	Offset to start of locked section (low-order 32 bits)
fileOffsetHigh	Offset to start of locked section (high-order 32 bits)
unlockLow	Number of bytes to unlock (low-order 32 bits)
unlockHigh	Number of bytes to unlock (high-order 32 bits)
Returns TRUE on success	

```
BOOL LockFileEx(
    HANDLE fileHandle,
    DWORD flags,
    DWORD reserved,
    DWORD numBytesLow,
    DWORD numBytesHigh,
    LPOVERLAPPED overlapped)
```

fileHandle	Handle to file created by **CreateFile**
flags	Access flags
reserved	Must be zero
numBytesLow	Number of bytes to lock (low order 32 bits)
numBytesHigh	Number of bytes to lock (high order 32 bits)
overlapped	Structure containing starting address of block

Returns TRUE on success

UnlockFileEx *Unlocks a locked range of bytes*

```
BOOL UnlockFileEx(
    HANDLE file,
    DWORD reserved,
    DWORD numBytesLow,
    DWORD numBytesHigh,
    LPOVERLAPPED overlapped)
```

fileHandle	Handle to file created by **CreateFile**
flags	Access flags
reserved	Must be zero
numBytesLow	Number of bytes to lock (low order 32 bits)

numBytesHigh	Number of bytes to lock (high order 32 bits)
overlapped	Structure containing starting address of block
Returns TRUE on success	

The **LockFileEx** function is slightly more bothersome to use because you have to create an OVERLAPPED structure (see Section 6.5) and place into it the starting address of the block that you want to lock (the rest of the fields in the structure are unused). However, **LockFileEx** offers more control over the locking process and it is therefore preferred in many cases.

Listing 2.15 contains code that demonstrates how to lock a structure in a file using the **LockFile** function. The program assumes the existence of a data file created by Listing 2.13, and locks record three in the file. The program then waits for the user to press return to unlock the record and continue.

```
// filelck1.cpp

#include <windows.h>
#include <iostream.h>

typedef struct
{
   int a, b, c;
} data;

void main()
{
   HANDLE fileHandle;
   BOOL success;
   char filename[MAX_PATH];
```

Listing 2.15
Locking a record with **LockFile**. Use Listing 2.13 to create the file (Page 1 of 2)

```
      char s[100];

      // get the file name
      cout << "Enter filename: ";
      cin.getline(filename, 100);

      // Open the file
      fileHandle = CreateFile(filename, GENERIC_READ,
         FILE_SHARE_READ,
         0, OPEN_EXISTING, 0, 0);
      if (fileHandle == INVALID_HANDLE_VALUE)
      {
         cout << "Error number " << GetLastError()
            << endl;
         return;
      }

      // Lock record 3, wait, and unlock
      success = LockFile(fileHandle, sizeof(data) * 2,
         0, sizeof(data), 0);
      if (!success)
         cout << "Lock error = " << GetLastError()
            << endl;
      cout << "Press return to continue: ";
      cin.getline(s, 100);
      UnlockFile(fileHandle, sizeof(data) * 2,
         0, sizeof(data), 0);

      // Close the file
      CloseHandle(fileHandle);
   }
```

Listing 2.15
Locking a record with **LockFile**. Use Listing 2.13 to create the file (Page 2 of 2)

Listing 2.15 shows how easy it is to lock and later unlock a range of bytes. You can see the effect of the lock by running a second instance of the program in a separate command shell. Run Listing 2.15, and then while it has the record locked, open a second command shell and run Listing 2.15 again. Since the first instance of the program has locked record three, the second instance of the program will fail with a lock violation—two programs cannot lock the same block simultaneously. Similarly, Windows will not allow any other process to read or write to the locked range.

The **LockFile** function forms an exclusive lock—no other process can read or write any part of the locked block until the program releases it with **UnlockFile**. Generally you will want to lock a range of bytes for the absolute minimum amount of time possible so that all other processes can access the record when they need it.

The **LockFileEx** function does the same thing as **LockFile**, but gives you more control over the process. In the **flags** parameter, you can use one of the following four combinations of flags:

0
LOCKFILE_FAIL_IMMEDIATELY
LOCKFILE_EXCLUSIVE_LOCK
LOCKFILE_FAIL_IMMEDIATELY |
LOCKFILE_EXCLUSIVE_LOCK

The LOCKFILE_FAIL_IMMEDIATELY flag controls the behavior of the function when it tries to lock a range of bytes that already has been locked by another process. If this flag is specified, then **LockFileEx** returns immediately with a lock violation. On the other hand, if it is not specified, then **LockFileEx** will wait for the requested block to become available. It will then lock the block and return. This process is demonstrated by Listing 2.16.

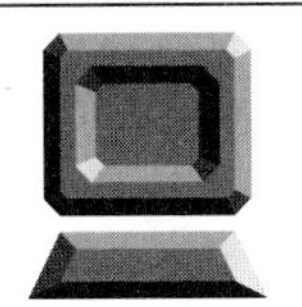

```
// filelck2.cpp

#include <windows.h>
#include <iostream.h>
```

Listing 2.16
Using the **LockFileEx** function in its waiting mode (Page 1 of 3)

```
typedef struct
{
   int a, b, c;
} data;

void main()
{
   HANDLE fileHandle;
   BOOL success;
   DWORD numRead;
   char filename[MAX_PATH];
   data dataRec;
   OVERLAPPED overlap;

   // get the file name
   cout << "Enter filename: ";
   cin >> filename;

   // Open the file
   fileHandle = CreateFile(filename, GENERIC_READ,
      FILE_SHARE_READ,
      0, OPEN_EXISTING, 0, 0);
   if (fileHandle == INVALID_HANDLE_VALUE)
   {
      cout << "Error number " << GetLastError()
         << endl;
      return;
   }

   // Seek and Read from the file until eof
   overlap.Offset = 0;
   overlap.OffsetHigh = 0;
   do
   {
```

Listing 2.16
Using the **LockFileEx** function in its waiting mode (Page 2 of 3)

```
            LockFileEx(fileHandle, 0, 0, sizeof(data), 0,
               &overlap);
            success = ReadFile(fileHandle, &dataRec,
               sizeof(dataRec), &numRead, 0);
            if (!success)
               cout << "Last error = " << GetLastError()
                  << endl;
            else
               cout << "Data = " << dataRec.a << endl;
            UnlockFileEx(fileHandle, 0, sizeof(data), 0,
               &overlap);
            overlap.Offset += sizeof(data);
         }
         while (numRead>0 && success);

         // Close the file
         CloseHandle(fileHandle);
      }
```

Listing 2.16
Using the **LockFileEx** function in its waiting mode (Page 3 of 3)

To demonstrate Listing 2.16, you should run 2.15 in one shell, and then 2.16 in another. Listing 2.16 tries to read through a file sequentially and output the data it finds. Since Listing 2.15 locks record three, Listing 2.16 will stall when it tries to lock record three. The **LockFileEx** function will not return until you press the return key in the instance of Listing 2.15. Then 2.16 will continue and read until end of file.

Now, modify Listing 2.16 so that the **LockFileEx** function uses the LOCKFILE_FAIL_IMMEDIATELY flag. Run Listings 2.15 and 2.16 again. When Listing 2.16 hits record 3, it will fail, and then the **ReadFile** function will fail as well. You can detect the failure in **LockFileEx** by looking at its return value and **GetLastError**, or detect it in **ReadFile** as shown in Listing 2.16.

The LOCKFILE_EXCLUSIVE_LOCK flag controls whether a locked block has an exclusive lock just like the one formed by **LockFile**, or a more permissive write lock. A write lock prevents other processes from writing to the block in question, but does allow them read from it. This mode is very common, especially in situations like the employee record example discussed earlier.

One process may lock a record because the user needs to modify it, but that should not necessarily exclude other users or processes from reading the record.

2.10 Compressed Files

The 32-bit API has a small extension library that works with compressed files. The `compress` command creates a compressed file that you can either decompress to a new file during your application's execution, or read from directly, without decompressing it at all. See Figure 2.3. Certain types of files compress very efficiently. For example, many different types of bitmap files compress at a 90% level or better, and most text files achieve a 50% compression factor. The ability to read compressed files directly allows you to keep certain files in a compressed format to save disk space.

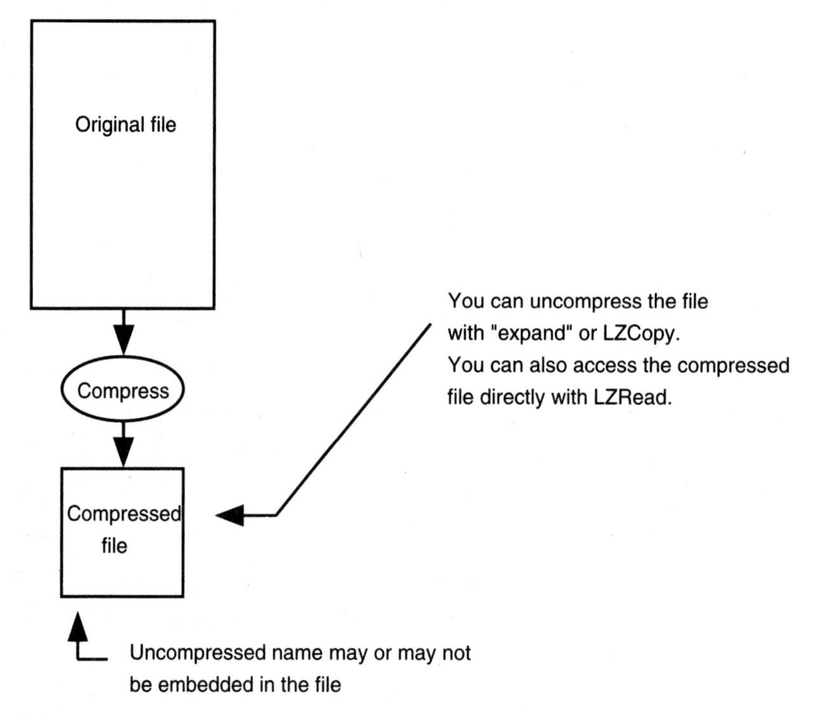

Figure 2.3
Creating and accessing a compressed file.

In order to test the compressed file facility, you need a file to compress. The code in Listing 2.17 is a very simple C++ program that creates a text file containing 10,000 lines of data. You can adjust the size of the file to suit your taste. The 10,000 line file requires about 238K of disk space.

```
// lztest.cpp

#include <windows.h>
#include <iostream.h>
#include <fstream.h>

void main()
{
   char filename[MAX_PATH];
   int x;

   cout << "Enter filename: ";
   cin >> filename;
   ofstream f(filename);
   if (f)
      for (x=0; x<10000; x++)
         f << "This is test line " << x << endl;
   f.close();
}
```

Listing 2.17
Creates a large text file for testing purposes

Assume that you name the file `xxx.txt`. You can compress this file to a new file named `xxx.lz` using the `compress` command:

```
compress xxx.txt xxx.lz
```

This file compressed from 238K in `xxx.txt` down to 42K in `xxx.lz`, a compression ratio of 83%. [For the sake of comparison, pkzip compressed it to 38K, or 84%, and was somewhat faster.] The main reason for the high compression ratio is the large amount of redundant data in the file. The compress command also has a /r option that embeds the original name of the file in the compressed file. The command that you use on the command line to uncompress a file is called expand.

The code in Listing 2.18 shows how to access a compressed file directly using the **LZOpenFile**, **LZSeek**, **LZRead**, and **LZClose** functions. Note that you must include the file lz32.lib in the list of link libraries in order for the code to compile.

LZOpenFile *Opens a compressed file for reading*

```
INT LZOpenFile(
    LPTSTR fileName,
    LPOFSTRUCT openBuf,
    WORD style)
```

fileName	The name of the file to open
openBuf	A pointer to a structure **LZOpenFile** loads with file information
style	One or more bit constants that control file access

Returns an integer value identifying the file, or a negative value indicating the error code

LZSeek *Seeks to a position in an lz file*

```
LONG LZSeek(
    INT fileHandle,
    LONG offset,
    INT origin)
```

fileHandle	Handle returned by **LZOpenFile**
offset	Byte offset into the file

origin	Reference point for offset: from beginning, end, or current.
Returns the offset of the file pointer, or a negative error code	

LZRead	*Reads from an lz file*

`INT LZRead(`
`INT fileHandle,`
`LPSTR buffer,`
`INT count)`	

fileHandle	Handle returned by **LZOpenFile**
buffer	Buffer to place data into
count	Number of bytes to read
Returns the number of bytes read, or a negative error code	

LZClose	*Closes an lz file*
`VOID LZClose(` `INT fileHandle)`	
fileHandle	Handle returned by **LZOpenFile**
Returns nothing	

It is important to recognize that the file handles returned by **LZFileOpen** can be used only by other **LZ** commands, as shown in the example program. Also note that the **info** parameter returned by **LZOpenFile** contains several pieces of information that may or may not be useful to you. See the documentation for details.

In Listing 2.18, the compressed file is a text file, but it can be any type of file that you can access at a byte level. The code in Listing 2.18 opens the file, seeks to the position 100,000 in the file, and then reads and displays 20 bytes from the file.

```
// lzread.cpp

#include <windows.h>
#include <iostream.h>
#include <stdio.h>

void main()
{
   char filename[MAX_PATH];
   OFSTRUCT info;
   INT fileHandle;
   LONG seekResult;
   INT readResult;
   char buffer[10];
   int x;

   cout << "Enter filename: ";
   cin >> filename;
   fileHandle = LZOpenFile(filename,
      &info, OF_READ);
   if (fileHandle < 0)
   {
      cout << "Source error = " << fileHandle
         << endl;
      return;
   }
   seekResult = LZSeek(fileHandle, 100000, 0);
   cout << "Seek result = " << seekResult << endl;
```

Listing 2.18
Reading from a compressed file (Page 1 of 2)

```
        for (x=0; x < 20; x++)
        {
           readResult = LZRead(fileHandle, buffer, 1);
           if (readResult >= 0)
              buffer[readResult] = 0;
           else
              buffer[0] = 0;
           cout << readResult << " " << buffer << endl;
        }
        cout << endl;
        LZClose(fileHandle);
    }
```

Listing 2.18
Reading from a compressed file (Page 2 of 2)

A fundamental question to ask at this point concerns performance. Although the capability shown in Listing 2.18 seems ideal, it is worthless if it takes 10 seconds to access each byte. If you do some tests on your own, you will probably find the following:

1. Sequential read speed on a compressed file is nearly indistinguishable from a normal file read.
2. Seeking and reading in a forward direction gives similarly good performance.
3. Backward seeking is a problem. When you seek from the end of the file toward the beginning, performance degrades by a factor of 50 or more compared to a normal file seek and read.

For example, the file created by Listing 2.17 contains 238K bytes. Write a program to seek to position 230,000, read 10 bytes, then to position 229,000, read 10 bytes, and so on, decrementing the file position by 1,000 each time until it hits the beginning of the file. Doing this with **SetFilePosition** and **ReadFile**, as shown in Listing 2.14, gives an almost instantaneous response. Using **LZSeek** and **LZRead**, however, will take quite awhile. If you need to do random or backward seeks in a file, you should test the **LZ** functions on some sample data first to make sure that the program's performance will be acceptable to your users. An important factor in the performance measurements that you make is the speed of your CPU.

The **LZCopy** function lets you copy a file from one place to another. If the file is compressed, it is expanded during the copy to its full size at the destination. Listing 2.19 demonstrates how to use the **LZCopy** command.

LZCopy	*Copies a compressed file and expands it in the process*

`LONG LZCopy(`
`INT sourceFile,`
`INT destFile)`	

sourceFile	Handle of the source file
destFile	Handle of the destination file
Returns the size of the expanded file, or a negative error code	

```
// lzcopy.cpp

#include <windows.h>
#include <iostream.h>
#include <stdio.h>

void main()
{
   char sourceFilename[MAX_PATH];
   char destFilename[MAX_PATH];
   OFSTRUCT sourceInfo, destInfo;
   INT sourceHandle, destHandle;
   // get source and dest file names
```

Listing 2.19
Copying a compressed file (Page 1 of 2)

```
        cout << "Enter source filename: ";
        cin >> sourceFilename;
        cout << "Enter destination filename: ";
        cin >> destFilename;

        // open both files
        sourceHandle = LZOpenFile(sourceFilename,
           &sourceInfo, OF_READ);
        if (sourceHandle < 0)
        {
           cout << "Source error = " << sourceHandle
              << endl;
           return;
        }
        destHandle = LZOpenFile(destFilename, &destInfo,
           OF_CREATE);
        if (destHandle < 0)
        {
           cout << "Dest error = " << destHandle
              << endl;
           return;
        }

        // perform the copy and close the files
        cout << "Result of copy = ";
        cout << LZCopy(sourceHandle, destHandle)
           << endl;
        LZClose(sourceHandle);
        LZClose(destHandle);
     }
```

Listing 2.19
Copying a compressed file (Page 2 of 2)

You can also use the **GetExpandedName** function to retrieve the name of the compressed file. If the original compression used the /r option, then the compressed file contains its original file name, and you can extract and use this name for the destination.

GetExpandedName	*Retrieves the name from a compressed file*

`INT GetExpandedName(`
`   LPSTR source,`
`   LPTSTR buffer)`	

source	The name of the compressed file
buffer	The buffer in which to place the name
Returns 1 on success or LZERROR_BADVALUE on failure	

You should make the buffer big enough to hold the file name (see Section 3.2 for information on obtaining the maximum file name length for a file system). On success, the **GetExpandedName** function returns TRUE. If the file is not compressed, or if it was not compressed with the `/r` option, the function returns LZERROR_BADVALUE.

2.11 File Mapping

The 32-bit API provides a feature called *file mapping* that allows you to map a file directly into the virtual memory space of an application. We will see in Chapter 5 that this capability is often used to implement interprocess communication schemes, but the technique is also useful for simplifying or speeding file access.

You can map a file either for read-only or read-write access. Once mapped, you access the file by address (using array or pointer syntax) rather than using file access functions such as **ReadFile** or **WriteFile** (See also **ReadProcessMemory** and **WriteProcessMemory**). When used in read-write mode, the technique is especially interesting because it gives you total control over when data gets flushed to disk.

For example, say that you need to access data in a file and you know that you will make a large number of writes to the file in rapid succession. Also imagine that, for performance reasons, you cannot afford the time it takes to perform all of those writes. Typically you would solve this problem by reading the file to an array, accessing the array, and then writing the array back to disk. File mapping does this automatically—it maps the file into memory for you. In addition, as discussed in Chapter 5, you can share the memory image among multiple processes, and the image will remain coherent to all viewers on a single machine.

Listing 2.20 shows how to use file mapping in read-only mode.

```
// mapfile.cpp

#include <windows.h>
#include <iostream.h>

void main()
{
   HANDLE fileHandle;
   char filename[MAX_PATH];
   HANDLE mapFileHandle;
   char *mapView;

   // get the file name
   cout << "Enter filename: ";
   cin >> filename;

   // open the file
   fileHandle = CreateFile(filename,
      GENERIC_READ, 0,
      0, OPEN_EXISTING, 0, 0);
   if (fileHandle == INVALID_HANDLE_VALUE)
   {
      cout << "Error number " << GetLastError()
```

Listing 2.20
Reading from a mapped file (Page 1 of 2)

```
            << endl;
         return;
      }

      // create the mapping
      mapFileHandle = CreateFileMapping(
         fileHandle, 0, PAGE_READONLY,
         0, 0, "mapfile");
      if (mapFileHandle <= 0)
      {
         cout << "Mapping error "
            << GetLastError() << endl;
         return;
      }

      // map the file to an address
      mapView = (char *)
         MapViewOfFile(mapFileHandle,
         FILE_MAP_READ, 0, 0, 0);

      // dump the file
      cout << mapView;

      // clean up
      if (!UnmapViewOfFile(mapView))
         cout << "problem unmapping\n";
      CloseHandle(mapFileHandle);
      CloseHandle(fileHandle);
   }
```

Listing 2.20
Reading from a mapped file (Page 2 of 2)

The program in Listing 2.20 begins by asking the user for a file name and opening the file with **CreateFile**, using the techniques described in Section 2.7. It then calls the **CreateFileMapping** function to create the mapping. This step determines the size of the mapping as well as its data, and gives the mapping a name so that other processes can view the same object. In this simple example the name "mapfile" is never used again, but in interprocess communication other processes can open the same mapping by using that name.

CreateFileMapping *Creates and names a mapping*

```
HANDLE CreateFileMapping(
    HANDLE fileHandle,
    LPSECURITY_ATTRIBUTES security,
    DWORD protect,
    DWORD sizeHigh,
    DWORD sizeLow,
    LPTSTR mapName)
```

fileHandle	Handle to the file, or 0xFFFFFFFF for a memory block
security	Security attributes. See Chapter 10
protect	Access protection (read-only vs. read-write)
sizeHigh	Maximum size of the mapping, high 32 bits
sizeLow	Maximum size of the mapping, low 32 bits
mapName	Name of the mapping

Returns a handle to the mapping or 0 on error

In Listing 2.20, the protection is set to read-only, and the size is set to the current file size by setting **sizeLow** and **sizeHigh** to zero.

The **MapViewOfFile** function actually loads the file data into the memory space of the process, and returns the new address of the data. In Listing 2.20, **mapView** is declared as a pointer to a character so that the data can be thought of text. You can declare **mapView** to be of any type. For example, if the file contains a set of structures, let **mapView** be a pointer to that type of structure.

MapViewOfFile — *Loads a file mapping into memory*

```
LPVOID MapViewOfFile(
   HANDLE mapHandle,
   DWORD access,
   DWORD offsetHigh,
   DWORD offsetLow,
   DWORD number)
```

mapHandle	Handle to the mapping
access	Type of access (read-only, read-write, etc.)
offsetHigh	Offset into the file, high 32 bits
offsetLow	Offset into the file, low 32 bits
number	Number of bytes to map

Returns the starting address of the view, or 0 on error

In Listing 2.20, the code maps the entire file with read-only access. Once mapped, **mapView** points to the address of the mapping, and you use it just like any other pointer or array. If you load a text file with this program, the **cout** statement writes the entire file to stdout, as shown. Once you have finished with the file, use **UnmapViewOfFile** to unload the memory and write any changes back to the original file. No changes were made here, but the next example makes use of this feature.

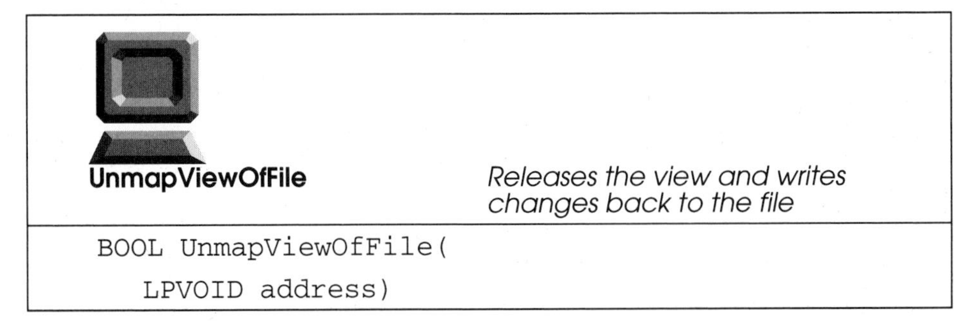

UnmapViewOfFile — *Releases the view and writes changes back to the file*

```
BOOL UnmapViewOfFile(
   LPVOID address)
```

address	Address of the mapping
Returns TRUE on success	

Listing 2.21 shows a second example of file mapping. Here the program opens the mapped file for read-write access and then writes to the file. The changes are flushed to disk only when the program calls **UnmapViewOfFile**.

```
// mapfilew.cpp

#include <windows.h>
#include <iostream.h>

void main()
{
   HANDLE fileHandle;
   char filename[MAX_PATH];
   HANDLE mapFileHandle;
   char *mapView;
   int i;

   // get the name of a file
   cout << "Enter filename: ";
   cin >> filename;

   // open the file
   fileHandle = CreateFile(filename,
      GENERIC_READ | GENERIC_WRITE, 0,
      0, OPEN_EXISTING, 0, 0);
   if (fileHandle == INVALID_HANDLE_VALUE)
   {
```

Listing 2.21
Reading and writing a mapped file (Page 1 of 2)

```
            cout << "Error number " << GetLastError()
               << endl;
            return;
        }

        // create the mapping
        mapFileHandle = CreateFileMapping(fileHandle, 0,
            PAGE_READWRITE, 0, 0, "mapfile");
        if (mapFileHandle <= 0)
        {
            cout << "Mapping error " << GetLastError()
               << endl;
            return;
        }

        // map the view to an address
        mapView = (char *) MapViewOfFile(mapFileHandle,
            FILE_MAP_WRITE, 0, 0, 0);

        // show the file
        cout << mapView;

        // modify the file
        for (i=0; i<20; i++)
            mapView[i] = 'x';

        // clean up
        if (!UnmapViewOfFile(mapView))
            cout << "problem unmapping\n";
        CloseHandle(mapFileHandle);
        CloseHandle(fileHandle);
    }
```

Listing 2.21
Reading and writing a mapped file (Page 2 of 2)

In Listing 2.21, **mapView** is treated like an array when the program writes characters to the mapping. The changes to the mapping get flushed to disk when the program calls **UnmapViewOfFile**. Alternatively, you can force file writes with the **FlushViewOfFile** function.

FlushViewOfFile	*Flushes changes in the view to disk*

`BOOL FlushViewOfFile(`
`   LPVOID address,`
`   DWORD number)`	

address	The base address of the bytes to flush
number	The number of bytes to flush
Returns TRUE on success	

When using **FlushViewOfFile**, you generally flush the entire file. The system is smart enough to write back to disk only those memory pages that actually contain modified data.

2.12 Conclusion

This chapter presents many of the individual concepts involved in handling and manipulating files. As you can see, in Windows file access is quite interesting because of all of the different techniques available in the API: normal file I/O, overlapped I/O, compressed files, file mapping, and so on.

The **CreateFile**, **ReadFile**, and **WriteFile** concepts discussed in this chapter apply not only to files, but also to several other I/O channels. For example, these same functions appear in Chapters 7, 11 and 12.

Chapter 6 discusses synchronization and contains several sections that discuss overlapped and extended overlapped I/O in detail. Section 5.11 discusses interprocess communication, and file mapping can be a very useful technique.

Chapters 3 and 4 show you how to access disk drives and directories. These concepts are important to the discussion of files because drives and directories hold the files that you access.

See Chapter 10 for information on securing files.

DRIVES

3

One of the neat things about studying operating systems is that they are built by *people*. That may or may not continue to be true in the future. If we ever come to the point where it is not true, OSs will probably become a lot more consistent, but somewhat more boring.

Since people design and build operating systems, operating systems are by their very nature quirky. People who are involved in an operating system early in its life have quite a bit of say in how the overall system ultimately works and what it includes. Their viewpoints and prejudices tend to influence both the user and programmer environments. These originators therefore contribute to a system's quirkiness far more than the legions of programmers who come along after the OS has become a standard.

You can easily see the effect of the originators in the user interface for UNIX. The creators of UNIX favored commands that are short and rich, so UNIX has commands like "ls," which lists files. It has a short and obscure name and 20 different options. Another very good example can be found in the "vi" editor that comes with every copy of UNIX. Vi is possibly the quirkiest editor ever built, is wildly frustrating to any new user, and takes hours and hours to master. But it will exist forever because it became part of the UNIX operating system early in its life.

Windows comes with its own historical quirks, because it has a very interesting pedigree. Windows comes from Windows 3.1, which is built on top of MS-DOS, which originally borrowed almost its entire interface from a system called CP/M. It is easy to imagine that CP/M was designed pretty much completely by a guy in a garage working on an early 8-bit microprocessor. Perhaps that is a slight exaggeration, but it is probably not far from the truth. That guy has had an invisible effect on a great many things in Windows.

One of the most obvious things born of this heritage is the subject of this chapter. The way Windows handles disk drives using *drive letters* comes straight out of CP/M. Drive letters are not a bad way to handle disk drives. However, people moving over from UNIX will find the concept bothersome because the UNIX scheme is somewhat more elegant. In UNIX, every drive on a system is *mounted* into a single directory tree. You might have 10 different physical drives on your UNIX machine, along with six connected over the network, but your view of those drives in UNIX is a single, homogeneous tree.

In MS-DOS, every drive—or *volume*—has a letter. This holds mostly true in Windows, although NT does allow multiple drives to connect together in *volume sets* or *stripe sets* that let single volumes contain many separate physical drives. Nonetheless, every Windows machine has a drive letter for each floppy drive, one or more drive letters for its hard disks, separate drive letters for things such as CD-ROM and cartridge drives, and then more letters for every drive mounted from the network. This configuration is shown in Figure 3.1.

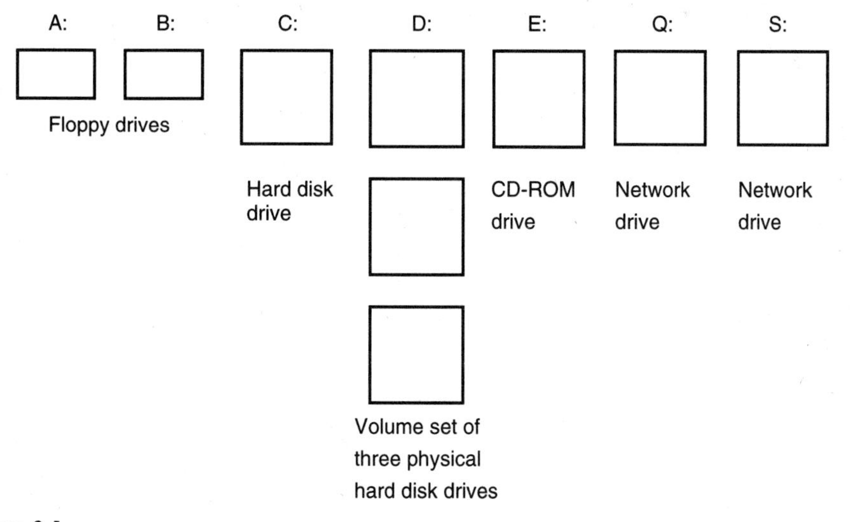

Figure 3.1
Drive letters on a typical Windows machine.

Since there are only 26 letters in the English alphabet, a machine can have at most 26 separate volumes.

The 32-bit API for Windows gives you several functions that you can use to access information about individual drives. You use these functions to find, for example, the maximum size and free space on a drive. Windows also contains a set of **WNet** functions that let you find and connect to network drives and printers shared by other machines.

Compatibility Note: All of the code in this chapter works identically in both Windows NT and Windows 95.

3.1 The Possibilities

The 32-bit API for Windows gives you several functions that you can use to access information about individual drives. You use these functions to find, for example:

- The maximum size and free space on a drive
- The type of the drive (network drive, CD-ROM drive, and so on)
- The file system used when the drive was formatted

Windows also contains a set of **WNet** functions that lets you find and connect to network drives and printers shared by other machines. With these functions you can:

- Enumerate all the domains on the network
- Enumerate all the machines in each domain
- Enumerate all the drives and printers on each machine
- Connect to any drive on the network
- Disconnect from any drive

All the connection options seen by a user in the File Manager are implemented using the **WNet** functions.

3.2 Getting Volume Information

You can obtain information about any volume available locally on your machine or mounted over the network using the **GetVolumeInformation** function. Listing 3.1 demonstrates this function.

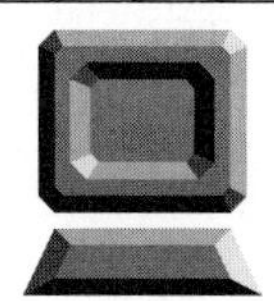

```
// drvgvi.cpp

#include <windows.h>
#include <iostream.h>

void main()
{
   BOOL success;
   char volumeName[MAX_PATH];
   DWORD volumeSerialNumber;
   DWORD maxNameLength;
   DWORD fileSystemFlags;
   char systemName[MAX_PATH];

   // get the volume information for drive C
   success = GetVolumeInformation("c:\\",
      volumeName, MAX_PATH,
      &volumeSerialNumber,
      &maxNameLength,
      &fileSystemFlags,
      systemName, MAX_PATH);

   // output information
   cout << "Volume name: " << volumeName << endl;
   cout << "Volume serial number: "
      << volumeSerialNumber << endl;

   cout << "File system type: " << systemName
      << endl;
   cout << "Maximum file name length:"
```

Listing 3.1
Results of the **GetVolumeInformation** function (Page 1 of 2)

```
           << maxNameLength << endl;

        cout << "File system characteristics: \n";
        if (fileSystemFlags & FS_CASE_IS_PRESERVED)
           cout << "    Case is preserved\n";
        else
           cout << "    Case is not preserved\n";

        if (fileSystemFlags & FS_CASE_SENSITIVE)
           cout << "    Case sensitive\n";
        else
           cout << "    Not case sensitive\n";

        if (fileSystemFlags & FS_UNICODE_STORED_ON_DISK)
           cout << "    Unicode stored\n";
        else
           cout << "    Unicode not stored\n";
     }
```

Listing 3.1
Results of the **GetVolumeInformation** function (Page 2 of 2)

GetVolumeInformation *Returns information about a drive*

```
BOOL GetVolumeInformation(
   LPTSTR rootName,
   LPTSTR volumeName,
   DWORD volumeNameSize,
   LPDWORD volumeSerialNumber,
   LPDWORD maximumNameLength,
   LPDWORD fileSystemFlags,
   LPTSTR fileSystemName,
   DWORD fileSystemNameSize)
```

rootName	The name of the logical drive

volumeName	The name of the volume
volumeNameSize	Size of the volume name
volumeSerialNumber	Volume serial number
maxNameLength	Maximum length of any file name
fileSystemFlags	Information flags for the file system
fileSystemName	Name of the file system (FAT, NTFS, and so on)
fileSystemNameSize	Size of the file system name
Returns TRUE on success	

As you can see in Listing 3.1, the **GetVolumeInformation** function returns the volume name and serial number, along with the type of file system used on the volume (FAT, NTFS, HPFS, or other) and the length of the maximum file name for the file system in use on that volume. The function also returns a flag word that gives you characteristics of the file system such as case sensitivity. The following flags are defined:

FS_CASE_IS_PRESERVED	The file system saves the case of characters when it stores file names on the disk
FS_CASE_SENSITIVE	The file system distinguishes upper- and lowercase characters in file names
FS_UNICODE_STORED_ON_DISK	File names support unicode

3.3 Getting Drive Types

You can use the **GetDriveType** function to determine the type of any drive connected to your system. Listing 3.2 shows you how to use this function.

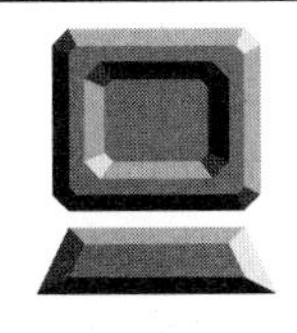

```
// drvtype.cpp
```

Listing 3.2
Checking the drive type with the **GetDriveType** function (Page 1 of 2)

```
#include <windows.h>
#include <iostream.h>

void main()
{
   UINT driveType;

   // Get the drive type for drive C
   driveType = GetDriveType("c:\\");
   switch (driveType)
   {
      case 0:
         cout << "error\n";
         break;
      case 1:
         cout << "Drive does not exist\n";
         break;
      case DRIVE_REMOVABLE:
         cout << "Media removable\n";
         break;
      case DRIVE_FIXED:
         cout << "Fixed disk\n";
         break;
      case DRIVE_REMOTE:
         cout << "Network drive\n";
         break;
      case DRIVE_CDROM:
         cout << "CD-ROM drive\n";
         break;
      case DRIVE_RAMDISK:
         cout << "RAM disk\n";
         break;
   }
   cout << endl;
```

Listing 3.2
Checking the drive type with the **GetDriveType** function (Page 2 of 2)

GetDriveType	*Returns information about a type of drive*
`UINT GetDriveType(` `   LPTSTR rootName)`	
rootName	The name of the logical drive
Returns a bit mask that should be compared against the DRIVE_ constants	

The **GetDriveType** function accepts a string that represents the logical drive. In Listing 3.2, drive C has been requested. The function returns an integer that can be matched against a set of predefined constants, as shown in the code and described next:

0	Unknown drive type
1	No root directory found on the drive
DRIVE_REMOVABLE	Disks can be removed from the drive, as in a floppy disk or cartridge disk
DRIVE_FIXED	Disk is permanently fixed in the drive
DRIVE_REMOTE	The drive is mounted over the network
DRIVE_CDROM	The drive is for CD-ROMs
DRIVE_RAMDISK	The drive is a RAM disk

3.4 Getting Free Space

You can find out the maximum size of any drive, along with its available free space, using the **GetDiskFreeSpace** function. Listing 3.3 demonstrates the use of this function.

```
// drvsize.cpp

#include <windows.h>
#include <iostream.h>

void main()
{
   BOOL success;
   unsigned long sectorsPerCluster, bytesPerSector,
      freeClusters, clusters;

   // Get disk space for drive C
   success = GetDiskFreeSpace( "c:\\",
      &sectorsPerCluster,
      &bytesPerSector, &freeClusters, &clusters);
   if (!success)
   {
      cout << "Error number: " << GetLastError()
         << endl;
      return;
   }

   // Output full disk size and free space
   cout << "Disk size: " << sectorsPerCluster *
      bytesPerSector * clusters << endl;
   cout << "Free space: " << sectorsPerCluster *
      bytesPerSector * freeClusters << endl;
   cout << endl;
}
```

Listing 3.3
Getting the size and free space on a disk

GetDiskFreeSpace	*Returns information about the size of a drive and its free space*

```
BOOL GetDiskFreeSpace(
    LPTSTR rootName,
    LPDWORD sectorsPerCluster,
    LPDWORD bytesPerSector,
    LPDWORD freeClusters,
    LPDWORD clusters)
```

rootName	The name of the logical drive
sectorsPerCluster	The number of sectors in each cluster
bytesPerSector	The number of bytes per sector
freeClusters	The number of unused clusters on the drive
clusters	The number of clusters per drive

Returns a Boolean indicating success

The **GetDiskFreeSpace** function returns information about the number of *clusters* or *free clusters* on a disk. Clusters are sets of sectors grouped together as a logical unit. The function also returns the number of sectors per cluster and the number of bytes per sector. Using this information, you can calculate the size of the drive and the amount of free space that it has available.

There are two ways that you might use this information. The most obvious use is to detect how much free space is available on a drive before writing a file to it. For example, if you know you are about to write 6 megabytes of information to a drive, you might check first and make sure that amount of space is available. This still is no guarantee: In a multi-tasking system two processes can write to the disk at the same time, so the disk space may get consumed by other processes before you completely write the file. However, if you check and see that only 12K of space is available, you can warn the user. The second way to use the information is to check for cluster size. No file can be smaller than the size of one cluster, so if the cluster size is very large on a drive, you might want to take some step to avoid writing a large number of very small files.

Note that the product of the sector size, the number of sectors per cluster, and the number of clusters can potentially overflow a 32-bit integer when the NT file system is in use. When checking the disk size, you may want to consider looking only at the free cluster number. The number of free clusters will certainly fall well below 4 billion for the foreseeable future. Alternatively, use Microsoft's 64-bit math library found in `largeint.h`.

3.5 Getting Logical Drives and Drive Strings

You can query Windows for the drive letters that are currently in use. Windows returns that information to you either as a bit array or as a set of strings. Listings 3.4 and 3.5 demonstrate the two functions that return this information.

```
// drvgld.cpp

#include <windows.h>
#include <iostream.h>

void main()
{
   DWORD drives;
   int x;

   drives = GetLogicalDrives();
   cout << "Logical drives on this machine: ";
   for (x=0; x<26; x++)
   {
      if (drives & 1!=0)
         cout << (char) ('A'+x) << ' ';
```

Listing 3.4
Getting the logical drives with **GetLogicalDrives** (Page 1 of 2)

```
            drives = drives >> 1;
        }
        cout << endl;
    }
```

Listing 3.4
Getting the logical drives with **GetLogicalDrives** (Page 2 of 2)

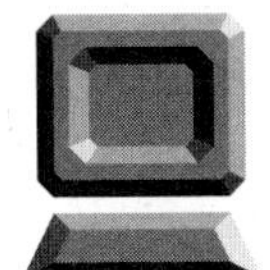

```
// drvglds.cpp

#include <windows.h>
#include <iostream.h>

void main()
{
    DWORD len;
    char buffer[1000];
    char *p;

    len = GetLogicalDriveStrings(1000, buffer);
    cout << "Logical drives on this machine: \n";
    for (p=buffer; *p != '\0'; p++)
    {
        cout << p << endl;
        while (*p != '\0') p++;
    }
}
```

Listing 3.5
Getting logical drive strings with **GetLogicalDriveStrings**

GetLogicalDrives	*Returns a bit array containing drives in use*
`DWORD GetLogicalDrives(void)`	
Returns a 32-bit bit string	

GetLogicalDriveStrings	*Returns all the logical drive strings in use*

`DWORD GetLogicalDriveStrings(`
`DWORD bufferSize,`
`LPTSTR buffer)`	

bufferSize	The size of the buffer
buffer	Buffer to hold the strings
Returns 0 on error or the length of the string in bytes	

In Listing 3.4, the **GetLogicalDrives** function returns a 32-bit value that contains 1 bit for each drive letter currently in use. Bit 0 represents drive A. The code looks at each bit up through bit 25 and prints out the corresponding drive letter for each bit that contains a 1.

In Listing 3.5, the **GetLogicalDriveStrings** function returns a set of strings, one for each drive letter currently in use. The strings are embedded in a single character array with NULL characters between them. Two NULL characters follow the final string to mark the end of the set. The program simply prints all these strings to stdout.

If the return value from **GetLogicalDriveStrings** is 0, it indicates failure, and you should use **GetLastError** to determine the problem. If the return value is greater than the size of the buffer, you should resize your buffer and call **GetLogicalDriveStrings** again.

3.6 Setting the Volume Label

You can change the label on a volume, provided your account has sufficient privilege to do so, using the **SetVolumeLabel** function as shown in Listing 3.6.

```
// drvsvl.cpp

#include <windows.h>
#include <iostream.h>

void main()
{
   BOOL success;
   char volumeName[MAX_PATH];

   cout << "Enter new volume label for drive C: ";
   cin >> volumeName;

   success = SetVolumeLabel("c:\\", volumeName);
   if (success)
      cout << "success\n";
   else
      cout << "Error code: " << GetLastError()
         << endl;
}
```

Listing 3.6
Setting the volume label

SetVolumeLabel	*Changes the label on a volume*

`BOOL SetVolumeLabel(`
`   LPTSTR rootName,`
`   LPTSTR volumeName)`	

rootName	The name of the logical drive

volumeName	New name for the volume
Returns TRUE on success	

The volume name is typically first set when the administrator or user formats the drive. For example, if you format a new floppy disk with the File Manager, you can set its volume label there. You can also change a volume label from the File Manager or with the `label` command from the command line. The **SetVolumeLabel** function simply provides a programmatic mechanism for doing the same thing. If the function does not succeed, **GetLastError** contains the appropriate error code.

3.7 WNet Functions

Windows is designed to work with networks. When several Windows machines exist on a net, they can easily share disk drives and printers with one another. Both the File Manager and the Print Manager provide easy ways for users to connect to these shared devices. The 32-bit API also gives you mechanisms to connect to these devices from within your applications.

Windows sees the network as a tree. Any Windows network is divided into a series of *domains*, each of which contains a set of machines. Each machine can share zero or more drives, directories, or printers on the network. This arrangement is shown in Figure 3.2.

The 32-bit API contains a set of functions that allows you to enumerate all the shared drives available throughout the network and then connect to any one of these drives. The network itself, its domains, and the machines in the domains are called *containers*. You open containers with the **WNetOpenEnum** function. A container can contain other containers (for example, domains contain machines), or it can contain actual drive and printer resources, called *objects*. You *enumerate* all the items in a container—that is, you request a list of everything that a container holds—using the **WNetEnumResources** function. Once you get down to the drive level, you can connect to a drive with the **WNetAddConnection2** function.

This section shows you how to walk through the resource tree and also how to gather information about connected resources.

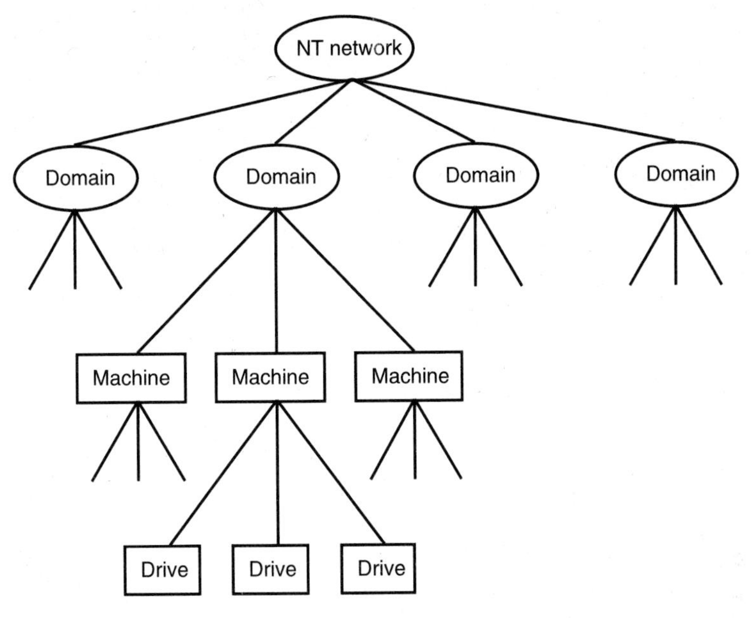

Figure 3.2
A typical Windows network.

3.7.1 Enumerating Drives

The code shown in Listing 3.7 demonstrates how to recursively walk through all the resources available on your network. It starts with the network itself and opens every container it finds until it reaches actual drives and printers that each machine shares on the network. It is these drive and printer objects that receive connections, as demonstrated in Section 3.7.2.

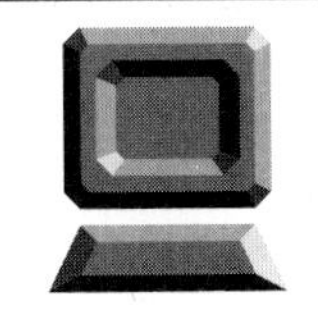

```
// drvenum.cpp

#include <windows.h>
#include <iostream.h>
```

Listing 3.7
Enumerating all shared resources on a network (Page 1 of 6)

```
///////////////////
// Needs mpr.lib
///////////////////

// This function handles WNet errors
void ErrorHandler(DWORD errorNum, char *s)
{
   DWORD result, error;
   char errorString[1000];
   char name[1000];

   if (errorNum != ERROR_EXTENDED_ERROR)
      cout << "Error number " << errorNum
         << " returned by " << s << endl;
   // If its an extended error, get the error.
   else
   {
      result = WNetGetLastError(&error,
         errorString, 1000, name, 1000);
      if (result != NO_ERROR)
         cout << "Failure in WNetGetLastError: "
            << result << endl;
      else
         cout << "Extended Error: " << errorString
            << ". Provider: " << name << endl;
   }
}

// This function displays the information in
// a NETRESOURCE structure
void DisplayStruct(NETRESOURCE l)
{
   cout << "Type: ";
   switch (l.dwType)
```

Listing 3.7
Enumerating all shared resources on a network (Page 2 of 6)

```
        {
            case RESOURCETYPE_DISK:
                cout << "disk\n";
                break;
            case RESOURCETYPE_PRINT:
                cout << "Printer\n";
                break;
        };

        cout << "Display type: ";
        switch (l.dwDisplayType)
        {
            case RESOURCEDISPLAYTYPE_DOMAIN:
                cout << "domain\n";
                break;
            case RESOURCEDISPLAYTYPE_GENERIC:
                cout << "generic\n";
                break;
            case RESOURCEDISPLAYTYPE_SERVER:
                cout << "server\n";
                break;
            case RESOURCEDISPLAYTYPE_SHARE:
                cout << "share\n";
                break;
        };

        if (l.lpLocalName)
            cout << "Local name: " << l.lpLocalName
                << endl;
        if (l.lpRemoteName)
            cout << "Remote name: " << l.lpRemoteName
                << endl;
        if (l.lpComment)
            cout << "Comment; " << l.lpComment << endl;
        if (l.lpProvider)
```

Listing 3.7
Enumerating all shared resources on a network (Page 3 of 6)

```
         cout << "Provider: " << l.lpProvider << endl;
      cout << endl;
   }

   // Recursive function to enumerate resources
   BOOL EnumerateResources(
      LPNETRESOURCE startingPoint)
   {
      DWORD result, resultEnum;
      HANDLE enumHandle;
      LPNETRESOURCE buffer;
      DWORD bufferSize = 16384;
      DWORD numEntries = 0xFFFFFFFF;
      DWORD i;

      // Open a container
      result = WNetOpenEnum(RESOURCE_GLOBALNET,
         RESOURCETYPE_ANY, 0, startingPoint,
         &enumHandle);

      if (result != NO_ERROR)
      {
         ErrorHandler( result, "WNetOpenEnum");
         return FALSE;
      }

      // allocate a buffer to hold resources
      buffer = (LPNETRESOURCE) GlobalAlloc(GPTR,
         bufferSize);

      // Loop through all the elements in the
      // container
      do
      {
         // reset bufferSize each time thru loop
```

Listing 3.7
Enumerating all shared resources on a network (Page 4 of 6)

```
         bufferSize = 16384;
         numEntries = 0xFFFFFFFF;

         // Get resources
         resultEnum = WNetEnumResource(enumHandle,
            &numEntries, buffer, &bufferSize);
         if (resultEnum == NO_ERROR)
         {
            // Loop through all entries
            for(i = 0; i < numEntries; i++)
            {
               DisplayStruct( buffer[i]);
               // if the entry is a container,
               // recursively open it
               if (buffer[i].dwUsage &
                  RESOURCEUSAGE_CONTAINER)
               {
                  if (!EnumerateResources(&buffer[i]))
                     cout << "Enumeration failed."
                        << endl;
               }
               // else add a connection.
               // See Section 3.7.2
            }
         }
         else if (resultEnum != ERROR_NO_MORE_ITEMS)
         {
            ErrorHandler(resultEnum,
               "WNetEnumResource");
            break;
         }
      }
      while(resultEnum != ERROR_NO_MORE_ITEMS);

      // Clean up
```

Listing 3.7
Enumerating all shared resources on a network (Page 5 of 6)

```
        GlobalFree((HGLOBAL) buffer);
        result = WNetCloseEnum(enumHandle);
        if (result != NO_ERROR)
        {
            ErrorHandler(result, "WNetCloseEnum");
            return FALSE;
        }
        return TRUE;
    }

    void main()
    {
        // Start the recursion at the net level
        EnumerateResources(NULL);
    }
```

Listing 3.7
Enumerating all shared resources on a network (Page 6 of 6)

The program in Listing 3.7 starts in its **main** function with a single call to the **EnumerateResources** function, which recursively traverses a container. Since this initial call passes a NULL parameter, the function will begin at the level of the network itself. Inside the **EnumerateResources** function, the program immediately calls **WNetOpenEnum**.

WNetOpenEnum *Opens a container*

```
DWORD WNetOpenEnum(
    DWORD scope,
    DWORD type,
    DWORD usage,
    LPNETRESOURCE resource,
    LPHANDLE enumHandle)
```

scope	Scope of the search
type	Type of items to enumerate

usage	Type of objects to open
resource	Specifies container to open. NULL for network
enumHandle	Returned handle to the opened container
Returns NO_ERROR on success or an error code	

The **WNetOpenEnum** function opens a container, returning a handle to that container so that you can enumerate its contents. The **resource** parameter specifies the container that you want to open. The **scope**, **type**, and **usage** parameters specify the type of objects that will be enumerated by the **WNetEnumResources** function.

Initially, the **WNetOpenEnum** function receives NULL for its **resource** parameter, indicating that it should start at the top level of the network tree (see Figure 3.2) and open up the network container itself. Once the container is open, Listing 3.7 enters a loop that calls **WNetEnumResources** to get all the objects inside the container.

WNetEnumResources — *Enumerates resources in an open container*

```
DWORD WNetEnumResource(
    HANDLE enumHandle,
    LPDWORD numEntries,
    LPVOID buffer,
    LPDWORD bufferSize)
```

enumHandle	Handle to an open container
numEntries	Number of entries desired/returned
buffer	Buffer to hold returned entries
bufferSize	Original/returned size of buffer
Returns NO_ERROR or ERROR_NO_MORE_ITEMS on success or an error code	

The **WNetEnumResources** function accepts the handle returned by **WNetOpenEnum**, the number of entries desired (or 0xFFFFFFFF if you want them all), a buffer to place the entries into (allocated by **GlobalAlloc**; see Chapter 15 for details), and the size of the buffer (the documentation specifies that 16K is a reasonable value). In the buffer the function returns an array of NETRESOURCE structures that contains information about each entry in the container.

```
typedef struct _NETRESOURCE {
    DWORD   dwScope;
    DWORD   dwType;
    DWORD   dwDisplayType;
    DWORD   dwUsage;
    LPTSTR lpLocalName;
    LPTSTR lpRemoteName;
    LPTSTR lpComment;
    LPTSTR lpProvider;
} NETRESOURCE;
```

Much useful information is contained in a NETRESOURCE structure. The **DisplayStruct** function near the top of Listing 3.7 displays most of this information. The **Scope** field tells the status of an enumeration:

RESOURCE_CONNECTED	The device is already connected
RESOURCE_GLOBALNET	The enumeration is not connected
RESOURCE_REMEMBERED	There is a persistent connection to the device

If connected or remembered, the enumeration must be a device, either a printer or a drive, and the **LocalName** field contains the local name of the device. An enumeration marked as USAGE_GLOBALNET gives more information about itself in the **Usage** field, which can have one of the following values:

RESOURCEUSAGE_CONNECTABLE	The enumeration is a connectable device
RESOURCEUSAGE_CONTAINER	The enumeration is a container (a domain or a machine)

In either case, the **RemoteName** field contains the name used to connect to or open the enumeration. The **Type** field tells whether a connectable object is a disk or a printer:

RESOURCETYPE_ANY
RESOURCETYPE_DISK
RESOURCETYPE_PRINT

The **DisplayType** field tells how to display the object. This field is used in Windows's connection dialogs to determine the icon placed next to each item:

RESOURCEDISPLAYTYPE_DOMAIN
RESOURCEDISPLAYTYPE_GENERIC
RESOURCEDISPLAYTYPE_SERVER
RESOURCEDISPLAYTYPE_SHARE

The NETRESOURCE structure also contains the comment and the name of the provider.

Following the call to **WNetEnumResources,** Listing 3.7 loops through all the NETRESOURCE structures in the buffer. First it displays each record's contents. Then it inspects each record to decide whether or not it is a container. If it is a container, the **EnumerateResources** function recursively calls itself so that it can open and display the container. If it is not a container, it is a drive or a printer and a connection can be formed to it. See Section 3.7.2 for details on adding connections. Once the code has examined all the entries in **buffer**, it cleans up and returns.

The first time that you call **WNetEnumResources** for any container it should return the error code NO_ERROR, as well as a buffer full of entries. However, there is no guarantee that the function was able to place all the entries for a given container into the buffer on the first call. Therefore, you should call it repeatedly until it returns ERROR_NO_MORE_ITEMS. This is the reason for the **do...while** loop in the code.

If something goes wrong, the **ErrorHandler** function seen in Listing 3.7 handles any **WNet** error. In cases where the network provider reports an error, the **ErrorHandler** function makes use of the special **WNetGetLastError** function, which returns extended error information.

WNetGetLastError	*Explains extended **WNet** errors*
`DWORD WNetGetLastError( LPDWORD errorCode, LPTSTR description, DWORD descriptionSize, LPTSTR name, DWORD nameSize)`	
errorCode	The error code returned by the provider
description	The provider's description of the error
descriptionSize	Buffer size for description
name	The name of the provider
nameSize	The size of the name buffer
Returns NO_ERROR on success or ERROR_INVALID_ADDRESS if the buffer address is invalid	

The **WNetGetLastError** function talks to the provider and retrieves an error code, an error string describing the problem, and the name of the provider.

3.7.2 Adding and Canceling Connections

In Listing 3.7, the code enumerates all the containers and objects found on the network, but does not really do anything with them except dump the information to stdout. If you look in the **EnumerateResources** function of Listing 3.7, however, it contains a comment that says "else add a connection." At this point in the program, the code has found a connectable object. You can call the function shown in Listing 3.8 to form a connection using the following call:

```
AddConnection(&buffer[i]);
```

This line passes a single NETRESOURCE structure to the function that forms the connection.

```
// drvcpmm.cpp
void AddConnection(LPNETRESOURCE nr)
{
   char localName[100];
   char s[100];
   DWORD result;

   cout << "Do you want to add a connection? ";
   cin.getline(s,100);
   if (s[0]!='y' && s[0]!='Y')
      return;
   cout << "Enter local name (eg 'f:'): ";
   cin.getline(localName, 100);
   nr->lpLocalName = localName;

   result = WNetAddConnection2(nr, 0, 0, 0);
   if (result != NO_ERROR)
      ErrorHandler(result, "WNetAddConnection2");
   else
      cout << "Success.\n";
   cout << endl;
}
```

Listing 3.8
Adding a connection to a drive or printer

The **AddConnection** function asks the user if it should form a connection. It then asks for the local name for the resource and adds this name to the NETRESOURCE structure. It then forms the connection using the **WNetAddConnection2** function.

WNetAddConnection2	*Adds a connection to a shared resource*

```
DWORD WNetAddConnection2(
    LPNETRESOURCE netResource,
    LPTSTR password,
    LPTSTR userName,
    DWORD connection)
```

netResource	NETRESOURCE structure holding connection info
password	Password string
userName	User name
connection	Flag controlling persistence of the connection

Returns NO_ERROR on success

Once you insert the local name into it, the NETRESOURCE structure contains all the information needed to form the connection. It lacks the name of the user and the password required for certain network objects shared by systems such as Windows for Workgroups or Netware. In the example code these values are set to NULL and this will work properly on homogeneous Windows networks. You will need to query the user for these fields on networks that require this information.

Modify Listing 3.7 so that it contains Listing 3.8 and run the program. Use the program to connect to a drive on the network. Once you connect to a drive, start up the File Manager (if it is already started, quit it and start again). The new connection will appear just like any other. You can cancel connections just as easily with the **WNetCancelConnection2** function.

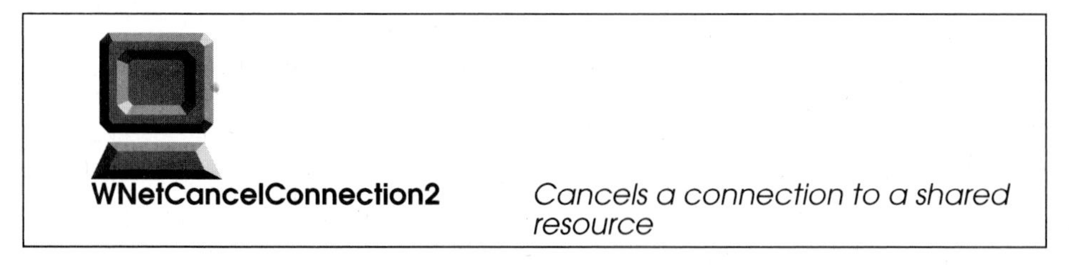

```
DWORD WNetCancelConnection2(
   LPTSTR name,
   DWORD flag,
   BOOL force)
```

name	Name of the resource (for example, "s:")
flag	Flag controlling persistence
force	Flag that forces disconnection
Returns NO_ERROR on success	

For example, if you pass the function a drive letter in the form "s:", the function will eliminate the connection "s" holds and free up the drive letter for another connection.

3.7.3 Getting Connection Names

You can learn the remote name of any connected resource using the **WNetGetConnection** function shown in Listing 3.9.

```
// drvgc.cpp

#include <windows.h>
#include <iostream.h>

void main()
{
   DWORD result;
   char name[256];
   DWORD bufferSize = 256;

   result = WNetGetConnection("s:", name,
```

Listing 3.9
Getting a connection's name with **WNetGetConnection** (Page 1 of 2)

```
            &bufferSize);
        if (result == NO_ERROR)
            cout << name << endl;
        else
            cout << "Error: " << result;
    }
```

Listing 3.9
Getting a connection's name with **WNetGetConnection** (Page 2 of 2)

WNetGetConnection	*Get the remote name for a local connection*

`DWORD WNetGetConnection(`
`    LPTSTR localName,`
`    LPTSTR remoteName,`
`    LPDWORD bufferSize)`	

localName	Name of the resource (for example, "s:")
remoteName	Buffer to hold the remote name
bufferSize	The size of the remoteName buffer
Returns NO_ERROR on success	

The **WNetGetConnection** function accepts the name of the local resource and a buffer to hold the remote name. It returns the remote name in the buffer. If it is unsuccessful, errors come back through the return value or **GetLastError**.

3.7.4 Getting User Names

You can retrieve the current user's name or the name used to connect to any network resource using the **WNetGetUser** function as shown in Listing 3.10.

```
// drvgetu.cpp

#include <windows.h>
#include <iostream.h>

void main()
{
   DWORD result;
   char name[256];
   DWORD bufferSize = 256;

   result = WNetGetUser(0, name, &bufferSize);
   if (result == NO_ERROR)
      cout << name << endl;
   else
      cout << "Error: " << result;
}
```

Listing 3.10
Using the **WNetGetUser** function to get the name of the current user. If you replace the 0 in the first parameter with a string like the one shown in Listing 3.9, it will return the name used to connect to that resource

WNetGetUser *Get the name of the current user or a resource's owner*

```
DWORD WNetGetUser(
LPTSTR localName,
LPTSTR userName,
LPDWORD bufferSize)
```

localName	Name of the resource (for example, "s:") or NULL for user
userName	Buffer to hold the user name
bufferSize	The size of the userName buffer
Returns NO_ERROR on success	

If you pass zero or NULL in for the **localName** parameter, the function returns the name of the current user. If you pass in a device name, the function returns the name used to attach to the device when **WNetAddConnection2** was called. The function returns an error code, or you can retrieve the error code with **GetLastError**.

3.8 Conclusion

There are many different and interesting ways to use the **WNet** functions described in this chapter. For example, you might want to make a tape backup program that scours the entire network and attaches to every shared drive it can find. Or you might want to create a Find program that searches every directory on every drive on every machine on the network. You might also want to create specialized applications that connect to specific drives during a run and then disconnect from them automatically to prevent users from accessing the drives randomly. You can create any of these capabilities using the functions described in this chapter.

4 DIRECTORIES

Every modern operating system currently in existence uses *hierarchical*, or *tree-structured*, directories to store its files. In Windows, these directory trees cap off the network-wide tree of domains and machines seen in Section 3.7. The functions used to traverse directory trees bear no resemblance to the network-walking functions seen previously however.

A directory tree in Windows starts with its root at a drive letter, for example `C:\`. This means that a Windows machine has multiple root directories, one for each drive letter. Each drive (or partition) potentially has a different file system, so individual directory trees can have slightly different characteristics. For example, the old FAT file system has much smaller file names than the NT file system, and a FAT partition has a much smaller potential size than an NTFS partition. None of the three file systems native to NT (FAT, NTFS, or HPFS) allow symbolic links, but other file systems may support this capability in the future. You can learn the characteristics for a given directory tree by using the drive information functions presented at the beginning of Chapter 3.

In all file systems, a directory can hold zero or more entries. The entries can be either files, or other directories, as shown in Figure 4.1. Because of this tree-like structure, functions that walk directory trees tend to be recursive.

Compatibility Note: All of the code in this chapter works identically in both Windows NT and Windows 95.

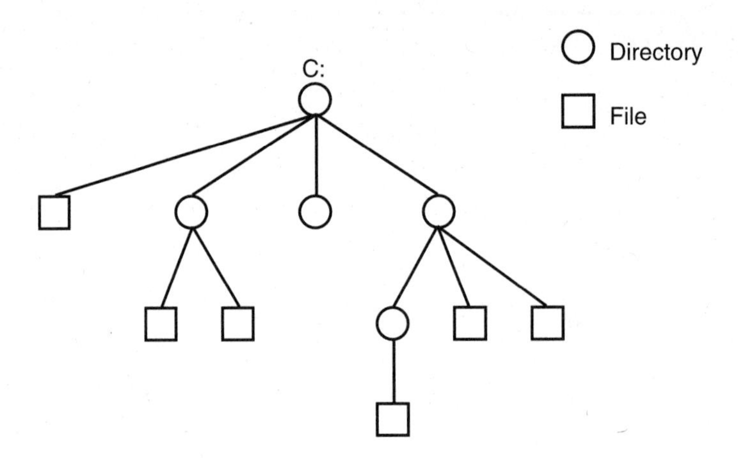

Figure 4.1
Directory trees in a Windows machine.

4.1 The Possibilities

This chapter discusses the routines available in the API to manipulate directories, and then turns to the directory-walking functions. You will learn how to:

- Create and delete directories
- Set the current directory or find out the current directory
- Search a directory for a file
- Recursively traverse all of the directories on a drive
- Asynchronously detect changes to files and directories. For example, if you are writing a text editor application, you can make the program detect when some other process has modified a file that the editor is currently editing, and warn the user of the change

The asynchronous detection functions in particular are quite unique and you will find many interesting ways to use them in applications.

4.2 Creating and Deleting Directories

Typically a user creates a directory either with the File Manager or with the `mkdir` command. There are many reasons why you might need to do the same thing inside of an application. For example, if you are writing an application that installs another application or a set of data files, you will need to create directories to hold the files that you are installing.

Listing 4.1 uses the **CreateDirectory** function to create a new directory.

```
// dircreat.cpp

#include <windows.h>
#include <iostream.h>

void main()
{
   char s[MAX_PATH];
   BOOL success;

   // get name of directory
   cout << "Enter path/name of new directory: ";
   cin >> s;

   success = CreateDirectory(s, 0);
   if (!success)
      cout << "Error code = " << GetLastError()
         << endl;
   else
      cout << "success.\n";
}
```

Listing 4.1
Creating a new directory

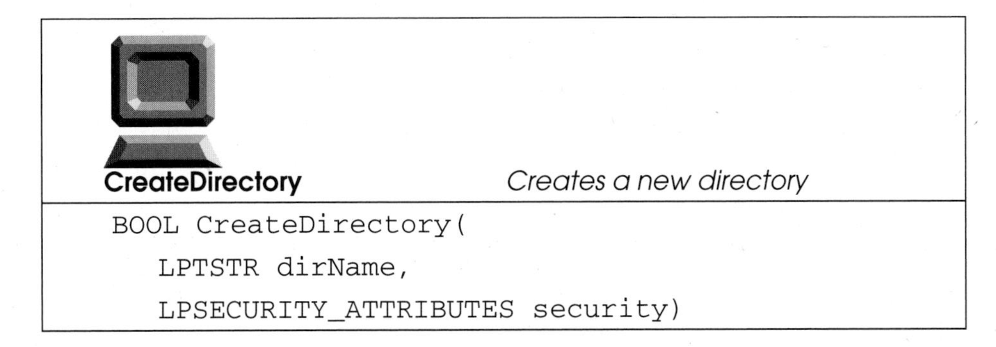

CreateDirectory *Creates a new directory*

```
BOOL CreateDirectory(
   LPTSTR dirName,
   LPSECURITY_ATTRIBUTES security)
```

dirName	Name/path of the directory to create
security	Security attributes. See Chapter 10
Returns TRUE on success	

The **dirName** parameter accepts either a name, or a path. If it receives just a name, it forms the new directory as a child of the current directory. If it receives a path (e.g. "C:\dos\temp\new"), it traverses the path ("c:\dos\temp") and creates the new directory ("new") there. If the path is invalid, it fails. The **GetLastError** function contains a detailed error code following any failure.

It is just as easy to delete a directory using the **RemoveDirectory** function as shown in Listing 4.2.

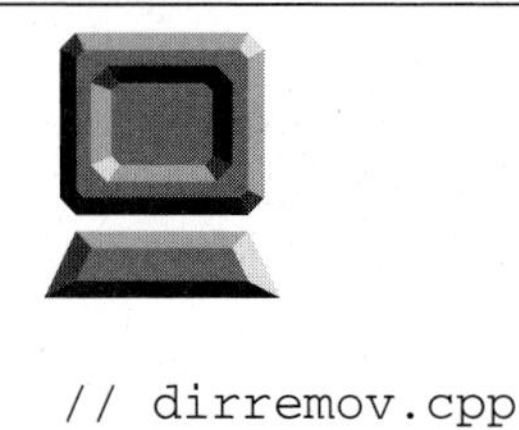

```
// dirremov.cpp

#include <windows.h>
#include <iostream.h>

void main()
{
   char s[MAX_PATH];
   BOOL success;

   // get name of directory
   cout << "Enter name of directory to remove: ";
   cin >> s;

   success = RemoveDirectory(s);
   if (!success)
      cout << "Error code = " << GetLastError()
         << endl;
```

Listing 4.2
Removing a directory (Page 1 of 2)

```
        else
            cout << "success.\n";
    }
```

Listing 4.2
Removing a directory (Page 2 of 2)

RemoveDirectory	*Removes an empty directory*
`BOOL RemoveDirectory(` `   LPTSTR dirName)`	
dirName	Name/path of the directory to remove
Returns TRUE on success	

The **RemoveDirectory** function can remove a directory only if it is empty. It accepts the same name and/or path information described for **CreateDirectory** above.

4.3 Getting and Setting the Current Directory

It is easy to get and set an application's current directory using the **GetCurrentDirectory** and **SetCurrentDirectory** functions, as demonstrated in Listing 4.3.

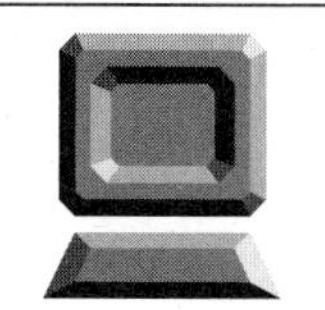

```
// dirget.cpp

#include <windows.h>
#include <iostream.h>
```

Listing 4.3
Getting and setting the current directory (Page 1 of 2)

```
void main()
{
   char s[MAX_PATH];
   char buffer[MAX_PATH];
   DWORD len;
   BOOL success;

   // print current directory
   len = GetCurrentDirectory(MAX_PATH, buffer);
   if (len == 0)
      cout << "Get error: " << GetLastError()
         << endl;
   else
      cout << "Current Directory = " << buffer
         << endl;

   // get name of new directory
   cout << "Enter path/name of directory to set: ";
   cin >> s;

   // change directory
   success = SetCurrentDirectory(s);
   if (!success)
      cout << "Set error: " << GetLastError()
         << endl;

   // print current directory
   len = GetCurrentDirectory(MAX_PATH, buffer);
   if (len == 0)
      cout << "Get error: " << GetLastError()
         << endl;
   else
      cout << "Current Directory = " << buffer
         << endl;
}
```

Listing 4.3
Getting and setting the current directory (Page 2 of 2)

Listing 4.3 starts by retrieving the current directory and printing it to stdout. It then requests a new directory name from the user and sets the current directory appropriately. It retrieves the current directory again to show that it has been set successfully. Note that changing the directory applies only to the application's perspective of things—the user's current directory in the command shell will not change.

GetCurrentDirectory	*Retrieves the current directory name*
`DWORD GetCurrentDirectory(`	
`DWORD bufferSize`	
`LPTSTR buffer`	
bufferSize	Size of the buffer
buffer	Buffer to hold the current directory string
Returns the number of characters in the buffer or 0 on error	

SetCurrentDirectory	*Sets the current directory*
`BOOL SetCurrentDirectory(`	
`LPTSTR newDir`	
newDir	String containing the new directory path
Returns TRUE on success	

If either of these functions detects an error, **GetLastError** contains the error value.

4.4 Searching for a File

The **SearchPath** function searches for a file either in the system path, or in an arbitrary directory or directory tree. Its use is demonstrated in Listing 4.4.

```
// dirsrch.cpp

#include <windows.h>
#include <iostream.h>

void main()
{
   char name[MAX_PATH];
   char pathName[MAX_PATH];
   char *pathPointer;
   char *p;
   char buffer[MAX_PATH];
   DWORD len;

   // get name of file
   cout << "Enter the name of the file to find: ";
   cin >> name;

   // get name of directory to start search
   cout << "Enter path to start search, or PATH: ";
   cin >> pathName;

   // Search named path, or system path
   if (strcmp(pathName, "PATH") == 0)
      pathPointer = NULL;
   else
      pathPointer = pathName;

   // do the search. It may take a while
   len = SearchPath(pathPointer, name, 0,
      MAX_PATH, buffer, &p);
   cout << "The search may take awhile...\n";

   if (len == 0)
```

Listing 4.4
Using the **SearchPath** function (Page 1 of 2)

```
            cout << "Not found: " << GetLastError()
               << endl;
         else
            cout << "Found in " << buffer << endl;
      }
```

Listing 4.4
Using the **SearchPath** function (Page 2 of 2)

The program in Listing 4.4 starts by asking for the name of the file to find. This file name must be specific—it cannot contain wild card characters. The program then asks for the directory in which to start the search. If you type "PATH" here, the program understands that to mean that you want to search the system path. It places the value NULL in the **pathPointer** parameter, which tells the **SearchPath** function to search a specific set of directories in the order given below:

1. The directory containing the application's executable
2. The current directory
3. The Windows system directory
4. The Windows main directory
5. Any directories contained in the PATH environment variable

The function stops on the first match and returns the path to the file if it finds it. If it does not find it, it returns an error code.

SearchPath *Searches for the specified file*

```
DWORD SearchPath(
   LPCTSTR path,
   LPCTSTR fileName,
   LPCTSTR fileExtension,
   DWORD bufferSize,
   LPTSTR buffer,
   LPTSTR *filePart)
```

path	NULL for system path, or a string indicating the starting directory for the search
fileName	Name of file to find
fileExtension	File extension appended if fileName has none
bufferSize	Size of the buffer
buffer	Buffer for path of found file
filePart	Pointer to start of filename in buffer
Returns the length of the path found, or 0 on error.	

The **SearchPath** function accepts in its first parameter either zero, or a string indicating the starting directory. Zero implies that the system should search the system path for the file. The **fileName** parameter may or may not contain the file extension. If it does not, you can place an extension in the **fileExtension** parameter and the function will append it to the file name before starting the search. The **bufferSize** and **buffer** parameters specify the buffer in which the function should return the result of the search, which is the path to the found file name. The **filePart** parameter returns a pointer to the first character of the actual file name in the buffer.

If an error occurs during the search, the function returns a zero and an error code can be obtained using the **GetLastError** function. It is also possible that the buffer size is inadequate to hold the entire path name. In this case, the returned value will be greater than the **bufferSize** parameter passed to the function.

The **SearchPath** function is a convenience. It returns the first instance of the file name requested. To do a more thorough search for duplicates, or to search for file names containing wildcards, you have to write code to do the search yourself, as described in the next section.

4.5 Traversing Directory Trees

Directory traversal is a very common activity in many different types of applications, and there are a number of good reasons to use this capability. For example, you might need to accomplish any of the following tasks:

1. Delete a directory and any subdirectories within it
2. Search a drive for the biggest, or 100 biggest, files

3. Get all of the file names held in a directory so that you can back them up to tape
4. Search for a file or group of files anywhere on a drive
5. Search through directories to find `.obj` or `.tmp` files to delete to free disk space
6. Find the total disk space consumed by a directory tree
7. Search for a specific word in any `.txt` file you find on a drive
8. Display the directory tree for a drive in a graphical way
9. Check a path to ensure that each directory it contains is indeed valid
10. Count the total number of files on a drive

The 32-bit API provides a set of three functions that let you easily traverse a directory. Using these same functions recursively you can traverse entire directory trees.

Listing 4.5 demonstrates the use of the directory walking functions in their simplest form. This code lists all of the file and directory names found in a single directory.

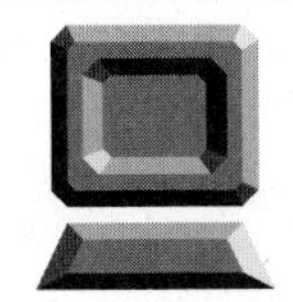

```
//dir1.cpp

#include <iostream.h>
#include <windows.h>

// Prints data in findData
void PrintFindData(WIN32_FIND_DATA *findData)
{
   // If it's a directory, print the name
   if( findData->dwFileAttributes &
      FILE_ATTRIBUTE_DIRECTORY )
   {
```

Listing 4.5
Listing the current directories contents (equivalent to the "dir" command) (Page 1 of 3)

```
        cout << "Directory: "
            << findData->cFileName << endl;
    }
    // else if it's a file, print name and size
    else
    {
        cout << findData->cFileName;
        cout << "\t(" << findData->nFileSizeLow
            << ")";
        cout << endl;
    }
}

// Lists the contents of the current directory
void ListDirectoryContents(char *fileMask)
{
    HANDLE fileHandle;
    WIN32_FIND_DATA findData;

    // get first file
    fileHandle = FindFirstFile( fileMask,
        &findData );
    if( fileHandle != INVALID_HANDLE_VALUE )
    {
        PrintFindData( &findData );

        // loop on all remeaining entries in dir
        while( FindNextFile( fileHandle,
            &findData ) )
        {
            PrintFindData( &findData );
        }
    }

    FindClose( fileHandle );
```

Listing 4.5
Listing the current directories contents (equivalent to the "dir" command) (Page 2 of 3)

```
}

int main(int argc, char *argv[])
{
   // List current directory's contents
   ListDirectoryContents( "*.*" );
   return( 0 );
}
```

Listing 4.5
Listing the current directories contents (equivalent to the "dir" command) (Page 3 of 3)

In Listing 4.5, the **ListDirectoryContents** function starts by calling the API's **FindFirstFile** function.

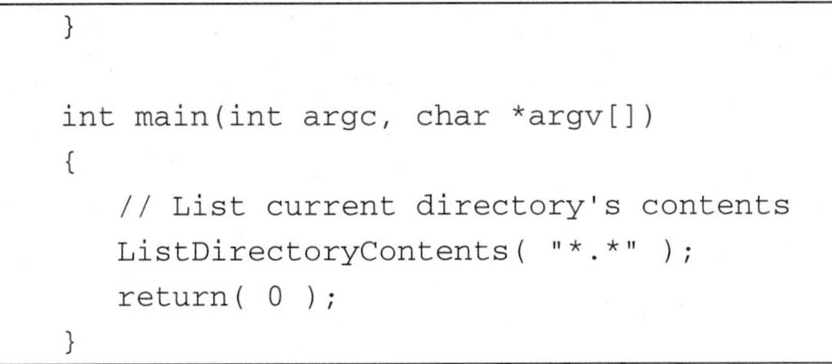

FindFirstFile	*Finds the specified file in the current directory*
`HANDLE FindFirstFile( LPTSTR searchFile, LPWIN32_FIND_DATA findData)`	
searchFile	The file to search for (wild cards are OK)
findData	Information about the file it finds
Returns a *search handle* to the first matching file found or INVALID_HANDLE_VALUE on failure	

The **FindFirstFile** function accepts the name of the file to find, and returns both a HANDLE to the file if it is found, as well as a structure describing the file. *The file handle is not a normal file handle like the ones produced by* ***CreateFile*** (see Chapter 2). It is specific to the **Find** functions described in this section. The WIN32_FIND_DATA structure returns the following information (from the API documentation):

```
typedef struct _WIN32_FIND_DATA {
    DWORD dwFileAttributes;
    FILETIME ftCreationTime;
```

```
    FILETIME ftLastAccessTime;
    FILETIME ftLastWriteTime;
    DWORD    nFileSizeHigh;
    DWORD    nFileSizeLow;
    DWORD    dwReserved0;
    DWORD    dwReserved1;
    TCHAR    cFileName[ MAX_PATH ];
    TCHAR    cAlternateFileName[ 14 ];
} WIN32_FIND_DATA;
```

A great deal of this information duplicates the information returned by the **GetFileInformationByHandle** function (see Section 2.4.4). It also returns the actual file name, as well as the alternative FAT file name.

You can pass to the **FindFirstFile** function a specific file name, a file name containing wild cards, or a path with or without a file name. If you include a path, the search starts in that directory. If not, it starts in the current directory. If it finds a file that matches the file name you have passed, it returns the HANDLE and information about the file. If it cannot find the file, it returns INVALID_FILE_HANDLE for the handle.

In Listing 4.5, the program is searching for every file in the current directory. It passes the structure returned by **FindFileFirst** to **PrintFindData**, which decides whether or not it is a directory name and prints out some of the information. The program then continues looking for other files in the directory using the **FindNextFile** function.

FindNextFile — *Finds the next file following a **FindFileFirst***

```
BOOL FindNextFile(
   HANDLE findFile,
   LPWIN32_FIND_DATA finData)
```

findFile	File handle returned by FindFileFirst or Next
findData	Information about the file it finds

Returns TRUE on success

FindNextFile accepts a handle produced by either **FindFirstFile** or a previous call to **FindNextFile**. It finds the next file in the directory that matches the file name description first passed to **FindFirstFile**, and returns a HANDLE and file information on the match. If no match is found, the returned Boolean value will be false, and the **GetLastError** function will contain the error code. Once no match is found, it means that the code has reached the end of the directory. At this point, the program calls **FindClose** to clean up the file handle used by the previous **Find** functions.

FindClose	*Closes the search handle*
`BOOL FindClose(` `   HANDLE findFile`	
findFile	File handle returned by FindFileFirst or Next
Returns TRUE on success	

The code in Listing 4.5 is suitable for examining all of the files in any single directory. If you want to look at entire directory trees, then you can make slight modifications to the code to make it recursive. In the recursive version, any directory it finds must in turn be traversed. Listing 4.6 demonstrates the process.

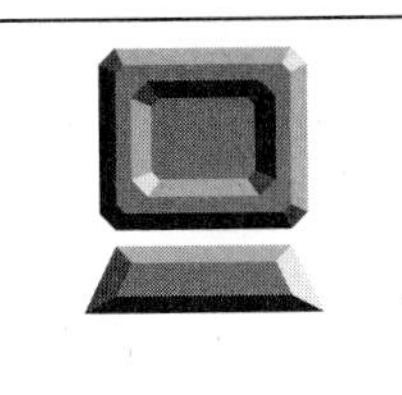

```
// dir2.cpp

#include <iostream.h>
#include <windows.h>
```

Listing 4.6
Recursively traversing a directory tree starting at the current directory (Page 1 of 4)

```
// prints information about a file
void PrintFindData(WIN32_FIND_DATA *findData)
{
   cout << "\t";
   cout << findData->cFileName;
   cout << "\t(" << findData->nFileSizeLow << ")";
   cout << endl;
}

// Recursively lists directories
void ListDirectoryContents(char *dirName,
   char *fileMask)
{
   char *fileName;
   char curDir[ 256 ];
   char fullName[ 256 ];
   HANDLE fileHandle;
   WIN32_FIND_DATA findData;

   // save current dir so it can restore it
   if( !GetCurrentDirectory( 256, curDir) )
      return;

   // if the directory name is neither . or .. then
   // change to it, otherwise ignore it
   if( strcmp( dirName, "." ) &&
      strcmp( dirName, ".." ) )
   {
      if( !SetCurrentDirectory( dirName ) )
         return;
   }
   else
      return;
```

Listing 4.6
Recursively traversing a directory tree starting at the current directory (Page 2 of 4)

```
    // print out the current directory name
    if( !GetFullPathName( fileMask, 256, fullName,
       &fileName ) )
       return;
    cout << endl << "Directory - " << fullName
       << endl;

    // Loop through all files in the directory
    fileHandle = FindFirstFile( fileMask,
       &findData );
    while ( fileHandle != INVALID_HANDLE_VALUE )
    {
       // If the name is a directory,
       // recursively walk it. Otherwise
       // print the file's data
       if( findData.dwFileAttributes &
          FILE_ATTRIBUTE_DIRECTORY )
       {
          ListDirectoryContents( findData.cFileName,
             fileMask );
       }
       else
          PrintFindData( &findData );

       // loop thru remaining entries in the dir
       if (!FindNextFile( fileHandle, &findData ))
          break;
    }

    // clean up and restore directory
    FindClose( fileHandle );
    SetCurrentDirectory( curDir );
 }

int main(int argc, char *argv[])
```

Listing 4.6
Recursively traversing a directory tree starting at the current directory (Page 3 of 4)

```
{
    char curDir[ 256 ];

    if( !GetCurrentDirectory( 256, curDir ) )
    {
        cerr << "Couldn't get the current directory."
            << endl;
        return( 1 );
    }

    // List all files, starting with the
    // current directory
    ListDirectoryContents( curDir, "*.*" );
    return( 0 );
}
```

Listing 4.6
Recursively traversing a directory tree starting at the current directory (Page 4 of 4)

The main differences between the code found in Listings 4.5 and 4.6 lies in the treatment of directories. The **ListDirectoryContents** function now accepts two parameters, one for the file name and one for the current directory. It changes into the specified directory and begins looking for files using **FindFileFirst** and **FindNextFile**. If it encounters any directories during its search, it recursively calls itself to probe the new directory. This process continues until all of the files in the subtree have been examined.

4.6 Combining Capabilities

It is possible to combine the concepts learned in this chapter with concepts learned in Chapter 3 and concepts from other chapters to create very interesting search capabilities. For example, you might want to use the recursive drive-walking code from Listing 3.7 along with the directory walking code demonstrated above to create a program that connects to every drive on the network and searches every directory on each one for a specific file.

The code in Listing 4.7 demonstrates an advanced searching program using capabilities from this chapter as well as Chapter 3. The program searches all directories on all drives connected to the current machine looking for the indicated file. When the program starts, it will ask you for the name of the file that you want to find. Wildcards are acceptable. It will then search each connected drive and list every matching file that it finds.

```
// dir3.cpp

#include <iostream.h>
#include <windows.h>

// prints information about a file
void PrintFindData(WIN32_FIND_DATA *findData,
   char *dirName)
{
   cout << dirName << '\\'
      << findData->cFileName;
   cout << endl;
}

// Recursively lists directories
void ListDirectoryContents(char *dirName,
   char *fileMask)
{
   char curDir[ 256 ];
   char printDir[ 256 ];
   HANDLE fileHandle;
   WIN32_FIND_DATA findData;

   // save current dir so it can restore it
   if( !GetCurrentDirectory( 256, curDir) )
      return;
```

Listing 4.7
Code that searches for the indicated file on all connected drives (Page 1 of 4)

```
// if the directory name is neither . or .. then
// change to it, otherwise ignore it
if( strcmp( dirName, "." ) &&
   strcmp( dirName, ".." ) )
{
   if( !SetCurrentDirectory( dirName ) )
      return;
   if( !GetCurrentDirectory( 256, printDir ) )
      return;
}
else
   return;

// Loop through all files in the looking for
// the file name of interest.
fileHandle = FindFirstFile( fileMask,
   &findData );
while ( fileHandle != INVALID_HANDLE_VALUE )
{
   PrintFindData( &findData, printDir );

   // loop thru remaining entries in the dir
   if (!FindNextFile( fileHandle, &findData ))
      break;
}
FindClose( fileHandle );

// Loop through all files in the directory
// looking for other directories
fileHandle = FindFirstFile( "*.*",
   &findData );
while ( fileHandle != INVALID_HANDLE_VALUE )
{
   // If the name is a directory,
   // recursively walk it.
```

Listing 4.7
Code that searches for the indicated file on all connected drives (Page 2 of 4)

```
            if( findData.dwFileAttributes &
               FILE_ATTRIBUTE_DIRECTORY )
            {
               ListDirectoryContents( findData.cFileName,
                  fileMask );
            }
            // loop thru remaining entries in the dir
            if (!FindNextFile( fileHandle, &findData ))
               break;
         }

         // clean up and restore directory
         FindClose( fileHandle );
         SetCurrentDirectory( curDir );
      }

      int main(int argc, char *argv[])
      {
         char curDir[ 256 ];
         char findName[ 256 ];
         DWORD drives;
         int x;

         cout << "Enter name to find: ";
         cin >> findName;

         drives = GetLogicalDrives();
         // Eliminate drives A and B
         drives = drives >> 2;

         for (x=0; x<24; x++)
         {
            if (drives & 1!=0)
            {
               cout << (char) ('C'+x) << endl;
```

Listing 4.7
Code that searches for the indicated file on all connected drives (Page 3 of 4)

```
                curDir[0] = (char) ('C'+x);
                curDir[1] = ':';
                curDir[2] = '\\';
                curDir[3] = '\0';
                ListDirectoryContents(curDir,
                    findName);
            }
            drives = drives >> 1;
        }
        cout << endl;

        return( 0 );
    }
```

Listing 4.7
Code that searches for the indicated file on all connected drives (Page 4 of 4)

The program in Listing 4.7 is structurally similar to Listing 4.6. It starts by asking the user for a file name. It then retrieves a bit mask that indicates all of the drive letters currently in use. It skips over drives A and B and starts searching on drive C if it exists.

The code has to run two separate find loops in order to accomplish its goal. The first find loop looks through one directory for any file names matching the user's requested file name. The code prints the path and name of every appropriate file. The program then uses a second find loop to look for subdirectories of the current directory so that it can recursively traverse them as well.

Two interesting improvements could be made to Listing 4.7. Using the concepts in Chapter 5, you can multi-thread the program. Most of the time spent during the search operation is spent waiting for data to arrive over the network from over drives. By extracting data from several drives simultaneously, the delays can be overlapped and therefore minimized. The advantage of this technique is that it speeds up the overall search operation, but the disadvantage is that it saturates the network.

An alternative is to place the search engine into an RPC server, and place a copy of that RPC server on each machine on the network that contains a searchable drive. The data needed for the search is therefore handled locally on each machine by the RPC servers, rather than being shipping over the network. The advantage of this approach is an increase in speed along with the minimization of network traffic. Chapter 8 contains an extensive discussion of RPCs and RPC strategies.

4.7 Detecting Changes to Directories and Files

The 32-bit API contains a set of functions that allow you to detect changes in files and directories. For example, if you set up a change notification handle on a certain directory and a new file appears in that directory, you can detect it in your application.

Two applications where you can see this capability in action are the File Manager and Visual C++. In VC++, if someone modifies a file that VC++ has open, then VC++ will recognize the change and advise you of it. For example, another user might attach to your drive over the network, open a file with notepad, modify it, and write it back to the disk. VC++ will post an error dialog when it detects the change, and ask you what to do. In the File Manager, if the contents of the drive change after a search operation and the search window is still visible, then the File Manager will ask if you want to re-search the drive to update the window.

To use the change notification functions, you indicate a directory for the functions to watch, specify whether you want them to watch the directory or the directory plus all of its subtrees, and what you want them to watch for. The change notification functions can detect any or all of the following changes to directories:

- FILE_NOTIFY_CHANGE_FILE_NAME: The functions notify you when any directory name change occurs due to renaming, creation, or deletion.
- FILE_NOTIFY_CHANGE_DIR_NAME: The functions notify you when any file name change occurs due to renaming, creation, or deletion.
- FILE_NOTIFY_CHANGE_ATTRIBUTES: The functions notify you when any file attribute changes.
- FILE_NOTIFY_CHANGE_SIZE: The functions notify you when any file changes size due to a file write operation
- FILE_NOTIFY_CHANGE_LAST_WRITE: The functions notify you when any file's last write time changes
- FILE_NOTIFY_CHANGE_SECURITY: The functions notify you when any file's security descriptor changes.

Section 6.6 contains an example and shows how to wait for the change notification both in a standard and an MFC program.

4.8 Conclusion

The concepts presented in this chapter allow you to manipulate and traverse the directory trees of any Windows drive. You can use these techniques to create search engines and installation programs, or to create your own directory-handling tools like those found in the File Manager.

See Chapter 10 for information on securing directories.

PROCESSES AND THREADS

5

Processes and threads are two of the most exciting and useful features in Windows. Processes give you the ability to run multiple programs on a Windows machine at one time. Threads let you break up a single program into multiple threads of execution. In this chapter you will learn how to create new threads within your applications so that your applications make better use of the system. Threads also let you take better advantage of the extra CPU power available in NT machines that contain multiple processors (see Section 1.8).

Compatibility Note: All of the code in this chapter works identically in both Windows NT and Windows 95. Note, however, that Windows 95 can use only one processor per machine, while Windows NT can make use of multiple CPUs. See Section 1.8 for details.

5.1 The Possibilities

There are a number of ways that you might use threads in your own programs. Here are some ideas:

- If you create an MDI (Multiple Document Interface) application, it is often useful to assign a separate thread to each window. For example, in an MDI communications program that lets you connect to multiple hosts via multiple modems simultaneously, it simplifies things considerably if each window has its own thread that communicates with just one host.

- In a program that takes a long time to refresh its display because of the complexity of the graphics involved (for example, a CAD/CAM program may have to draw 10,000 line segments to refresh the display in a complicated drawing), it is useful to create a separate thread to handle the redrawing. The user interface, with its own thread, remains active for the user while the redrawing takes place in the background. See Section 5.4 for details.
- In a complicated simulation program, (for example a program that simulates the activity of organisms in an environment), the design of the program is often conceptually simpler if each entity has its own thread. The entities are then fully independent of one another and can respond to their own simulation events individually.
- If you have part of a program that needs to respond to certain high-priority events very quickly, the problem is easily solved using thread priorities. The high-priority portion of the code is placed in its own thread, and that thread is given a higher priority than other threads running on the machine. The high-priority thread then waits for the necessary events. When it senses one, it will awaken and receive almost all of the CPU cycles available until it completes its task. It can then go back to sleep waiting for the next event to arrive. See Section 5.7.
- If you are using an NT machine with multiple processors and you want to take full advantage of all of the CPU power available, then you need to break the application into multiple threads. NT's unit of division across CPUs is the thread, so if you have an application that contains only one thread it will, by default, use only one CPU out of those available. If the program breaks up its work into multiple threads, however, NT can run each thread on a different CPU. See Section 5.5 for details.
- Any task that needs to happen in the background while the user continues to work with the application is easily handled with threads. For example, you might place lengthy recalculations, page formatting operations, file reading and writing, and so forth in separate threads that let the activities proceed in the background without disturbing the user.

As you go through the examples in this chapter and the next, you will come up with many other ideas of your own. The thread concept turns out to be quite useful and flexible once you grasp its capabilities.

5.2 Introduction

If you are moving to Windows from UNIX, VMS, or a mainframe, then multi-processing is a familiar concept. Multi-threading may be new to you however. If you are moving from MS-DOS, then both multi-processing and multi-threading are probably new to you. Let's start by looking at what multi-processing and multi-threading actually mean from an operating system standpoint.

The MS-DOS operating system is a *single-tasking* operating system. It can run one program at a time. You load a program, work with it, quit it, and then run another. TSRs can, in certain situations, give an impression of multi-processing. However, the problems that TSRs normally cause show that they are at best an illusion that MS-DOS was never intended to support.

Microsoft Windows 3.1, as well as Apple's Macintosh system, are *cooperative multi-tasking* operating environments. Both can run multiple programs (processes), at the same time. For example, you can run a word processor in one window, a spreadsheet in another window, and download a file from a BBS in a third window. The word *cooperative* is used because it is up to each program to properly relinquish control at appropriate times so that all of the processes appear to be working simultaneously. Cooperative multi-tasking works to some degree. However, a lengthy disk access or other undividable task performed by one program will tend to monopolize the entire system for a moment and the cooperation breaks down. This makes cooperative multi-tasking systems seem jerky in many cases. Cooperative systems also have a fatal flaw: if one program locks up, the whole system often dies with it. As soon as one program locks, it cannot relinquish control to the others and everything stops.

UNIX is a *preemptive multi-tasking* operating system. The operating system, rather than individual applications, is in charge of giving CPU time to all of the running processes, and it does so as it best sees fit. UNIX gives a process a *time slice* of CPU time—perhaps 20 milliseconds or so—and when that amount of time expires the operating system *preempts* the process and gives the next slice of CPU time to another process. A UNIX machine can therefore have literally hundreds of processes running at one time and still feel very smooth to the user. If one process locks it has no effect on the others because the operating system is still in control of slicing up the CPU time.

Windows is a *preemptive multi-tasking, multi-threaded* operating system. Because it uses preemptive multi-tasking, it shares with UNIX the same smoothness of operation and process independence. Multi-threading goes one step further however. An individual program by default contains one thread, but it can break itself into several independent threads of execution so that, for example, one thread of an application can send a file to the printer while another is responding to user input. This simple change in the a program's design can significantly reduce any waiting that the user normally has to worry about during lengthy recalculations, screen painting, file reading and writing, and so on.

Multi-threading also lets you take advantage of multiple CPUs available in many high-end NT machines. Say, for example, that you purchase an advanced RISC machine capable of using up to ten CPU chips, but initially you purchase only one CPU for it. As part of your learning cycle you write a simple Mandelbrot set program, and you find that for a window of a certain size it takes 15 seconds to redraw the image of the Mandelbrot set.

Now you add nine more CPU chips to the machine. When you rerun the Mandelbrot program, you will find that it still takes almost 15 seconds to execute. NT has the ability to run different threads on different CPUs, but it cannot do anything with a single-threaded program but devote one CPU to it. There is no way for NT to divide a single thread across CPUs. Since NT is itself multi-threaded, the Mandelbrot program will speed up slightly because it is not competing with NT's system threads for CPU time. However, any one program cannot harness more than one tenth of the CPU power in a ten-CPU machine unless it is multi-threaded.

If you multi-thread your Mandelbrot program, NT can run the separate threads on separate CPUs, and this allows it to take full advantage of all of the available CPU power. For example, if the Mandelbrot program breaks itself into ten threads, then one thread will run on each CPU and the program will run ten times faster. There is no reason, from a performance standpoint, to use more than ten threads on a 10-CPU machine, because each thread incurs a very slight amount of overhead, and it is therefore wasteful to have more than ten. However, you could break the program into 100 threads if you like, or use one thread for each scan-line of the drawing, if that makes things conceptually easier. The overhead incurred by a thread is minimal. There are many cases where breaking an application into multiple threads actually makes the whole program much easier to understand, and threads turn out to be remarkably easy to create.

Processes in Windows are not nearly as interesting as threads. A program can create a separate process, but the new process is completely and totally separate from the original program. Unlike UNIX, where a new process obtains a complete copy of the variable space of the original process, a new process in Windows can at most inherit copies of specifically indicated handles. Generally you use a process when you want to start another independent program from within a running program. For example, if you wanted to write your own version of the Program Manager or File Manager, you would use processes to launch other applications from your program.

When any process starts in Windows, it by default contains one thread of execution. For example, when you type "notepad" on the command line or double click on notepad's icon, Windows creates a process and that process has one thread that "runs" notepad's code. The process is essentially a container for the global variables, environment strings, the heap owned by the application, and the thread. The thread is what actually executes the code.

All threads in one process *share* the global variable space of their parent process. Each thread also has its own stack. When you create a new thread within a process, it has access to all of the global variables and the heap of the parent process. See Figures 5.1 and 5.2. All of the problems that arise from the careless use of globals in a normal program are therefore compounded in a multithreaded program, because now several different threads can modify the same global variables independently of one another. To solve the problems that tend to arise in such situations, there are *synchronization mechanisms* built in to Windows that help you to guarantee exclusive access to global values. See Chapter 6 for more information.

5.3 Simple Examples

For many people, the whole idea of creating multiple threads within a single process requires some mental adjustment. Let's start by looking at several extremely simple examples to see how threads work in Windows.

Listing 5.1 contains an extremely simple program. In this program, the code prints the value of the global variable named **count** each time the user presses the return key. Nothing in the program changes **count**, so the program always prints 0. There is no magic here.

Now let's add a *thread* to Listing 5.1, as shown in Listing 5.2 and Figure 5.3. A thread in Windows is simply a function that executes in the background.

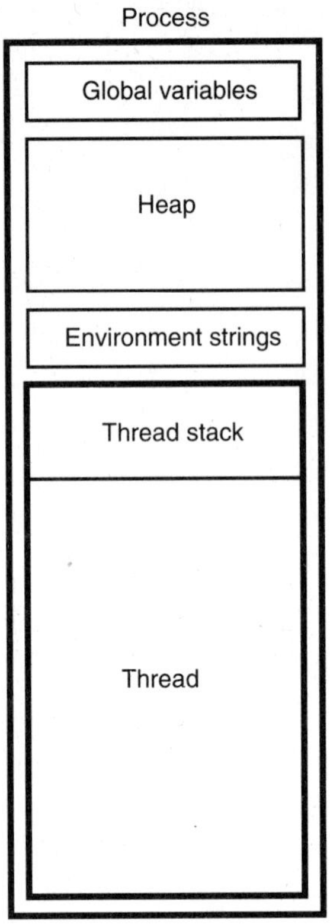

Process

Global variables

Heap

Environment strings

Thread stack

Thread

Figure 5.1
A process just after creation, with one thread. The process holds the global variables, heap, and environment strings, while the thread owns its stack (and therefore any local variables).

The function **CountThread** in Listing 5.2 increments the global variable **count** and then *sleeps* for 100 milliseconds. When you run the program, you will find that each time you press the enter key, **count** has increased. The thread runs in the background incrementing **count**, while the original thread is responding to user input. The program is doing two things at once.

Process

Global variables

Heap

Environment strings

Thread stack | Thread stack | Thread stack

Thread 1 | Thread 2 | Thread 3

Figure 5.2
A process holding three threads. The threads share the globals, heap, and environment strings, while each thread has its own stack (and therefore its own local variables).

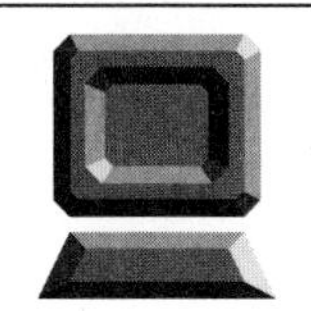

```
//nothread.cpp
#include <windows.h>
#include <iostream.h>

UINT count;
```

Listing 5.1
A very simple single-threaded program (Page 1 of 2)

```
void main(void)
{
  CHAR retStr[100];

  count=0;
  while(1)
  {
    cout
      << "Press <ENTER> to display the count... ";
    cin.getline(retStr, 100);
    cout << "The count is: " << count << endl
      << endl;
  }
}
```

Listing 5.1
A very simple single-threaded program (Page 2 of 2)

```
// thread1a.cpp

#include <windows.h>
#include <iostream.h>

volatile UINT count;

void CountThread()
{
  while(1)
  {
    count++;
    Sleep(100);
```

Listing 5.2
A very simple thread (Page 1 of 2)

```
    }
  }

  void main(void)
  {
    HANDLE countHandle;
    DWORD threadID;
    CHAR retStr[100];

    count=0;

    // create a thread which
    // executes the "CountThread" function
    countHandle=CreateThread(0, 0,
      (LPTHREAD_START_ROUTINE) CountThread,
      0, 0, &threadID);
    if (countHandle==0)
      cout << "Cannot create thread: "
        << GetLastError() << endl;

    while(1)
    {
      cout
        << "Press <ENTER> to display the count... ";
      cin.getline(retStr, 100);
      cout << "The count is: " << count << endl
        << endl;
    }
  }
```

Listing 5.2
A very simple thread (Page 2 of 2)

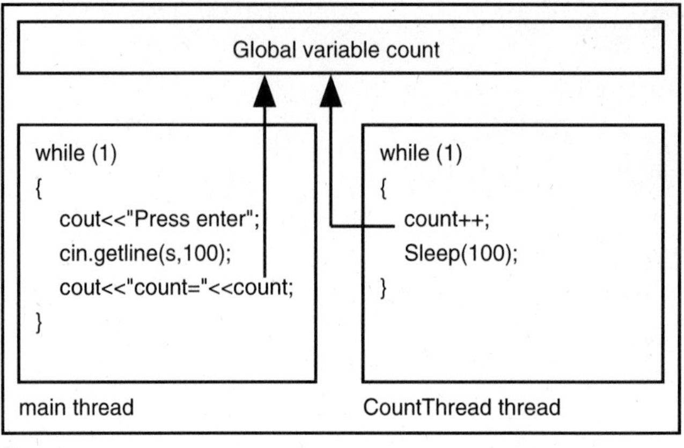

Figure 5.3
The arrangement of the main thread, the counting thread, and the global variable in Listing 5.2.

The code in Listing 5.2 starts by creating the thread using the **CreateThread** function.

CreateThread — *Creates a new thread in the parent process*

```
HANDLE CreateThread(
    LPSECURITY_ATTRIBUTES security,
    DWORD stack,
    LPTHREAD_START_ROUTINE function,
    LPVOID param,
    DWORD flags,
    LPDWORD threadID)
```

security	Security attributes. See Chapter 10
stack	The initial size of the thread's stack
function	The name of the function that the thread starts
param	A four-byte value that the thread function receives at startup
flags	Pass in 0 or CREATE_SUSPENDED

threadID	A pointer to a DWORD to receive the thread's ID
Returns a handle to the new thread or 0 on error.	

The **CreateThread** function accepts the name of the *thread function*, the function to execute in the new thread. Here, the thread function is **CountThread**. The thread function can optionally accept one four-byte parameter. In Listing 5.2 the function uses no parameters, but if it did the parameter that the thread function receives is passed to **CreateThread** in the **param** parameter, and **CreateThread** in turn passes it on to the thread function (see thread2.cpp). **CreateThread** returns both a thread ID and a handle to the thread. The thread ID is used to uniquely identify the thread system-wide, and is also accepted by a few functions such as **AttachThreadInput**.

You can control the initial size of the thread's stack using the **stack** parameter. Setting **stack** to 0 causes the thread to start with a stack of the same size as its parent thread. The stack will grow as necessary, but growth is a wasteful activity; if you know that the thread will need a certain amount of space in its stack because of the size of its local variables, you should try to accommodate that from the start. It is also possible to start a thread so that it is originally suspended. In this case, the thread will consume no CPU time until some other thread unsuspends it with **ResumeThread**.

The **Sleep** function in Listing 5.2 provides an efficient way for a thread to delay itself. In a previous life you may have used a **for** loop or some similar mechanism to cause a delay, but as you know **for** loops are unreliable and also extremely wasteful. As the **for** loop is spinning it consumes CPU cycles that could be put to better use. The **Sleep** function lets a thread delay itself without consuming any CPU cycles. A thread is totally suspended during a sleep.

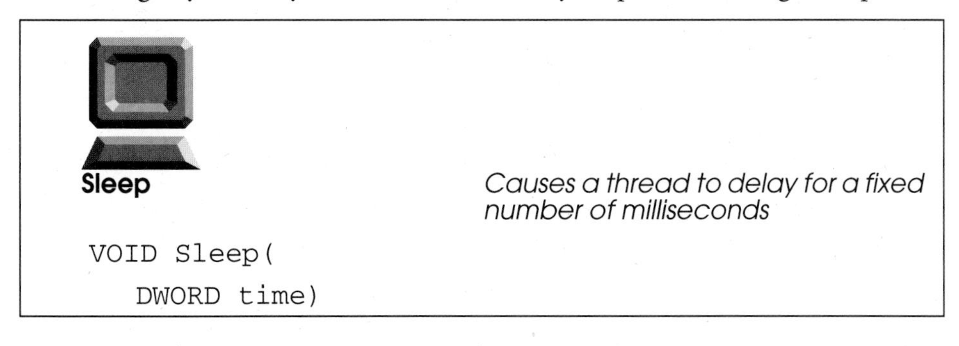

Sleep — *Causes a thread to delay for a fixed number of milliseconds*

```
VOID Sleep(
    DWORD time)
```

time	The amount of time to sleep, in milli-seconds
Returns nothing	

Note the use of the **volatile** modifier on the **count** global variable. If you comment out the **Sleep** function in the thread and remove the **volatile** modifier, **count** may always be zero when you press the enter key. This phenomenon occurs because of strange side effects resulting from compiler optimizations. The compiler, for example, may use a register to store the **count** variable in the main thread, so changes to the value by the second thread are ignored. The **volatile** modifier is a way of telling the compiler that you do not want any optimizations applied to the variable, that you do not want it placed in a register, and that the value may change due to outside influences during evaluation. You will find it to be a very important modifier for global variables referenced by multiple threads.

The code shown in Listing 5.3 is another simple example of a background thread running separately from the main thread. This thread beeps in the background while the main thread waits for it to finish. The code shows how to pass an integer parameter to a thread, and also how to wait for a thread to complete.

```
// thread1.cpp

#include <windows.h>
#include <stdlib.h>
#include <iostream.h>

// The function to run in a thread
void HonkThread(DWORD iter)
{
  DWORD i;
```

Listing 5.3
A simple thread that beeps in the background (Page 1 of 3)

```
    for (i=0; i<iter; i++)
    {
      Beep(200, 50);
      Sleep(1000);
    }
  }

  void main(void)
  {
    HANDLE honkHandle;
    DWORD threadID;
    DWORD iterations;
    CHAR iterStr[100];

    cout << "Enter the number of beeps to produce: ";
    cin.getline(iterStr, 100);

    // convert string into integer
    iterations=atoi(iterStr);

    // create a thread which
    // executes the "HonkThread" function
    honkHandle=CreateThread(0, 0,
      (LPTHREAD_START_ROUTINE) HonkThread,
      (VOID *) iterations, 0, &threadID);

    // wait until the thread has finished
    int count=0;
    while ( WaitForSingleObject(honkHandle, 0)
      == WAIT_TIMEOUT)
    {
      cout
        << "waiting for the thread to finish "
        << count++
```

Listing 5.3
A simple thread that beeps in the background (Page 2 of 3)

```
            << endl;
        }
    }
```

Listing 5.3
A simple thread that beeps in the background (Page 3 of 3)

When you run Listing 5.3, you should enter an integer value such as 5. The main program will start the thread, passing it the value 5 through the parameter. The thread will run in the background, beep five times, and quit. Meanwhile, the main program is waiting for the thread to quit using the **WaitForSingleObject** function in a loop. Each time through the loop it increments an integer and prints it to stdout.

WaitForSingleObject *Causes a thread to wait for a signal*

```
DWORD WaitForSingleObject(
    HANDLE object,
    DWORD timeout)
```

object	The object to wait for
timeout	The maximum amount of time to wait, in milliseconds

Returns an error code or the event that caused it to stop waiting.

The **WaitForSingleObject** function is waiting on the thread handle for the thread to terminate. See Section 6.4 for details. The value 0 passed in as the timeout value causes **WaitForSingleObject** to return immediately and indicate that either the thread has or has not completed. If the thread has not completed, **WaitForSingleObject** returns the value WAIT_TIMEOUT. See Chapter 6 for more information on this function—it has many different uses. Here we are using it simply to detect whether or not the background thread has finished.

It is possible to pass structures into a thread function by passing a pointer to the structure through the parameter, as shown in Listing 5.4. The structure should be stable. That is, it should be a global variable, a static local variable, or a block allocated from the heap. The structure should not be a local variable to a function that might cease to exist during the run of the thread.

```
// thread2.cpp

#include <windows.h>
#include <stdlib.h>
#include <iostream.h>

typedef struct
{
  DWORD frequency;
  DWORD duration;
  DWORD iterations;
} honkParams;

void HonkThread(honkParams *params)
{
  DWORD i;

  for (i=0; i<params->iterations; i++)
  {
    Beep(params->frequency, params->duration);
    Sleep(1000);
  }
}

void main(void)
{
  HANDLE honkHandle;
  DWORD threadID;
```

Listing 5.4
Passing a structure to a thread (Page 1 of 2)

```
    honkParams params;
    CHAR freqStr[100];
    CHAR durStr[100];
    CHAR iterStr[100];

    cout << "Enter the beep frequency to produce: ";
    cin.getline(freqStr, 100);
    params.frequency=atoi(freqStr);

    cout << "Enter the beep duration to produce: ";
    cin.getline(durStr, 100);
    params.duration=atoi(durStr);

    cout << "Enter the number of beeps to produce: ";
    cin.getline(iterStr, 100);
    params.iterations=atoi(iterStr);

    // create a thread and pass it the address of
    //the "params" structure
    honkHandle=CreateThread(0, 0,
      (LPTHREAD_START_ROUTINE) HonkThread,
      &params, 0, &threadID);

    WaitForSingleObject(honkHandle, INFINITE);
}
```

Listing 5.4
Passing a structure to a thread (Page 2 of 2)

In Listing 5.4, the three values entered by the user are placed in a structure that is then passed to the thread. The main function calls **WaitForSingleObject** to keep from terminating before the thread has completed. Without this call, the main function would return immediately, killing off both the main process and the threads. With it in place, the main function efficiently waits for thread completion. Compare to Listing 5.3.

Listing 5.5 takes Listing 5.4 a step further, and shows that it is possible to create multiple background threads using either multiple-thread functions or a single-thread function that is called several times.

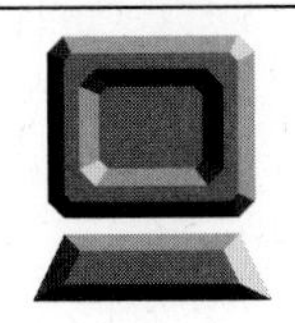

```
// thread3.cpp

#include <windows.h>
#include <stdlib.h>
#include <iostream.h>

typedef struct
{
  DWORD frequency;
  DWORD duration;
  DWORD iterations;
} honkParams;

void HonkThread(honkParams *params)
{
  DWORD i;

  for (i=0; i<params->iterations; i++)
  {
    Beep(params->frequency, params->duration);
    Sleep(1000);
  }

  GlobalFree(params);
}

void main(void)
{
  HANDLE honkHandles[3];
  DWORD threadID;
```

Listing 5.5
Creating multiple threads (Page 1 of 2)

```
    honkParams *params;
    DWORD count;
    CHAR freqStr[100];
    CHAR durStr[100];
    CHAR iterStr[100];

    for (count=0; count<3; count++)
    {
      // allocate memory for a "params" structure
      params=(honkParams *) GlobalAlloc(GPTR,
        sizeof(honkParams));

      cout << "Enter the beep frequency: ";
      cin.getline(freqStr, 100);
      params->frequency=atoi(freqStr);

      cout << "Enter the beep duration: ";
      cin.getline(durStr, 100);
      params->duration=atoi(durStr);

      cout << "Enter the number of beeps: ";
      cin.getline(iterStr, 100);
      params->iterations=atoi(iterStr);

      // create a thread and pass it the pointer
      // to its "params" struct
      honkHandles[count]=CreateThread(0, 0,
        (LPTHREAD_START_ROUTINE) HonkThread,
        params, 0, &threadID);
    }

    // wait for all threads to finish execution
    WaitForMultipleObjects(3, honkHandles,
      TRUE, INFINITE);
  }
```

Listing 5.5
Creating multiple threads (Page 2 of 2)

When you run Listing 5.5, the program asks you to enter a frequency and duration as well as the number of beeps. You can do this three times, so you will hear beeps from all three threads simultaneously, if you set the number of beeps for each thread high enough to cause an overlap.

In Listing 5.5, a wait function is again used to keep the main function, and therefore the process, from completing before all three threads have finished. The **WaitForMultipleObjects** does the same thing that **WaitForSingleObject** does, but it waits for all of the specified events to occur. **WaitForMultipleObjects** accepts an array of object handles, in this case handles from the three threads. See Section 6.4 for details.

WaitForMultipleObjects — *Causes a thread to delay waiting for one-of-many or all-of-many signals to occur*

```
DWORD WaitForMultipleObjects(
    DWORD numObjects,
    CONST HANDLE * objectArray,
    BOOL waitForAll,
    DWORD timeout)
```

numObjects	Number of objects in objectArray
objectArray	An array of object handles to wait on
waitForAll	If TRUE, the function waits for all events to occur, otherwise for any one of them
timeout	The maximum amount of time to wait, in milliseconds

Returns an error code or the event that caused it to stop waiting.

You can see from the examples given in this chapter that the use of threads, at least at a simple level, is not much more difficult than calling a normal function. The thread function executes as you expect, but it returns immediately and executes in the background, in parallel with the main thread of the application.

5.4 Using Threads in GUI Applications

The book entitled *Visual C++: Creating Professional Applications for Windows 95 and Windows NT using MFC* by Marshall Brain and Lance Lovette (ISBN 0-13-305145-5) shows how to use C++ and the Microsoft Foundation Class library to create GUI applications for Windows. In this section we will look at two different ways to use threads in a typical GUI application.

Listing 5.6 contains the code for a simple Mandelbrot set program that does not use threads. See Appendix A for compilation instructions. When you run this program, you can choose the **Draw** option in the **File** menu to cause the window to redraw. Unless you are working with a very zippy machine, do not make the window any larger than its default size initially. Now resize the window so that redrawing takes between 10 and 15 seconds.

```
// mandel0.cpp

#include <afxwin.h>
#include "menus.h"

#define NUM_ITERATIONS 64

const double left = -1.0;
const double right = 1.0;
const double top = -1.0;
const double bottom = 1.0;

DWORD colors[64];

typedef struct
{
```

Listing 5.6
A simple Mandelbrot set program created with the MFC class hierarchy and C++ (Page 1 of 6)

```
                    z.imag * z.imag;
                if (spread > 4.0)
                    break;
            }
            ((CManWindow *)manApp.m_pMainWnd)->
                SetPix(i, j, iter);
        }
    }
}

// The message map
BEGIN_MESSAGE_MAP(CManWindow, CFrameWnd)
    ON_WM_PAINT()
    ON_COMMAND(IDM_DODRAW, OnDoDraw)
    ON_COMMAND(IDM_EXIT, OnExit)
END_MESSAGE_MAP()

// Handler for the Draw menu option
void CManWindow::OnDoDraw()
{
    // clear the window
    CClientDC dc(this);
    CRect r;
    GetClientRect(&r);
    dc.PatBlt(0, 0, r.Width(), r.Height(),
        WHITENESS);
    // Redraw the set
    RunMandel();
}

// Handler for WM_PAINT messages
void CManWindow::OnPaint()
{
    // Do not do anything in response to
    // paint events
```

Listing 5.6
A simple Mandelbrot set program created with the MFC class hierarchy and C++
(Page 4 of 6)

```
      ValidateRect(NULL);
   }

   // Handler for the Exit menu option
   void CManWindow::OnExit()
   {
      DestroyWindow();
   }

   // CManWindow constructor
   CManWindow::CManWindow()
   {
      WORD x;
      BYTE red=0, green=0, blue=0;

      Create( NULL, "Normal Mandel Example",
         WS_OVERLAPPEDWINDOW,
         CRect(0,0,150,150), NULL, "MainMenu" );
      for (x=0; x<64; x++)
      {
         colors[x] = RGB(red, green, blue);
         if (!(red += 64))
            if (!(green += 64))
               blue += 64;
      }
      colors[63] = RGB(255,255,255);
   }

   // Initialize the CManApp m_pMainWnd data member
   BOOL CManApp::InitInstance()
   {
      m_pMainWnd = new CManWindow();
      m_pMainWnd -> ShowWindow( m_nCmdShow );
      m_pMainWnd -> UpdateWindow();
```

Listing 5.6
A simple Mandelbrot set program created with the MFC class hierarchy and C++
(Page 5 of 6)

```
    return TRUE;
}
```

Listing 5.6
A simple Mandelbrot set program created with the MFC class hierarchy and C++ (Page 6 of 6)

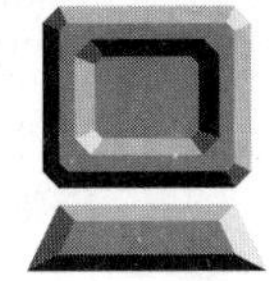

```
// menus.h

#define IDM_DODRAW   1001
#define IDM_EXIT     1002
```

Listing 5.7
The menus.h file used by Listing 5.6

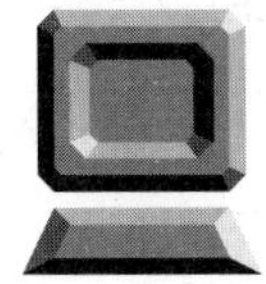

```
// mandel.rc

#include <windows.h>
#include <afxres.h>

#include "menus.h"

MainMenu MENU
{
   POPUP "&File"
   {
      MENUITEM "&Draw", IDM_DODRAW
      MENUITEM "E&xit", IDM_EXIT
   }
}
```

Listing 5.8
The menus.rc resource file used to create the menus for Listing 5.6

When you run the code shown in Listing 5.6, you will notice a serious problem with the application. Once the user selects the Draw option from the menu, the user cannot do anything because the redrawing code prevents the event loop from running. The user cannot use the menu, quit the program, or minimize the program until the redrawing step completes. If the user does happen to click on anything, the event queue stores the clicks and plays them all rapidly once the redraw completes. If the application's window is full-screen and the machine is slow, it may be several minutes before a redraw completes and the user can do anything with the application.

The situation presented here is common in any program that creates sophisticated displays. For example, a CAD/CAM program may have to extract 10,000 vectors from a database to refresh the screen for a complex drawing. Mapping programs, three-dimensional rendering programs, complex mathematical visualization programs, and so on, all suffer from the same problem.

Threads offer an easy solution to this problem. By placing all redrawing activity in its own thread, you allow the user to continue to use the program while redrawing takes place in the background. From the user's standpoint, this is a major improvement over being locked out of the interface. From a programmer's standpoint, the thread solution is significantly easier to work with than the **OnIdle** capability that MFC provides for solving this problem in non-threaded environments.

Listing 5.9 contains a version of the Mandelbrot program that contains a separate thread to handle redrawing. It works just like the code in Listing 5.6, except that the menus function properly during redrawing. You can use the **Exit** option to terminate the program even when redrawing is taking place.

```
// mandel1.cpp
```

Listing 5.9
A multi-threaded version of the Mandelbrot program that uses a thread to handle redrawing (Page 1 of 7)

```
#include <afxwin.h>
#include "menus.h"

#define NUM_ITERATIONS 64

const double left = -1.0;
const double right = 1.0;
const double top = -1.0;
const double bottom = 1.0;

DWORD colors[64];

typedef struct
{
   double real;
   double imag;
} complex;

typedef struct
{
   WORD height;
   WORD width;
} mandelParams;

// Define the application object class
class CManApp : public CWinApp
{
public:
   virtual BOOL InitInstance();
};

// Define the edit window class
class CManWindow : public CFrameWnd
{
private:
```

Listing 5.9
A multi-threaded version of the Mandelbrot program that uses a thread to handle redrawing (Page 2 of 7)

```
    HANDLE threadHandle;
    mandelParams params;
public:
    CManWindow();
    void RunMandel();
    void SetPix(int x, int y, WORD iter);
    afx_msg void OnPaint();
    afx_msg void OnDoDraw();
    afx_msg void OnExit();
    DECLARE_MESSAGE_MAP()
};

// Create an instance of the application object
CManApp manApp;

// member function used to set pixel colors
// in the window
void CManWindow::SetPix(int x, int y, WORD iter)
{
    CClientDC dc(this);
    dc.SetPixel(x, y, colors[iter]);
}

// the thread function which does the drawing
DWORD MandelThread(mandelParams *params)
{
    double xstep, ystep;
    double x, y;
    int i,j;
    WORD iter;
    complex k;
    complex z;
    double real, imag, spread;

    ystep = (double) (bottom - top) /
```

Listing 5.9
A multi-threaded version of the Mandelbrot program that uses a thread to handle redrawing (Page 3 of 7)

```
            params->height;
        xstep = (double) (right - left) / params->width;

        for (y=top, j=0; y <= bottom; y += ystep, j++)
        {
            for (x=left, i=0; x<=right; x += xstep, i++)
            {
                k.real = x;
                k.imag = y;
                z.real=z.imag=0.0;

                for (iter=0; iter<NUM_ITERATIONS-1;
                    iter++)
                {
                    real = z.real + k.real;
                    imag = z.imag + k.imag;
                    z.real = real * real -
                        imag * imag;
                    z.imag = 2 * real * imag;
                    spread = z.real * z.real +
                        z.imag * z.imag;
                    if (spread > 4.0)
                        break;
                }
                ((CManWindow *)manApp.m_pMainWnd)->
                    SetPix(i, j, iter);
            }
        }
        return(0);
    }

    // member function used to instigate
    // the drawing thread
    void CManWindow::RunMandel()
    {
```

Listing 5.9
A multi-threaded version of the Mandelbrot program that uses a thread to handle redrawing (Page 4 of 7)

```
    DWORD threadID;
    CRect r;

    GetClientRect(&r);
    params.height=r.Height();
    params.width=r.Width();

    threadHandle=CreateThread(NULL, 0,
       (LPTHREAD_START_ROUTINE) MandelThread,
       &params, 0, &threadID);
}

// The message map
BEGIN_MESSAGE_MAP(CManWindow, CFrameWnd)
    ON_WM_PAINT()
    ON_COMMAND(IDM_DODRAW, OnDoDraw)
    ON_COMMAND(IDM_EXIT, OnExit)
END_MESSAGE_MAP()

// Handler for the Start/Stop menu option
void CManWindow::OnDoDraw()
{
    DWORD threadStatus;
    BOOL status;

    status = GetExitCodeThread(threadHandle,
       &threadStatus);
    if (threadStatus == STILL_ACTIVE)
    {
       // stop the existing thread
       TerminateThread(threadHandle, 0);
       CloseHandle(threadHandle);
    }
    // clear the window
    CClientDC dc(this);
```

Listing 5.9
A multi-threaded version of the Mandelbrot program that uses a thread to handle redrawing (Page 5 of 7)

```
        CRect r;
        GetClientRect(&r);
        dc.PatBlt(0, 0, r.Width(), r.Height(),
           WHITENESS);
        // redraw
        RunMandel();
     }

     // Handler for WM_PAINT messages
     void CManWindow::OnPaint()
     {
        ValidateRect(NULL);
     }

     // Handler for the Exit menu option
     void CManWindow::OnExit()
     {
        CloseHandle(threadHandle);
        DestroyWindow();
     }

     // CManWindow constructor
     CManWindow::CManWindow()
     {
        WORD x;
        BYTE red=0, green=0, blue=0;

        Create( NULL, "Threaded Mandel Example",
           WS_OVERLAPPEDWINDOW,
           CRect(0,0,150,150), NULL, "MainMenu" );
        for (x=0; x<64; x++)
        {
           colors[x] = RGB(red, green, blue);
           if (!(red += 64))
              if (!(green += 64))
```

Listing 5.9
A multi-threaded version of the Mandelbrot program that uses a thread to handle redrawing (Page 6 of 7)

```
                blue += 64;
        }
        colors[63] = RGB(255,255,255);
    }

    // Initialize the CManApp m_pMainWnd data member
    BOOL CManApp::InitInstance()
    {
        m_pMainWnd = new CManWindow();
        m_pMainWnd -> ShowWindow( m_nCmdShow );
        m_pMainWnd -> UpdateWindow();

        return TRUE;
    }
```

Listing 5.9
A multi-threaded version of the Mandelbrot program that uses a thread to handle redrawing (Page 7 of 7)

If you compare the code in Listing 5.6 and Listing 5.9, you will find only minor differences. First, the **OnDoDraw** function in Listing 5.9 must check to see if a redrawing thread is active before it starts a new one. The **GetExitCodeThread** function is used here, but the **WaitForSingleObject** function seen in the previous section would work just as well. If the **OnDoDraw** function finds an active thread, it kills the thread. It then clears the window and calls **RunMandel,** just as Listing 5.6 does.

The **RunMandel** function now has two pieces. The first piece, **RunMandel** itself, sets up a parameter structure and calls **CreateThread** to start the thread function. The thread function is called **MandelThread** and it contains all of the actual redrawing code. The code is not any different from the redrawing code seen in Listing 5.6, except that the threaded version takes its width and height from the parameter structure.

You can see here that the addition of a thread to an MFC program is fairly straightforward. In any application that you create, you can place the redrawing step in the background by following the same pattern seen in this code. It is also easy to place any sort of recalculation code in a thread using the same techniques.

5.5 Matching the Number of Threads to the Number of CPUs

When you run a compute-bound program on an NT machine that has multiple CPUs, You want to split the computation portion of the program into a set of threads whose number matches the number of CPUs. For example, in the Mandelbrot program seen in the previous section, you would like to create one redrawing thread for each CPU that is available. Each redrawing thread can handle a portion of the image. NT will run each separate thread on a different CPU, so the program will make maximum use of the CPU power available. Listing 5.10 demonstrates how to make the Mandelbrot program split into multiple threads.

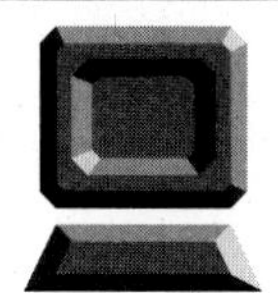

```
// mandel2.cpp

#include <afxwin.h>
#include "menus.h"

#define NUM_ITERATIONS 64

const double left = -1.0;
const double right = 1.0;
const double top = -1.0;
const double bottom = 1.0;

DWORD colors[64];
BOOL quit;

typedef struct
{
```

Listing 5.10
A multi-threaded implementation that will create one thread for each processor found on the machine (if it finds only one processor it creates four threads by default) (Page 1 of 8)

```
      double real;
      double imag;
   } complex;

   typedef struct
   {
      double xstep;
      double ystep;
      WORD height;
      double startpoint;
      WORD startpos;
   } mandelParams;

   // Define the application object class
   class CManApp : public CWinApp
   {
   public:
      virtual BOOL InitInstance();
   };

   // Define the edit window class
   class CManWindow : public CFrameWnd
   {
   private:
      DWORD numThreads;
      HANDLE *threadHandles;
      BOOL initialized;
   public:
      CManWindow();
      void RunMandel();
      void SetPix(int x, int y, WORD iter);
      afx_msg void OnPaint();
      afx_msg void OnDoDraw();
      afx_msg void OnExit();
```

Listing 5.10
A multi-threaded implementation that will create one thread for each processor found on the machine (if it finds only one processor it creates four threads by default) (Page 2 of 8)

```
    DECLARE_MESSAGE_MAP()
};

// Create an instance of the application object
CManApp manApp;

// member function which sets pixel colors
// in the window
void CManWindow::SetPix(int x, int y, WORD iter)
{
    CClientDC dc(this);
    dc.SetPixel(x, y, colors[iter]);
}

// thread function which draws on the window
DWORD MandelThread(mandelParams *p)
{
    double x, y;
    int i,j;
    WORD iter;
    complex k;
    complex z;
    double real, imag, spread;

    for (y=p->startpoint, j=p->startpos;
        y <= (p->startpoint + p->height*p->ystep);
            y += p->ystep, j++)
    {
        for (x=left, i=0; x<=right; x += p->xstep,
            i++)
        {
            k.real = x;
            k.imag = y;
            z.real=z.imag=0.0;
```

Listing 5.10
A multi-threaded implementation that will create one thread for each processor found on the machine (if it finds only one processor it creates four threads by default) (Page 3 of 8)

```
            for (iter=0; iter<NUM_ITERATIONS-1;
               iter++)
            {
               real = z.real + k.real;
               imag = z.imag + k.imag;
               z.real = real * real -
                  imag * imag;
               z.imag = 2 * real * imag;
               spread = z.real * z.real +
                  z.imag * z.imag;
               if (spread > 4.0)
                  break;
            }
            ((CManWindow *)manApp.m_pMainWnd)->
               SetPix(i, j, iter);
            if (quit)
            {
               GlobalFree(p);
               return(0);
            }
         }
      }
      return(0);
   }

   // member function which instigates the thread(s)
   void CManWindow::RunMandel()
   {
      DWORD threadID;
      SYSTEM_INFO sysInfo;
      CRect r;
      WORD n;
      WORD height;
```

Listing 5.10
A multi-threaded implementation that will create one thread for each processor found on the machine (if it finds only one processor it creates four threads by default) (Page 4 of 8)

```
        double xstep, ystep;
        mandelParams *params;

        GetSystemInfo(&sysInfo);

        numThreads=sysInfo.dwNumberOfProcessors;
        if (numThreads==1) numThreads=4;

        quit=FALSE;

        threadHandles=(HANDLE *) GlobalAlloc(GPTR,
            (sizeof(HANDLE)*numThreads));

        GetClientRect(&r);
        xstep=(right - left)/double(r.Width());
        ystep=(bottom - top)/double(r.Height());
        height=r.Height()/(WORD)numThreads;

        for(n=0; n<numThreads; n++)
        {
            params=(mandelParams *) GlobalAlloc(GPTR,
                sizeof(mandelParams));
            params->xstep=xstep;
            params->ystep=ystep;
            params->height=height;
            params->startpoint=top + height*ystep*n;
            params->startpos=height*n;
            threadHandles[n]=CreateThread(0, 0,
                (LPTHREAD_START_ROUTINE) MandelThread,
                params, 0, &threadID);
        }
    }

    // The message map
```

Listing 5.10
A multi-threaded implementation that will create one thread for each processor found on the machine (if it finds only one processor it creates four threads by default) (Page 5 of 8)

```
BEGIN_MESSAGE_MAP(CManWindow, CFrameWnd)
   ON_WM_PAINT()
   ON_COMMAND(IDM_DODRAW, OnDoDraw)
   ON_COMMAND(IDM_EXIT, OnExit)
END_MESSAGE_MAP()

// Handler for the Start/Stop menu option
void CManWindow::OnDoDraw()
{
   if (!initialized)
   {
      initialized=TRUE;
      RunMandel();
   }
   else
   {
      WORD n;

      // wait for and stop all existing threads
      quit=TRUE;
      WaitForMultipleObjects(numThreads,
         threadHandles, TRUE,
         INFINITE);
      for (n=0; n<numThreads; n++)
         CloseHandle(threadHandles[n]);
      GlobalFree(threadHandles);
      // clear the window
      CClientDC dc(this);
      CRect r;
      GetClientRect(&r);
      dc.PatBlt(0, 0, r.Width(), r.Height(),
         WHITENESS);
      // start over again
      RunMandel();
```

Listing 5.10
A multi-threaded implementation that will create one thread for each processor found on the machine (if it finds only one processor it creates four threads by default) (Page 6 of 8)

```
   }}

void CManWindow::OnPaint()
{
   ValidateRect(NULL);
}

// Handler for the Exit menu option
void CManWindow::OnExit()
{
   WORD n;

   quit=TRUE;
   WaitForMultipleObjects(numThreads,
      threadHandles,
      TRUE, INFINITE);
   for (n=0; n<numThreads; n++)
      CloseHandle(threadHandles[n]);

   GlobalFree(threadHandles);

   DestroyWindow();
}

// CManWindow constructor
CManWindow::CManWindow()
{
   WORD x;
   BYTE red=0, green=0, blue=0;

   Create( NULL, "Multi-Threaded Mandel Example",
      WS_OVERLAPPEDWINDOW,
      CRect(0,0,150,150), NULL, "MainMenu" );
   for (x=0; x<64; x++)
```

Listing 5.10
A multi-threaded implementation that will create one thread for each processor found on the machine (if it finds only one processor it creates four threads by default) (Page 7 of 8)

```
        {
            colors[x] = RGB(red, green, blue);
            if (!(red += 64))
                if (!(green += 64))
                    blue += 64;
        }
        colors[63] = RGB(255,255,255);

        initialized=FALSE;
    }

// Initialize the CManApp m_pMainWnd data member
BOOL CManApp::InitInstance()
{
    m_pMainWnd = new CManWindow();
    m_pMainWnd -> ShowWindow( m_nCmdShow );
    m_pMainWnd -> UpdateWindow();

    return TRUE;
}
```

Listing 5.10
A multi-threaded implementation that will create one thread for each processor found on the machine (if it finds only one processor it creates four threads by default) (Page 8 of 8)

If you compare Listing 5.10 to Listing 5.9, you will find most of the differences in the **RunMandel** and **MandelThread** functions. The **RunMandel** function determines the number of threads to create by calling the **GetSystemInfo** function:

```
GetSystemInfo(&sysInfo);

numThreads=sysInfo.dwNumberOfProcessors;
if (numThreads==1) numThreads=4;
```

See Chapter 13 for more information on this function. One of the things that **GetSystemInfo** returns is the number of processors in the machine. If the program finds only one processor, it arbitrarily chooses to think that it has four processors simply to create an interesting display.

RunMandel next sets the global variable **quit** to FALSE. This variable will control the threads: if a thread sees **quit** change to TRUE, it cleans up its allocated memory and terminates immediately. This technique lets threads manage their own termination, which greatly simplifies a multi-threaded application like this one.

The **RunMandel** function next allocates a block of memory big enough to hold all of the thread handles it needs to create. This array will hold a copy of the handles so that the program can later wait on all of the threads to complete.

```
threadHandles=(HANDLE *) GlobalAlloc(GPTR,
    (sizeof(HANDLE)*numThreads));
```

Next **RunMandel** determines the area of the picture that each of the threads will manage, and then creates a parameter structure to hold the coordinates. Once it has calculated the area for a thread, it starts the thread and assigns it an area.

```
    GetClientRect(&r);
    xstep=(right - left)/double(r.Width());
    ystep=(bottom - top)/double(r.Height());
    height=r.Height()/(WORD)numThreads;

    for(n=0; n<numThreads; n++)
    {
        params=(mandelParams *) GlobalAlloc(GPTR,
            sizeof(mandelParams));
        params->xstep=xstep;
        params->ystep=ystep;
        params->height=height;
        params->startpoint=top + height*ystep*n;
        params->startpos=height*n;
        threadHandles[n]=CreateThread(0, 0,
            (LPTHREAD_START_ROUTINE) MandelThread,
            params, 0, &threadID);
    }
}
```

Perhaps a simpler way to implement this portion of the program would be to create a separate thread for each scan line in the image. For example, if the image is 100 pixels high, the program could create 100 threads. The advantage of this approach is simplicity. The disadvantage is a slight inefficiency that comes from the operating system overhead of managing the threads and swapping between them. Section 6.2.3 demonstrates how to use semaphores to limit the actual number of threads that are running while keeping the simplicity of having one thread per scan line.

The **MandelThread** function contains two changes. First, it paints only the indicated portion of the image rather than the entire image. Second, it looks at the global **quit** variable each time it draws a pixel. If it notices **quit** change to TRUE, it cleans up space allocated for the parameters on the heap and kill itself off.

The **OnExit** function is one place where the global **quit** variable gets set:

```
// Handler for the Exit menu option
void CManWindow::OnExit()
{
    WORD n;

    quit=TRUE;
    WaitForMultipleObjects(numThreads,
        threadHandles,
        TRUE, INFINITE);
    for (n=0; n<numThreads; n++)
        CloseHandle(threadHandles[n]);

    GlobalFree(threadHandles);

    DestroyWindow();
}
```

The function sets **quit**, and then waits for all of the threads to terminate. Once they terminate, it closes their handles and frees the memory used to hold all of the thread handles.

The **OnDoDraw** function contains the only other significant modification to the code. It starts by checking to see whether or not the program has redrawn itself once. If not, it redraws immediately. If it has already redrawn once, then it uses the same technique seen in **OnExit** to clean up any running threads.

5.6 Using Thread Local Storage

The 32-bit API contains a unique feature called Thread Local Storage (TLS) that you can use in processes and DLLs in a variety of ways. The capability itself is very straightforward, but some of its extended ramifications are what make it interesting.

The TLS capability consists of four very simple functions: **TlsAlloc**, **TlsFree**, **TlsSetValue**, and **TlsGetValue**. You use TLS by first calling the **TlsAlloc** function, as shown below:

```
DWORD tlsIndex;// probably a global variable

...

// allocate a thread local storage index
tlsIndex=TlsAlloc();
```

The call to **TlsAlloc** creates a block of memory that contains one 32-bit storage location for each existing thread in a process. Any new threads created after the call to **TlsAlloc** also receive a unique 32-bit storage location. **TlsAlloc** returns an index value that the process uses when referring to this particular set of 32-bit thread storage locations. The process can call **TlsAlloc** as many times as it likes as long as it uses a different variable each time. See Figure 5.4.

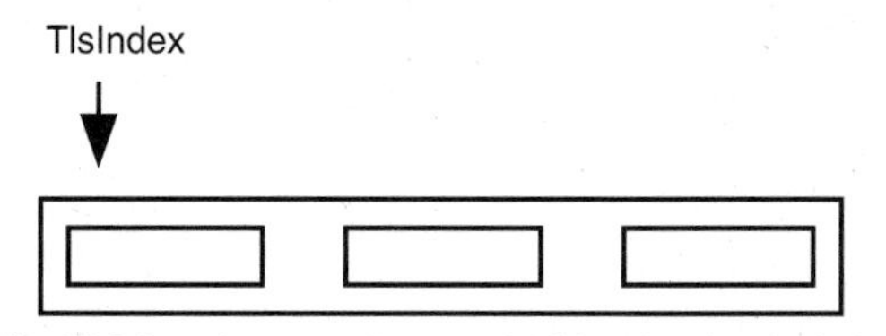

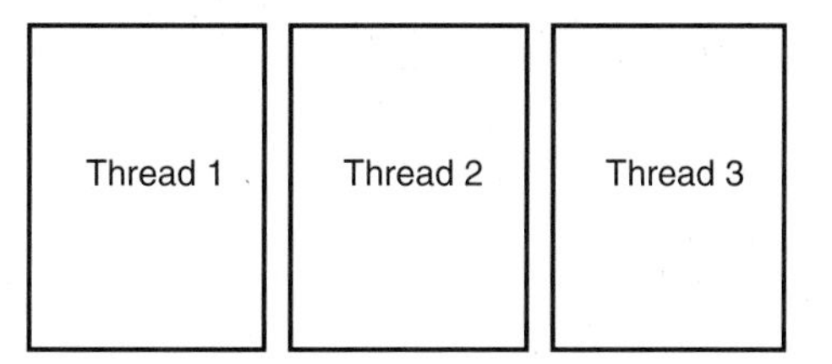

Figure 5.4
The relationship between TLS and the threads in a process. TlsIndex references a block of storage that contains one 32-bit value for each thread in the process.

Inside any thread, a call to the function **TlsGetValue** with the **TlsIndex** value returns the 32-bit value from TLS storage associated with that particular thread. That is, the value returned by **TlsGetValue** is context sensitive based on whatever thread is calling the function. The same goes for **TlsSetValue**.

The **TlsFree** function frees up the space occupied by all of the storage locations.

The TLS capability is frequently used inside of DLLs to store pointers to blocks of memory associated with the different threads calling the DLL. See Chapter 14 for details.

Listing 5.11 demonstrates TLS in a simple program. You should compare this program with Listing 5.5 because both do approximately the same thing in two different ways.

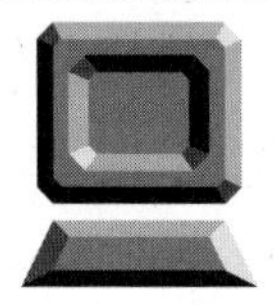

```
// thread4.cpp

#include <windows.h>
#include <stdlib.h>
#include <iostream.h>

DWORD tlsIndex;

typedef struct
{
  DWORD frequency;
  DWORD duration;
} honkParams;

void ParamsAlloc()
{
  honkParams *params;

  params=(honkParams *) GlobalAlloc(GPTR,
```

Listing 5.11
Using Thread Local Storage (TLS). Compare with Listing 5.5 (Page 1 of 4)

```
      sizeof(honkParams));

    // generate a randomish value for the frequency
    params->frequency=GetTickCount() & 0x00000FFF;
    cout << "Using frequency: "
      << params->frequency << endl;
    params->duration=100;

    // save the pointer value relevant
    // for the calling thread
    TlsSetValue(tlsIndex, params);
  }

  void ParamsFree()
  {
    honkParams *params;

    // retrieve the pointer value relevant
    // for the calling thread
    params=(honkParams *) TlsGetValue(tlsIndex);

    GlobalFree(params);
  }

  void Honk(void)
  {
    honkParams *params;

    // retrieve the pointer value relevant
    // for the calling thread
    params=(honkParams *) TlsGetValue(tlsIndex);

    Beep(params->frequency, params->duration);
  }
```

Listing 5.11
Using Thread Local Storage (TLS). Compare with Listing 5.5 (Page 2 of 4)

```
void HonkThread()
{
  DWORD i;

  // use a general purpose "params"
  // allocation function
  ParamsAlloc();

  for (i=0; i<8; i++)
  {
    Honk();
    Sleep(1000);
  }

  // use a general purpose "params" free function
  ParamsFree();
}

void main(void)
{
  HANDLE honkHandles[3];
  DWORD threadID;
  DWORD count;

  // allocate a thread local storage index
  tlsIndex=TlsAlloc();

  for (count=0; count<3; count++)
  {
    // create a thread which beeps
    honkHandles[count]=CreateThread(NULL, 0,
      (LPTHREAD_START_ROUTINE) HonkThread, 0, 0,
      &threadID);
    Sleep(1500);
  }
```

Listing 5.11
Using Thread Local Storage (TLS). Compare with Listing 5.5 (Page 3 of 4)

```
    WaitForMultipleObjects(3, honkHandles, TRUE,
      INFINITE);

    // free the thread local storage index
    TlsFree(tlsIndex);
}
```

Listing 5.11
Using Thread Local Storage (TLS). Compare with Listing 5.5 (Page 4 of 4)

The code in Listing 5.11 declares a global variable named **TlsIndex**. The program's first action in the main function is to allocate a TLS storage block pointed to by **TlsIndex**. The main function then creates three threads and waits for their completion before freeing the TLS storage space.

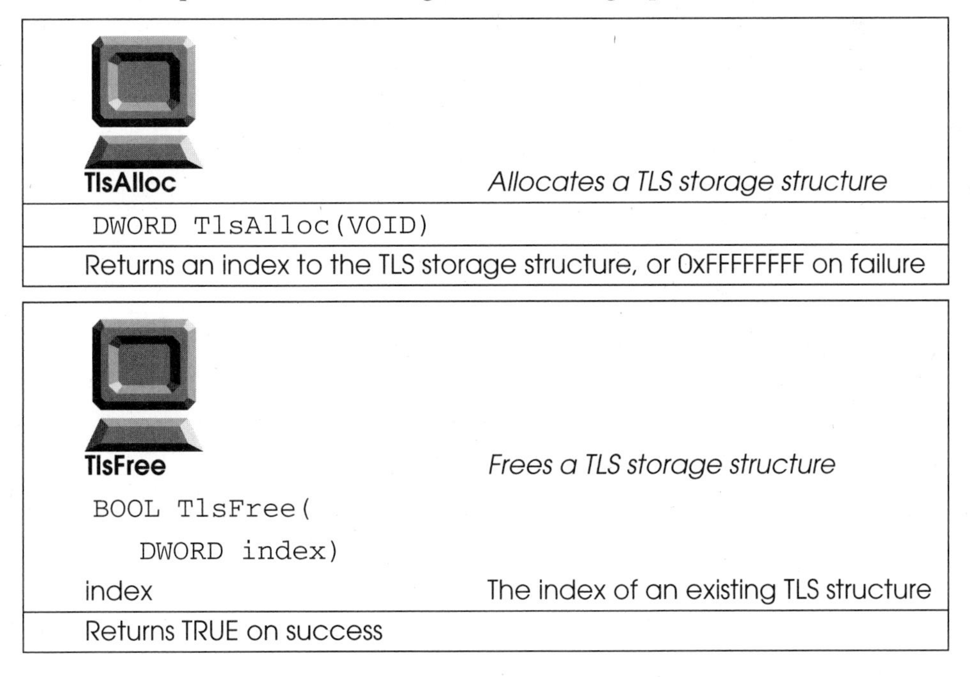

TlsAlloc *Allocates a TLS storage structure*

```
DWORD TlsAlloc(VOID)
```

Returns an index to the TLS storage structure, or 0xFFFFFFFF on failure

TlsFree *Frees a TLS storage structure*

```
BOOL TlsFree(
   DWORD index)
```

index The index of an existing TLS structure

Returns TRUE on success

Each thread calls the **ParamsAlloc** function, which allocates a parameter structure on the heap and fills it with values for the thread. The pointer to the parameter block is placed into the TLS area using **TlsSetValue. TlsSetValue** chooses the location in the TLS to place the pointer based on the thread that calls the function. To later free up its parameter storage block, each thread calls

ParamsFree. This function retrieves the pointer from the TLS and frees the block.

TlsGetValue	*Retrieves a value from a TLS structure based on the thread making the call*
`LPVOID TlsGetValue(` `    DWORD index)`	
index	The index of an existing TLS structure
Returns the value for the thread on success, or 0 on failure	

TlsSetValue	*Sets a value into a TLS structure based on the thread making the call*

`BOOL TlsSetValue(`
`    DWORD index,`
`    LPVOID value)`	

index	The index of an existing TLS structure
value	The value to store
Returns TRUE on success	

The TLS capability could have been used to implement the parameter storage for the multi-threaded Mandelbrot program shown in Listing 5.10, especially since each thread is in charge of cleaning up its allocated memory in that program. The TLS capability is also frequently used in DLLs to keep memory allocations in the DLL separated on a thread-by-thread basis. See Chapter 14 for details.

5.7 Thread Priorities

Windows uses a round-robin priority queue structure to schedule CPU time among available threads. In order to understand thread priorities and how to set them, you need to be familiar with the priority and scheduling mechanisms used by Windows. This section contains a brief overview.

All of the threads in a process have a priority relative to their parent process. The priority of the threads determines the amount of CPU time they receive relative to one another and relative to other threads in other processes. You set a thread's priority using the **SetThreadPriority** function and retrieve it using the **GetThreadPriority** function.

GetThreadPriority	*Retrieves the priority of a thread*
`int GetThreadPriority(` `   HANDLE threadHandle)`	
threadHandle	The handle of the thread
Returns the priority or THREAD_PRIORITY_ERROR_RETURN	

SetThreadPriority	*Sets the priority of a thread*

`BOOL SetThreadPriority(`
`   HANDLE threadHandle,`
`   int priority)`	

threadHandle priority	The handle of the thread The new priority
Returns TRUE on success	

Every process in Windows starts with a base priority determined by its *priority class*. Windows defines four different classes:

Class	Base priority
IDLE_PRIORITY_CLASS	4
NORMAL_PRIORITY_CLASS	9 foreground, 7 background
HIGH_PRIORITY_CLASS	13
REALTIME_PRIORITY_CLASS	24

A regular process, such as one launched from the Program Manager or the command line, is "normal." The threads within a process can then adjust their priority relative to the base priority of the process. When you call **SetThreadPriority**, it accepts one of the following values:

THREAD_PRIORITY_LOWEST	-2
THREAD_PRIORITY_BELOW_NORMAL	-1
THREAD_PRIORITY_NORMAL	+0
THREAD_PRIORITY_ABOVE_NORMAL	+1
THREAD_PRIORITY_HIGHEST	+2

For example, if a foreground process has a normal priority class and one of its threads sets its priority to THREAD_PRIORITY_LOWEST, then the thread's priority value is 7 (9 - 2 = 7).

Two additional thread priorities set a thread's priority value to an absolute number:

THREAD_PRIORITY_TIME_CRITICAL	15 or 31 absolute
THREAD_PRIORITY_IDLE	1 or 16 absolute

Setting a thread's priority to THREAD_PRIORITY_IDLE makes the thread's priority value 16 if its process's class is REALTIME_ PRIORITY_ CLASS, and makes it 1 otherwise. Setting a thread's priority to THREAD_ PRIORITY_TIME_CRITICAL makes the thread's priority value 31 if its process's class is REALTIME_PRIORITY_CLASS, and makes it 15 otherwise (Find the **SetPriorityClass** description in the API help file for a complete chart).

Based on the different base priorities of processes and the possible thread priorities, there are a total of 22 different priority values possible, ranging between 1 and 31. Windows's scheduler uses the priority value of all of the threads currently in existence to determine which thread gets the next slice of CPU time.

Think about a typical Windows system in the middle of operation on a typical day. It has all sorts of threads running. If you get out the Performance Monitor in NT and look at the **Threads** counter under the **Objects** object, it will tell you exactly how many threads currently exist on your machine. On my machine at this particular moment there are 155. By killing off all of the extraneous windows, I can get it down to 138. These are threads associated with different background services, operating system tasks and so on.

At any given moment, a thread can be in any of several states. Some threads are *suspended*. For example, you might have called the **SuspendThread** function on a thread. Some threads are *sleeping* because they called the **Sleep** function. Some of the threads are *waiting* for something. For example one thread might need user input from the keyboard to continue, while another is waiting for a network packet, and another is waiting for a sector from the hard disk.

The rest of the threads are *ready*. They have something to do, and the only thing preventing them from doing it is the fact that there is only one CPU and perhaps five threads needing to share it (on a multi-CPU NT machine, there might be three CPUs and five threads waiting for one of them).

Windows, like most preemptive operating systems, picks a ready thread and lets it use the CPU for a specified amount of time, a *time slice*, of perhaps 20 milliseconds. The thread will normally end up requesting something that is not available, like a keystroke or a disk sector, before its time slice completes. The operating system will then stop it and let it wait for what it needs. Otherwise the time slice will elapse and Windows will preempt the thread. It then picks another ready thread and gives it the next time slice.

Windows picks the thread that will receive the next time slice using a set of ready queues arranged by priority. Figure 5.5 shows a typical arrangement. Each queue works in a round-robin fashion, so a thread that is ready gets put on the end of one of the priority queues. The queue chosen is determined by the priority of the thread. The operating system services all of the threads in a given queue in order. If a thread uses up its time slice and is still ready, it gets put onto the end of its ready queue again. All of the ready threads in the highest priority queue get serviced until that queue is empty. The system then moves down to the next lower queue and begins servicing its threads, and so on.

Given this description of the Windows priority structure, it is easy to see how one can easily wreak havoc with it. For example, say that you take Listing 5.2, remove the call to **Sleep** in the thread function, and then set the thread's priority just one level up by changing it to THREAD_PRIORITY_ABOVE_NORMAL after you create the thread. This

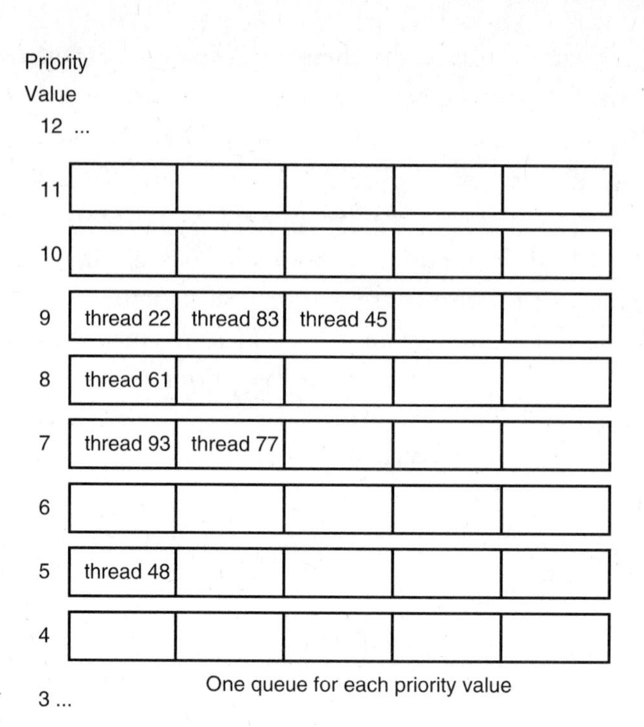

Figure 5.5
The priority queue structure used by the scheduler, here with seven different threads ready and waiting for CPU time. The three threads with priority value 9 will be serviced until they are all waiting for something and there are no ready threads at priority 9. Then the thread at priority 8 will be serviced, and so on.

simple act will essentially lock up all of the other normal processes currently running. Once you remove the call to **Sleep**, the thread function in Listing 5.2 contains an endless counting loop, so it never needs to wait for anything. It is always ready. It is *compute-bound.* Windows therefore services it continually, at the expense of *all* threads below it. The operating system threads that are in higher classes still run so the whole machine does not lock up, but all of the normal processes appear to die. While there is a safety value—lower priority threads do get an occasional time slice—the frequency of these spurious time slices is so low (perhaps one slice every two seconds) that for all practical purposes they do not occur.

There is an important lesson here. If you have a thread that you know will always be ready—that is, a thread that is compute-bound—you should probably lower its priority so that it does not stall all of the threads below it in the scheduler. Alternatively, you can cause it to sleep occasionally or frequently to give the threads below it some time slices. An idle thread with priority value 1 *never* gets a time slice unless *all* threads above it are waiting for something. Therefore, it may be a reasonable practice to set your compute-bound threads to the absolute priority THREAD_PRIORITY_IDLE so that they don't cut off any other processes. If every application did that, things would work well.

You should never give a thread a high priority unless you *know* that it will frequently wait, and that it will not use much CPU time when it becomes ready. For example, you might place a call to **WaitCommEvent** in a high priority thread waiting for a certain communications event such as the arrival of a character. The thread can then quickly process that character and wait again. Design the application so that a normal priority thread actually does something with the character retrieved, or set the priority of the high-priority thread back to normal during processing so that you do not starve everything else.

5.8 Other Thread Functions

There are several thread functions not demonstrated in the above examples that are useful in certain situations. Each of these functions is briefly described below:

The **SuspendThread** and **ResumeThread** functions let you temporarily stop and restart the execution of a thread. If you start a thread in a suspended state by setting the creation flags in **CreateThread** to CREATE_SUSPENDED, then **ResumeThread** is the only way to get the thread running at a later time. There are also cases where the use of suspension and resumption is the easiest way to control a thread. See, for example, Chapter 9 where the Pause and Continue features of a service are implemented this way.

Each thread keeps track of a suspend count. Calling **SuspendThread** increments the count, so if several different pieces of code suspend the thread the count will rise. The **ResumeThread** function looks at the count. If it is greater than zero, it decrements the count. If the new count equals zero it resumes the thread. The suspend counter ensures that multiple suspend requests are handled properly. It also means that your calls to suspend and resume must match.

DWORD SuspendThread(HANDLE threadHandle)	
threadHandle	The handle of the thread to suspend
Returns the suspend count or 0xFFFFFFFF on failure	

ResumeThread	*Resumes a thread's execution*
DWORD ResumeThread(HANDLE threadHandle)	
threadHandle	The handle of the thread to suspend
Returns the suspend count or 0xFFFFFFFF on failure	

Inside of a thread, you can exit immediately using the **ExitThread** function. It accepts an exit code. Calling **ExitThread** and calling **return** from within the thread function are equivalent actions. If the thread function calls another function, then **ExitThread** lets you terminate the thread that called the function.

ExitThread	*Exits a thread*
VOID ExitThread(DWORD exitCode)	
exitCode	The exit code of the thread, retrievable by **GetExitCodeThread**
Returns nothing	

The **GetCurrentThread** function returns a pseudohandle for the current thread. A pseudohandle is valid when used inside of the thread it represents. Otherwise it is invalid. Do not pass copies of pseudohandles off to other threads. To turn a pseudohandle into a real handle, duplicate it with **DuplicateHandle** and then use the duplicate.

GetCurrentThread *Retrieves a pseudohandle for a thread*

```
HANDLE GetCurrentThread(VOID)
```

Returns a pseudohandle to the current thread

If you need to retrieve a thread's ID within the thread, call the **GetCurrentThreadID** function. The thread ID is used by the following functions: **GetThreadDesktop**, **AttachThreadInput**, **PostThreadMessage**, and **SetWindowsHookEx**.

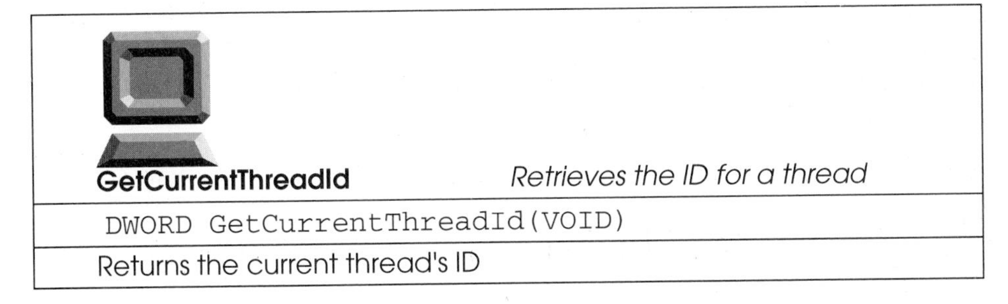

GetCurrentThreadId *Retrieves the ID for a thread*

```
DWORD GetCurrentThreadId(VOID)
```

Returns the current thread's ID

5.9 Processes

Windows' Threads give you an extremely easy way to create multiple execution streams within an application. It is also easy for the threads to communicate with one another because they share the same global variable space. Since the system does not copy any global or environment areas when creating a thread, threads also have a very low creation overhead.

Because of these advantages, you will generally create threads when you need multiple streams of execution. There are situations, however, where it is useful to be able to spawn an entirely new process. For example, if you want to create your own version of the File Manager, you need a way to launch other applications from within your application. The launched applications need to be created as stand-alone processes.

It is also sometimes useful to design a single application as several independent shells. You might do this to make a project more segmentable during construction (several teams work independently on completely separate applications), or because you want to sell different modules to different clients. An application like this often has a "main window" that is able to launch the other applications. The other applications need to be started as independent processes.

Listing 5.12 demonstrates how to start a separate process from within a running application using the **CreateProcess** function. The program in Listing 5.12 is nearly identical to the `start` command used in the MS-DOS prompt, except that it asks for the name of the application to start rather than accepting a command line argument.

```
// proc1.cpp

#include <windows.h>
#include <iostream.h>

void main(void)
{
  CHAR cmdStr[100];
  STARTUPINFO startUpInfo;
  PROCESS_INFORMATION procInfo;
  BOOL success;

  // Get the name of the child process to run
  cout << "Enter the command to execute: ";
  cin.getline(cmdStr, 100);

  // Retrieve the STARTUPINFOR structure for
  // the current process
```

Listing 5.12
Creating a separate process from within an application (Page 1 of 2)

```
    GetStartupInfo(&startUpInfo);

    // Create the child process
    success=CreateProcess(
      0, cmdStr, 0, 0, FALSE,
      CREATE_NEW_CONSOLE,
      0, 0, &startUpInfo, &procInfo);
    if (!success)
      cout << "Error creating process: "
        << GetLastError() << endl;

    // Wait for the child process to complete
    WaitForSingleObject(procInfo.hProcess,
      INFINITE);
}
```

Listing 5.12
Creating a separate process from within an application (Page 2 of 2)

The program in Listing 5.12 starts by asking for the name of the executable. You can enter the name followed by command line arguments. The way that the program calls **CreateProcess** in Listing 5.12 causes the program to search the path, as well as several other directories, for the executable. You can enter any executable command name in response to the program's prompt. Note that you cannot enter shell commands like "dir" unless you say `cmd -c dir` (in NT) or `command /c dir` (in Windows 95).

The program next retrieves the current process's startup information using the **GetStartupInfo** function. Calling this function is simply a convenience to shorten the code. There are a number of fields you can set in the startup structure, as seen below in this description copied from the Win32 help file:

```
typedef struct _STARTUPINFO { /* si */
    DWORD   cb; // number of bytes in structure
    LPTSTR  lpReserved;
    LPTSTR  lpDesktop;  // 0 for curr. desktop
    LPTSTR  lpTitle; // title for consoles
    DWORD   dwX; // X,Y offset of new window
    DWORD   dwY;
    DWORD   dwXSize; // W,H of new window
```

```
      DWORD    dwYSize;
      DWORD    dwXCountChars; // size of new consoles
      DWORD    dwYCountChars;
      DWORD    dwFillAttribute; // colors in consoles
      DWORD    dwFlags; // one or more of many flags
      WORD     wShowWindow; SW_ constants
      WORD     cbReserved2;
      LPBYTE   lpReserved2;
      HANDLE   hStdInput; // Stdin handle
      HANDLE   hStdOutput; // stdout handle
      HANDLE   hStdError; // stderr handle
  } STARTUPINFO, *LPSTARTUPINFO;
```

Listing 5.12 next starts the new process by calling the **CreateProcess** function. The function accepts 10 parameters.

CreateProcess *Creates a new stand-alone process*

```
BOOL CreateProcess(
   LPCTSTR imageName,
   LPCTSTR commandLine
   LPSECURITY_ATTRIBUTES processSecurity,
   LPSECURITY_ATTRIBUTES threadSecurity,
   BOOL inherit,
   DWORD create,
   LPVOID environment,
   LPCTSTR currDir,
   LPSTARTUPINFO startInfo,
   LPPROCESS_INFORMATION procInfo)
```

imageName	An explicit path to the executable
commandLine	Command line parameters, led if desired by an executable name
processSecurity	Security attributes for the process

threadSecurity	Security attributes for the first thread
inherit	If true, inheritable handles in the parent process are inherited by the child
create	Possible values (one or more of): DEBUG_PROCESS, DEBUG_ONLY_THIS_PROCESS, CREATE_SUSPENDED, DETACHED_PROCESS, CREATE_NEW_CONSOLE, CREATE_NEW_PROCESS_GROUP, plus one of IDLE_PRIORITY_CLASS, NORMAL_PRIORITY_CLASS, HIGH_PRIORITY_CLASS, REALTIME_PRIORITY_CLASS
environment	Points to an array of strings containing environment variables
currDir	Starting drive and directory for the process
startInfo	Appearance Information about the process's window when it starts
procInfo	Returned information for a process
Returns TRUE on success	

You can create the new process using **CreateProcess** in one of two ways:

1. You can supply an explicit path to the executable in the first parameter and then supply command line parameters for it in the second parameter.
2. You can supply the name of the program to execute along with its command line options in the second parameter. The function will search the original program's load directory, the current directory, the Windows and Windows system directories, and then all directories in the PATH for the file specified.

The first option is generally faster because it minimizes search times.

Using the parameters, there are eight important things you can control about the way the new process starts:

1. The process will automatically start in a new window if it is a GUI application. If it is a console application it will either use the current console or create its own, depending on the value of the creation flags. The

CREATE_NEW_CONSOLE flag indicates that the system should create a new console for the application.

2. You indicate the priority class in the creation flags.
3. You determine whether the process should start in an active or suspended state using the CREATE_SUSPENDED flag.
4. The initial security attributes of the new process and its thread are controlled by the **security** parameter.
5. You can control whether or not the parent's handles are inherited by the child process using the **inherit** parameter.
6. The new process can receive new environment variables if desired using the **environment** parameter.
7. The default drive and directory for the new process is determined by the **currDir** parameter.
8. The startup state of the new process is controlled by the startup structure. It controls things like window size and position.

Once the process starts, it is completely independent of the parent process.

5.10 Inheriting Handles

When a process creates a child process, the child is completely independent of the parent. By default the parent and child have absolutely no connection to one another. However, it is possible for the child process to inherit handles from the parent if the parent marks any of its handles as inheritable. For example, if the parent creates a file handle, or a handle to a thread, or an event handle, it is possible for it to share those handles with child processes it creates. Listings 5.13 and 5.14 show a parent and child process that share a file handle.

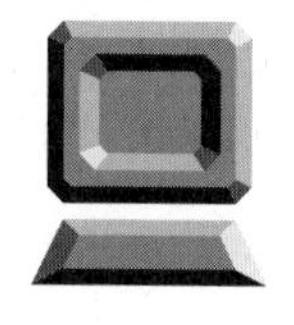

```
// parent.cpp
```

Listing 5.13
The parent process that will share a file handle with an appropriately designed child. Listing 5.14 contains the child process (Page 1 of 3)

```
#include <windows.h>
#include <iostream.h>
#include <stdlib.h>

HANDLE sample;

void main(void)
{
  STARTUPINFO startUpInfo;
  PROCESS_INFORMATION procInfo;
  BOOL success;
  char s[100];
  SECURITY_ATTRIBUTES sa;

  // Set up security attributes to allow
  // inheritance of the file handle
  sa.nLength = sizeof(SECURITY_ATTRIBUTES);
  sa.lpSecurityDescriptor = 0;
  sa.bInheritHandle=TRUE;

  // Create a file handle
  sample = CreateFile("parent.cpp", GENERIC_READ,
    FILE_SHARE_READ, &sa, OPEN_EXISTING,
    FILE_ATTRIBUTE_NORMAL, 0);
  if (sample==INVALID_HANDLE_VALUE)
    cout << "In CreateFile" << GetLastError()
      << endl;

  // Init a startup structure
  GetStartupInfo(&startUpInfo);

  // convert the sample handle to a string
  _itoa((DWORD)sample, s, 10);
```

Listing 5.13
The parent process that will share a file handle with an appropriately designed child. Listing 5.14 contains the child process (Page 2 of 3)

```
        // Create the child process, specifying
        // inherited handles. Pass the value of the
        // handle as a command line parameter
        success=CreateProcess("child.exe", s, 0, 0, TRUE,
          CREATE_NEW_CONSOLE,
          0, 0, &startUpInfo, &procInfo);
        if (!success)
          cout << "Error creating process: "
            << GetLastError() << endl;

        // wait for the child to return (this
        // is not a requirement since the child
        // is its own independent process)
        WaitForSingleObject(procInfo.hProcess, INFINITE);
    }
```

Listing 5.13
The parent process that will share a file handle with an appropriately designed child. Listing 5.14 contains the child process (Page 3 of 3)

```
// child.cpp

#include <windows.h>
#include <iostream.h>
#include <stdlib.h>

HANDLE sample;

void main(int argc, char *argv[])
{
  char str[200];
```

Listing 5.14
The child process that inherits the file handle from the parent shown is Listing 5.13 (Page 1 of 2)

```
    DWORD numRead;
    BOOL success;

    // Get the handle value off of the command line
    sample = (HANDLE) atoi(argv[0]);

    // Now use it like a normal file handle to
    // read the file
    success = ReadFile(sample, str, 100,
      &numRead, 0);
    if (!success)
      cout << "In ReadFile: " << GetLastError()
        << endl;

    // Output the string read from the file
    str[numRead] = '\0';
    cout << str << endl;

    Sleep(2000);
  }
```

Listing 5.14
The child process that inherits the file handle from the parent shown is Listing 5.13 (Page 2 of 2)

The parent process in Listing 5.13 has to do three things to allow the child process in Listing 5.14 to share the file handle:

1. When it calls **CreateFile** to create the file handle, it must supply security attributes that indicate that its handle should be inheritable. It does this by setting the **bInheritHandle** field of the security parameter to TRUE.
2. It must communicate the value of the handle to the child. Here this communication is done by converting the handle value to a string using **_itoa** and then passing the string to the child on the command line.
3. The **inherit** parameter passed to **CreateProcess** must be set to TRUE so that the child process is allowed to inherit handles.

The child process receives a copy of the parent's *handle table.* This handle table contains all of the parent's handles. You can declare a handle in the child as usual.

```
HANDLE sample;
```

When you do this, you are declaring a variable that holds an index that points into the handle table. When the parent passes the value of that index to the child, the child can load the index into a handle variable of its own. Since the child has a copy of the parent's handle table, it can gain access to one of the parent's handles. Listing 5.14 shows the process. The child in Listing 5.14 can read from the file that the parent opened.

In Listings 5.13 and 5.14, the handle value is passed as a string on the command line. It is also possible to pass the handle value using any other interprocess communication method. See Section 5.11 for more information on interprocess communication.

If the handle is not marked as inheritable in the parent, then the child will get an error the first time it tries to use the handle. The child cannot access one of the parent's handles in the handle table unless it is marked as inheritable when the parent created it.

5.11 Interprocess Communication

There are some situations where you want a new process to be able to communicate with other processes on its system, or on other systems on the network. For example, you might want to create a Control Panel applet to control a service (See Chapter 9). Or several processes might want to share information so that they can chop up a problem among themselves. There are three preferred mechanisms that you can use for interprocess communication:

1. Named Pipes: In situations where one process knows that another will probably be there when it starts up, named pipes are useful. For example, if you want to use a Control Panel applet to control a service then named pipes are appropriate. The applet knows that the service should be there and that it should respond. Therefore, the service can listen for connections on a specific named pipe and the Control Panel applet can automatically try to attach to it. See Chapter 7 for information on named pipes. It is just as easy to transmit data across the network to remote processes as it is to transmit data to a local process on the same machine when you use named pipes.

2. Mailslots: If several processes need to share information among the group, mailslots are useful. All of the processes can open a known mailslot name and send data to it, or all can both listen and send. Mailslots limit you to messages with a maximum size, but also work over the network just as well as they do on a single machine. See Chapter 7 for details.
3. File Mapping: File mapping allows a file of a specified name to map itself into a process's address space, as discussed in Section 2.11. It is possible for multiple processes to access the same mapped file by name, and in that way share data with one another. File mapping is faster than either named pipes or mailslots, and it is also as secure as any file is. However, it does not work over the network. It is also possible to share memory, without using an interceding file on the hard disk, by using the handle 0xFFFFFFFF when first calling the **CreateFileMapping** function. This memory is mapped into the normal swap file, and has no real advantage over a mapped file except that you do not have to create an actual file on the file system to use it.

If you are designing an application or a set of applications in which multiple processes must communicate, you should use shared memory if you will need to transmit a large amount of data between processes on a single machine. Since file mapping is efficient, this is the quickest way to move the data. If you have two processes that need to form a connection, then named pipes are useful. If many processes need to communicate, use mailslots.

There are several other far more complicated communication options for GUI programs, including OLE, DDE, and the clipboard. These topics are discussed in the following book in the series.

5.12 Conclusion

When you use threads in your own program, you make it possible for the application to simultaneously perform two or more tasks. For example, the application can recalculate an equation in the background while servicing user requests in the foreground.

Chapter 7 contains a number of thread examples as it demonstrates multithreaded servers and clients using named pipes. The chapter also demonstrates the use of the **_beginthread** function as an alternative for starting threads.

See Chapter 10 for information on securing threads.

Synchronization

6

The previous chapter discusses threads and processes. Threads in particular tend to be extremely useful because they give your applications the ability to do many things at once. After a little practice, you start to think of a thread function as nothing more than a normal function that returns immediately and executes in the background.

There is one minor problem with thread functions, however. Because you can have several threads running at the same time, it is possible for them to compete with each other, or for them to run into each other, in ways that are often quite unexpected. A single-threaded application is something like a car driving around in a completely empty parking lot. Because the lot is empty, the car cannot run into anything. If you let just two cars drive around in the lot, however, they will eventually run into each other. It is inevitable unless you create mechanisms that prevent collisions.

In this chapter you will learn about the problems that can arise when multiple processes and threads compete for resources. You will also learn about the mechanisms provided by the 32-bit API to eliminate these problems.

Compatibility Note: All of the code in this chapter works identically in both Windows NT and Windows 95, with the exception of the overlapped file demonstrations in Section 6.5.

6.1 Understanding the Problem

If you have never worked in a preemptive multi-threaded environment before, it may be hard to imagine that anything peculiar can happen. If you *have* worked in such an environment, then you know the problems all too well. Let's look at two very simple examples of the problems that can arise when you use multiple threads in Windows.

Listing 6.1 contains a simple program. The program starts and immediately creates four identical threads. Each thread increments the same global variable 250,000 times, so **count** is incremented a total of 1,000,000 times. The main program waits for the four threads to complete, and then prints out the global **count** variable. See Chapter 5 for an explanation of threads, thread functions, and the `volatile` keyword.

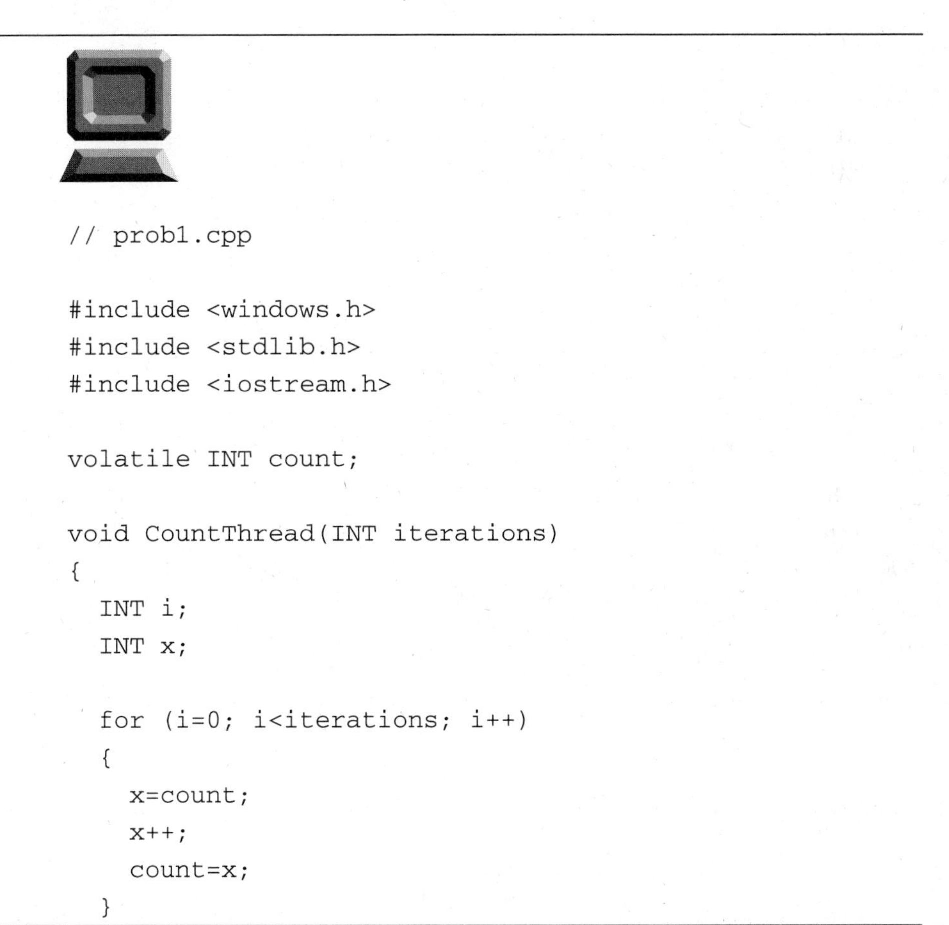

```
// prob1.cpp

#include <windows.h>
#include <stdlib.h>
#include <iostream.h>

volatile INT count;

void CountThread(INT iterations)
{
  INT i;
  INT x;

  for (i=0; i<iterations; i++)
  {
    x=count;
    x++;
    count=x;
  }
```

Listing 6.1
A simple program in which four identical threads increment a count variable 250,000 times each (Page 1 of 2)

```
}

const INT numThreads=4;

void main(void)
{
  HANDLE handles[numThreads];
  DWORD threadID;
  INT i;

  for (i=0; i<numThreads; i++)
  {
    // create the threads
    handles[i]=CreateThread(0, 0,
      (LPTHREAD_START_ROUTINE) CountThread,
      (VOID *) 250000, 0, &threadID);
  }

  // wait for all threads to finish execution
  WaitForMultipleObjects(numThreads, handles,
    TRUE, INFINITE);

  cout << "Global count = " << count << endl;
}
```

Listing 6.1
A simple program in which four identical threads increment a count variable 250,000 times each (Page 2 of 2)

Run this program on your own machine and you will immediately see the problem. I ran it 10 times on my machine, and each time got different output. Here are my results:

Global Count = 469459

Global Count = 520484

Global Count = 459216

Global Count = 508529

Global Count = 710670

Global Count = 588914

Global Count = 584157
Global Count = 462185
Global Count = 508553
Global Count = 720819

None of these numbers are close to the expected value. Since the four threads increment the global variable 250,000 times each, the global count should always be 1,000,000 at the end of each run. Instead, we get apparently random output. The output is, in fact, totally and truly random. Try changing the counter to 25,000 and 25,000,000 as well, and note the results.

The random output is occurring because the four threads are running "simultaneously." On a machine with one processor, the operating system is periodically stopping one thread and giving the CPU to another one. On a machine with four or more processors, the four threads are truly running concurrently. We will discuss the single CPU case here because it is more common.

When the operating system starts thread 1, it gives it a "slice" of CPU time, perhaps 20 milliseconds at most. When that slice of time runs out, the operating system stops the thread and gives CPU time to another thread on the system, sharing the CPU very rapidly among all of the threads to give the impression that they are running simultaneously. See Section 5.7 for a discussion of thread priorities and how they affect scheduling. When all four copies of the thread function are running, the CPU is giving each one a time slice in a round-robin fashion.

Let's say that the global **count** value is currently 100, that thread 1 is running, and that it has just executed the "x=count" statement in the thread function of Listing 6.1. Thread 1 places the value 100 in its local variable **x**. At this moment its time slice runs out and the operating system preempts it to let another thread run.

Thread 2 gets the next time slice. Let's say it is just starting, so it also copies the value 100 into its local copy of **x**, increments **x**, and stores the result, 101, back into the global **count** variable. Thread 2 may get through its loop hundreds of times, raising the value of the global count to 400, before its time slice ends and the CPU is given to another thread.

Eventually thread 1 gets another time slice, and it picks up exactly where it left off. It increments its copy of **x**, which happens to be 100 from the previous time slice, and stores 101 into **count**. This obliterates the work of the other threads. When four threads are doing the same thing hundreds of times per second, you get results like those seen in the sample output above. In order to get correct output, something must be done to prevent the threads from stepping on each other like this.

As a second example, say that you have two threads sharing a common, global data structure, in this case a stack. One thread writes to the stack, while the other reads from it. The code in Listing 6.2 illustrates a possible implementation for the push and pop operations using pointers. There is no error checking in the code to simplify things.

```
typedef struct _NODE
{
  int data;
  _NODE *next;
} NODE;

NODE *top = 0;

void push(int value)
{
  NODE *temp;

  temp = new NODE;
  temp->data = value;
  temp->next = top;
  top = temp;
}

int pop()
```

Listing 6.2
Sample code demonstrating possible implementations of the push and pop operations (Page 1 of 2)

```
    {
      NODE *temp;
      int value;

      if (top == 0)
        return 0;
      temp = top;
      value = top->data;
      top = top->next;
      delete temp;
      return value;
    }
```

Listing 6.2
Sample code demonstrating possible implementations of the push and pop operations (Page 2 of 2)

Say that thread 1 is pushing a value onto the stack. It gets down to the line "top = temp" in the **push** function of Listing 6.2, but is unable to execute the line before it gets preempted. Figure 6.1a illustrates the situation.

Now thread 2 starts and performs a complete **pop**, as shown in Figure 6.1b. Thread 1 then gets another time slice and completes its push operation. The final result is shown in Figure 6.1c. Because the two threads were working simultaneously in a preemptive environment, the stack is corrupted in a way that is impossible in a single-tasking environment.

What is so sad about this particular stack example is that the code *looks* fine. It may *appear* to work correctly for quite some time as you test it. It is often very difficult to track the problem because it may manifest itself quite subtly and infrequently. However, the code is clearly wrong unless something is done to prevent separate threads from colliding as demonstrated here.

These are very simple examples, but they clearly illustrate the problem. You can imagine what might happen when ten threads are competing for 20 global resources. What you need is a way to control access to shared global resources so that threads can access them only in controlled ways. In both cases illustrated above, there needs to be a way to prevent multiple access to the glo-

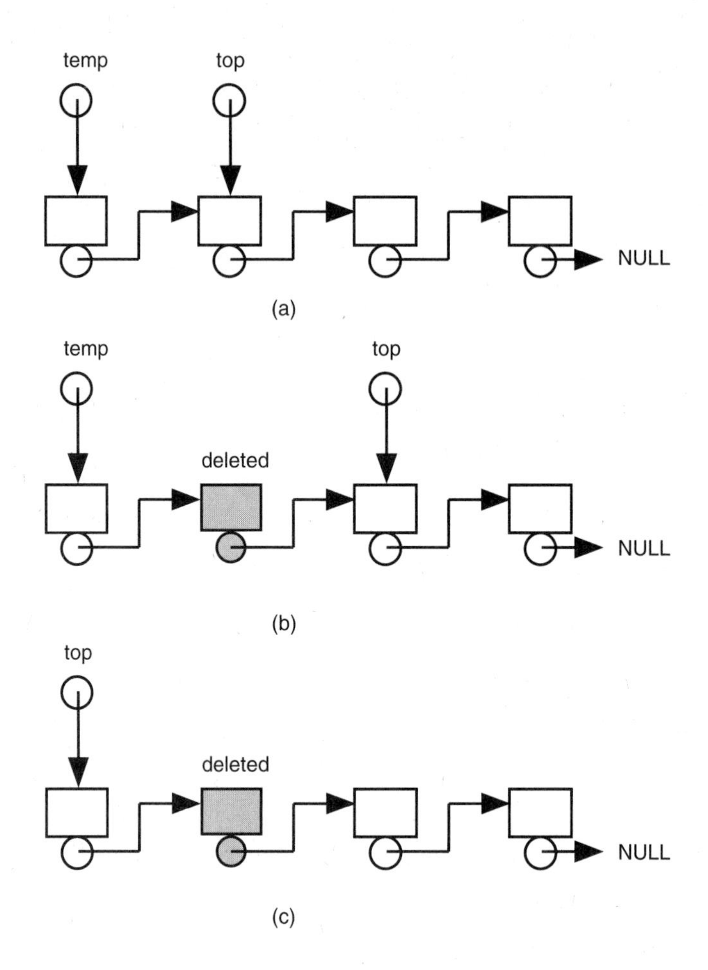

Figure 6.1
The state of the stack when preemptive multi-tasking allows the pushing thread to be preempted in the middle of a push operation. See text for a description.

bal resources. People will often use a variety of different ways to speak about this concept:

- "We need to serialize the access to the global **count** variable so only one thread can access it at a time."
- "We should synchronize the threads so that only one can access the global **count** variable at any given time."
- "Access to the **count** variable should be mutually exclusive—no two threads should be able to use it at the same time."

- "That incrementing code for the global **count** variable is a critical section. We cannot let more than one thread run it at one time."

The terminology differs depending on what book the particular person was using when he or she learned about process synchronization. Different operating system researchers who studied synchronization came up with different ways to talk about and solve the problem. The 32-bit API tries to accommodate these different ways of thinking.

6.2 Four Different Synchronization Methods

The 32-bit API provides four different *synchronization mechanisms*:

1. Critical sections
2. Mutexes
3. Semaphores
4. Events

All four mechanisms might be used to solve the two problems described above, although once you understand them you will see that either critical sections or mutexes would be the logical choices for these particular problems. Semaphores and events have more advanced applications. The following four sections look at each of the techniques and show you how they can be used to solve the simple counting problem demonstrated by Listing 6.1, as well as other more important problems.

One thing that you will notice in the following examples is that all of the synchronization mechanisms implement *efficient waiting*. That is, the synchronization mechanisms built into the 32-bit API all suspend a waiting thread so that the thread requires little or no CPU time while it is waiting. Also note that all of the mechanisms are totally under operating system control, and therefore they do not compromise the system's reliability in any way. For example, in some environments you ensure that a thread has mutually exclusive access to something by turning off interrupts, thereby preventing any type of preemption. Windows does not allow you to do this for obvious system integrity reasons. The mechanisms discussed here also work regardless of the number of processors that the machine uses.

Another thing you will notice is that the mechanisms described here all provide implicit queuing. For example, say that you want to control access to a communication port so that only one thread accesses it at a time. As you will see in the following, you can use a *mutex* to control access. All of the threads "wait on the mutex," and once one owns the mutex it can safely access the communications port. The operating system queues the waiting threads for you, so if five threads are waiting they wait efficiently in a queue and the operating system releases them one at a time based on arrival order.

6.2.1 Critical Sections

The term *critical section* refers to a section of code that should be executed by only one thread at a time. In Listing 6.1, the critical section is the three lines of code that increment the count in the thread function. In the example, both the **push** and **pop** functions contain critical sections, and they are linked. If the **push** function is executing, other pushes *as well as other pops* should be prevented because both functions use the same global data structure. You would therefore mark the contents of both the **push** and **pop** functions with the same critical section variable.

In the 32-bit API, four functions implement critical sections. To create a critical section, you declare a variable of type CRITICAL_SECTION. Call the **InitializeCriticalSection** function to initialize that variable. At the beginning of a critical piece of code, use the **EnterCriticalSection** function and at the end call **LeaveCriticalSection**. When you are done with the critical section variable call **DeleteCriticalSection.**

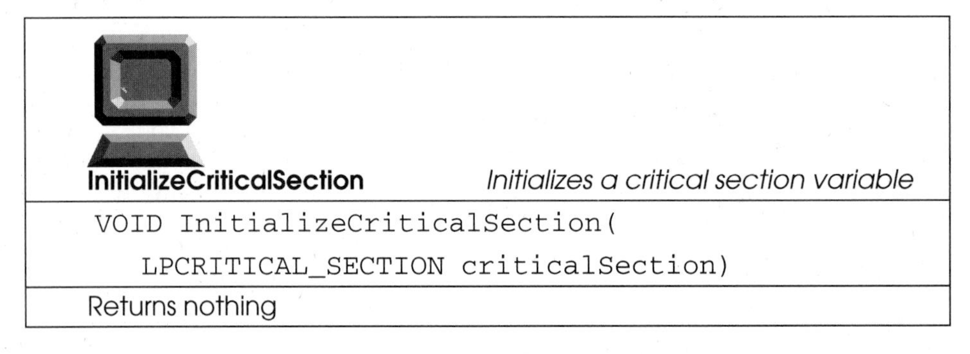

InitializeCriticalSection	*Initializes a critical section variable*

```
VOID InitializeCriticalSection(
   LPCRITICAL_SECTION criticalSection)
```

Returns nothing

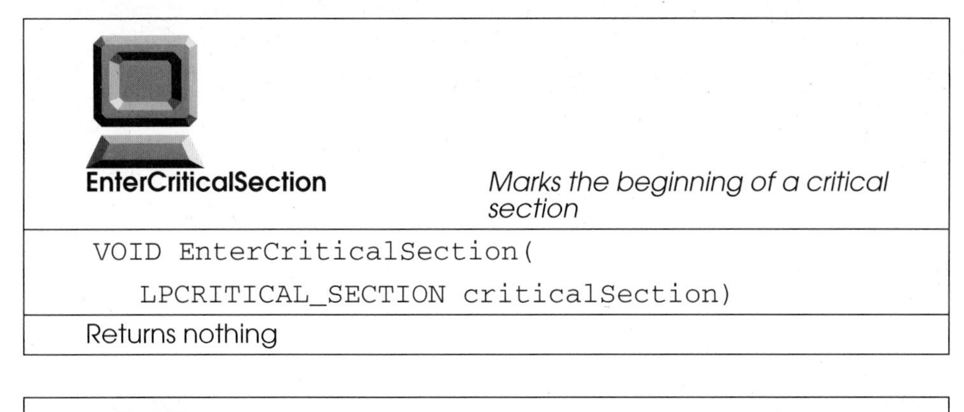

EnterCriticalSection *Marks the beginning of a critical section*

```
VOID EnterCriticalSection(
   LPCRITICAL_SECTION criticalSection)
```

Returns nothing

LeaveCriticalSection *Marks the end of a critical section*

```
VOID LeaveCriticalSection(
   LPCRITICAL_SECTION criticalSection)
```

Returns nothing

DeleteCriticalSection *Releases any allocation for the critical section*

```
VOID DeleteCriticalSection(
   LPCRITICAL_SECTION criticalSection)
```

Returns nothing

Listing 6.3 demonstrates the use of the critical section functions to solve the problem with the global **count** variable demonstrated in Listing 6.1. The critical section variable **critSec** appears globally. The main thread initializes it and then later deletes it just before it quits. The thread function marks the three increment lines as the critical section of code in this program. When you run

Listing 6.3, it will produce the correct answer but will require quite a bit longer (perhaps 50 times longer) to execute.

```
// critsec.cpp

#include <windows.h>
#include <stdlib.h>
#include <iostream.h>

volatile INT count;
CRITICAL_SECTION critSec;

void CountThread(INT iterations)
{
  INT i;
  INT x;

  for (i=0; i<iterations; i++)
  {
    EnterCriticalSection(&critSec);
    x=count;
    x++;
    count=x;
    LeaveCriticalSection(&critSec);
  }
}

const INT numThreads=4;

void main(void)
{
```

Listing 6.3
Applying the critical section code to Listing 6.1 (Page 1 of 2)

```
    HANDLE handles[numThreads];
    DWORD threadID;
    INT i;

    InitializeCriticalSection(&critSec);

    for (i=0; i<numThreads; i++)
    {
      // create a thread and pass it the pointer
      // to its "params" struct
      handles[i]=CreateThread(0, 0,
        (LPTHREAD_START_ROUTINE) CountThread,
        (VOID *) 25000, 0, &threadID);
    }

    // wait for all threads to finish execution
    WaitForMultipleObjects(numThreads, handles,
      TRUE, INFINITE);

    DeleteCriticalSection(&critSec);

    cout << "Global count = " << count << endl;
}
```

Listing 6.3
Applying the critical section code to Listing 6.1 (Page 2 of 2)

The marking for the **push** and **pop** functions of Listing 6.2 is shown in Listing 6.4. Note that they both use the same critical section variable.

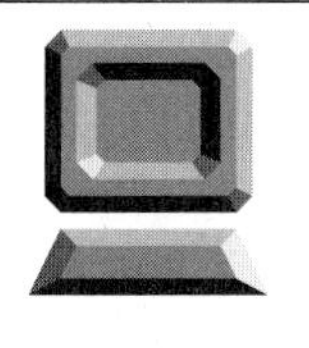

```
typedef struct _NODE
{
```

Listing 6.4
Marking the push and pop functions with a single critical section (Page 1 of 3)

```
  int data;
  _NODE *next;
} NODE;

CRITICAL_SECTION critSec;
NODE *top = 0;

void push(int value)
{
  NODE *temp;

  EnterCriticalSection(&critSec);
  temp = new NODE;
  temp->data = value;
  temp->next = top;
  top = temp;
  LeaveCriticalSection(&critSec);
}

int pop()
{
  NODE *temp;
  int value;

  EnterCriticalSection(&critSec);
  if (top == 0)
  {
    LeaveCriticalSection(&critSec);
    return 0;
  }
  temp = top;
  value = top->data;
  top = top->next;
  delete temp;
  LeaveCriticalSection(&critSec);
```

Listing 6.4
Marking the push and pop functions with a single critical section (Page 2 of 3)

```
        return value;
    }
```

Listing 6.4
Marking the push and pop functions with a single critical section (Page 3 of 3)

The **InitializeCriticalSection** function initializes the critical section variable specified. Do not call this function more than once for the given variable.

A call to **EnterCriticalSection** causes the system to check the specified critical section variable. If the critical section is not in use, the system marks the variable as in-use and returns. If it is in use, the operating system suspends the thread calling **EnterCriticalSection**. Later, when a thread calls **LeaveCriticalSection**, the operating system wakes up the suspended thread and allows it to proceed into the critical section code. Multiple threads can be waiting to enter the critical section at one time. They are serviced on a first-come-first-served basis each time another thread calls **LeaveCriticalSection**.

Here are some points to keep in mind about critical sections:

- A thread can call **EnterCriticalSection** on the same critical section variable multiple times without harm. The system will not block it, making it impossible for a thread to deadlock itself. The thread must call **LeaveCriticalSection** an equal number of times.
- A program can have multiple critical sections by declaring multiple critical section variables. You might do this, for example, if you have two global variables to increment, or two stacks that are active. Two threads should be able to access two independent stacks simultaneously.
- A critical section variable should not be initialized more than once, nor should it be moved or copied. Declare it as a global or member variable and use it that way exclusively.
- Critical section variables are only valid for threads in the same process. Use a mutex (Section 6.2.2) to provide mutual exclusion between multiple processes.
- Do not call **LeaveCriticalSection** unless it has been preceded by a call to **EnterCriticalSection**. The results of an unmatched **Leave** are unpredictable.

With critical sections and all other synchronization techniques, you need to guard against deadlock when there is more than one critical section being used in a single process. See Section 6.3 for details.

Critical sections should be kept short, and should never contain non-deterministic code. For example, a critical section should never contain a read statement that accepts input from the user, because it is impossible to predict how long it will take for the user to respond. In the meantime, all other threads waiting on the critical section are blocked indefinitely.

If you have a large block of code, or a block of code that contains a non-deterministic section, then break up the critical section. For example:

```
EnterCriticalSection
... Deterministic, short-duration code ...
LeaveCriticalSection

... Non-deterministic code ...
EnterCriticalSection
... Deterministic, short-duration code ...
LeaveCriticalSection
```

A critical section should never contain a loop unless you know that the number of iterations is *always* small. It is better to enter and leave the critical section each time through the loop as shown in Listing 6.3.

Note that it is *extremely* easy to create faulty code by not exactly matching your Enters and Leaves, and this code is extremely hard to debug. For example, forgetting the second Leave in the **if** block of the **Pop** function in Listing 6.4 is an easy mistake to make, but is very hard to debug.

6.2.2 Mutexes

A mutex provides mutually exclusive access to a piece of code or a variable in a way that is valid across multiple processes. You often think of a mutexes differently than you do a critical section. Usually you associate a mutex with a global resource, whereas you think of a critical section as referring to a piece of code.

For example, you might assign a mutex to a global variable, or a communications port, or a printer, or a file, to make sure that only one thread uses that resource at a time. The thread accessing the resource "owns" the mutex until it is done with the resource. Then it "releases" the mutex. Other threads wanting to use the resource are "waiting" for the mutex, and as soon as it is released it is acquired by one of the waiting threads.

Listing 6.5 demonstrates a simple use of a mutex. It does the same thing that Listing 6.3 does, except that it uses a mutex instead of a critical section to serialize access to the shared global counter.

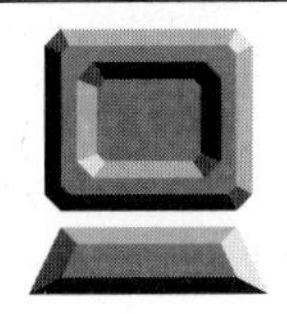

```
// mutex.cpp

#include <windows.h>
#include <stdlib.h>
#include <iostream.h>

volatile INT count;
HANDLE mutex;

void CountThread(INT iterations)
{
  INT i;
  INT x;

  for (i=0; i<iterations; i++)
  {
    WaitForSingleObject(mutex, INFINITE);
    x=count;
    x++;
    count=x;
    ReleaseMutex(mutex);
  }
}

const INT numThreads=4;

void main(void)
```

Listing 6.5
Using a mutex to provide mutual exclusion. Compare to Listing 6.3 (Page 1 of 2)

```
    {
      HANDLE handles[numThreads];
      DWORD threadID;
      INT i;

      mutex = CreateMutex(0, FALSE, 0);

      for (i=0; i<numThreads; i++)
      {
        // create the threads
        handles[i]=CreateThread(0, 0,
          (LPTHREAD_START_ROUTINE) CountThread,
          (VOID *) 25000, 0, &threadID);
      }

      // wait for all threads to finish execution
      WaitForMultipleObjects(numThreads, handles,
        TRUE, INFINITE);

      CloseHandle(mutex);

      cout << "Global count = " << count << endl;
    }
```

Listing 6.5
Using a mutex to provide mutual exclusion. Compare to Listing 6.3 (Page 2 of 2)

The program in Listing 6.5 starts by creating a mutex using the **CreateMutex** function. A mutex is an object (see Sections 1.4 and 10.5), so **CreateMutex** returns a handle to it.

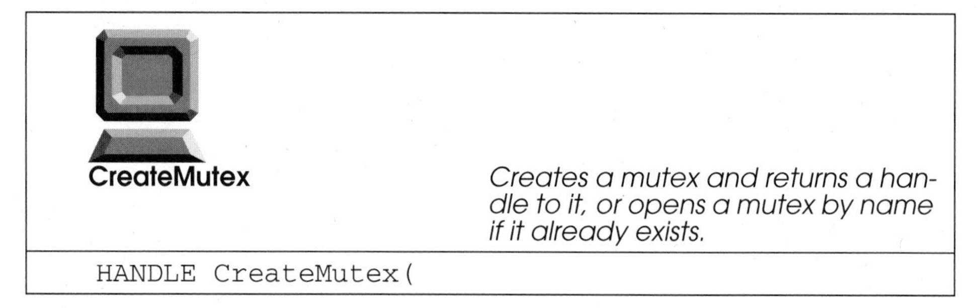

CreateMutex

Creates a mutex and returns a handle to it, or opens a mutex by name if it already exists.

```
HANDLE CreateMutex(
```

```
    LPSECURITY_ATTRIBUTES security,
    BOOL initialOwner,
    LPCTSTR name)
```

security	Security attributes. See Chapter 10
initialOwner	Set to TRUE if you want to initially own the mutex
name	The name of the mutex, or 0 if nameless

Returns a handle to the mutex, or 0 on error. If a mutex of the specified name already exists, then **GetLastError** will return ERROR_ALREADY_EXISTS but the handle will be valid.

OpenMutex *Opens a mutex by name if it already exists*

```
HANDLE OpenMutex(
    DWORD access,
    BOOL inherit,
    LPCTSTR name)
```

access	SYNCHRONIZE and/or MUTEX_ALL_ACCESS
inherit	Set to TRUE if you want the mutex handle to be inheritable
name	The name of the mutex to open

Returns a handle to the mutex, or 0 on error

The mutex object can be named or unnamed. In Listing 6.5 it is unnamed because it is used in only one process. If you want to use it in multiple processes, then you can name it and other processes can open handles to access it using either **CreateMutex** or **OpenMutex**. When you use **CreateMutex** with the name of a mutex that already exists, then it simply opens the existing mutex and returns a handle just like **OpenMutex** would.

The main function in Listing 6.5 then creates the four threads. The threads wait for the mutex by calling the **WaitForSingleObject** function. See Section 6.4 for details.

WaitForSingleObject	*Waits for the mutex to be released*

`DWORD WaitForSingleObject(`
`   HANDLE object,`
`DWORD timeout)`	

object	The mutex to wait for
timeout	0, a number of milliseconds, or INFINITE
Returns WAIT_FAILED, WAIT_ABANDONED, WAIT_TIMEOUT, or WAIT_OBJECT_0	

The **WaitForSingleObject** function waits for the specified object to be "signaled." A mutex is initially set to the signaled state (unless **initialOwner** is TRUE), so the first thread to call **WaitForSingleObject** gets the mutex immediately. Multiple threads can efficiently wait on a single mutex, which will remain "unsignaled" until the owning thread releases it. As soon as the mutex is released, the operating system gives it to one of the waiting threads.

If a thread already owns a mutex and calls **WaitForSingleObject** again, then it continues execution so that a thread cannot block itself. The thread must release the mutex an equivalent number of times.

The **WaitForSingleObject** function accepts a timeout value. If the value is 1,000, then the function returns when the mutex is signaled, or when 1,000 milliseconds elapses, whichever comes first. If the timeout value is 0, then the function returns immediately regardless of the state of the mutex and provides an easy way to test the mutex's state. If the timeout value is set to INFINITE, the function does not return until the mutex is signaled.

The **WaitForSingleObject** function returns WAIT_FAILED on an error. It returns WAIT_TIMEOUT if the timeout period elapsed. It returns WAIT_OBJECT_0 if the mutex is signaled. It returns WAIT_ABANDONED if the thread owning the mutex died before calling the **ReleaseMutex** function to formally release the mutex. Abandonment implies an error, and the thread receiving a mutex in this state should assume that the resource that the mutex guards is in an unstable state. It is a good design practice to provide a function that the thread can call to restabilize the resource whenever it detects an abandoned mutex.

When a thread is done with the resource, it should call the **ReleaseMutex** function. This allows another thread waiting on the mutex to access the resource.

ReleaseMutex	*Releases a mutex so another thread can use it*
`BOOL ReleaseMutex(` `   HANDLE mutex)`	
mutex	The mutex to release
Returns TRUE on success	

Mutexes are often used when mutual exclusion between multiple processes is needed. By naming the mutex, another process can open a handle to it. Listing 6.6 demonstrates the use of a named mutex.

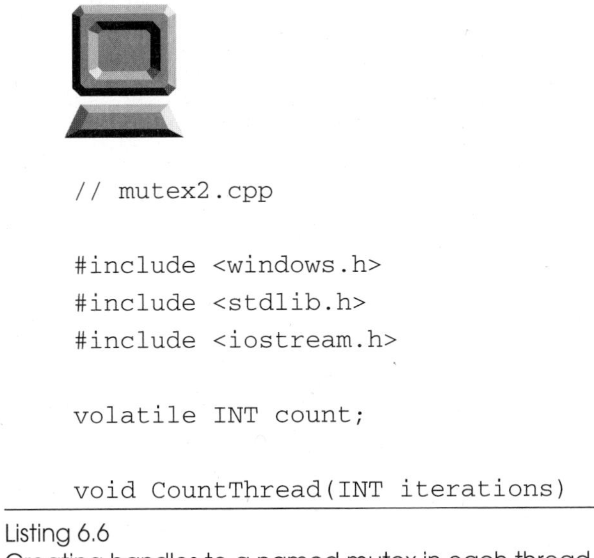

```
// mutex2.cpp

#include <windows.h>
#include <stdlib.h>
#include <iostream.h>

volatile INT count;

void CountThread(INT iterations)
```

Listing 6.6
Creating handles to a named mutex in each thread rather than using a single handle (Page 1 of 3)

```
{
  INT i;
  INT x;
  HANDLE mutex;

  mutex = CreateMutex(0, FALSE, "counterMutex");

  for (i=0; i<iterations; i++)
  {
    WaitForSingleObject(mutex, INFINITE);
    x=count;
    x++;
    count=x;
    ReleaseMutex(mutex);
  }

  CloseHandle(mutex);
}

const INT numThreads=4;

void main(void)
{
  HANDLE handles[numThreads];
  DWORD threadID;
  INT i;

  for (i=0; i<numThreads; i++)
  {
    // create the threads
    handles[i]=CreateThread(0, 0,
      (LPTHREAD_START_ROUTINE) CountThread,
      (VOID *) 25000, 0, &threadID);
  }
```

Listing 6.6
Creating handles to a named mutex in each thread rather than using a single handle (Page 2 of 3)

```
    // wait for all threads to finish execution
    WaitForMultipleObjects(numThreads, handles,
      TRUE, INFINITE);

    cout << "Global count = " << count << endl;
}
```

Listing 6.6
Creating handles to a named mutex in each thread rather than using a single handle (Page 3 of 3)

In Listing 6.6, each thread calls **CreateMutex** using the name "counter-Mutex." The first thread to call **CreateMutex** actually creates the mutex. All other calls to **CreateMutex** with the same name perform an open operation and return a handle to the existing mutex. Each thread keeps a local handle pointing to the mutex, so four handles point to the same mutex once all four threads have started. If the threads happened to be in different processes, the effect would be the same.

When a thread is done using a mutex, it should close the handle to it with **CloseHandle**. The thread should release the mutex first if it owns it. When all handles pointing to the mutex are closed, the operating system automatically deletes the mutex object.

6.2.3 Semaphores

A semaphore is a superset of a mutex. It works just like a mutex, but in addition it has a counter associated with it. The counter always has a value between zero and a maximum that you set when you create the semaphore. When the counter is greater than zero, the semaphore is signaled, and any Wait function will proceed (see Section 6.4 for details). When the counter is zero the semaphore is not signaled and any Wait function blocks until the count rises above zero due to another thread releasing the semaphore. When you call the release function you specify a value to be added to the semaphore's counter, generally 1. You set the initial value of the semaphore's counter when you create the semaphore.

By setting a semaphore's maximum value to 1 and initial value to 1, you get behavior that is identical to a mutex. Listing 6.7 duplicates Listing 6.5 using a semaphore in place of a mutex.

```
// sema.cpp

#include <windows.h>
#include <stdlib.h>
#include <iostream.h>

volatile INT count;
HANDLE semaphore;

void CountThread(INT iterations)
{
  INT i;
  INT x;
  LONG semaCount;

  for (i=0; i<iterations; i++)
  {
    WaitForSingleObject(semaphore, INFINITE);
    x=count;
    x++;
    count=x;
    ReleaseSemaphore(semaphore, 1, &semaCount);
  }
}

const INT numThreads=4;
```

Listing 6.7
A duplication of Listing 6.5 using a semaphore with a maximum value of 1 in place of the mutex (Page 1 of 2)

```
void main(void)
{
  HANDLE handles[numThreads];
  DWORD threadID;
  INT i;

  semaphore = CreateSemaphore(0, 1, 1, 0);

  for (i=0; i<numThreads; i++)
  {
    // create the threads
    handles[i]=CreateThread(0, 0,
      (LPTHREAD_START_ROUTINE) CountThread,
      (VOID *) 25000, 0, &threadID);
  }

  // wait for all threads to finish execution
  WaitForMultipleObjects(numThreads, handles,
    TRUE, INFINITE);

  CloseHandle(semaphore);

  cout << "Global count = " << count << endl;
}
```

Listing 6.7
A duplication of Listing 6.5 using a semaphore with a maximum value of 1 in place of the mutex (Page 2 of 2)

You can see that the functions used when working with a semaphore are nearly identical to those used with mutexes. The **CreateSemaphore** function accepts an initial and maximum count.

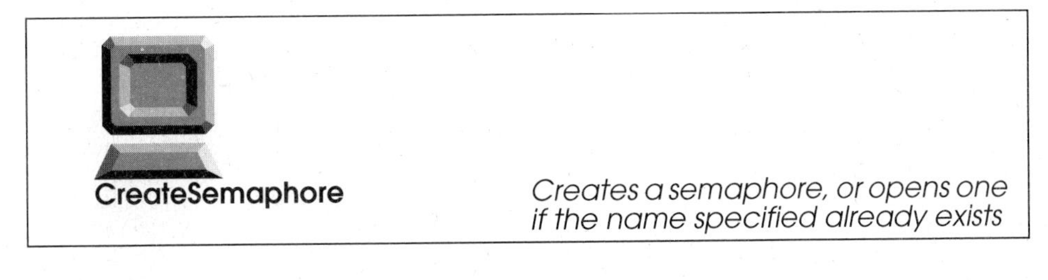

```
HANDLE CreateSemaphore(
    LPSECURITY_ATTRIBUTES security,
    LONG initialValue,
    LONG maxValue,
    LPCTSTR name)
```

security	Security attributes. See Chapter 10
initialValue	The initial value of the semaphore's count
maxValue	The maximum value of the semaphore's count
name	The name of the semaphore, or 0 if nameless

Returns a handle to the semaphore, or NULL on error. If a semaphore of the specified name already exists, then **GetLastError** will return ERROR_ALREADY_EXISTS but the handle will be valid.

OpenSemaphore *Opens an existing semaphore by name*

```
HANDLE OpenSemaphore(
    DWORD access,
    BOOL inherit,
    LPCTSTR name)
```

access	SEMAPHORE_MODIFY_STATE, SYNCHRONIZE, and/or SEMAPHORE_ALL_ACCESS
inherit	Set to TRUE if handle should be inheritable
name	The name of the semaphore to open

Returns a handle to the named semaphore, or NULL if it does not exist

Semaphores, like mutexes, can be named or unnamed. If named, processes can share them by opening an existing semaphore.

Threads wait on a semaphore using **WaitForSingleObject**, as shown in the previous section. If the value of the semaphore is zero, the thread blocks when it calls the Wait function. Any non-zero value lets the thread proceed. Because of this, semaphores can allow a limited number of threads to use a resource simultaneously. In Listing 6.7, with the maximum value of the count set to one, only one thread can access the global counter. However, if the maximum value and initial value were set to three, then three threads could access the resource together. As with a mutex, you can specify a timeout value for the Wait function.

To release a semaphore, call the **ReleaseSemaphore** function.

ReleaseSemaphore — *Increments the count of the semaphore by the specified value.*

```
BOOL ReleaseSemaphore(
    HANDLE semaphore,
    LONG incrementValue,
    LPLONG count)
```

Parameter	Description
semaphore	The semaphore to release
incrementValue	The value to add to the semaphore's counter, generally 1
count	A variable to hold the returned count prior to incrementing. Set to 0 if you don't need the count

Returns TRUE on success

Generally you pass in 1 as the increment value, although other values are possible.

Listing 6.7's use of a semaphore is something of a waste. With the maximum value of the semaphore set to 1, the semaphore behaves just like a mutex. The count value associated with semaphores makes them useful in a variety of situations, however. For example, it is easy to solve the "bounded buffer" problem using semaphores.

The bounded buffer problem assumes that there is a single buffer shared by two threads. One thread is filling the buffer, while the other is emptying it. The buffer might hold messages passed between the two threads, queuing them when the reader cannot keep up with the writer. The buffer, however, is "bounded." It cannot hold more than some fixed number of messages. Once the buffer reaches its maximum size, the writer should stop adding messages until there is again room available in the buffer. If the buffer becomes empty, the reader should stop until something appears in the buffer again.

To solve the bounded buffer problem with semaphores, assume that you create two of them. One semaphore is called **empty** and starts with the value N, where N is the maximum size of the buffer. The other is called **full** and starts with the value 0.

The writer thread waits on the **empty** semaphore. Since **empty** starts with the value N, the writer proceeds through the wait and puts a value in the buffer. The writer then increments the **full** semaphore to signal that the buffer contains one value. For example:

```
WaitForSingleObject(empty);
... add to the buffer ...
ReleaseSemaphore(full, 1);
```

The reader thread is doing just the opposite, waiting on **full** and then incrementing **empty**. For example:

```
WaitForSingleObject(full);
... remove from the buffer ...
ReleaseSemaphore(empty, 1);
```

As the writer places values in the buffer, it decrements empty toward zero. Once the buffer is full, **empty** will hit zero and the writer will be blocked until the reader removes a value and releases **empty**, thereby incrementing it. On the other hand, the reader decrements **full** each time it reads a value. Since **full** starts at zero, the reader is initially blocked, but becomes unblocked each time the writer increments **full** by releasing it. The value of **full** never rises above the maximum because the writer has to wait on **empty** first.

Listing 6.8 shows an implementation of the bounded buffer problem using two semaphores. It uses the stack code discussed in Listings 6.2 and 6.4 to add and remove values from the buffer, with a critical section to prevent faulty access to the stack's global variables. A second critical section is also used for the **cout** statements because they sometimes do odd things when called simultaneously.

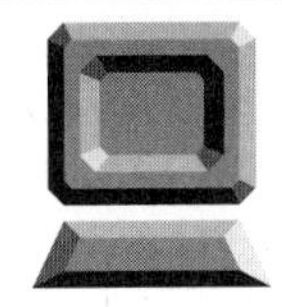

```
// buffer.cpp

#include <windows.h>
#include <iostream.h>

typedef struct _NODE
{
  int data;
  _NODE *next;
} NODE;

NODE *top = 0;
HANDLE empty, full;
CRITICAL_SECTION critSec;
CRITICAL_SECTION coutCritSec;
const MAX_BUFFERS = 5;

void push(int value)
{
  NODE *temp;

  EnterCriticalSection(&critSec);
  temp = new NODE;
  temp->data = value;
  temp->next = top;
  top = temp;
  LeaveCriticalSection(&critSec);
}
```

Listing 6.8
A solution to the bounded-buffer problem using semaphores (Page 1 of 4)

```
int pop()
{
  NODE *temp;
  int value;

  EnterCriticalSection(&critSec);
  if (top == 0)
  {
    LeaveCriticalSection(&critSec);
    return 0;
  }
  temp = top;
  value = top->data;
  top = top->next;
  delete temp;
  LeaveCriticalSection(&critSec);
  return value;
}

VOID ReadThread(VOID)
{
  int x, p;
  LONG count;

  for (x=0; x<10; x++)
  {
    WaitForSingleObject(full, INFINITE);
    p = pop();
    ReleaseSemaphore(empty, 1, &count);
    EnterCriticalSection(&coutCritSec);
    cout << "Read iteration: " << x
      << " value popped: " << p
      << " empty count: " << count << endl;
    LeaveCriticalSection(&coutCritSec);
```

Listing 6.8
A solution to the bounded-buffer problem using semaphores (Page 2 of 4)

```
    Sleep(200);
  }
}

VOID WriteThread(VOID)
{
  int x;
  LONG count;

  for (x=0; x<10; x++)
  {
    WaitForSingleObject(empty, INFINITE);
    push(x);
    ReleaseSemaphore(full, 1, &count);
    EnterCriticalSection(&coutCritSec);
    cout << "Write iteration: " << x
      << " full count: " << count << endl;
    LeaveCriticalSection(&coutCritSec);
    Sleep(100);
  }
}

const INT numThreads=2;

void main(void)
{
  HANDLE handles[numThreads];
  DWORD threadID;

  // Init synchronization
  InitializeCriticalSection(&critSec);
  InitializeCriticalSection(&coutCritSec);
  full = CreateSemaphore(0, 0, MAX_BUFFERS, 0);
  empty = CreateSemaphore(0, MAX_BUFFERS,
    MAX_BUFFERS, 0);
```

Listing 6.8
A solution to the bounded-buffer problem using semaphores (Page 3 of 4)

```
    // create a thread to read from the buffer
    handles[0]=CreateThread(0, 0,
      (LPTHREAD_START_ROUTINE) ReadThread,
      0, 0, &threadID);

    // create a thread to write to the buffer
    handles[1]=CreateThread(0, 0,
      (LPTHREAD_START_ROUTINE) WriteThread,
      0, 0, &threadID);

    // wait for all threads to finish execution
    WaitForMultipleObjects(numThreads, handles,
      TRUE, INFINITE);

    // Clean up
    CloseHandle(empty);
    CloseHandle(full);
    DeleteCriticalSection(&critSec);
    DeleteCriticalSection(&coutCritSec);
}
```

Listing 6.8
A solution to the bounded-buffer problem using semaphores (Page 4 of 4)

In Listing 6.8, the writer will produce 10 values and push them onto the stack. The reader reads 10 values by popping them off of the stack. You can adjust the sleep times in the reader and writer to let the writer outpace the reader, or to let the reader outpace the writer. With the values shown in Listing 6.8, I received the following output from the program:

```
H:\users\brain\nt\internal\code\sync>buffer
Write iteration: 0 full count: 0
Read iteration: 0 value popped: 0 empty count: 4
Write iteration: 1 full count: 0
Read iteration: 1 value popped: 1 empty count: 4
Write iteration: 2 full count: 0
Write iteration: 3 full count: 1
Read iteration: 2 value popped: 3 empty count: 3
```

```
Write iteration: 4 full count: 1

Write iteration: 5 full count: 2

Read iteration: 3 value popped: 5 empty count: 2

Write iteration: 6 full count: 2

Write iteration: 7 full count: 3

Read iteration: 4 value popped: 7 empty count: 1

Write iteration: 8 full count: 3

Write iteration: 9 full count: 4

Read iteration: 5 value popped: 9 empty count: 0

Read iteration: 6 value popped: 8 empty count: 1

Read iteration: 7 value popped: 6 empty count: 2

Read iteration: 8 value popped: 4 empty count: 3

Read iteration: 9 value popped: 2 empty count: 4
```

Here the writer is working twice as fast as the reader, so it fills the buffer quickly and then finishes, while the reader empties the buffer.

Semaphores are useful in many similar situations where you want to limit access to a resource to a fixed number of threads. For example, you might want to create a different thread to calculate each scan line in a Mandelbrot set (see Section 5.4 for details) because this makes the problem conceptually easy to multi-thread. However, you may want to limit the number of threads running simultaneously to the number of available processors for maximum efficiency. Semaphores solve this problem easily using the techniques seen in Listing 6.8.

6.2.4 Events

Events are a general-purpose signaling system that you can use when one process or thread needs to signal another process or thread. Events are also used inside of overlapped structures (see Section 6.5). They come in two flavors: manual and automatic. In automatic mode they have the same functionality as a mutex, as demonstrated in Listing 6.9.

```
// event.cpp

#include <windows.h>
#include <stdlib.h>
#include <iostream.h>

volatile INT count;
HANDLE event;

void CountThread(INT iterations)
{
  INT i;
  INT x;

  for (i=0; i<iterations; i++)
  {
    WaitForSingleObject(event, INFINITE);
    x=count;
    x++;
    count=x;
    SetEvent(event);
  }
}

const INT numThreads=4;

void main(void)
{
  HANDLE handles[numThreads];
```

Listing 6.9
Using events like a mutex. Compare to Listing 6.3 (Page 1 of 2)

```
    DWORD threadID;
    INT i;

    event = CreateEvent(0, FALSE, TRUE, 0);

    for (i=0; i<numThreads; i++)
    {
      // create a thread and pass it the pointer
      // to its "params" struct
      handles[i]=CreateThread(0, 0,
        (LPTHREAD_START_ROUTINE) CountThread,
        (VOID *) 25000, 0, &threadID);
    }
    // wait for all threads to finish execution
    WaitForMultipleObjects(numThreads, handles,
      TRUE, INFINITE);

    CloseHandle(event);

    cout << "Global count = " << count << endl;
}
```

Listing 6.9
Using events like a mutex. Compare to Listing 6.3 (Page 2 of 2)

Listing 6.9 starts by creating an event. An event can be thought of as a general purpose signaling mechanism. You generally use it to cause a thread to wait efficiently for something to happen.

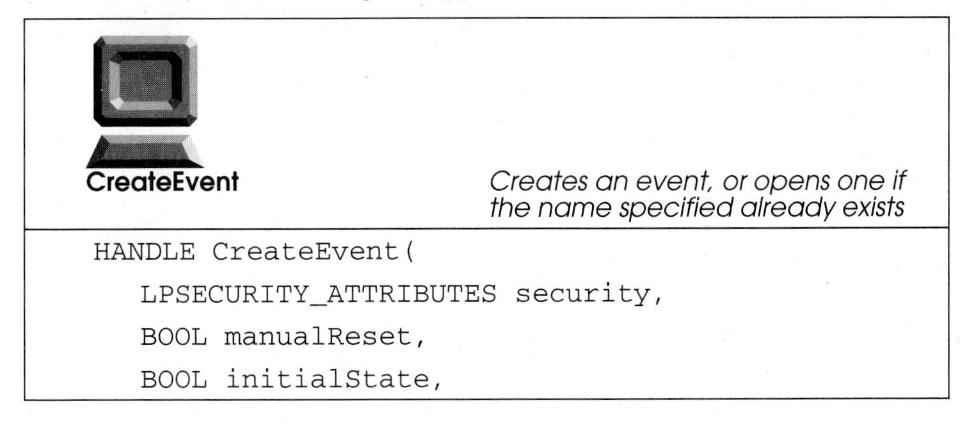

CreateEvent

Creates an event, or opens one if the name specified already exists

```
HANDLE CreateEvent(
   LPSECURITY_ATTRIBUTES security,
   BOOL manualReset,
   BOOL initialState,
```

```
    LPCTSTR name)
```

security	Security attributes. See Chapter 10
manualReset	TRUE for manual reset, FALSE for automatic reset
initialState	The initial state of the event: TRUE if signaled
name	The name of the event, or 0 if nameless

Returns a handle to the event, or 0 on error. If a event of the specified name already exists, then **GetLastError** will return ERROR_ALREADY_EXISTS but the handle will be valid.

OpenEvent *Opens an existing event by name*

```
HANDLE OpenEvent(
    DWORD access,
    BOOL inherit,
    LPCTSTR name)
```

access	EVENT_MODIFY_STATE, SYNCHRONIZE, and/or EVENT_ALL_ACCESS
inherit	Set to TRUE if handle should be inheritable
name	The name of the event to open

Returns a handle to the named event, or NULL if it does not exist

When you wait on an automatic event using, for example, **WaitForSingleObject**, the thread blocks until the event is in a signaled state. When the event is signaled the Wait function returns and the thread proceeds. The event becomes unsignaled automatically by the Wait function, and the thread "owns" the event. When the thread is finished with the event it calls **SetEvent**, which signals the event for another thread. As you can see, an automatic event acts just like a mutex.

SetEvent	*Sets an event to the signaled state*
`BOOL SetEvent(` `    HANDLE event)`	
event	The event to set
Returns TRUE on success	

Events also come in a manual flavor. In manual mode each thread must set the event to signaled or reset it to unsignaled on its own. A Wait function has no automatic effect on the event.

ResetEvent	*Resets an event to the unsignaled state*
`BOOL ResetEvent(` `    HANDLE event)`	
event	The event to reset
Returns TRUE on success	

You use manual events when you want to allow one thread to signal another, and the other thread needs to wait efficiently until it receives the signal. For example, say that one thread is calculating a result and a second thread needs to wait for the answer. The second thread can wait efficiently on an event, and the first thread can signal the event when it is ready.

In manual mode you can also "pulse" an event. When you pulse an event, the event becomes signaled long enough to release all waiting threads, and then it becomes unsignaled again.

PulseEvent	*Sets an event to the signaled state long enough to release all waiting threads, and then resets the event*
`BOOL PulseEvent(` `   HANDLE event)`	
event	The event to pulse
Returns TRUE on success	

Events are also used in overlapped structures. See Section 6.5 for examples and more information.

6.2.5 Interlocked Operations

The 32-bit API supplies three low-level functions that can be used in special situations or as primitives for building your own synchronization mechanisms. These are called the *interlocked* functions. The **InterlockedIncrement** function increments a value of type LONG and returns a result that is zero, positive or negative. If the value of the variable becomes zero as a result of the increment operation, then the returned result is zero. Otherwise, the result has the same sign, but not necessarily the same value, as the variable that was incremented. **InterlockedDecrement** decrements a variable in the same way. The **InterlockedExchange** function replaces one value with another value and returns the replaced value. All three of these functions are atomic: they will not be interrupted once they start.

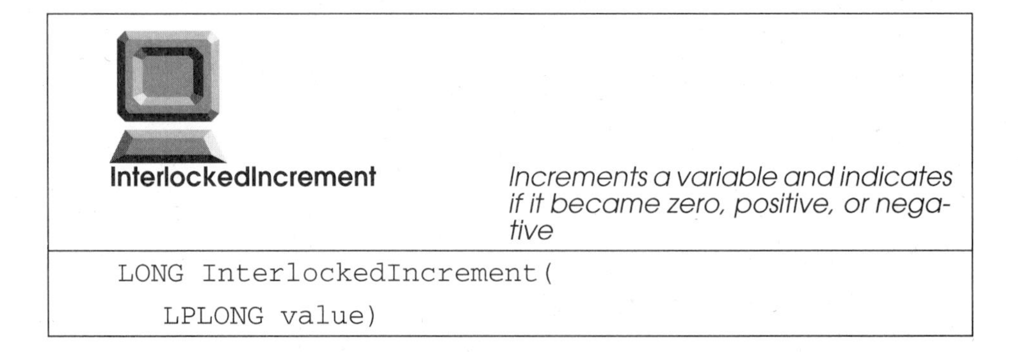

InterlockedIncrement	*Increments a variable and indicates if it became zero, positive, or negative*
`LONG InterlockedIncrement(` `   LPLONG value)`	

value	The value to increment
Returns 0 if the value became zero, or a value with the appropriate sign	

InterlockedDecrement	*Decrements a variable and indicates if it became zero, positive, or negative*

```
LONG InterlockedDecrement(
    LPLONG value)
```

value	The value to increment
Returns 0 if the value became zero, or a value with the appropriate sign	

InterlockedExchange	*Replaces a variable with the value indicated*

```
LONG InterlockedExchange(
    LPLONG target,
    LONG value)
```

target	The variable to replace
value	The value to use as the replacement
Returns the value of target prior to the exchange	

6.3 Deadlocks, Starvation, and Other Synchronization Bugs

The reason you use the synchronization mechanisms described in the preceding sections is to prevent threads from colliding with one another when they access global resources. When used properly, they accomplish this goal. Unfortunately, one of the problems with synchronization mechanisms is that they can breed their own special variety of bugs, both simple and complex. Several of these bugs are demonstrated in this section.

One classic synchronization problem is called the "dining philosophers" problem. You will find a solution to this problem in every textbook on operating systems. It may initially seem a bit contrived if this is the first time you have seen it, but it is a metaphor for general multi-resource allocation problems. Framing the problem as a group of philosophers makes it very easy to see and understand the concepts of *deadlock* and *starvation*.

Imagine that you have a square or round table with several people sitting around it. Typically the people are characterized as Chinese philosophers, hence the name of the problem. Each philosopher has a large bowl of food in front of him, and one chopstick to his left and right. However, there is only one chopstick for each philosopher: the chopstick to the right of one philosopher is the same chopstick that is to the left of the next. See Figure 6.2. Ignore the sanitary issues of this arrangement for the moment, and also assume that there will be no cooperation or communication among the philosophers to modify their dilemma.

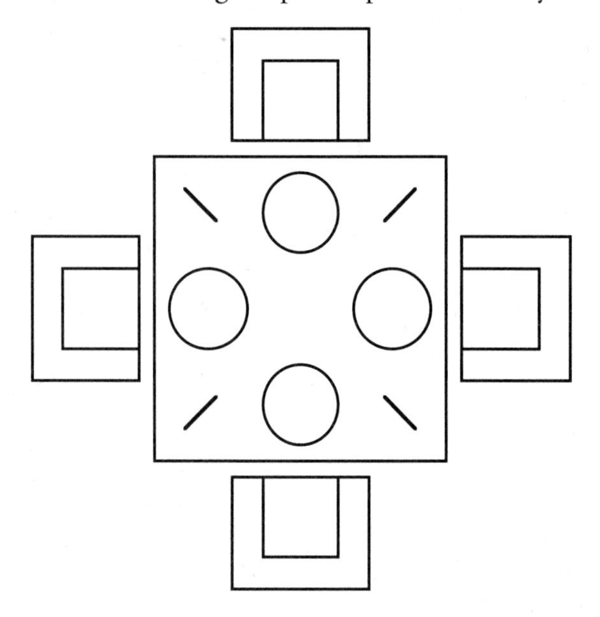

Figure 6.2
The table arrangement for the dining philosophers problem with four philosophers.

The philosophers either think or eat. Each philosopher sits back in his chair and thinks for awhile, and then gets hungry and decides to eat. In order to eat the philosopher must pick up the chopsticks on his left and right side. However, because of the chopstick arrangement, if either chopstick is in use then the philosopher must wait for his neighbor to finish eating. Assume that each philosopher picks up his left chopstick first, and then his right chopstick.

As you can see, the problem is conceptually simple. However, it represents a number of real life problems in which threads must share global resources. Each philosopher represents a thread, and each chopstick represents a resource. Each thread must have two resources to complete its job, and different threads are competing for the resources they need. For example, one thread might need the communications port and the printer to complete its task. Another might need the printer and exclusive access to a file. Yet another might need the same file and the communications port. This is exactly the sort of scenario that the dining philosophers problem portrays.

Listing 6.10 shows an implementation of the dining philosophers problem using mutexes to represent the chopsticks and threads to represent the philosophers.

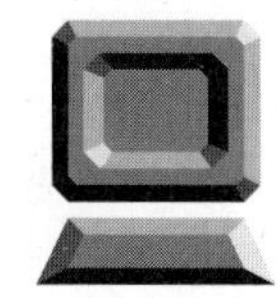

```
// dinphil.cpp

#include <windows.h>
#include <stdlib.h>
#include <iostream.h>

const INT numPhilosophers=3;
HANDLE chopsticks[numPhilosophers];
CHAR csStat[numPhilosophers+1];
CHAR pStat[numPhilosophers+1];

void PhilosopherThread(INT id)
{
  while (1)
  {
```

Listing 6.10
An implementation of the dining-philosophers problem (Page 1 of 3)

```
        //thinking
        Sleep(GetTickCount() % 50);

        // hungry, so picks up chopsticks
        WaitForSingleObject(chopsticks[id],
          INFINITE);
        csStat[id]='1';
        WaitForSingleObject(
          chopsticks[(id+1)%numPhilosophers],
          INFINITE);
        csStat[(id+1)%numPhilosophers]='1';
        pStat[id]='1';

        // eating
        cout << csStat << "   " << pStat << endl;
        Sleep(GetTickCount() % 50);

        pStat[id]='0';
        // done eating
        ReleaseMutex(chopsticks[id]);
        csStat[id]='0';
        ReleaseMutex(
          chopsticks[(id+1)%numPhilosophers]);
        csStat[(id+1)%numPhilosophers]='0';
      }
    }

    void main(void)
    {
      HANDLE handles[numPhilosophers];
      DWORD threadID;
      INT i;

      csStat[numPhilosophers]='\0';
      pStat[numPhilosophers]='\0';
```

Listing 6.10
An implementation of the dining-philosophers problem (Page 2 of 3)

```
    // Create the chopstick mutexes
    for (i=0; i<numPhilosophers; i++)
      chopsticks[i] = CreateMutex(0, FALSE, 0);

    // Create the philosopher threads
    for (i=0; i<numPhilosophers; i++)
    {
      // create the philosopher threads
      handles[i]=CreateThread(0, 0,
        (LPTHREAD_START_ROUTINE) PhilosopherThread,
        (VOID *) i, 0, &threadID);
    }

    // wait for all threads to finish execution
    WaitForMultipleObjects(numPhilosophers, handles,
      TRUE, INFINITE);

    for (i=0; i<numPhilosophers; i++)
      CloseHandle(chopsticks[i]);

    cout << "Done" << endl;
}
```

Listing 6.10
An implementation of the dining-philosophers problem (Page 3 of 3)

In Listing 6.10, the main program starts by initializing the mutexes and then creating the threads. As shown, the code will create three philosophers and three chopsticks. In each thread, the code simulates thinking by sleeping for a random amount of time. The thread then attempts to pick up two chopsticks using **WaitForSingleObject** on the left and right chopstick. As soon as it has both, the thread sleeps for a random amount of time to simulate eating, and then puts down its two chopsticks using **ReleaseMutex**.

The program in Listing 6.10 contains two arrays that help you see what is going on inside the program. When you run the program it will print out the contents of both arrays. The **chStat** array is the chopstick status array. It shows which chopsticks are currently allocated to a philosopher. That is, **chStat** indicates which chopsticks are currently in somebody's hand because somebody either wants to eat or is in the process of eating. The **pStat** array indicates which philosophers are actually eating. In the three philosopher case shown in Listing 6.10, only one philosopher can eat at a time.

This program seems simple enough, but when you run it there is a problem. It will run for a bit and then stop. Run it again and it stops again. It may run for quite some time in certain cases, but eventually it will stop every time.

What is happening here is called *deadlock*. In this program a deadlock occurs when every philosopher has one of the chopsticks in his left hand. No one can proceed because there are no right chopsticks to pick up, so everyone waits infinitely and the program locks up. In the three-philosopher case the probability of a deadlock is fairly high, so the program locks quickly.

There are two other problems with the code in Listing 6.10. Increase the number of philosophers to 20 and run the program again. The first problem you should notice is that the program probably does not lock up. With this many people eating, the probability of all 20 picking up their left chopsticks at the same time is very small, so the deadlock problem is *hidden*. You could test the program for quite some time and never see anything wrong, but the possibility of deadlock is still there. The fact that the program runs correctly for three days does not prove it to be bug-free—it just proves that you are lucky. It also shows how synchronization problems can lurk in code and avoid detection for quite some time.

You can see another problem by looking at the output, a sample of which is shown below for the 20-philosopher case:

```
11000111110011110111  00001000000000100000
11100111110011110111  01001000000000100000
11111011110011110111  01010000000000100000
11111111110011111111  01010000000001000000
11011111110011111111  10010000000001000000
11111111110011001111  10010000000010000000
11111111110011001111  00010000000010000001
01111111110010001111  00100000000010000001
00111111110010101111  00100000000100000001
00101111110010101111  01000000000100000001
00111111110011101111  01000000000100000010
10111111110101101100  01000000001000000000
10111111111001101100  01000000010000000000
10111111111011101110  01000000010000000100
```

```
10111111111111101111  00000000100000000100
11111111111111101111  10000000100000000100
11111111101111101111  10000000100000001000
11111111100111101001  00000000100000001001
11111111100111101011  00000001000000001001
11111111010111101111  00000001000000010001
11111111010111101111  00000010000000010001
01111111010111101111  00000010000000010010
```

The left side shows the number of chopsticks held by philosophers, while the right side shows how many people are actually eating. Many people are waiting, but only two or three eat at one time because a lot of mini-deadlocks occur at different points on the table.

Probably the easiest way to solve the deadlock problem here is to require each philosopher to not pick up any chopsticks unless he can pick up both at the same time. There are several ways to implement this behavior, but Windows makes it easy with the **WaitForMultipleObjects** function. **WaitForMultipleObjects**, when configured with its **waitAll** parameter set to TRUE, does not return until all of the requested objects are available. See Listing 6.11.

```
// dinphil2.cpp

#include <windows.h>
#include <stdlib.h>
#include <iostream.h>

const INT numPhilosophers=20;
HANDLE chopsticks[numPhilosophers];
CHAR csStat[numPhilosophers+1];
CHAR pStat[numPhilosophers+1];
```

Listing 6.11
An improved version of the dining-philosophers problem that eliminates deadlock (Page 1 of 3)

```
void PhilosopherThread(INT id)
{
  HANDLE cs[2];
  while (1)
  {
    //thinking
    Sleep(GetTickCount() % 50);

    // hungry, so picks up chopsticks
    cs[0] = chopsticks[id];
    cs[1] = chopsticks[(id+1)%numPhilosophers];
    WaitForMultipleObjects(2, cs, TRUE, INFINITE);
    csStat[id]='1';
    csStat[(id+1)%numPhilosophers]='1';
    pStat[id]='1';

    // eating
    cout << csStat << "  " << pStat << endl;
    Sleep(GetTickCount() % 50);

    pStat[id]='0';
    // done eating
    ReleaseMutex(chopsticks[id]);
    csStat[id]='0';
    ReleaseMutex(
      chopsticks[(id+1)%numPhilosophers]);
    csStat[(id+1)%numPhilosophers]='0';
  }
}

void main(void)
{
  HANDLE handles[numPhilosophers];
  DWORD threadID;
```

Listing 6.11
An improved version of the dining-philosophers problem that eliminates deadlock (Page 2 of 3)

```
    INT i;

    csStat[numPhilosophers]='\0';
    pStat[numPhilosophers]='\0';

    // Create the chopstick mutexes
    for (i=0; i<numPhilosophers; i++)
      chopsticks[i] = CreateMutex(0, FALSE, 0);

    // Create the philosopher threads
    for (i=0; i<numPhilosophers; i++)
    {
      // create the philosopher threads
      handles[i]=CreateThread(0, 0,
        (LPTHREAD_START_ROUTINE) PhilosopherThread,
        (VOID *) i, 0, &threadID);
    }

    // wait for all threads to finish execution
    WaitForMultipleObjects(numPhilosophers, handles,
      TRUE, INFINITE);

    for (i=0; i<numPhilosophers; i++)
      CloseHandle(chopsticks[i]);

    cout << "Done" << endl;
}
```

Listing 6.11
An improved version of the dining-philosophers problem that eliminates deadlock (Page 3 of 3)

In the three philosopher case (and all other cases), the code in Listing 6.11 eliminates deadlock. In the 20-philosopher case it improves throughput tremendously, as shown in the output sample below:

```
00001101101111110000  00001001001010100000
00001101101111110011  00001001001010100010
00001101101111111111  00001001001010101010
00001101101111110000  00001001001010100000
```

```
00001101101111110000  00001001001010100000
00001101101111110000  00001001001010100000
01111001110011111111  01010001010010101010
01111111110011111111  01010101010010101010
01111001110011111111  01010001010010101010
01111111110011111111  01010101010010101010
01111111110111001111  01010101010100001010
01111001110011111111  01010001010010101010
01111111110011111111  01010101010010101010
01111111110111001111  01010101010100001010
01101101101111111111  01001001001010101010
01111111110100001100  01010101010100001000
01111111110100011100  01010101010100010000
01111111110111001111  01010101010100001010
01101101101111111111  01001001001010101010
01101101111111111111  01001001010010101010
01111111110100001100  01010101010100001000
01111111110100001100  01010101010100001000
```

As you can see, about the same number of chopsticks are held by philosophers, but many more philosophers eat at one time.

This new implementation has the potential for a problem of its own. Imagine that you are looking at a group of three philosophers at the 20-philosopher table. Let's call them A, B, and C for simplicity. Both A and C are eating. B would like to eat but has no utensils. A finishes and puts down his chopsticks. Later, A starts eating again. Now C finishes and puts down his chopsticks. Before A finishes, C starts eating again. Now before C finishes A starts eating again, and so on. If A and C get in a cycle like this, perhaps because they are sharing another resource that synchronizes their behavior, philosopher B starves to death.

There is no particularly simple way to prevent starvation in the dining philosophers problem. One technique that you can use is to put a timeout value in the call to **WaitForMultipleObjects** that represents a tolerable wait time. If B times out while waiting to eat, he can then revert to picking up his chopsticks one at a time to break the cycle of A and C.

Another problem that you should be aware of when working with synchronized threads is called a *race condition*. Like deadlocks and starvation, race conditions are subtle and can lie hidden in code for quite some time before they manifest themselves.

Let's say that you have three threads accessing a resource. These three threads can access the resource simultaneously. Perhaps these three threads all want to read a certain data structure, and because they are only reading it, it is acceptable for them to access the data structure simultaneously. Now a fourth thread wants to write to the data structure. Because of the changes it has to make, any readers need to be eliminated so that the writer has exclusive access to the data structure during the write operation. Once the writer finishes, the readers can resume their activity.

The scenario described in the previous paragraph is known as the "readers/writers problem." Let's say that you think about this problem and you come up with code for the reader thread that looks like this:

```
Wait(writerEvent);
numReaders++;
if (numReaders==1)
  Reset(readerEvent);

... read the data structure ...

numReaders--;
if (numReaders==0)
  Set(readerEvent);
```

Each reader checks the **writerEvent** to make sure that the writer is not writing. If not, the reader increments the number of readers, and if it is one resets the **readerEvent** to advise the writer that readers are working. When the last reader finishes reading, it sets the writer event so that the writer can work if it needs to.

You also create corresponding code for the writer that looks like this:

```
Wait(readerEvent);
Reset(writerEvent);

... write for awhile ...

Set(writerEvent);
```

The writer waits on the **readerEvent** so that it has exclusive access, then it locks out readers by resetting the **writerEvent**.

This code looks good, but there are two problems. The first is that if multiple readers arrive continuously, **readerEvent** will never reach zero and the writer starves. Let's ignore that problem. The second problem involves the way that the incrementing is done in the reader code. Assume that one reader is reading, and that reader thread is about to finish. A second reader thread has just barely started: it has finished the line that waits on **WriterEvent**, but gets preempted just before the line that increments **numReaders**. Now the first reader thread gets a time slice, decrements **numReaders** to zero, and sets **readerEvent**. At this moment a writer starts and begins writing.

You can see the problem: now the reader just getting started will increment **numReaders**, but it is too late. A reader and a writer are in the data structure at the same time colliding with each other. This situation is called a *race condition* because the two threads are racing each other for control. One thread usually has a much higher probability of winning so the code *seems* OK when you test it, but every once in awhile conditions line up just right and the program dies.

You prevent race conditions by firmly tying together competing threads with the *same* synchronizing mechanism. Listing 6.12 shows a solution to the readers/writers problem that uses a semaphore *shared by the reader and the writer.* This solution completely prevents race conditions because the readers and writers are interlocked with one another using a single synchronization mechanism.

```
// rw.cpp

#include <windows.h>
#include <stdlib.h>
#include <iostream.h>

volatile INT readerCount=0;
HANDLE mutex;
```

Listing 6.12
A valid solution to the readers-writers problem (Page 1 of 4)

```
HANDLE write;

void ReaderThread(INT id)
{
  while (1)
  {
    // Simulate the reader processing
    Sleep(GetTickCount() % 100);

    // The reader needs to read
    WaitForSingleObject(mutex, INFINITE);
    readerCount++;
    if (readerCount==1)
      WaitForSingleObject(write, INFINITE);
    ReleaseMutex(mutex);

    // The reader is reading
    cout << readerCount << " readers"
      << endl;
    Sleep(GetTickCount() % 100);

    // The reader is done reading
    WaitForSingleObject(mutex, INFINITE);
    readerCount--;
    cout << readerCount << " readers"
      << endl;
    if (readerCount==0)
      ReleaseSemaphore(write, 1, 0);
    ReleaseMutex(mutex);
  }
}

void WriterThread(INT id)
{
  while (1)
```

Listing 6.12
A valid solution to the readers-writers problem (Page 2 of 4)

```
    {
      // Simulate the write processing
      Sleep(GetTickCount() % 1000);

      // The writer needs to write
      cout << "writer " << id << " waiting"
        << endl;
      WaitForSingleObject(write, INFINITE);

      // The writer is writing
      cout << id << " writing\n";
      Sleep(GetTickCount() % 1000);
      cout << "writer " << id << " done"
        << endl;

      // The writer is done
      ReleaseSemaphore(write, 1, 0);
    }
  }

const INT numReaders=6;
const INT numWriters=3;

void main(void)
{
  HANDLE handles[numReaders+numWriters];
  DWORD threadID;
  INT i;

  mutex = CreateMutex(0, FALSE, 0);
  write = CreateSemaphore(0, 1, 1, 0);

  // start readers
  for (i=0; i<numReaders; i++)
  {
    handles[i]=CreateThread(0, 0,
```

Listing 6.12
A valid solution to the readers-writers problem (Page 3 of 4)

```
            (LPTHREAD_START_ROUTINE) ReaderThread,
            (VOID *) i, 0, &threadID);
    }

    // start writers
    for (i=0; i<numWriters; i++)
    {
      handles[i+numReaders]=CreateThread(0, 0,
            (LPTHREAD_START_ROUTINE) WriterThread,
            (VOID *) i, 0, &threadID);
    }

    // wait for all threads to finish execution
    WaitForMultipleObjects(numReaders+numWriters,
      handles, TRUE, INFINITE);

    CloseHandle(mutex);
    CloseHandle(write);
  }
```

Listing 6.12
A valid solution to the readers-writers problem (Page 4 of 4)

A good operating system book will discuss deadlocks, starvation, and race conditions in detail, and you might consider getting one if this material is new to you.

6.4 Wait Functions

Windows provides two wait functions, **WaitForSingleObject** and **WaitForMultipleObjects,** that allow you to "wait on handles." See Section 1.5 for a description of objects and handles in the 32-bit API. We have used these two functions extensively in the previous sections to wait on events, mutexes, and semaphores.

All handles have two states: *signaled* and *unsignaled.* The **WaitForSingleObject** function waits efficiently (blocks) until the handle it is waiting on becomes signaled.

WaitForSingleObject *Causes a thread to wait for a signal*

```
DWORD WaitForSingleObject(
    HANDLE object,
    DWORD timeout)
```

object	The object to wait for
timeout	The maximum amount of time to wait, in milliseconds

Returns an error code or the event that caused it to stop waiting

WaitForSingleObject accepts a single object handle and a timeout value, and returns either when the object switches to the signaled state or the timeout elapses. It returns with one of four values:

1. WAIT_FAILED on an error
2. WAIT_TIMEOUT if the timeout period elapsed
3. WAIT_OBJECT_0 if the object is signaled.
4. WAIT_ABANDONED if the object is a mutex and the thread owning the mutex died before calling the **ReleaseMutex** function to formally release the mutex. See Section 6.2.2.

The **WaitForMultipleObjects** function waits for multiple objects either in a one-of-many way or an all-of-many way.

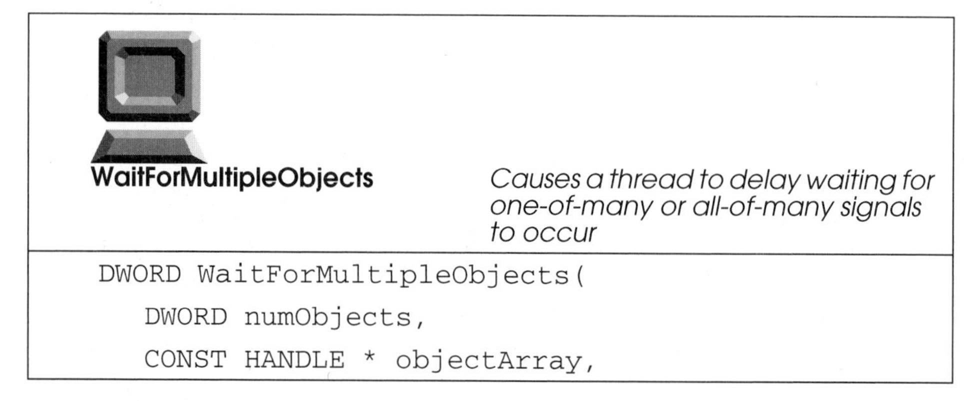

WaitForMultipleObjects *Causes a thread to delay waiting for one-of-many or all-of-many signals to occur*

```
DWORD WaitForMultipleObjects(
    DWORD numObjects,
    CONST HANDLE * objectArray,
```

```
    BOOL waitForAll,
    DWORD timeout)
```

Parameter	Description
numObjects	Number of objects in objectArray
objectArray	An array of object handles to wait on
waitForAll	If TRUE, the function waits for all events to occur, otherwise for any one of them
timeout	The maximum amount of time to wait, in milliseconds

Returns an error code or the event that caused it to stop waiting.

The **WaitForMultipleObjects** function accepts an array of object handles and the number of handles in the array, a timeout value, and a boolean that switches it between one-of-many and all-of-many behavior. It returns the same values as **WaitForSingleObject**, but in addition it can indicate which of the several objects signaled in the one-of-many case.

It is possible to wait on many objects in Windows, and each one tells you something different when it changes state. The list below summarizes the different objects and what they mean to the wait functions:

- *Change function handle:* Section 6.6 describes the **FindFirstChangeNotification** function. The handle returned by this function changes to signaled when a change occurs in the specified directory.
- *Console input:* Chapter 11 describes consoles. A console input handle changes to signaled when there is input available in the console's input buffer.
- *Event:* An event object is signaled when the event is Set, and unsignaled when it is Reset. An event object can start in a signaled or unsignaled state. An automatic event reverts to unsignaled as soon as a Wait function unblocks because of it being in the signaled state. Manual events must be set and reset manually. See Section 6.2.4.
- *Mutex:* A mutex object is signaled when no thread owns it, and is unsignaled when it is owned. A thread calls **ReleaseMutex** to give up ownership and signal it. See Section 6.2.2.
- *Process:* A process object is unsignaled while the process is active, and signals when the process terminates. See Chapter 5.

- *Semaphore:* A semaphore object is signaled if its count is greater than zero, and unsignaled when the count equals zero. See Section 6.2.3.
- *Thread:* A thread object is unsignaled while the thread is active, and signaled when the thread terminates. See Chapter 5.

Certain other handles signal in some cases. For example, a file handle returned by **CreateFile** can signal when used in overlapped mode and the overlapped structure's event is set to NULL. However, the documentation clearly discourages such use. You should use only the handles listed above with the Wait functions.

The SYNCHRONIZE standard right enables an object to work with a Wait function. See Chapter 10 for information on standard rights.

6.5 Overlapped I/O

*Compatibility Note: The code in this section works properly in Windows NT but does not work in Windows 95 because the overlapped concept does not apply to files. See the **ReadFile** and **ReadFileEx** functions in the Win32 help file for further information.*

The API supports an asynchronous form of file access that allows you to start an I/O operation and then proceed with other activities. The technique is referred to as *overlapped I/O.* This capability exists in Windows for two reasons:

1. Overlapped I/O lets you create the impression of multi-threading without actually implementing a separate thread. In certain situations this makes the code more compact, or it lets you handle asynchronous file I/O more easily than a second thread would.
2. Overlapped I/O makes it possible for separate threads in a single program to manipulate the same file handle simultaneously. With overlapped I/O, each thread can keep track of its file position independently of other threads, and this lets threads simultaneously access the same pipe, file, and so on.

Asynchronous operations are extremely useful when you want to perform multiple file operations on the same file handle simultaneously. For example, in Section 7.5.2 a single named pipe is read in one thread and written in another. Overlapped I/O is the only way to handle this situation.

Overlapped file operations rely on events. See Section 6.2.4 for details on this object. Events are used with overlapped file operations to let the operation signal that the I/O request has completed.

To implement an asynchronous file operation, you must do the following:

1. Create the file, specifying a FILE_FLAG_OVERLAPPED flag when calling **CreateFile**
2. Create and initialize a synchronizing event (see Section 6.2.4)
3. Create and initialize an OVERLAPPED structure
4. Attempt to read from the file
5. If the read is successful, continue
6. If not, and the I/O operation is pending, continue, and check the event or **GetOverlappedResult** to know when it completes

The key step is step 6. Once you set up everything, you have a way to access the file that is non-blocking, and that also allows the operation to complete on its own. Listing 6.13 shows an implementation of the six steps described above.

```
// fileovlp.cpp

#include <windows.h>
#include <iostream.h>

void main()
{
   HANDLE fileHandle;
   BOOL success;
   char s[300000];
   DWORD numRead;
   char filename[1000];
   OVERLAPPED overlappedInfo;
```

Listing 6.13
Overlapped file access (Page 1 of 3)

```
HANDLE event;
BOOL waitSuccess;

// get the file name
cout << "Enter filename: ";
cin >> filename;

// Open the file
fileHandle = CreateFile(filename,
   GENERIC_READ, FILE_SHARE_WRITE,
   0, OPEN_EXISTING, FILE_FLAG_OVERLAPPED, 0);
if (fileHandle == INVALID_HANDLE_VALUE)
{
   cout << "Error number " << GetLastError()
      << endl;
   return;
}

// set up the overlapped structure
overlappedInfo.Offset = 0;
overlappedInfo.OffsetHigh = 0;
event = CreateEvent(0, TRUE, FALSE, 0);
overlappedInfo.hEvent = event;

// Read from the file
success = ReadFile(fileHandle, s, 100000,
   &numRead, &overlappedInfo);

// wait for the operation to finish
if (!success &&
   GetLastError() == ERROR_IO_PENDING)
{
   cout << "Error number = " << GetLastError()
      << endl;  //just to see it
   do
   {
```

Listing 6.13
Overlapped file access (Page 2 of 3)

```
                cout << "waiting...\n";
                // check for completion
                waitSuccess =
                    WaitForSingleObject(event, 0);
            }
            while (waitSuccess == WAIT_TIMEOUT);
            // find out how many bytes were read
            GetOverlappedResult(fileHandle,
                &overlappedInfo, &numRead, FALSE);
        }
        // update the file pointer
        overlappedInfo.Offset += numRead;
        cout << numRead << endl;

        // Close the file
        CloseHandle(event);
        CloseHandle(fileHandle);
    }
```

Listing 6.13
Overlapped file access (Page 3 of 3)

To demonstrate this code, use it to open and read any existing file. Try it both on the hard disk and the floppy disk drive. Since the **ReadFile** statement in Listing 6.13 requests 100,000 bytes, the file needs to be fairly large but it does not matter what the file contains. The program starts by requesting a file name and opening the file in the normal way. It then reads from the file asynchronously. This means that the program can go off and do whatever it likes while the I/O operation completes. In Listing 6.13, the code loops waiting for completion, printing a message to stdout each time through the loop to show that it could be doing useful work. When working inside a normal event loop in a GUI application, you can have the event loop check for completion each time through. In an MFC program, you can handle the event in several different ways. See Section 6.7 for details.

Overlapped file access requires the use of an OVERLAPPED structure. This structure contains information about the starting file position for the operation, and also contains the synchronizing event. The OVERLAPPED structure contains the file position because **SetFilePointer** has no meaning for an asynchronous file access. In an asynchronously opened file, each process or thread maintains its own position information in its overlapped structure, and must update the information manually after each read or write operation. Multiple overlapped operations can occur simultaneously in the same file.

The program in Listing 6.13 initializes the **overlapped** structure just after it creates the file. It starts with the file offset at zero (it is permissible to start anywhere), and also creates the synchronizing event using the **CreateEvent** function. See Section 6.2.4. It is important that any synchronizing event used in an overlapped file operation be a manual event, and start in a reset (FALSE) state, as shown in Listing 6.13.

The program passes the OVERLAPPED structure to the **ReadFile** function, which attempts to read from the file starting at the indicated position. If the read operation can return immediately with the requested data it does so, but if it cannot it signals that the I/O operation is pending and returns. The program is now free to do whatever it wants—the requested operation will complete in the background, and the program can access the results in the buffer whenever it needs to.

The system signals that the I/O operation has finished by setting the synchronizing event in the OVERLAPPED structure. You can check the state of the event with the **GetOverlappedResult** function or alternatively use the **WaitForSingleObject** function on the event itself (see Section 6.4 for details). The **GetOverlappedResult** function also determines how many bytes the I/O operation transferred. This number indicates the new file position for sequential reads.

GetOverlappedResult	*Gets the result of the overlapped operation*

```
BOOL GetOverlappedResult(
   HANDLE fileHandle,
   LPOVERLAPPED overlapped,
   LPDWORD numTransfered,
   BOOL wait)
```

fileHandle	Handle to the file

overlapped	OVERLAPPED structure
numTransferred	Number of bytes transferred
wait	Whether or not the function should wait for completion
Returns TRUE on success. The function will return FALSE and ERROR_IO_PENDING if the I/O operation has not completed yet.	

If you were reading sequentially in a loop, the **numTransferred** parameter returned by **GetOverlappedResult** should be added to the **Offset** field in the OVERLAPPED structure as shown in the example code. If you are reading random records, then this step is not necessary since the next read operation will set the **Offset** field to a new random location anyway.

Chapters 7, 11, and 12 contain good examples of the usefulness of overlapped I/O. You can gain a better understanding of overlapping by examining these examples closely.

Chapter 7 discusses network communications. Section 7.5.2 discusses a multi-threaded network client for a named pipe server. One thread of the client reads from the pipe, while the other one writes to the pipe. The implementation *must* use overlapped I/O because the client process can open only one connection to the named pipe. Overlapped I/O allows two threads to access the same pipe object simultaneously. In Listing 7.11, the core of the writing thread looks like this:

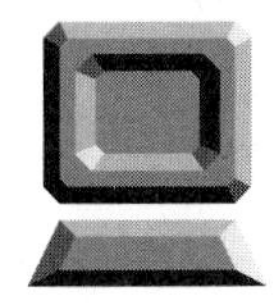

```
while(1)
{
  cout << "Type text to send: ";
  cin.getline(textToSend, BUFSIZE);

  // Write message to named pipe
  WriteFile(msnpPipe,
```

Listing 6.14
A code fragment from Listing 7.11 that demonstrates the writing thread of a multi-threaded network client using overlapped I/O (Page 1 of 2)

```
      textToSend, strlen(textToSend) + 1,
      &numBytesWritten, &overlappedWrite)
    GetOverlappedResult(msnpPipe,
      &overlappedWrite, &numBytesWritten,
      TRUE);
    overlappedWrite.Offset += numBytesWritten;

  } // while
```

Listing 6.14
A code fragment from Listing 7.11 that demonstrates the writing thread of a multi-threaded network client using overlapped I/O (Page 2 of 2)

It gets a line of text from the user and writes it to the pipe using overlapped I/O. The core of the reading thread looks like this:

```
  while (1)
  {
    // Read a message from the server
    ReadFile(msnpPipeDup,
      textBuffer, BUFSIZE,
      &numBytesRead, &overlappedRead)
    GetOverlappedResult(msnpPipeDup,
      &overlappedRead, &numBytesRead,
      TRUE);
    overlappedRead.Offset += numBytesRead;

    // send the message to the screen
    cout << textBuffer << endl;
  } /* while */
```

Listing 6.15 A code fragment from Listing 7.11 that demonstrates the reading thread of a multi-threaded network client using overlapped I/O

Note that the code in both threads calls the **GetOverlappedResult** function immediately after the read and write operations, so it might as well use synchronous calls to read and write. The overlapped I/O capability is important here not because of background operation, but because it allows both threads to work with a single pipe at the same time. See Section 7.5.2 for details.

Section 12.7 discusses a simple terminal emulator. It uses overlapped I/O in a completely different way. Here the core of the program needs to be able to accept characters from either the keyboard or the modem asynchronously. If a character arrives from the modem, the program must post it to the screen immediately. At the same time, if the user types a character on the keyboard then the program must send it to the modem immediately. The main loop of the program uses overlapped I/O on a communications port, along with console signaling (see Section 6.4) to implement this behavior.

The program first calls **SetUpCommPort** to initialize the communications port for overlapped I/O. It then sets up read and write OVERLAPPED structures for the port, as shown in the code fragment from Listing 12.3 below:

```
comHandle = SetupCommPort(portString);

// Set up for overlapped reading and
// writing on the port
overlappedRead.Offset =
   overlappedWrite.Offset = 0;
overlappedRead.OffsetHigh =
   overlappedWrite.OffsetHigh = 0;
readEvent = CreateEvent(0, TRUE, FALSE, 0);
writeEvent = CreateEvent(0, FALSE, FALSE, 0);
overlappedRead.hEvent = readEvent;
overlappedWrite.hEvent = writeEvent;
```

Listing 6.16
A code fragment from Listing 12.3 that shows overlapped I/O being used to read in the background from a communications port (Page 1 of 3)

```
// Set up handles array
// for WaitForMultipleObjects
handles[0] = consoleStdin;
handles[1] = readEvent;

// Prime the pump by getting the read
// process started
success = ReadFile(comHandle, &readBuffer, 1,
   &numRead, &overlappedRead);
do
{
   // Wait for either a keystroke or a
   // modem character. Time out after
   // 1000 seconds
   s = WaitForMultipleObjects(2, handles,
      FALSE, 1000000);
   if (s==WAIT_TIMEOUT)
      break;
   // If it is a character from the
   // keyboard then...
   else if (s==WAIT_OBJECT_0)
   {
   ... read from console and write to port ...
   }
   // If the character is coming in from
   // the comm port, then...
   else if (s==WAIT_OBJECT_0 + 1)
   {
      // Get the character from the port
      // and send it to the console
      success = GetOverlappedResult(comHandle,
         &overlappedRead, &numRead, TRUE);
      overlappedRead.Offset += numRead;
      WriteFile(consoleStdout, &readBuffer, 1,
```

Listing 6.16
A code fragment from Listing 12.3 that shows overlapped I/O being used to read in the background from a communications port (Page 2 of 3)

```
                &numWrite, 0);
            ResetEvent(readEvent);
            // Wait for the next character
            // from the comm port
            ReadFile(comHandle, &readBuffer, 1,
                &numRead, &overlappedRead);
        }
    // Terminate when the user types an 'X'
    } while  (writeBuffer != 'X');
```

Listing 6.16
A code fragment from Listing 12.3 that shows overlapped I/O being used to read in the background from a communications port (Page 3 of 3)

The code in Listing 6.16 uses the **WaitForMultipleObjects** function to detect an arriving character from either the keyboard or the modem. A character arriving from the keyboard causes the console handle to signal (see Section 11.4 for a discussion of raw input from consoles). A character arriving from the modem triggers the read event in the OVERLAPPED structure. The incoming modem character is counted with the **GetOverlappedResult** function and written to the console. The code then calls another overlapped **ReadFile** operation so that it can wait for the next character from the modem. See Section 12.7 for details.

You can see in these two examples two different ways to use overlapped I/O. Be certain that you use overlapped I/O whenever two threads need to access the same file or pipe simultaneously.

The 32-bit API supports a second and completely separate form of overlapped I/O that uses *completion routines.* Five functions support this facility: **ReadFileEx**, **WriteFileEx**, **WaitForSingleObjectEx**, **WaitForMultipleObjectsEx**, and **SleepEx**. A completion routine is a function that the **ReadFileEx** or **WriteFileEx** function calls when an I/O operation completes and the thread enters an *alertable wait* via the **WaitForSingleObjectEx**, **WaitForMultipleObjectsEx**, or **SleepEx** functions.

Listing 6.17 demonstrates the use of completion routines. When you run this program it will ask you for a file name. Use a file that is at least 10,000 bytes long, because the read statement attempts to read 10,000 bytes. Once the program finishes reading the data you will see output from the completion routine and then the main function will print a message and terminate.

```
// fileovex.cpp

#include <windows.h>
#include <iostream.h>

VOID WINAPI CompletionRoutine(
   DWORD error, DWORD transferred,
   LPOVERLAPPED overlapped)
{
   if (error != 0)
   {
      cout << "Completion Error = "
         << error << endl;
      return;
   }
   // update the file pointer
   overlapped->Offset += transferred;
   cout << "Inside completion routine. \n";
   cout << "Number of bytes read = ";
   cout << transferred << endl;
}

void main()
{
   HANDLE fileHandle;
   BOOL success;
   char s[300000];
   char filename[1000];
```

Listing 6.17
Using completion routines (Page 1 of 3)

```
    OVERLAPPED overlappedInfo;
    HANDLE event;

    // get the file name
    cout << "Enter filename: ";
    cin >> filename;

    // Open the file
    fileHandle = CreateFile(filename, GENERIC_READ,
       0, 0, OPEN_EXISTING,
       FILE_FLAG_OVERLAPPED, 0);
    if (fileHandle == INVALID_HANDLE_VALUE)
    {
       cout << "Error number " << GetLastError()
          << endl;
       return;
    }

    // set up the overlapped structure
    overlappedInfo.Offset = 0;
    overlappedInfo.OffsetHigh = 0;
    event = CreateEvent(0, TRUE, FALSE, 0);
    overlappedInfo.hEvent = event;

    // Read from the file
    success = ReadFileEx(fileHandle, s, 10000,
       &overlappedInfo, CompletionRoutine);
    if (!success)
    {
       cout << "Error number " << GetLastError()
          << endl;
       return;
    }

    // Sleep until I/O is complete
```

Listing 6.17
Using completion routines (Page 2 of 3)

```
    SleepEx(INFINITE, TRUE);
    cout << "\nSleep complete.\n";

    // Close the file
    CloseHandle(event);
    CloseHandle(fileHandle);
}
```

Listing 6.17
Using completion routines (Page 3 of 3)

In Listing 6.17, the code uses the **CreateFile** function to open the file in overlapped mode. It then initializes an overlapped structure as described earlier. The call to **ReadFileEx** specifies the completion routine, which you will find at the top of the listing.

ReadFileEx — *Reads bytes from a file and calls a completion routine when the read operation is complete*

```
BOOL ReadFileEx(
    HANDLE file,
    LPVOID buffer,
    DWORD requestedBytes,
    LPOVERLAPPED overlapped,
    LPOVERLAPPED_COMPLETION_ROUTINE compRoutine)
```

file	File handle created with **CreateFile**
buffer	Buffer to hold the read bytes
requestedBytes	The number of bytes desired
overlapped	Pointer to overlapped structure. See Section 6.5
compRoutine	The address of the completion routine to call

Returns TRUE on success

The call to **ReadFileEx** is very similar to a call to **ReadFile** (See Section 2.7). **ReadFileEx** does not return the number of bytes read (this value is instead passed to the completion routine), and it also accepts the address of the completion routine it should call when its I/O operation finishes.

After calling **ReadFileEx**, the main function calls **SleepEx**. This function causes the main thread to sleep until the timeout value expires or the I/O operation completes.

SleepEx	*Causes a thread to delay for a fixed number of milliseconds or until an I/O operation completes*

```
DWORD SleepEx(
    DWORD time,
    BOOL alertable)
```

time	The amount of time to sleep, in milliseconds
alertable	Set to TRUE if the function should return after an I/O completion

Returns 0 on timeout or WAIT_IO_COMPLETION if an I/O operation completed

Since the code in Listing 6.17 passes TRUE to **SleepEx**, the main thread is in an *alertable wait* state. If either a **ReadFileEx** or **WriteFileEx** operation completes, then the **SleepEx** function will return once the completion routine finishes execution. In Listing 6.17, the call to **SleepEx** returns once **CompletionRoutine** finishes.

Completion routines have a standard format.

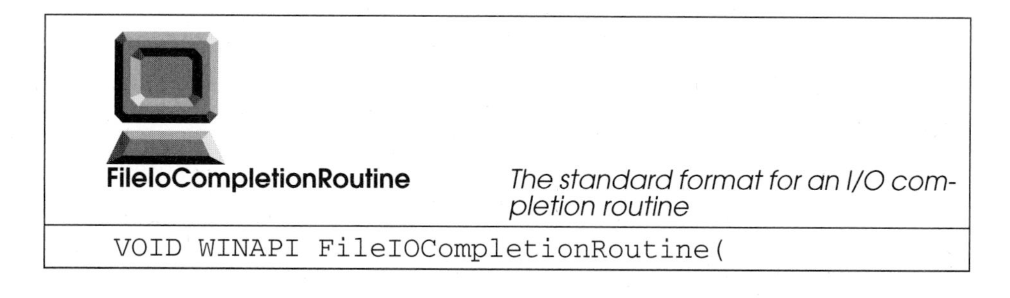

FileIoCompletionRoutine	*The standard format for an I/O completion routine*

```
VOID WINAPI FileIOCompletionRoutine(
```

```
        DWORD error,
        DWORD transferred,
        LPOVERLAPPED overlapped)
```

error	An error code
transferred	Number of bytes transferred in the I/O operation
overlapped	An overlapped structure
Returns nothing	

As shown in Listing 6.17, the completion routine receives an error code from the I/O operation, the number of bytes transferred during the operation, and a pointer to the overlapped structure used in the call to **ReadFileEx** or **WriteFileEx** so that the completion routine can update the structure.

When do you use completion routines? The facility accomplishes approximately the same thing as normal overlapped I/O does. However, in certain situations where many overlapped operations are in-process at once, completion routines can simplify your code. For example, imagine that you are designing a server that must talk to several clients simultaneously, and each client can be in one of several states. With completion routines, you can read from the client, specify a completion routine that will handle the client's response appropriately, and then forget about that client. With normal overlapped I/O you would have to build a case statement instead, and that can be structurally annoying. However, the two techniques accomplish the same goal, and you should pick the one with which you feel most comfortable.

6.6 Change Functions

The 32-bit API supports a facility called *change notification* that allows an application to detect changes in files and directories. Please see Section 4.7 for a description of the facility and its uses.

The change notification facility uses *change handles* to notify the program of changes. A change handle is initially unsignaled but changes to signaled when the appropriate directory is modified. You use the Wait functions (Section 6.4) in your code to detect when a change handle signals.

Listing 6.18 demonstrates change handles. When you run this program, it will display a line that indicates that it is waiting. If you use the File Manager or a second DOS shell to rename a file in c:\, then the program will indicate that a change occurred and then wait for a second change. Once the second change occurs the program terminates.

```
//filefind.cpp

#include <iostream.h>
#include <windows.h>

int main(int argc, char *argv[])
{
   HANDLE changeHandle;

   // Wait for a file name change in the
   // current directory
   changeHandle = FindFirstChangeNotification("c:\\",
      FALSE, FILE_NOTIFY_CHANGE_FILE_NAME);
   cout << "Waiting for a change ..."
      << endl;
   WaitForSingleObject(changeHandle, INFINITE);
   cout << "A file name changed." << endl;

   // Wait for a second change
   FindNextChangeNotification(changeHandle);
   cout << "Waiting for a 2nd change ..."
      << endl;
   WaitForSingleObject(changeHandle, INFINITE);
   cout << "A file name changed." << endl;

   // quit
   FindCloseChangeNotification(changeHandle);
   return( 0 );
```

Listing 6.18
A demonstration of the change notification facility (Page 1 of 2)

```
    }
```

Listing 6.18
A demonstration of the change notification facility (Page 2 of 2)

The program in Listing 6.18 starts by calling the **FindFirstChangeNotification** function.

FindFirstChangeNotification	*Returns a change handle that signals when the specified change occurs in the specified directory*

```
HANDLE FindFirstChangeNotification(
    LPCTSTR path,
    BOOL watchSubTree,
    DWORD flags)
```

path	The path of the directory to watch
watchSubTree	Indicates whether or not to watch all subtrees of the specified directory
flags	Indicates the changes to watch for

Returns a change handle or INVALID_HANDLE_VALUE on error

The **FindFirstChangeNotification** function can detect any or all of the following changes in the specified directory or in the specified directory and all of its subtrees:

- FILE_NOTIFY_CHANGE_FILE_NAME: renames, creations, and deletions of files
- FILE_NOTIFY_CHANGE_DIR_NAME: renames, creations, and deletions of directories
- FILE_NOTIFY_CHANGE_ATTRIBUTES: changes to attribute bits in any file
- FILE_NOTIFY_CHANGE_SIZE: changes to file size of any file
- FILE_NOTIFY_CHANGE_LAST_WRITE: changes to the last write time of any file

- FILE_NOTIFY_CHANGE_SECURITY: changes to the security descriptors of any file or directory

The function returns a *change handle*. You can use this handle in any Wait function. Once one of the specified changes occurs the change handle is signaled.

The program next calls the **FindNextChangeNotification** function. This function resets the change handle so that it can signal again on the next change.

FindNextChangeNotification	*Resets a change handle so that it signals again when the specified change occurs in the specified directory*
`BOOL FindNextChangeNotification( HANDLE changeHandle)`	
changeHandle	Handle created by FindFirstChangeNotification
Returns TRUE on success	

When you are finished using a change handle, call the **FindCloseChangeNotification** function.

FindCloseChangeNotification	*Closes a change handle*
`BOOL FindCloseChangeNotification( HANDLE changeHandle)`	
changeHandle	Handle created by FindFirstChangeNotification to be closed
Returns TRUE on success	

The following section demonstrates how to integrate the change functions into a normal MFC program.

6.7 Integrating Synchronization into MFC Programs

All of the sample code in this chapter uses simple text programs to demonstrate synchronization. In these examples, the blocking behavior of functions like **WaitForSingleObject** is acceptable. In a GUI application using the 32-bit API or MFC however, blocking is a problem because it shuts down the event loop.

For example, if you want to create an MFC program that waits for a file change as demonstrated in Section 6.6, you cannot simply call **WaitForSingleObject** with an infinite timeout value and wait. An MFC program must return to the event loop frequently so that it can continue processing user events. One solution is to use the **OnIdle** member function of **CWinApp** and poll the change handle using a timeout value of 0 in **WaitForSingleObject**. However, this misses the whole point of the Wait functions. The **WaitForSingleObject** function waits efficiently if you let it, and polling destroys that efficiency.

The code in Listing 6.19 demonstrates how to efficiently wait using **WaitForSingleObject** in an MFC program. When you run this program, it will display a button that you can push at any time. The application will beep and display a message box in response to a button click. The program also contains a call to **FindFirstChangeNotification**, so if you rename a file in the current directory, a dialog will appear telling you that the program detected the change. The program monitors the change handle returned by **FindFirstChangeNotification** efficiently and recognizes the change immediately.

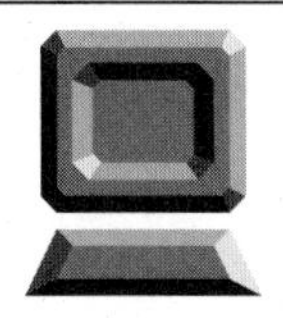

```
// mfc.cpp

#include <afxwin.h>

#define IDB_BUTTON 100
#define FIND_MSG "find change message"
```

Listing 6.19
An MFC program that uses **WaitForSingleObject** to efficiently wait on a change handle (Page 1 of 5)

```
// Declare the application class
class CButtonApp : public CWinApp
{
public:
   virtual BOOL InitInstance();
};

// Create an instance of the application class
CButtonApp ButtonApp;

// Declare the main window class
class CButtonWindow : public CFrameWnd
{
   CButton *button;
   static UINT findMsg;
public:
   CButtonWindow();
   ~CButtonWindow();
   afx_msg void HandleButton();
   afx_msg LONG FindHandler( UINT param1,
      LONG param2 );

   DECLARE_MESSAGE_MAP()
};

// declare the static variable in CButtonWindow
UINT CButtonWindow::findMsg =
   ::RegisterWindowMessage(FIND_MSG);

// The message handler function
void CButtonWindow::HandleButton()
{
   Beep(700,100);
   MessageBox("Button pushed", "Dialog", MB_OK);
```

Listing 6.19
An MFC program that uses **WaitForSingleObject** to efficiently wait on a change handle (Page 2 of 5)

```
}

// The message handler for file changes
LONG CButtonWindow::FindHandler( UINT wParam,
   LONG lParam )
{
   Beep(500,500);
   MessageBox( "A file changed",
      "Find Dialog", MB_ICONINFORMATION );
   return 0;
}

// The message map
BEGIN_MESSAGE_MAP(CButtonWindow, CFrameWnd)
   ON_COMMAND(IDB_BUTTON, HandleButton)
   ON_REGISTERED_MESSAGE( findMsg, FindHandler )
END_MESSAGE_MAP()

// The InitInstance function is called once
// when the application first executes
BOOL CButtonApp::InitInstance()
{
   m_pMainWnd = new CButtonWindow();
   m_pMainWnd->ShowWindow(m_nCmdShow);
   m_pMainWnd->UpdateWindow();

   return TRUE;
}

// The thread that waits for the file change
// in the background
VOID FindThread(VOID)
{
   HANDLE changeHandle;
   UINT threadMsg;
```

Listing 6.19
An MFC program that uses **WaitForSingleObject** to efficiently wait on a change handle (Page 3 of 5)

```
        Beep(1000, 1000);

        // Register a custom message that the message
        // map will recognize
        threadMsg = RegisterWindowMessage(
            FIND_MSG );
        // wait for the first change
        changeHandle = FindFirstChangeNotification("c:\\",
            TRUE, FILE_NOTIFY_CHANGE_FILE_NAME);
        WaitForSingleObject(changeHandle, INFINITE);
        // inform the main event loop of the change
        ::SendMessage( ButtonApp.m_pMainWnd->m_hWnd,
            threadMsg, 0, 0 );
    }

    // The constructor for the window class
    CButtonWindow::CButtonWindow()
    {
        CRect r;
        DWORD threadId;

        // Create the window itself
        Create(NULL,
            "CButton Tests",
            WS_OVERLAPPEDWINDOW,
            CRect(0,0,200,200));

        // Get the size of the client rectangle
        GetClientRect(&r);
        r.InflateRect(-20,-20);

        // Create a button
        button = new CButton();
        button->Create("Push me",
```

Listing 6.19
An MFC program that uses **WaitForSingleObject** to efficiently wait on a change handle (Page 4 of 5)

```
        WS_CHILD|WS_VISIBLE|BS_PUSHBUTTON,
        r,
        this,
        IDB_BUTTON);

     findMsg = RegisterWindowMessage(
        FIND_MSG );
     CreateThread(0, 0,
        (LPTHREAD_START_ROUTINE)FindThread,
        0, 0, &threadId);
  }

  // The destructor for the window class
  CButtonWindow::~CButtonWindow()
  {
     delete button;
     CFrameWnd::~CFrameWnd();
  }
```

Listing 6.19
An MFC program that uses **WaitForSingleObject** to efficiently wait on a change handle (Page 5 of 5)

The code in Listing 6.19 creates a separate thread and a custom message to efficiently wait. The program creates the thread in the window's constructor, but you can create it anywhere in your own applications. The thread registers a custom window message, requests a file change notification in the current directory, and then waits on the change handle. When a change occurs, the thread sends a message to the message map and terminates.

The message map for the **CButtonWindow** class contains an ON_REGISTERED_MESSAGE handler for the custom message generated by the thread. When the message map sees the thread's message, it calls the **FindHandler** function. This function simply displays a message box.

You can apply the technique demonstrated here to efficiently wait on any object in an MFC program. For example, you might want to wait on the event returned by an overlapped I/O operation, or wait for a mutex to change to signaled. The separate thread shown above allows the event loop to proceed while the Wait function blocks. The custom message lets the thread inject a message into the program's event loop when the object is signaled, so that the program can respond appropriately.

For more information on MFC programming, see the book *Visual C++: Developing Professional Applications with Windows 95 and NT using MFC* by Marshall Brain and Lance Lovette, ISBN 0-13-305145-5.

6.8 Conclusion

This chapter has covered several diverse but related topics, including Windows synchronization mechanisms, synchronization bugs, the wait functions, and file overlapping.

This chapter also demonstrates how to integrate the Wait functions into normal MFC applications. Chapters 7, 11, and 12 use these concepts extensively and contain further examples.

7 NETWORK COMMUNICATIONS

Windows is meant to be used on a network. It is designed from the ground up to interact with other Windows machines. The 32-bit API therefore offers several different software abstractions for communicating over the net, both with other Windows machines and with other TCP/IP machines.

In this chapter you will learn about the four different techniques that are used for network communications: mailslots, named pipes, UDP, and TCP. Sample code demonstrates both simple connections and more advanced application ideas. You can use the capabilities discussed here in your own applications to provide full network interconnectivity on simple local nets as well as on worldwide TCP/IP networks. You can also use the techniques discussed in Section 6.7 to integrate these concepts into MFC code.

Compatibility Note: All of the code in this chapter works identically in both Windows NT and Windows 95 with one exception. At the time of publication, it is not possible to create a named pipe server in Windows 95.

7.1 The Possibilities

If you have never programmed with a network operating system before, you may have trouble imagining what is possible, or why network programming is so exciting and versatile. The following list describes five different programs and shows how each makes use of the network.

1. *A multi-player game:* Say that you want to create a multi-player game that runs on a network. For example, you might create a flight simulator

that lets several people fly separate airplanes and have dogfights with one another. Or you might want to have several players run a dungeon-type adventure game on their machines, and then link the machines through the network so that the different players can "see" and "talk to" each other in the dungeon. One easy way to implement games like these is to have each copy of the game broadcast packets of information to all other copies of the game running on the network.

2. *Finger:* All UNIX machines support a program called **finger** which lets you list information about other users on other machines on the network. For example, if you type "finger brain@iftech.com" from a UNIX machine connected to the Internet, you will receive information about the user named "brain" on the specified machine. The finger program forms a point-to-point connection using TCP packets to a finger server on the remote machine and retrieves the data.
3. *Chat:* The Chat program that comes with Windows NT forms a point-to-point connection to the machine that you wish to chat with, and then sends the characters typed by both users back and forth over the network.
4. *Client/server applications:* Many database engines act as "servers" that allow multiple "clients" to connect to them through the network. The client forms a connection to the server, and then sends a packet requesting information from the database. The server responds to the request by sending the data back over the network. Client/server architectures like this are becoming very popular not only for databases but also for graphical information, conferencing, information distribution, and so on.
5. *Bulletin boards:* A network-based bulletin board system would also act in a client/server relationship, with the bulletin board itself as the server. A user wanting to access the bulletin board would run a special client that would connect to the server and begin making requests for information from the bulletin board.

You will find that network connections tend to come in three general forms, as shown in Figure 7.1:

1. Two programs can form a direct connection between one another and send data back and forth, as with the Chat program.

2. In client/server relationships, a central server accepts multiple connections and responds to all clients simultaneously.
3. In broadcast mode, several or many programs listen on the network simultaneously. When one of the programs wants to signal the others, it broadcasts a single packet that is heard by all listeners. Many game programs use this configuration.

Each mode has advantages and disadvantages, but one approach is generally best for any given application.

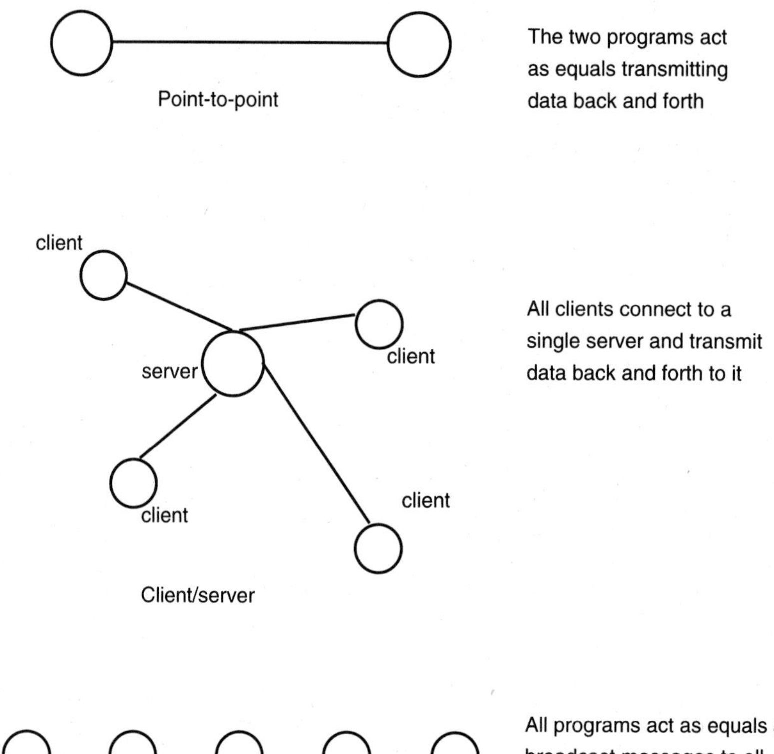

Figure 7.1
The three different connection topologies.

7.2 Understanding Your Options

There are many different ways for you to access the network from the programs that you write, and one of these techniques involves absolutely no work at all on your part. It is important that you recognize that the trivial technique is a viable way to perform network communications, because it often simplifies program design immensely. More advanced techniques let you form dedicated network connections between specific programs running on different machines, and therefore give you better control over when and how data flows between the source and destination. This section will help you to understand all of the options that are available.

The word *network* is normally used to mean several different things. For example, you might refer to "the network" to mean a collection of interconnected machines that act together as a single, amorphous system. You might say, "Let me log into the network and print that file for you." On the other hand, the word "network" often refers to the cable and adapter cards that make up the interconnection scheme between all of the individual machines. For example, you might say, "I've installed an Ethernet network," or "The network is down today. You can still use your machine but it cannot talk to anybody else." Another way to think of a network is as a set of specific software protocols used to standardize communications between machines. For example, UNIX machines normally communicate over "TCP/IP networks," while Windows machines natively communicate on "NetBEUI networks." We tend to use these words interchangeably, but it is important to recognize the differences. In this chapter the word "network" is generally used in the second and third senses, to imply specific interconnections between individual machines either at a wiring or protocol level.

Figure 7.1 shows a typical small network. Each machine on the net has a network adapter and a cable that connects it to the other machines. Note two things from this diagram. First, each machine has a name, and this name uniquely identifies it on the network. Second, in any small Windows network, all machines can communicate with any other. If you know a machine's name, then you can form an immediate network connection to it. Please see the third book in this series, *Windows NT Administration: Single Systems to Heterogeneous Networks,* for more information about setting up machines on a Windows NT network and configuring the network.

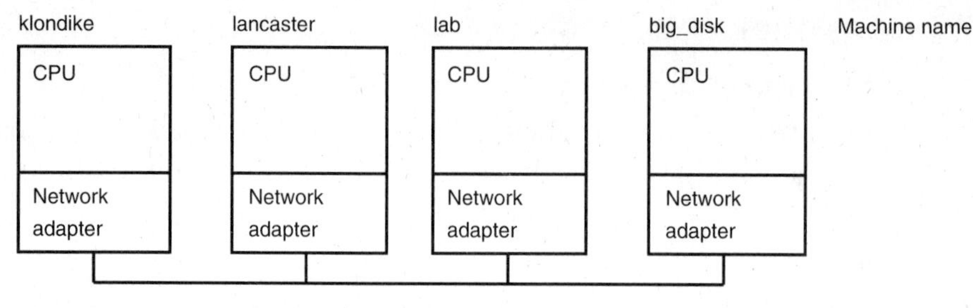

Figure 7.2
A typical small network. Each machine has a name and can communicate with any other.

Data is transmitted on the network in *packets*. For example, if the machine named "klondike" in Figure 7.1 wants to send 100K bytes of data specifically to the machine called "lancaster," it first communicates with lancaster to establish a connection, and then sends the data in packets of perhaps 1K bytes each. Each packet contains a header that identifies the packet and the recipient. The network adapter on klondike waits for an opportunity to access the network cable (in Ethernet systems it waits for the cable to become idle and then transmits, while in token ring systems it waits for an empty token to arrive and fills it), and then transmits the packet. The recipient receives the packet, recognizes itself as the recipient by examining the packet's header, and uses the data in the packet appropriately. Many machines can access the net simultaneously by interleaving their packets, giving the impression of many simultaneous network conversations happening at once.

Network connections come is two flavors: point-to-point and broadcast. In a point-to-point connection, you indicate a specific recipient machine and communicate only with it. This type of connection has two advantages: it is secure, and it is dependable. Once you have established a point-to-point connection, the delivery of the packets is guaranteed. If the connection breaks, (for example because the application on the recipient machine terminates), the transport mechanism responsible for sending the packets realizes the problem and informs you. Client/server systems use multiple point-to-point connections to the server.

Broadcast connections allow you to send packets to many machines at once, but the link is in one direction only. You have no way of knowing which machines actually receive any packet without having them all transmit a packet back. Unfortunately, the network traffic created by such an arrangement makes acknowledgment impractical. You will therefore use point-to-point connections for bidirectional communications where you need to know that the data actually arrived. You will use broadcast communications when you need to send one packet to many recipients and guaranteed delivery is not important.

There are at least four different ways to communicate over a network in Windows:

1. The simplest way is through a normal file. If you use the File Manager to connect to a hard disk on another system and then copy a file to that hard disk, you have effectively communicated over the network using almost no code at all. If many other machines are also connected to that same hard disk, then you can essentially broadcast the contents of the file to many machines at once. Windows completely abstracts away the network in this case, and all that you have to do is call the **CopyFile** function discussed in Chapter 2 to use the network. The advantage of this scheme is its simplicity. The disadvantage is the relative slowness that comes from opening a file and writing to a hard disk. If all that you want to do is transmit a few characters, then the overhead of opening, closing and erasing many small files becomes quite large. However, if you want to move several megabytes of data around on the network and many machines need to be able to see it, then the file approach is probably best.
2. RPCs also communicate over the network, and they do all the work for you as well. RPCs use an abstraction based on function calls, so a normal function call that you make in an application ends up getting transmitted over the network and executed on another machine. It is extremely easy to set up client/server systems using RPCs, and this is the preferred way to create such systems not only because it is easy, but because it allows both Windows and UNIX machines to intercommunicate. See Chapter 8 for details on RPCs.
3. Another way to transmit data on the network is called a "mailslot." Mailslots are one directional and are generally used as a broadcast mechanism. One machine sends a message, and the message appears on all other machines on the network. Any machine that is running a program listening to the appropriate mailslot gets the message. The advantage of mailslots is ease of use and speed. To get a message to 20 different machines, you simply send it once and all recipients receive it. The disadvantage is that

you have no way to know that the message was received. In network parlance, mailslots form an unreliable connection, and data delivery is not guaranteed. In many different applications however, reliable delivery is not important and mailslots are appropriate and easy to use.

4. A named pipe forms point-to-point connections between two programs. Named pipes are also used to implement client/server connections. The advantage of a named pipe is that it forms a reliable connection. You specifically form the connection, and if it breaks you learn about it as soon as you try to use the pipe. For example, if the server goes down, the client gets official notification of it when it next tries to access the pipe. The client therefore knows about the problem immediately. The disadvantage of a named pipe is that the point-to-point nature of the connections can lead to inefficiencies. For example, if a server wants to send the same message to 20 connected clients, it must do so by sending the message 20 times, once down each pipe.

Named pipes and mailslots are the two native and preferred mechanisms for communicating between Windows machines. If you need to communicate on TCP/IP networks, however, and particularly networks of UNIX machines, you will want to use the TCP or UDP connection mechanisms. Generally speaking, TCP is a point-to-point scheme similar to a named pipe, while UDP is a connectionless system that works in broadcast mode like a mailslot. You use TCP for the same applications that you would named pipes, while UDP and mailslots perform the same tasks. See Section 7.6 for details.

7.3 Mailslots

One of the simplest ways to perform network communications in Windows is called a mailslot. Mailslots provide a one-directional communication path from the sender to one or more recipients on the same network segment. You use mailslots when you do not particularly care whether or not the data actually arrives, or when you want to send one piece of data to many recipients at once.

For example, say that you want to create a status board application. You have probably seen a status board in many office environments, but they are particularly common in large real estate or law firms. The board lists everyone in the office and whether each person is currently "in" or "out." If the person is out, the board normally says where the person has gone and when he or she expects to return. This system helps the secretary and other employees know where everyone is.

You can easily create a program with status board functionality using mailslots. Figure 7.3 shows a view of the application. Each user would run a copy of the program on his or her workstation to see where everyone is.

Name	In	Out	Reason
Marshall Brain	X		
Kelly Campbell		X	Meeting in Raleigh, back at 2:00
Lance Lovette	X		
Leigh Clarke	X		
Shay Woodard		X	Gone with Kelly

Name: Marshall Brain Status: In Out

Reason:

Figure 7.3
A status board application.

This application would use mailslots in the following way. Whenever a copy of the program begins execution, it would broadcast a message onto the network using a well-known mailslot name. For example, all copies of the program might automatically broadcast to a mailslot named "status." The startup message would indicate that a new copy of the program is running and needs to be updated. All other copies of the program on the network would have *mailslot servers* open on their machines, using the well-known name for the name of the mailslot. Each copy of the program would hear the message from the new copy that has just started, and they would each send back a response containing their user's name and status.

During the day, whenever the user changes his or her status, the application would broadcast a message indicating the change onto the net. All other copies of the program would receive the message and update their displays appropriately.

Mailslots are extremely easy to create, and reading and writing are done using the normal **ReadFile** and **WriteFile** file commands discussed in Chapter 2. When creating the mailslot, a special path name passed to the **CreateMailslot** function causes the system to create a mailslot rather than a normal file. The following example demonstrates how to use a mailslot in a very simple program.

Listing 7.1 shows a piece of code that opens and reads from a mailslot. This piece of code demonstrates a *mailslot server.* Listing 7.2 demonstrates how to create and write to a mailslot as a *mailslot client.* If you run these two programs simultaneously on one workstation, the writer will send a message every five seconds and the reader will receive it. The writer broadcasts to all machines on the network, so if you run multiple copies of the reader on different machines, all of them will see the message produced by the writer. Alternatively, you can run multiple writers on the net and any copies of the reader will see the messages from all of them.

```
// sms_recv.cpp

// Usage: sms_recv

#include <windows.h>
#include <iostream.h>

int main()
{
  char toDisptxt[80];
  HANDLE hSMS_Slot;
  DWORD nextSize;
  DWORD Msgs;
  DWORD NumBytesRead;
  BOOL Status;
```

Listing 7.1
A program that creates a mailslot server and reads from it (Page 1 of 3)

```
/* Create a mailslot for receiving messages */
hSMS_Slot=CreateMailslot("\\\\.\\mailslot\\sms",
  0, 0, (LPSECURITY_ATTRIBUTES) NULL);

/* Check and see if the mailslot was created */
if (hSMS_Slot == INVALID_HANDLE_VALUE)
{
  cerr << "ERROR: Unable to create mailslot"
    << endl;
  return (1);
}

/* Repeatedly check for messages until the
   program is terminated */
while(1)
{
  Status=GetMailslotInfo(hSMS_Slot,
    (LPDWORD) NULL, &nextSize, &Msgs,
    (LPDWORD) NULL);
  if (!Status)
  {
    cerr << "ERROR: Unable to get status."
      << endl;
    CloseHandle(hSMS_Slot);
    return (1);
  }

  /* If messages are available, then get them */
  if (Msgs)
  {

    /* Read the message and check to see if
       read was successful */
    if (!ReadFile(hSMS_Slot, toDisptxt, nextSize,
```

Listing 7.1
A program that creates a mailslot server and reads from it (Page 2 of 3)

```
            &NumBytesRead, (LPOVERLAPPED) NULL))
          {
            cerr
              << "ERROR: Unable to get status."
              << endl;
            CloseHandle(hSMS_Slot);
            return (1);
          }

          /* Display the Message */
          cout << toDisptxt << endl;
        }
        else
          /* Check for new messages twice a second */
          Sleep(500);
      } /* while */
    }
```

Listing 7.1
A program that creates a mailslot server and reads from it (Page 3 of 3)

```
// sms_send.c

// Usage: sms_send

#include <windows.h>
#include <iostream.h>
#include <string.h>

int main()
{
  char toSendTxt[100], buffer[100];
```

Listing 7.2
A program that writes to a mailslot every five seconds (Page 1 of 3)

```
    DWORD bufferLen=100;
    HANDLE hSMS_Slot;
    BOOL Status;
    DWORD NumBytesWritten;

    /* Create the mailslot file handle for
       sending messages */
    hSMS_Slot=CreateFile("\\\\*\\mailslot\\sms",
      GENERIC_WRITE, FILE_SHARE_READ,
      (LPSECURITY_ATTRIBUTES) NULL,
      OPEN_EXISTING,
      FILE_ATTRIBUTE_NORMAL,
      (HANDLE) NULL);

    /* Check and see if the mailslot file was
       opened, if not terminate program */
    if (hSMS_Slot == INVALID_HANDLE_VALUE)
    {
      cerr << "ERROR: Unable to create mailslot"
        << endl;
      return (1);
    }

    /* form string to send */
    GetComputerName(buffer, &bufferLen);
    strcpy(toSendTxt, "Test string from ");
    strcat(toSendTxt, buffer);

    /* Repeatedly send message until program
       is terminated */
    while(1)
    {
      cout << "Sending..." << endl;
      /* Write message to mailslot */
      Status=WriteFile(hSMS_Slot,
```

Listing 7.2
A program that writes to a mailslot every five seconds (Page 2 of 3)

```
          toSendTxt, (DWORD) strlen(toSendTxt)+1,
          &NumBytesWritten, (LPOVERLAPPED) NULL);

        /* If error occurs when writing to mailslot,
           terminate program */
        if (!Status)
        {
          cerr << "ERROR: Unable to write to mailslot"
            << endl;
          CloseHandle(hSMS_Slot);
          return (1);
        }

        /* Wait sending the message again */
        Sleep(4800);
      } /* while*/
    }
```

Listing 7.2
A program that writes to a mailslot every five seconds (Page 3 of 3)

The programs shown in Listing 7.1 and 7.2 are as simple as possible so that you can easily see the steps necessary to transmit and receive data through a mailslot. Listing 7.1 shows how to create a mailslot and read from it. This form of mailslot is referred to as a *server*. The **CreateMailslot** function creates the server.

CreateMailslot — *Creates a mailslot that you can then read from*

```
HANDLE CreateMailslot(
   LPTSTR name,
   DWORD maxMsg,
   DWORD readTimeout,
   LPSECURITY_ATTRIBUTES security)
```

name	The name of the mailslot

maxMsg	Max message size, or 0 for no max
readTimeout	Zero or MAILSLOT_WAIT_FOREVER
security	Security attributes. See Chapter 10
Returns a handle to the mailslot or INVALID_HANDLE_VALUE	

The **CreateMailslot** function creates a mailslot server on the local machine. The server is a queue that holds messages received until you read them using the **ReadFile** function. The queue stores messages in the order of their arrival. You can read from the handle returned by **CreateMailslot**.

If you want to create a group of programs that all communicate through the same mailslot, you must make sure that all of them are using the same name. The name of the mailslot must be of the form "\\.\mailslot\[path]name." This looks like a file name, and it acts like a file name in that the normal **ReadFile** command works to read from the mailslot. Messages that arrive are buffered in a first-in-first-out queue. However, no actual file is created by the function: The mailslot is held in memory. A typical mailslot name is shown in Listing 7.1. It is also possible to add paths to further categorize mailslots, and you will see an example of this below.

When you create the mailslot, you can specify the maximum message length, as well as the **readTimeout**. Mailslots can send no more than 400 bytes over the network at one time. You can set the timeout value to 0, in which case any read operations will be non-blocking. That is, as soon as you call **ReadFile**, the function will return immediately whether or not there is anything in the buffer. You can set the timeout to a specific number of milliseconds to cause any read operation to fail if that amount of time elapses before a message arrives. You can also create a blocking read by passing the MAILSLOT_WAIT_FOREVER constant.

Listing 7.1 takes the non-blocking approach, and then additionally demonstrates the **GetMailslotInfo** function to make sure that messages exist in the queue before performing a read. This function returns the maximum length of messages in the mailslot queue, the length of the next message in the queue, and the number of messages waiting.

GetMailslotInfo	*Gets information about the given mailslot*

```
BOOL GetMailslotInfo(
    HANDLE mailslot,
    LPDWORD maxMsgLen,
    LPDWORD nextMsgLen,
    LPDWORD numMsgs,
    LPDWORD readTimeout)
```

mailslot	Handle to the mailslot
maxMsgLen	Max message size
nextMsgLen	Length of next message
numMsgs	The number of messages in the queue
readTimeout	The timeout value

Returns TRUE on success

Listing 7.1 uses **GetMailslotInfo** to determine if messages exist in the mailslot. If there are any, then it reads the first one. Reading from a mailslot is just like reading from a file. See Section 2.7 for details. A corresponding **SetMailslotInfo** function lets you change the timeout value of an existing mailslot at any time.

Any message, sent from any computer on the network to a machine running Listing 7.1, will be received provided that the mailslot names of the sender and the receiver match. There are two limits on message size however. Messages sent from a sender to a receiver running on the *same* machine can be no longer than 64K bytes, while messages sent over the network between machines have a 400 byte limit.

Listing 7.2 shows how to send messages to a mailslot. It starts by using the **CreateFile** function discussed in Section 2.7 to open a writeable connection to the mailslot. You use **CreateFile** whenever you want to create a program that writes to a mailslot. The program is referred to as a mailslot *client* because it writes to mailslot servers already running on the network. The **CreateFile** function understands, because of the use of the special mailslot file name, that you are not creating a file but instead wish to communicate with a mailslot. Four different formats for the file name are typically used:

1. \\.\mailslot\[path]name
2. *\mailslot\[path]name
3. \\domain\mailslot\[path]name
4. \\machine\mailslot\[path]name

In the first and last cases, the name specifies the local machine or a specific machine on the net, respectively. The second form specifies a broadcast operation to all machines in the local machine's primary domain. The third form specifies all machines in the indicated domain. See the book *Windows NT Administration: Single Systems to Heterogeneous Networks* for more information on domains and domain controllers. In order for the code in Listing 7.2 to function appropriately, there must be a mailslot with the same name on the specified machine or machines.

After opening the mailslot, Listing 7.2 gets the local computer's name using **GetComputerName** (see Section 13.2), and then proceeds to broadcast the name to all mailslots in the current domain every five seconds. The code uses the normal **WriteFile** function seen in Section 2.7 to perform the write operation.

When you run the programs, note that termination of either the reader or the writer has no effect on the other end of the pair. A mailslot program can broadcast packets on the network even if no machine has created a server to receive them. Also, a server can exist in the absence of any clients. You will see that named pipes, discussed in the following section, are much more specific when forming connections. In both Listings 7.1 and 7.2, also note the presumption that the program will be terminated externally. You can formally close a either a mailslot server or client using the **CloseHandle** function discussed in Chapter 2.

Listing 7.1 uses a polling technique to check for messages. Every half second it calls **GetMailslotInfo** and checks to see if any messages are waiting in the slot. This approach works well in certain cases. In general, however, polling is not a good technique to use in a multi-threaded environment because it is inefficient. An efficient way to wait on a mailslot is to *specify a timeout value* when you call **CreateMailslot**. You may want the value to be infinite if waiting forever is appropriate, or you may want to make it shorter if, for example, you want the server to time out if it does not receive any messages during a certain period of time. In the **while** loop seen in Listing 7.1 set up code that looks like this in order to eliminate the polling:

```
while (1)
{
  /* Block waiting for input */
  ReadFile(hSMS_Slot, toDisptxt, 0,
    &NumBytesRead, (LPOVERLAPPED) NULL))
  if (GetLastError() !=
      ERROR_INSUFFICIENT_BUFFER)
  {
     ... handle error
     ... it may be a timeout, so check
  }

  Status=GetMailslotInfo(hSMS_Slot,
    (LPDWORD) NULL, &nextSize, &Msgs,
    (LPDWORD) NULL);
  if (!Status)
  {
    ... handle errror
  }

  /* If messages are available, then get them */
  if (Msgs)
  {
    /* Read the message and check to see if
       read was successful */
    if (!ReadFile(hSMS_Slot, toDisptxt, nextSize,
      &NumBytesRead, (LPOVERLAPPED) NULL);
    {
      ... handle error
```

```
        }
        ... handle message
    {
```

The first call to **ReadFile** is there simply to wait efficiently. It requests 0 bytes from the mailslot. As soon as anything arrives in the mailslot, **ReadFile** will unblock. You still have to call **GetMailslotInfo** to find out how big the message is, but then you can read it and proceed using the second **ReadFile**.

Listings 7.3, 7.4, and 7.5 present a more involved and realistic use of mailslots in a facility called Ranmon, or the "Run and Notify MONitor" system. This system lets you run a program on one machine and then receive notification of the program's completion on other machines. You might use this facility to run a program on one machine in the lab, and then receive a message indicating its completion on your personal machine in your office. You can run any executable using the Ranmon system.

The "ran" program, shown in Listing 7.5, is used to run a program. For example, you might type the following command on the command line:

```
ran labtest data1.db
```

The command `ran` is used like the command `start` on the command line: it simply precedes a normal command and its command line options. "labtest" is the name of an application and "data1.db" is a dataset used by that application. The "ran" program records the start time, and then runs labtest. When the program finishes execution, ran uses a mailslot to broadcast a message on the net indicating this fact.

Ranmon, shown in Listing 7.4, listens to a mailslot and when it hears a message from ran pops up a dialog indicating that labtest has completed. Note that you must use the same login ID on both machines. Ranmon creates separate mailslots for specific users, as described below, and the login ID of the current user determines the separation.

```
// ran.h

typedef struct
{
  char AppName[10];
  char WkstnName[MAX_COMPUTERNAME_LENGTH + 1];
  long RunHrs;
  long RunMin;
  long RunSec;
  int stopMonitors;
} RANData;
```

Listing 7.3
The common header file ran.h for ran and ranmon

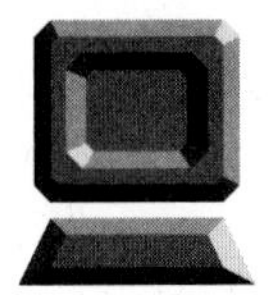

```
// ranmon.cpp

// Usage: ranmon

#include <windows.h>
#include <string.h>
#include "ran.h"

#define TITLE_NAME "Run And Notify MONitor"
#define MAX_USERNAME 15
```

Listing 7.4
The ranmon program waits for messages produced by ran (Listing 7.5) and pops up a message box when it receives one (Page 1 of 3)

```
int WINAPI WinMain(HANDLE ghInstance,
  HANDLE hPrevInstance, LPSTR lpCmdLine,
  int nCmdShow)
{
  HANDLE RANSlot;
  DWORD NumBytesRead;
  DWORD length;
  RANData randata;
  char slotPath[MAX_PATH];
  char msgString[255];
  char tmp[85];
  char userName[MAX_USERNAME + 1];

  strcpy(slotPath, "\\\\.\\mailslot\\ran\\");
  length=sizeof(userName);
  GetUserName(userName, &length);
  strcat(slotPath, userName);

  /* Create a mailslot for receiving messages */
  RANSlot=CreateMailslot(slotPath, sizeof(RANData),
    MAILSLOT_WAIT_FOREVER,
    (LPSECURITY_ATTRIBUTES) NULL);

  /* Check and see if the mailslot was created */
  if (RANSlot == INVALID_HANDLE_VALUE)
  {
    MessageBox(NULL,
      "ERROR: Unable to create mailslot.",
      TITLE_NAME, MB_OK | MB_ICONHAND);
    return(1);
  }

  /* Repeatedly check for messages until
     the program terminates */
  while(1)
```

Listing 7.4
The ranmon program waits for messages produced by ran (Listing 7.5) and pops up a message box when it receives one (Page 2 of 3)

```
    {
      /* Read a message and check to see if
         read was successful */
      if (!ReadFile(RANSlot, &randata,
        sizeof(RANData),
        &NumBytesRead, (LPOVERLAPPED) NULL))
      {
        MessageBox(NULL,
          "ERROR: Unable to read from mailslot.",
          TITLE_NAME, MB_OK | MB_ICONHAND);
        CloseHandle(RANSlot);
        return(1);
      }

      if (randata.stopMonitors == 1) return(0);

      strcpy(msgString, "The application \"");
      strcat(msgString, randata.AppName);
      strcat(msgString, "\" executing on ");
      strcat(msgString, randata.WkstnName);
      strcat(msgString, " has finished.\n\n");
      wsprintf(tmp, "It executed for: %ld hours,\
        %ld minutes, and %ld seconds.",
        randata.RunHrs, randata.RunMin,
        randata.RunSec);
      strcat(msgString, tmp);
      MessageBox(NULL, msgString,
        TITLE_NAME, MB_SETFOREGROUND | MB_OK
        | MB_ICONINFORMATION);
    } /* while */
  }
```

Listing 7.4
The ranmon program waits for messages produced by ran (Listing 7.5) and pops up a message box when it receives one (Page 3 of 3)

```
// ran.cpp

// Usage: ran <executable|batch file|-stopmon>

#include <windows.h>
#include <process.h>
#include <iostream.h>
#include <stdlib.h>
#include <string.h>
#include <time.h>
#include "ran.h"

#define MAX_USERNAME 15

int main(int argc, char *argv[])
{
  HANDLE RANSlot;
  BOOL Status;
  DWORD NumBytesWritten;
  DWORD length;
  RANData randata;
  char cmdLine[MAX_PATH];
  char slotPath[MAX_PATH];
  char userName[MAX_USERNAME + 1];
  int i;
  long elapsedTime;
  time_t startTime;
  time_t stopTime;
  char *timeString;
```

Listing 7.5
The ran portion of the ranmon system. This program runs a program and then signals ranmon when it is complete (Page 1 of 4)

```
    if (argc < 2)
    {
      cout <<
        "Usage: ran <executable|batch file|-\
stopmon>\n"
        << endl;
      return(1);
    }


    /* If -stopmon, stop ranmon */
    if (!strcmp(argv[1], "-stopmon"))
    {
      randata.stopMonitors=1;
      cout << "Sending Ranmon the stop signal..."
        << endl;
    }
    /* otherwise, run the requested program */
    else
    {
      /* Get the comp name and record it */
      randata.stopMonitors=0;
      strcpy(randata.AppName, argv[1]);
      length=sizeof(randata.WkstnName);
      GetComputerName(randata.WkstnName, &length);
      strcpy(cmdLine, argv[1]);
      for (i=2; i<argc; i++)
      {
        strcat(cmdLine, " ");
        strcat(cmdLine, argv[i]);
      }

      /* Get the start time */
      time(&startTime);
      timeString=ctime(&startTime);
```

Listing 7.5
The ran portion of the ranmon system. This program runs a program and then signals ranmon when it is complete (Page 2 of 4)

```
    cout << argv[1] << " started: " << timeString
      << endl;

    /* run the program */
    system(cmdLine);

    /* Record the stop time */
    time(&stopTime);
    timeString=ctime(&stopTime);
    cout << argv[1] << " exited: " << timeString
      << endl;

    elapsedTime=stopTime-startTime;
    randata.RunHrs=elapsedTime / 3600;
    elapsedTime-=(randata.RunHrs * 3600);
    randata.RunMin=elapsedTime / 60;
    elapsedTime-=(randata.RunMin * 60);
    randata.RunSec=elapsedTime;

    cout << argv[1] << " executed: "
      << randata.RunHrs
      << " hours, " <<  randata.RunMin
      << " minutes, and "
      << randata.RunSec << " seconds\n" << endl;
  }

  /* Set up mailslot path */
  strcpy(slotPath, "\\\\*\\mailslot\\ran\\");
  length=sizeof(userName);
  GetUserName(userName, &length);
  strcat(slotPath, userName);
  /* Create the mailslot file handle
     for sending messages */
  RANSlot=CreateFile(slotPath,
    GENERIC_WRITE, FILE_SHARE_READ,
```

Listing 7.5
The ran portion of the ranmon system. This program runs a program and then signals ranmon when it is complete (Page 3 of 4)

```
      (LPSECURITY_ATTRIBUTES) NULL,
      OPEN_EXISTING, FILE_ATTRIBUTE_NORMAL,
      (HANDLE) NULL);

    /* Check and see if the mailslot file was opened,
       if not terminate program */
    if (RANSlot == INVALID_HANDLE_VALUE)
    {
      cerr << "ERROR: Unable to create a mailslot"
        << endl;
      return (1);
    }

    /* Send message that program has terminated */
    /* Write message to mailslot */
    Status=WriteFile(RANSlot,
      &randata, sizeof(RANData),
      &NumBytesWritten, (LPOVERLAPPED) NULL);

    /* If error occurs when writing to mailslot,
       terminate program */
    if (!Status)
    {
      cerr << "ERROR: Unable to write message"
        << endl;
      CloseHandle(RANSlot);
      return (1);
    }

    CloseHandle(RANSlot);
    return(0);
}
```

Listing 7.5
The ran portion of the ranmon system. This program runs a program and then signals ranmon when it is complete (Page 4 of 4)

The ran program in Figure 7.5 is straightforward. It first checks for proper usage, and then for the `-stopmon` option. If `-stopmon` is seen, it signals the fact by setting the **stopMonitors** value to 1. Ranmon will interpret this value as a signal to terminate itself. Otherwise, ran notes the time, uses the **system** function to execute the requested application, and when it finishes notes the stop time. All of the time data, along with the application and machine name, is stored in the **randata** structure (see Listing 7.3 for its definition).

Ran then creates the client side of a mailslot. Note that the mailslot name here includes the path "ran" as well as the user name, for example:

```
\\*\mailslot\ran\smith
```

This allows multiple users to use ranmon on the same network and keep their messages separate. Once the mailslot is created, ran broadcasts the **randata** structure onto the network and exits.

The ranmon application is fairly simple. Its job is to run in the background and wait for messages from copies of the ran program. The messages will contain a **randata** structure, and will always have a fixed size, so you can use **ReadFile** without having to call **GetMailslotInfo** first to determine the message size. When ranmon sees a message, it either terminates itself if **stopMonitors** is 1, or it pops up a message box containing the data.

Note than ranmon creates an infinite loop in its **WinMain** function. The fact that the program uses **WinMain** (see Appendix A) means that you cannot kill it with ctrl-C on the command line, hence the backdoor `-stopmon` option in ran that allows you to kill off ranmon when necessary. You can start ranmon by placing an icon for it in your startup group in the Program Manager if you want it to run every time you log in.

Note: If you have both the NetBEUI and TCP/IP drivers loaded and active in the Network applet of the Control Panel, you will probably get two copies of every packet sent to a mailslot. If you find that your machine receives multiple copies of mailslot messages, that is probably why. You should therefore design any mailslot protocol that you create so that you can detect duplicates of a message and ignore them.

7.4 Named Pipes

Compatibility Note: At the time of publication, it is not possible to create a named pipe server in Windows 95 because of a ***ConnectNamedPipe*** *failure.*

While the mailslot facility discussed in the previous section is easy to use, it has one handicap that often makes it unacceptable: it does not guarantee delivery. For example, if two programs on different machines communicate via mailslots, the following problem arises: When machine one sends a message to machine two, it has no way to know that the data actually arrived. You could code the programs so that machine two sends back an acknowledgment, but then you could argue that it has no way of knowing if the acknowledgment arrived. This problem means that if machine one has sent a command to machine two and machine two does not respond, it has no way to know what happened. Should it send the packet again, wait for awhile, or give up? Guaranteed delivery solves this problem.

Named pipes provide a guaranteed delivery mechanism. Instead of broadcasting the packet onto the network, you form a distinct connection with another machine using a named pipe. If the connection ever breaks, for example because a machine goes down or a portion of the network fails, both parties to the connection find out as soon as they try to send or receive anything. Packets are also guaranteed to arrive in sequence through a named pipe. The only problem with named pipes is that you lose the ability to broadcast packets. To broadcast anything, all of the target machines must have a connection to a central server, and the server must separately transmit the message to each one. This limitation is actually an advantage in large networks, because it forces you to discipline yourself in your use of network bandwidth. You cannot afford to broadcast packets across multiple domains with mailslots: If you had many programs doing this the network would rapidly saturate. By forcing the server to converse only with directly connected machines, you limit network traffic.

You use named pipes to form point-to-point connections between pairs of processes (on the same or separate machines), or to create client/server systems where many machines connect to a single, central server. For example, say that you want to create a conference system, something like a multi-user chat program. Each user can type a message, and sees in a scrolling window the comments of everyone else. See Figure 7.4.

One easy way to implement this program is with mailslots, but if the users are hundreds of miles apart on a giant network, this approach won't work. What you might do instead is set up a conference server at a known location on the network. At the appointed time everyone starts their conference appli-

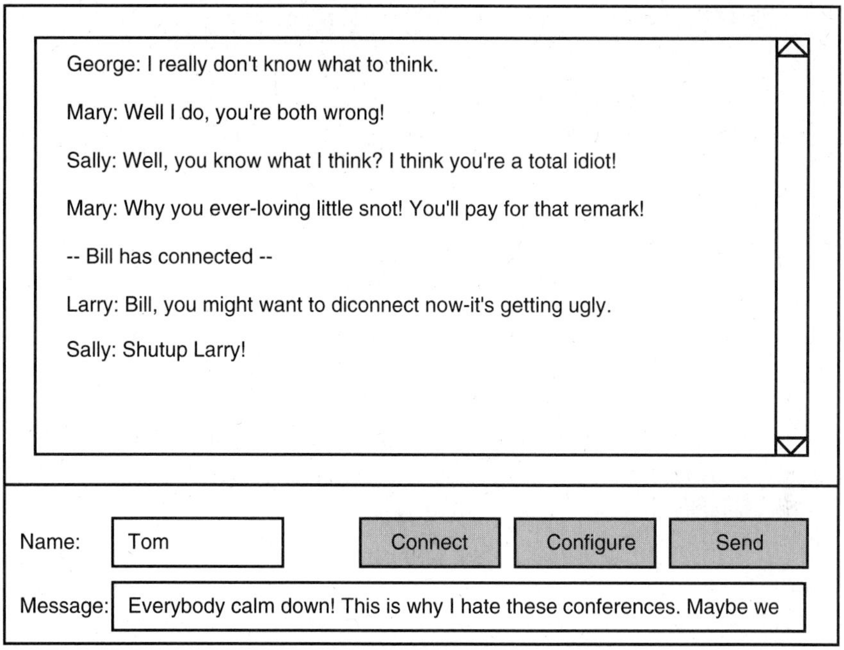

George: I really don't know what to think.

Mary: Well I do, you're both wrong!

Sally: Well, you know what I think? I think you're a total idiot!

Mary: Why you ever-loving little snot! You'll pay for that remark!

-- Bill has connected --

Larry: Bill, you might want to diconnect now-it's getting ugly.

Sally: Shutup Larry!

Name: Tom

Connect Configure Send

Message: Everybody calm down! This is why I hate these conferences. Maybe we

Figure 7.4
A multi-user conferencing system.

cation and connects to the server. The application connects using a named pipe. Whenever a user types a message and presses the send button, the message gets transmitted to the server. The server then resends the message to each of the connected users one at a time. Since named pipes are used, the server can monitor and announce connections and disconnections.

Named pipes are only slightly more difficult to create than mailslots. Listings 7.6 and 7.7 show how to create a simple point-to-point connection between two applications using named pipes. If you run the receiving program shown in Listing 7.6 first, and then on the same machine run the sending program in 7.7, the program will query you for the name of the machine to connect to. Since you are running the sender and the receiver on the same machine, type "." or enter your machine name. You will see a message sent from sender to receiver every five seconds or so. When you kill off the sender, notice that you immediately see a message in the receiver indicating that it has detected the break in the pipe. If you try to start up the sender without the receiver running, the sender will fail immediately because it cannot connect. Unlike mailslots, pipes can tell when the other end is not working properly.

A named pipe connection can occur across the network as simply as it occurs on the same machine. For example, if the server program in Listing 7.6 is running on a machine named "orion," log in to a different machine *using an account with the exact same login ID and password as the one you are using on "orion."* Run the sender in Listing 7.7 on the new machine and enter the name "orion" when it asks for the machine name to connect to. The connection will occur properly. Note that, with named pipes, you *must* know the name of the machine running the server.

Also note that if you have a different user try to connect to the receiver, then the connection fails. For example, if the user "jones" is running the receiver on the machine "orion" and the user "smith" tries to connect using the sender on another machine, the connection fails with an "access denied" error. This is the NT security system at work. See Chapter 10 and Section 10.9 for explanations and solutions.

```
// ssnprecv.cpp

// Usage: ssnprecv

#include <windows.h>
#include <iostream.h>

int main()
{
  char toDisptxt[80];
  HANDLE ssnpPipe;
  DWORD NumBytesRead;
```

Listing 7.6
A simple program that creates a named pipe server. The server will wait and accept one connection, and then receive messages from it (Page 1 of 3)

```
/* Create a named pipe for receiving messages */
ssnpPipe=CreateNamedPipe("\\\\.\\pipe\\ssnp",
  PIPE_ACCESS_INBOUND,
  PIPE_TYPE_MESSAGE | PIPE_WAIT,
  1, 0, 0, 150,
  (LPSECURITY_ATTRIBUTES) NULL);

/* Check and see if the named pipe was created */
if (ssnpPipe == INVALID_HANDLE_VALUE)
{
  cerr << "ERROR: Unable to create a named pipe."
    << endl;
  return (1);
}

/* Allow a client to connect to the name pipe,
   terminate if unsuccessful */
if(!ConnectNamedPipe(ssnpPipe,
  (LPOVERLAPPED) NULL))
{
  cerr << "ERROR: Unable to connect a named pipe"
    << endl;
  CloseHandle(ssnpPipe);
  return (1);
}

/* Repeatedly check for messages until the program
   is terminated */
while(1)
{
  /* Read the message and check to see if read
     was successful */
  if (!ReadFile(ssnpPipe, toDisptxt,
    sizeof(toDisptxt),
```

Listing 7.6
A simple program that creates a named pipe server. The server will wait and accept one connection, and then receive messages from it (Page 2 of 3)

```
          &NumBytesRead, (LPOVERLAPPED) NULL))
        {
          cerr
            << "ERROR: Unable to read from named pipe"
            << endl;
          CloseHandle(ssnpPipe);
          return (1);
        }

        /* Display the Message */
        cout << toDisptxt << endl;

      } /* while */
    }
```

Listing 7.6
A simple program that creates a named pipe server. The server will wait and accept one connection, and then receive messages from it (Page 3 of 3)

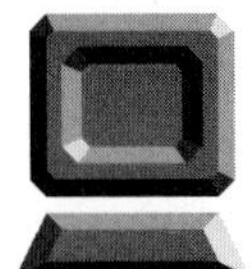

```
// ssnpsend.cpp

// Usage: ssnpsend

#include <windows.h>
#include <iostream.h>

int main()
{
  char *toSendtxt="Test String";
  HANDLE ssnpPipe;
  DWORD NumBytesWritten;
  char machineName[80];
```

Listing 7.7
A named pipe client able to connect to Listing 7.6 and send it messages (Page 1 of 3)

```
char pipeName[80];

cout << "Enter name of server machine: ";
cin >> machineName;
wsprintf(pipeName, "\\\\%s\\pipe\\ssnp",
  machineName);

/* Create the named pipe file handle for sending
   messages */
ssnpPipe=CreateFile(pipeName,
  GENERIC_WRITE, FILE_SHARE_READ,
  (LPSECURITY_ATTRIBUTES) NULL,
  OPEN_EXISTING, FILE_ATTRIBUTE_NORMAL,
  (HANDLE) NULL);

/* Check and see if the named pipe file was
   opened, if not terminate program */
if (ssnpPipe == INVALID_HANDLE_VALUE)
{
  cerr << "ERROR: Unable to create a named pipe"
    << endl;
  cerr << GetLastError() << endl;
  return (1);
}

/* Repeatedly send message until program is
   terminated */
while(1)
{
  cout << "Sending..." << endl;
  /* Write message to the pipe */
  if (!WriteFile(ssnpPipe,
        toSendtxt, (DWORD) strlen(toSendtxt)+1,
        &NumBytesWritten, (LPOVERLAPPED) NULL))
  {
```

Listing 7.7
A named pipe client able to connect to Listing 7.6 and send it messages (Page 2 of 3)

```
          /* If error occurs when writing to named
             pipe, terminate program */
          cerr << "ERROR: Unable to write to named pipe"
            << endl;
          CloseHandle(ssnpPipe);
          return (1);
        }

        /* Wait before sending the message again */
        Sleep(4800);
      } /* while*/
    }
```

Listing 7.7
A named pipe client able to connect to Listing 7.6 and send it messages (Page 3 of 3)

In Listing 7.6, the program starts by creating a named pipe server using the **CreateNamedPipe** function.

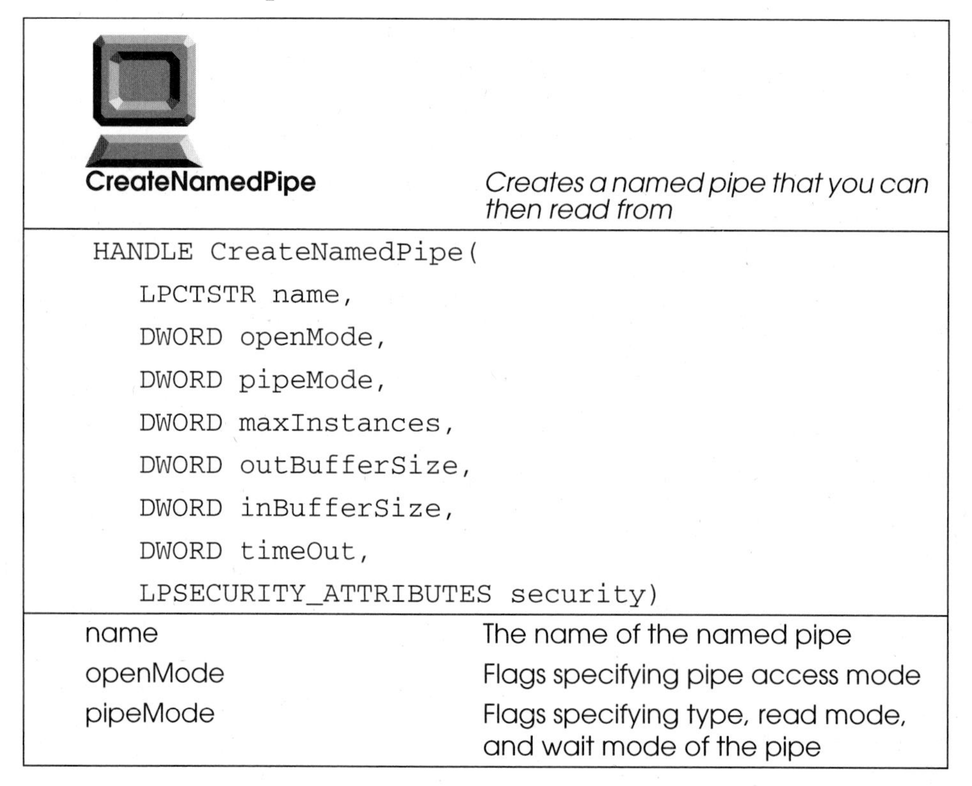

CreateNamedPipe *Creates a named pipe that you can then read from*

```
HANDLE CreateNamedPipe(
   LPCTSTR name,
   DWORD openMode,
   DWORD pipeMode,
   DWORD maxInstances,
   DWORD outBufferSize,
   DWORD inBufferSize,
   DWORD timeOut,
   LPSECURITY_ATTRIBUTES security)
```

name	The name of the named pipe
openMode	Flags specifying pipe access mode
pipeMode	Flags specifying type, read mode, and wait mode of the pipe

maxInstances	Maximum number of instances, 1 through PIPE_UNLIMITED_INSTANCE. Must be the same for all instances
outBufferSize	The output buffer size
inBufferSize	The input buffer size
timeOut	The time out value for the pipe. All instances must have the same value
security	Security attributes. See Chapter 10
Returns a handle to the named pipe or INVALID_HANDLE_VALUE.	

The name used with the **CreateNamedPipe** function will always have the same form:

\\.\pipe\[path]name

As with mailslots, you can specify a path before the name of the pipe to clearly distinguish it from other pipes on the system.

The **openMode** parameter passed to **CreateNamedPipe** lets you determine the direction of the pipe. Named pipes can be one directional or bi-directional, depending on the following constants used with the **openMode** parameter:

PIPE_ACCESS_DUPLEX
PIPE_ACCESS_INBOUND
PIPE_ACCESS_OUTBOUND

You can also specify the buffering and overlap behavior of the pipe with two other constants:

FILE_FLAG_WRITE_THROUGH
FILE_FLAG_OVERLAPPED

On byte-type pipes (described later), write-through causes all bytes sent to a pipe to be transmitted immediately, rather than being held in a buffer. The write function does not return until all bytes are sent. If write-through is not specified, then bytes are placed in a buffer and collected until the system can send a reasonably sized network packet. The overlapped flag enables overlapped reads on a pipe (see Section 6.5). Overlapped operations on a pipe allow asynchronous operations just as they do in a file. They also allow simultaneous reading and writing on the same pipe, and this is very important in multi-threaded servers and clients that use pipes. See the example that follows.

The **pipeMode** parameter of **CreateNamedPipe** determines whether the pipe works with a pure stream of bytes, or with packets of bytes called messages. A stream of bytes has no logical boundaries that group the bytes together, so bytes can be broken up anywhere when forming network packets. Messages contain a group of bytes that must be kept together as a unit. You can declare byte or message behavior in both the read and write directions:

PIPE_TYPE_MESSAGE
PIPE_TYPE_BYTE
PIPE_READMODE_MESSAGE
PIPE_READMODE_BYTE

You also specify the PIPE_WAIT constant as shown, unless you are using overlapped I/O. In Listing 7.6, the different constants in the open and pipe mode parameters are used to create a pipe that is one-directional inbound, message oriented, and blocking.

A pipe can have more than one instance on a single machine. This capability allows multiple server threads to service multiple clients, each in different threads. An example appears in Section 7.5. Since the example in Listings 7.6 and 7.7 is a simple point-to-point connection, only one instance is necessary, so a maximum of 1 instance is specified in the call to **CreateNamedPipe** in Listing 7.6. The call to **CreateNamedPipe** also uses 0 for the buffer sizes to pick default values, and finally specifies a timeout value of 150 milliseconds. The timeout value is relevant only when the **WaitNamedPipe** function is used.

Listing 7.6 next waits for a connection on the named pipe using the **ConnectNamedPipe** function.

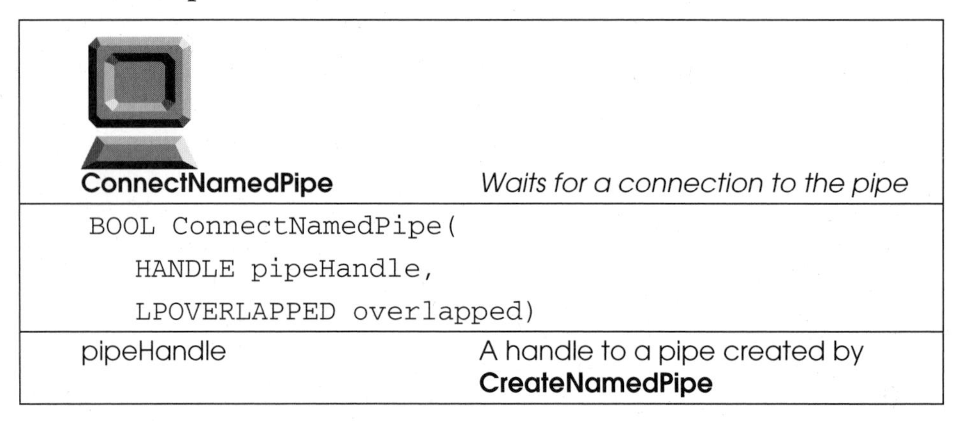

ConnectNamedPipe	*Waits for a connection to the pipe*

`BOOL ConnectNamedPipe(`
`HANDLE pipeHandle,`
`LPOVERLAPPED overlapped)`	

pipeHandle	A handle to a pipe created by **CreateNamedPipe**

overlapped	A pointer to an overlapped structure
Returns TRUE on success	

A connection is formed in the server when a client program calls **CreateFile** with named pipe specified in the server as its destination. Upon connection, the **ConnectNamedPipe** function returns. Alternatively you can specify an overlapped structure (See Section 6.5) and **ConnectNamedPipe** will return immediately and later signal the event in the overlapped structure upon connection.

Listing 7.6 then enters a loop, waiting for data to arrive with a **ReadFile** function as described in Chapter 2.7. The **ReadFile** function behaves slightly differently here than it does with files, communications ports, and so on. Because this named pipe is in message mode, the **ReadFile** function will return as soon as it receives a complete message, regardless of how many bytes the message contains. It is possible to use a blocking read as shown, or to use an overlapped read. Overlapped reads are discussed in Section 6.5.

Listing 7.7 is a simple client for Listing 7.6. Listing 7.7 starts by creating a connection to the named pipe with the **CreateFile** function. See Chapter 2.7 for details on **CreateFile**. It is also possible to create a connection to a message-based pipe using the **CallNamedPipe** convenience function, which contains a call to **CreateFile**.

Listing 7.7 then writes messages to the pipe continuously, one every five seconds, using the **WriteFile** function. See Chapter 2 for details on this function. Each individual call to **WriteFile** constitutes a message at the receiving end of the named pipe, so the receiver's **ReadFile** function will unblock when it receives the message. Each time the client writes, the server produces a message on the screen.

If two copies of the client try to connect to the server shown above at the same time, then the server will reject the second client. Only one connection is allowed on a named pipe. The following section shows how to create multiple instances of the same pipe to handle multiple clients in a server.

7.5 Named Pipe Client/Server Systems

If you need to create a client/server system in Windows, where multiple clients connect to a single server somewhere on the network, you have three choices. You can use RPCs, TCP communications, or named pipes. RPCs (see

Chapter 8) are easier to use in many cases because they handle all of the connection problems for you. Many of the remote services that NT offers are implemented with RPCs. There are certain cases, however, where named pipes are more appropriate. For example, if you need to stream 10 megabytes of data across the network, then a named pipe is appropriate. In that case, it might be suitable to create a hybrid system, where an RPC server sets up the connection and then a point-to-point named pipe handles the data flow. The advantage of a named pipe is reduced overhead.

In a client/server system using named pipes, the server resides on a known machine on the network, and multiple clients can connect to it. The server machine may respond to each client individually, for example when the server is managing a database. The clients connect, make requests of the database, and then disconnect. Although many clients may be connected at once, their activities are unrelated. On the other hand, the server may exist to allow intercommunication between clients. The conversation system described earlier is an example of this architecture. Each client connects, and the server broadcasts messages received from the client to all of the other clients currently connected.

This section demonstrates these two different client/server architectures using named pipes. In both systems, multiple clients can connect to the server and send and receive messages. In the first example, the clients are managed independently of one another. In the second example, clients talk to one another through the server, and the clients are multi-threaded to demonstrate the technique of multi-threading a named pipe application to handle reading and writing to the pipe in separate threads.

Please note that when you run these examples, all clients and the server must have the same login ID and password. If they do not, you will get access denied errors when a client tries to connect to the server. See Chapter 10 and Section 10.9 for explanations and solutions.

7.5.1 A Simple Client/Server System

Listings 7.8 and 7.9 contain the code for a typical server and client. The server treats each client independently. You should run the server code on one machine. You can then run multiple copies of the client code on the same machine or on other machines on the network. *When running over the network, be sure all clients have the same login ID and password as the server.* See Chapter 10 and Section 10.9 and for an explanation of the NT security system.

When you run a client, it will connect and then request a line of text from the user. Type something and press return. The server will receive the line, convert it to upper case, and return it to the client, which will display the line received from the server on the screen. The MAX_INSTANCES constant in the server controls how many clients can connect at any one time. Set it to any value you like.

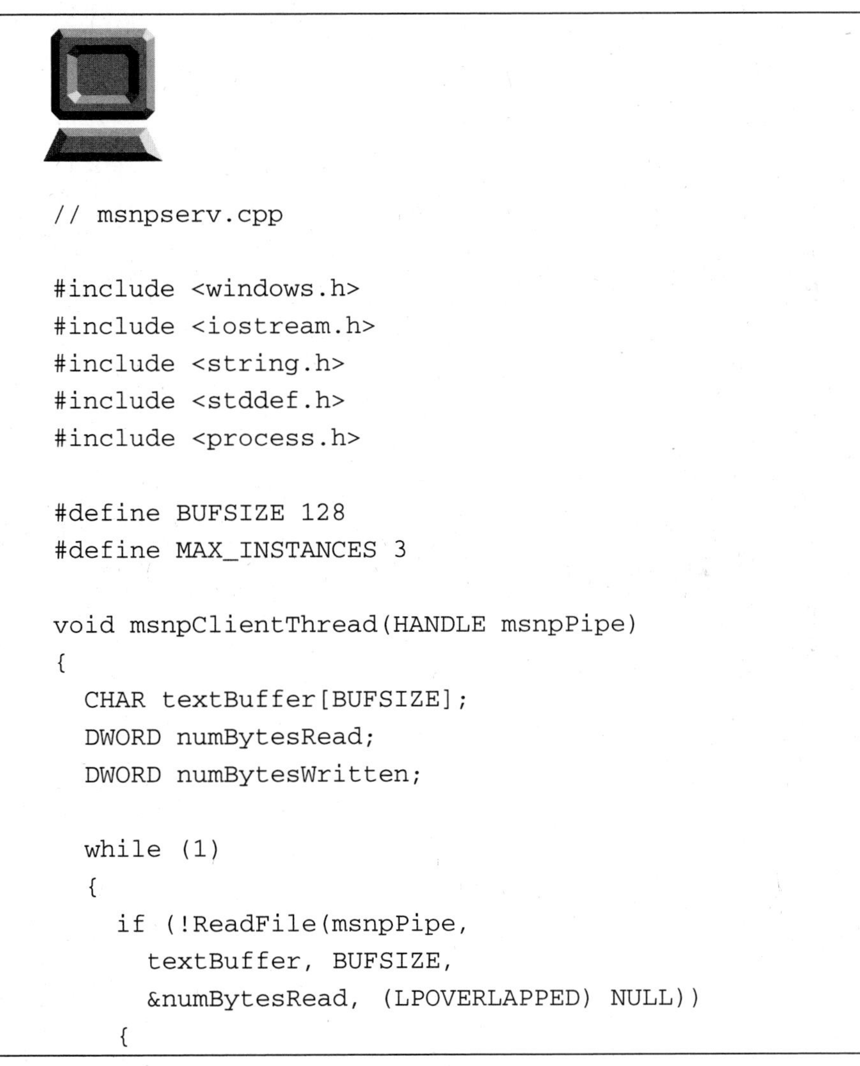

```
// msnpserv.cpp

#include <windows.h>
#include <iostream.h>
#include <string.h>
#include <stddef.h>
#include <process.h>

#define BUFSIZE 128
#define MAX_INSTANCES 3

void msnpClientThread(HANDLE msnpPipe)
{
  CHAR textBuffer[BUFSIZE];
  DWORD numBytesRead;
  DWORD numBytesWritten;

  while (1)
  {
    if (!ReadFile(msnpPipe,
      textBuffer, BUFSIZE,
      &numBytesRead, (LPOVERLAPPED) NULL))
    {
```

Listing 7.8
A server that uses named pipes. Multiple clients can connect to the server, and it handles each one separately (Page 1 of 4)

```
            cerr
              << "ERROR: Unable to read from named pipe"
              << endl;
            break;
          }

          _strupr(textBuffer);

          if (!WriteFile(msnpPipe,
            textBuffer, strlen(textBuffer) + 1,
            &numBytesWritten, (LPOVERLAPPED) NULL))
          {
            cerr
              << "ERROR: Unable to write to named pipe"
              << endl;
            break;
          }

          cout << textBuffer << endl;
        } /* while */

        FlushFileBuffers(msnpPipe);
        DisconnectNamedPipe(msnpPipe);
        CloseHandle(msnpPipe);
      }

      INT main(VOID)
      {
        HANDLE msnpPipe;
        DWORD msnpThread;

        while (1)
        {
          /* Create a named pipe for receiving
             messages */
```

Listing 7.8
A server that uses named pipes. Multiple clients can connect to the server, and it handles each one separately (Page 2 of 4)

```
msnpPipe=CreateNamedPipe("\\\\.\\pipe\\msnp",
  PIPE_ACCESS_DUPLEX,
  PIPE_TYPE_BYTE | PIPE_WAIT,
  MAX_INSTANCES, 0, 0, 150,
  (LPSECURITY_ATTRIBUTES) NULL);

/* Check and see if the named pipe was
   created */
if (msnpPipe == INVALID_HANDLE_VALUE)
{
  cerr
    << "ERROR: Unable to create a named pipe"
    << endl;
  continue;
}

/* Allow a client to connect to the name pipe,
   terminate if unsuccessful */
if (!ConnectNamedPipe(msnpPipe,
  (LPOVERLAPPED) NULL))
{
  cerr
    << "ERROR: Unable to connect a named pipe."
    << endl;
  CloseHandle(msnpPipe);
  return (1);
}

msnpThread=_beginthread(msnpClientThread,
  0, (HANDLE) msnpPipe);
if (msnpThread == -1)
{
  cerr << "ERROR: Unable to create thread"
    << endl;
  CloseHandle(msnpPipe);
```

Listing 7.8
A server that uses named pipes. Multiple clients can connect to the server, and it handles each one separately (Page 3 of 4)

```
            }

        } /* while */
    }
```

Listing 7.8
A server that uses named pipes. Multiple clients can connect to the server, and it handles each one separately (Page 4 of 4)

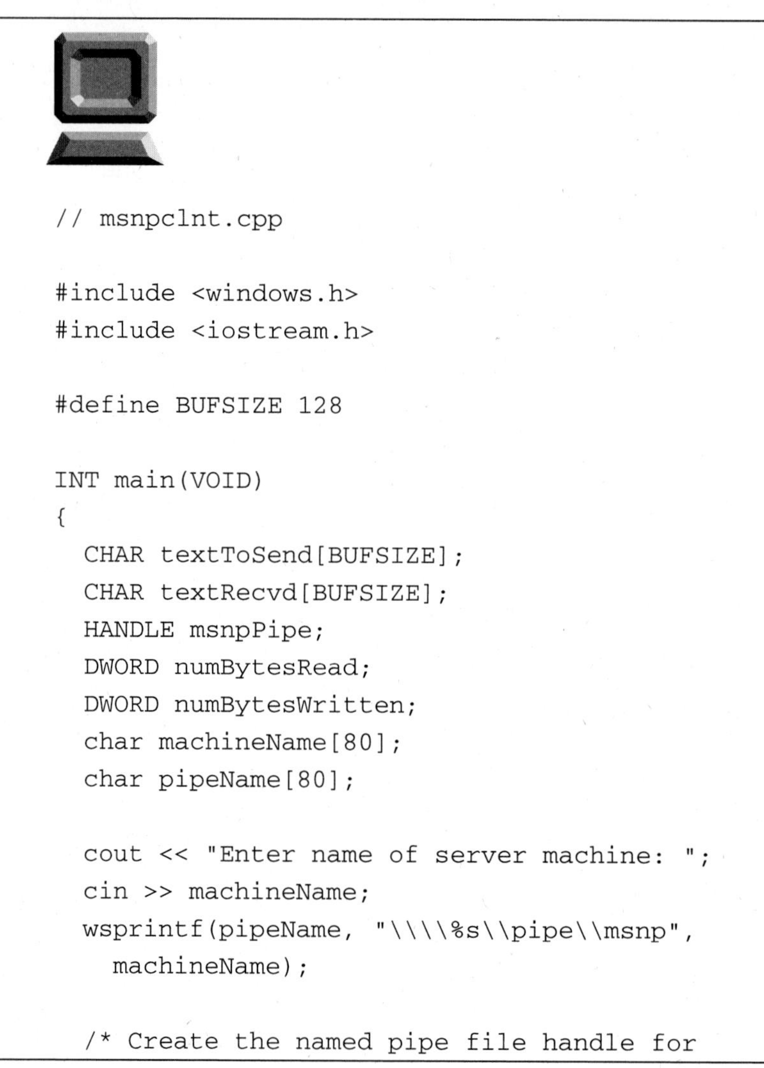

```
// msnpclnt.cpp

#include <windows.h>
#include <iostream.h>

#define BUFSIZE 128

INT main(VOID)
{
  CHAR textToSend[BUFSIZE];
  CHAR textRecvd[BUFSIZE];
  HANDLE msnpPipe;
  DWORD numBytesRead;
  DWORD numBytesWritten;
  char machineName[80];
  char pipeName[80];

  cout << "Enter name of server machine: ";
  cin >> machineName;
  wsprintf(pipeName, "\\\\%s\\pipe\\msnp",
    machineName);

  /* Create the named pipe file handle for
```

Listing 7.9
A typical client for Listing 7.8's server (Page 1 of 3)

```
      sending messages */
    msnpPipe=CreateFile(pipeName,
      GENERIC_READ | GENERIC_WRITE,
      0, (LPSECURITY_ATTRIBUTES) NULL,
      OPEN_EXISTING, FILE_ATTRIBUTE_NORMAL,
      (HANDLE) NULL);

    /* Check and see if the named pipe file was
       opened, if not terminate program */
    if (msnpPipe == INVALID_HANDLE_VALUE)
    {
      cerr << "ERROR: Unable to create a named pipe"
        << endl;
      return (1);
    }

    /* Repeatedly send message until program
       terminates */
    while(1)
    {
      cout << "Type text to send: ";
      cin.getline(textToSend, BUFSIZE);

      /* Write message to named pipe */
      if (!WriteFile(msnpPipe,
        textToSend, strlen(textToSend) + 1,
        &numBytesWritten, (LPOVERLAPPED) NULL))
      {
        cerr << "ERROR: Unable to write to pipe."
          << endl;
        CloseHandle(msnpPipe);
        return (1);
      }

      if (!ReadFile(msnpPipe,
```

Listing 7.9
A typical client for Listing 7.8's server (Page 2 of 3)

```
          textRecvd, BUFSIZE,
          &numBytesRead, (LPOVERLAPPED) NULL))
        {
          cerr << "ERROR: Unable to read from pipe"
            << endl;
          CloseHandle(msnpPipe);
          return (1);
        }

        cout << "Received: " << textRecvd << endl;

    } /* while*/
  }
```

Listing 7.9
A typical client for Listing 7.8's server (Page 3 of 3)

In the **main** function of Listing 7.8, you will find a loop that starts by creating an instance of the msnp pipe. There will be one instance for each connected client, along with one instance waiting for the next connection. The code then calls **ConnectNamedPipe** to wait for a client to connect. This process is identical to that described in Section 7.4. After it receives a connection, the server then creates a new thread to handle the new client. The thread receives the instance of the pipe as a parameter. Therefore, the system will contain one independent thread for each connected client, and the thread knows of the pipe instance of its specific client. Once the new thread exists, the server loops to create a new instance of the same pipe so that it can wait for another connection. This is how the server is able to allow several client connections to the "same" pipe.

The code here uses **_beginthread**, from the MSC library (see the Run-time Routines help file), to start the thread. It is used simply for variety. It does the same thing that **CreateThread** does, and **CreateThread** (see Chapter 5) would work just as well here.

The thread, once created, is responsible for all interaction with its client using the pipe handle that it received as a parameter. Here the interaction is very simple: The thread waits for the client to send it a string, converts the string to upper case, and then sends the new string back to the client.

When the client terminates, the **ReadFile** or **WriteFile** function will fail immediately, breaking out of the thread's loop. At that point the thread cleans up the pipe and disconnects gracefully before terminating. When creating a system of your own, you will probably have a message the client can send to force normal termination, but your server should always handle the unplanned death of a client gracefully, as shown here.

The client program in Listing 7.9 is very simple. It opens a handle to the server's pipe and then enters a loop. The loop requests a string from the user, sends it to the server, waits for the server's response, and then prints the response. See Listing 7.11 for an example of a multi-threaded client.

There is a small but finite chance that the call to **CreateFile** in the client can fail because the server is in the middle of creating one client thread but has not yet cycled around to create a new instance of its pipe to handle the next client. In this case you will receive an ERROR_PIPE_BUSY error code and you may want to cycle through **CreateFile** again to retry the connection.

The code shown in this section is simple because the server can deal with each client independently. Therefore, the client threads in the server do not need to interact with one another. The next section demonstrates the case in which clients interact.

7.5.2 Intercommunicating Clients

Compatibility Note: Be sure that you specify the multi-threaded libraries in the project file when compiling this code. See the diskette for details.

There are many situations where you create a server to allow multi-client interaction. Mailslots implicitly allow this sort of activity, but have problems because they are unreliable and insecure. Mailslots also broadcast their messages on the net, so they are inappropriate for inter-segment routing. Named pipes solve all of these problems, and a server that uses named pipes is able to let multiple clients interact in a authenticated way no matter how far apart they are on the network.

Listings 7.10 and 7.11 demonstrate a very simple conversation server. Run the server on one machine. As in Section 7.5.1, clients can run on the server machine or on other machines on the network. *Be sure that you are logged in under the same login ID and password on the server and all client machines,* or the server will reject the client connections. See Chapter 10 and Section 10.9 for explanations and suggestions. The maximum number of clients is controlled by

MAX_INSTANCES. See the description at the beginning of Section 7.5.1 for details.

When the server receives a message from any client, it converts the message to upper case and then sends it out to all of the connected clients. The clients use a multi-threaded design so that they can accept input from the pipe asynchronously, but the same thing can also be accomplished using overlapped I/O (See Section 6.5).

```
// mtnpserv.cpp

#include <windows.h>
#include <iostream.h>
#include <string.h>
#include <stddef.h>
#include <process.h>

#define BUFSIZE 128
#define MAX_INSTANCES 3

// Information needed for each connection
// to a client
typedef struct _CLIENT_INFO
{
  HANDLE h;
  OVERLAPPED overlappedRead;
  OVERLAPPED overlappedWrite;
} CLIENT_INFO;

// The array holds one entry for
// each client
```

Listing 7.10
A named pipe server that broadcasts any messages it receives back to all connected clients (Page 1 of 6)

```
CLIENT_INFO clients[MAX_INSTANCES];
volatile int numClients=0;

// There is one thread for each client
// attached to the server
void mtnpClientThread(HANDLE id)
{
  CHAR textBuffer[BUFSIZE];
  DWORD numBytesRead;
  DWORD numBytesWritten;
  int x;
  int ID = (int) id;

  while (1)
  {
    // Get input from the client
    if (!ReadFile(clients[ID].h,
      textBuffer, BUFSIZE,
      &numBytesRead,
      &(clients[ID].overlappedRead)))
    {
      if (GetLastError() != ERROR_IO_PENDING)
      {
        cerr <<
          "ERROR: Unable to read from named pipe "
          << GetLastError()
          << endl;
        break;
      }
    }
    GetOverlappedResult(clients[ID].h,
      &(clients[ID].overlappedRead), &numBytesRead,
      TRUE);
    clients[ID].overlappedRead.Offset +=
      numBytesRead;
```

Listing 7.10
A named pipe server that broadcasts any messages it receives back to all connected clients (Page 2 of 6)

```
        // Convert the client's string to
        // upper case to show server is
        // doing something
        _strupr(textBuffer);

        // Send the message to ALL clients
        // in the client array
        for (x=0; x<numClients; x++)
        {
          if (!WriteFile(clients[x].h,
            textBuffer, strlen(textBuffer) + 1,
            &numBytesWritten,
            &(clients[ID].overlappedWrite)))
          {
            if (GetLastError() != ERROR_IO_PENDING)
            {
              cerr
                << "ERROR: Unable to write to pipe "
                << GetLastError()
                << endl;
              break;
            }
          }
          GetOverlappedResult(clients[ID].h,
            &(clients[ID].overlappedWrite),
            &numBytesWritten,
            TRUE);
          clients[ID].overlappedWrite.Offset +=
            numBytesWritten;
        }

        // Echo the string in the server's window
        cout << textBuffer << endl;
      } // while
```

Listing 7.10
A named pipe server that broadcasts any messages it receives back to all connected clients (Page 3 of 6)

```
      // Clean up the pipe on termination
      // of the thread
      FlushFileBuffers(clients[ID].h);
      DisconnectNamedPipe(clients[ID].h);
      CloseHandle(clients[ID].h);
    }

    INT main(VOID)
    {
      HANDLE mtnpPipe;
      DWORD mtnpThread;

      while (1)
      {
        // Create a named pipe for receiving messages
        mtnpPipe=CreateNamedPipe("\\\\.\\pipe\\mtnp",
          PIPE_ACCESS_DUPLEX | FILE_FLAG_OVERLAPPED,
          PIPE_TYPE_MESSAGE |PIPE_READMODE_MESSAGE|
          PIPE_WAIT,
          MAX_INSTANCES, 0, 0, 150,
          (LPSECURITY_ATTRIBUTES) NULL);

        // Check and see if the named pipe was created
        if (mtnpPipe == INVALID_HANDLE_VALUE)
        {
          cerr << "ERROR: Unable to create pipe"
            << endl;
          return (1);
        }

        // Allow a client to connect to the name pipe,
        // terminate if unsuccessful
        if (!ConnectNamedPipe(mtnpPipe,
          (LPOVERLAPPED) NULL))
```

Listing 7.10
A named pipe server that broadcasts any messages it receives back to all connected clients (Page 4 of 6)

```
    {
      cerr << "ERROR: Unable to connect a pipe."
        << endl;
      CloseHandle(mtnpPipe);
      return (1);
    }

    // Init a client data structure. It contains
    // a handle to the pipe and overlapped structs
    clients[numClients].h = mtnpPipe;
    clients[numClients].overlappedRead.Offset =
      clients[numClients].overlappedWrite.Offset =
        0;
    clients[numClients].overlappedRead.OffsetHigh =
      clients[numClients].overlappedWrite.
        OffsetHigh = 0;
    clients[numClients].overlappedWrite.hEvent =
      CreateEvent(0, TRUE, FALSE, 0);
    clients[numClients].overlappedRead.hEvent =
      CreateEvent(0, TRUE, FALSE, 0);

    // Create a new thread to accept messages
    // from the new client
    mtnpThread=_beginthread(mtnpClientThread,
      0, (HANDLE) numClients);
    if (mtnpThread == -1)
    {
      cerr << "ERROR: Unable to create thread"
        << endl;
      CloseHandle(mtnpPipe);
    }

    // increment the number of clients
    numClients++;
```

Listing 7.10
A named pipe server that broadcasts any messages it receives back to all connected clients (Page 5 of 6)

```
    } /* while */
  }
```

Listing 7.10
A named pipe server that broadcasts any messages it receives back to all connected clients (Page 6 of 6)

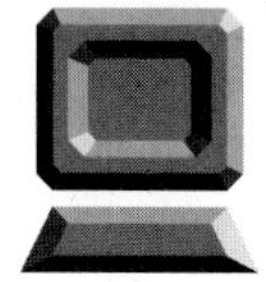

```
// mtnpclnt.cpp

#include <windows.h>
#include <iostream.h>
#include <stddef.h>
#include <process.h>

#define BUFSIZE 128

// The thread receives all messages from
// from the server
void mtnpServerThread(HANDLE mtnpPipeDup)
{
  CHAR textBuffer[BUFSIZE];
  DWORD numBytesRead;
  OVERLAPPED overlappedRead;

  // Init the overlapped structure
  overlappedRead.Offset =
    overlappedRead.OffsetHigh = 0;
  overlappedRead.hEvent =
    CreateEvent(0, TRUE, FALSE, 0);

  while (1)
  {
```

Listing 7.11
A multi-threaded client for Listing 7.10 (Page 1 of 5)

```
        // Read a message from the server
        if (!ReadFile(mtnpPipeDup,
          textBuffer, BUFSIZE,
          &numBytesRead, &overlappedRead))
        {
          if (GetLastError() != ERROR_IO_PENDING)
          {
            cerr <<
              "ERROR: Unable to read from named pipe"
              << endl;
            break;
          }
        }
        GetOverlappedResult(mtnpPipeDup,
          &overlappedRead, &numBytesRead,
          TRUE);
        overlappedRead.Offset += numBytesRead;

        // send the message to the screen
        cout << textBuffer << endl;
      } /* while */

      // clean up the pipe
      FlushFileBuffers(mtnpPipeDup);
      DisconnectNamedPipe(mtnpPipeDup);
      CloseHandle(mtnpPipeDup);
    }

    // The main function opens a handle
    // to the pipe and then writes to it
    INT main(VOID)
    {
      CHAR textToSend[BUFSIZE];
      HANDLE mtnpPipe;
      DWORD mtnpThread;
      DWORD numBytesWritten;
```

Listing 7.11
A multi-threaded client for Listing 7.10 (Page 2 of 5)

```
    BOOL success;
    OVERLAPPED overlappedWrite;
    char machineName[80];
    char pipeName[80];

    cout << "Enter name of server machine: ";
    cin.getline(machineName,80);
    wsprintf(pipeName, "\\\\%s\\pipe\\mtnp",
      machineName);

    // init overlapped structure
    overlappedWrite.Offset =
      overlappedWrite.OffsetHigh = 0;
    overlappedWrite.hEvent =
      CreateEvent(0, TRUE, FALSE, 0);

    // Create the named pipe file handle for
    // sending messages
    mtnpPipe=CreateFile(pipeName,
      GENERIC_WRITE | GENERIC_READ,
      0,
      (LPSECURITY_ATTRIBUTES) NULL,
      OPEN_EXISTING,
      FILE_ATTRIBUTE_NORMAL|FILE_FLAG_OVERLAPPED,
      (HANDLE) NULL);
    // Check and see if the named pipe file was
    // opened, if not terminate program
    if (mtnpPipe == INVALID_HANDLE_VALUE)
    {
      cerr << "ERROR: Unable to create a named pipe "
        << GetLastError()
        << endl;
      return (1);
    }

    // Set the pipe into message mode
```

Listing 7.11
A multi-threaded client for Listing 7.10 (Page 3 of 5)

```
DWORD mode = PIPE_READMODE_MESSAGE | PIPE_WAIT;
success = SetNamedPipeHandleState(mtnpPipe,
  &mode, 0, 0);
if (!success)
{
  cerr << "ERROR: Unable to set pipe mode"
    << endl;
  return (1);
}

// Begin a separate thread to read from
// the pipe
mtnpThread = _beginthread(mtnpServerThread,
  0, (HANDLE) mtnpPipe);
if (mtnpThread == -1)
{
  cerr << "ERROR: Unable to create thread"
    << endl;
  CloseHandle(mtnpPipe);
}

// Repeatedly send messages to the pipe
// until program is terminated
while(1)
{
  cout << "Type text to send: ";
  cin.getline(textToSend, BUFSIZE);

  // Write message to named pipe
  if (!WriteFile(mtnpPipe,
    textToSend, strlen(textToSend) + 1,
    &numBytesWritten, &overlappedWrite))
  {
    if (GetLastError() != ERROR_IO_PENDING)
    {
      cerr
```

Listing 7.11
A multi-threaded client for Listing 7.10 (Page 4 of 5)

```
                << "ERROR: Unable to write to pipe "
                << GetLastError() << endl;
              CloseHandle(mtnpPipe);
              return (1);
            }
          }
          GetOverlappedResult(mtnpPipe,
            &overlappedWrite, &numBytesWritten,
            TRUE);
          overlappedWrite.Offset += numBytesWritten;

        } // while
        return (0);
      }
```

Listing 7.11
A multi-threaded client for Listing 7.10 (Page 5 of 5)

You will notice that both the server and client now use overlapped I/O structures (see Section 6.5) even though they do not use asynchronous I/O. The overlapped I/O structures are used here because they are required when multiple threads access the same pipe handle. Since both server and client are multi-threaded, and reading and writing occur in different threads, overlapped I/O is a necessity.

The server's job in Listing 7.10 is to accept connections from multiple clients, just as in Listing 7.8. That portion of the code is no different. The server code now contains an array, however, that holds the pipes and overlapped structures for each client connection. The server initializes one element of the array for each connection it receives.

This array allows the different client threads in the server to broadcast all messages received to all of the connected clients. You will see in the **ClientThread** thread function a **for** loop that sends each capitalized string out to all of the clients. The overlapped I/O structures are required because of the **for** loop: Since it is possible for two threads to be reading or writing the same pipe simultaneously, the overlapped structures prevent conflict.

The server shown here does not handle disconnection very well. Ideally the server should update the array whenever a client disconnects, deleting the client's entry to allow another client to connect. This implementation detail is left as an exercise for the reader. In its current form, expect problems to arise if you kill off one client and try to connect another.

The client side of the system appears in Listing 7.11. The client here is nearly identical to Listing 7.9, except that it is multi-threaded. The main thread interacts with the user and writes to the pipe, while the **ServerThread** function reads from the pipe and writes messages to the screen. Because the two threads use the same pipe, you must use overlapped I/O structures. The program initializes the overlapped structures in the two different threads and then uses **ReadFile** and **WriteFile** normally. Again, the non-blocking behavior of overlapped I/O is not used here: the overlapped structures are necessary because the code is using the same pipe in two separate threads. The code passes the overlapped structures to **ReadFile** and **WriteFile** to make these functions compliant with the cross-thread reading and writing.

Typically a client program will handle pipe I/O in a more elegant manner than shown here. See Section 6.7 for ideas on integrating asynchronous pipe I/O into an MFC program.

7.6 Connecting with UNIX and Other TCP/IP Machines

In the previous sections you have learned about network communications using Windows' native communication protocol. Mailslots and named pipes work well when you want to communicate with other Windows machines on a homogeneous Windows network.

Windows also supports the TCP/IP protocol. This is the protocol used by UNIX machines and the Internet. If you load the TCP/IP drivers in the Network applet of the Control Panel (see the book *Windows NT Administration: Single Systems to Heterogeneous Networks* for more information), a number of TCP/IP commands (ftp, telnet, finger, etc.) become available on the command line. You can also create code that can read and write packets on the network using the TCP/IP protocol. There are at least three reasons for creating code using this protocol:

1. You want to write code that connects to an existing network service on a UNIX machine.
2. You want to create a network service (see Chapter 9) on an NT machine that UNIX machines will be able to access.

3. You want to create programs that allow widely-separated Windows machines on the Internet to communicate with one another, and you want to make sure the packets will route correctly on the Internet.

For example, if you want to create a Finger service that allows UNIX users to finger your NT machine, you must use the TCP/IP communications functions when you write the code.

Windows supplies a complete library of functions for creating TCP/IP code. The library is called the Windows Sockets API, or "winsock." All winsock functions are documented in the Win32 help file. UNIX programmers will find that the functions are very similar to the functions they are accustomed to for writing socket code on UNIX machines. There is also a another API called the Microsoft Windows Sockets Asynchronous Extensions that supplies TCP/IP support in a cooperative multi-tasking (non-threaded) environment such as Windows 3.1. These functions work in a manner similar to overlapped I/O. Because Windows NT and Windows 95 are multi-threaded, the extension functions are not necessarily needed here, but they can be useful in some situations.

There are several vocabulary words and concepts that you need to understand in order to use the TCP/IP functions:

1. Any machine, whether on the world-wide Internet or on an isolated TCP/IP network has both an *IP address* and a *fully-qualified domain name*. An IP address is of the form `152.1.45.17`, while a name has the form `server.iftech.com`. Both are unique to a particular machine network-wide. In your code you use IP addresses to connect to a machine, but there are functions that let you convert names to addresses. A typical small TCP/IP network consisting of several Windows machines and a UNIX machine is shown in Figure 7.5.

2. The Berkeley flavor of UNIX popularized the concept of a *socket*. A socket is a bi-directional communication device. A socket is similar to a file handle or a pipe in a sense. When you open a file handle to an existing file, you create an entity that you can read from and write to. When you create a socket, you can also read from it and write to it, but it is associated with the network rather than the file system.

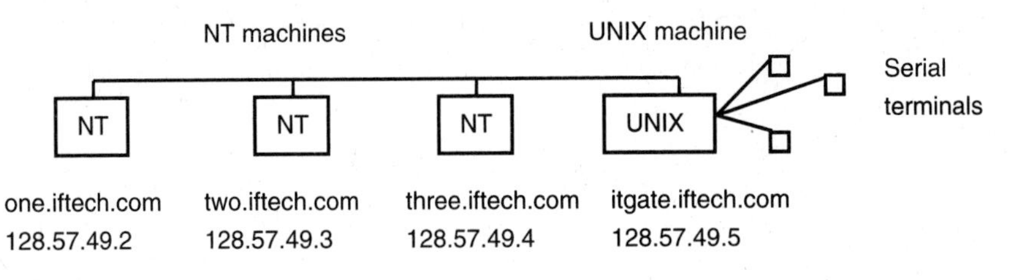

Figure 7.5
A typical small TCP/IP network consisting of three NT machines and one UNIX machine.

3. You can do one of two things with a socket: You can *bind* it to a *port* on the local machine, or, in TCP mode, you can *connect* it to a port on another machine. Ports are referred to by positive integer numbers. When you bind a socket to a port, you are claiming a port with a specific number on the local machine. Programs on other machines can connect to that port. Figure 7.6 shows a simplified representation of the different pieces.

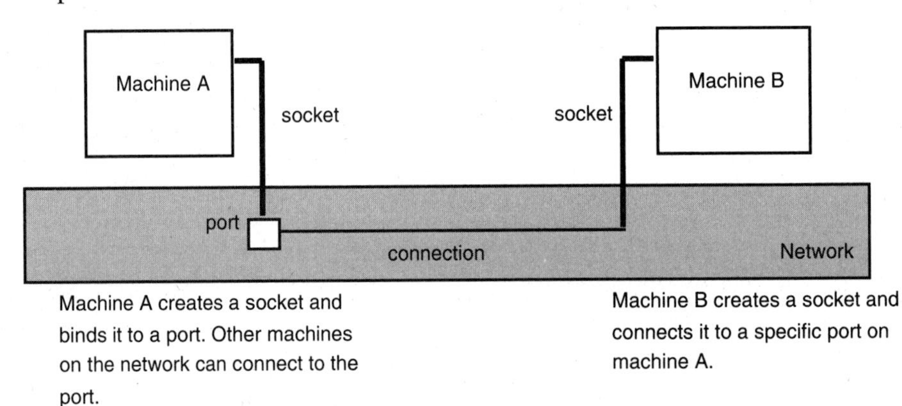

Figure 7.6
TCP connections using ports and sockets.

4. A port, when used in TCP mode, has the ability to *accept* connections. First you give it the ability to *listen*, and then you let it start accepting connections. Letting a port listen enables it. Other machines can now start connecting to the port. Each time a program *accepts* a connection, data can start to flow across the network. A port has a queue that holds connections waiting to be accepted. You define the maximum size of the queue when you tell the port to start listening.

TCP/IP networks support both mailslot-like (unreliable) communications with the potential for broadcasting, as well as point-to-point connections used in client/server architectures. Point-to-point connections, like named pipes, have guaranteed delivery, error correction, and sequencing. Point-to-point connections are referred to as TCP connections. UDP connections, on the other hand, are unreliable but permit broadcasting. TCP connections are far more common in the UNIX world than UDP connections are.

To be a server using the TCP protocol, a program must create a socket, bind it to a port, let the port begin listening, and then accept connections. Each time it accepts a connection, the server can communicate over the new connection with a different client. A client must create a socket and connect it to a port on another machine. Once it has a connection, it can communicate. See Figure 7.7.

TCP/IP networks support three different types of network packets.

1. IP packets are raw packets and are rarely seen. Raw packets are directed to a specific machine or are broadcast, but they bypass the port system and therefore must be handled as generic packets. You will never use IP packets yourself.
2. UDP packets are very similar in concept to mailslot packets. They can be directed to a port on a machine or broadcast, just like a mailslot. UDP packets are always sent to a specific port number. UDP packets are not very common in the UNIX world because they cannot travel farther than the local network segment and their use tends to lead to large traffic loads on that segment.
3. TCP packets are similar in concept to named pipe packets, and are used for point-to-point or client/server communications. They are sent to a specific port on a specific machine. TCP communications are properly sequenced, reliable, and error-corrected, just like named pipes. Almost all UNIX network communications use TCP packets.

One of the most significant advantages of TCP/IP is its routability. A *router* is a device that sits between two separate network *segments*, as shown in Figure 7.8. It examines the TCP/IP header in each packet and decides whether or not a packet on one of the segments should be copied to the other segment. In the diagram below, an administrator has created two separate subnets (128.57.49.xxx and 128.57.50.xxx) and would configure the router to recog-

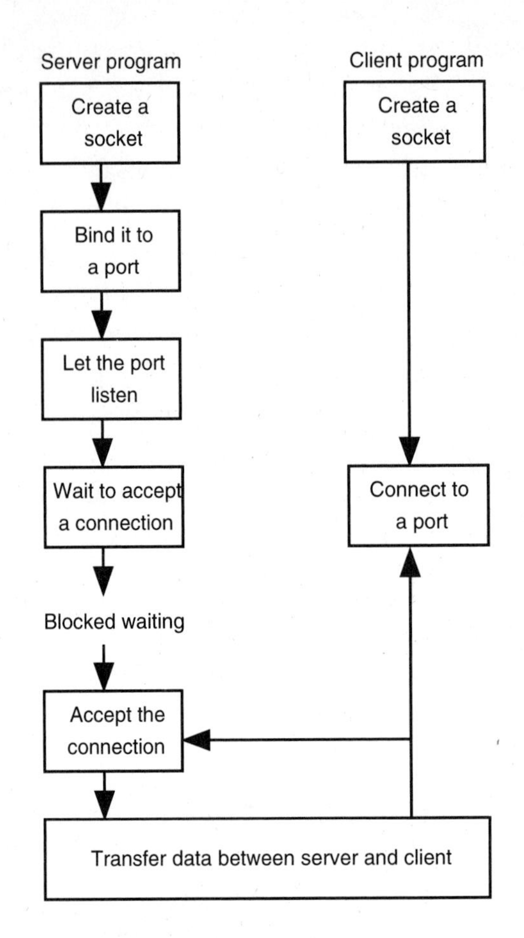

Figure 7.7
The steps involved in connecting a TCP client to a TCP server.

nize and route packets appropriately. If a machine on network segment 1 sends a packet to another machine on network segment 1, the router ignores it because both machines have the same subnet number. On the other hand, the router would detect a packet on network segment 1 intended for network segment 2 because of the difference in the subnet number. It would echo the packet onto network segment 2 so that the appropriate machine can receive it.

The following sections demonstrate how to write both UDP and TCP code.

7.7 UDP Connections

The most common example of a program using UDP is the `rwho` command in UNIX. The `who` command tells you who is logged onto the local UNIX machine. The `rwho` command does the same thing for all of the ma-

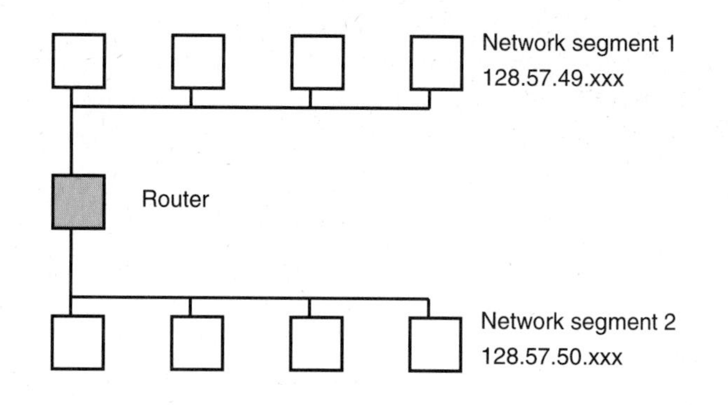

Figure 7.8
A router routing packets between two network segments.

chines on the local network segment. The `rwho` command is made possible by the rwho daemon, which runs on every machine that supports rwho (a daemon is like an NT service—it starts at boot time and runs continuously regardless of who is logged in. See Chapter 9). This daemon periodically broadcasts a UDP packet containing the machine's status information onto the network. The packet includes a list of who is currently logged in, the machine's load, the uptime for the machine, and so on. The daemon also listens for the status messages from other rwho daemons and caches the information it receives.

The `rwho` command has gone out of favor on most networks because it tends to generate a huge quantity of spurious network traffic. However, it does demonstrate both the pros and cons of broadcasting packets using UDP. As a side note, it is important to recognize that routers will not pick up broadcast packets, so UDP communications are limited to a single segment.

The programs in Listings 7.12 and 7.13 demonstrate a simple UDP sender and receiver. If you run Listing 7.12, it will wait for UDP packets on port 44,966. The port number used here is arbitrary. Numbers below 1,000 should be avoided because they tend to be pre-defined, but numbers between 1,000 and 64,000 are generally fair game. You will get an error in the server if the port is already in use.

You can run as many senders and receivers as you like on the local machine or on any other machine on the network. They all use port 44,966, and each receiver will print any messages that it receives.

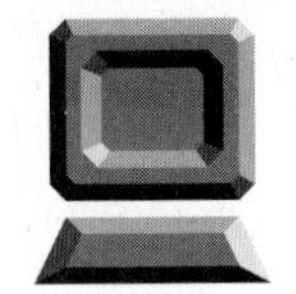

```
// mciprecv.cpp

#include <windows.h>
#include <iostream.h>
#include <winsock.h>

#define NO_FLAGS_SET 0

#define PORT (u_short) 44966
#define MAXBUFLEN 256

INT main(VOID)
{
  WSADATA Data;
  SOCKADDR_IN recvSockAddr;
  SOCKET recvSocket;
  int status;
  int numrcv;
  char buffer[MAXBUFLEN];

  /* initialize the Windows Socket DLL */
  status=WSAStartup(MAKEWORD(1, 1), &Data);
  if (status != 0)
    cerr << "ERROR: WSAStartup unsuccessful"
      << endl;

  /* zero the sockaddr_in structure */
  memset(&recvSockAddr, 0, sizeof(recvSockAddr));
  /* specify the port portion of the address */
```

Listing 7.12
A UDP receiver (Page 1 of 3)

```
    recvSockAddr.sin_port=htons(PORT);
    /* specify the address family as Internet */
    recvSockAddr.sin_family=AF_INET;
    /* specify that the address does not matter */
    recvSockAddr.sin_addr.s_addr=htonl(INADDR_ANY);

    /* create a socket */
    recvSocket=socket(AF_INET, SOCK_DGRAM, 0);
    if (recvSocket == INVALID_SOCKET)
      cerr << "ERROR: socket unsuccessful" << endl;

    /* associate the socket with the address */
    status=bind(recvSocket,
      (LPSOCKADDR) &recvSockAddr,
      sizeof(recvSockAddr));
    if (status == SOCKET_ERROR)
      cerr << "ERROR: bind unsuccessful" << endl;

    while(1)
    {
      numrcv=recvfrom(recvSocket, buffer, MAXBUFLEN,
        NO_FLAGS_SET, NULL, NULL);
      if (numrcv == SOCKET_ERROR)
      {
        cerr << "ERROR: recvfrom unsuccessful"
          << endl;
        status=closesocket(recvSocket);
        if (status == SOCKET_ERROR)
          cerr << "ERROR: closesocket unsuccessful"
            << endl;
        status=WSACleanup();
        if (status == SOCKET_ERROR)
          cerr << "ERROR: WSACleanup unsuccessful"
            << endl;
        return(1);
```

Listing 7.12
A UDP receiver (Page 2 of 3)

```
      }
      cout << buffer << endl;
    } /* while */
  }
```

Listing 7.12
A UDP receiver (Page 3 of 3)

```
// mcipsend.cpp

#include <windows.h>
#include <iostream.h>
#include <winsock.h>

#define NO_FLAGS_SET 0

#define PORT (u_short) 44966

INT main(VOID)
{
  WSADATA Data;
  SOCKADDR_IN destSockAddr;
  SOCKET destSocket;
  int status;
  int numsnt;
  int enable=1;
  char *toSendtxt="Test String";

  /* initialize the Windows Socket DLL */
  status=WSAStartup(MAKEWORD(1, 1), &Data);
  if (status != 0)
    cerr << "ERROR: WSAStartup unsuccessful"
```

Listing 7.13
A UDP sender (Page 1 of 3)

```
        << endl;

    /* specify the IP address */
    destSockAddr.sin_addr.s_addr=
      htonl(INADDR_BROADCAST);
    /* specify the port portion of the address */
    destSockAddr.sin_port=htons(PORT);
    /* specify the address family as Internet */
    destSockAddr.sin_family=AF_INET;

    /* create a socket */
    destSocket=socket(AF_INET, SOCK_DGRAM, 0);
    if (destSocket == INVALID_SOCKET)
    {
      cerr << "ERROR: socket unsuccessful" << endl;
      status=WSACleanup();
      if (status == SOCKET_ERROR)
        cerr << "ERROR: WSACleanup unsuccessful"
          << endl;
      return(1);
    }

    /* permit broadcasting on the socket */
    status=setsockopt(destSocket, SOL_SOCKET,
      SO_BROADCAST, (char *) &enable,
        sizeof(enable));
    if (status != 0)
      cerr << "ERROR: setsockopt unsuccessful"
        << endl;

    while(1)
    {
      cout << "Sending..." << endl;
      numsnt=sendto(destSocket, toSendtxt,
        strlen(toSendtxt) + 1, NO_FLAGS_SET,
```

Listing 7.13
A UDP sender (Page 2 of 3)

```
            (LPSOCKADDR) &destSockAddr,
              sizeof(destSockAddr));
        if (numsnt != (int)strlen(toSendtxt) + 1)
        {
          cerr << "ERROR: sendto unsuccessful" << endl;
          status=closesocket(destSocket);
          if (status == SOCKET_ERROR)
            cerr << "ERROR: closesocket unsuccessful"
              << endl;
          status=WSACleanup();
          if (status == SOCKET_ERROR)
            cerr << "ERROR: WSACleanup unsuccessful"
              << endl;
          return(1);
        }

      /* Wait before sending the message again */
      Sleep(4800);
      } /* while */
  }
```

Listing 7.13
A UDP sender (Page 3 of 3)

The code in Listing 7.12 starts by initializing winsock using the **WSAStartup** function (look in the Win32 help file for more information on these functions).

WSAStartup	*Initializes the winsock library*
`int PASCAL FAR WSAStartup ( WORD version, LPWSADATA data );`	
version	Version number of the winsock library this code uses

data	Pointer to a struct that lets WSAStart-up return data
Returns 0 on success.	

This step is mandatory. In this call you initialize the winsock DLL for your process and make sure that the DLL can support your code by passing in the version number you are using.

Listing 7.12 next initializes a SOCKADDR_IN structure. This structure is required to bind a socket to a port (the following is copied from the Win32 help file):

```
struct sockaddr_in {
        short   sin_family;
        u_short sin_port;
        struct  in_addr sin_addr;
        char    sin_zero[8];
};
```

The structure specifies the port that the socket will bind to in **sin_port**, the protocol family in **sin_family**, and the machine it will accept messages from in **sin_addr**. In this case, the receiver will accept messages on the port specified in the PORT constant (44966) and will accept messages from any sender.

The calls to the **htonl** and **htons** functions convert values to *network byte order*. Everything put on the network should always be in network byte order. Individual machines then convert values back to their *host byte order*. This step ensures that machines with different byte orders can communicate without difficulty.

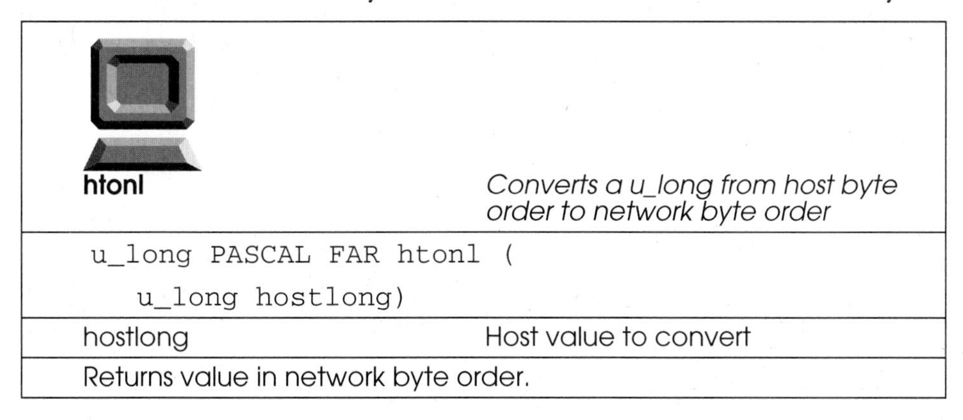

htonl	*Converts a u_long from host byte order to network byte order*
`u_long PASCAL FAR htonl ( u_long hostlong)`	
hostlong	Host value to convert
Returns value in network byte order.	

htons — *Converts a u_short from host byte order to network byte order*

```
u_short PASCAL FAR htons (
   u_short hostshort)
```

Parameter	Description
hostshort	Host value to convert

Returns value in network byte order.

Listing 7.12 next creates the socket using the **socket** function. When you create a socket you specify the address format, the type of socket (UDP or TCP), and the protocol. The library currently supports only one address format, and generally you pass 0 for the protocol, so all that this function call does here is choose between UDP and TCP packets. It will create the socket or return an error code.

The next line binds the socket to the specified port using the **bind** function.

socket — *Creates a socket*

```
SOCKET PASCAL FAR socket (
   int af,
   int type,
   int protocol)
```

Parameter	Description
af	Address format
type	Type: SOCK_STREAM (TCP) or SOCK_DGRAM (UDP)
protocol	Network protocol, or 0 if don't care

Returns socket descriptor or INVALID_SOCKET on failure

bind	*binds a socket to a port*
`int PASCAL FAR bind ( SOCKET socket, const struct sockaddr FAR * name, int nameLen)`	
socket	The socket to bind
name	The port to bind to
nameLen	Length of the port information
Returns 0 on success or SOCKET_ERROR	

The **bind** function accepts the socket to bind, and the structure containing the port name, and binds the socket to the port.

Listing 7.12 then enters a loop where it waits for messages to arrive. The **recvfrom** function blocks until a UDP packet arrives on the port. If there is an error the code cleans up gracefully, calling **closesocket** and **WSACleanup**. Otherwise, it prints the message received.

recvfrom	*Receives a packet from a UDP socket*
`int PASCAL FAR recvfrom ( int socket, char FAR * buffer, int bufferLen, int flags, struct sockaddr FAR * from, int FAR * fromLen)`	
socket	The socket to receive from
buffer	The buffer to place the received message in

bufferLen	Length of the buffer
flags	MSG_PEEK and/or MSG_OOB
from	Sender information
fromLen	Length of sender info
Returns the number of bytes received on success, 0 if the connection was closed, or SOCKET_ERROR	

closesocket	*Closes a socket*

```
int FAR PASCAL closesocket (
   SOCKET socket)
```

socket	The socket to close
Returns 0 on success or SOCKET_ERROR	

WSACleanup	*Terminates the WSA DLL cleanly*

```
int PASCAL FAR WSACleanup ( void )
```

Returns 0 on success or SOCKET_ERROR

This is all fairly simple: if you were to strip out the error handling code the program is only 11 lines long. It may take a few days to get used to the terminology, but once you do you do not have to write an immense amount of code to create simple network interactions on heterogeneous networks using UDP packets.

The sender code in Listing 7.13 follows the same general pattern. It initializes WSA, creates a UDP socket, and then sets options on the socket so that it can send in broadcast mode using the **setsockopt** function.

setsockopt	*Sets options on a socket*

```
int PASCAL FAR setsockopt (
   SOCKET socket,
   int level,
   int optName,
   const char FAR * optVal,
   int optLen)
```

socket	The socket
level	SOL_SOCKET or IPPROTO_TCP
optName	The option to set
optVal	The value to set on the option
optLen	The length of the value

Returns 0 on success or SOCKET_ERROR

You can set a wide range of options, as described in the Win32 help file. Here the goal is to tell the socket to permit broadcast transmissions, so the SO_BROADCAST option is set to TRUE (1).

With the socket established and set to broadcast mode, the sender can start transmitting messages to any receivers on the network. It uses the **sendto** function to do this.

sendto	*Sends messages*

```
int PASCAL FAR sendto (
   SOCKET socket,
   const char FAR * buffer,
   int bufferLen,
   int flags,
```

```
    const struct sockaddr FAR * to,
    int toLen)
```

Parameter	Description
socket	The socket
buffer	The message to send
bufferLen	The length of the message
flags	Flags
to	The machine to send it to
toLen	The length of the to buffer

Returns 0 on success or SOCKET_ERROR

The **sendto** function sends the contents of the buffer to the port on the machine specified. The **destSockAddr** structure here specifies a broadcast transmission, so all receivers on the network receive the packet.

Listing 7.14 contains a file named `unixsend.c`. It is a version of Listing 7.13 for UNIX machines, and you can use it to demonstrate that UNIX machines can talk to Windows machines using UDP packets. Compile Listing 7.14 with a C compiler on a UNIX machine. The UNIX machine needs to be on the same network segment as a Windows machine running the receiver. When first testing this version of Listing 7.14, it failed on the **sendto** statement. Our UNIX machine simply will not accept the IP address 255.255.255.255. Our UNIX machine's IP address is 152.1.100.100 however (type `hostname -i` on the UNIX machine to find its address), and all of our test machines are on the segment 152.1.100.xxx, so by changing the IP address in the `sendto` statement to 152.1.100.255 we solved the problem. The octet 255 has the meaning "broadcast" in an IP address, here implying "broadcast on the segment 152.1.100.xxx." If the code fails on the **sendto** statement when you run it, suspect the IP address and work with it.

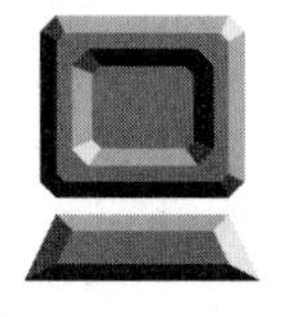

```
/* unixsend.c */
```

Listing 7.14
A UNIX version of the sender in Listing 7.13 (Page 1 of 3)

```
#include <stdio.h>
#include <netinet/in.h>
#include <sys/socket.h>

#define NO_FLAGS_SET 0

#define PORT (unsigned short) 44966

int main()
{
  struct sockaddr_in destSockAddr;
  int destSocket;
  int status;
  int numsnt;
  int enable=1;
  char *toSendtxt="Test String";

  /* specify the IP address */
  destSockAddr.sin_addr.s_addr=
    inet_addr("255.255.255.255");
  /* specify the port portion of the address */
  destSockAddr.sin_port=htons(PORT);
  /* specify the address family as Internet */
  destSockAddr.sin_family=AF_INET;

  /* create a socket */
  destSocket=socket(AF_INET, SOCK_DGRAM, 0);
  if (destSocket == -1)
    printf("Error creating socket\n");

  /* permit broadcasting on the socket */
  status=setsockopt(destSocket, SOL_SOCKET,
    SO_BROADCAST, (char *) &enable,
    sizeof(enable));
```

Listing 7.14
A UNIX version of the sender in Listing 7.13 (Page 2 of 3)

```
        if (status == -1)
          printf("Error setting socket opts\n");

        while(1)
        {
          printf("Sending...\n");
          numsnt=sendto(destSocket, toSendtxt,
            strlen(toSendtxt) + 1, NO_FLAGS_SET,
            &destSockAddr, sizeof(destSockAddr));
          if (numsnt != (int)strlen(toSendtxt) + 1)
          {
            printf("ERROR: sendto unsuccessful\n");
            status=close(destSocket);
            return(1);
          }

        /* Wait before sending the message again */
        sleep(5);
        } /* while */
      }
```

Listing 7.14
A UNIX version of the sender in Listing 7.13 (Page 3 of 3)

Compare the code in Listing 7.14 to the code in Listing 7.13 and you will find that they are nearly identical except for a few minor declaration changes and the loss of the WSA functions. The winsock library follows the UNIX standards very closely. It would be equally easy to create a UNIX version of Listing 7.12 and have the receiver run on a UNIX machine as well.

7.8 TCP Connections

TCP connections are used almost exclusively for network connections in the UNIX world. TCP packets, unlike UDP packets, are automatically sequenced and error checked by the network drivers, and the system can detect when the connection terminates automatically. The `telnet`, `ftp`, `finger` and `talk` commands all rely on point-to-point TCP connections. You can `talk` to someone on a machine in the next room or halfway around the world if you are connected to the Internet.

TCP connections are very similar to Windows named pipes, but they allow you to connect to a wide variety of machines on heterogeneous networks. This section demonstrates both point-to-point and client/server architectures. Many parts of the code demonstrated here are similar to code demonstrated in the previous section, so you may want to review that code as a starting point. You should also note that the concepts here are very similar to those seen in the named pipe discussion earlier in this chapter.

Listings 7.15 and 7.16 demonstrate a simple one-directional point-to-point TCP connection. Listing 7.15 contains the receiver, while Listing 7.16 contains the sender. Run the receiver first, and then run the sender on the same machine. You will see a "Test String" message at the receiver every five seconds. Find out the IP address of the receiver machine (use the Network applet in the Control Panel and use the Configure button on the TCP/IP module) and use it to modify the DEST_IP_ADDR constant in the sender. You can then run the sender program on any machine on the network.

```
// ssiprecv.cpp

#include <windows.h>
#include <iostream.h>
#include <winsock.h>

#define NO_FLAGS_SET 0

#define PORT (u_short) 44965
#define MAXBUFLEN 256

INT main(VOID)
{
  WSADATA Data;
```

Listing 7.15
A single TCP receiver for point-to-point connections (Page 1 of 3)

```
SOCKADDR_IN serverSockAddr;
SOCKADDR_IN clientSockAddr;
SOCKET serverSocket;
SOCKET clientSocket;
int addrLen=sizeof(SOCKADDR_IN);
int status;
int numrcv;
char buffer[MAXBUFLEN];

/* initialize the Windows Socket DLL */
status=WSAStartup(MAKEWORD(1, 1), &Data);
if (status != 0)
  cerr << "ERROR: WSAStartup unsuccessful"
    << endl;

/* zero the sockaddr_in structure */
memset(&serverSockAddr, 0,
  sizeof(serverSockAddr));
/* specify the port portion of the address */
serverSockAddr.sin_port=htons(PORT);
/* specify the address family as Internet */
serverSockAddr.sin_family=AF_INET;
/* specify that the address does not matter */
serverSockAddr.sin_addr.s_addr=htonl(INADDR_ANY);

/* create a socket */
serverSocket=socket(AF_INET, SOCK_STREAM, 0);
if (serverSocket == INVALID_SOCKET)
  cerr << "ERROR: socket unsuccessful" << endl;

/* associate the socket with the address */
status=bind(serverSocket,
  (LPSOCKADDR) &serverSockAddr,
  sizeof(serverSockAddr));
if (status == SOCKET_ERROR)
```

Listing 7.15
A single TCP receiver for point-to-point connections (Page 2 of 3)

```
      cerr << "ERROR: bind unsuccessful" << endl;

    /* allow the socket to take connections */
    status=listen(serverSocket, 1);
    if (status == SOCKET_ERROR)
      cerr << "ERROR: listen unsuccessful" << endl;

    /* accept the connection request when one
       is received */
    clientSocket=accept(serverSocket,
      (LPSOCKADDR) &clientSockAddr,
      &addrLen);

    cout << "Got the connection..." << endl;

    while(1)
    {
      numrcv=recv(clientSocket, buffer,
        MAXBUFLEN, NO_FLAGS_SET);
      if ((numrcv == 0) || (numrcv == SOCKET_ERROR))
      {
        cout << "Connection terminated." << endl;
        status=closesocket(clientSocket);
        if (status == SOCKET_ERROR)
          cerr << "ERROR: closesocket unsuccessful"
            << endl;
        status=WSACleanup();
        if (status == SOCKET_ERROR)
          cerr << "ERROR: WSACleanup unsuccessful"
            << endl;
        return(1);
      }
      cout << buffer << endl;
    } /* while */
}
```

Listing 7.15
A single TCP receiver for point-to-point connections (Page 3 of 3)

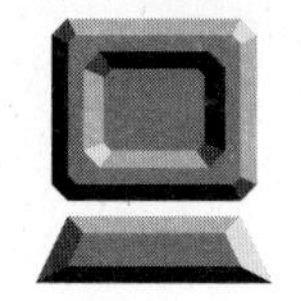

```
// ssipsend.cpp

#include <windows.h>
#include <iostream.h>
#include <winsock.h>

#define NO_FLAGS_SET 0

#define PORT (u_short) 44965
#define DEST_IP_ADDR "127.0.0.1"

INT main(VOID)
{
  WSADATA Data;
  SOCKADDR_IN destSockAddr;
  SOCKET destSocket;
  unsigned long destAddr;
  int status;
  int numsnt;
  char *toSendtxt="Test String";

  /* initialize the Windows Socket DLL */
  status=WSAStartup(MAKEWORD(1, 1), &Data);
  if (status != 0)
    cerr << "ERROR: WSAStartup unsuccessful"
      << endl;

  /* convert IP address into in_addr form */
  destAddr=inet_addr(DEST_IP_ADDR);
  /* copy destAddr into sockaddr_in structure */
  memcpy(&destSockAddr.sin_addr,
```

Listing 7.16
A simple TCP sender for point-to-point connections (Page 1 of 3)

```
    &destAddr, sizeof(destAddr));
  /* specify the port portion of the address */
  destSockAddr.sin_port=htons(PORT);
  /* specify the address family as Internet */
  destSockAddr.sin_family=AF_INET;

  /* create a socket */
  destSocket=socket(AF_INET, SOCK_STREAM, 0);
  if (destSocket == INVALID_SOCKET)
  {
    cerr << "ERROR: socket unsuccessful" << endl;
    status=WSACleanup();
    if (status == SOCKET_ERROR)
      cerr << "ERROR: WSACleanup unsuccessful"
        << endl;
    return(1);
  }

  cout << "Trying to connect to IP Address: "
    << DEST_IP_ADDR << endl;

  /* connect to the server */
  status=connect(destSocket,
    (LPSOCKADDR) &destSockAddr,
    sizeof(destSockAddr));
  if (status == SOCKET_ERROR)
  {
    cerr << "ERROR: connect unsuccessful" << endl;
    status=closesocket(destSocket);
    if (status == SOCKET_ERROR)
      cerr << "ERROR: closesocket unsuccessful"
        << endl;
    status=WSACleanup();
    if (status == SOCKET_ERROR)
      cerr << "ERROR: WSACleanup unsuccessful"
```

Listing 7.16
A simple TCP sender for point-to-point connections (Page 2 of 3)

```
            << endl;
        return(1);
      }

      cout << "Connected..." << endl;

      while(1)
      {
        cout << "Sending..." << endl;
        numsnt=send(destSocket, toSendtxt,
          strlen(toSendtxt) + 1, NO_FLAGS_SET);
        if (numsnt != (int)strlen(toSendtxt) + 1)
        {
          cout << "Connection terminated" << endl;
          status=closesocket(destSocket);
          if (status == SOCKET_ERROR)
            cerr << "ERROR: closesocket unsuccessful"
              << endl;
          status=WSACleanup();
          if (status == SOCKET_ERROR)
            cerr << "ERROR: WSACleanup unsuccessful"
              << endl;
          return(1);
        }

      /* Wait before sending the message again */
      Sleep(4800);
      } /* while */
    }
```

Listing 7.16
A simple TCP sender for point-to-point connections (Page 3 of 3)

The TCP receiver program in Listing 7.15 starts just like the UDP receiver in Listing 7.12 does. It initializes the library, creates a socket, and binds the socket to a port. The socket here is in SOCK_STREAM mode, which causes it to use TCP rather than UDP packets. Listing 7.15 then calls the **listen** function.

listen — *Enables a socket to listen for connections*

```
int PASCAL FAR listen(
   SOCKET socket,
   int queue)
```

socket	The socket to enable
queue	The number of pending connections it can hold

Returns 0 on success or SOCKET_ERROR

The **listen** function creates a connection queue on the port attached to the socket. The queue specifies how many *pending connections* the port can support. When another machine tries to connect to the port, its connection request is held in the queue. If the queue is full, or if the port's queue does not exist because the **listen** function has not been called on the port, then the connection request is rejected. If space exists in the queue, then the connection is held in the queue until it is *accepted.* The connecting machine will probably time out if the queued connection is not accepted within 30 seconds or so.

The call to **listen** specifies the size of the queue. In Listing 7.15 the size is set to 1, but a typical server program might set it to five to handle multiple incoming requests.

Listing 7.15 next calls the **accept** function. This program is able to accept just one connection. The **accept** function will block until a copy of the send program in Listing 7.16 tries to connect.

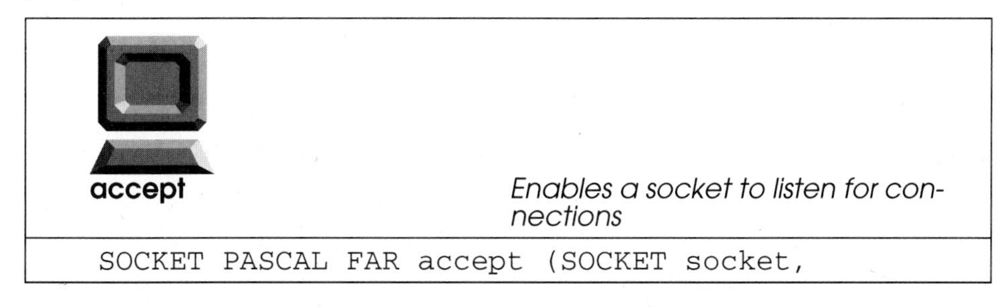

accept — *Enables a socket to listen for connections*

```
SOCKET PASCAL FAR accept (SOCKET socket,
```

```
    struct sockaddr FAR * addr,
    int FAR * addrLen)
```

socket	The socket to accept from
addr	Pointer to a structure that identifies the connector
addrLen	Size of the returned structure

Returns a socket number on success or INVALID_SOCKET

The **accept** function removes the first connection request from the pending connection queue for the port. It then chooses an unused port number and assigns the connection to that port. The program can then receive on that port, while the space in the queue on the well-known port number is freed up for other connection requests. The **accept** function returns a structure that identifies the connecting machine.

With the connection properly established, Listing 7.15 enters a loop to receive messages from the sender. It uses the **recv** function, which is nearly identical to the **recvfrom** function seen earlier. The **recv** function does not return information about the sender like **recvfrom** does, and this information is not needed here because the connection is point-to-point.

recv *Receives a packet from a socket*

```
int PASCAL FAR recv (
    int socket,
    char FAR * buffer,
    int bufferLen,
    int flags)
```

socket	The socket to receive from
buffer	The buffer to place the received message in
bufferLen	Length of the buffer
flags	MSG_PEEK and/or MSG_OOB

Returns the number of bytes received on success, 0 if the connection was closed, or SOCKET_ERROR

Note that this receiver can accept just one connection because it calls the **accept** function once. If you try to create multiple connections from multiple senders, they will fail. The following example handles multiple connections.

The sender code in Listing 7.16 is nearly identical to Listing 7.13, except that it connects to a specific machine rather than broadcasting. TCP connections do not allow broadcast packets—only UDP connections do.

The second example, shown in Listings 7.17 and 7.18, demonstrates a client/server pair like the pair shown for named pipes. The server accepts connections from clients. When a client sends a string, the server converts it to upper case and sends it back to the client. Clients can connect from any machine on the network world-wide because this system uses TCP packets. This is the same sort of technology you would use to create an FTP or talk server.

Run the server on an Windows machine. Test the server by running the client on the same machine. The current IP address for the sender, 127.0.0.1 in the DEST_IP_ADDR constant of the client, is a loopback connection to the local machine. The client should connect automatically. Now replace 127.0.0.1 with the actual IP address for the server machine. Recompile the client and you should be able to run multiple copies of it on any machine on the network.

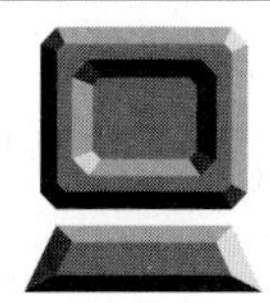

```
// msipserv.cpp

#include <windows.h>
#include <iostream.h>
#include <winsock.h>
#include <process.h>

#define NO_FLAGS_SET 0
```

Listing 7.17
A multi-client server using TCP (Page 1 of 5)

```
#define PORT (u_short) 44965
#define MAXBUFLEN 256

VOID talkToClient(VOID *cs)
{
  char buffer[MAXBUFLEN];
  int status;
  int numsnt;
  int numrcv;
  SOCKET clientSocket=(SOCKET)cs;

  while(1)
  {
    numrcv=recv(clientSocket, buffer,
      MAXBUFLEN, NO_FLAGS_SET);
    if ((numrcv == 0) || (numrcv == SOCKET_ERROR))
    {
      cout << "Connection terminated" << endl;
      break;
    }

    _strupr(buffer);

    numsnt=send(clientSocket, buffer,
      strlen(buffer) + 1, NO_FLAGS_SET);
    if (numsnt != (int)strlen(buffer) + 1)
    {
      cout << "Connection terminated." << endl;
      break;
    }

  } /* while */

  /* terminate the connection with the client
```

Listing 7.17
A multi-client server using TCP (Page 2 of 5)

```
      (disable sending/receiving) */
    status=shutdown(clientSocket, 2);
    if (status == SOCKET_ERROR)
      cerr << "ERROR: shutdown unsuccessful" << endl;

    /* close the socket */
    status=closesocket(clientSocket);
    if (status == SOCKET_ERROR)
      cerr << "ERROR: closesocket unsuccessful"
        << endl;
  }

  INT main(VOID)
  {
    WSADATA Data;
    SOCKADDR_IN serverSockAddr;
    SOCKADDR_IN clientSockAddr;
    SOCKET serverSocket;
    SOCKET clientSocket;
    int addrLen=sizeof(SOCKADDR_IN);
    int status;
    DWORD threadID;

    /* initialize the Windows Socket DLL */
    status=WSAStartup(MAKEWORD(1, 1), &Data);
    if (status != 0)
    {
      cerr << "ERROR: WSAStartup unsuccessful"
        << endl;
      return(1);
    }

    /* zero the sockaddr_in structure */
    memset(&serverSockAddr, 0,
      sizeof(serverSockAddr));
```

Listing 7.17
A multi-client server using TCP (Page 3 of 5)

```
    /* specify the port portion of the address */
    serverSockAddr.sin_port=htons(PORT);
    /* specify the address family as Internet */
    serverSockAddr.sin_family=AF_INET;
    /* specify that the address does not matter */
    serverSockAddr.sin_addr.s_addr=htonl(INADDR_ANY);

    /* create a socket */
    serverSocket=socket(AF_INET, SOCK_STREAM, 0);
    if (serverSocket == INVALID_SOCKET)
    {
      cerr << "ERROR: socket unsuccessful"
        << endl;
      status=WSACleanup();
      if (status == SOCKET_ERROR)
        cerr << "ERROR: WSACleanup unsuccessful"
          << endl;
      return(1);
    }

    /* associate the socket with the address */
    status=bind(serverSocket,
      (LPSOCKADDR) &serverSockAddr,
      sizeof(serverSockAddr));
    if (status == SOCKET_ERROR)
      cerr << "ERROR: bind unsuccessful" << endl;

    /* allow the socket to take connections */
    status=listen(serverSocket, 1);
    if (status == SOCKET_ERROR)
      cerr << "ERROR: listen unsuccessful" << endl;

    while(1)
    {
      /* accept the connection request when
```

Listing 7.17
A multi-client server using TCP (Page 4 of 5)

```
            one is received */
        clientSocket=accept(serverSocket,
          (LPSOCKADDR) &clientSockAddr,
          &addrLen);
        if (clientSocket == INVALID_SOCKET)
        {
          cerr << "ERROR: Unable to accept connection."
            << endl;
          return(1);
        }

        threadID=_beginthread(talkToClient,
          0, (VOID *)clientSocket);
        if (threadID == -1)
        {
          cerr << "ERROR: Unable to create thread"
            << endl;
          /* close the socket */
          status=closesocket(clientSocket);
          if (status == SOCKET_ERROR)
            cerr << "ERROR: closesocket unsuccessful"
              << endl;
        }

      } /* while */
    }
```

Listing 7.17
A multi-client server using TCP (Page 5 of 5)

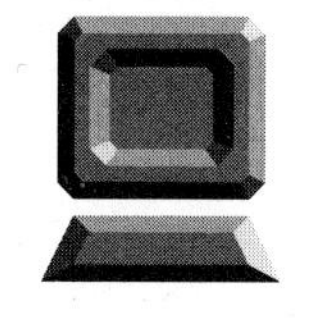

```
// msipclnt.cpp
```

Listing 7.18
A TCP client for the server in Listing 7.17 (Page 1 of 5)

```
#include <windows.h>
#include <iostream.h>
#include <winsock.h>

#define NO_FLAGS_SET 0

#define PORT (u_short) 44965
#define DEST_IP_ADDR "127.0.0.1"
#define MAXBUFLEN 256

INT main(VOID)
{
  WSADATA Data;
  SOCKADDR_IN destSockAddr;
  SOCKET destSocket;
  unsigned long destAddr;
  int status;
  int numsnt;
  int numrcv;
  char sendText[MAXBUFLEN];
  char recvText[MAXBUFLEN];

  /* initialize the Windows Socket DLL */
  status=WSAStartup(MAKEWORD(1, 1), &Data);
  if (status != 0)
    cerr << "ERROR: WSAStartup unsuccessful"
      << endl;

  /* convert IP address into in_addr form*/
  destAddr=inet_addr(DEST_IP_ADDR);
  /* copy destAddr into sockaddr_in structure */
  memcpy(&destSockAddr.sin_addr, &destAddr,
    sizeof(destAddr));
  /* specify the port portion of the address */
  destSockAddr.sin_port=htons(PORT);
```

Listing 7.18
A TCP client for the server in Listing 7.17 (Page 2 of 5)

```
    /* specify the address family as Internet */
    destSockAddr.sin_family=AF_INET;

    /* create a socket */
    destSocket=socket(AF_INET, SOCK_STREAM, 0);
    if (destSocket == INVALID_SOCKET)
    {
      cerr << "ERROR: socket unsuccessful" << endl;
      status=WSACleanup();
      if (status == SOCKET_ERROR)
        cerr << "ERROR: WSACleanup unsuccessful"
          << endl;
      return(1);
    }

    cout << "Trying to connect to IP Address: "
      << DEST_IP_ADDR << endl;

    /* connect to the server */
    status=connect(destSocket,
      (LPSOCKADDR) &destSockAddr,
      sizeof(destSockAddr));
    if (status == SOCKET_ERROR)
    {
      cerr << "ERROR: connect unsuccessful"
        << endl;
      status=closesocket(destSocket);
      if (status == SOCKET_ERROR)
        cerr << "ERROR: closesocket unsuccessful"
          << endl;
      status=WSACleanup();
      if (status == SOCKET_ERROR)
        cerr << "ERROR: WSACleanup unsuccessful"
          << endl;
      return(1);
```

Listing 7.18
A TCP client for the server in Listing 7.17 (Page 3 of 5)

```
    }

    cout << "Connected..." << endl;

    while(1)
    {
      cout << "Type text to send: ";
      cin.getline(sendText, MAXBUFLEN);

      /* Send the message to the server */
      numsnt=send(destSocket, sendText,
        strlen(sendText) + 1, NO_FLAGS_SET);
      if (numsnt != (int)strlen(sendText) + 1)
      {
        cout << "Connection terminated." << endl;
        status=closesocket(destSocket);
        if (status == SOCKET_ERROR)
          cerr << "ERROR: closesocket unsuccessful"
            << endl;
        status=WSACleanup();
        if (status == SOCKET_ERROR)
          cerr << "ERROR: WSACleanup unsuccessful"
            << endl;
        return(1);
      }

      /* Wait for a response from server */
      numrcv=recv(destSocket, recvText,
        MAXBUFLEN, NO_FLAGS_SET);
      if ((numrcv == 0) || (numrcv == SOCKET_ERROR))
      {
        cout << "Connection terminated.";
        status=closesocket(destSocket);
        if (status == SOCKET_ERROR)
          cerr << "ERROR: closesocket unsuccessful"
```

Listing 7.18
A TCP client for the server in Listing 7.17 (Page 4 of 5)

```
            << endl;
          status=WSACleanup();
          if (status == SOCKET_ERROR)
            cerr << "ERROR: WSACleanup unsuccessful"
              << endl;
          return(1);
        }

        cout << "Received: " << recvText << endl;

      } /* while */
    }
```

Listing 7.18
A TCP client for the server in Listing 7.17 (Page 5 of 5)

The server code in Listing 7.17 bears a strong resemblance to Listing 7.15. The main difference occurs around the **accept** function in Listing 7.17. Right after accepting a connection, the program creates a new and independent thread to manage the new client. Each client will have its own thread (see the Run-time Routines help file for information on **_beginthread**).

Inside the **talkToClient** thread function, the program simply accepts client messages as they arrive, converts them to upper case, and then sends them back. The client in Listing 7.18, in the meantime, is accepting strings from the user, sending them to the server, and then displaying the upper case result to the user. If the server dies, the client code correctly detects it and terminates.

In all of the client code demonstrated above, one thing that would improve the code would be a way to connect to the server by name rather than by IP address. The function that does the translation from name to IP address is called **gethostbyname**. The following code demonstrates how to use the function:

```
struct hostent *serverHostent;

serverHostent = gethostbyname("itgate.iftech.com");
if (serverHostent == 0)
  ... error
else
{
  memcpy(&destSockAddr.sin_addr,
```

```
        serverHostent->h_addr,
        serverHostent->h_length);
}
```

gethostbyname	*Converts a machine name to its IP address*
`struct hostent FAR * PASCAL FAR gethostbyname( const char FAR * name)`	
name	The machine name
Returns a pointer to a structure or 0 on failure	

The pointer returned by **gethostbyname** points to a single copy of the structure that is maintained by the library. *Do not* modify or delete this structure.

7.9 Conclusion

This chapter contains an example of every network communication arrangement possible in Windows. It uses threads in a number of different ways, and you may therefore want to review Chapter 5 for more information on this topic.

Chapter 8 presents Remote Procedure Calls, or RPCs. RPCs automatically work in a client/server fashion and hide most of the network details, so you may want to use them to automate the process of creating client/server applications.

Serial communications over modems is another way for Windows machines to talk to one other. Chapter 12 discusses this topic.

See Chapter 10 for information on security and impersonation in pipes.

8 REMOTE PROCEDURE CALLS

Remote Procedure Calls (RPCs) allow you to call a function that, instead of being executed on your local machine, is executed on a machine somewhere else on the network. The RPC concept gives you tremendous flexibility in using the computing resources on your network, and allows you to optimize different machines for specific tasks. In this chapter you will learn how to design and implement your own RPC servers and clients, and you will also learn how to create and configure RPC servers and clients properly.

Compatibility Note: All of the code in this chapter works in Windows NT. At the time of publication, you can run both RPC servers and clients on Windows 95 provided that: 1) you do not use the ncacn_np (named pipe) protocol, and 2) that you implicitly bind to a specific machine rather than using the name server features. The code in Section 8.9 is configured to use ncacn_ip_tcp and a specific machine name so it will work in Windows 95 without modification.

8.1 The Possibilities

There are many ways to use remote procedure calls to improve the speed of your applications and to better use specialized resources available on the network. Listed below are several examples that will help you to see the possibilities.

- *Compute servers:* Say that your company has purchased a new machine that contains ten high-speed RISC processors, and you want to spread the power of that machine across the network when running certain in-house applications. One easy way to do it is to place RPC servers for CPU-intensive functions onto the new machine. You can then modify your in-house applications slightly so that they call the RPC servers for those functions.

For example, if you have a rotation operation in a graphics program and the operation takes a tremendous amount of CPU power to execute, it would be a perfect candidate for an RPC. Or you might build libraries of math-intensive functions (FFTs, fractal calculations, etc.) and make the entire library available to every machine on the network using an RPC server for the library.

- *Data management:* You might have a machine containing a large and fast hard disk that holds an extremely large data set. Say that certain operations on the data set require scanning it from one end to the other. You don't want to perform those operations on any other machine on the network because it means transmitting the entire data set over the net. However, you can put an RPC server on the machine containing the data set, and perform the data-intensive operations locally. When another machine performs the operation, it calls the RPC and all of the data is handled directly on the machine containing the hard disk. Only the results are transmitted back over the network.

  A good example of this situation can be found in the Search capability in the File Manager. When you search a hard disk on your local machine, it is fairly quick. It slows down significantly when you perform the search on a network drive because all of the file name information is transmitted over the network and scanned on your machine. If each machine had an RPC server that handled the searching, then your machine could call the RPC server, which would scan the file names on the machine where it resides and return just the result. A system like this would reduce network traffic significantly during search operations.
- *Memory-intensive operations:* If you have an application that occasionally requires 100 megabytes of physical memory to perform an operation, it might not be practical to give every user on the net 100 megabytes of RAM. However, you can make one machine possessing the required RAM the RPC server for that operation, and then let other machines perform the operation remotely.
- *Combinations:* Say you have a single application that occasionally needs 100 megabytes of physical memory and also uses an extremely large data

set and a lot of very CPU-intensive math functions. You want 10 people on the network to be able to run it from inexpensive, low-end machines. If you have RPC servers on suitably optimized high-end machines, then the low-end machines will be able to run the application at an acceptable rate. All of the real work is farmed out to the big machines, and the low end machines simply pull the pieces together.

You can see from these examples that the RPC mechanism is simply a standardized way to implement client/server architectures. The RPC facility gives you the ability to create your own servers very easily and share them over the network.

8.2 The Basic Idea

Once everything is set up and working properly, a remote procedure call looks trivial. In your code you simply call a function just like you normally would. Looking at the code, there is no way to distinguish an RPC from a normal function. For example, in a graphics program you might have a function named **CalcPixel** that calculates the value for a pixel in a ray-traced image. In any ray-tracing application, **CalcPixel** would represent a fairly CPU-intensive function call. A typical call might look like this:

```
color = CalcPixel(x,y);
```

In a normal program, when you call the function the program branches off to execute the function, calculates the result, and returns with the answer. In an RPC program, however, the computer instead acts as an *RPC client* and sends a network packet containing the x and y parameters to another machine running the *RPC server* for that function. The function executes on the second machine, and when it is done that machine sends a network packet containing the function's result back to the caller. See Figure 8.1.

There is nothing magical about RPCs. For example, it is possible for you to implement most of an RPC's functionality yourself using the network commands discussed in Chapter 7. However, it would take a lot of code, and it would not be nearly as clean as the RPC implementation. The advantage of using RPCs is that the syntax is so delightfully simple. You just call a function like you always do, and everything else is automatic. All of the network details are hidden from view and you can ignore them.

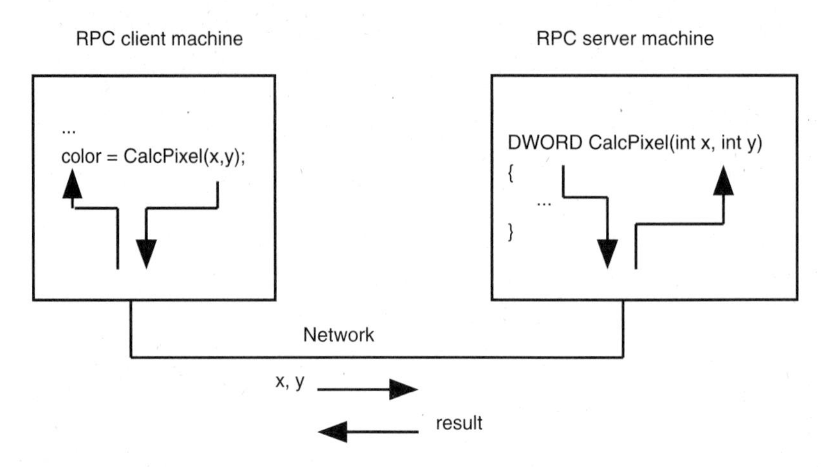

Figure 8.1
Remote procedure calls send parameters to a remote machine, where the function executes. Any results are sent back to the caller through the network as well.

The most important advantage of RPCs is the ability they give you to optimize the use of the hardware resources available on your network. For example, if you have a machine that contains a board that is very good at calculating ray-traced pixels, you can put the RPC server for **CalcPixel** on that machine. Now anyone on the network, regardless of the type of machine they are using, can run the ray-tracing program and take advantage of the speed of that special board. RPCs give you an extremely powerful tool for creating client/server applications.

8.3 Design Issues

As with anything else, RPCs have trade-offs. RPC's disadvantages stem primarily from the fact that the network is being used to transport parameters and results back and forth. This tends to give RPCs high latencies. RPCs also have a fairly significant per-call overhead because of the amount of coordinating that the system is doing behind the scenes. It is important for you to understand the overhead and trade-offs involved with RPCs so that you can design effective RPC architectures.

The best way to get a feel for the trade-offs involved with RPCs is to walk through the design of a simple RPC application. For example, let's walk through the design of a simple Mandelbrot set application and see if RPCs can speed up its execution time. This is a good sample application because it is easy to understand, and because it can be broken down in several different ways.

A Mandelbrot set program produces an image of the Mandelbrot set as its output (See Section 5.4). It has to perform one independent calculation to produce each pixel in the image. This calculation is a fairly involved floating point operation. Let's call the calculation function **CalcPixel**. The program has to call this function once for each pixel in the image it creates, so the function has the following prototype:

```
int CalcPixel(double x, double y);
```

The function accepts double precision floating point values that represent the pixel's location on a complex number plane. For example, the plane might stretch from -1.0 to 1.0 in both the X and Y directions. The program simply divides the real number distance (2.0 in this case) by the number of pixels in the display window and passes those coordinates to the **CalcPixel** function one at a time.

Let's say that you want to run this Mandelbrot program on an inexpensive machine that does not have a floating point co-processor. It will take quite awhile to generate an image if you do the floating point calculations locally. Therefore, you want to execute **CalcPixel** using an RPC so that the RPC server can reside on a faster machine that does have floating point capabilities. To demonstrate the design issues involved in this problem, we created an isolated demonstration network with three NT machines on it. Two of the machines are 33MHZ 486SX machines, and the third is a 66MHZ 486DX2. For those of you not schooled in Intel nomenclature, the 66MHZ CPU is nearly twice as fast as the 33MHZ CPU. The DX portion of a name implies that the CPU contains a built-in floating point co-processor, while the SX CPUs do not. Otherwise the computers placed on the demonstration network are identical—same manufacturer, same network cards, and so on.

We then created two versions of the Mandelbrot program. The first is "normal:" it uses a normal function call to perform the **CalcPixel** function. The second version is presented in Section 8.11 and uses an RPC for **CalcPixel**. We set the window size of the two programs to 150 by 150 pixels, yielding a 142 by 104 pixel drawing area for the Mandelbrot set itself. Therefore, the programs execute 14,768 calls to the **CalcPixel** function to produce a complete frame.

The normal version of the program, using normal function calls rather than RPCs, takes 70 seconds to execute on the 33MHZ 486SX machines, and 15 seconds to execute on the 66MHZ DX machine. We would have expected it to take about 35 seconds on the 66MHZ machine since the CPU is twice as fast, but the floating point co-processor gave it an extra boost and brought the execution time down significantly. Our design goal is to use RPCs to bring the execution time on the SX machines down to the level of the DX machine.

When designing with RPCs, it is important to take the overhead of an RPC call into account. To determine the overhead of the RPC calls themselves, we placed both the RPC server and the RPC client *on the same machine*. In this configuration, the network has no effect on the execution time. Only the overhead of the RPC call itself is added to the execution time. The **CalcPixel** function was placed in an RPC server and called 14,768 times on the local machine. On the 33MHZ machines, the execution time rose from 70 to 147 seconds, and on the 66MHZ machine it went up to 66 seconds from the original 15 seconds. In other words, the 14,768 RPC calls have a fairly significant overhead:

(147 - 70) / 14,768 = 5.2 milliseconds per RPC call on the 33MHZ machine

(66 - 15) /14,768 = 3.4 milliseconds per RPC call on the 66MHZ machine

The time on your machine will vary of course, but for comparison purposes a normal function call to **CalcPixel** with a null body (the function does nothing but return immediately) on the 33MHZ machine requires about one microsecond. In other words, an RPC call is roughly 5,000 times more expensive than a normal function call.

When you add in network delay, things get worse. We ran the RPC server on one of the 33MHZ machine, and the RPC client on the other. The network is a stock Ethernet (10 Mbits/second) network with no other traffic. The run time for the Mandelbrot program increased to 234 seconds. The time required to transmit the parameters on the network and send the result back was therefore 87 seconds, or almost 6 milliseconds per call.

As a final experiment we ran the RPC server on the 66MHZ machine and the client on a 33MHZ machine. The client completed in 149 seconds, or 85 seconds faster than it did when the server ran on the 33MHZ machine. This is almost exactly what you would expect: The 66MHZ machine was able to complete the RPC version of the program 81 seconds faster than the 33MHZ machine when both were using local RPC servers.

	33MHZ	66MHZ	Difference
Normal function calls	70	15	55
Local RPC servers	147	66	81
33MHZ client with remote server	234	149	85

(Time in seconds)

There is one fundamental conclusion that you should draw from all of these comparisons: each remote procedure call incurs a penalty of roughly 10 milliseconds. Six milliseconds of that is network delay, and it will increase when network traffic is high. The remaining four or so milliseconds is hardware-dependent, and will decrease on faster hardware. However, it will never go away completely.

Given this conclusion, you can formulate a design rule: You should not use an RPC function call for any function unless you expect to get more than a 10 millisecond speedup by running it on a different machine. For example, if you have a function that takes 30 seconds to run on one machine but only five seconds to run on another, then this function call can be made into an RPC call with great benefit. The savings of 25 seconds significantly overshadows the 10 millisecond delay of the RPC call. If you are only going to save only a few milliseconds on the call, you should not use an RPC.

From the results cited above, we can conclude that RPCs were a dismal failure in the Mandelbrot program *because the design of the program used RPCs incorrectly.* The original program took 70 seconds to execute on the 33MHZ machine, and we wanted to decrease that time. Instead, the current design, which makes an RPC call for each pixel in the image, doubles or triples the execution time. Adding in an RPC call for every single pixel made the program run more slowly because the time savings gained from calculating one pixel on the 66MHZ machine is less than 10 milliseconds.

By redesigning the **CalcPixel** function, RPCs might still be useful in the Mandelbrot application. For example, if the RPC calculated an entire scan line instead of a single pixel, only 104 RPC calls, instead of 14,768, would be made. 104 RPC calls require only about one second of total CPU and network overhead to execute, but the expected savings is 55 seconds, so the 33MHZ client would take 16 rather than 70 seconds to complete. RPCs would be very worthwhile in this situation.

In designing your own programs, keep this simple design rule in mind. Design your RPC functions so that you gain more time from operating on a faster remote machine than you are losing due to RPC call overhead. You can perform experiments on your own network to determine what the exact RPC overhead is at your site and on your equipment, but the 10 millisecond number is a good rule of thumb.

8.4 Creating RPCs

The steps that you must follow to create an RPC server and an RPC client that can communicate with it are fairly involved. The first time you see it, the whole sequence can be rather intimidating. In this section we will walk through the steps using a simple example program. This will let you try the process once and get the whole thing working on your network (or on a single machine). The next section explains all of the terminology and steps in detail.

Start by creating the code for the RPC server. In this example, the server will contain one function called **SumUp**. This function accepts an integer, and calculates the sum of all of the integers between 1 and that value. Therefore, if you call **SumUp** with the value 5 it will return 15 (5 + 4 + 3 + 2 + 1 = 15). The server will run continuously on a machine and make the **SumUp** function available to RPC clients who need to execute that function. You create the server in four separate parts:

1. The server's **SumUp** function itself (sum.cpp)
2. The server body (autoserv.cpp)
3. An IDL (Interface Definition Language) file (sum.idl)
4. An ACF (Attribute Control File) (sum.acf)

The same IDL and ACF files are also used by the client program. Listing 8.1 shows the **SumUp** function, Listing 8.2 shows the server body, Listing 8.3 shows the IDL file, and Listing 8.4 shows the ACF.

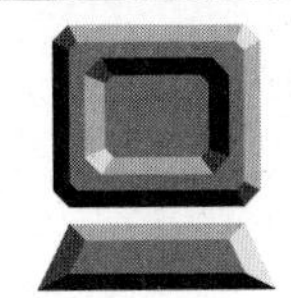

```
// sum.cpp

#include <windows.h>
#include "sum.h"

long SumUp(short sumVal)
{
  short iter;
  long theSum;

  theSum=0;
  for (iter=1; iter<=sumVal; theSum+=iter, iter++);

  Beep(300, 30);

  return(theSum);
}
```

Listing 8.1
The **SumUp** function (sum.cpp)

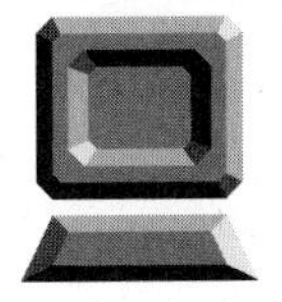

```
// autoserv.cpp

#include <windows.h>
```

Listing 8.2
The server body (autoserv.cpp) (Page 1 of 3)

```
#include <iostream.h>
#include <rpc.h>
#include "sum.h"
#include "memstub"

INT main(VOID)
{
  RPC_BINDING_VECTOR *bindVector;

  // use the protocols specified in the
  // IDL file for this interface
  if (RpcServerUseAllProtseqsIf(1,
    sumup_v1_0_s_ifspec, NULL))
  {
    cerr << "ERROR: Could not specify protocols"
      << endl;
    return(1);
  }

  // register the interface
  if (RpcServerRegisterIf(sumup_v1_0_s_ifspec,
    NULL, NULL))
  {
    cerr <<
      "ERROR: Could not register interface handle"
      << endl;
    return(1);
  }

  // get binding handles for the interface
  if (RpcServerInqBindings(&bindVector))
  {
    cerr
      << "ERROR: Could not inquire about bindings"
      << endl;
```

Listing 8.2
The server body (autoserv.cpp) (Page 2 of 3)

```
        return(1);
    }

    // add an entry in the name service
    // for the interface
    if (RpcNsBindingExport(RPC_C_NS_SYNTAX_DEFAULT,
        (UCHAR *) "/.:/autorpc",
        sumup_v1_0_s_ifspec, bindVector, NULL))
    {
        cerr
          << "ERROR: Could not export binding" << endl;
        return(1);
    }

    // listen for and service RPC requests
    if (RpcServerListen(1, 5, FALSE))
    {
        cerr <<
          "ERROR: Server cant listen for RPC requests"
          << endl;
        return(1);
    }

    return(0);
}
```

Listing 8.2
The server body (autoserv.cpp) (Page 3 of 3)

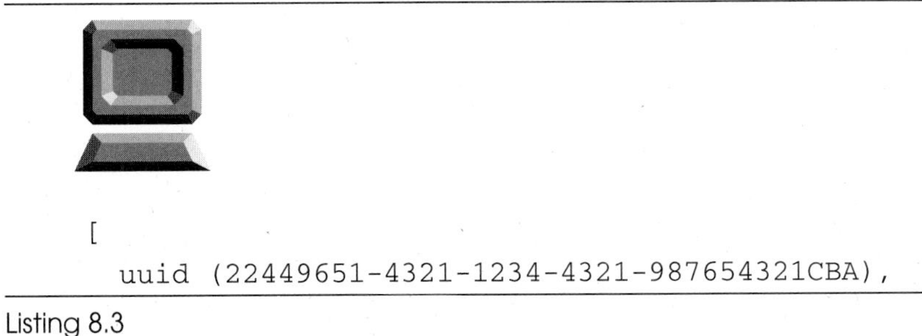

```
[
  uuid (22449651-4321-1234-4321-987654321CBA),
```

Listing 8.3
The IDL file (sum.idl)

```
    version(1.0),
    endpoint ("ncacn_np:[\\pipe\\autorpc]")
  ]
  interface sumup
  {
    long SumUp([in] short sumVal);
  }
```

Listing 8.3
The IDL file (sum.idl)

```
  [
    auto_handle
  ]
  interface sumup
  {
  }
```

Listing 8.4
The ACF file (sum.acf)

The client side of things is much simpler. Shown in Listing 8.5 is a simple client that uses the **SumUp** function.

```
  // autoclnt.cpp

  /*
  This program uses an autobinding RPC call to
  calculate a running sum.
```

Listing 8.5
A simple RPC client that calls **SumUp** (autoclnt.cpp) (Page 1 of 2)

```
*/

#include <windows.h>
#include <iostream.h>
#include <rpc.h>
#include <stdlib.h>
#include "sum.h"
#include "memstub"

INT main(VOID)
{
  CHAR sumUpToStr[10];
  long theSum;

  cout << "Enter a value to compute running sum: ";
  cin.getline(sumUpToStr, 10);

  theSum=SumUp((short)atoi(sumUpToStr));

  cout << "The running sum is: " << theSum << endl;

  return(0);
}
```

Listing 8.5
A simple RPC client that calls **SumUp** (autoclnt.cpp) (Page 2 of 2)

Finally, you need a "memstub" file that defines how the RPC runtime libraries will allocate and deallocate memory, as well as a makefile. These are shown in Listings 8.6 and 8.7.

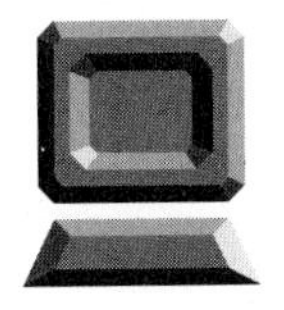

```
void __RPC_FAR * __RPC_API midl_user_allocate(
```

Listing 8.6
A memstub file. Replace with **malloc** and **free** if you are writing C code (memstub)

```
   size_t len)
{
   return(new(unsigned char [len]));
}

void __RPC_API midl_user_free(void __RPC_FAR * ptr)
{
   delete(ptr);
}
```

Listing 8.6
A memstub file. Replace with **malloc** and **free** if you are writing C code (memstub)

```
NODEBUG=1
CLIENT=autoclnt
SERVER=autoserv
RPCFILE=sum

!include <ntwin32.mak>

.SUFFIXES: .cpp

.c.obj:
   $(cc) -J $(cflags) $(cvars) $(cdebug) $<

.cpp.obj:
   $(cc) -J $(cflags) $(cvars) $(cdebug) $<

all: $(CLIENT).exe $(SERVER).exe


$(SERVER).exe: $(SERVER).obj $(RPCFILE).obj \
```

Listing 8.7
A makefile for both client and server (makefile) (Page 1 of 2)

```
$(RPCFILE)_s.obj
    $(link) $(conlflags) $(ldebug) $(conlibs) \
        rpcrt4.lib rpcns4.lib -out:$(SERVER).exe \
        $(SERVER).obj $(RPCFILE).obj \
        $(RPCFILE)_s.obj


$(CLIENT).exe: $(CLIENT).obj $(RPCFILE)_c.obj
    $(link) $(conlflags) $(ldebug) $(conlibs) \
        rpcrt4.lib rpcns4.lib -out:$(CLIENT).exe \
        $(CLIENT).obj $(RPCFILE)_c.obj


$(SERVER).obj: $(SERVER).cpp $(RPCFILE).h

$(CLIENT).obj: $(CLIENT).cpp $(RPCFILE).h

$(RPCFILE).obj: $(RPCFILE).cpp $(RPCFILE).h

$(RPCFILE)_c.obj: $(RPCFILE)_c.c $(RPCFILE).h
$(RPCFILE)_s.obj: $(RPCFILE)_s.c $(RPCFILE).h

$(RPCFILE).h $(RPCFILE)_c.c \
$(RPCFILE)_s.c: $(RPCFILE).idl \
$(RPCFILE).acf
    midl $(RPCFILE).idl
```

Listing 8.7
A makefile for both client and server (makefile) (Page 2 of 2)

The above code looks rather messy, especially the first time you see it. Here are two things to keep in mind:

1. Note how simple Listing 8.5, the client, is. Once the server is set up and running, creating clients is easy. The only thing that tells you that the client even contains an RPC is the `rpc.h` and `memstub` include files—the code itself looks absolutely normal.
2. Everything except Listing 8.1, 8.3 and 8.5 is mostly boilerplate, so you won't have to modify it very much for your own applications.

Get all of this code set up on your machine, and then make the makefile (See Appendix A). You will get two useful pieces of output: `autoserv.exe`, and `autoclnt.exe`.

To run the RPC server and client on a single machine, first make sure that the RPC services in the Services applet of the Control Panel have started. Both the RPC Locator and the RPC service must be active. Set them for automatic startup if they are not already configured that way. Then run the server on your machine by opening an MS-DOS prompt and typing:

```
autoserv
```

The server will run continuously waiting for connection attempts from clients. If it fails to run, look at its error messages. They will help you to debug the problem. See the Win32 API help file for help decoding error messages. You should have no problems if you enter the code exactly as shown above.

Now run the client by opening a second MS-DOS window on the same machine and typing:

```
autoclnt
```

When you input a value at the client's prompt, you should experience a several-second pause, followed by a beep from the server and the result.

RPCs are not really useful unless you are working on a network. If you want to try running the server and client on separate machines, take the following steps:

1. If the server and client machines use different CPU architectures, you will need to recompile the server and client for their appropriate machines. It is best to compile both server and client on both architectures and try running the pairs on their own machines to make sure they work. As you will learn in the next section, it is safe for a client on one architecture to call a server on another architecture, because the design of RPCs goes to great lengths to ensure cross-architecture compatibility.
2. On NT, make sure the RPC services (in the Services applet of the Control Panel) are running.
3. Now, on the RPC server machine, start the server by typing:

```
autoserv
```

4. Make sure no other copies of the server are running anywhere else on the network.
5. On the client machine, run the client by typing:

```
autoclnt
```

You should see a several-second delay once you type in the number, followed by a beep on the server machine and the result on the client machine. If you run the client a second time, its result should appear somewhat more quickly. The first run takes a hit due to network locator and binding delays.

If your RPC server or client will not run, first make sure that your code exactly matches Listings 8.1 through 8.7. Check the Services applet in the Control Panel and make sure both RPC services have started. If you experience memory problems, close several applications or add memory to your machine.

Now that you have successfully created and used an RPC server and client, we will examine the details.

8.5 Understanding RPCs at a High Level

Microsoft's RPC mechanism was originally designed by the Open Software Foundation (OSF) as an open standard for RPC functionality on heterogeneous networks. It is the standard for UNIX DCE (Distributed Computing Environment) RPC implementation, and is already in widespread use on the UNIX side because of that. OSF had several goals for its design:

1. Allow machines with different architectures to communicate without the problems that normally arise from differing word sizes, byte sexes, and so on.
2. Allow the use of most normal C types without difficulty. These types include integer and real types, strings, arrays, pointers, structures, and unions
3. Support multiple network protocols
4. Hide the underlying network protocols as much as possible with high-level functions
5. Allow the programmer flexibility in determining the amount of control he/she wants over the network connections. The programmer generally can trade convenience for efficiency.

To a large extent, the OSF specification accomplishes these goals. For example, you can place an RPC server on an NT machine and connect to it from an RPC client on a UNIX machine with a completely different CPU architecture, and it will work. It also works in the other direction, with the client on a Windows machine and the server on the UNIX machine. The RPC server can exist on a Cray computer 200 miles away from any of its clients and the system will work.

To meet these goals, the OSF RPC design has to demand certain information from the programmer when creating both servers and clients. For example, in order to eliminate word-size and byte-sex problems, a programmer has to carefully describe how he/she is planning to use parameters in function calls. These descriptions go far beyond the normal prototype descriptions used in C or C++. The IDL file seen in Listing 8.3 contains these parameter specifications. To handle multiple network protocols, the programmer must specify the protocols desired, and must set up endpoints in the RPC server for RPC clients to attach to. This information can come from the IDL file, or can be hard coded in the server code. In order to publicize the existence of an RPC server on the network, the programmer must write code that tells the RPC name server about the RPC server. None of these steps are particularly difficult, but they are new and require some education before you can work with them.

Let's start by looking at how an RPC client connects to an RPC server at a high level. This will allow you to see some of the options available.

8.5.1 The Server

Compatibility Note: See Section 8.8 for a discussion of RPC name services.

The server must always start first. In the preceding example you explicitly started the server at an MS-DOS prompt. In a production version of an RPC server, you generally wrap it in a service (Chapter 9) so that it starts automatically when the machine boots.

When the RPC server begins running, it does several things. First, it informs the machine it is running on which network protocols it will use for communication with clients. It also tells the machine the names of the endpoints for the different protocols. Clients will then connect to these endpoints.

NT's RPCs support eight different protocols (Windows 95 does not support ncacn_np):

Name	Description
ncacn_dnet_nsp	DECnet on DOS and Windows 3.1
ncacn_ip_tcp	TCP/IP
ncacn_nb_nb	NetBIOS over NetBEUI
ncacn_nb_tcp	NetBIOS over TCP
ncacn_np	Named pipes
ncacn_spx	SPX (Novell)
ncalrpc	Local

Each supported protocol has a different sort of name for its endpoint. For example, when using the TCP/IP protocol, you specify a port number. When using the named pipe protocol, you specify a pipe name such as \pipe\pipe-name (as shown in Listing 8.3, see also Section 7.4 for general information on named pipes). As you can see, you need to have a little knowledge of how the different protocols work in order to pick appropriate endpoint names. If you are working strictly with NT machines on your network, use named pipes for simplicity. If you are using Windows 95 use strictly TCP/IP. See Chapter 7 for information on both TCP/IP and NetBEUI network communications.

With the protocols and endpoints established, the RPC server next registers an *interface* for the functions it supports. The interface defines exactly how parameters will flow through the supported functions, and guarantees compatibility across architectures. The IDL file specifies the interface for all of the functions supported by a server. In this simple example, the server supports just one function named **SumUp**.

The RPC server can optionally register itself with a name server. The name server allows RPC clients to quickly find appropriate servers anywhere on the network. If the RPC server does not publicize itself through a name server, then the client must implicitly know the name of the machine running the server, the supported protocol(s), and the name of the endpoint(s). With a name server on the network, the client can obtain all of this information at run time.

On a domain-controlled network, the domain controller normally acts as the name server. In the absence of a domain controller, you can arbitrarily pick a machine on a peer-to-peer network and use it as the name server. If you do not pick a specific name server machine, then RPC clients have a way to scan a peer-to-peer network looking for servers on a machine-by-machine basis. On a heterogeneous network of Windows and UNIX machines, a UNIX machine can act as a name server. In this case, the UNIX name server is called the *cell directory server.* We will ignore this heterogeneous case in our examples, but it works just the same way as NT's locator service. See Section 8.8 for details.

On an NT machine, the RPC Locator service acts as the name server. If you are using a name server on your network, only the name server machine needs to be running the RPC Locator. If you do not have a specific name server machine, then all machines running RPC servers must run the RPC Locator so that RPC clients can hunt on the network for RPC servers.

Having said all of this, you can see that any RPC server performs the following tasks as it begins running:

1. Specifies the protocols it will use and the endpoint names for those protocols
2. Registers the interfaces for the functions it supports
3. Optionally registers itself with a name server

Once these tasks are complete, the RPC server is ready to accept function calls from RPC clients.

8.5.2 The Client

An RPC client that wants to perform a remote procedure call first needs to *bind* with the appropriate RPC server. It can do this either automatically or manually. In *manual binding*, the RPC client must know the machine name, protocol, and endpoint name for the RPC server it wants to use. It binds to the server and calls the functions it needs. It then unbinds itself. The programmer must write code to perform the binding, and the programmer or the user must know the binding information.

Optionally, an RPC client can manually query the name server (see **RpcNsBindingImportBegin**) and obtain the machine name, protocol, and endpoint name for an RPC server. It can then manually bind to the server. Again the programmer must write code to perform the binding, but the name server provides the needed connection information.

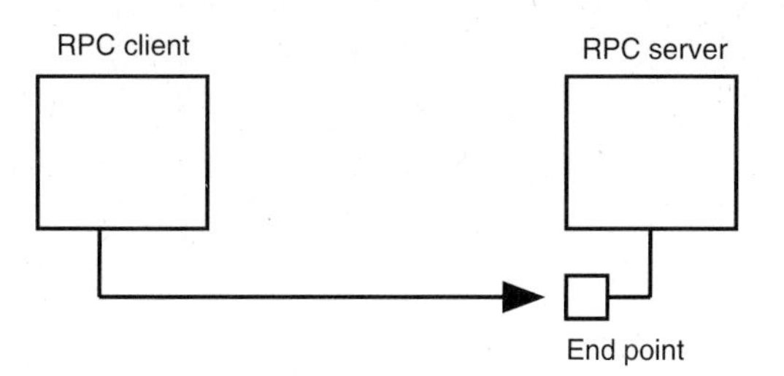

Figure 8.2
A pure manual binding. The RPC client knows the machine, the protocol, and the endpoint for the RPC server, binds to it, and then performs the remote function call(s).

In *automatic binding*, the programmer for the client code does nothing. Each time the client program calls an RPC server function, the RPC runtime library automatically queries the network's RPC name server, finds an appropriate RPC server, binds to it, performs the remote function call, and then unbinds from the server. As you can imagine, this is much easier to implement, but executes slowly if you need to make many remote calls to a server. Manual binding is preferred when the program needs to make numerous remote calls because the RPC client can bind to the server just once before making all of the calls.

Figures 8.2, 8.3, and 8.4 illustrate the three different binding modes.

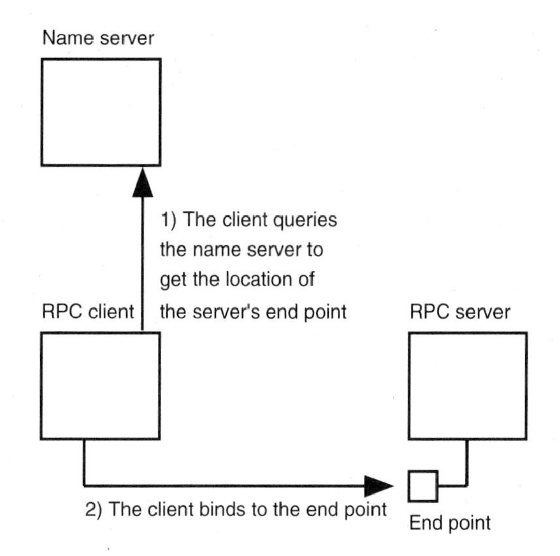

Figure 8.3
An assisted manual binding. The RPC client manually queries the name server to obtain the machine, protocol, and endpoint for the server, and then binds to the server manually as in Figure 8.2.

8.6 Parameter Passing

During an RPC call between an RPC client and an RPC server, the network acts as a transport mechanism for all parameters to, and all results from, the RPC function in the server. The interface specification for each function in the IDL file describes how parameters and return values get passed. IDL specifications are extremely specific so that you can minimize the amount of network traffic generated by an RPC call.

Windows RPCs support the following basic types:

boolean	TRUE or FALSE
byte	8-bit value
char	8-bit value, unsigned
double	64-bit real number
float	32-bit real number
long	32-bit integer value, signed or unsigned
short	16-bit integer value, signed or unsigned
small	8-bit integer value, signed or unsigned
wchar_t	Wide character type

When you declare a function's interface, you declare the type of each parameter as well as the direction that the data flows. For example, the **CalcPixel** function seen in Section 8.2 accepts two parameters but does not modify them. Therefore, the parameters need to be transmitted to the RPC server, but not back from the server. The interface description in the IDL file in Listing 8.3 therefore looks like this:

```
long CalcPixel([in] double x, [in] double y);
```

Parameters that do not need to be transmitted to the server but that are modified by the server and do need to be transmitted back are declared as **[out]** parameters. Parameters that need to move in both directions are declared as **[in, out]**.

Arrays pose different problems. With an array, the contents of the array must get passed to or returned from the server. You therefore need a way to describe the size of the array and the number of elements to pass. Sometimes you need to pass the entire array, but other times you may need to pass only a few values to complete a computation. Function parameters can specify sizes dynamically. For example:

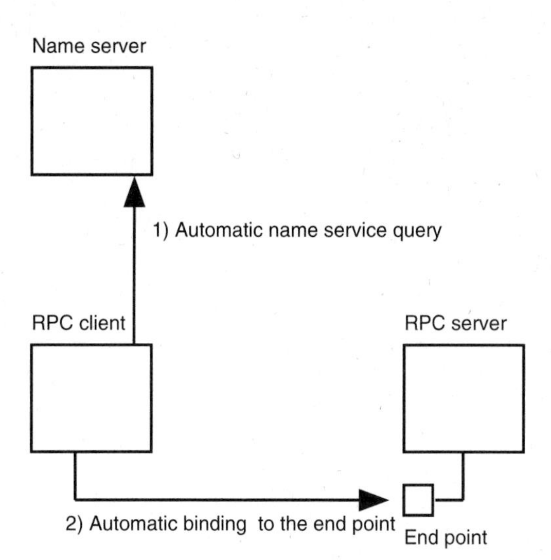

Figure 8.4
Automatic binding. The RPC client code automatically queries the name server, binds to the RPC server, makes one remote function call, and then unbinds from the RPC server.

```
long sumArray([in] long arraySize,

   [in, size_is(arraySize)] long array[]);
```

Here, the number of elements specified by **arraySize** are transferred. The **first_is**, **last_is**, and **length_is** keywords can additionally let you specify exactly how much of the array needs to be passed on each call.

Strings are handled by passing all characters up to the '\0' over the network, and allocating enough space on the server to handle them. For example:

```
long strlen([in, string] char str[]);
```

In this call, the characters in the string up to the first '\0' are passed to the server and used as **str**.

It is also possible to pass pointers, although this is slightly more difficult because the system also must pass enough of the memory pointed to by the pointer in order for the pointer to work. See the topic "Attributes, Arrays and Pointers" in the RPC help file in the SDK for details, or see the MIDL on-line help file (in win32 helpfile). The following table summarizes different parameter options in the IDL file:

first_is	Specifies the first array element to transfer
in	Specifies that the value should be transmitted when the function is called
last_is	Specifies the last array element to transfer
length_is	Specifies the length of a variable length array
max_is	Specifies the maximum value of an array index
min_is	Specifies the minimum value of an array index
out	Specifies that the value should be transmitted when the function returns
ptr	Designates a full pointer
ref	Designates a reference pointer
size_is	Specifies the amount of memory to allocate for an array
string	Specifies that the parameter is a string and characters up to the first \0 should be copied
unique	Designates a unique pointer

8.7 Understanding the Code

To understand the code in Section 8.4, start with the IDL file shown in Listing 8.3, duplicated here:

```
[
  uuid (22449651-4321-1234-4321-987654321CBA),
  version(1.0),
  endpoint ("ncacn_np:[\\pipe\\autorpc]")
]
interface sumup
{
  long SumUp([in] short sumVal);
}
```

Each RPC server will have a unique IDL file that identifies the server and defines all of the functions it supports. The example file shown here, like all IDL files, contains a *uuid* (universally unique identifier) value that uniquely identifies this server. The uuid number is generated, along with the stub for the IDL file, by a program named `uuidgen`. For example, if you type:

```
uuidgen -i
```

You will get a new IDL stub file containing a new uuid number. The ID number is formed from both the current time and the machine ID, so it is unique on the network.

The version number in the IDL file starts at 1.0 but can be changed, allowing you to have multiple versions of the same server running on the network simultaneously without conflict.

The endpoint line defines the protocol and the appropriate name for the endpoint. It is possible for a single server to support multiple protocols, for example:

```
endpoint ("ncacn_np:[\\pipe\\autorpc]",
        "ncacn_ip_tcp:[1050]")
```

This definition specifies that the server should use the named pipe protocol with the endpoint named `\pipe\autorpc`, as well as the TCP/IP protocol with the endpoint at port number 1050. The interface line names the server, here as "sumup," and is then followed by the parameter descriptions for all of the functions in the server. Here the server supports only one function.

If you look at the last part of the makefile seen in Listing 8.7, you can see a line that resolves to this:

```
midl sum.idl
```

The MIDL program is the *IDL compiler.* It accepts the IDL file, looks at the name of it (here it is "sum" from "sum.idl"), automatically opens a file named "sum.acf" if it exists (in this case, the ACF file tells the MIDL compiler that auto binding should be used), and produces the following files:

sum.h

sum_c.c

sum_s.c

These files contain "behind the scenes" code that make the RPC server and client work correctly. The makefile eventually compiles the code in these files and links them to the code you write. Because this example uses auto binding, this supplemental code contains everything necessary to query the name server and bind the client to the server. You can learn quite a bit about the binding process by looking through the code. The ACF file specifies the binding type and therefore controls how the binding takes place in this code.

Given the three files generated by the MIDL compiler, the normal C++ compiler can compile and link both the server and client. The client code in Listing 8.5 is trivial. There really is no indication, beyond the header files, that it uses RPCs. All of the details of the network interaction were generated automatically by the MIDL compiler and appear in the `sum_c.c` file.

On the server side there are two files. The `sum.cpp` file in Listing 8.1 looks normal, and it contains the code for the **SumUp** function itself. The `autoserv.cpp` file in Listing 8.2 is a different story, and will look totally foreign to you. The functions called here are described in the 32-bit API help file. If you strip out the error checking, there really are only five lines in this file:

```
RpcServerUseAllProtseqsIf(1,
  sumup_v1_0_s_ifspec, NULL);
RpcServerRegisterIf(sumup_v1_0_s_ifspec,
  NULL, NULL);
RpcServerInqBindings(&bindVector);
RpcNsBindingExport(RPC_C_NS_SYNTAX_DEFAULT,
  (UCHAR *) "/.:/autorpc",
  sumup_v1_0_s_ifspec, bindVector, NULL);
RpcServerListen(1, 5, FALSE);
```

The first function call to **RpcServerUseAllProtseqsIf** tells the server to use all of the protocols specified in the IDL file. It is also possible to use protocols individually.

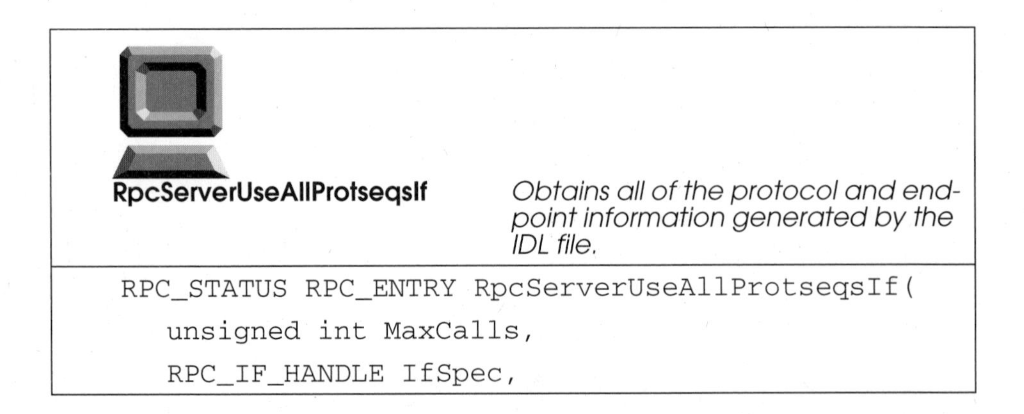
RpcServerUseAllProtseqsIf *Obtains all of the protocol and endpoint information generated by the IDL file.*

```
RPC_STATUS RPC_ENTRY RpcServerUseAllProtseqsIf(
   unsigned int MaxCalls,
   RPC_IF_HANDLE IfSpec,
```

```
    void * SecurityDescriptor)
```

MaxCalls	The maximum number of concurrent calls the server will accept at one time
IfSpec	The protocol and endpoint information
SecurityDescriptor	NT Security descriptor. See Chapter 10

Returns a status code

The **sumup_v1_0_s_ifspec** name comes from `sum.h`, which the MIDL compiler generated from the IDL file you supplied. The word "sumup" in the variable name is the name you supplied for the interface in the IDL file.

The second function call to **RpcServerRegisterIf** lets the server know about the interfaces that clients can call.

RpcServerRegisterIf *Registers an interface*

```
RPC_STATUS RPC_ENTRY RpcServerRegisterIf(
    RPC_IF_HANDLE IfSpec,
    UUID * MgrTypeUuid,
    RPC_MGR_EPV * MgrEpv)
```

IfSpec	The interface to register
MgrTypeUuid	UUID or NULL
MgrEpv	Entry-point vector or NULL

Returns a status code

The third call to **RpcServerInqBindings** returns a list enumerating all of the bindings that this server provides. The list is used in the following call so that the name server can publicize these bindings.

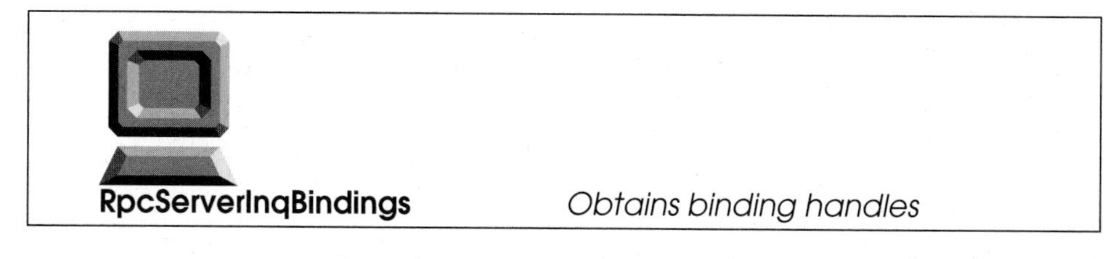

```
RPC_STATUS RPC_ENTRY RpcServerInqBindings(
   RPC_BINDING_VECTOR** BindingVector)
```

BindingVector	The binding vector retrieved
Returns a status code	

The fourth call to **RpcNsBindingExport** tells the name server about this RPC server and gives it the name "autorpc" (the name is required, but is irrelevant in the case of auto binding). The name server now starts publicizing this RPC server.

RpcNsBindingExport — *Registers the RPC server with the name server, telling the name server its name and valid bindings*

```
RPC_STATUS RPC_ENTRY RpcNsBindingExport(
   unsigned long EntryNameSyntax,
   unsigned char* EntryName,
   RPC_IF_HANDLE IfSpec,
   RPC_BINDING_VECTOR* BindingVec,
   UUID_VECTOR* ObjectUuidVec)
```

EntryNameSyntax	Use RPC_C_NS_SYNTAX_DEFAULT
EntryName	The name of the RPC server
IfSpec	The interface for the server
BindingVec	The bindings for the server
ObjectUuidVec	Vector of object UUIDs, or NULL
Returns a status code	

The last call to **RpcServerListen** causes the server to begin listening for connection requests from RPC clients.

RpcServerListen — *Allows the server to begin listening for requests from clients*

```
RPC_STATUS RPC_ENTRY RpcServerListen(
   unsigned int MinCallThreads,
   unsigned int MaxCalls,
   unsigned int DontWait)
```

MinCallThreads	Minimum number of threads
MaxCalls	Maximum number of concurrent calls the server will accept at one time
DontWait	If TRUE this function returns immediately. If FALSE it blocks until shutdown

Returns a status code when the server stops listening

It is helpful to read the descriptions of each of these functions in the RPC help in the SDK file to gain a better understanding of what each function does. On the other hand, if you use auto binding for all of your RPC servers, the code shown in Listing 8.2 is generic and will work in many different situations. You should change the name "autorpc" passed to the **RpcNsBindingExport** function for each different server you create.

The last piece of code shown in Section 8.4 is the stub file in Listing 8.6. These two routines are used by the hidden code generated by the MIDL compiler to allocate and deallocate memory.

All of these pieces work together to form a working RPC server and client. The following sections explore other options through several different example programs and descriptions.

8.8 Setting up a Name Server in the Registry

Compatibility Note: At the time of publication, RPC name services as described in this section do not work in Windows 95.

By default, the NT RPC mechanism uses a distributed architecture for name services. When an RPC client starts, it will first look on the local machine for any RPC servers it needs, then on the domain controller if there is one, and then it will begin enumerating machines on the network, talking with their RPC locators and searching for the appropriate RPC servers. This latter process can be time consuming. By declaring one machine on the network to be the RPC name server, you centralize all RPC server information and make the search process much faster. If you have a domain controller on the network, then it is normally chosen for the responsibility of being the name server. However, you can arbitrarily choose any machine on the network for this role. The chosen machine is the only one on the network required to run the RPC Locator service.

To specify the name server, go to each machine that will run an RPC client and open the registry (use `regedt32.exe` in NT and `regedit.exe` in Windows 95). Find the key named HKEY_LOCAL_MACHINE\Software\Microsoft\RPC\NameService. Change the **NetworkAddress** and **ServerNetworkAddress** values to hold the name of the chosen name server machine. For example, if the name server machine is called "nts," then fill the values with "\\nts." Now RPC clients will automatically go to \\NTS when they want to use the name server.

If you are working on a heterogeneous network that uses a UNIX machine as the name server for RPCs, then that UNIX machine is called the *cell directory service.* You can tell NT to use the cell directory service by opening the Network applet in the Control Panel. Find the RPC Name Service Provider module in the list of installed network software, and click the **Configure** button. Select **DCE Cell Directory Server** from the list, and enter the IP address of the machine supplying the service in **Network Address** field. The address will appear in the registry automatically.

If at some point you find that RPC clients that formerly worked begin failing for no apparent reason, you should check on the health of the name server machine. Also, if somebody randomly changes the name of the name server machine, it can play havoc with a network using RPCs because all of the registries on the client machines must change. One advantage of not using a centralized name server is that you don't have any dependency on a single machine.

8.9 Manual Binding with Implicit Handles

Compatibility Note: All of the code in this section is configured so that it will work identically in Windows 95, Windows NT, and any combination of Windows 95 and NT pairs on a TCP/IP network. Note that you must change the machine name in conclnt.cpp (Listing 8.12) from "localhost" to a specific machine name and recompile in order for this code to work across the network.

Auto handles, which were used in the example code described previously, are nice because they make the client code extremely simple. However, auto handles are inefficient when you need to make multiple calls to the RPC server. With auto handles, each call to the server means that the RPC client binds to the RPC server, calls the remote function it needs, and then unbinds. The binding and unbinding is expensive. Manual binding allows you to bind once and then make numerous function calls before unbinding.

Listings 8.8 though 8.14 demonstrate the pieces of code necessary to implement manual binding with the **SumUp** function seen previously.

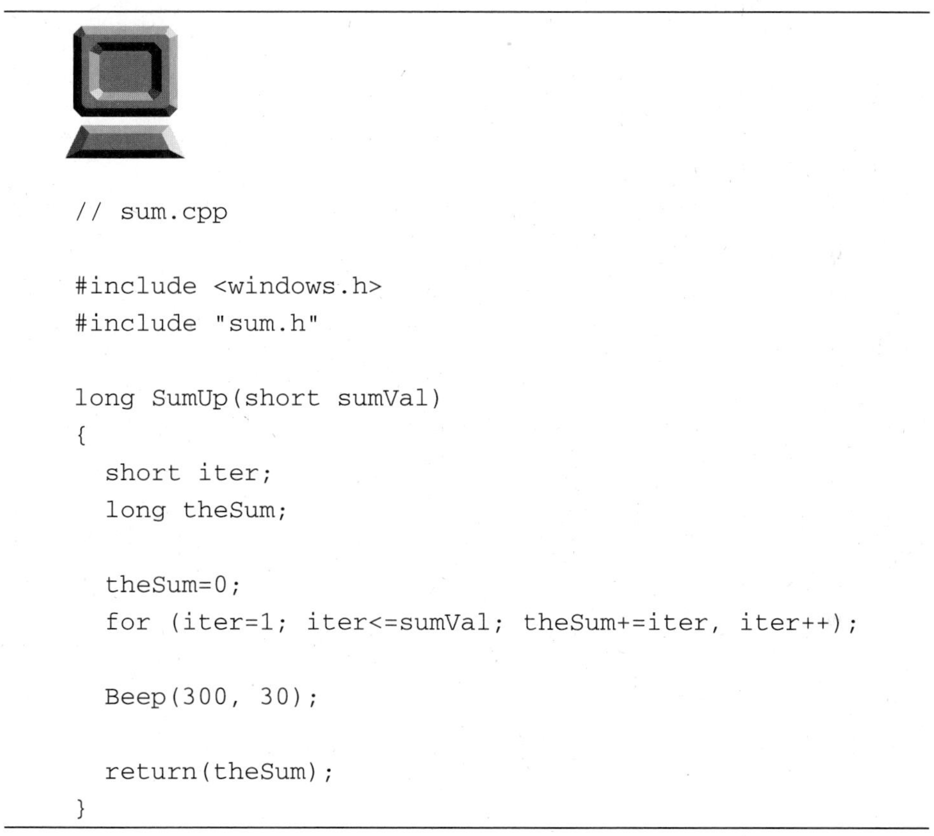

```
// sum.cpp

#include <windows.h>
#include "sum.h"

long SumUp(short sumVal)
{
  short iter;
  long theSum;

  theSum=0;
  for (iter=1; iter<=sumVal; theSum+=iter, iter++);

  Beep(300, 30);

  return(theSum);
}
```

Listing 8.8
The **SumUp** function (sum.cpp), identical to Listing 8.1

```
// conserv.cpp

#include <windows.h>
#include <iostream.h>
#include <rpc.h>
#include "sum.h"
#include "memstub"

INT main(VOID)
{
  // use the specified protocol and endpoint
  if (RpcServerUseProtseqEp(
    (UCHAR *) "ncacn_ip_tcp", 1,
    (UCHAR *) "55449", NULL))
  {
    cerr << "ERROR: Could not specify protocol"
      << endl;
    return(1);
  }

  // register the interface
  if (RpcServerRegisterIf(sumup_v1_0_s_ifspec,
    NULL, NULL))
  {
    cerr <<
      "ERROR: Could not register interface handle"
      << endl;
    return(1);
```

Listing 8.9
The server body (conserv.cpp). Because the client uses direct manual binding, there is no need to register with the name server and that code is left out. Otherwise it is identical to Listing 8.2 (Page 1 of 2)

```
    }

    // listen for and service RPC requests
    if (RpcServerListen(1, 5, FALSE))
    {
      cerr <<
        "ERROR: Server unable to listen for requests"
        << endl;
      return(1);
    }

    return(0);
  }
```

Listing 8.9
The server body (conserv.cpp). Because the client uses direct manual binding, there is no need to register with the name server and that code is left out. Otherwise it is identical to Listing 8.2 (Page 2 of 2)

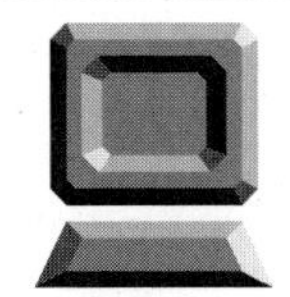

```
[
  uuid (55449658-4321-1234-4321-987654321CBA),
  version(1.0)
]
interface sumup
{
  long SumUp([in] short sumVal);
}
```

Listing 8.10
The IDL file (sum.idl), is the same as Listing 8.3 but does not contain the protocol or endpoint information because it appears in the client code

```
[
  implicit_handle(handle_t SumUpHandle)
]
interface sumup
{
}
```

Listing 8.11
The ACF file (sum.acf) declaring an implicit handle

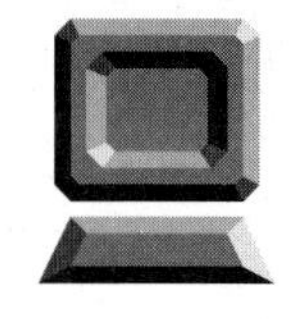

```
// conclnt.cpp

/*
This program calls an RPC function
using a manual handle.
*/

#include <windows.h>
#include <iostream.h>
#include <rpc.h>
#include <stdlib.h>
#include "sum.h"
#include "memstub"

INT main(VOID)
```

Listing 8.12
The RPC client (conclnt.cpp) that calls SumUp, containing the code to perform the manual binding (Page 1 of 3)

```
{
  CHAR sumUpToStr[10];
  long theSum;
  UCHAR *stringBinding;

  cout << "Enter a value to compute running sum: ";
  cin.getline(sumUpToStr, 10);

  // put together string binding
  if (RpcStringBindingCompose(NULL,
    (UCHAR *) "ncacn_ip_tcp",
    (UCHAR *) "localhost", // Change to specific machine
    (UCHAR *) "55449", NULL, &stringBinding))
  {
    cerr <<
      "ERROR: Unable to compose string binding"
      << endl;
    return(1);
  }

  // bind to server using string binding info
  if (RpcBindingFromStringBinding(stringBinding,
    &SumUpHandle))
  {
    cerr << "ERROR: Unable to bind" << endl;
    return(1);
  }

  // free the string binding info
  if (RpcStringFree(&stringBinding))
  {
    cerr
      << "ERROR: Unable to free string binding"
      << endl;
    return(1);
```

Listing 8.12
The RPC client (conclnt.cpp) that calls SumUp, containing the code to perform the manual binding (Page 2 of 3)

```
    }

    theSum=SumUp((short)atoi(sumUpToStr));

    cout << "The running sum is: " << theSum << endl;

    // release binding to server
    if (RpcBindingFree(&SumUpHandle))
    {
      cerr
        << "ERROR: Unable to free binding"
        << endl;
      return(1);
    }

    return(0);
  }
```

Listing 8.12
The RPC client (conclnt.cpp) that calls SumUp, containing the code to perform the manual binding (Page 3 of 3)

```
void __RPC_FAR * __RPC_API midl_user_allocate
    (size_t len)
{
    return(new(unsigned char [len]));
}
void __RPC_API midl_user_free(void __RPC_FAR * ptr)
{
    delete(ptr);
}
```

Listing 8.13
The memstub file. Replace with malloc and free if you are using C rather than C++

```
NODEBUG=1
CLIENT=conclnt
SERVER=conserv
RPCFILE=sum

!include <ntwin32.mak>

.SUFFIXES: .cpp

.c.obj:
   $(cc) -J $(cflags) $(cvars) $(cdebug) $<

.cpp.obj:
   $(cc) -J $(cflags) $(cvars) $(cdebug) $<

all: $(CLIENT).exe $(SERVER).exe


$(SERVER).exe: $(SERVER).obj $(RPCFILE).obj \
$(RPCFILE)_s.obj
   $(link) $(conlflags) $(ldebug) $(conlibs) \
     rpcrt4.lib rpcns4.lib -out:$(SERVER).exe \
     $(SERVER).obj $(RPCFILE).obj \
     $(RPCFILE)_s.obj


$(CLIENT).exe: $(CLIENT).obj $(RPCFILE)_c.obj
   $(link) $(conlflags) $(ldebug) $(conlibs) \
     rpcrt4.lib rpcns4.lib -out:$(CLIENT).exe \
```

Listing 8.14
A makefile for both client and server (Page 1 of 2)

```
        $(CLIENT).obj $(RPCFILE)_c.obj \


$(SERVER).obj: $(SERVER).cpp $(RPCFILE).h

$(CLIENT).obj: $(CLIENT).cpp $(RPCFILE).h

$(RPCFILE).obj: $(RPCFILE).cpp $(RPCFILE).h

$(RPCFILE)_c.obj: $(RPCFILE)_c.c $(RPCFILE).h
$(RPCFILE)_s.obj: $(RPCFILE)_s.c $(RPCFILE).h

$(RPCFILE).h $(RPCFILE)_c.c \
$(RPCFILE)_s.c: $(RPCFILE).idl \
$(RPCFILE).acf
   midl $(RPCFILE).idl
```

Listing 8.14
A makefile for both client and server (Page 2 of 2)

You can see by comparing the seven listings above with the seven listings from Section 8.3 that there are many similarities. The main difference is the extra code added to the client program in Listing 8.12. The following is a complete list of the similarities and differences:

1. Listing 8.8 (the **SumUp** function) and 8.1 are identical.
2. Listing 8.9 (the server code) is very similar to Listing 8.2, but 8.9 declares the protocol and endpoint within the server itself. It is also missing the two calls (**RpcServerInqBindings** and **RpcNsBindingExport)** seen in Listing 8.2 that register the RPC server with the name server. These changes were made to simplify the work that the client has to do to perform the manual binding. The client in this example will bind to the server directly, rather than requesting server information from the name server, so there is no need for the server to register with the name server. However, you could use the version of the server shown in Listing 8.2 and query the name server in the client if you choose.
3. Listing 8.10 (the IDL file) is the same as Listing 8.3, but it is missing the declaration of the protocol and endpoint seen in Listing 8.3. The server

and client code in Listings 8.9 and 8.12 both contain this information rather than reading it from the IDL file. Either technique is valid.

4. Listing 8.11 (the ACF file) declares an implicit handle, which implies manual binding, rather than the auto handle seen in Listing 8.4. The name **SumUpHandle** is used by the MIDL compiler as an internal variable name when calling RPC functions. The client code will initialize this handle.
5. The RPC client seen in Listing 8.12 is significantly more complicated than its counterpart seen in Listing 8.5. The client now contains the code to perform the manual binding. The client contains within it the name of the machine, the protocol, and the endpoint for the RPC server it needs. The client first creates a binding string containing all of the information about the server. It then creates the actual binding to the server. It calls the RPC function it needs, and then releases the binding. There could potentially be hundreds of RPC function calls between the formation and release of the binding, and this approach is significantly more efficient than auto binding, which binds and releases individually for every function call it makes.
6. The stub files and makefiles are identical. Change the name of the CLIENT and SERVER in the makefile.

The name "localhost" seen in Listing 8.12 implies that the server and client are running on the same machine (useful for initial testing), but can be changed to any machine on the network provided that that machine is running the RPC server. You could also modify the client code so that the machine name comes in through a command line parameter.

If you strip out the error-handling code in the RPC client program, it is only a few lines long:

```
cout << "Enter a value to compute running sum: ";
cin.getline(sumUpToStr, 10);

// Form the manual binding
RpcStringBindingCompose(NULL,
   (UCHAR *) "ncacn_ip_tcp",
   (UCHAR *) "localhost", // change to machine name
   (UCHAR *) "55449", NULL, &stringBinding)
```

```
    RpcBindingFromStringBinding(stringBinding,
      &SumUpHandle);
    RpcStringFree(&stringBinding);

    // Call the RPC function
    theSum=SumUp((short)atoi(sumUpToStr));
    cout << "The running sum is: " << theSum << endl;

    // Release the manual binding
    RpcBindingFree(&SumUpHandle);
```

To create a manual binding, the first step is to *compose* a string containing the binding information from its components. This string specifies the binding. The client needs to know the name of the machine on which the RPC server is running, the protocol the RPC server uses, and the name of the endpoint. The **RpcStringBindingCompose** function handles this task, returning to you a pointer to a block of memory containing the string. This pointer is called a *string-binding handle*. In this example all binding information appears explicitly in the code. It is also possible to extract it from the IDL file as shown in several other examples that follow.

RpcStringBindingCompose — *Composes a string-binding handle from its components*

```
RPC_STATUS RPC_ENTRY
   RpcStringBindingCompose(
   unsigned char* ObjUuid,
   unsigned char* ProtSeq,
   unsigned char* NetworkAddr,
   unsigned char* EndPoint,
   unsigned char* Options,
   unsigned char** StringBinding)
```

Parameter	Description
ObjUuid	A UUID, or NULL to use the one from the IDL file
ProtSeq	The network protocol

NetworkAddr	The name of the machine holding the server, or "localhost" for the local machine
EndPoint	The name of the endpoint
Options	Options, or NULL for none
StringBinding	The function returns a pointer to a block containing the binding string
Returns a status code	

Given a string-binding handle, the client can bind to the server using the **RpcBindingFromStringBinding** function. The binding is returned in the variable **SumUpHandle**, which the MIDL compiler has created in the `sum.h` file. The name **SumUpHandle** is user-definable and is specified in the ACF file. The run-time library will use this name implicitly whenever the client code calls **SumUp**.

RpcBindingFromStringBinding *Binds the client to the RPC server*

```
RPC_STATUS RPC_ENTRY RpcBindingFromStringBinding(
    unsigned char* StringBinding,
    RPC_BINDING_HANDLE* Binding)
```

StringBinding	A string-binding handle
Binding	A binding handle
Returns a status code	

If successful, the **RpcBindingFromStringBinding** function returns a binding handle and the client can talk to the RPC server. The client should free up the block of memory pointed to by the string-binding handle using the **RpcStringFree** function.

RpcStringFree	*Frees memory associated with a string-binding handle*
`RPC_STATUS RPC_ENTRY RpcStringFree(` `unsigned char** String)`	
String	A string-binding handle
Returns a status code	

In this example, the client calls the RPC function just once. In a production program you would normally make many RPC function calls after forming the binding. If you need to make just one function call, you should use automatic binding instead to simplify the client.

Once the client is done using the RPC server, it should release the binding to the server by calling the **RpcBindingFree** function.

RpcBindingFree	*Releases the binding to the RPC server*
`RPC_STATUS RPC_ENTRY RpcBindingFree(` `RPC_BINDING_HANDLE* Binding)`	
Binding	The binding to release
Returns a status code	

In Listings 8.9 (the RPC server) and 8.12 (the RPC client), both the protocol and endpoint are declared directly in the code. This information can remain in the IDL file when using manual binding—the choice is yours. For example, if you change the IDL file, the server file, and the client file as shown in Listings 8.15, 8.16, and 8.17, then both the server and client will pull the protocol and endpoint name from the IDL file.

```
// conserv2.cpp

#include <windows.h>
#include <iostream.h>
#include <rpc.h>
#include "sum.h"
#include "memstub"

INT main(VOID)
{
  // use the specified protocol and
  // get endpoint from IDL file
  if (RpcServerUseProtseqIf(
    (UCHAR *) "ncacn_ip_tcp", 1,
    sumup_v1_0_s_ifspec, NULL))
  {
    cerr
      << "ERROR: Could not specify protocol"
      << endl;
    return(1);
  }

  // register the interface
  if (RpcServerRegisterIf(sumup_v1_0_s_ifspec,
    NULL, NULL))
```

Listing 8.15
A replacement for Listing 8.9. This code uses the endpoint in the IDL file rather than declaring it explicitly in the code. It is also possible to use **RpcServerUseAppProtseqsIf** rather than naming the protocol explicitly—see Section 8.10 for an example
(Page 1 of 2)

```
    {
      cerr
        << "ERROR: Could not register interface"
        << endl;
      return(1);
    }

    // listen for and service RPC requests
    if (RpcServerListen(1, 5, FALSE))
    {
      cerr
        << "ERROR: Unable to listen for requests"
        << endl;
      return(1);
    }

    return(0);
}
```

Listing 8.15
A replacement for Listing 8.9. This code uses the endpoint in the IDL file rather than declaring it explicitly in the code. It is also possible to use **RpcServerUseAppProtseqsIf** rather than naming the protocol explicitly—see Section 8.10 for an example
(Page 2 of 2)

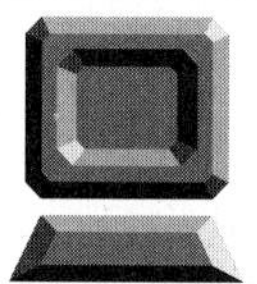

```
[
  uuid (55449651-4321-1234-4321-987654321CBA),
  version(1.0),
  endpoint ("ncacn_ip_tcp:[55465]")
]
interface sumup
```

Listing 8.16
A replacement for Listing 8.10 that contains the TCP/IP endpoint

```
{
  long SumUp([in] short sumVal);
}
```

Listing 8.16
A replacement for Listing 8.10 that contains the TCP/IP endpoint

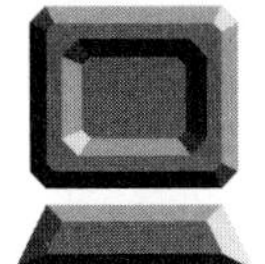

```
// conclnt2.cpp

#include <windows.h>
#include <iostream.h>
#include <rpc.h>
#include <stdlib.h>
#include "sum.h"
#include "memstub"

INT main(VOID)
{
  CHAR sumUpToStr[10];
  long theSum;
  UCHAR *stringBinding;

  cout << "Enter a value to compute running sum: ";
  cin.getline(sumUpToStr, 10);

  // put together string binding
  if (RpcStringBindingCompose(NULL,
    (UCHAR *) "ncacn_ip_tcp",
    (UCHAR *) "localhost",
    NULL, NULL, &stringBinding))
  {
```

Listing 8.17
A replacement for Listing 8.12 that uses the IDL file's endpoint (Page 1 of 3)

```
    cerr
      << "ERROR: Unable to compose string binding"
      << endl;
    return(1);
  }

  // bind to server using string binding info
  if (RpcBindingFromStringBinding(stringBinding,
    &SumUpHandle))
  {
    cerr << "ERROR: Unable to bind" << endl;
    return(1);
  }

  // free the string binding info
  if (RpcStringFree(&stringBinding))
  {
    cerr
      << "ERROR: Unable to free string binding"
      << endl;
    return(1);
  }

  theSum=SumUp((short)atoi(sumUpToStr));

  cout << "The running sum is: " << theSum << endl;

  // release binding to server
  if (RpcBindingFree(&SumUpHandle))
  {
    cerr
      << "ERROR: Unable to free binding"
      << endl;
    return(1);
  }
```

Listing 8.17
A replacement for Listing 8.12 that uses the IDL file's endpoint (Page 2 of 3)

```
   return(0);
}
```

Listing 8.17
A replacement for Listing 8.12 that uses the IDL file's endpoint (Page 3 of 3)

8.10 An RPC Server for Mandelbrot Sets

Chapter 5 demonstrates a simple Mandelbrot set program and shows how to multi-thread it. It is fairly easy to add RPCs to the Mandelbrot program, and this idea was the basis for the discussion of RPC design issues in Section 8.3.

This section presents the Mandelbrot set code using a single RPC call for each pixel in the image. The following section shows how to significantly improve the speed of the Mandelbrot program by using one RPC call for each scan line of the image rather than for each pixel.

Listings 8.18 through 8.26 contain all of the code and auxiliary files necessary to create the Mandelbrot program's RPC server and client.

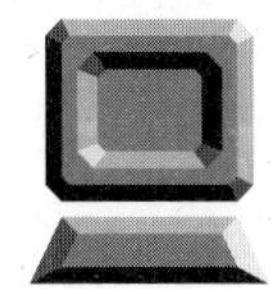

```
// ccrpc.cpp

#include <windows.h>
#include "ccrpc.h"

#define NUM_ITERATIONS 64

short CalcColor(complex k)
{
   complex z;
   double real, imag, spread;
   WORD iter;
```

Listing 8.18
The work function of the RPC server (ccrpc.cpp) (Page 1 of 2)

```
    z.real=z.imag=0.0;

    for (iter=0; iter<NUM_ITERATIONS-1; iter++)
    {
       real = z.real + k.real;
       imag = z.imag + k.imag;
       z.real = real * real - imag * imag;
       z.imag = 2 * real * imag;
       spread = z.real * z.real + z.imag * z.imag;
       if (spread > 4.0)
          break;
    }

    return(iter);
}
```

Listing 8.18
The work function of the RPC server (ccrpc.cpp) (Page 2 of 2)

```
// mandels.cpp

#include <windows.h>
#include <iostream.h>
#include <rpc.h>
#include "ccrpc.h"
#include "memstub"

INT main(VOID)
{
  // use the protocols specified in
```

Listing 8.19
The RPC server body (mandels.cpp). The server uses manual binding and pulls the protocols and endpoints from the IDL file (Page 1 of 2)

```
    // the IDL file for this interface
    if (RpcServerUseAllProtseqsIf(1,
      calcclr_v1_0_s_ifspec,
      NULL))
    {
      cerr
        << "ERROR: Could not specify protocols"
        << endl;
      return(1);
    }

    // register the interface
    if (RpcServerRegisterIf(calcclr_v1_0_s_ifspec,
      NULL, NULL))
    {
      cerr <<
        "ERROR: Could not register interface handle"
        << endl;
      return(1);
    }

    // listen for and service RPC requests
    if (RpcServerListen(1, 5, FALSE))
    {
      cerr <<
        "ERROR: Unable to listen for RPC requests"
        << endl;
      return(1);
    }

    return(0);
  }
```

Listing 8.19
The RPC server body (mandels.cpp). The server uses manual binding and pulls the protocols and endpoints from the IDL file (Page 2 of 2)

```
[
  uuid (87654321-4321-1234-4321-987654321CBA),
  version(1.0),
  endpoint ("ncacn_np:[\\pipe\\ccrpc]")
]
interface calcclr
{
  typedef struct
  {
    double real;
    double imag;
  } complex;

  short CalcColor([in] complex k);
}
```

Listing 8.20
The IDL file (ccrpc.idl). Note the use of a structure as a parameter

```
[
  implicit_handle(handle_t calcclrHandle)
]
interface calcclr
{
}
```

Listing 8.21
The ACF file (ccrpc.acf) specifying implicit handles and manual binding

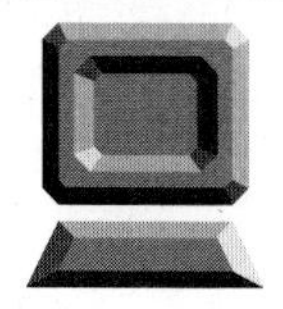

```
// mandelc.cpp

#include <afxwin.h>
#include <rpc.h>
#include "ccrpc.h"
#include "menus.h"

const double left = -1.0;
const double right = 1.0;
const double top = -1.0;
const double bottom = 1.0;

DWORD colors[64];

typedef struct
{
   WORD height;
   WORD width;
} mandelParams;

// Define the application object class
class CManApp : public CWinApp
{
public:
   virtual BOOL InitInstance();
};

// Define the edit window class
class CManWindow : public CFrameWnd
```

Listing 8.22
The RPC client (mandelc.cpp). Note that the binding occurs once in the window's constructor and is released in **OnExit** (Page 1 of 7)

```
{
private:
   HANDLE threadHandle;
   BOOL running;
   BOOL initialized;
   mandelParams params;
public:
   CManWindow();
   void RunMandel();
   void SetPix(int x, int y, WORD iter);
   afx_msg void OnPaint();
   afx_msg void OnStartStop();
   afx_msg void OnExit();
   DECLARE_MESSAGE_MAP()
};

// Create an instance of the application object
CManApp manApp;

// member function used to set pixel colors
// in the window
void CManWindow::SetPix(int x, int y, WORD iter)
{
   CClientDC dc(this);
   dc.SetPixel(x, y, colors[iter]);
}

// the thread function which does the drawing
DWORD MandelThread(mandelParams *params)
{
   double xstep, ystep;
   double x, y;
   int i,j;
   WORD iter;
   complex k;
```

Listing 8.22
The RPC client (mandelc.cpp). Note that the binding occurs once in the window's constructor and is released in **OnExit** (Page 2 of 7)

```
      ystep = (double) (bottom - top) /
         params->height;
      xstep = (double) (right - left) /
         params->width;

      for (y=top, j=0; y <= bottom; y += ystep, j++)
      {
         for (x=left, i=0; x<=right; x += xstep, i++)
         {
            k.real = x;
            k.imag = y;
            RpcTryExcept
            {
               iter=CalcColor(k);
            }
            RpcExcept(1)
            {
               MessageBox(NULL,
                  "Unable to call CalcColor( ).\n\
Click OK and then Exit.",
                  "ERROR", MB_SETFOREGROUND |
                     MB_OK | MB_ICONSTOP);
               ExitThread(1);
            }
            RpcEndExcept;

            ((CManWindow *)manApp.m_pMainWnd)->
               SetPix(i, j, iter);
         }
      }
      return(0);
   }

   // member function used to instigate the
```

Listing 8.22
The RPC client (mandelc.cpp). Note that the binding occurs once in the window's constructor and is released in **OnExit** (Page 3 of 7)

```
// drawing thread
void CManWindow::RunMandel()
{
   DWORD threadID;
   CRect r;

   GetClientRect(&r);
   params.height=r.Height();
   params.width=r.Width();

   threadHandle=CreateThread(NULL, 0,
      (LPTHREAD_START_ROUTINE) MandelThread,
      &params, 0, &threadID);

   running=TRUE;
}

// The message map
BEGIN_MESSAGE_MAP(CManWindow, CFrameWnd)
   ON_WM_PAINT()
   ON_COMMAND(IDM_STARTSTOP, OnStartStop)
   ON_COMMAND(IDM_EXIT, OnExit)
END_MESSAGE_MAP()

// Handler for the Start/Stop menu option
void CManWindow::OnStartStop()
{
   if(running)
      SuspendThread(threadHandle);
   else
      ResumeThread(threadHandle);

   running=!running;
}
```

Listing 8.22
The RPC client (mandelc.cpp). Note that the binding occurs once in the window's constructor and is released in **OnExit** (Page 4 of 7)

```
// Handler for WM_PAINT messages
void CManWindow::OnPaint()
{
   ValidateRect(NULL);
   if (!initialized)
   {
      initialized=TRUE;
      RunMandel();
   }
   else
   if (running)
   {
      // stop the existing thread
      TerminateThread(threadHandle, 0);
      CloseHandle(threadHandle);
      // clear the window
      CClientDC dc(this);
      CRect r;
      GetClientRect(&r);
      dc.PatBlt(0, 0, r.Width(), r.Height(),
      WHITENESS);
      // start over again
      RunMandel();
   }
}

// Handler for the Exit menu option
void CManWindow::OnExit()
{
   SuspendThread(threadHandle);
   CloseHandle(threadHandle);
   RpcBindingFree(&calcclrHandle);
   DestroyWindow();
}
```

Listing 8.22
The RPC client (mandelc.cpp). Note that the binding occurs once in the window's constructor and is released in **OnExit** (Page 5 of 7)

```
// CManWindow constructor
CManWindow::CManWindow()
{
   WORD x;
   BYTE red=0, green=0, blue=0;
   UCHAR *stringBinding;
   CHAR serverName[MAX_PATH];

   Create( NULL, "RPC Mandel Example",
      WS_OVERLAPPEDWINDOW,
      CRect(0,0,150,150), NULL, "MainMenu" );
   // Set up a set of colors
   for (x=0; x<64; x++)
   {
      colors[x] = RGB(red, green, blue);
      if (!(red += 64))
         if (!(green += 64))
      blue += 64;
   }
   colors[63] = RGB(255,255,255);

   if (strlen(manApp.m_lpCmdLine))
      strcpy(serverName, manApp.m_lpCmdLine);
   else
      strcpy(serverName, "\\\\.");

   RpcStringBindingCompose(NULL,
      (UCHAR *) "ncacn_np", (UCHAR *) serverName,
      (UCHAR *) "\\pipe\\ccrpc", NULL,
      &stringBinding);

   RpcBindingFromStringBinding(stringBinding,
      &calcclrHandle);

   RpcStringFree(&stringBinding);
```

Listing 8.22
The RPC client (mandelc.cpp). Note that the binding occurs once in the window's constructor and is released in **OnExit** (Page 6 of 7)

```
        initialized=FALSE;
    }

    // Initialize the CManApp m_pMainWnd data member
    BOOL CManApp::InitInstance()
    {
        m_pMainWnd = new CManWindow();
        m_pMainWnd -> ShowWindow( m_nCmdShow );
        m_pMainWnd -> UpdateWindow();

        return TRUE;
    }
```

Listing 8.22
The RPC client (mandelc.cpp). Note that the binding occurs once in the window's constructor and is released in **OnExit** (Page 7 of 7)

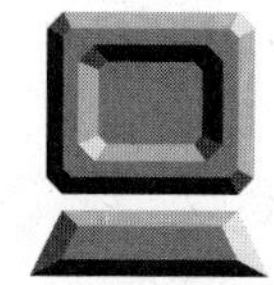

```
void __RPC_FAR * __RPC_API
    midl_user_allocate(size_t len)
{
    return(new(unsigned char [len]));
}

void __RPC_API midl_user_free(void __RPC_FAR * ptr)
{
    delete(ptr);
}
```

Listing 8.23
The stub file (memstub)

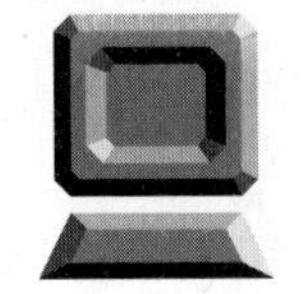

```
NODEBUG=1
SERVER=mandels
RPCFILE=ccrpc

!include <ntwin32.mak>

.SUFFIXES: .cpp

.c.obj:
   $(cc) -J $(cflags) $(cvars) $(cdebug) $<

.cpp.obj:
   $(cc) -J $(cflags) $(cvars) $(cdebug) $<

all: $(SERVER).exe

$(SERVER).exe: $(SERVER).obj $(RPCFILE).obj \
$(RPCFILE)_s.obj
   $(link) $(conlflags) $(ldebug) $(conlibs) \
   rpcrt4.lib \
     rpcns4.lib -out:$(SERVER).exe \
     $(SERVER).obj $(RPCFILE).obj \
     $(RPCFILE)_s.obj


$(SERVER).obj: $(SERVER).cpp $(RPCFILE).h

$(RPCFILE).obj: $(RPCFILE).cpp $(RPCFILE).h
```

Listing 8.24
The makefile (Page 1 of 2)

```
$(RPCFILE)_c.obj: $(RPCFILE)_c.c $(RPCFILE).h
$(RPCFILE)_s.obj: $(RPCFILE)_s.c $(RPCFILE).h

$(RPCFILE).h $(RPCFILE)_c.c \
$(RPCFILE)_s.c: $(RPCFILE).idl \
$(RPCFILE).acf
   midl $(RPCFILE).idl
```

Listing 8.24
The makefile (Page 2 of 2)

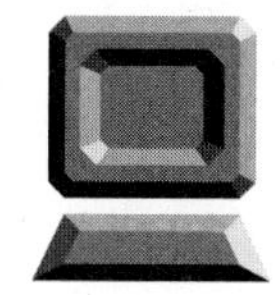

```
// mandelc.rc

#include <afxres.h>

#include "menus.h"

MainMenu MENU
{
   POPUP "&File"
   {
      MENUITEM "&Start/Stop", IDM_STARTSTOP
      MENUITEM "E&xit", IDM_EXIT
   }
}
```

Listing 8.25
The RC file for the menus (mandelc.rc)

```
// menus.h

#define IDM_STARTSTOP      1001
#define IDM_EXIT           1002
```

Listing 8.26
The menu constants (menus.h)

Listings 8.18 through 8.24 have been ordered so that they exactly correspond to Listings 8.1 through 8.7 and 8.8 through 8.14. The Mandelbrot program uses manual binding for efficiency, as duplicated below from Listing 8.22:

```
// CManWindow constructor
CManWindow::CManWindow()
{
   WORD x;
   BYTE red=0, green=0, blue=0;
   UCHAR *stringBinding;
   CHAR serverName[MAX_PATH];

   Create( NULL, "RPC Mandel Example",
      WS_OVERLAPPEDWINDOW,
      CRect(0,0,150,150), NULL, "MainMenu" );
   // Set up a set of colors
   for (x=0; x<64; x++)
   {
      colors[x] = RGB(red, green, blue);
      if (!(red += 64))
         if (!(green += 64))
      blue += 64;
   }
   colors[63] = RGB(255,255,255);
```

```
    if (strlen(manApp.m_lpCmdLine))
        strcpy(serverName, manApp.m_lpCmdLine);
    else
        strcpy(serverName, "\\\\.");

    RpcStringBindingCompose(NULL,
        (UCHAR *) "ncacn_np", (UCHAR *) serverName,
        (UCHAR *) "\\pipe\\ccrpc", NULL,
        &stringBinding);

    RpcBindingFromStringBinding(stringBinding,
        &calcclrHandle);

    RpcStringFree(&stringBinding);

    initialized=FALSE;
}
```

Note that the machine name for the RPC server comes from the command line. As an experiment you might want to change this code and the RPC server code over to automatic binding and see how badly performance degrades on your network.

Note how the manual binding code occurs once, unobtrusively, in the main window's constructor. The binding is released in the **OnExit** function. Beyond that, the code is almost identical to the code seen earlier. In the **MandelThread** function in Listing 8.22 you can see the call to the RPC server, duplicated below:

```
            RpcTryExcept
            {
                iter=CalcColor(k);
            }
            RpcExcept(1)
            {
                MessageBox(NULL,
                    "Unable to call CalcColor( ).\n\
Click OK and then Exit.",
```

```
                "ERROR", MB_SETFOREGROUND |
                    MB_OK | MB_ICONSTOP);
            ExitThread(1);
        }
        RpcEndExcept;
```

This code uses RPC exceptions to detect errors in the RPC call (see Chapter 15 for more information on Windows' exception handling mechanisms). Because the binding occurs early in the program and the computations take a long time (on the order of several minutes), there really is no guarantee that the RPC server and network will remain stable throughout the program's execution. If a problem arises, the RPC runtime library will raise an exception during the call to the RPC server. In the code shown here, the exception generates a message box to tell the user about the problem, and the thread terminates.

To run this RPC client and server at your own site, take the following steps:

1. Compile the client and server initially on a single machine to make sure everything is working. You should simply have to type "nmake" to get everything set up.
2. Run the server in one window by typing:

   `mandels`
3. Run the client in another window by typing:

   `mandelc`

   If you look in the window's constructor function in Listing 8.22, you will find that the RPC client program looks to the local machine for the RPC server if no command line parameters are given.
4. Now compile and run the server on a different machine on the network.
5. Run the client by typing:

   `mandelc machinename`

   Where machinename is the name of the machine running the server.

The mandelc program will run significantly slower than the version presented in Chapter 5. As noted in Section 8.3, this occurs because of poor use of RPC functions here. The overhead of the RPC call is not justified by the savings garnered by a single pixel calculation. This problem is remedied in the following section.

8.11 Improving the Mandelbrot RPC Server

As discussed in Section 8.3, the key to an efficient RPC client/server arrangement is to make sure that the overhead inherent in an RPC call is appropriately balanced by the amount of time saved by making the call. The arrangement for the Mandelbrot program shown in Section 8.10 is not really appropriate because one RPC call is made for each pixel in the image. The overhead penalty incurred by these thousands of RPC calls has a devastating effect on the program's overall performance.

To solve this problem and make RPCs useful in the Mandelbrot program, you must somehow create batches of pixels that are calculated in a single function call to the RPC server. The batches need to be broken up so that the returned pixel values form a reasonably sized network packet, but at the same time you want to minimize the number of calls to the RPC server. One extreme was shown in Section 8.10: network packet size is at a minimum and the number of RPC calls is at a maximum. This created a problem due to RPC call overhead.

At the other extreme, you could call the RPC server once for the entire frame, and pass back all of the pixel values at the same time. There are two problems with this approach:

1. On a 1000x1000 image, the two megabyte network packet returned by the call bogs down the network. Actually the system would end up transmitting back about two thousand network packs of about 1K bytes each.
2. There is a long (up to several minutes) lag time between the user's request for the image and its appearance on the screen.

What is desired is some midpoint between these two extremes. An easy solution is to calculate entire lines of pixels in a single RPC call. A line is a good increment to use because the results returned by a call form a nicely sized network packet, and the user is informed of progress in reasonable time increments.

The program shown in Section 8.10 must be modified in several different ways to complete the conversion:

1. The server function `ccrpc.cpp` shown in Listing 8.18 must be modified to handle lines of pixels rather than single pixels. See Listing 8.27.
2. The IDL file shown in Listing 8.20 must be changed to reflect the change in Listing 8.18. See Listing 8.28.

3. The **MandelThread** function in Listing 8.22 needs to change slightly to reflect the change in Listing 8.18 as well. Several other minor naming and declaration changes are also required. See Listing 8.29.

After you make these modifications, you will find that the performance of the Mandelbrot program is only degraded by about one second per 100 scan lines due to RPC call overhead.

```
// ccrpc2.cpp

#include <windows.h>
#include "ccrpc2.h"

#define NUM_ITERATIONS 64

void CalcLine(double left, double right, double y,
   long width, short line[])
{
   complex k, z;
   double x, xstep, real, imag, spread;
   WORD i, iter;

   xstep = (double) (right - left) / width;

   for (x=left, i=0; x<=right; x += xstep, i++)
   {
      k.real = x;
      k.imag = y;
      z.real=z.imag=0.0;

      for (iter=0; iter<NUM_ITERATIONS-1; iter++)
```

Listing 8.27
The new server function ccrpc2.cpp, modified to handle pixels one line of the image at a time. Compare with Listing 8.18 (Page 1 of 2)

```
        {
           real = z.real + k.real;
           imag = z.imag + k.imag;
           z.real = real * real - imag * imag;
           z.imag = 2 * real * imag;
           spread = z.real * z.real + z.imag *
              z.imag;
           if (spread > 4.0)
              break;
        }
        line[i]=iter;
     }
     return;
  }
```

Listing 8.27
The new server function ccrpc2.cpp, modified to handle pixels one line of the image at a time. Compare with Listing 8.18 (Page 2 of 2)

```
[
  uuid (87654329-4321-1234-4321-987654321CBA),
  version(1.0),
  endpoint ("ncacn_np:[\\pipe\\ccrpc2]")
]
interface calcline
{
  typedef struct
  {
    double real;
    double imag;
```

Listing 8.28
The new IDL file, reflecting the changes seen in Listing 8.27. Compare with Listing 8.20 (Page 1 of 2)

```
    } complex;

    void CalcLine([in] double left,
     [in] double right,
     [in] double y, [in] long width,
     [out, size_is(width)] short line[]);
}
```

Listing 8.28
The new IDL file, reflecting the changes seen in Listing 8.27. Compare with Listing 8.20 (Page 2 of 2)

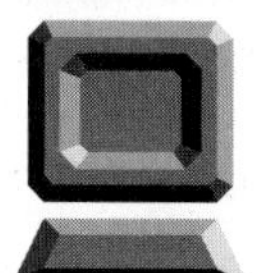

```
// mandelc2.cpp

#include <afxwin.h>
#include <rpc.h>
#include "ccrpc2.h"
#include "menus.h"

const double left = -1.0;
const double right = 1.0;
const double top = -1.0;
const double bottom = 1.0;

DWORD colors[64];

typedef struct
{
   WORD height;
   WORD width;
```

Listing 8.29
The new client program. All important changes appear in the **MandelThread** function. Compare with Listing 8.22 (Page 1 of 7)

```
} mandelParams;

// Define the application object class
class CManApp : public CWinApp
{
public:
   virtual BOOL InitInstance();
};

// Define the edit window class
class CManWindow : public CFrameWnd
{
private:
   HANDLE threadHandle;
   BOOL running;
   BOOL initialized;
   mandelParams params;
public:
   CManWindow();
   void RunMandel();
   void SetPix(int x, int y, WORD iter);
   afx_msg void OnPaint();
   afx_msg void OnStartStop();
   afx_msg void OnExit();
   DECLARE_MESSAGE_MAP()
};

// Create an instance of the application object
CManApp manApp;

// member function used to set pixel colors
// in the window
void CManWindow::SetPix(int x, int y, WORD iter)
{
   CClientDC dc(this);
```

Listing 8.29
The new client program. All important changes appear in the **MandelThread** function. Compare with Listing 8.22 (Page 2 of 7)

```
        dc.SetPixel(x, y, colors[iter]);
    }

    // the thread function which does the drawing
    DWORD MandelThread(mandelParams *params)
    {
        double ystep;
        double y;
        int i,j;
        short line[150];

        ystep = (double) (bottom - top) /
            params->height;

        for (y=top, j=0; y <= bottom; y += ystep, j++)
        {
            RpcTryExcept
            {
                CalcLine(left, right, y,
                    params->width, line);
            }
            RpcExcept(1)
            {
                MessageBox(NULL,
                    "Unable to call CalcLine( ).\n\
    Click OK and then Exit.",
                    "ERROR", MB_SETFOREGROUND |
                    MB_OK | MB_ICONSTOP);
                ExitThread(1);
            }
            RpcEndExcept;

            for (i=0; i<params->width; i++)
                ((CManWindow *)manApp.m_pMainWnd)->
                    SetPix(i, j, line[i]);
```

Listing 8.29
The new client program. All important changes appear in the **MandelThread** function. Compare with Listing 8.22 (Page 3 of 7)

```
    }
    return(0);
}

// member function used to instigate
// the drawing thread
void CManWindow::RunMandel()
{
    DWORD threadID;
    CRect r;

    GetClientRect(&r);
    params.height=r.Height();
    params.width=r.Width();

    threadHandle=CreateThread(NULL, 0,
        (LPTHREAD_START_ROUTINE) MandelThread,
        &params, 0, &threadID);

    running=TRUE;
}

// The message map
BEGIN_MESSAGE_MAP(CManWindow, CFrameWnd)
    ON_WM_PAINT()
    ON_COMMAND(IDM_STARTSTOP, OnStartStop)
    ON_COMMAND(IDM_EXIT, OnExit)
END_MESSAGE_MAP()

// Handler for the Start/Stop menu option
void CManWindow::OnStartStop()
{
    if(running)
        SuspendThread(threadHandle);
    else
```

Listing 8.29
The new client program. All important changes appear in the **MandelThread** function. Compare with Listing 8.22 (Page 4 of 7)

```
        ResumeThread(threadHandle);

    running=!running;
}

// Handler for WM_PAINT messages
void CManWindow::OnPaint()
{
    ValidateRect(NULL);
    if (!initialized)
    {
        initialized=TRUE;
        RunMandel();
    }
    else
    if (running)
    {
        // stop the existing thread
        TerminateThread(threadHandle, 0);
        CloseHandle(threadHandle);
        // clear the window
        CClientDC dc(this);
        CRect r;
        GetClientRect(&r);
        dc.PatBlt(0, 0, r.Width(), r.Height(),
            WHITENESS);
        // start over again
        RunMandel();
    }
}

// Handler for the Exit menu option
void CManWindow::OnExit()
{
    SuspendThread(threadHandle);
```

Listing 8.29
The new client program. All important changes appear in the **MandelThread** function. Compare with Listing 8.22 (Page 5 of 7)

```
      CloseHandle(threadHandle);
      RpcBindingFree(&calclineHandle);
      DestroyWindow();
   }

   // CManWindow constructor
   CManWindow::CManWindow()
   {
      WORD x;
      BYTE red=0, green=0, blue=0;
      UCHAR *stringBinding;
      CHAR serverName[MAX_PATH];

      Create( NULL, "RPC Mandel Example 2",
         WS_OVERLAPPED,
         CRect(0,0,150,150), NULL, "MainMenu" );
      for (x=0; x<64; x++)
      {
         colors[x] = RGB(red, green, blue);
         if (!(red += 64))
            if (!(green += 64))
               blue += 64;
      }
      colors[63] = RGB(255,255,255);

      if (strlen(manApp.m_lpCmdLine))
         strcpy(serverName, manApp.m_lpCmdLine);
      else
         strcpy(serverName, "\\\\.");

      RpcStringBindingCompose(NULL,
         (UCHAR *) "ncacn_np", (UCHAR *) serverName,
         (UCHAR *) "\\pipe\\ccrpc2", NULL,
            &stringBinding);
```

Listing 8.29
The new client program. All important changes appear in the **MandelThread** function. Compare with Listing 8.22 (Page 6 of 7)

```
        RpcBindingFromStringBinding(stringBinding,
           &calclineHandle);

        RpcStringFree(&stringBinding);

        initialized=FALSE;
    }

    // Initialize the CManApp m_pMainWnd data member
    BOOL CManApp::InitInstance()
    {
        m_pMainWnd = new CManWindow();
        m_pMainWnd -> ShowWindow( m_nCmdShow );
        m_pMainWnd -> UpdateWindow();

        return TRUE;
    }
```

Listing 8.29
The new client program. All important changes appear in the **MandelThread** function. Compare with Listing 8.22 (Page 7 of 7)

You can see in the IDL file shown in Listing 8.28 that the RPC server now accepts the x,y coordinate of the start of a line of pixels, the x coordinate of the end of the line of pixels, and the number of pixels in the line, and then returns an array that contains all of the desired pixels.

It is very interesting to compare the performance of the single-line version with the single-pixel version in a quantitative way. You can do this with a stop watch, but you can also use the Performance Meter found in the Administrative Tools group of the Program Manager. On the server machine, get out the Performance Meter and look at the Processor Time item in the Processor object, the Packets/sec item in the NetBEUI object, and the Frame Bytes/sec item in the NetBEUI object. Run both servers (single pixel and single line) independently using a client on a different machine. When you run the single-pixel version, you can see that the number of bytes per packet (divide frame bytes/sec by packets/sec), hovers right at 100 bytes or so per packet. Most of that 100 bytes is wasted packet overhead, because the code sends at most 16 bytes per packet. You will also notice that the total frame bytes/sec remains fairly low because of all of the network processing overhead involved with sending a packet.

You will see a very different picture when you run the second implementation using scan lines. The packet overhead bytes remain constant no matter how big a packet is, so their percentage declines. The number of packets per second declines noticeably as well. The network is working much more efficiently in the second case.

8.12 Explicit Handles

The previous examples have used either *auto-binding* or *implicit manual binding* to bind the RPC client to the RPC server. In auto-binding, the MIDL compiler generates code that lets the client bind to the server automatically. In implicit manual binding, the client code creates the binding to the server, but stores the binding handle in a variable that the MIDL compiler generated using the ACF file. Once the initialization of the binding handle is complete, the client can call RPC functions implicitly.

Auto-binding is the easiest to implement. The client code looks exactly like normal code. However, auto-binding is slow if the client needs to make a large number of function calls to the RPC server. The client binds to the server and releases for each function call it makes. Implicit manual binding is more efficient, but it requires slightly more work in the client code to manually bind to the server and then release.

In *explicit manual binding*, the RPC client goes one step further. Now in each function call, the client code specifies explicitly which server it wants to talk to. You use explicit handles when you want to open the same RPC server on several different machines and call all of them simultaneously. For example, a Mandelbrot RPC client program might open the same Mandelbrot RPC server on four different machines, and then multi-thread itself (See Chapter 5) so that it can call all four servers simultaneously. In this situation, each of the four threads must explicitly state which server they want to talk to when they make RPC calls.

Listings 8.30 through 8.34 show how to modify the **SumUp** RPC server and client demonstrated previously so that they use explicit handles. You will notice the following changes in the code when you compare Listing 8.30 through 8.34 with Listings 8.8 through 8.12:

- In Listing 8.30, the **SumUp** function accepts an explicit handle as its first parameter. Otherwise, the function is unchanged. The parameter is actually used in `sum_c.c` (generated by the MIDL compiler) to determine which server gets called when the client uses the **SumUp** function.
- The server body in Listing 8.31 is unchanged from previous versions.
- The IDL file in Listing 8.32 is similar to previous IDL files, but contains the extra parameter needed by **SumUp**.
- The ACF file is empty and actually unneeded for explicit handles.
- The client code in Listing 8.34 is very similar to the client code for implicit handles seen in Listing 8.12. The main difference is that the client code now declares its own copy of **SumUpHandle** to hold the binding information. It initializes this handle as it binds to the server and then uses it when it calls **SumUp** to direct the call to a specific server.

The explicit handle should *always* appear as the first parameter in any RPC function that uses explicit manual binding.

The client code could bind to the same RPC server running on several different machines by declaring and initializing multiple binding handles like **SumUpHandle**. Then it could call the same function named **SumUp** but direct it at different servers in each call.

```
// sum.cpp

#include <windows.h>
#include "sum.h"

long SumUp(handle_t SumUpHandle,
  short sumVal)
{
  short iter;
```

Listing 8.30
The implementation of the **SumUp** function using explicit handles (sum.cpp) (Page 1 of 2)

```
    long theSum;

    theSum=0;
    for (iter=1; iter<=sumVal; theSum+=iter, iter++);

    Beep(300, 30);

    return(theSum);
  }
```

Listing 8.30
The implementation of the **SumUp** function using explicit handles (sum.cpp) (Page 2 of 2)

```
// explserv.cpp

#include <windows.h>
#include <iostream.h>
#include <rpc.h>
#include "sum.h"
#include "memstub"

INT main(VOID)
{
  // use the protocols specified in the IDL file
  // for this interface
  if (RpcServerUseAllProtseqsIf(1,
    sumup_v1_0_s_ifspec,
    NULL))
  {
    cerr << "ERROR: Could not specify protocols"
```

Listing 8.31
The server body for explicit handles (explserv.cpp) (Page 1 of 2)

```
            << endl;
          return(1);
        }

        // register the interface
        if (RpcServerRegisterIf(sumup_v1_0_s_ifspec,
          NULL, NULL))
        {
          cerr
            << "ERROR: Could not register intf handle"
            << endl;
          return(1);
        }

        // listen for and service RPC requests
        if (RpcServerListen(1, 5, FALSE))
        {
          cerr
            << "ERROR: nable to listen for RPC requests"
            << endl;
          return(1);
        }

        return(0);
      }
```

Listing 8.31
The server body for explicit handles (explserv.cpp) (Page 2 of 2)

```
[
  uuid (22449651-4321-1234-4321-987654321000),
```

Listing 8.32
The IDL file for explicit handles (sum.idl) (Page 1 of 2)

```
    version(1.0),
    endpoint ("ncalrpc:[explrpc]")
]
interface sumup
{
    long SumUp([in] handle_t SumUpHandle,
      [in] short sumVal);
}
```

Listing 8.32
The IDL file for explicit handles (sum.idl) (Page 2 of 2)

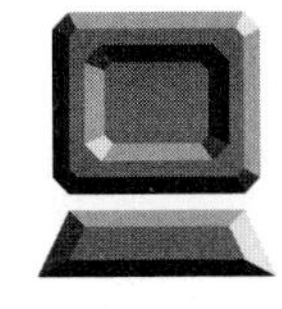

```
interface sumup
{
}
```

Listing 8.33
The ACF file for explicit handles (sum.acf)

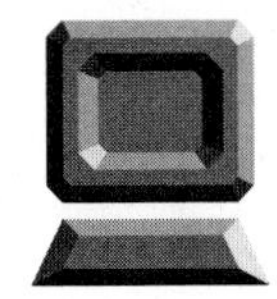

```
// explclnt.cpp

#include <windows.h>
#include <iostream.h>
#include <rpc.h>
#include <stdlib.h>
#include "sum.h"
```

Listing 8.34
A client program that calls **SumUp** using explicit handles (explclnt.cpp) (Page 1 of 3)

```
#include "memstub"

INT main(VOID)
{
  CHAR sumUpToStr[10];
  long theSum;
  UCHAR *stringBinding;
  handle_t SumUpHandle;

  cout << "Enter a value to compute running sum: ";
  cin.getline(sumUpToStr, 10);

  // put together string binding
  if (RpcStringBindingCompose(NULL,
    (UCHAR *) "ncalrpc", NULL,
    NULL, NULL, &stringBinding))
  {
    cerr
      << "ERROR: Unable to compose string binding"
      << endl;
    return(1);
  }

  // bind to server using string binding info
  if (RpcBindingFromStringBinding(stringBinding,
    &SumUpHandle))
  {
    cerr << "ERROR: Unable to bind" << endl;
    return(1);
  }

  // free the string binding info
  if (RpcStringFree(&stringBinding))
  {
    cerr << "ERROR: Unable to free string binding"
      << endl;
```

Listing 8.34
A client program that calls **SumUp** using explicit handles (explclnt.cpp) (Page 2 of 3)

```
        return(1);
    }

    theSum=SumUp(SumUpHandle,
        (short)atoi(sumUpToStr));

    cout << "The running sum is: " << theSum << endl;

    // release binding to server
    if (RpcBindingFree(&SumUpHandle))
    {
        cerr << "ERROR: Unable to free binding"
            << endl;
        return(1);
    }

    return(0);
}
```

Listing 8.34
A client program that calls **SumUp** using explicit handles (explclnt.cpp) (Page 3 of 3)

The makefile and memstub files for this code are identical to those seen in Listings 8.13 and 8.14.

8.13 Context Handles

There are many situations where you would like to maintain context information in the RPC server's memory space and then be able to refer to that context from call to call. For example, you might want to build and maintain a linked list on the RPC server using many different calls to the RPC server. If you want all clients to be able to access a single linked list, then you can declare global variables in the server and use appropriate synchronization mechanisms (Chapter 6) so that clients don't collide. However, if you want each client to be able to create and refer to its own linked list, then each client needs its own context on the RPC server.

As another example, say that you would like clients to be able to open a file on the server, and then read that file line-by-line using RPC calls. The client needs to be able to open a file handle and refer to that handle from call to call.

RPCs allow you to preserve context information in individual clients by using *context handles*. Context handles are an extension of explicit handles. They contain an explicit handle, but they also allow the RPC server and client to pass one 32-bit value back and forth to each other. This value is normally a pointer to a structure. The pointer points to memory *in the server's address space* and is therefore valid only when used by the RPC server.

Listings 8.35 through 8.39 contain a very simple example that uses context handles. In this code, the context handle points to a structure that contains an integer. Each call to the RPC server adds a value to the integer. Because it uses context handles, multiple clients can maintain their own running sums independently of one another.

If you look at the client code in Listing 8.39 and the server implementation of the **SumUp** and supporting functions in Listing 8.35, you can get a good idea of how context handles work. Here is a summary of the interaction between client and server in the example program:

1. The client program in Listing 8.39 binds to the RPC server.
2. The client program calls **InitSum**. This function's implementation appears in Listing 8.35. Two things happen during this call. The first is made obvious in Listing 8.35: the server allocates memory for a structure. The pointer to this structure is returned in the context handle. The second occurs behind-the-scenes: the implicit handle **SumUpHandle** is copied into the context handle in code generated by the MIDL compiler. The context handle therefore becomes an explicit handle to a specific server. This occurs because the context handle contains a pointer that applies to the address space of a specific RPC server on the network.
3. The client program in Listing 8.39 now calls **SumUp** repeatedly, passing it the context handle. In Listing 8.35, the implementation of **SumUp** uses the pointer in the context handle to refer to the block of memory allocated to its particular client. The Server adds a value to the integer in the structure pointed to by the context handle.
4. When the client is done, it calls **UnInitSum**, which frees the context structure in the server's memory space.

The structure that appears in the server can be as big as you like. It can contain integers, file handles, pointers to other blocks of memory allocated in the server, and so on.

Note that the server implementation in Listing 8.35 contains an extra function named **SumUpContext_rundown**. This function does not appear in the IDL file. Instead, it is used by the server if contact is lost with a client. It allows the server to clean up the client's memory allocations. There will be one rundown function for each structure declared in the IDL file, and these functions are named by taking each structure name and appending "_rundown" to it.

The IDL file in Listing 8.37 contains the three functions used in the client, along with a declaration for the context structure.

```
[
  uuid (22449651-4321-1234-4321-987654321010),
  version(1.0),
  endpoint ("ncalrpc:[ctxtrpc]")
]
interface sumup
{
  typedef [context_handle] void *SumUpContext;

  void InitSum([out, ref]
    SumUpContext *contextHandle);

  long SumUp([in] SumUpContext contextHandle,
    [in] short sumVal);

  void UnInitSum([in, out, ref]
    SumUpContext *contextHandle);
}
```

The context handle is declared in the IDL file as a **void** pointer marked as a context handle using the `[context_handle]` key word. The IDL file does not care about what the pointer points to: it cares only about the name and the fact that it is a context handle. The IDL file specifies that the **InitSum** function returns the pointer by marking it as `[out,ref]`. The **out** key word means that the function returns the pointer value, and the **ref** key word means "pass by reference." Only the pointer's value gets returned. When the RPC client calls **InitSum**, it passes in the address of a pointer (the **SumUpContext** type is a pointer), and the value returned by the RPC server fills this pointer. Each time the client program calls the **SumUp** function, it passes this pointer back in to the server. The server can use this pointer to refer to the structure for that client allocated in the server's memory space. The **UnInitSum** function accepts the pointer so that it can free the memory block, and also returns it so it can set it to NULL in the client.

Note that the implementation of **InitSum** and **UnInitSum** in Listing 8.35 use **midl_user_allocate** and **midl_user_free**. These functions come from the memory stub file seen in Listing 8.6.

An RPC server can have multiple context structures in a single IDL file, and each one should have its own rundown function.

```
// sum.cpp

#include <windows.h>
#include "sum.h"

typedef struct
{
  long currentSum;
} sumContext;

// function to initialize sum context
void InitSum(SumUpContext *contextHandle)
{
  sumContext *tmpSum;
```

Listing 8.35
The implementation of the **SumUp** function using context handles (sum.cpp) (Page 1 of 3)

```
  tmpSum=(sumContext *)
    midl_user_allocate(sizeof(sumContext));

  tmpSum->currentSum=0;

  *contextHandle=(SumUpContext)tmpSum;
}

long SumUp(SumUpContext contextHandle,
  short sumVal)
{
  short iter;
  long theSum;

  theSum=((sumContext *)contextHandle)->currentSum;

  for (iter=1; iter<=sumVal; theSum+=iter, iter++);

  ((sumContext *)contextHandle)->currentSum=theSum;

  Beep(300, 30);

  return(theSum);
}

// function to uninitialize sum context
void UnInitSum(SumUpContext *contextHandle)
{
  midl_user_free(*contextHandle);

  *contextHandle=NULL;
}

// function which gets called if client
```

Listing 8.35
The implementation of the **SumUp** function using context handles (sum.cpp)
(Page 2 of 3)

```
// looses contact with server
void __RPC_USER SumUpContext_rundown
  (SumUpContext contextHandle)
{
  midl_user_free(contextHandle);
}
```

Listing 8.35
The implementation of the **SumUp** function using context handles (sum.cpp) (Page 3 of 3)

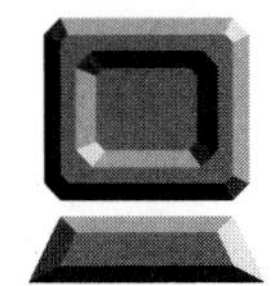

```
// ctxtserv.cpp

#include <windows.h>
#include <iostream.h>
#include <rpc.h>
#include "sum.h"
#include "memstub"

INT main(VOID)
{
  // use the protocols specified in the IDL file
  // for this interface
  if (RpcServerUseAllProtseqsIf(1,
    sumup_v1_0_s_ifspec,
    NULL))
  {
    cerr << "ERROR: Could not specify protocols"
      << endl;
    return(1);
  }
```

Listing 8.36
The server body for context handles (ctxtserv.cpp) (Page 1 of 2)

```
    // register the interface
    if (RpcServerRegisterIf(sumup_v1_0_s_ifspec,
      NULL, NULL))
    {
      cerr
        << "ERROR: Could not register intf handle"
        << endl;
      return(1);
    }

    // listen for and service RPC requests
    if (RpcServerListen(1, 5, FALSE))
    {
      cerr
        << "ERROR: Unable to listen for RPC requests"
        << endl;
      return(1);
    }

    return(0);
  }
```

Listing 8.36
The server body for context handles (ctxtserv.cpp) (Page 2 of 2)

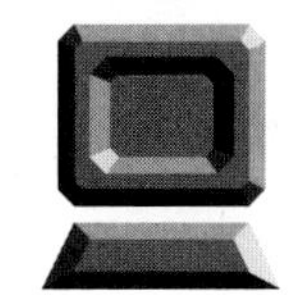

```
  [
    uuid (22449651-4321-1234-4321-987654321010),
    version(1.0),
    endpoint ("ncalrpc:[ctxtrpc]")
  ]
```

Listing 8.37
The IDL file for context handles (sum.idl) (Page 1 of 2)

```
interface sumup
{
  typedef [context_handle] void *SumUpContext;

  void InitSum([out, ref]
    SumUpContext *contextHandle);

  long SumUp([in] SumUpContext contextHandle,
    [in] short sumVal);

  void UnInitSum([in, out, ref]
    SumUpContext *contextHandle);
}
```

Listing 8.37
The IDL file for context handles (sum.idl) (Page 2 of 2)

```
[
  implicit_handle(handle_t SumUpHandle)
]
interface sumup
{
}
```

Listing 8.38
The ACF file for context handles (sum.acf)

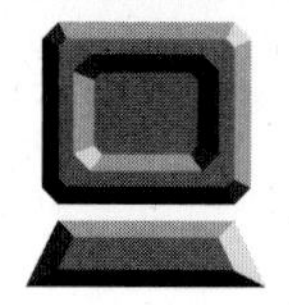

```
// ctxtclnt.cpp

#include <windows.h>
#include <iostream.h>
#include <rpc.h>
#include <stdlib.h>
#include "sum.h"
#include "memstub"

INT main(VOID)
{
  long theSum;
  UCHAR *stringBinding;
  SumUpContext sumupContext;

  // put together string binding
  if (RpcStringBindingCompose(NULL,
    (UCHAR *) "ncalrpc", NULL,
    NULL, NULL, &stringBinding))
  {
    cerr
      << "ERROR: Unable to compose string binding"
      << endl;
    return(1);
  }

  // bind to server using string binding info
  if (RpcBindingFromStringBinding(stringBinding,
    &SumUpHandle))
```

Listing 8.39
A client program that calls **SumUp** using context handles (ctxtclnt.cpp) (Page 1 of 3)

```
    {
      cerr << "ERROR: Unable to bind" << endl;
      return(1);
    }

    // free the string binding info
    if (RpcStringFree(&stringBinding))
    {
      cerr << "ERROR: Unable to free string binding"
        << endl;
      return(1);
    }

    // establish sum context
    InitSum(&sumupContext);

    // release initial binding to server
    if (RpcBindingFree(&SumUpHandle))
    {
      cerr << "ERROR: Unable to free binding"
        << endl;
      return(1);
    }

    do
    {
      theSum=SumUp(sumupContext, 5);

      cout << "The running sum is: "
        << theSum << endl;

      Sleep(1000);
    } while (theSum < 150);

    // release sum context
```

Listing 8.39
A client program that calls **SumUp** using context handles (ctxtclnt.cpp) (Page 2 of 3)

```
    UnInitSum(&sumupContext);

    return(0);
}
```

Listing 8.39
A client program that calls **SumUp** using context handles (ctxtclnt.cpp) (Page 3 of 3)

The makefile and memstub files for this code are identical to those seen in Listings 8.13 and 8.14.

8.14 Common Questions

This chapter only scratches the surface of RPCs—you could easily write an entire book on the subject. The RPC help file that comes with the SDK is useful as a reference, as are the MIDL and Win32 API on-line help files. Here are some questions commonly asked about RPCs, along with answers that will help you to find the material you need in the available documentation.

Can an RPC server handle more than one RPC client at a time?
Yes. An RPC server can accept multiple function calls from multiple clients simultaneously. The number of concurrent clients that an RPC server can accept is controlled by the **RpcServerUseAllProtseqsIf** and **RpcServerListen** functions.

Can an RPC server contain global variables?
Yes. Declare them as `extern` in the server functions (e.g., Listing 8.1), and then declare their instances in the server itself (e.g., Listing 8.2). See question 3 also. Since multiple server functions can execute simultaneously, you need to guard global variables with appropriate synchronization calls. See Chapter 6.

What if I want to implement an operation that needs to retain information across calls to the RPC server? For example, I want to open a file on the server and then read from it with multiple calls, so I need the server's file handle. How do I implement that?
Global variables are a bad solution to this problem because of the number of potential clients and the problem with identifying clients. Instead you should use a manually bound *context* handle instead, which can

return context information like a file handle in the binding handle. See Section 8.13 above for more information and an example.

Is there a way for a manual handle to retrieve information from the name server so that the client program does not need to know where the server is?
Yes. Use **RpcNsBindingImportBegin**, **RpcNsBindingImportNext**, and **RpcNsBindingImportDone** to enumerate servers in the name server.

What is the optimal size for a network packet sent to or returned from an RPC server?
1K bytes is a good, optimal packet size to aim for. Ethernet will not accept packets larger than about 1,500 bytes, so if you go above that limit multiple packets will be generated anyway.

The exception handling code seen in Section 8.10 seems fairly generic. Is it possible to get more detailed exception information.
Yes. The **RpcExceptionCode** function works somewhat like **GetLastError** to identify the specific cause of the exception.

Walking over to the server machine and manually starting an RPC server from the command line seems fairly primitive. How do I make an RPC server available all of the time, starting when the machine boots?
Place the RPC server in a service. See Chapter 9.

Do I have to do anything special to shut down an RPC server?
The code shown in these examples does nothing explicit to shut down the server, but to close a server cleanly you should call **RpcMgmtStopServerListening** and **RpcServerUnregisterIf**, as shown below:

```
void ShutdownServer(void)
{
    RPC_STATUS stat;
    status = RpcMgmtStopServerListening(0);
    status = RpcServerUnregisterIf(0, 0, FALSE);
}
```

You can add this function to the available functions for the RPC server and let an RPC client call it to terminate the server, or you can place it in the Stop code for the RPC server's service. The latter is preferred. See the previous question.

What do I need to give to a programmer who wants to create a client program to access one of my servers?
You need to give the programmer a copy of the IDL and ACF files, along with documentation on the RPC server's available functions. The programmer should be able to create the client with just that information.

Presumably a network will have all sorts of RPC servers running all of the time. How do I find out what all of them do?
Word of mouth, or published details on servers at your site, are the only way to truly know about RPC servers that are available on your network. You can enumerate all of the RPC servers registered with the name server (see the question regarding a manual handle retrieving information from the name server) and then try to hunt down their owners, but there is no way to know what the servers do or how to call them without some sort of documentation.

We keep running into name conflicts on endpoints. Two people will pick the same endpoint name or port number and it makes a mess. Is there a way around this problem?
Yes, using *dynamic endpoints* and *partially bound handles.* If you leave endpoint names out of the IDL file and use **RpcServerUseAllProtseqs** instead of **RpcServerUseAllProtseqsIf** in the RPC server, and if you are using a name server, then the name server and RPC server will pick endpoint names dynamically and eliminate these conflicts.

Can an RPC server handle requests from both Windows and UNIX machines simultaneously?
Yes. Register multiple protocols in the IDL file to handle both. Also, since UNIX machines cannot interrogate NT locators, but NT machines *can* interrogate a UNIX cell directory service, you will have to use the cell directory service running on a UNIX machine as the name server. See section 8.8.

Is there a way to prevent someone from accessing a RPC server?
Yes. When you specify the protocol sequences for the server (e.g.—**RpcServerUseAllProtseqsIf**), you can pass a security descriptor. See Chapter 10 for details on security descriptors.

I want to run the same RPC server on 10 different machines on the network, and then create a program that splits itself into 10 threads and talks to all ten servers at once. Is this possible?

Yes. The client will need to manually bind to all ten machines. You will also have to use *explicit handles*, so that when the client calls the remote function it can pass one of the 10 binding handles and in that way specify which of the ten machines it wants to use. See Section 8.12 for an example.

8.15 Conclusion

RPCs are an easy and very effective way to create client/server applications that work on heterogeneous networks. Almost all of the details of the network interactions are hidden from view. When using automatic binding, client program's that use RPCs look no different from normal programs except for the addition of sever include files.

If you want to create RPC servers that run all the time, starting when the machine boots, then you need to look at NT services. They are described in detail in Chapter 9.

If you want to learn more about the network to get a better understanding of network protocols and endpoints, see Chapter 7.

To learn more about threads and the Mandelbrot program discussed in this chapter, see Chapter 5.

SERVICES

9

Any operating system needs a way to start up processes when the system boots, and then leave them running while the system is on-line. For example, The Messenger service that comes with Windows NT monitors the network continuously and displays a dialog box whenever it receives a message. An application that receives faxes needs to start up at boot time and then continuously monitor the fax modem for fax machines dialing in. A home or office security system needs to continuously monitor sensors and respond to them, regardless of who is currently using the machine.

In UNIX, this functionality is handled by Daemons. Daemons are loaded as the system boots and receive CPU time as background tasks. Typical UNIX daemons handle mail coming in over the network, cron jobs (similar to jobs scheduled with the `at` command in NT), `finger` requests, and so on. In DOS, background processing is handled by TSR (Terminate and Stay Resident) programs that are invoked through the `autoexec.bat` file. In Windows 3.1, the Startup group of the Program Manager can start background processes. Windows 3.1 automatically invokes this group as soon as it starts up, unlike Windows NT, which invokes it only when someone logs in. If you have a FAX board in a normal Windows 3.1 computer, you can place the FAX program's icon in the Startup group and the fax board can start receiving faxes as soon as Windows starts.

In NT, you need a way to create processes that automatically start as the system boots, and then remain running as background processes no matter who is currently logged in. This functionality is handled by *services*. In this chapter you will learn how to create, install, and control your own services.

Compatibility Note: All of the code in this chapter works in Windows NT, while none of it works in Windows 95.

9.1 The Possibilities

The Service mechanism in Windows NT provides an extremely elegant way to create background tasks for NT machines. NT itself uses services in quite a few ways. At least fifteen services are available after you install the base system, and add-on modules like the Remote Access Server and the FTP server add new services of their own.

Probably the simplest existing service provided by NT is the Messenger service. When it starts, it creates a mailslot and monitors it. When it sees a message in the mailslot's queue, it retrieves it and displays a message box containing the message on the screen.The Schedule service is slightly more advanced. When someone types the `at` command, the requested task is stored in a task list. The Schedule service periodically looks at the list and decides if there are pending jobs that it needs to execute. If it finds one, it executes it, and potentially updates the task list.

The FTP server offers a good example of an advanced service. The service automatically starts when NT boots (you can also change its behavior so that it manually starts instead). It monitors the network, and when it sees another machine trying to make an FTP connection it accepts the connection and validates the user's login ID. Then it accepts commands from the remote user to get and put files. All of these operations occur in the background.

The FTP server also places an icon in the Control Panel during installation. A service control process like this one is able to send a signal to the service to tell it to update its current status (see Section 9.5 for an example of how to send a signal to a service). The control process can also use named pipes or other inter-process communication techniques (see Chapter 5) to communicate with the service in a pre-arranged way.

There are many good reasons for you to create your own services. For example:

- If you have an NT machine attached to and controlling a piece of manufacturing equipment on the factory floor, you may want the controller software to run all of the time. By implementing the software as a service, you can cause it to start as soon as the machine boots, and it will run no matter who is logged in to the machine. You can set thread priorities (see Section 5.7) on the service's threads so that the service can appropriately respond to high-priority events coming back from the equipment it monitors and controls.

- If you want to create a bulletin board system that runs all of the time, you can implement it as a service. When the machine boots the BBS will start and begin monitoring the appropriate communications port(s) for incoming calls. When it receives a call, it can process the user's requests without interrupting the person currently logged onto the machine. See Chapter 12 for information on communication ports.
- If you want an RPC server (Chapter 8) to be available all of the time, you can place it inside a service so that it starts when the machine boots. See Section 9.11.
- If you want to create an inventory system that periodically polls a number of separate stores to download their inventory status, you can implement the in-store portion of the system using services. The service in each store runs in the background waiting for a connection request. The central machine at the warehouse can call to each store, and the service there will respond appropriately regardless or who, or whether, anyone is logged in.

Any task that you want to run continuously and in the background, regardless of who is logged in, should be handled using a service.

9.2 Understanding Services

You can learn a great deal about the fundamentals of services simply by working with the Services applet in the Control Panel. If you start up the Control Panel and open the Services applet on your machine now, you will find a number of standard services that come with NT. For example, the Alerter, Clipbook Server, Computer Browser, and Directory Replicator services are all preinstalled when you load NT onto your system. You may also find services that have been loaded by your administrator to handle special tasks, or that came with different applications to handle background processing for them.

Any new service that you create needs to be installed in this applet's list of services. Installation creates an entry for the service in the Registry (specifically in HKEY_LOCAL_MACHINE\System\CurrentControlSet\ Services), so that the machine knows about it each time it boots. NT provides an installation function that handles the creation of this entry automatically.

Every service must be able to respond to a set of standard events that the Services applet can pass to it. These events are represented in the applet as buttons:

- Start: Starts the service if it is of the manual start variety, if the user stopped it, or if it failed to start at boot time
- Stop: Stops the service
- Pause: Suspends the service temporarily
- Continue: Restarts a suspended service

Using the Services applet, the administrator can select how a given service will start up each time the machine boots. The service can start automatically, it can start manually, or the administrator can mark it as disabled. If a service is disabled, then no one but the administrator or a power user can manipulate the service. The administrator can also assign an account under which the service logs in when it starts. A service normally runs under the **LocalSystem** account unless another account is specified. An account other than **LocalSystem** might be used to restrict a service in some way.

If you look at the bottom of the Services applet window, you will see a text area labeled "Startup Parameters." These parameters allow you to pass special values into the service when it manually starts. The parameters come into the service through the **ServiceMain** function in an **argv** list just as command line parameters would. Startup parameters apply only to manual start services.

9.3 Service Choreography

All services are managed by a system called the *Service Control Manager*. The SCM maintains the list of known services in the registry and starts them either automatically at boot time or when requested by a user. The SCM keeps a list of services and their start-up status in the registry. New services are added to the list by installing them, as described in Section 9.5. It is also possible to later remove services.

A program that acts as a service is a normal EXE file, but it must meet special requirements so that it interfaces properly with the Service Control Manager. Microsoft has carefully choreographed the flow of these functions, and you must follow that plan closely or the service will not work. The requirements follow:

- The service's EXE must have a normal **main** or **WinMain** function. This function should immediately (or in special cases within 30 seconds—see Section 9.7) call the **StartServiceCrtlDispatcher** function. By calling this function, you register the EXE with the Service Control Manager and give the SCM a pointer to a **ServiceMain** function to call when it wants to start the service. You can name the **ServiceMain** function anything you like, but you will find its description in the documentation under **ServiceMain**. The **main** function should return after registering **ServiceMain** with the SCM.

  You would never run a service's EXE from a command line. Instead, you install it in the services list known to the SCM and the SCM starts the EXE itself by calling the **main** function. If you do accidentally execute a service on the command line, it will fail because it cannot connect to the SCM.
- The Service Control Manager will call the **ServiceMain** function when it wants to start the service. For example, if the administrator presses the **Start** button in the Services applet of the Control Panel, then the SCM will execute the **ServiceMain** function in a separate thread.

  The **ServiceMain** function has several responsibilities. The main one is to immediately call the **RegisterServiceCtrlHandler** function, which registers a **Handler** function with the SCM for it to call with control requests. See the following section for details on the **Handler** function. You can name the **Handler** function anything you like, but it is listed in the documentation under **Handler**. The **RegisterServiceCtrlHandler** function will return a handle that the service can use when it wants to send status messages to the SCM.

  The **ServiceMain** function must also start the thread that does the actual work of the service itself. Once this thread has started, the **ServiceMain** function generally waits on an event. The **ServiceMain** function should not return until it is time for the service to stop. When it returns, the service has stopped, and the SCM restarts it by calling **ServiceMain** again.
- The **Handler** function contains a switch statement that parses control requests received from the Service Control Manager. By default the SCM can send any of the following control constants:

- SERVICE_CONTROL_STOP: Tells the service to stop.
- SERVICE_CONTROL_PAUSE: Tells the service to pause.
- SERVICE_CONTROL_CONTINUE: Tells the service to resume.
- SERVICE_CONTROL_INTERROGATE: Tells the service immediately report its status.
- SERVICE_CONTROL_SHUTDOWN: Tells the service that shutdown is imminent.

It is also possible to create custom constants (with values between 128 and 255) and send them through the SCM to the service. See Section 9.5 for details.

When you create an EXE that contains the **main**, **ServiceMain**, and **Handler** functions described above, as well as a function that contains the thread for the service itself, you have a complete service. Figure 9.1 summarizes the interactions between these different functions and the SCM.

The following section gives an example of the simplest possible service so that you can see how the different pieces shown in the EXE file of Figure 9.1 work together.

9.4 The Simplest Service

Listing 9.1 shows the simplest service possible. This service simply beeps. By default it beeps every two seconds. Optionally you can modify the beep interval with startup parameters. This service is complete in that it will appropriately respond to the Service Control Manager for every control signal possible. Because of that, this program can act as a good template for creating your own services. See Appendix A for compilation instructions.

```
// beepserv.cpp

#include <windows.h>
#include <stdio.h>
```

Listing 9.1
A complete service that beeps at a fixed or user-controlled interval (Page 1 of 11)

```
#include <iostream.h>
#include <stdlib.h>

// Global variables

// The name of the service
char *SERVICE_NAME = "BeepService";
// Event used to hold ServiceMain from completing
HANDLE terminateEvent = NULL;
// Handle used to communicate status info with
// the SCM. Created by RegisterServiceCtrlHandler
SERVICE_STATUS_HANDLE serviceStatusHandle;
// The beep interval in ms.
int beepDelay = 2000;
// Flags holding current state of service
BOOL pauseService = FALSE;
BOOL runningService = FALSE;
// Thread for the actual work
HANDLE threadHandle = 0;

void ErrorHandler(char *s, DWORD err)
{
   cout << s << endl;
   cout << "Error number: " << err << endl;
   ExitProcess(err);
}

DWORD ServiceThread(LPDWORD param)
{
   while (1)
   {
      Beep(200,200);
      Sleep(beepDelay);
   }
   return 0;
```

Listing 9.1
A complete service that beeps at a fixed or user-controlled interval (Page 2 of 11)

```
}

// Initializes the service by starting its thread
BOOL InitService()
{
   DWORD id;

   // Start the service's thread
   threadHandle = CreateThread(0, 0,
      (LPTHREAD_START_ROUTINE) ServiceThread,
      0, 0, &id);

   if (threadHandle==0)
      return FALSE;
   else
   {
      runningService = TRUE;
      return TRUE;
   }
}

// Resumes a paused service
VOID ResumeService()
{
   pauseService=FALSE;
   ResumeThread(threadHandle);
}

// Pauses the service
VOID PauseService()
{
   pauseService = TRUE;
   SuspendThread(threadHandle);
}
```

Listing 9.1
A complete service that beeps at a fixed or user-controlled interval (Page 3 of 11)

```
// Stops the service by allowing ServiceMain to
// complete
VOID StopService()
{
   runningService=FALSE;
   // Set the event that is holding ServiceMain
   // so that ServiceMain can return
   SetEvent(terminateEvent);
}

// This function consolidates the activities of
// updating the service status with
// SetServiceStatus
BOOL SendStatusToSCM (DWORD dwCurrentState,
   DWORD dwWin32ExitCode,
   DWORD dwServiceSpecificExitCode,
   DWORD dwCheckPoint,
   DWORD dwWaitHint)
{
   BOOL success;
   SERVICE_STATUS serviceStatus;

   // Fill in all of the SERVICE_STATUS fields
   serviceStatus.dwServiceType =
      SERVICE_WIN32_OWN_PROCESS;
   serviceStatus.dwCurrentState = dwCurrentState;

   // If in the process of something, then accept
   // no control events, else accept anything
   if (dwCurrentState == SERVICE_START_PENDING)
      serviceStatus.dwControlsAccepted = 0;
   else
      serviceStatus.dwControlsAccepted =
         SERVICE_ACCEPT_STOP |
         SERVICE_ACCEPT_PAUSE_CONTINUE |
```

Listing 9.1
A complete service that beeps at a fixed or user-controlled interval (Page 4 of 11)

```
            SERVICE_ACCEPT_SHUTDOWN;

    // if a specific exit code is defines, set up
    // the win32 exit code properly
    if (dwServiceSpecificExitCode == 0)
        serviceStatus.dwWin32ExitCode =
            dwWin32ExitCode;
    else
        serviceStatus.dwWin32ExitCode =
            ERROR_SERVICE_SPECIFIC_ERROR;
    serviceStatus.dwServiceSpecificExitCode =
        dwServiceSpecificExitCode;

    serviceStatus.dwCheckPoint = dwCheckPoint;
    serviceStatus.dwWaitHint = dwWaitHint;

    // Pass the status record to the SCM
    success = SetServiceStatus (serviceStatusHandle,
        &serviceStatus);
    if (!success)
        StopService();

    return success;
}

// Dispatches events received from the service
// control manager
VOID ServiceCtrlHandler (DWORD controlCode)
{
    DWORD  currentState = 0;
    BOOL success;

    switch(controlCode)
    {
        // There is no START option because
```

Listing 9.1
A complete service that beeps at a fixed or user-controlled interval (Page 5 of 11)

```
// ServiceMain gets called on a start

// Stop the service
case SERVICE_CONTROL_STOP:
   currentState = SERVICE_STOP_PENDING;
   // Tell the SCM what's happening
   success = SendStatusToSCM(
      SERVICE_STOP_PENDING,
      NO_ERROR, 0, 1, 5000);
   // Not much to do if not successful

   // Stop the service
   StopService();
   return;

// Pause the service
case SERVICE_CONTROL_PAUSE:
   if (runningService && !pauseService)
   {
      // Tell the SCM what's happening
      success = SendStatusToSCM(
         SERVICE_PAUSE_PENDING,
         NO_ERROR, 0, 1, 1000);
      PauseService();
      currentState = SERVICE_PAUSED;
   }
   break;

// Resume from a pause
case SERVICE_CONTROL_CONTINUE:
   if (runningService && pauseService)
   {
      // Tell the SCM what's happening
      success = SendStatusToSCM(
         SERVICE_CONTINUE_PENDING,
```

Listing 9.1
A complete service that beeps at a fixed or user-controlled interval (Page 6 of 11)

```
                NO_ERROR, 0, 1, 1000);
            ResumeService();
            currentState = SERVICE_RUNNING;
         }
         break;

      // Update current status
      case SERVICE_CONTROL_INTERROGATE:
         // it will fall to bottom and send status
         break;

      // Do nothing in a shutdown. Could do cleanup
      // here but it must be very quick.
      case SERVICE_CONTROL_SHUTDOWN:
         // Do nothing on shutdown
         return;
      default:
         break;
   }
   SendStatusToSCM(currentState, NO_ERROR,
      0, 0, 0);
}

// Handle an error from ServiceMain by cleaning up
// and telling SCM that the service didn't start.
VOID terminate(DWORD error)
{
   // if terminateEvent has been created, close it.
   if (terminateEvent)
      CloseHandle(terminateEvent);

   // Send a message to the scm to tell about
   // stopage
   if (serviceStatusHandle)
      SendStatusToSCM(SERVICE_STOPPED, error,
```

Listing 9.1
A complete service that beeps at a fixed or user-controlled interval (Page 7 of 11)

```
            0, 0, 0);

      // If the thread has started kill it off
      if (threadHandle)
         CloseHandle(threadHandle);

      // Do not need to close serviceStatusHandle
   }

   // ServiceMain is called when the SCM wants to
   // start the service. When it returns, the service
   // has stopped. It therefore waits on an event
   // just before the end of the function, and
   // that event gets set when it is time to stop.
   // It also returns on any error because the
   // service cannot start if there is an eror.
   VOID ServiceMain(DWORD argc, LPTSTR *argv)
   {
      BOOL success;

      // immediately call Registration function
      serviceStatusHandle =
         RegisterServiceCtrlHandler(
            SERVICE_NAME,
            (LPHANDLER_FUNCTION)ServiceCtrlHandler);
      if (!serviceStatusHandle)
      {
         terminate(GetLastError());
         return;
      }

      // Notify SCM of progress
      success = SendStatusToSCM(
         SERVICE_START_PENDING,
         NO_ERROR, 0, 1, 5000);
```

Listing 9.1
A complete service that beeps at a fixed or user-controlled interval (Page 8 of 11)

```
    if (!success)
    {
        terminate(GetLastError());
        return;
    }

    // create the termination event
    terminateEvent = CreateEvent (0, TRUE, FALSE,
        0);
    if (!terminateEvent)
    {
        terminate(GetLastError());
        return;
    }

    // Notify SCM of progress
    success = SendStatusToSCM(
        SERVICE_START_PENDING,
        NO_ERROR, 0, 2, 1000);
    if (!success)
    {
        terminate(GetLastError());
        return;
    }

    // Check for startup params
    if (argc == 2)
    {
        int temp = atoi(argv[1]);
        if (temp < 1000)
            beepDelay = 2000;
        else
            beepDelay = temp;
    }
```

Listing 9.1
A complete service that beeps at a fixed or user-controlled interval (Page 9 of 11)

```
        // Notify SCM of progress
        success = SendStatusToSCM(
           SERVICE_START_PENDING,
           NO_ERROR, 0, 3, 5000);
        if (!success)
        {
           terminate(GetLastError());
           return;
        }

        // Start the service itself
        success = InitService();
        if (!success)
        {
           terminate(GetLastError());
           return;
        }

        // The service is now running.
        // Notify SCM of progress
        success = SendStatusToSCM(
           SERVICE_RUNNING,
           NO_ERROR, 0, 0, 0);
        if (!success)
        {
           terminate(GetLastError());
           return;
        }

        // Wait for stop signal, and then terminate
        WaitForSingleObject (terminateEvent, INFINITE);

        terminate(0);
     }
```

Listing 9.1
A complete service that beeps at a fixed or user-controlled interval (Page 10 of 11)

```
VOID main(VOID)
{
   SERVICE_TABLE_ENTRY serviceTable[] =
   {
   { SERVICE_NAME,
      (LPSERVICE_MAIN_FUNCTION) ServiceMain},
   { NULL, NULL }
   };
   BOOL success;

   // Register with the SCM
   success =
      StartServiceCtrlDispatcher(serviceTable);
   if (!success)
      ErrorHandler("In StartServiceCtrlDispatcher",
         GetLastError());
}
```

Listing 9.1
A complete service that beeps at a fixed or user-controlled interval (Page 11 of 11)

The following sections describe what each of the functions in Listing 9.1 does.

9.4.1 Main

The main function calls **StartServiceCtrlDispatcher** to register the **ServiceMain** function for this service with the SCM. The registration is performed using an array of SERVICE_TABLE_ENTRY structures. In this case, the program contains just one service, so there is only one entry in the table. However, it is possible for there to be several services contained in a single EXE file, and in that case the table identifies the appropriate **ServiceMain** function that the SCM should use to start each of the services. See Section 9.7 for details. In the case of a single-service EXE like this one, the SERVICE_NAME constant is irrelevant, and the service picks up its name during the installation process as described in the next section.

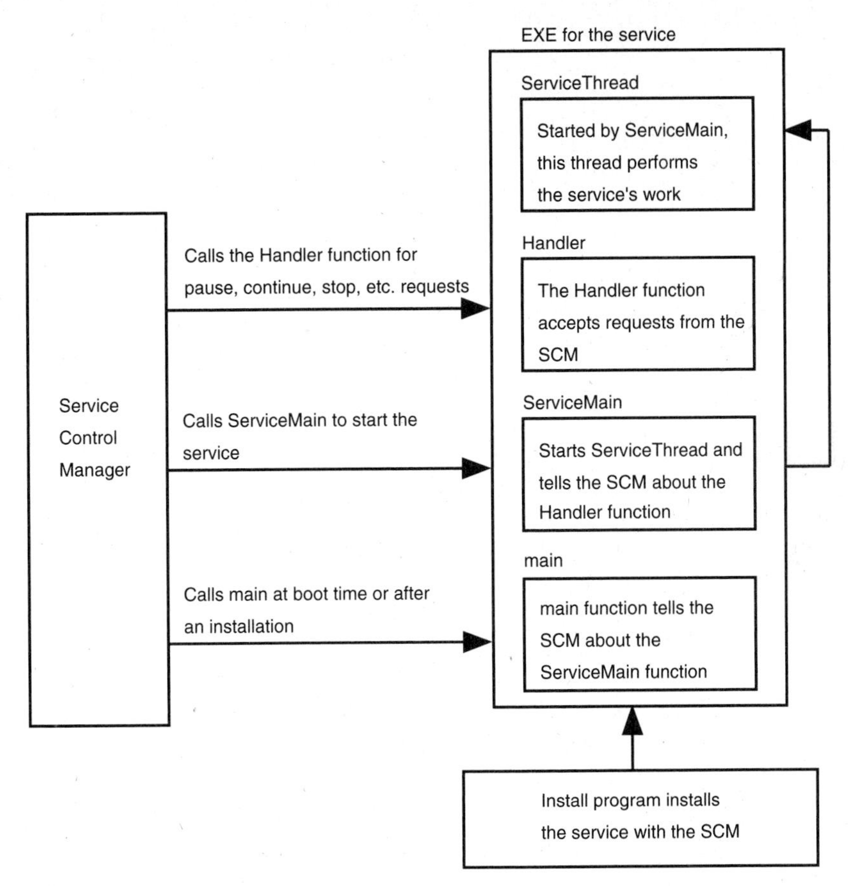

Figure 9.1
The relationship between the SCM, the service's EXE, and the Install program.

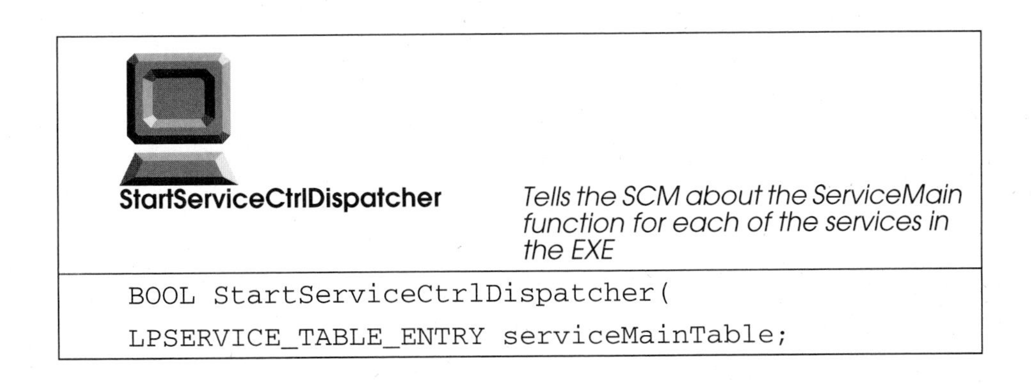

StartServiceCtrlDispatcher *Tells the SCM about the ServiceMain function for each of the services in the EXE*

```
BOOL StartServiceCtrlDispatcher(
LPSERVICE_TABLE_ENTRY serviceMainTable;
```

serviceMainTable	A table of ServiceMain entry points for each service in the EXE
returns TRUE on success	

If the call to **StartServiceCtrlDispatcher** fails, it will return an error code and the program prints it to stdout. The user will see this only if the program is accidentally executed from the command line. If properly started by the SCM, there is no way to output the failure except to create an entry in the event log, as described in Chapter 15.

It is possible to put initialization code in the **main** function prior to the call to **StartServiceCtrlDispatcher**, but this code must complete in less than 30 seconds. If it takes longer than 30 seconds the SCM times out and aborts the service on the assumption that something went wrong. If there is only one service in the EXE as shown in Listing 9.1, there is no reason to do the initialization in **main**, and the initialization code should be placed in **ServiceMain** instead. If the EXE contains multiple services and you need to perform global initializations for all services, place them in **main**.

9.4.2 ServiceMain

The SCM calls the **ServiceMain** function when it wants to start the service either during the boot process or because of a manual start. **ServiceMain** will always contain the following steps:

1. It immediately calls **RegisterServiceCtrlHandler** to register the **ServiceCtrlHandler** function with the SCM as this service's Handler function. The Handler function handles requests from the SCM to stop, pause, resume or interrogate the service. The **RegisterServiceCtrlHandler** function also returns a handle that the service uses to send status information back to the SCM.
2. The **ServiceMain** function then calls the **SendStatusToSCM** function (created in Listing 9.1). It does this to notify the SCM of progress. The fourth parameter to **SendStatusToSCM** is a click count value, which increments each time the program updates the status. The SCM and other programs can look at the click count and see that progress is being made during initialization. The last parameter passed to **SendStatusToSCM** is a wait hint, which tells the SCM how long it should expect to

wait before the click count next gets updated. This number is rather subjective—someone running the service on a 20MHZ 386 with 8 megabytes or RAM will experience a somewhat longer delay than someone running on an Alpha, so it is better to err on the high side. The five seconds shown in this example is adequate for most situations.

3. The **ServiceMain** function next creates an event (Chapter 6) that it will use at the bottom of the function to prevent it from returning until the SCM issues a STOP request. After it creates the event, the function again updates the SCM on progress by calling **SendStatusToSCM** with an incremented click count.

4. Next, **ServiceMain** checks for startup parameters. These parameters can be passed in by the user during a manual start, using the Startup Parameters line in the Service applet of the Control Panel. Any parameters typed on the Startup Parameters line in the Services applet come into the **ServiceMain** function exactly like they would come in to the main function of a normal program from the command line. In this example, the program checks to make sure that the user has typed just one parameter. If so, the program converts it to an integer, validates it, and then uses it if appropriate. You can use startup parameters in your own services in any way that you like. The code then updates its status with the SCM.

5. If your service needs to perform other initialization tasks, they should go here just prior to the call to **InitService**.

6. The **ServiceMain** function now, finally, gets to the heart of the matter and calls the **InitService** function, which will start the thread that does the actual work of the service. If this call succeeds, then **ServiceMain** lets the SCM know that the service has successfully started.

7. **ServiceMain** now calls **WaitForSingleObject**, which waits efficiently for the **terminateEvent** event object to be set. This object gets set in the **StopService** function. Once it does get set, **ServiceMain** calls the **terminate** function to clean up, and then returns to stop the service.

As you can see, there is not a lot of flexibility in this function. With the exception of step 5, you must perform each of the tasks mentioned in the order mentioned for the service to start properly.

ServiceMain	*The standard form for any **Service-Main** function*

`VOID ServiceMain(`
`    DWORD argc,`
`    LPTSTR *argv)`	

argc	A count of the number of startup parameters, plus 1
argv	An array of pointers to strings containing the parameters
No return value	

RegisterServiceCtrlHandler	*Registers the control handler for the service with the SCM*

`SERVICE_STATUS_HANDLE RegisterServiceCtrlHandler(`
`    LPCTSTR serviceName,`
`    LPHANDLER_FUNCTION handler)`	

serviceName	The name of the service for the SCM
handler	A pointer to the handler function
Returns the handle used to send status info back to the SCM	

9.4.3 Terminate

The **terminate** function is called by **ServiceMain** if the service fails to start, or when stopping the service. The **terminate** function cleans up any open handles, and sends a status message to the SCM to tell it that the service is stopped. This function should also place an entry in the event log to notify the administrator of any error. The event log is really the only way that a service has to emit an error message. See Chapter 15 for details on event logging.

9.4.4 ServiceCtrlHandler

The SCM calls the **ServiceCtrlHandler** function whenever it wants to pause, resume, interrogate, or stop the service. This function accepts integer control codes and uses a switch statement to parse them. Five standard control constants are recognized in this implementation:

- SERVICE_CONTROL_STOP: Tells the service to stop.
- SERVICE_CONTROL_PAUSE: Tells the service to pause.
- SERVICE_CONTROL_CONTINUE: Tells the service to resume.
- SERVICE_CONTROL_INTERROGATE: Tells the service immediately report its status.
- SERVICE_CONTROL_SHUTDOWN: Tells the service that shutdown is imminent.

It is also possible to create new constants, as described in Section 9.5.

To stop the service, the handler tells the SCM that the stop is pending, and then sets **terminateEvent**. By doing this, it causes **ServiceMain**, which is executing as a separate thread, to terminate and return. Once **ServiceMain** returns, the service is stopped, and the only way to restart it is for the SCM to call **ServiceMain** again.

To pause or continue the service, the handler tells the SCM that the operation is pending, and then calls the appropriate function.

An interrogation request simply asks the service to update its status immediately with the SCM.

During a shutdown, each service gets a signal telling it that the shutdown is imminent. Any file cleanup or variable storage can be performed at this point provided that it occurs very quickly.

Handler	*The standard form for any service* ***Handler*** *function*
`VOID Handler(` `   DWORD control)`	
control	A constant indicating the action to perform
No return value	

9.4.5 SendStatusToSCM

The **SendStatusToSCM** function consolidates all of the statements necessary to send the service's current status to the SCM. To send a status message, this function takes seven values and places them in a SERVICE_STATUS structure. It then passes that structure to the **SetServiceStatus** function. In Listing 9.1, five of the seven fields in the SERVICE_STATUS structure vary from call to call, while two are constant:

- **serviceType**: Indicates the type of service. Possible values: SERVICE_WIN32_OWN_PROCESS, SERVICE_WIN32_SHARE_PROCESS, SERVICE_KERNEL_DRIVER, SERVICE_FILE_SYSTEM_DRIVER
- **currentState**: Indicates the current state of the service. Possible values: SERVICE_STOP_PENDING, SERVICE_RUNNING, SERVICE_CONTINUE_PENDING, SERVICE_PAUSE_PENDING, SERVICE_PAUSED
- **controlsAccepted**: Indicates which control-signals another process can send with the **ControlService** function. Possible values, any or all of the following: SERVICE_ACCEPT_STOP, SERVICE_ACCEPT_PAUSE_CONTINUE, SERVICE_ACCEPT_SHUTDOWN. A service always accepts an interrogate request. There is no way to block service-defined codes except in your own code.
- **win32ExitCode**: If an error occurs while the service is starting or stopping, the service can pass the value retrieved from **GetLastError** back through this field. If there is no error, set this field to NO_ERROR. If you want to create your own specific error constants for your service, set this field to ERROR_SERVER_SPECIFIC_ERROR and pass the service-defined code back in the following field.
- **serviceSpecificExitCode**: If the previous field is appropriately marked, then you can send back a service-defined error constant in this field.
- **checkPoint**: During a start, stop, or continue operation, the SCM needs to be able to tell if the service is making progress. You signal

progress by incrementing this field and updating the status of the service to the SCM.

- **waitHint**: This field tells the SCM an amount of time, in milliseconds, that it should expect to wait before seeing **checkPoint** increment.

9.4.6 StopService

The **StopService** function gets called by **ServiceCtrlHandler** whenever the SCM requests the service to stop. It sets the event that allows **ServiceMain** to return. **ServiceMain** therefore returns, killing off the service's thread in the process and stopping the service.

9.4.7 PauseService

The **PauseService** function gets called by **ServiceCtrlHandler** whenever the SCM requests the service to pause. It simply pauses the thread that does the work of the service by calling **SuspendService**.

9.4.8 ResumeService

The **ResumeService** function gets called by **ServiceCtrlHandler** whenever the SCM requests the service to resume. It resumes the service's thread by calling **ResumeThread**.

9.4.9 InitService

The **InitService** function gets called by **ServiceMain** when it needs to start the service's thread. This function calls **CreateThread** (Chapter 5) to create a new thread for the service.

It is also possible to start a new process instead of a thread in **InitService**. The process might be a stand-alone application or command-line program that you want to run in the service. For example, if you have a normal application that you need to start running as soon as the machine boots, you can start it by calling **CreateProcess** here.

9.4.10 ServiceThread

The **ServiceThread** function contains the actual work that is to be performed by the service. In this case, the thread consists of an infinite loop that beeps and then sleeps for a predetermined interval. When creating your own services, you can place any normal function call in this thread, either to Win32 functions or to your own functions.

This thread works independently of all of the other code in Listing 9.1, although any changes made to global variables can affect the thread if the thread's code is written that way.

9.4.11 ErrorHandler

The **ErrorHandler** function prints error messages.

9.5 Installing and Removing a Service

In order to use the beep service described in the previous section, you have to install it. Installation makes the SCM aware of the service, and causes the SCM to add it to the list of services that appears in the Services Applet of the Control Panel. The code shown in Listing 9.2 demonstrates how to install a service.

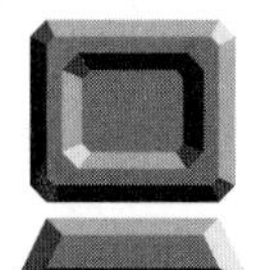

```
// install.cpp

#include <windows.h>
#include <iostream.h>

void ErrorHandler(char *s, DWORD err)
{
   cout << s << endl;
   cout << "Error number: " << err << endl;
   ExitProcess(err);
}

void main(int argc, char *argv[])
{
   SC_HANDLE newService, scm;
```

Listing 9.2
Installing a service (Page 1 of 3)

```
    if (argc != 4)
    {
       cout << "Usage:\n";
       cout << "   install service_name \
service_label executable\n";
       cout << "           service_name is the \
name used internally by the SCM\n";
       cout << "           service_label is the \
name that appears in the Services applet\n";
       cout << "               (for multiple \
words, put them in double quotes)\n";
       cout << "           executable is the \
full path to the EXE\n";
       cout << endl;
       return;
    }

    cout << "Starting...\n";
    // open a connection to the SCM
    scm = OpenSCManager(0, 0,
       SC_MANAGER_CREATE_SERVICE);
    if (!scm)
       ErrorHandler("In OpenScManager",
          GetLastError());

    // Install the new service
    newService = CreateService(
       scm, argv[1], // eg "beep_srv"
       argv[2],      // eg "Beep Service"
       SERVICE_ALL_ACCESS,
       SERVICE_WIN32_OWN_PROCESS,
       SERVICE_DEMAND_START,
       SERVICE_ERROR_NORMAL,
       argv[3],      // eg "c:\winnt\xxx.exe"
```

Listing 9.2
Installing a service (Page 2 of 3)

```
            0, 0, 0, 0, 0);
        if (!newService)
            ErrorHandler("In CreateService",
                GetLastError());
        else
            cout << "Service installed\n";

        // clean up
        CloseServiceHandle(newService);
        CloseServiceHandle(scm);
        cout << "Ending...\n";
    }
```

Listing 9.2
Installing a service (Page 3 of 3)

Listing 9.2 starts by opening a connection to the service control manager using the **OpenSCManager** function.

OpenSCManager	*opens a connection to the SCM*

`SC_HANDLE OpenSCManager(`
`    LPCTSTR machine,`
`    LPCTSTR database,`
`    DWORD access)`	

machine	The name of the machine, NULL for the current machine
database	The name of the database to open. Set to NULL
access	Specifies the desired access
Returns a handle to the SCM or NULL on error	

In Listing 9.2, the call to the **OpenSCManager** function specifies that the database on the current machine be opened so that the program can create a new service. In the call to **OpenSCManager**, you must also specify what you want to do so that it can validate that activity. If the account you are logged in under when you execute Listing 9.2 does not have sufficient privilege to perform the requested activity, then the call will return NULL.

The call to **CreateService** actually installs the new service.

CreateService — *Installs a service in the SCM database*

```
SC_HANDLE CreateService(
    SC_HANDLE scm,
    LPCTSTR name,
    LPCTSTR displayName,
    DWORD access,
    DWORD serviceType,
    DWORD start,
    DWORD errorSeverity,
    LPCTSTR exePath,
    LPCTSTR loadOrderGroup,
    LPDWORD ID,
    LPCTSTR dependencies,
    LPCTSTR serviceAccount,
    LPCTSTR password)
```

scm	A handle to the SCM from **OpenSCManager**
name	The name of the service used internally
displayName	The name of the service displayed in the Service applet
access	Desired access to the service
serviceType	The type of service, i.e. process or driver
start	The start type: auto or manual
errorSeverity	Specifies the severity of a failure to start

exePath	The full path to the executable containing the service
loadOrderGroup	A string containing NULL or one of the load ordering groups from the registry
ID	An ID value for the ordering group used
dependencies	A pointer to an array of strings containing the names of services that must start before this one
account	The account the service uses when it starts. If NULL, LocalSystem is used. Otherwise use "domain\account"
password	Password of the account. Pass NULL for no password
Returns a handle to the new service or NULL on an error.	

In the case shown in Listing 9.2, the call to **CreateService** uses the pointer to the SCM returned by **OpenSCManager**, the name, label, and EXE file specified on the command line, along with a set of standard parameters to fill in all of the other values. The use of SERVICE_WIN32_OWN_PROCESS indicates that the service's EXE file contains just one service, and SERVICE_DEMAND_START indicates that the service is initially tagged as manual start rather than automatic start.

A typical invocation of the install program at the command line is shown below:

```
install BeepService "Beeper" c:\winnt\beep.exe
```

The first parameter specifies the name of the service used internally by the SCM. This name is later used to remove the service. The second parameter specifies the label used to display the service in the Services Applet of the Control Panel. The third parameter gives the fully qualified path to the service's executable. When you run the install program, it will either succeed or print an error number that you can look up in the on-line help file for the Win32 API.

To remove a service, you follow the steps shown in Listing 9.3.

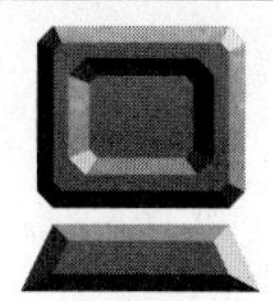

```
// remove.cpp

#include <windows.h>
#include <iostream.h>

void ErrorHandler(char *s, DWORD err)
{
   cout << s << endl;
   cout << "Error number: " << err << endl;
   ExitProcess(err);
}

void main(int argc, char *argv[])
{
   SC_HANDLE service, scm;
   BOOL success;
   SERVICE_STATUS status;

   if (argc != 2)
   {
      cout << "Usage:\n";
      cout << "   remove service_name\n";
      return;
   }

   cout << "Starting...\n";
   // Open a connection to the SCM
   scm = OpenSCManager(0, 0,
      SC_MANAGER_CREATE_SERVICE);
   if (!scm)
```

Listing 9.3
Removing a service from the SCM (Page 1 of 3)

```
      ErrorHandler("In OpenScManager",
         GetLastError());

   // Get the service's handle
   service = OpenService(
      scm, argv[1],
      SERVICE_ALL_ACCESS | DELETE);
   if (!service)
      ErrorHandler("In OpenService",
         GetLastError());

   // Stop the service if necessary
   success = QueryServiceStatus(service, &status);
   if (!success)
      ErrorHandler("In QueryServiceStatus",
         GetLastError());
   if (status.dwCurrentState != SERVICE_STOPPED)
   {
      cout << "Stopping service...\n";
      success = ControlService(service,
         SERVICE_CONTROL_STOP,
         &status);
      if (!success)
         ErrorHandler("In ControlService",
            GetLastError());
      Sleep(500);
   }

   // Remove the service
   success = DeleteService(service);
   if (success)
      cout << "Service removed\n";
   else
      ErrorHandler("In DeleteService",
         GetLastError());
```

Listing 9.3
Removing a service from the SCM (Page 2 of 3)

```
        // Clean up
        CloseServiceHandle(service);
        CloseServiceHandle(scm);
        cout << "Ending...\n";
    }
```

Listing 9.3
Removing a service from the SCM (Page 3 of 3)

Listing 9.3 starts by opening a connection to the service control manager, as described with Listing 9.2. It then opens a connection to the service using the **OpenService** function.

OpenService	*Opens a connection to the specified service*

`SC_HANDLE OpenService(`
`    SC_HANDLE scm,`
`    LPCTSTR name,`
`    DWORD access)`	

scm	A handle to the SCM from **OpenSCManager**
name	The name of the service used internally
access	The desired access
Returns a handle to the service or NULL on error	

The **OpenService** function accepts a handle to the SCM and the name of the service to open, along with a set of flags representing the requested level of access. If the user running the remove program has sufficient privilege to gain that access to the service in question, then the function returns a pointer that can be used to communicate with the service. Otherwise it returns NULL.

Listing 9.3 next queries the service to find out if it is currently stopped. If it is not, it stops it. This is a courtesy to the user removing the service: If the service is running at the time of the removal, then the Services applet will retain a link to the service and the service will, in fact, remain running. When someone tries to stop the orphaned service, the Services applet sometimes complains. By stopping the service first, these problems are avoided.

The **QueryServiceStatus** function gets the current SERVICE_STATUS record from the SCM. To guarantee freshness, you might first send an interrogation request to the service (using **ControlService**), but that is not necessary in this case. **QueryServiceStatus** fills a status record.

QueryServiceStatus — *Retrieves the current status from the service*

```
BOOL QueryServiceStatus(
    SC_HANDLE service,
    LPSERVICE_STATUS status)
```

service	A handle to the service
status	A pointer to a SERVICE_STATUS structure

Returns TRUE on success

QueryServiceStatus fills a status record. The **dwCurrentState** field of the structure contains the state of the service, and the program in Listing 9.3 checks this field to make sure the service is stopped. If it is not, the program uses the **ControlService** function to attempt to stop the service.

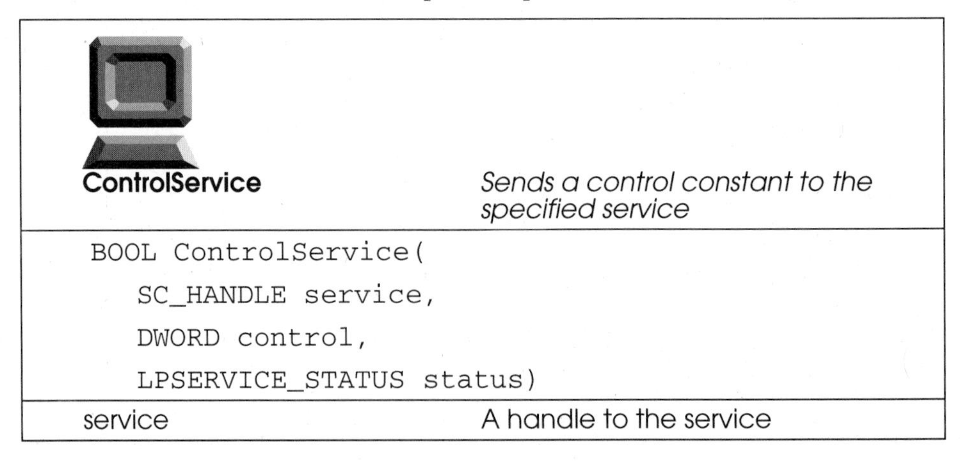

ControlService — *Sends a control constant to the specified service*

```
BOOL ControlService(
    SC_HANDLE service,
    DWORD control,
    LPSERVICE_STATUS status)
```

service	A handle to the service

control	Control constant telling the service what to do
status	A pointer to a SERVICE_STATUS structure
Returns TRUE on success	

The call to **ControlService** function accepts a handle to the service, a control constant, and a pointer to a SERVICE_STATUS record so that it can return the current status after the requested action. If the service was opened using SERVICE_ALL_ACCESS or SERVICE_USER_DEFINED_CONTROL access, then it is possible to send a user-defined control constant (between 128 and 255) to the service. Otherwise, the following constants are understood:

SERVICE_CONTROL_STOP

SERVICE_CONTROL_PAUSE

SERVICE_CONTROL_CONTINUE

SERVICE_CONTROL_INTERROGATE

SERVICE_CONTROL_SHUTDOWN

Now that the service has stopped, the program deletes it using the **DeleteService** function.

DeleteService	*Deletes the specified service*
`BOOL DeleteService( SC_HANDLE service)`	
service	A handle to the service to delete
Returns TRUE on success	

The **DeleteService** function removes the service from the **Services** applet in the Control Panel. A typical invocation of the removal program shown in Listing 9.3 would look like this:

```
remove BeepService
```

If desired, you can immediately reinstall the service.

9.6 Displaying Dialogs from within a Service

Frequently it is useful to display simple message boxes from within a service. For example, the Messenger service listens on the network for messages sent with the `net send` command and displays a message box for any messages that arrive. It is easy to modify the beep service shown in Section 9.4 to emulate this behavior. Any more advanced user interface to a service requires that you write a separate GUI front end and hook it to the service with something like a named pipe. Note the use of MB_DEFAULT_DESKTOP_ONLY.

As an example, you might want to create a "logon announcement" service that announces people when they log onto an NT machine on your network. In order to do this, the service will want to create a mailslot (Chapter 7) with a specific name so that it can listen for logon messages. When a logon message arrives at the mailslot, the service can display a message box. Users who want to announce themselves would place a command in their logon script that announces them (or the service could be made smart enough to sense when people log in and announce it automatically—see Section 9.7 for an example).

Listing 9.4 contains a simple console program that performs the announcement operation needed by the logon announcement service. Compile it and call it any time:

```
announce "John has logged in"
```

If you place this command in your logon script it will send the announcement as soon as you log on.

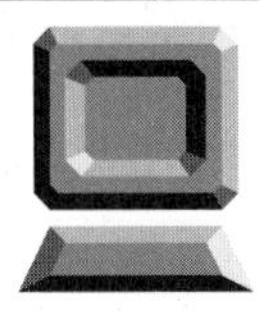

```
// announce.cpp

#include <windows.h>
#include <stdio.h>
#include <iostream.h>
```

Listing 9.4
A console program to send a logon announcement to the logon announcing service (Page 1 of 3)

```
#include <stdlib.h>

void ErrorHandler(char *s, DWORD err)
{
   cout << s << endl;
   cout << "Error number: " << err << endl;
   ExitProcess(err);
}

VOID main(int argc, char *argv[])
{
   HANDLE mailslot;
   DWORD numWrite;
   BOOL success;

   if (argc != 2)
   {
      cout << "Usage: announce message\n";
      cout << "  if message > 1 word, put it \
in quotes\n";
      return;
   }

   // create a mailslot to write to
   mailslot = CreateFile(
      "\\\\*\\mailslot\\logonann",
      GENERIC_WRITE, FILE_SHARE_READ, 0,
      OPEN_EXISTING, FILE_ATTRIBUTE_NORMAL, 0);
   if (mailslot == INVALID_HANDLE_VALUE)
      ErrorHandler("In CreateFile",
         GetLastError());

   // Write the message to the new slot
   success = WriteFile(mailslot, argv[1],
      strlen(argv[1]), &numWrite, 0);
```

Listing 9.4
A console program to send a logon announcement to the logon announcing service (Page 2 of 3)

```
        if (!success)
            ErrorHandler("In WriteFile", GetLastError());
        else
            cout << "success\n";

        CloseHandle(mailslot);
    }
```

Listing 9.4
A console program to send a logon announcement to the logon announcing service (Page 3 of 3)

The service that receives the messages from Listing 9.4 needs to create a mailslot server (Chapter 7) so that it receives the logon messages. It then needs to produce the message boxes that announce each logon message. To do that, you need to change only three functions in the beepserver program shown in Listing 9.1. The **main** function needs to turn into a **WinMain** function so that message boxes can appear. The **ServiceThread** function needs to change so that it creates the mailslot server and reads from it properly. The **terminate** function needs to change so that it properly closes the **mailslot** handle. The modified **main** function is shown in Listing 9.5, while the modified **ServiceThread** function appears in Listing 9.6.

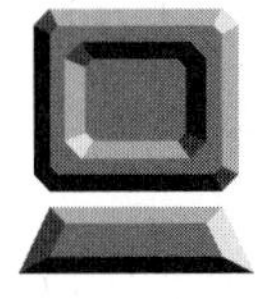

```
int WINAPI WinMain(HANDLE ghInstance,
   HANDLE hPrevInstance, LPSTR lpCmdLine,
   int nCmdShow)
{
   SERVICE_TABLE_ENTRY serviceTable[] =
   {
   { SERVICE_NAME,
      (LPSERVICE_MAIN_FUNCTION) ServiceMain},
```

Listing 9.5
The **main** function in Listing 9.1 should be replaced by this **WinMain** function (Page 1 of 2)

```
        { NULL, NULL }
    };
    BOOL success;

    // Create the mailslot
    // Another place for this is in ServiceMain
    mailslot = CreateMailslot(
        "\\\\.\\mailslot\\logonann",
        200, MAILSLOT_WAIT_FOREVER, 0);

    // Connect to the SCM
    success = StartServiceCtrlDispatcher(
        serviceTable);
    if (!success)
        ErrorHandler("In StartServiceCtrlDispatcher",
            GetLastError());

    return 0;
}
```

Listing 9.5
The **main** function in Listing 9.1 should be replaced by this **WinMain** function (Page 2 of 2)

The code in the **WinMain** function shown in Listing 9.5 contains two modifications to the original **main** function:

1. It is a **WinMain** function rather than a **main** function, which means that **MessageBox** calls will work. It needs to be compiled differently, however. See Appendix A for compilation instructions.
2. Listing 9.5 contains a call to **CreateMailslot**, where **mailslot** is a new global variable. A better place to put the initialization code in this particular example is in the **ServiceMain** function, the advantage being that it is possible to detect and then report errors through the SCM from inside of **ServiceMain**.

The new **ServiceThread** function in Listing 9.6 continuously checks the mailslot for new messages, displays them in a message box if any are found, or waits a second before checking again. See Chapter 7 for more information on mailslots.

```
DWORD ServiceThread(LPDWORD param)
{
   char buffer[2000];
   DWORD numRead;
   DWORD maxMsg, nextMsg, numMsg, timeout;

   Beep(200,200); // Announce success
   while (1)
   {
      // Check for waiting messages
      GetMailslotInfo(mailslot, &maxMsg,
         &nextMsg, &numMsg, &timeout);
      // if messages are available, read them
      // and display in a message box.
      // Otherwise wait 1 second.
      if (numMsg > 0)
      {
         Beep(200,200);
         ReadFile(mailslot, buffer, nextMsg,
            &numRead, 0);
         buffer[numRead]='\0';
         MessageBox(0, buffer,
            "Logon Announcement", MB_OK |
            MB_SETFOREGROUND | MB_DEFAULT_DESKTOP_ONLY);
      }
      else
         Sleep(1000);
   }
   return 0;
}
```

Listing 9.6
The **ServiceThread** function in Listing 9.1 should be replaced by this **ServiceThread** function

Once these two functions are in place in Listing 9.1 and the service is compiled and installed as described in Section 9.5, you will see nothing until someone on the network uses the `announce` command shown at the beginning of this section. Then you will see a message box containing the announcement message. You can test the service by typing announce commands on your own workstation.

9.7 Multiple Services in an Executable

It is possible and sometimes useful to put more than one service into a single executable. Generally you do this so that the separate service threads can communicate with one another through shared global variables. Because each of the services is a separate thread that shares the same data space, you can create global variables that are accessible by all of the services. The only requirement is that you use proper synchronization methods (see Chapter 6) to insure valid access to the shared data.

When you create a multi-service EXE, you have to duplicate everything seen in Listing 9.1 except the **main** function. See Figure 9.2. During installation and when reporting status with **SendStatusToSCM**, you must indicate that multiple services are sharing the same process using the SERVICE_WIN32_SHARE_PROCESS flag (an EXE that contains just one service marks itself as SERVICE_WIN32_OWN_PROCESS during installation and when reporting status information). As shown in Listing 9.7, the **main** or **WinMain** function must also change. The service entry table must contain the name of the service and the name of the **ServiceMain** function for each of the services in the EXE.

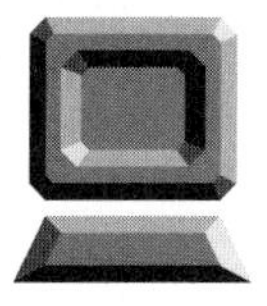

```
int WINAPI WinMain(HANDLE ghInstance,
    HANDLE hPrevInstance, LPSTR lpCmdLine,
```

Listing 9.7
A typical **WinMain** function for a service EXE containing two services. The table indicates the name of each service and the **ServiceMain** function for each (Page 1 of 2)

```
        int nCmdShow)
    {
        SERVICE_TABLE_ENTRY serviceTable[] =
        {
        { "Service1",
           (LPSERVICE_MAIN_FUNCTION) ServiceMain1},
        { "Service2",
           (LPSERVICE_MAIN_FUNCTION) ServiceMain2},
        { NULL, NULL }
        };
        BOOL success;

        success =
           StartServiceCtrlDispatcher(serviceTable);
        if (!success)
           ErrorHandler("In StartServiceCtrlDispatcher",
              GetLastError());
        return 0;
    }
```

Listing 9.7
A typical **WinMain** function for a service EXE containing two services. The table indicates the name of each service and the **ServiceMain** function for each (Page 2 of 2)

The Service Entry Table in Listing 9.7 is much more important in a multi-service EXE than it is in a single-service EXE like the beep service shown in Listing 9.1. In Listing 9.1, the system ignores the service name in the entry table. You can install the service under any name using the install code shown in Section 9.5 and the service will still start properly. It works because the SCM defaults to using the first **ServiceMain** function in the table if it cannot find a name match or if the EXE is marked as SERVICE_WIN32_OWN_PROCESS during installation. In a multi-service EXE, the SCM looks for the name of the service in the table when it tries to start it, and uses the **ServiceMain** function indicated in the table.

As a very simple example of multiple services in a single service EXE, say that you want to modify the beep service code shown in Listing 9.1. For example, you might want to have one service beep, and another one increment a global counter than controls the beep frequency. Change the **main** function to

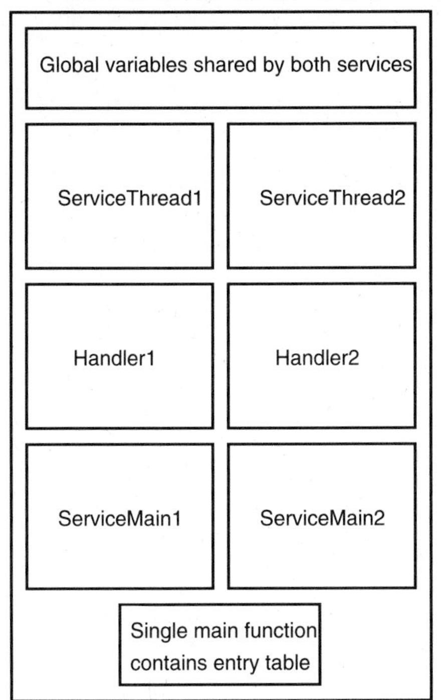

Figure 9.2
A typical EXE containing two services. Most of the code for each service is duplicated, but they share a single main function and global variables.

contain an entry table like the one shown in Listing 9.7. Duplicate the **ServiceMain** function and name the two versions **ServiceMain1** and **ServiceMain2**. Duplicate the **Handler** function and name them **Handler1** and **Handler2**. Duplicate the other peripheral pieces of code and the necessary global variables such as **terminateEvent**, **serviceStatusHandle**, and so on, and rename all of them appropriately. Then create two threads and a shared integer variable as shown in Listing 9.8.

```
int frequency = 100;

DWORD ServiceThread1(LPDWORD param)
{
   while (1)
   {
      Beep(frequency,200);
      Sleep(beepDelay);
   }
   return 0;
}

DWORD ServiceThread2(LPDWORD param)
{
   while (1)
   {
      frequency += 50;
      Sleep(5000);
   }
   return 0;
}
```

Listing 9.8
The two service threads for a simple two-service EXE

Compile the program to an EXE named `multbeep.exe`. Place this EXE in `c:\winnt` or other suitable directory. Then use the install command seen in Listing 9.2, *modified so that it contains SERVICE_WIN32_SHARE_PROCESS rather than SERVICE_WIN32_OWN_PROCESS.* Type the following two commands on the command line:

```
install Service1 "Beeper" c:\winnt\multbeep.exe
install Service2 "Beepfreq" c:\winnt\multbeep.exe
```

Note that the same EXE file is specified for both installs, but the two service names, Service1 and Service2, are different. In the Services applet of the Control Panel, you will find the two services. Start "Beeper" first. The SCM will execute the **main** function, and the entry table tells it to run **ServiceMain1** because the service name of "Beeper" is Service1. Now start "Beepfreq." The SCM will *not* execute **main** this time because the process is already running, but it will start the **ServiceMain2** thread in that process. You will hear the beep's frequency rise every five seconds.

Three things can prevent this from working:

1. If you forget to specify SERVICE_WIN32_SHARE_PROCESS in the install program and in the **SendStatusToSCM** function, then it will not be possible to start Service2.
2. If, during the installation of the service, you use service names that do not appear in the entry table, then the misnamed service will not start.
3. If you have an existing service named "Beeper" service from the previous examples, you will not be allowed to install this version of the beeper. Remove the previous instance using the code in Section 9.5.

In more complicated services that share a single EXE, you commonly need to initialize shared global variables or perform other initialization tasks used by all of the services in the EXE. If shared initializations need to take place in a multi-service EXE file, you can:

1. Place global initialization code in the **main** function prior to the call to **StartServiceCtrlDispatcher,** as long as it takes less than 30 seconds to complete.
2. Place a **CreateThread** call prior to the call to **StartServiceCtrlDispatcher** and do initializations taking longer than 30 seconds in the thread. You then need to make sure that none of the services start working prior to the completion of that initialization thread by using synchronization mechanisms (see Chapter 6).
3. Place a call to the initialization code in one of the services and make sure that only one service executes it using a semaphore or other control mechanism. Also make sure that none of the other services try to start before the initialization is complete.

As another example of a multi-service EXE, we use a logon service similar to the one described previously on our own network at the office. The only difference between our service and the one shown in Listing 9.4 is the fact that the EXE contains two services. The first senses when someone logs on, and the second performs the normal announcement activity seen in Listing 9.4. There is no advantage or disadvantage to placing these two services in a single EXE because they do not share any global variables, but they are related and it is nice to have them copied as a pair when the EXE file gets copied. Listing 9.9 shows the code for the two threads.

```
DWORD AnnounceThread(LPDWORD param)
{
   char buffer[2000];
   DWORD numRead;
   DWORD maxMsg, nextMsg, numMsg, timeout;
   HANDLE mailslot;

   mailslot = CreateMailslot(
      "\\\\.\\mailslot\\logonann", 200,
      MAILSLOT_WAIT_FOREVER, 0);

   while (1)
   {
      GetMailslotInfo(mailslot, &maxMsg,
         &nextMsg, &numMsg, &timeout);
      if (numMsg > 0)
      {
         ReadFile(mailslot, buffer, nextMsg,
            &numRead, 0);
         buffer[numRead]='\0';
```

Listing 9.9
Multiple threads in a single service to announce and sense logins (Page 1 of 3)

```
            MessageBox(0, buffer,
               "Logon Announcement", MB_OK |
               MB_SETFOREGROUND | MB_DEFAULT_DESKTOP_ONLY);
         }
         else
            Sleep(1000);
      }
      return 0;
   }

   BOOL CALLBACK EnumWindowsProc(HANDLE win,
      LPARAM param)
   {
      char buffer[100];
      DWORD numWrite;

      GetWindowText(win, buffer, 100);
      if (strncmp(buffer, "Program Manager", 15)==0 &&
         strcmp((buffer+18),currentUser) != 0)
      {
         HANDLE writeMailslot = CreateFile(
            "\\\\*\\mailslot\\logonann",
            GENERIC_WRITE, FILE_SHARE_READ, 0,
            OPEN_EXISTING, FILE_ATTRIBUTE_NORMAL, 0);
         WriteFile(writeMailslot, (buffer+18),
            strlen(buffer+18), &numWrite, 0);
         CloseHandle(writeMailslot);
         strcpy(currentUser, (buffer+18));
         return FALSE;
      }
      else
         return TRUE;
   }
```

Listing 9.9
Multiple threads in a single service to announce and sense logins (Page 2 of 3)

```
DWORD SenseThread(LPDWORD param)
{
   BOOL success;

   while (1)
   {
      success = EnumWindows(
         (WNDENUMPROC) EnumWindowsProc, 0);
      Sleep(10000);
   }
   return 0;
}
```

Listing 9.9
Multiple threads in a single service to announce and sense logins (Page 3 of 3)

9.8 Getting and Setting Configuration Information

The information passed in the call to **CreateService** in Section 9.5 gets stored in the registry when the SCM creates the service. You can view the information directly using the normal registry viewer, `regedt32.exe`, or you can run the `winmsd` command and view all service information there. Inside a program, it is possible to both retrieve a copy of this information, and to modify it. The **QueryServiceConfig** function lets you obtain a copy of the configuration information.

QueryServiceConfig — *Retrieves configuration information in the registry for the specified service*

```
BOOL QueryServiceConfig(
   SC_HANDLE service,
   LPQUERY_SERVICE_CONFIG config,
   DWORD bufSize,
   LPDWORD sizeNeeded)
```

service	A handle to the service to query

config	A pointer to a buffer for the returned information
bufSize	The size of the buffer
sizeNeeded	The amount of space needed for the buffer
Returns TRUE on success	

You must first open the service using the **OpenService** function as seen in Section 9.5. Listing 9.10 demonstrates the process.

```
// getcon.cpp

#include <windows.h>
#include <iostream.h>

void ErrorHandler(char *s, DWORD err)
{
   cout << s << endl;
   cout << "Error number: " << err << endl;
   ExitProcess(err);
}

void main(int argc, char *argv[])
{
   SC_HANDLE service, scm;
   BOOL success;
   LPQUERY_SERVICE_CONFIG buffer;
   DWORD sizeNeeded;

   if (argc != 2)
   {
```

Listing 9.10
Using the **QueryServiceConfig** function (Page 1 of 3)

```
      cout << "Usage:\n";
      cout << "   getcon service_name\n";
      return;
   }

   // Open a connection to the SCM
   scm = OpenSCManager(0, 0,
      SC_MANAGER_ALL_ACCESS);
   if (!scm)
      ErrorHandler("In OpenScManager",
         GetLastError());

   // Get the service's handle
   service = OpenService(
      scm, argv[1],
      SERVICE_QUERY_CONFIG);
   if (!service)
      ErrorHandler("In OpenService",
         GetLastError());

   // Find out how big the buffer needs to be
   success = QueryServiceConfig(service, 0, 0,
      &sizeNeeded);

   // Allocate space for the buffer
   buffer = (LPQUERY_SERVICE_CONFIG)
      LocalAlloc (LPTR, sizeNeeded);

   // Get the buffer
   success = QueryServiceConfig(service, buffer,
      sizeNeeded, &sizeNeeded);
   if (!success)
      ErrorHandler("In QueryServiceConfig",
         GetLastError());
```

Listing 9.10
Using the **QueryServiceConfig** function (Page 2 of 3)

```
        // Print the contents of the buffer
        cout << "Service type: "
            << buffer->dwServiceType << endl;
        cout << "Start type: "
            << buffer->dwStartType << endl;
        // and so on

        // Clean up
        LocalFree(buffer);
        CloseServiceHandle(service);
        CloseServiceHandle(scm);
    }
```

Listing 9.10
Using the **QueryServiceConfig** function (Page 3 of 3)

The code in Listing 9.10 first opens a connection to the SCM, and then to a specific service. It then calls **QueryServiceConfig** once to get the size of the buffer it needs. This buffer size changes because of the variable-size strings that hold the EXE path, dependencies, and so on. Once the size is known, the appropriate amount of space is allocated and the function is called again to retrieve the data.

Changing configuration information in the registry using **ChangeServiceConfig** follows a similar path, but you must lock the database before you modify it to ensure that no other process tries to use the database during modification. Generally you would either get the current configuration values for a service using the code shown in Listing 9.10 and then modify that information, or alternatively you could specify field values in the call to **ChangeServiceConfig** that causes them to remain unchanged. The parameters for **ChangeServiceConfig** follow those of **CreateService** almost exactly.

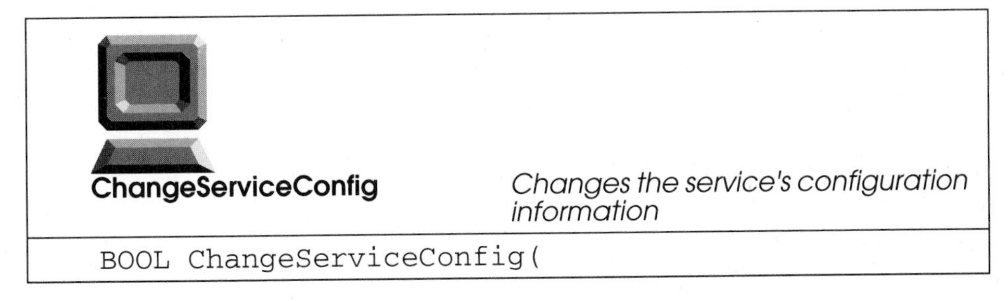

```
    SC_HANDLE service,
    DWORD serviceType,
    DWORD start,
    DWORD errorSeverity,
    LPCTSTR exePath,
    LPCTSTR loadOrderGroup,
    LPDWORD ID,
    LPCTSTR dependencies,
    LPCTSTR serviceAccount,
    LPCTSTR password,
    LPCTSTR displayName)
```

service	A handle to the service to change
serviceType	The type of service, i.e. process or driver
start	The start type: auto or manual
errorSeverity	Specifies the severity of a failure to start
exePath	The full path to the executable containing the service
loadOrderGroup	A string containing NULL or one of the load ordering groups from the registry
ID	An ID value for the ordering group used
dependencies	A pointer to an array of strings containing the names of services that must start before this one
account	The account the service uses when it starts. If NULL, LocalSystem is used. Otherwise use "domain\account"
password	Password of the account. Pass NULL for no password
displayName	The name of the service displayed in the Service applet

Returns TRUE on success

On the **serviceType**, **start**, and **errorSeverity** fields, the SERVICE_NO_CHANGE value indicates that you want to make no change to the field. A zero in any other field indicates no change. Listing 9.11 demonstrates the use of this function.

```
// setcon.cpp

#include <windows.h>
#include <iostream.h>

void ErrorHandler(char *s, DWORD err)
{
   cout << s << endl;
   cout << "Error number: " << err << endl;
   ExitProcess(err);
}

void main(int argc, char *argv[])
{
   SC_HANDLE service, scm;
   BOOL success;
   SC_LOCK lock;

   if (argc != 2)
   {
      cout << "Usage:\n";
      cout << "   setcon service_name\n";
      return;
   }

   // Open a connection to the SCM
```

Listing 9.11
Changing a service's configuration (Page 1 of 3)

```
    scm = OpenSCManager(0, 0,
        SC_MANAGER_ALL_ACCESS | GENERIC_WRITE);
    if (!scm)
        ErrorHandler("In OpenScManager",
            GetLastError());

    lock = LockServiceDatabase(scm);
    if (lock == 0)
        ErrorHandler("In LockServiceDatabase",
            GetLastError());

    // Get the service's handle
    service = OpenService(
        scm, argv[1],
        SERVICE_ALL_ACCESS);
    if (!service)
    {
        DWORD err = GetLastError();
        UnlockServiceDatabase(lock);
        ErrorHandler("In ChangeServiceConfig", err);
    }

    // Change the service to automatic start mode
    success = ChangeServiceConfig(
        service,
        SERVICE_NO_CHANGE,
        SERVICE_AUTO_START,
        SERVICE_NO_CHANGE,
        0, 0, 0, 0, 0, 0, 0);
    if (!success)
    {
        DWORD err = GetLastError();
        UnlockServiceDatabase(lock);
        ErrorHandler("In ChangeServiceConfig", err);
    }
```

Listing 9.11
Changing a service's configuration (Page 2 of 3)

```
        // unlock the database
        success = UnlockServiceDatabase(lock);
        if (!success)
            ErrorHandler("In UnlockServiceDatabase",
                GetLastError());

        // Clean up
        CloseServiceHandle(service);
        CloseServiceHandle(scm);
    }
```

Listing 9.11
Changing a service's configuration (Page 3 of 3)

The code in Listing 9.11 starts by opening a connection to the Service Control Manager and then locks the database using **LockServiceDatabase**. If this function fails, it is either because the database is already locked by someone else, or because the call to **OpenSCManager** did not request access to lock the database.

LockServiceDatabase	*Locks the service database to guarantee exclusive access during a configuration change*
`SC_LOCK LockServiceDatabase(` `    SC_HANDLE scm)`	
scm	A handle to the scm
Returns a lock or 0 on error	

The function then proceeds to open a specific service and to change its configuration. In this case, it sets the service to start automatically. The code then unlocks the database.

UnlockServiceDatabase	*Unlocks the service database*
`BOOL UnlockServiceDatabase(` `SC_LOCK lock)`	
lock	A lock created by LockServiceDatabase
Returns TRUE on success	

You can also use the **QueryServiceLockStatus** function to check on a lock's current status. Call it using the same technique shown in Listing 9.10 for the call to **QueryServiceConfig**.

9.9 Controlling Services

Generally you control a service using the Services applet in the Control Panel. This service allows you to start, stop, pause, and resume any service. There are some cases, however, where it is useful to be able to control a service either from a separate program or from another service. The **ControlService** and **StartService** functions allow you to control services in your code.

ControlService	*Sends a control constant to the specified service*

`BOOL ControlService(`
`SC_HANDLE service,`
`DWORD control,`
`LPSERVICE_STATUS status)`	

service	A handle to the service
control	Control constant telling the service what to do
status	A pointer to a SERVICE_STATUS structure
Returns TRUE on success	

The **ControlService** function accepts a handle to the service, a control constant, and a pointer to a SERVICE_STATUS record so that it can return the current status after the requested action. If the service was opened using SERVICE_ALL_ACCESS or SERVICE_USER_DEFINED_CONTROL access, then it is possible to send a user defined control constant (between 128 and 255) to the service. Otherwise, the following constants are understood:

SERVICE_CONTROL_STOP
SERVICE_CONTROL_PAUSE
SERVICE_CONTROL_CONTINUE
SERVICE_CONTROL_INTERROGATE
SERVICE_CONTROL_SHUTDOWN

The user-defined constants provide a very limited communication path between outside programs and a service. For example, one program might send in the special value 132 and the service could respond by sending back a special, service-defined error code. More complicated forms of communication are normally accomplished using named pipes.

Starting a service is different from stopping, pausing, or resuming a service as shown in Listing 9.12. The latter three work through the **Handler** function in the service, while a start operation requires that the SCM to start a thread that executes the **ServiceMain** function for the service. A separate call to the **StartService** function tells the SCM to perform a start operation.

StartService	*Starts the indicated service*

`BOOL StartService(`
`    SC_HANDLE service,`
`    DWORD argc,`
`    LPCTSTR *argv)`	

service	A handle to the service created by **OpenService**
argc	The number of strings in argv
argv	A standard argv array of pointers to character
Returns TRUE on success	

The **argc** and **argv** values allow you to pass startup parameters to the service as you can from the Services applet in the Control Panel. Pass zero in both parameters if you do not wish to pass any parameters.

```
// startsvc.cpp

#include <windows.h>
#include <iostream.h>

void ErrorHandler(char *s, DWORD err)
{
   cout << s << endl;
   cout << "Error number: " << err << endl;
   ExitProcess(err);
}

void main(int argc, const char *argv[])
{
   SC_HANDLE service, scm;
   BOOL success;

   if (argc < 2)
   {
      cout << "Usage:\n";
      cout << "   start service_name arguments\n";
      cout << "   the arguments are passed as \
startup arguments to the service\n";
      return;
   }

   // Open a connection to the SCM
```

Listing 9.12
Starting a service (Page 1 of 2)

```
    scm = OpenSCManager(0, 0,
       SC_MANAGER_ALL_ACCESS | GENERIC_WRITE);
    if (!scm)
       ErrorHandler("In OpenScManager",
          GetLastError());

    // Get the service's handle
    service = OpenService(
       scm, argv[1],
       SERVICE_ALL_ACCESS);
    if (!service)
       ErrorHandler("In OpenService",
          GetLastError());

    // Start the service, passing
    // it startup parameters
    success = StartService(service,
       argc-2, &argv[2]);
    if (!success)
       ErrorHandler("In StartService",
          GetLastError());

    // Clean up
    CloseServiceHandle(service);
    CloseServiceHandle(scm);
}
```

Listing 9.12
Starting a service (Page 2 of 2)

9.10 Enumerating Services

NT offers two ways to enumerate services. Using the **EnumServicesStatus** function you can enumerate all of the available services. Using **EnumDependentServices** you can enumerate the services that a specific service expects to have started before it starts. Listing 9.13 demonstrates the **EnumServicesStatus** function.

```
// enum.cpp

#include <windows.h>
#include <iostream.h>

void ErrorHandler(char *s, DWORD err)
{
   cout << s << endl;
   cout << "Error number: " << err << endl;
   ExitProcess(err);
}

void main(int argc, const char *argv[])
{
   SC_HANDLE scm;
   BOOL success;
   LPENUM_SERVICE_STATUS status;
   DWORD numServices=0, sizeNeeded=0, resume=0;

   // Open a connection to the SCM
   scm = OpenSCManager(0, 0,
      SC_MANAGER_ALL_ACCESS);
   if (!scm)
      ErrorHandler("In OpenScManager",
         GetLastError());

   // get the number of bytes to allocate
   // MAKE SURE resume starts at 0
   resume = 0;
   success = EnumServicesStatus(scm,
```

Listing 9.13
Enumerating available services (Page 1 of 2)

```
            SERVICE_WIN32 | SERVICE_DRIVER,
            SERVICE_ACTIVE | SERVICE_INACTIVE,
            0, 0, &sizeNeeded, &numServices, &resume);
        if (GetLastError() != ERROR_MORE_DATA)
            ErrorHandler("In EnumServicesStatus1",
                GetLastError());
        // Allocate space
        status = (LPENUM_SERVICE_STATUS)
            LocalAlloc(LPTR, sizeNeeded);

        // Get the status records. Making an assumption
        // here that no new services get added during
        // the allocation (could lock the database to
        // guarantee that...)
        resume = 0;
        success = EnumServicesStatus(scm,
            SERVICE_WIN32 | SERVICE_DRIVER,
            SERVICE_ACTIVE | SERVICE_INACTIVE,
            status, sizeNeeded, &sizeNeeded,
                &numServices, &resume);
        if (!success)
            ErrorHandler("In EnumServicesStatus",
                GetLastError());

        DWORD i;
        for (i=0; i < numServices; i++)
            cout << i << " "
                << status[i].lpServiceName << " "
                << status[i].lpDisplayName << endl;

        // Clean up
        LocalFree(status);
        CloseServiceHandle(scm);
    }
```

Listing 9.13
Enumerating available services (Page 2 of 2)

The code in Listing 9.13 starts by opening a connection to the SCM. It then calls **EnumServicesStatus** once to get the amount of memory needed to store all of the service entries in the database. Here it requests all services in existence by requesting SERVICE_WIN32 and SERVICE_DRIVER in the **serviceType** field and SERVICE_ACTIVE and SERVICE_INACTIVE in the **serviceState** field.

EnumServicesStatus — *Retrieves the names and status records of all requested services*

```
BOOL EnumServicesStatus(
    SC_HANDLE scm,
    DWORD serviceType,
    DWORD serviceState,
    LPENUM_SERVICE_STATUS buffer,
    DWORD bufferSize,
    LPDWORD sizeNeeded,
    LPDWORD numServices,
    LPDWORD resume)
```

Parameter	Description
scm	A handle to the scm
serviceType	The types of services to retrieve (normal and/or drivers)
serviceState	The service state to filter on (active and/or inactive)
buffer	A buffer to hold the retrieved information
bufferSize	Number of bytes available in the buffer
sizeNeeded	Amount of space needed to complete
numServices	Number of services placed in buffer
resume	A pointer to the next service to retrieve on multiple retrievals. Must start at zero

Returns TRUE on success. If FALSE and GetLastError returns ERROR_MORE_DATA then the buffer was not big enough and a second call should be made

In this particular program, all of the required space is allocated at once, but it is also possible to use a fixed size buffer and call **EnumServicesStatus** multiple times. The program then walks through the returned array and prints out the name and display name of each service. By passing different flags into the **serviceType** and **serviceState** parameters, you can control the types of services returned in the array.

The **EnumDependentServices** function works in the same way, but you open a specific service and the function returns a status array for all of the services it is dependent on. You set the dependent services by passing an array of service names to **CreateService** or **ChangeServiceConfig**.

9.11 Placing an RPC Server in a Service

Chapter 8 describes RPCs and RPC servers. Once you have created and debugged an RPC server, you will often want to place it in a service so that it is always available on the network.

Listings 9.14 through 9.19 demonstrate the files necessary to create an RPC server service. These listings combine the simple service shown in Listing 9.1 with the auto-binding RPC server for **SumUp** demonstrated in Listings 8.1 through 8.4. You can use the RPC client in Listing 8.5 to test the new service. *Use the installation program in Section 9.5 to install the RPC server service in the Services Applet of the Control Panel.* See Chapter 8 for a complete description of this process.

```
// sum.cpp

#include <windows.h>
```

Listing 9.14
The implementation of **SumUp,** identical to Listing 8.1 (Page 1 of 2)

```
#include "sum.h"

long SumUp(short sumVal)
{
  short iter;
  long theSum;

  theSum=0;
  for (iter=1; iter<=sumVal; theSum+=iter, iter++);

  Beep(300, 30);

  return(theSum);
}
```

Listing 9.14
The implementation of **SumUp,** identical to Listing 8.1 (Page 2 of 2)

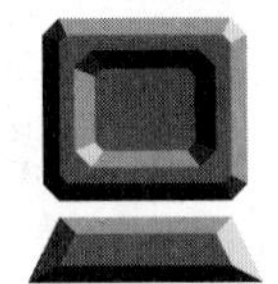

```
// sumserv.cpp

#include <windows.h>
#include <iostream.h>
#include <rpc.h>
#include "sum.h"
#include "memstub"

// Global variables

// The name of the service
char *SERVICE_NAME = "SumService";
```

Listing 9.15
The Service implementing the RPC server. Compare to Listings 9.1 and 8.2 (Page 1 of 11)

```
// Event used to hold ServiceMain from completing
HANDLE terminateEvent = NULL;
// Handle used to communicate status info with
// the SCM. Created by RegisterServiceCtrlHandler
SERVICE_STATUS_HANDLE serviceStatusHandle;
// Flags holding current state of service
BOOL pauseService = FALSE;
BOOL runningService = FALSE;

// Initializes the service
BOOL InitService()
{
   RPC_BINDING_VECTOR *bindVector;

   runningService = TRUE;

   // use protocols specified by interface
   if (RpcServerUseAllProtseqsIf(1,
      sumup_v1_1_s_ifspec,
      NULL))
      return FALSE;

   // register the interface
   if (RpcServerRegisterIf(sumup_v1_1_s_ifspec,
      NULL, NULL))
      return FALSE;

   // get binding handles available
   if (RpcServerInqBindings(&bindVector))
      return FALSE;

   // export binding info
   if (RpcNsBindingExport(RPC_C_NS_SYNTAX_DEFAULT,
      (UCHAR *) "/.:/autorpc",
      sumup_v1_1_s_ifspec,
```

Listing 9.15
The Service implementing the RPC server. Compare to Listings 9.1 and 8.2
(Page 2 of 11)

```
            bindVector, NULL))
        {
            // release memory used by binding vectors
            RpcBindingVectorFree(&bindVector);
            return FALSE;
        }

        // release memory used by binding vectors
        if (RpcBindingVectorFree(&bindVector))
            return FALSE;

        // activate this server
        if (RpcServerListen(1, 5, TRUE))
            return FALSE;

        return TRUE;
    }

    // Resumes a paused service
    VOID ResumeService()
    {
        pauseService=FALSE;
        // reactivate this server
        RpcServerListen(1, 5, TRUE);
    }

    // Pauses the service
    VOID PauseService()
    {
        pauseService = TRUE;
        // stop accepting new calls
        RpcMgmtStopServerListening(NULL);
        // wait for existing calls to finish
        RpcMgmtWaitServerListen();
    }
```

Listing 9.15
The Service implementing the RPC server. Compare to Listings 9.1 and 8.2
(Page 3 of 11)

```
// Stops the service by allowing ServiceMain
// to complete
VOID StopService()
{
   runningService=FALSE;
   // Set the event that is holding ServiceMain
   // so that ServiceMain can return
   SetEvent(terminateEvent);
}

// This function consolidates the activities of
// updating the service status
// with SetServiceStatus
BOOL SendStatusToSCM (DWORD dwCurrentState,
   DWORD dwWin32ExitCode,
   DWORD dwServiceSpecificExitCode,
   DWORD dwCheckPoint,
   DWORD dwWaitHint)
{
   BOOL success;
   SERVICE_STATUS serviceStatus;

   // Fill in all of the SERVICE_STATUS fields
   serviceStatus.dwServiceType =
      SERVICE_WIN32_OWN_PROCESS;
   serviceStatus.dwCurrentState = dwCurrentState;

   // If in the process of starting, then accept
   // no control events, else accept anything
   if (dwCurrentState == SERVICE_START_PENDING)
      serviceStatus.dwControlsAccepted = 0;
   else
      serviceStatus.dwControlsAccepted =
         SERVICE_ACCEPT_STOP |
```

Listing 9.15
The Service implementing the RPC server. Compare to Listings 9.1 and 8.2
(Page 4 of 11)

```
              SERVICE_ACCEPT_PAUSE_CONTINUE |
              SERVICE_ACCEPT_SHUTDOWN;

   // if a specific exit code is defines, set up
   // the win32 exit code properly
   if (dwServiceSpecificExitCode == 0)
      serviceStatus.dwWin32ExitCode =
      dwWin32ExitCode;
   else
      serviceStatus.dwWin32ExitCode =
         ERROR_SERVICE_SPECIFIC_ERROR;
   serviceStatus.dwServiceSpecificExitCode =
      dwServiceSpecificExitCode;

   serviceStatus.dwCheckPoint = dwCheckPoint;
   serviceStatus.dwWaitHint = dwWaitHint;

   // Pass the status record to the SCM
   success = SetServiceStatus (serviceStatusHandle,
      &serviceStatus);
   if (!success)
      StopService();

   return success;
}

// Dispatches events received from the service
// control manager
VOID ServiceCtrlHandler (DWORD controlCode)
{
   DWORD  currentState = 0;
   BOOL success;

   switch(controlCode)
   {
```

Listing 9.15
The Service implementing the RPC server. Compare to Listings 9.1 and 8.2
(Page 5 of 11)

```
        // There is no START option because
        // ServiceMain gets called on a start

        // Stop the service
        case SERVICE_CONTROL_STOP:
           currentState = SERVICE_STOP_PENDING;
           // Tell the SCM what's happening
           success = SendStatusToSCM(
              SERVICE_STOP_PENDING,
              NO_ERROR, 0, 1, 5000);
           // Not much to do if not successful

           // Allow ServiceMain to return
           SetEvent(terminateEvent);
           return;

        // Pause the service
        case SERVICE_CONTROL_PAUSE:
           if (runningService && !pauseService)
           {
              // Tell the SCM what's happening
              success = SendStatusToSCM(
                 SERVICE_PAUSE_PENDING,
                 NO_ERROR, 0, 1, 1000);
              PauseService();
              currentState = SERVICE_PAUSED;
           }
           break;

        // Resume from a pause
        case SERVICE_CONTROL_CONTINUE:
           if (runningService && pauseService)
           {
              ResumeService();
              // Tell the SCM what's happening
```

Listing 9.15
The Service implementing the RPC server. Compare to Listings 9.1 and 8.2
(Page 6 of 11)

```
                success = SendStatusToSCM(
                    SERVICE_CONTINUE_PENDING,
                    NO_ERROR, 0, 1, 1000);
                currentState = SERVICE_RUNNING;
            }
            break;

        // Update current status
        case SERVICE_CONTROL_INTERROGATE:
            // it will fall to bottom and send status
            break;

        // Do nothing in a shutdown. Could do cleanup
        // here, but it must be very quick.
        case SERVICE_CONTROL_SHUTDOWN:
            // Do nothing on shutdown
            return;
        default:
            break;
    }
    SendStatusToSCM(currentState, NO_ERROR,
        0, 0, 0);
}

// Handle an error from ServiceMain by cleaning up
// and telling SCM that the service didn't start.
VOID terminate(DWORD error)
{
    if (!error)
    {
        // stop accepting new calls
        RpcMgmtStopServerListening(NULL);

        // remove binding info
        RpcNsBindingUnexport(RPC_C_NS_SYNTAX_DEFAULT,
```

Listing 9.15
The Service implementing the RPC server. Compare to Listings 9.1 and 8.2 (Page 7 of 11)

```
            (UCHAR *) "/.:/autorpc",
            sumup_v1_1_s_ifspec,
            NULL);

         // unregister interface and wait
         // for existing calls to finish
         RpcServerUnregisterIf(NULL, NULL, TRUE);
      }

      // if terminateEvent has been created, close it.
      if (terminateEvent)
         CloseHandle(terminateEvent);

      // Send a message to the SCM to tell about
      //stopage
      if (serviceStatusHandle)
         SendStatusToSCM(SERVICE_STOPPED, error,
            0, 0, 0);

      // Do not need to close serviceStatusHandle
   }

   // ServiceMain is called when the SCM wants
   // to start the service. When it returns,
   // the service has stopped. It
   // Therefore waits on an event just before the end
   // of the function, and that event gets set
   // when it is time to stop. It also returns
   // on any error because the
   // service cannot start if there is an eror.
   VOID ServiceMain(DWORD argc, LPTSTR *argv)
   {
      BOOL success;

      // immediately call Registration function
```

Listing 9.15
The Service implementing the RPC server. Compare to Listings 9.1 and 8.2
(Page 8 of 11)

```
        serviceStatusHandle =
           RegisterServiceCtrlHandler(SERVICE_NAME,
              (LPHANDLER_FUNCTION)ServiceCtrlHandler);
        if (!serviceStatusHandle)
        {
           terminate(GetLastError());
           return;
        }

        // Notify SCM of progress
        success = SendStatusToSCM(
           SERVICE_START_PENDING,
           NO_ERROR, 0, 1, 5000);
        if (!success)
        {
           terminate(GetLastError());
           return;
        }

        // create the termination event
        terminateEvent = CreateEvent (0, TRUE,
           FALSE, 0);
        if (!terminateEvent)
        {
           terminate(GetLastError());
           return;
        }

        // Notify SCM of progress
        success = SendStatusToSCM(
           SERVICE_START_PENDING,
           NO_ERROR, 0, 2, 1000);
        if (!success)
        {
           terminate(GetLastError());
```

Listing 9.15
The Service implementing the RPC server. Compare to Listings 9.1 and 8.2
(Page 9 of 11)

```
        return;
    }

    // Start the service itself
    success = InitService();
    if (!success)
    {
        terminate(GetLastError());
        return;
    }

    // The service is now running.
    // Notify SCM of progress
    success = SendStatusToSCM(
        SERVICE_RUNNING,
        NO_ERROR, 0, 0, 0);
    if (!success)
    {
        terminate(GetLastError());
        return;
    }

    // Wait for stop signal, and then terminate
    WaitForSingleObject (terminateEvent, INFINITE);

    terminate(0);
}

VOID main(VOID)
{
    SERVICE_TABLE_ENTRY serviceTable[] =
    {
    { SERVICE_NAME,
        (LPSERVICE_MAIN_FUNCTION) ServiceMain},
    { NULL, NULL }
```

Listing 9.15
The Service implementing the RPC server. Compare to Listings 9.1 and 8.2
(Page 10 of 11)

```
    };
    BOOL success;

    // Register with the SCM
    success =
       StartServiceCtrlDispatcher(serviceTable);
    if (!success)
       ExitProcess(GetLastError());
}
```

Listing 9.15
The Service implementing the RPC server. Compare to Listings 9.1 and 8.2 (Page 11 of 11)

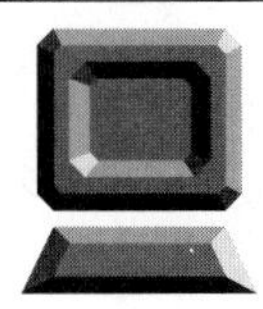

```
[
  uuid (22449651-4321-1234-4321-987654321CBA),
  version(1.1),
  endpoint ("ncacn_np:[\\pipe\\autorpc]")
]
interface sumup
{
  long SumUp([in] short sumVal);
}
```

Listing 9.16
The IDL file, identical to Listing 8.3

```
[
  auto_handle
```

Listing 9.17
The ACF file, identical to Listing 8.4 (Page 1 of 2)

```
]
interface sumup
{
}
```

Listing 9.17
The ACF file, identical to Listing 8.4 (Page 2 of 2)

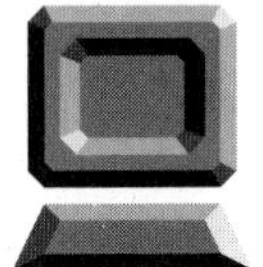

```
void __RPC_FAR * __RPC_API
   midl_user_allocate(size_t len)
{
   return(new(unsigned char [len]));
}

void __RPC_API midl_user_free(void __RPC_FAR * ptr)
{
   delete(ptr);
}
```

Listing 9.18
The memstub file

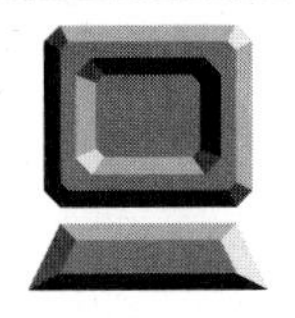

```
NODEBUG=1
SERVER=sumserv
RPCFILE=sum

!include <ntwin32.mak>

.SUFFIXES: .cpp
```

Listing 9.19
The makefile (Page 1 of 2)

```
.c.obj:
   $(cc) -J $(cflags) $(cvars) $(cdebug) $<

.cpp.obj:
   $(cc) -J $(cflags) $(cvars) $(cdebug) $<

all: $(SERVER).exe


$(SERVER).exe: $(SERVER).obj $(RPCFILE).obj \
$(RPCFILE)_s.obj
   $(link) $(conlflags) $(ldebug) $(conlibs) \
   rpcrt4.lib \
   rpcns4.lib advapi32.lib -out:$(SERVER).exe \
   $(SERVER).obj $(RPCFILE).obj \
   $(RPCFILE)_s.obj


$(SERVER).obj: $(SERVER).cpp $(RPCFILE).h

$(RPCFILE).obj: $(RPCFILE).cpp $(RPCFILE).h

$(RPCFILE)_s.obj: $(RPCFILE)_s.c $(RPCFILE).h

$(RPCFILE).h $(RPCFILE)_s.c: \
$(RPCFILE).idl $(RPCFILE).acf
   midl -client none $(RPCFILE).idl
```

Listing 9.19
The makefile (Page 2 of 2)

The RPC server demonstrated here uses auto handles. In Listing 9.15, the **InitService** function starts the RPC server and registers with the name server. Once it calls **RpcServerListen** the RPC server is available (note that **RpcServerListen**'s last parameter is TRUE so the function returns). The **PauseService** function in Listing 9.15 causes the RPC server to stop listening. The server waits for all pending function calls to clear, and then **PauseService** returns. The

ResumeService function resumes the RPC server by letting it listen for connections again.

The service formally stops the RPC server in the **terminate** function by first calling **RpcMgmtStopServerListening**. It then unregisters the server with the name server and unregisters the interface. The service can then proceed with its normal termination activities.

Compile the RPC server service code to create the service's EXE file. Install the service using the installation program in Section 9.5. You should then be able to start the service using the Services applet in the Control Panel. Once started, run the client in Listing 8.5 to test the server.

You may want to modify the installation program so that this service is dependent on the RPC locator or other services that it needs to execute properly.

By following the pattern shown above, you can successfully adapt any RPC server so that it runs as a service.

9.12 Conclusion

As discussed in the first section of this chapter, you can use services in a variety of ways to create programs that run constantly on an NT machine. By using the beep service in Listing 9.1 as a template, you can easily add in your own code and quickly create a wide variety of services.

Services depend heavily on threads. See Chapter 5 and 6 for information on threads and thread synchronization. Services also rely on the registry, which is described in Chapter 15.

SECURITY

10

One of the most fascinating parts of Windows NT is its security system. As demonstrated in the last nine chapters, it is possible to almost completely ignore this part of the 32-bit API if you don't care to secure things. However, there are many situations where the security features built into NT can help to solve some very interesting problems. In this chapter you will learn about the intent of NT's security system, the concepts that help you to understand what is going on, and the techniques used to manipulate it.

Please note that some of the code in this chapter will not work as described unless you log in as the administrator. Only administrators have the rights necessary to perform some of the system security tasks demonstrated here.

Compatibility Note: All of the code in this chapter works in Windows NT. None of it works in Windows 95 at the time of publication due to unimplemented functions.

10.1 The Possibilities

Most people have never seen or worked with a security system as complete and intricate as NT's. Experienced UNIX programmers are familiar with UNIX's file security system and with the idea of root privileges, but these systems are primitive compared to NT. The following examples give you some feeling for the scope and preciseness of NT's security system.

- People using the NT File System can see the security features built into it because of the Security menu and security editor in the File Manager. You can write your own code that modifies the security information in an NT File System volume at that same level of detail. From programs that you write, you can control who has what type of access to any file on an NTFS volume, just like the File Manager does.

- You can create a named pipe server on one system that, for example, only administrators on other systems can access. When people try to connect to the server, the security system will check to make sure they have the proper access authority and reject users who do not have administrative privileges. You might do this so that administrators on different machines can send information to one another in a way that guarantees authenticity. You can write code so that it selectively allows or denies access to any user or group of users, or to all users.
- You can create a mutex with security attributes that allow only certain users or groups to access it. This capability applies to any object in the system: files, semaphores, threads, events, shared memory in file mappings, and so on. In the case of a mutex, you can use this facility to guard against unauthorized access to the synchronization mechanism of an application.
- You can give any object (for example, a thread, mutex, pipe, file, or registry key) the ability to create an entry in the event log whenever it is accessed. You can specify individual types of access, and individual users, that generate an event log entry. For example, you can cause a specific file to generate an event log entry whenever the user "smith" successfully reads that file.

The above examples show that NT allows you to give precise security access to specific objects in the system, and it also allows you to monitor and record how objects are used.

10.2 Understanding the Terminology and Concepts of the NT Security System

One of the most interesting and frustrating parts of the NT security system is the huge number of new concepts that it contains, along with the vocabulary that describes these concepts. The goal of this section is to put those concepts into simple terms so that you can understand them.

By now you are already familiar with the most visible part of the security system: passwords. You can think of the password system as the lock on the front door of a building. The password system keeps people out of an NT system just like a lock on a building keeps people from wandering around in the lobby. Your password gives you a key to the building that is an NT system.

If one of your hard disks is formatted with the NT File System, then you know that there is a second layer of security in NT as well. You can think of this second layer as locks on individual rooms inside of the building. Some rooms are wide open and anyone can walk in, while others have locks on them. The locks on an individual room can be *very* specific in NT. For example, you can create a file on a volume formatted with the NT File System and you can let any combination of people access it:

- You can let no one but the owner access it
- You can let a single user access it
- You can let several individual users access it
- You can name an NT group and let any member of that group access it
- You can name an NT group and let any member of that group access it, but then specifically deny access to individual members of the group
- You can name multiple groups that can access it
- You can let anyone access it

Think of a secured file as a room. The security permissions that you put on the file are like a lock that determines who is allowed into the room. You can also control what a person is allowed to do once they get into a room. For example, with a file you can give one user read access, another user write access, and so on. See the Permissions dialog in the Security menu of the File Manager for examples.

You can also put a sentry at the door of any of the rooms. The sentry's job is to monitor who uses the room, and how they use it. This is called *auditing* in NT. When you attach an auditing request to an NT object, the object writes entries in the security portion of the event log whenever certain users access the object in specified ways. For example, if you have access to an NT file system volume and have administrative privileges, open the File Manager and select a file that you own. Then select the Auditing option in the Security menu. For any individual user or group, you can detect when they successfully or unsuccessfully (or both) read the file, write to the file, execute the file, and so on.

The most obvious place to see these security features is in the NT File System. The security editor in the File Manager lets you easily and graphically ma-

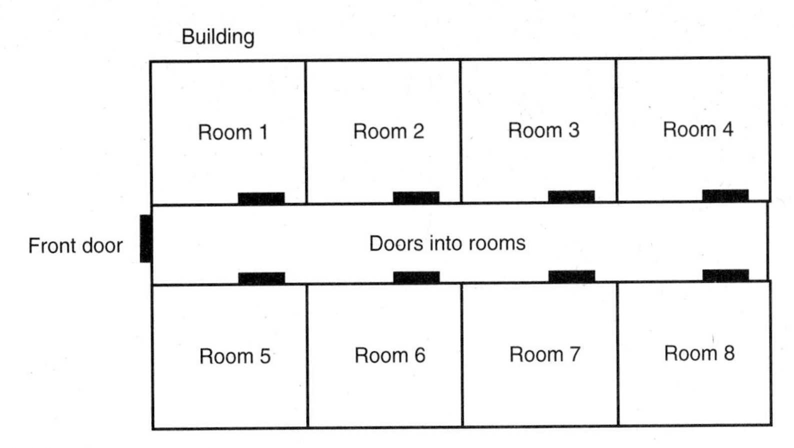

Figure 10.1
Think of NT as a building full of rooms. Your password gives you a key that lets you into the building. Once inside, you can then use your key to enter individual rooms. Some rooms have no locks, while others are locked and will let you in, and still others will refuse you entry. The rooms are individual objects in the NT system: files, registry keys, thread and mutex objects, and so on.

nipulate all of the different security features available for files. This same level of security detail applies to many different objects in NT. For example, you can secure items in the Registry with this level of detail, and in fact the registry editor contains the same sort of visual security editor that the File Manager contains. You can also specify security attributes on many internal system objects. For example, you can limit access to a named pipe (see Section 10.9) in this way.

Here is a brief summary of these concepts:

- An NT system is like a building. Your password gives you a key into the building.
- Once you are inside you find potentially thousands of rooms. A file is like a room, and so is a registry entry, a named pipe, a thread, and so on.
- Each room can be secured by its owner with a lock that is keyed for user and group IDs. That is, the owner of the room can let just one person use the room, or a collection of users and groups, or everyone.
- Each room can also be manned with a sentry who detects and records who enters the room and what each person does once they are inside.

Now that you understand the general concepts, let's look at some of NT's specific vocabulary for discussing security.

10.3 NT Security Vocabulary

When you log in to an NT system, the system gives you an *access token*. The access token is your key to all of the locks found in an NT system. Your key will turn some locks, but it will not work in all of them unless you log in as the administrator. Each process that you create contains a copy of your access token.

The access token does two different things. First, it identifies *who you are*. For example, if you logged in as the user "smith," then your access token contains your identity as that user. The access token also identifies you by all of the groups you belong to. For example, in the User Manager you may be a member of the Power User group, the Backup Operator group, and a custom group named Programmers. Your access token identifies you as a member of these different groups.

Your access token also contains all of your *user rights*. Each group you belong to can have user rights, or *privileges*, associated with it. If you open the User Manager you can look at the list of rights with the User Rights menu option. For example, power users and administrators have the right to set the system time, while normal users do not. Some users can shut down the system while others cannot, and so on. The system builds up the list of rights in your access token by combining all of the individual rights found in each group you belong to. Individual users can also have special rights granted to them specifically by the administrator with the User Manager.

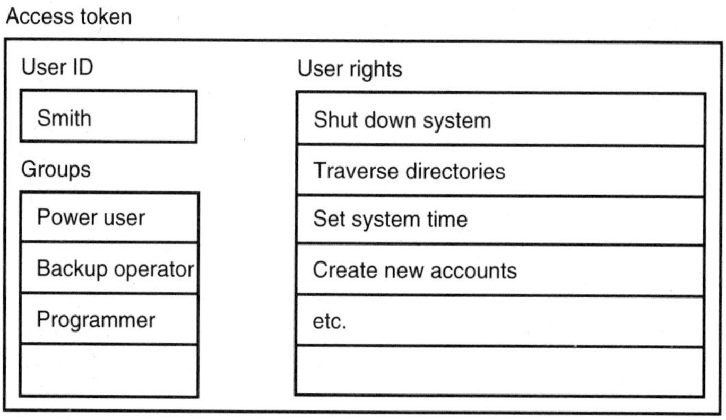

Access token

User ID
Smith
Groups
Power user
Backup operator
Programmer

User rights
Shut down system
Traverse directories
Set system time
Create new accounts
etc.

Figure 10.2
An access token contains a user ID, the names of the groups the user belongs to, and the combined user rights from all of those groups.

Most of the objects in the system can have locks on them. In NT, a lock is called a *security descriptor*. If the **Create** function for an object contains a security parameter, you can lock it. The following objects can have locks:

- Files (if they exist on an NT File System volume)
- Directories (if they exist on an NT File System volume)
- Registry keys
- Processes
- Threads
- Mutexes
- Semaphores
- Events
- Named pipes (on the system *and* over the network)
- Anonymous pipes (on the system only)
- Mailslots (on the system only)
- Console screen buffers
- File mappings
- Services
- Private objects

To lock an object, you create a security descriptor and pass it to the object when you create it. In all of the previous sections in this book, the example code has passed a zero in for the security attributes parameter to functions such as **CreateFile** or **CreateThread**. The zero indicates to the system that it should create a default security descriptor that allows you to access the object. See Section 10.8 for a description of default security descriptors.

A security descriptor contains four things:

1. An owner identifier that identifies the current owner of the object
2. A primary group identifier
3. A *system access control list*, or SACL, that contains auditing information
4. A *discretionary access control list*, or DACL, that determines which users and groups can and cannot access the object

The owner of an NT object can always set its security information. For example, if you own a file and accidentally set it so that no one can access it, you can still go back and change its security because you are the owner. It is like breaking the lock to your house: Even though the lock is broken, you can always replace it with a new one because you own the house.

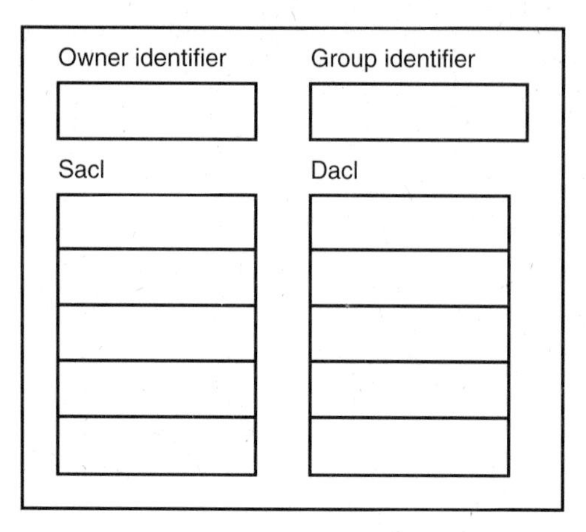

Figure 10.3
The security descriptor for any object contains the owner and group IDs, the discretionary access control list that determines who can and cannot access the object, and the system access control list that controls who gets audited when they use the object.

The DACL (Discretionary Access Control List) is the heart of the actual lock. It controls who can and cannot access the object. It is an *access control list*, or ACL, that contains *access control entries*, or ACEs. Each ACE indicates one user or group, along with what they can or cannot do to the object. For example, if the object is a file and the user "smith" is allowed to read from the file, then there will be an ACE that indicates that user "smith" has read access. This is called an *access allowed ACE* because it allows a user or group to do something. There is one access allowed ace for each person or group allowed to access the object. Similarly, there are *access denied ACEs* which deny specific users or groups access. For example, if you have given the Power Users group access to an object, but "smith" is a power user and you don't want him to have access, an access denied ACE keeps him out.

The SACL (System Access Control List) also contains ACEs, but these ACEs determine who will be audited and why. An ACE in a SACL is called an *audit access ACE*. For example, if the system is supposed to create an audit entry whenever the user "smith" successfully reads a file, one ACE in the SACL states that.

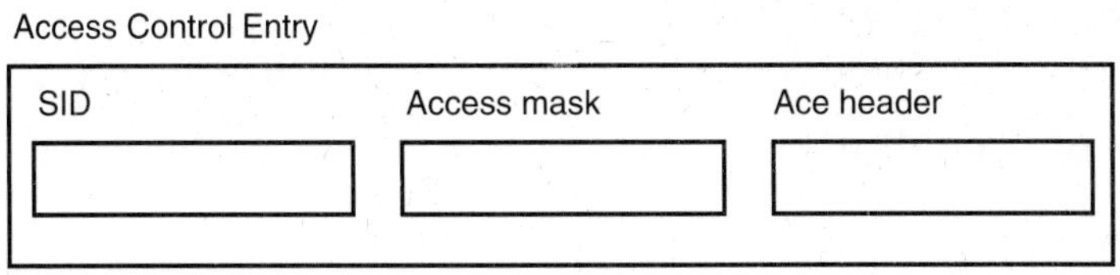

Access Control Entry

SID	Access mask	Ace header

Figure 10.4
An Access Control Entry (ACE) specifies one user or group (the SID identifies the user or group) and the type of access allowed. ACEs are stored in ACLs (see Figure 10.3).

To convey its information, each ACE in an ACL consists of three parts: a *Security Identifier*, or SID, an *access mask*, and an *ACE header*. The SID is a value stored in the registry (and also available through function calls) that uniquely identifies each user or group that exists in the User Manager. The ACE header determines the type of ACE: access allowed, access denied, and so on. An access mask is a 32-bit mask that determines what the user can do with the object. There are standard rights that apply to all objects on the system. Some objects also have a variety of special access rights that apply only to them. For example, you can apply the following specific and standard access rights to a file object:

specific:
FILE_READ_DATA
FILE_WRITE_DATA
FILE_APPEND_DATA
FILE_READ_EA
FILE_WRITE_EA
FILE_EXECUTE
FILE_READ_ATTRIBUTES
FILE_WRITE_ATTRIBUTES
FILE_ALL_ACCESS

standard:
DELETE
READ_CONTROL
STANDARD_RIGHTS_ALL
STANDARD_RIGHTS_EXECUTE
STANDARD_RIGHTS_READ
STANDARD_RIGHTS_REQUIRED
STANDARD_RIGHTS_WRITE

SYNCHRONIZE
WRITE_DAC
WRITE_OWNER

generic:
GENERIC_ALL
GENERIC_EXECUTE
GENERIC_READ
GENERIC_WRITE

The generic rights are pre-defined combinations of standard and specific rights and change from object to object. See Section 10.5 for more information on securable objects and their access rights.

An access mask is simply a 32-bit bit-mask. Each of the standard, specific, and generic rights has a bit associated with it in the access mask. The first 16 bits hold specific rights and are keyed to the object that the access mask refers to (for example, the FILE_ constants above). The next eight bits hold standard rights. The high-order four bits hold generic rights.

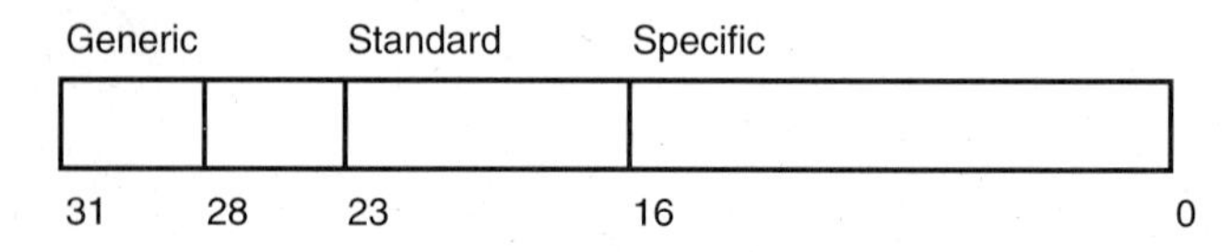

Figure 10.5
The bit layout of an access mask.

As you can see, there is a whole cornucopia of new terminology used to describe NT's security features. However, you will become intimately familiar with all of these words as you work through the sample code, and all of the concepts are easy to understand. Here is a quick summary:

- When users log in, they receive *access tokens.* An access token contains the user's ID, the user's groups, and the user's privileges culled from the groups.
- Each object has a *security descriptor* that acts as its lock. A security descriptor contains an owner and group identifier, a *System ACL,* and a *Discretionary ACL.*
- A *DACL* controls who is allowed to do what to the object
- A *SACL* controls who is audited for doing what to an object

- *ACLs* consist of *ACEs*. Each ACE contains a *SID* that identifies the user or group, an *access mask* that determines the actions allowed to the user or group, and an *ACE header* that determines the type of ACE.

The following section presents three simple examples to show how the security functions and all of this vocabulary fit together.

10.4 Simple Examples

The purpose of this section is to walk through the creation and application of a security descriptor for a file object. A file object is chosen for this example because it is common and easily understood, and also because it is easy to view the results with the security editor in the File Manager to prove that the code works. However, if your hard disk is not formatted with the NT File System, this code will not do anything and the security editor is disabled. You have three options if this is the case:

1. Convert your hard disk to NTFS
2. Install a new hard disk and format it with the NT File System
3. Partition off a small section (say 10 megabytes) of your existing hard disk and format it with NTFS. This means that you will have to reformat and reload the original partition as well

Alternatively, you can wait a moment and we will apply this same security code to a registry key. You will be able to see the security editor in the registry editor regardless of the file system that you are using.

Listing 10.1 contains a program that creates a new file. The security descriptor for the new file is set up so that only the user "guest" can use the file, and the user can do nothing but read it. The program contains absolutely no error checking so that the essentials are easy to see. When you run Listing 10.1, it should create a file on `c:\` named `testfile`. Select the file in the File Manager and then choose the **Permissions** option in the **Security** menu. You will find that there is one entry in the list: The user "guest" can read the file. Feel free to change the name of the file or the name of the user when you run the code yourself.

```
// filesec.cpp

#include <windows.h>
#include <iostream.h>

SECURITY_ATTRIBUTES sa;
SECURITY_DESCRIPTOR sd;
BYTE aclBuffer[1024];
PACL pacl=(PACL)&aclBuffer;
BYTE sidBuffer[100];
PSID psid=(PSID) &sidBuffer;
DWORD sidBufferSize = 100;
char domainBuffer[80];
DWORD domainBufferSize = 80;
SID_NAME_USE snu;
HANDLE file;

void main(void)
{
  InitializeSecurityDescriptor(&sd,
    SECURITY_DESCRIPTOR_REVISION);
  InitializeAcl(pacl, 1024, ACL_REVISION);
  LookupAccountName(0, "guest", psid,
    &sidBufferSize, domainBuffer,
    &domainBufferSize, &snu);
  AddAccessAllowedAce(pacl, ACL_REVISION,
    GENERIC_READ, psid);
  SetSecurityDescriptorDacl(&sd, TRUE, pacl,
    FALSE);
```

Listing 10.1
A simple security program (without any error checking) that creates a file that only the user "guest" can read. This code will not work unless you have formatted your hard disk with the NT File System (Page 1 of 2)

```
    sa.nLength= sizeof(SECURITY_ATTRIBUTES);
    sa.bInheritHandle = FALSE;
    sa.lpSecurityDescriptor = &sd;

    file = CreateFile("c:\\testfile",
      GENERIC_READ | GENERIC_WRITE,
      0, &sa, CREATE_NEW,
      FILE_ATTRIBUTE_NORMAL, 0);
    CloseHandle(file);
}
```

Listing 10.1
A simple security program (without any error checking) that creates a file that only the user "guest" can read. This code will not work unless you have formatted your hard disk with the NT File System (Page 2 of 2)

Start by looking at the bottom of the program. Here you will find a call to **CreateFile** that creates a file named `c:\testfile`. However, this call to **CreateFile**, unlike all of the previous calls that you have seen in this book, has a security parameter at location four in the parameter list. In all previous code we have used a zero in this location. The zero tells the operating system to use a default security descriptor when it creates the object (see Section 10.8). The zero value also disables inheritance (see Chapter 5). In Listing 10.1, the code instead creates a SECURITY_ATTRIBUTES structure that contains a valid security descriptor.

The creation of a security descriptor starts with a call to the **InitializeSecurityDescriptor** function seen at the first line of Listing 10.1.

InitializeSecurityDescriptor	*Initializes a security descriptor*

`BOOL InitializeSecurityDescriptor(`
`   PSECURITY_DESCRIPTOR psd,`
`   DWORD revision)`	

psd	A pointer to a security descriptor

revision	Revision level. Must be SECURITY_DESCRIPTOR_REVISION
Returns TRUE on success	

This step creates a security descriptor in absolute format (there is also a second format called the self-relative format, and the differences are described in Section 10.6). The new security descriptor initially contains no information besides the revision level: no owner identifier, no group identifier, no SACL, and no DACL.

The next line calls **InitializeAcl** to create the ACL that will become the DACL for the security descriptor.

InitializeAcl *Initializes an ACL*

```
BOOL InitializeAcl(
   PACL pacl,
   DWORD bufferLen,
   DWORD revision)
```

pacl	A pointer to an ACL
bufferLen	The length of the ACL buffer supplied
revision	Revision level. Must be ACL_REVISION
Returns TRUE on success	

When the **InitializeAcl** function returns, **pacl** points to an empty ACL. That is, the ACL contains no ACEs. If you were to comment out the next two lines so that this empty ACL was placed into the security descriptor, and that security descriptor was applied to the file, then no one would be able to access the file. In the absence of any ACEs in the discretionary ACL, no one has access. Alternatively, if you were to create no DACL at all and pass NULL in during the DACL installation step below, then everyone could access the file. The total absence of a DACL gives access to everyone.

The next two lines of Listing 10.1 create an ACE and add it to the ACL. The **LookupAccountName** function returns a SID for the specified account name.

LookupAccountName	*Returns a SID for the specified account*

```
BOOL LookupAccountName(
    LPCTSTR system,
    LPCTSTR accountName,
    PSID psid,
    LPDWORD sidBufferSize,
    LPTSTR domainName,
    LPDWORD domainNameLen,
    PSID_NAME_USE psnu)
```

system	Name of a remote system or 0 for local
accountName	The name of the account to look up
psid	A pointer to a buffer for the returned SID
sidBufferSize	The size of the psid buffer
domainName	A pointer to a buffer for the returned domain name
domainNameLen	Size of the domain name buffer
psnu	Returned enumerated type indicating the type of account

Returns TRUE on success

The **LookupAccountName** function looks up the account name specified on the system specified or on the local system. If it is not found locally the function looks on the domain controller or trusted domain controllers if appropriate. The function returns a SID for the account, the domain where it was found if the SID came from a domain controller, and an enumerated value that indicates the type of account:

SidTypeUser
SidTypeGroup
SidTypeDomain
SidTypeAlias
SidTypeWellKnownGroup
SidTypeDeletedAccount
SidTypeInvalid
SidTypeUnknown

A SID is a *security identifier*. It uniquely identifies a user or a group to the system.

The SID returned by the **LookupAccountName** function is used in a call to the **AddAccessAllowedAce** function to create an access allowed (as opposed to access denied) ACE and add it to the currently-empty ACL.

AddAccessAllowedAce — *Creates an access allowed ACE and adds it to the specified ACL*

```
BOOL AddAccessAllowedAce(
    PACL pacl,
    DWORD revision,
    DWORD accessMask,
    PSID psid)
```

pacl	A pointer to an ACL
revision	Revision level. Must be ACL_REVISION
accessMask	Access mask bits
psid	A SID

Returns TRUE on success

The **AddAccessAllowedAce** function creates the ACE with the SID and access mask specified and adds it to the ACL specified. The GENERIC_READ access mask grants read access to the file and its attributes. See Section 10.5 for a list of the specific and standard rights that GENERIC_READ adds to the access mask.

Now the code in Listing 10.1 has an ACL containing one ACE that specifies that the user "guest" should have read access. This ACL needs to be placed into the Discretionary ACL of the security descriptor using the **SetSecurityDescriptorDacl** function.

SetSecurityDescriptorDacl — *Sets the DACL in a security descriptor*

```
BOOL SetSecurityDescriptorDacl(
   PSECURITY_DESCRIPTOR psd,
   BOOL daclPresent,
   PACL pacl,
   BOOL daclDefaulted)
```

psd	A pointer to a security descriptor
daclPresent	A boolean that if TRUE says pacl contains an ACL. If it is FALSE, the function ignores anything in pacl and sets the DACL in the security descriptor to NULL.
pacl	A pointer to the ACL to add
daclDefaulted	A boolean indicating the source of the DACL

Returns TRUE on success

Now the security descriptor contains a valid DACL with one ACE in it. Listing 10.1 places this security descriptor in a security attributes structure and then passes it to the **CreateFile** function (see Chapter 2).

Compile and run Listing 10.1. Make sure that the file name specified in the program does not already exist when you run it. When you look at the new file with the File Manager's security editor, you will find that its permissions are set as specified in the code.

You can easily modify Listing 10.1 to experiment with security descriptors. For example, try giving write access to a certain group, or add several ACEs to the DACL, or create an access denied ACE using **AddAccessDenied-Ace**. *Be sure that access denied ACEs precede access allowed ACEs.* Use the **SetSe-**

curityDescriptorOwner function to modify the owner in the security descriptor.

This exact same security descriptor code can be applied to any other securable NT object, because the security system is uniform across all objects. For example, you can use it to create a key in the registry, as demonstrated in Listing 10.2. See Chapter 15 for information on the registry and registry keys. If you compare Listing 10.2 with Listing 10.1, you will find that they are exactly the same except that Listing 10.2 uses **RegCreateKeyEx** to create a registry key instead of a file.

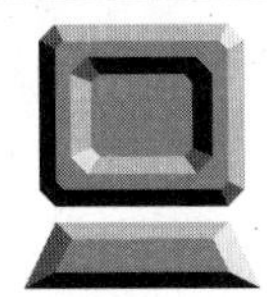

```
// regsec.cpp

#include <windows.h>
#include <iostream.h>

SECURITY_ATTRIBUTES sa;
SECURITY_DESCRIPTOR sd;
BYTE aclBuffer[1024];
PACL pacl=(PACL)&aclBuffer;
BYTE sidBuffer[100];
PSID psid=(PSID) &sidBuffer;
DWORD sidBufferSize = 100;
char domainBuffer[80];
DWORD domainBufferSize = 80;
SID_NAME_USE snu;
LONG result;
HKEY regKey;
DWORD disposition;

void main(void)
```

Listing 10.2
Code to create a registry key that only the user "guest" can access (Page 1 of 2)

```
{
  InitializeSecurityDescriptor(&sd,
    SECURITY_DESCRIPTOR_REVISION);
  InitializeAcl(pacl, 1024, ACL_REVISION);
  LookupAccountName(0, "guest", psid,
    &sidBufferSize, domainBuffer,
    &domainBufferSize, &snu);
  AddAccessAllowedAce(pacl, ACL_REVISION,
    GENERIC_READ, psid);
  SetSecurityDescriptorDacl(&sd, TRUE, pacl,
    FALSE);

  sa.nLength= sizeof(SECURITY_ATTRIBUTES);
  sa.bInheritHandle = FALSE;
  sa.lpSecurityDescriptor = &sd;

  result = RegCreateKeyEx(HKEY_CURRENT_USER,
    "junk", 0, 0, REG_OPTION_VOLATILE,
    KEY_ALL_ACCESS, &sa, &regKey,
    &disposition);
  cout << result << endl;
  RegCloseKey(regKey);
}
```

Listing 10.2
Code to create a registry key that only the user "guest" can access (Page 2 of 2)

Before running Listing 10.2, run the registry editor (`regedt32.exe`) and look at the HKEY_CURRENT_USER window to make sure HKEY_CURRENT_USER does not already contain a key named "junk." If it does, delete it, or modify the code in Listing 10.2 to create a different key. Now run Listing 10.2. Refresh the registry editor display if it is not set to automatically refresh, and you will see a new key named "junk." When you check its permissions using the Permissions option in the Security menu, you will find that you or "administrator" owns the key and that "guest" is the only user who has access to it. Change the name of the key or the user as you desire. Since the code in Listing 10.2 creates volatile keys, they will disappear when you log off or reboot the system.

You can apply the same security descriptor code to a named pipe to control who can access the pipe, as shown in Listing 10.3. The code in Listing 10.3 is a modification to the simple named pipe receiver seen in Listing 7.6. When applied to a named pipe like this, the security code causes the pipe to reject connections from any user other than "guest." Change "guest" to any user that you prefer. It is probably wise to use your own user ID in this code. See Section 10.9 for a complete description of how named pipes use security descriptors.

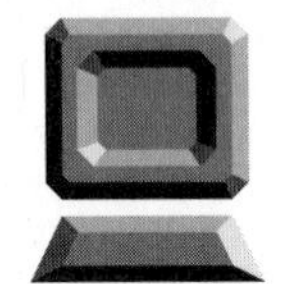

```
// pipesec.cpp

#include <windows.h>
#include <iostream.h>

SECURITY_ATTRIBUTES sa;
SECURITY_DESCRIPTOR sd;
BYTE aclBuffer[1024];
PACL pacl=(PACL)&aclBuffer;
BYTE sidBuffer[100];
PSID psid=(PSID) &sidBuffer;
DWORD sidBufferSize = 100;
char domainBuffer[80];
DWORD domainBufferSize = 80;
SID_NAME_USE snu;
HANDLE file;

int main(void)
{
  InitializeSecurityDescriptor(&sd,
    SECURITY_DESCRIPTOR_REVISION);
  InitializeAcl(pacl, 1024, ACL_REVISION);
```

Listing 10.3
Code demonstrating how to secure a named pipe. Only the user "guest" running a program such as Listing 7.7 can connect to this pipe (Page 1 of 4)

```
LookupAccountName(0, "guest", psid,
  &sidBufferSize, domainBuffer,
  &domainBufferSize, &snu);
AddAccessAllowedAce(pacl, ACL_REVISION,
  GENERIC_READ|GENERIC_WRITE, psid);
SetSecurityDescriptorDacl(&sd, TRUE, pacl,
  FALSE);

sa.nLength= sizeof(SECURITY_ATTRIBUTES);
sa.bInheritHandle = FALSE;
sa.lpSecurityDescriptor = &sd;

// Print out the allowed connector
char domainBuffer[80];
DWORD domainBufferSize = 80;
char name[80];
DWORD nameSize= 80;
LookupAccountSid(0, psid, name, &nameSize,
  domainBuffer, &domainBufferSize, &snu);
cout << "allowing " << domainBuffer
  << "\\" << name
  << " to access pipe" << endl;

char toDisptxt[80];
HANDLE ssnpPipe;
DWORD NumBytesRead;

/* Create a named pipe for receiving messages */
ssnpPipe=CreateNamedPipe("\\\\.\\pipe\\ssnp",
  PIPE_ACCESS_INBOUND,
  PIPE_TYPE_MESSAGE | PIPE_WAIT,
  1, 0, 0, 150, &sa);

/* Check and see if the named pipe was created */
if (ssnpPipe == INVALID_HANDLE_VALUE)
```

Listing 10.3
Code demonstrating how to secure a named pipe. Only the user "guest" running a program such as Listing 7.7 can connect to this pipe (Page 2 of 4)

```
    {
      cerr << "ERROR: Unable to create a named pipe."
        << endl;
      return (1);
    }

    /* Allow a client to connect to the name pipe,
       terminate if unsuccessful */
    if(!ConnectNamedPipe(ssnpPipe,
      (LPOVERLAPPED) NULL))
    {
      cerr << "ERROR: Unable to connect a named pipe"
        << endl;
      CloseHandle(ssnpPipe);
      return (1);
    }

    /* Repeatedly check for messages
       until the program is terminated */
    while(1)
    {
      /* Read the message and check to see if read
         was successful */
      if (!ReadFile(ssnpPipe, toDisptxt,
        sizeof(toDisptxt),
        &NumBytesRead, (LPOVERLAPPED) NULL))
      {
        cerr << "ERROR: Unable to read from pipe"
          << endl;
        CloseHandle(ssnpPipe);
        return (1);
      }

      /* Display the Message */
      cout << toDisptxt << endl;
```

Listing 10.3
Code demonstrating how to secure a named pipe. Only the user "guest" running a program such as Listing 7.7 can connect to this pipe (Page 3 of 4)

```
    } /* while */
}
```

Listing 10.3
Code demonstrating how to secure a named pipe. Only the user "guest" running a program such as Listing 7.7 can connect to this pipe (Page 4 of 4)

Run Listing 10.3 in one command window. The program will output the identity of the user allowed to connect to the pipe. As shown in Listing 10.3, only "guest" can connect, but you can change that if you like. Now open another command window and run Listing 7.7, which will connect to the pipe and send messages to it. If you are logged in as "guest" when you run Listing 7.7, then the two programs will connect. If not, then Listing 7.7 will receive an "Access Denied" error code via **GetLastError**. You will see this same behavior if you try to connect over the network. See Section 7.4 for details on network connections with named pipes. See Section 10.9 for further information on named pipe security.

10.5 Securable Objects and Access Rights

When you create an access mask in an ACE you can specify standard rights which apply to any NT object, and you can also pick extremely specific rights that apply to individual objects. For example, if you want to give the user "smith" the right to delete an object, then create an ACE giving "smith" the standard right DELETE. If, on the other hand, you want the user "jones" to be able to modify the state of a semaphore object, create an ACE giving "jones" the semaphore-specific right SEMAPHORE_MODIFY_STATE.

All of the different access rights are simply bit definitions that get ORed into the 32-bit access mask. The first 16 bits hold specific rights and are keyed to the object that the access mask refers to (for example, the FILE_ constants). The next eight bits hold standard rights. The high-order four bits hold generic rights.

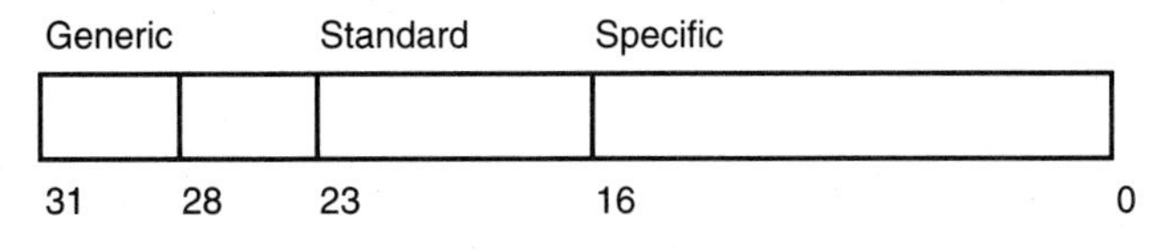

Figure 10.6
The bit layout of an access mask.

The standard rights available on all objects, along with their bit definitions, are listed below:

DELETE	(0x00010000) Can delete the object
READ_CONTROL	(0x00020000) Can Read the security descriptor except the SACL
WRITE_DAC	(0x00040000) Can write to the DACL in a security descriptor
WRITE_OWNER	(0x00080000) Can write to the owner in a security descriptor
SYNCHRONIZE	(0x00100000) A thread can wait for the object using a Wait function. Not supported for all objects. See Section 6.4.
STANDARD_RIGHTS_ALL	DELETE | READ_CONTROL | WRITE_DAC | WRITE_OWNER | SYNCHRONIZE
STANDARD_RIGHTS_EXECUTE	READ_CONTROL
STANDARD_RIGHTS_READ	READ_CONTROL
STANDARD_RIGHTS_REQUIRED	DELETE | READ_CONTROL | WRITE_DAC | WRITE_OWNER
STANDARD_RIGHTS_WRITE	READ_CONTROL

The specific rights that apply to the different securable system objects available in Windows NT are listed in the following sections, along with the names of the functions that let you create or modify the security descriptor for the objects.

The "Security Overview" section of the Win32 help file contains complete descriptions of all of the specific rights listed in the following sections.

10.5.1 Files

CreateFile: The handle returned has **SYNCHRONIZE, FILE_READ_ATTRIBUTES**, and the requested combination of **GENERIC_READ** and/or **GENERIC_WRITE**

GetFileSecurity

SetFileSecurity

Specific:

FILE_READ_DATA	(0x0001)
FILE_WRITE_DATA	(0x0002)
FILE_APPEND_DATA	(0x0004)
FILE_READ_EA	(0x0008)
FILE_WRITE_EA	(0x0010)
FILE_EXECUTE	(0x0020)
FILE_READ_ATTRIBUTES	(0x0080)
FILE_WRITE_ATTRIBUTES	(0x0100)
FILE_ALL_ACCESS	(0x1FF | STANDARD_RIGHTS_REQUIRED | SYNCHRONIZE)

Generic:

FILE_GENERIC_READ	(STANDARD_RIGHTS_READ | FILE_READ_DATA | FILE_READ_ATTRIBUTES | FILE_READ_EA | SYNCHRONIZE)
FILE_GENERIC_WRITE	(STANDARD_RIGHTS_WRITE | FILE_WRITE_DATA | FILE_WRITE_ATTRIBUTES | FILE_WRITE_EA | FILE_APPEND_DATA | SYNCHRONIZE)

FILE_GENERIC_EXECUTE	(STANDARD_RIGHTS_EXECUTE | FILE_READ_ATTRIBUTES | FILE_EXECUTE | SYNCHRONIZE)

10.5.2 Directories

CreateDirectory: The handle returned has **SYNCHRONIZE** and **FILE_ LIST_DIRECTORY**

CreateDirectoryEx

GetFileSecurity

SetFileSecurity

Specific:

FILE_LIST_DIRECTORY	(0x0001)
FILE_ADD_FILE	(0x0002)
FILE_ADD_SUBDIRECTORY	(0x0004)
FILE_READ_EA	(0x0008)
FILE_WRITE_EA	(0x0010)
FILE_TRAVERSE	(0x0020)
FILE_DELETE_CHILD	(0x0040)
FILE_READ_ATTRIBUTES	(0x0080)
FILE_WRITE_ATTRIBUTES	(0x0100)
FILE_ALL_ACCESS	(0x1FF | STANDARD_RIGHTS_REQUIRED | SYNCHRONIZE)

Generic:

FILE_GENERIC_READ	(STANDARD_RIGHTS_READ | FILE_READ_DATA | FILE_READ_ATTRIBUTES | FILE_READ_EA | SYNCHRONIZE)
FILE_GENERIC_WRITE	(STANDARD_RIGHTS_WRITE |

	FILE_WRITE_DATA |
	FILE_WRITE_ATTRIBUTES |
	FILE_WRITE_EA |
	FILE_APPEND_DATA |
	SYNCHRONIZE)
FILE_GENERIC_EXECUTE	(STANDARD_RIGHTS_EXECUTE |
	FILE_READ_ATTRIBUTES |
	FILE_EXECUTE |
	SYNCHRONIZE)

10.5.3 Pipes

CreateNamedPipe: The rights of the handle returned depend on the access requested:

PIPE_ACCESS_DUPLEX	GENERIC_READ |
	GENERIC_WRITE |
	SYNCHRONIZE
PIPE_ACCESS_INBOUND	GENERIC_READ |
	SYNCHRONIZE
PIPE_ACCESS_OUTBOUND	GENERIC_WRITE |
	SYNCHRONIZE

CreatePipe
GetFileSecurity
SetFileSecurity

Specific:

FILE_READ_DATA	(0x0001)
FILE_WRITE_DATA	(0x0002)
FILE_CREATE_PIPE_INSTANCE	(0x0004)
FILE_READ_ATTRIBUTES	(0x0080)
FILE_WRITE_ATTRIBUTES	(0x0100)
FILE_ALL_ACCESS	(0x1FF |

	STANDARD_RIGHTS_REQUIRED | SYNCHRONIZE)

Generic:

FILE_GENERIC_READ	(STANDARD_RIGHTS_READ | FILE_READ_DATA | FILE_READ_ATTRIBUTES | SYNCHRONIZE)
FILE_GENERIC_WRITE	(STANDARD_RIGHTS_WRITE | FILE_WRITE_DATA | FILE_WRITE_ATTRIBUTES | SYNCHRONIZE)

10.5.4 Mailslots

CreateMailslot: The handle returned has SYNCHRONIZE, GENERIC_READ, and WRITE_DAC

GetFileSecurity
SetFileSecurity
Same rights as files. Only GENERIC_READ applies

10.5.5 Consoles

CreateConsoleScreenBuffer

10.5.6 Processes

CreateProcess: The handle returned has PROCESS_ALL_ACCESS rights
SetKernelObjectSecurity
GetKernelObjectSecurity

Specific:

PROCESS_TERMINATE	(0x0001)
PROCESS_CREATE_THREAD	(0x0002)
PROCESS_VM_OPERATION	(0x0008)
PROCESS_VM_READ	(0x0010)

PROCESS_VM_WRITE	(0x0020)
PROCESS_DUP_HANDLE	(0x0040)
PROCESS_CREATE_PROCESS	(0x0080)
PROCESS_SET_INFORMATION	(0x0200)
PROCESS_QUERY_INFORMATION	(0x0400)
PROCESS_ALL_ACCESS	(STANDARD_RIGHTS_REQUIRED | SYNCHRONIZE | 0xFFF)

10.5.7 Threads

CreateThread: The handle returned has THREAD_ALL_ACCESS rights
SetKernelObjectSecurity
GetKernelObjectSecurity

Specific:

THREAD_TERMINATE	(0x0001)
THREAD_SUSPEND_RESUME	(0x0002)
THREAD_GET_CONTEXT	(0x0008)
THREAD_SET_CONTEXT	(0x0010)
THREAD_SET_INFORMATION	(0x0020)
THREAD_QUERY_INFORMATION	(0x0040)
THREAD_SET_THREAD_TOKEN	(0x0080)
THREAD_IMPERSONATE	(0x0100)
THREAD_DIRECT_IMPERSONATION	(0x0200)
THREAD_ALL_ACCESS	(STANDARD_RIGHTS_REQUIRED | SYNCHRONIZE | 0x3FF)

10.5.8 File Mappings

CreateFileMapping: The rights of the handle returned depends on the access requested:

PAGE_READWRITE	SECTION_QUERY | SECTION_MAP_READ | SECTION_MAP_WRITE
PAGE_READONLY	SECTION_QUERY | SECTION_MAP_READ

SetKernelObjectSecurity
GetKernelObjectSecurity

Specific:

SECTION_QUERY	0x0001
SECTION_MAP_WRITE	0x0002
SECTION_MAP_READ	0x0004
SECTION_MAP_EXECUTE	0x0008
SECTION_EXTEND_SIZE	0x0010
SECTION_ALL_ACCESS	(STANDARD_RIGHTS_REQUIRED| SECTION_QUERY| SECTION_MAP_WRITE | SECTION_MAP_READ | SECTION_MAP_EXECUTE | SECTION_EXTEND_SIZE)

10.5.9 Access Tokens

OpenProcessToken
OpenThreadToken
SetKernelObjectSecurity
GetKernelObjectSecurity

Specific:

TOKEN_ASSIGN_PRIMARY	(0x0001)
TOKEN_DUPLICATE	(0x0002)
TOKEN_IMPERSONATE	(0x0004)
TOKEN_QUERY	(0x0008)
TOKEN_QUERY_SOURCE	(0x0010)
TOKEN_ADJUST_PRIVILEGES	(0x0020)
TOKEN_ADJUST_GROUPS	(0x0040)
TOKEN_ADJUST_DEFAULT	(0x0080)
TOKEN_ALL_ACCESS	(STANDARD_RIGHTS_REQUIRED | TOKEN_ASSIGN_PRIMARY | TOKEN_DUPLICATE | TOKEN_IMPERSONATE | TOKEN_QUERY | TOKEN_QUERY_SOURCE | TOKEN_ADJUST_PRIVILEGES | TOKEN_ADJUST_GROUPS | TOKEN_ADJUST_DEFAULT)
TOKEN_READ	(STANDARD_RIGHTS_READ | TOKEN_QUERY)
TOKEN_WRITE	(STANDARD_RIGHTS_WRITE | TOKEN_ADJUST_PRIVILEGES | TOKEN_ADJUST_GROUPS | TOKEN_ADJUST_DEFAULT)
TOKEN_EXECUTE	

10.5.10 Registry Objects

RegCreateKeyEx: The handle returned has the access rights requested in the call

RegSaveKey
RegGetKeySecurity
RegSetKeySecurity

Specific:

KEY_QUERY_VALUE	(0x0001)
KEY_SET_VALUE	(0x0002)
KEY_CREATE_SUB_KEY	(0x0004)
KEY_ENUMERATE_SUB_KEYS	(0x0008)
KEY_NOTIFY	(0x0010)
KEY_CREATE_LINK	(0x0020)
KEY_READ	((STANDARD_RIGHTS_READ | KEY_QUERY_VALUE | KEY_ENUMERATE_SUB_KEYS | KEY_NOTIFY) & (~SYNCHRONIZE))
KEY_WRITE	((STANDARD_RIGHTS_WRITE | KEY_SET_VALUE | KEY_CREATE_SUB_KEY) & (~SYNCHRONIZE))
KEY_EXECUTE	((KEY_READ) & (~SYNCHRONIZE))
KEY_ALL_ACCESS	((STANDARD_RIGHTS_ALL | KEY_QUERY_VALUE | KEY_SET_VALUE | KEY_CREATE_SUB_KEY | KEY_ENUMERATE_SUB_KEYS | KEY_NOTIFY | KEY_CREATE_LINK) & (~SYNCHRONIZE))

10.5.11 Service Objects

OpenService
OpenSCManager
QueryServiceObjectSecurity
SetServiceObjectSecurity

Specific:

SC_MANAGER_CONNECT	(0x0001)
SC_MANAGER_CREATE_SERVICE	(0x0002)
SC_MANAGER_ENUMERATE_SERVICE	(0x0004)
SC_MANAGER_LOCK	(0x0008)
SC_MANAGER_QUERY_LOCK_STATUS	(0x0010)
SC_MANAGER_MODIFY_BOOT_CONFIG	(0x0020)
SC_MANAGER_ALL_ACCESS	(STANDARD_RIGHTS_REQUIRED | SC_MANAGER_CONNECT | SC_MANAGER_CREATE_SERVICE | SC_MANAGER_ENUMERATE_SERVICE | SC_MANAGER_LOCK | SC_MANAGER_QUERY_LOCK_STATUS | SC_MANAGER_MODIFY_BOOT_CONFIG)

SERVICE_QUERY_CONFIG	(0x0001)
SERVICE_CHANGE_CONFIG	(0x0002)
SERVICE_QUERY_STATUS	(0x0004)
SERVICE_ENUMERATE_DEPENDENTS	(0x0008)
SERVICE_START	(0x0010)
SERVICE_STOP	(0x0020)
SERVICE_PAUSE_CONTINUE	(0x0040)
SERVICE_INTERROGATE	(0x0080)
SERVICE_USER_DEFINED_CONTROL	(0x0100)
SERVICE_ALL_ACCESS	(STANDARD_RIGHTS_REQUIRED |

	SERVICE_QUERY_CONFIG | SERVICE_CHANGE_CONFIG | SERVICE_QUERY_STATUS | SERVICE_ENUMERATE_ DEPENDENTS | SERVICE_START | SERVICE_STOP | SERVICE_PAUSE_CONTINUE | SERVICE_INTERROGATE | SERVICE_USER_DEFINED_ CONTROL)

10.5.12 Events

CreateEvent: The handle returned has EVENT_ALL_ACCESS rights

SetKernelObjectSecurity

GetKernelObjectSecurity

Specific:

EVENT_MODIFY_STATE	0x0002
EVENT_ALL_ACCESS	(STANDARD_RIGHTS_REQUIRED | SYNCHRONIZE | 0x3)

10.5.13 Mutexes

CreateMutex: The handle returned has MUTEX_ALL_ACCESS rights

SetKernelObjectSecurity

GetKernelObjectSecurity

Specific:

MUTEX_MODIFY_STATE	0x0002
MUTEX_ALL_ACCESS	(STANDARD_RIGHTS_REQUIRED | SYNCHRONIZE | 0x3)

10.5.14 Semaphores

CreateSemaphore: The handle returned has SEMAPHORE_ALL_ ACCESS rights

SetKernelObjectSecurity

GetKernelObjectSecurity

Specific:

SEMAPHORE_MODIFY_ STATE	0x0002
SEMAPHORE_ALL_ACCESS	(STANDARD_RIGHTS_ REQUIRED| SYNCHRONIZE| 0x3)

10.5.15 Private Objects

CreatePrivateObjectSecurity

DestroyPrivateObjectSecurity

GetPrivateObjectSecurity

SetPrivateObjectSecurity

10.6 Examining Existing Access Tokens and Security Descriptors

You can learn quite a bit about access tokens and security descriptors by writing and running code that dumps the contents of existing tokens and descriptors. This section contains two different dumping programs. The first dumps an existing process's security descriptor. The second examines the access token of any existing process.

Processes (along with files and registry keys) are one of the few Windows NT objects that you can easily access without creating the code that creates the object. The process viewer `(pview.exe)` will give you a list of processes along with their IDs.

10.6.1 Dumping a Process's Security Descriptor

The code in Listing 10.4 requests a process ID and then obtains and dumps the security descriptor for that process. A process, like any other NT object, has a security descriptor that controls who can access it.

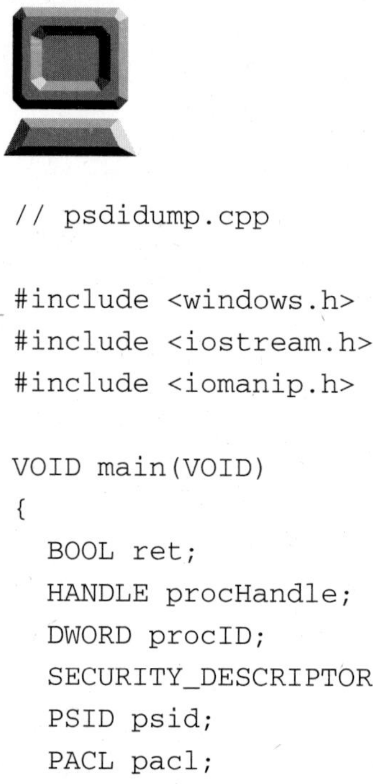

```
// psdidump.cpp

#include <windows.h>
#include <iostream.h>
#include <iomanip.h>

VOID main(VOID)
{
  BOOL ret;
  HANDLE procHandle;
  DWORD procID;
  SECURITY_DESCRIPTOR *sdData;
  PSID psid;
  PACL pacl;
  BOOL byDef;
  BOOL haveDACL;
  DWORD sizeRqd;
  CHAR str[80];
  DWORD strSize;
  CHAR str2[80];
  DWORD str2Size;
  SID_NAME_USE sidType;
  UINT x;
  ACL_SIZE_INFORMATION aclSize;
  ACCESS_ALLOWED_ACE *pace;
```

Listing 10.4
Code that dumps the security descriptor of a process (Page 1 of 7)

```
cout << "Enter process ID to query: ";
cin >> procID;

// get a handle for the process
procHandle=OpenProcess(READ_CONTROL,
  FALSE, procID);
if (procHandle == NULL)
{
  cerr << "Unable to open the process for query."
    << endl;
  return;
}

// find out how much mem is needed
ret=GetKernelObjectSecurity(procHandle,
  OWNER_SECURITY_INFORMATION |
  GROUP_SECURITY_INFORMATION |
  DACL_SECURITY_INFORMATION,
  NULL, 0,
  &sizeRqd);

// allocate that memory
sdData=(SECURITY_DESCRIPTOR *)
  GlobalAlloc(GPTR, sizeRqd);
if (sdData == NULL)
{
  cerr << "Unable to allocate memory." << endl;
  return;
}

// actually get the SD info
ret=GetKernelObjectSecurity(procHandle,
  OWNER_SECURITY_INFORMATION |
  GROUP_SECURITY_INFORMATION |
```

Listing 10.4
Code that dumps the security descriptor of a process (Page 2 of 7)

```
    DACL_SECURITY_INFORMATION,
    sdData, sizeRqd,
    &sizeRqd);
  if (!ret)
  {
    cerr << "Unable to get SD info." << endl;
    return;
  }

  // close process handle
  CloseHandle(procHandle);

  // get the owner info
  ret=GetSecurityDescriptorOwner(sdData, &psid,
    &byDef);
  if (!ret)
  {
    cerr << "Unable to get owner info." << endl;
    return;
  }

  if (psid == NULL)
  {
    cout << "SD Owner: NULL"
      << " (No owner)" << endl;
  }
  else
  {
    // specify size of string buffers
    strSize=str2Size=80;

    // convert owner SID into a name and domain
    ret=LookupAccountSid(NULL, psid,
      str, &strSize, str2, &str2Size, &sidType);
    if (!ret)
```

Listing 10.4
Code that dumps the security descriptor of a process (Page 3 of 7)

```
        {
          cerr << "Unable to look up SID." << endl;
          return;
        }

        cout << "SD owner: \"" << str << "\" from \""
          << str2 << "\"." << endl;
      }

      // get the group info
      ret=GetSecurityDescriptorGroup(sdData, &psid,
        &byDef);
      if (!ret)
      {
        cerr << "Unable to get group info." << endl;
        return;
      }

      if (psid == NULL)
      {
        cout << "SD Group: NULL"
          << " (No group)" << endl;
      }
      else
      {
        // specify size of string buffers
        strSize=str2Size=80;

        // convert group SID into a name and domain
        ret=LookupAccountSid(NULL, psid,
          str, &strSize, str2, &str2Size, &sidType);
        if (!ret)
        {
          cerr << "Unable to look up SID." << endl;
          return;
```

Listing 10.4
Code that dumps the security descriptor of a process (Page 4 of 7)

```
      }

      cout << "SD group: \"" << str << "\" from \""
        << str2 << "\"." << endl;
    }

    // get the DACL info
    ret=GetSecurityDescriptorDacl(sdData,
      &haveDACL, &pacl, &byDef);
    if (!ret)
    {
      cerr << "Unable to get DACL info." << endl;
      return;
    }

    if (!haveDACL)
    {
      cout << "SD DACL: NULL"
        << " (Unrestricted Access)" << endl;
    }
    else
    {
      // get size info about this DACL
      ret=GetAclInformation(
        pacl, &aclSize, sizeof(ACL_SIZE_INFORMATION),
        AclSizeInformation);
      if (!ret)
      {
        cerr << "Unable to get ACL size info."
          << endl;
        return;
      }

      for (x=0; x<aclSize.AceCount; x++)
      {
```

Listing 10.4
Code that dumps the security descriptor of a process (Page 5 of 7)

```
        // get ACE info
        ret=GetAce(
          pacl, x, (LPVOID *) &pace);

        // specify size of string buffers
        strSize=str2Size=80;

        // convert ACE SID into a name and domain
        ret=LookupAccountSid(NULL,
          &pace->SidStart,
          str, &strSize, str2, &str2Size, &sidType);
        if (!ret)
        {
          strcpy(str, "      !UNKNOWN!");
          strcpy(str2, "");
        }

        cout << "SD DACL ACE: Type 0x"
          << setiosflags(ios::internal)
          << hex << setw(2) << setfill('0')
          << pace->Header.AceType
          << ", Mask 0x" << setw(8) << pace->Mask
          << resetiosflags(ios::internal)
          << setfill(' ')
          << endl << "                           for \""
          << setw(18) << setiosflags(ios::left)
          << str << "\" from \""
          << setw(12) << str2 << "\"." << endl;
      }
    }

    // release memory
    if(GlobalFree(sdData))
    {
      cerr << "Unable to free memory." << endl;
```

Listing 10.4
Code that dumps the security descriptor of a process (Page 6 of 7)

```
            return;
        }

    }
```

Listing 10.4
Code that dumps the security descriptor of a process (Page 7 of 7)

To run Listing 10.4, first start a copy of the pview application by opening a command window and typing “pview.” In the Process list you will see the names of processes followed by process IDs as hex values in parentheses. Pick a process and note its ID (for example, I picked WINLOGON with an ID of 0x11. If you are not logged in as administrator, pick a process that you own, such as your program manager). Now run Listing 10.4 and enter the process ID when the program prompts for it. I received the following output for WINLOGON:

```
SD owner: "Administrators" from "BUILTIN".

SD group: "SYSTEM" from "NT AUTHORITY".

SD DACL ACE: Type 0x00, Mask 0x001f0fff
                        for "SYSTEM" from "NT AUTHORITY".

SD DACL ACE: Type 0x00, Mask 0x00120410
                        for "Administrators" from "BUILTIN".
```

Listing 10.4 retrieves the security descriptor from the specified process and dumps the owner, the group, and the ACEs in the DACL. Each ACE contains a header that specifies the type of ACE (access allowed, access denied, audit access), the user it applies to, and the access mask. You can see from the mask of first ACE in the sample shown above that the SYSTEM user has full access to the process, while in the second ACE administrators have only partial access.

You can determine exactly what administrators are able to do by looking at the access mask and comparing it with the mask bits in Sections 10.5 and 10.5.6. The access mask contains the 32-bit mask value 0x00120410. The administrator therefore has the specific right to read the memory of the process (PROCESS_VM_READ, 0x0010) and can also query the process (PROCESS_QUERY_INFORMATION, 0x0400). The administrator can, from the standard rights, read the security descriptor for the process (READ_CONTROL, 0x00020000) and use Wait functions on the process (SYNCHRONIZE, 0x00010000).

From the DACL shown above, you can see that unless you log in as the administrator you will not be able to view the security descriptor for the WINLOGON process because the security descriptor does not contain an ACE for anyone other than administrators and SYSTEM. However, you will be able to view security descriptors for any process that you own, such as your Program Manager.

The code in Listing 10.4 is straightforward, and demonstrates several security functions that are useful for examining security descriptors. The program first asks the user for the ID of a process to dump, and uses it to open the process. It can then obtain a copy of the process's security descriptor using the **GetKernelObjectSecurity** function. The code uses a two-step process: it calls the function once to figure out how big the security descriptor is, then allocates the needed memory and calls the function again.

GetKernelObjectSecurity — *Obtains the security descriptor for a kernel object (process, thread, file mapping or token)*

```
BOOL GetKernelObjectSecurity(
    HANDLE objectHandle,
    SECURITY_INFORMATION security,
    PSECURITY_DESCRIPTOR buffer,
    DWORD bufferSize,
    LPDWORD requiredBufferSize)
```

Parameter	Description
objectHandle	A handle to the kernel object
security	Mask identifying the desired information
buffer	Buffer to hold the returned self-relative security descriptor
bufferSize	The size of buffer
requiredBufferSize	The size of a buffer needed to hold the security descriptor

Returns TRUE on success

The program next retrieves the owner from the security descriptor returned by **GetKernalObjectSecurity**. The **GetSecurityDescriptorOwner** function extracts the SID of the owner from the security descriptor, and the **LookupAccountSid** function converts the SID into a user name.

GetSecurityDescriptorOwner *Obtains the owner SID from a security descriptor*

```
BOOL GetSecurityDescriptorOwner(
    PSECURITY_DESCRIPTOR psd,
    PSID *sid,
    LPBOOL ownerDefaulted)
```

psd	A pointer to the security descriptor
sid	A pointer to a pointer to a SID structure
ownerDefaulted	Returns a copy of the SE_OWNER_DEFAULTED flag in the boolean pointed to.

Returns TRUE on success

LookupAccountSid *Looks up the account name of a SID*

```
BOOL LookupAccountSid(
    LPCTSTR system,
    PSID psid,
    LPTSTR accountName,
    LPDWORD accountNameLen,
    LPTSTR domain,
    LPDWORD domainLen,
    PSID_NAME_USE psnu)
```

system	Name of system to look up SID on
psid	A pointer to a SID structure
accountName	A buffer to hold the account name
accountNameLen	The size of the account name buffer
domain	A buffer to hold the name of the domain
domainLen	The size of the domain buffer
psnu	A buffer to hold the SID type
Returns TRUE on success	

The **LookupAccountSid** function accepts a system name (or NULL for the local system) and a SID. It returns the name of the account that the SID refers to and the length of the name. It also returns the name of the domain and its length. Finally it returns a constant identifying the type of SID it is.

Once Listing 10.4 has printed the security descriptor's owner's name, it next does the same thing for the security descriptor's group. It calls the **GetSecurityDescriptorGroup** function and then **LookupAccountSid** again.

GetSecurityDescriptorGroup *Obtains the primary group SID from a security descriptor*

```
BOOL GetSecurityDescriptorOwner(
   PSECURITY_DESCRIPTOR psd,
   PSID *sid,
   LPBOOL groupDefaulted)
```

psd	A pointer to the security descriptor
sid	A pointer to a pointer to a SID structure
groupDefaulted	Returns a copy of the SE_GROUP_DEFAULTED flag in the boolean pointed to.
Returns TRUE on success	

Finally, the program retrieves the DACL and loops through each ACE in it, printing its contents. It starts by calling the **GetSecurityDescriptorDacl** function to get a pointer to the DACL.

GetSecurityDescriptorDacl *Obtains a pointer to the DACL*

```
BOOL GetSecurityDescriptorDacl(
   PSECURITY_DESCRIPTOR psd,
   LPBOOL daclPresent,
   PACL *pacl,
   LPBOOL daclDefaulted)
```

psd	A pointer to the security descriptor
daclPresent	Returns a boolean indicating that the security descriptor contains a DACL.
pacl	The returned pointer to the DACL
daclDefaulted	Returns a copy of the SE_DACL_DEFAULTED flag in the boolean pointed to.

Returns TRUE on success

It then gets the number of entries in the DACL by calling the **GetAclInformation** function.

GetAclInformation *Obtains information about the ACL*

```
BOOL GetAclInformation(
   PACL pacl,
   LPVOID buffer,
   DWORD bufferLen,
   ACL_INFORMATION_CLASS aclClass)
```

pacl	A pointer to the ACL

buffer	The buffer to hold the returned ACL information
bufferLen	The size of the buffer
aclClass	The class of information requested: **AclRevisionInformation** or **AclSize-Information** are valid values.
Returns TRUE on success	

The **GetAce** function returns the information in each ACE: A type, a SID, and an access mask. The **for** loop calls **GetAce** once for each ACE in the ACL. The program looks up the SID in each ACE as described above.

GetAce — *Retrieves the information in one ACE in the ACL*

```
BOOL GetAce(
   PACL pacl,
   DWORD aceIndex,
   LPVOID *ace)
```

pacl	A pointer to the ACL
aceIndex	The ACE to retrieve
ace	A pointer to a pointer: The function points the pointer to the ace
Returns TRUE on success	

Once it has a pointer to the ACE, Listing 10.4 prints out all of the information contained in the ACE and loops back for the next one.

10.6.2 Dumping a Process's Access Token

Listing 10.5 dumps the access token of a process. All of your processes (see Chapter 5 for information on processes) contain a copy of your access token, so this is a way to look at your own access token.

Before you log in, a process called WINLOGON has control of the machine. The WINLOGON process is a SYSTEM process: it runs under the well-known identity SYSTEM, which gives it access to all resources on the machine.

Most services run under this same identity. When you log in, the WINLOGON process authenticates you, creates your access token, and creates your Program Manager window.

Each process running on the system contains an access token which gives it the right to access certain resources. When WINLOGON creates your Program Manager, it gives it your access token. Every process that you create while you are logged in will be a child of your Program Manager in some way, and every process inherits its copy of the access token from its parent. Therefore, every one of your processes contains a copy of your access token. When you run Listing 10.5 on one of your processes, you are dumping a copy of your access token. Follow the same procedure listed in the previous section for obtaining a process ID from pview, and use it when you run Listing 10.5.

```
// patidump.cpp

#include <windows.h>
#include <iostream.h>
#include <iomanip.h>

VOID main(VOID)
{
  BOOL ret;
  HANDLE procToken;
  HANDLE procHandle;
  DWORD procID;
  TOKEN_INFORMATION_CLASS tic;
  VOID *tokenData;
  DWORD sizeRqd;
  CHAR str[80];
  DWORD strSize;
```

Listing 10.5
Code that dumps the access token associated with a process (Page 1 of 12)

```
    CHAR str2[80];
    DWORD str2Size;
    SID_NAME_USE sidType;
    UINT x;
    DWORD langID;
    ACL_SIZE_INFORMATION aclSize;
    ACCESS_ALLOWED_ACE *pace;

    cout << "Enter process ID to query: ";
    cin >> procID;

    // get a handle for the process
    procHandle=OpenProcess(PROCESS_QUERY_INFORMATION,
      FALSE, procID);
    if (procHandle == NULL)
    {
      cerr << "Unable to open the process for query."
        << endl;
      return;
    }

    // get a handle for the access token used
    // by the process
    ret=OpenProcessToken(procHandle,
      TOKEN_QUERY, &procToken);
    if (!ret)
    {
      cerr
        << "Unable to open the access token."
        << endl;
      return;
    }

    // close process handle
    CloseHandle(procHandle);
```

Listing 10.5
Code that dumps the access token associated with a process (Page 2 of 12)

```
// ----- Get user information -----

// specify to return user info
tic=TokenUser;

// find out how much mem is needed
ret=GetTokenInformation(procToken, tic, NULL, 0,
  &sizeRqd);

// allocate that memory
tokenData=(TOKEN_USER *) GlobalAlloc(GPTR,
  sizeRqd);
if (tokenData == NULL)
{
  cerr << "Unable to allocate memory." << endl;
  return;
}

// actually get the user info
ret=GetTokenInformation(procToken, tic,
  tokenData, sizeRqd, &sizeRqd);
if (!ret)
{
  cerr << "Unable to get user info." << endl;
  return;
}

// specify size of string buffers
strSize=str2Size=80;

// convert user SID into a name and domain
ret=LookupAccountSid(NULL,
  ((TOKEN_USER *)tokenData)->User.Sid,
  str, &strSize, str2, &str2Size, &sidType);
```

Listing 10.5
Code that dumps the access token associated with a process (Page 3 of 12)

```
if (!ret)
{
  cerr << "Unable to look up SID." << endl;
  return;
}

// release memory
if(GlobalFree(tokenData))
{
  cerr << "Unable to free memory." << endl;
  return;
}

cout << "Token user: \"" << str << "\" from \""
  << str2 << "\"." << endl;

// ----- Get group information -----

// specify to return group info
tic=TokenGroups;

// find out how much mem is needed
ret=GetTokenInformation(procToken, tic, NULL, 0,
  &sizeRqd);

// allocate that memory
tokenData=(TOKEN_GROUPS *) GlobalAlloc(GPTR,
  sizeRqd);
if (tokenData == NULL)
{
  cerr << "Unable to allocate memory." << endl;
  return;
}

// actually get the group info
```

Listing 10.5
Code that dumps the access token associated with a process (Page 4 of 12)

```
ret=GetTokenInformation(procToken, tic,
  tokenData, sizeRqd, &sizeRqd);
if (!ret)
{
  cerr << "Unable to get group info." << endl;
  return;
}

for (x=0;
  x<((TOKEN_GROUPS *)tokenData)->GroupCount;
  x++)
{
  // specify size of string buffers
  strSize=str2Size=80;

  // convert group SID into a name and domain
  ret=LookupAccountSid(NULL,
    ((TOKEN_GROUPS *)tokenData)->Groups[x].Sid,
    str, &strSize, str2, &str2Size, &sidType);
  if (!ret)
  {
    if (((TOKEN_GROUPS *)
      tokenData)->Groups[x].Attributes &
      SE_GROUP_LOGON_ID)
    {
      strcpy(str, "Logon Identifier");
      strcpy(str2, "");
    }
    else
    {
      strcpy(str, "     !UNKNOWN!");
      strcpy(str2, "");
    }
  }
```

Listing 10.5
Code that dumps the access token associated with a process (Page 5 of 12)

```
        cout << "Token group: \"" << setw(18)
          << setiosflags(ios::left) << str
          << "\" from \""
          << setw(12) << str2 << "\" w/ attributes 0x"
          << setiosflags(ios::internal)
          << hex << setw(8) << setfill('0')
          << ((TOKEN_GROUPS *)
                tokenData)->Groups[x].Attributes
          << resetiosflags(ios::internal)
          << setfill(' ') << endl;
      }

      // release memory
      if(GlobalFree(tokenData))
      {
        cerr << "Unable to free memory." << endl;
        return;
      }

      // ----- Get privilege information -----

      // specify to return privilege info
      tic=TokenPrivileges;

      // find out how much mem is needed
      ret=GetTokenInformation(procToken, tic, NULL, 0,
        &sizeRqd);

      // allocate that memory
      tokenData=(TOKEN_PRIVILEGES *)
        GlobalAlloc(GPTR, sizeRqd);
      if (tokenData == NULL)
      {
        cerr << "Unable to allocate memory." << endl;
        return;
```

Listing 10.5
Code that dumps the access token associated with a process (Page 6 of 12)

```
}

// actually get the privilege info
ret=GetTokenInformation(procToken, tic,
  tokenData, sizeRqd, &sizeRqd);
if (!ret)
{
  cerr << "Unable to get privilege info."
    << endl;
  return;
}

for (x=0;
  x<((TOKEN_PRIVILEGES *)
      tokenData)->PrivilegeCount;
  x++)
{
  // specify size of string buffers
  strSize=str2Size=80;

  // convert privilege LUID into a name and desc
  ret=LookupPrivilegeName(NULL,
    &((TOKEN_PRIVILEGES *)
    tokenData)->Privileges[x].Luid,
    str, &strSize);
  if (!ret)
  {
    cerr << "Unable to look up LUID." << endl;
    return;
  }

  ret=LookupPrivilegeDisplayName(NULL, str,
    str2, &str2Size, &langID);
  if (!ret)
  {
```

Listing 10.5
Code that dumps the access token associated with a process (Page 7 of 12)

```
        cerr << "Unable to look up desc." << endl;
        return;
      }

      cout << setiosflags(ios::left)
        << "Token privilege: \""
        << setw(26) << str << "\" w/ attributes 0x"
        << setiosflags(ios::internal)
        << hex << setw(8) << setfill('0')
        << ((TOKEN_PRIVILEGES *)
          tokenData)->Privileges[x].Attributes
        << setfill(' ')
        << resetiosflags(ios::internal)
        << endl << "           Desc: \"" << str2
        << "\""
        << endl;
    }

    // release memory
    if(GlobalFree(tokenData))
    {
      cerr << "Unable to free memory." << endl;
      return;
    }

    // ----- Get default user information -----

    // specify to return owner info
    tic=TokenOwner;

    // find out how much mem is needed
    ret=GetTokenInformation(procToken, tic, NULL, 0,
      &sizeRqd);

    // allocate that memory
```

Listing 10.5
Code that dumps the access token associated with a process (Page 8 of 12)

```
tokenData=(TOKEN_OWNER *) GlobalAlloc(GPTR,
  sizeRqd);
if (tokenData == NULL)
{
  cerr << "Unable to allocate memory." << endl;
  return;
}

// actually get the owner info
ret=GetTokenInformation(procToken, tic,
  tokenData, sizeRqd, &sizeRqd);
if (!ret)
{
  cerr << "Unable to get owner info." << endl;
  return;
}

// specify size of string buffers
strSize=str2Size=80;

// convert owner SID into a name and domain
ret=LookupAccountSid(NULL,
  ((TOKEN_OWNER *)tokenData)->Owner,
  str, &strSize, str2, &str2Size, &sidType);
if (!ret)
{
  cerr << "Unable to look up SID." << endl;
  return;
}

// release memory
if(GlobalFree(tokenData))
{
  cerr << "Unable to free memory." << endl;
  return;
```

Listing 10.5
Code that dumps the access token associated with a process (Page 9 of 12)

```
}

cout << "Token default owner: \""
  << str << "\" from \""
  << str2 << "\"." << endl;

// ----- Get default group information -----

// specify to return def DACL info
tic=TokenDefaultDacl;

// find out how much mem is needed
ret=GetTokenInformation(procToken, tic, NULL, 0,
  &sizeRqd);

// allocate that memory
tokenData=(TOKEN_DEFAULT_DACL *)
  GlobalAlloc(GPTR, sizeRqd);
if (tokenData == NULL)
{
  cerr << "Unable to allocate memory." << endl;
  return;
}

// actually get the def DACL info
ret=GetTokenInformation(procToken, tic,
  tokenData, sizeRqd, &sizeRqd);
if (!ret)
{
  cerr << "Unable to get default DACL info."
    << endl;
  return;
}

if (((TOKEN_DEFAULT_DACL *)tokenData)->
```

Listing 10.5
Code that dumps the access token associated with a process (Page 10 of 12)

```
    DefaultDacl == NULL)
  {
    cout << "Token default DACL: NULL"
      << " (Unrestricted Access)" << endl;
  }
  else
  {
    // get size info about this DACL
    ret=GetAclInformation(
      ((TOKEN_DEFAULT_DACL *)tokenData)->
        DefaultDacl,
      &aclSize, sizeof(ACL_SIZE_INFORMATION),
      AclSizeInformation);
    if (!ret)
    {
      cerr << "Unable to get ACL size info."
        << endl;
      return;
    }

    for (x=0; x<aclSize.AceCount; x++)
    {
      // get ACE info
      ret=GetAce(
        ((TOKEN_DEFAULT_DACL *)tokenData)->
          DefaultDacl,
        x, (LPVOID *) &pace);

      // specify size of string buffers
      strSize=str2Size=80;

      // convert ACE SID into a name and domain
      ret=LookupAccountSid(NULL, &pace->SidStart,
        str, &strSize, str2, &str2Size, &sidType);
      if (!ret)
```

Listing 10.5
Code that dumps the access token associated with a process (Page 11 of 12)

```
        {
          strcpy(str, "      !UNKNOWN!");
          strcpy(str2, "");
        }

        cout << "Token default DACL ACE: Type 0x"
          << setiosflags(ios::internal)
          << hex << setw(2) << setfill('0')
          << pace->Header.AceType
          << ", Mask 0x" << setw(8) << pace->Mask
          << resetiosflags(ios::internal)
          << setfill(' ')
          << endl << "                              for\""
          << setw(18) << setiosflags(ios::left)
          << str << "\" from \""
          << setw(12) << str2 << "\"." << endl;
      }
    }

    // release memory
    if(GlobalFree(tokenData))
    {
      cerr << "Unable to free memory." << endl;
      return;
    }

    // close handle to access token
    CloseHandle(procToken);
  }
```

Listing 10.5
Code that dumps the access token associated with a process (Page 12 of 12)

When I ran Listing 10.5 on my Program Manager process, I received the following information:

```
Enter process ID to query: 0xa3
Token user: "brain" from "IT".
Token group: "Domain Users      " from "IT          "
        w/ attributes 0x00000007
```

```
Token group: "Everyone           " from "              "
        w/ attributes 0x00000007
Token group: "Users              " from "BUILTIN       "
        w/ attributes 0x00000007
Token group: "Administrators     " from "BUILTIN       "
        w/ attributes 0x0000000f
Token group: "Domain Admins      " from "IT            "
        w/ attributes 0x00000007
Token group: "Logon Identifier   " from "              "
        w/ attributes 0xc0000007
Token group: "LOCAL              " from "              "
        w/ attributes 0x00000007
Token group: "INTERACTIVE        " from "NT AUTHORITY"
        w/ attributes 0x00000007
Token privilege: "SeChangeNotifyPrivilege   "
           w/ attributes 0x00000003
           Desc: "Bypass traverse checking"
Token privilege: "SeShutdownPrivilege       "
           w/ attributes 0x00000000
           Desc: "Shut down the system"
Token privilege: "SeSecurityPrivilege       "
           w/ attributes 0x00000000
           Desc: "Manage auditing and security log"
Token privilege: "SeBackupPrivilege         "
           w/ attributes 0x00000000
           Desc: "Back up files and directories"
Token privilege: "SeRestorePrivilege        "
           w/ attributes 0x00000000
           Desc: "Restore files and directories"
Token privilege: "SeSystemtimePrivilege     "
           w/ attributes 0x00000000
           Desc: "Change the system time"
Token privilege: "SeRemoteShutdownPrivilege "
           w/ attributes 0x00000000
           Desc: "Force shutdown from a remote system"
Token privilege: "SeTakeOwnershipPrivilege  "
           w/ attributes 0x00000000
           Desc: "Take ownership of files or other objects"
Token privilege: "SeDebugPrivilege          "
           w/ attributes 0x00000000
           Desc: "Debug programs"
Token privilege: "SeSystemEnvironmentPrivilege"
           w/ attributes 0x00000000
           Desc: "Modify firmware environment values"
Token privilege: "SeSystemProfilePrivilege  "
```

```
            w/ attributes 0x00000000
            Desc: "Profile system performance"
Token privilege: "SeProfileSingleProcessPrivilege"
            w/ attributes 0x00000000
            Desc: "Profile single process"
Token privilege: "SeIncreaseBasePriorityPrivilege"
            w/ attributes 0x00000000
            Desc: "Increase scheduling priority"
Token default owner: "Administrators" from "BUILTIN".
Token default DACL ACE: Type 0x00, Mask 0x10000000
                              for "Administrators" from "BUILTIN     ".
Token default DACL ACE: Type 0x00, Mask 0x10000000
                              for "SYSTEM         " from "NT AUTHORITY".
```

An access token, as described in Section 10.3, contains a user ID, a list of groups that the user belongs to, and a set of privileges collected from those groups. The user "brain" is fairly well endowed in terms of privileges and groups, but if you login as "guest" and dump its Program Manager access token, you will find that it is much more sparse.

Listing 10.5 also dumps the default owner and default DACL. These are used when the process creates an object with a default security descriptor. For example, if this user were to run a program that called **CreateFile** and pass it a NULL security attributes structure, then the default owner and DACL are used to create a default security descriptor for the new file.

You can see in the sample output that both the groups and privileges have *attributes* associated with them. Group attributes are defined as follows:

SE_GROUP_MANDATORY	(0x01) Cannot disable the group
SE_GROUP_ENABLED_BY_DEFAULT	(0x02) Group enabled by default
SE_GROUP_ENABLED	(0x04) Group enabled
SE_GROUP_OWNER	(0x08) Group is owned by user
SE_GROUP_LOGON_ID	(0xC0000000) Group is logon identifier

Privilege attributes are as follows, and are explained in greater detail in the following section:

SE_PRIVILEGE_ENABLED_BY_DEFAULT	(0x01)
SE_PRIVILEGE_ENABLED	(0x02)
SE_PRIVILEGE_USED_FOR_ACCESS	(0x80000000)

The code in Listing 10.5 is long but straightforward, and follows the same pattern seen in Listing 10.4. For example, to list the groups in the access token, the code in Listing 10.5 does the following (the error handling code has been removed for clarity):

```
// specify to return group info
tic=TokenGroups;

// find out how much mem is needed
ret=GetTokenInformation(procToken, tic, NULL, 0,
  &sizeRqd);

// allocate that memory
tokenData=(TOKEN_GROUPS *) GlobalAlloc(GPTR,
  sizeRqd);

// actually get the group info
ret=GetTokenInformation(procToken, tic,
  tokenData, sizeRqd, &sizeRqd);

for (x=0;
  x<((TOKEN_GROUPS *)tokenData)->GroupCount;
  x++)
{
  // specify size of string buffers
  strSize=str2Size=80;

  // convert group SID into a name and domain
  ret=LookupAccountSid(NULL,
    ((TOKEN_GROUPS *)tokenData)->Groups[x].Sid,
    str, &strSize, str2, &str2Size, &sidType);

  cout << "Token group: \"" << setw(18)
    << setiosflags(ios::left) << str
    << "\" from \""
    << setw(12) << str2 << "\" w/ attributes 0x"
    << setiosflags(ios::internal)
    << hex << setw(8) << setfill('0')
    << ((TOKEN_GROUPS *)
          tokenData)->Groups[x].Attributes
    << resetiosflags(ios::internal)
```

```
        << setfill(' ') << endl;
    }
    // release memory
    if(GlobalFree(tokenData))
```

First the code determines how much space is required to store the group information, allocates that much space, and then retrieves the information. It then calls **GetTokenInformation** to find out how many groups exist in the list. The **for** loop cycles through the list, getting the group name of each group with the **LookupAccountSid** function and then printing all of the information for that group.

10.7 Privileges

Access to certain capabilities of the Windows NT system is limited by *privileges*. For example, in order to shut down the system, your access token must contain the SE_SHUTDOWN_NAME privilege. To set the system time it must contain the SE_SYSTEMTIME_NAME privilege. The list below shows all of the privileges available in Windows NT:

SE_ASSIGNPRIMARYTOKEN_NAME	Can assign a process's primary token
SE_AUDIT_NAME	Can create audit-log entries
SE_BACKUP_NAME	Can perform backups
SE_CHANGE_NOTIFY_NAME	Can receive file and directory change notifications. Enabled by default for all users
SE_CREATE_PAGEFILE_NAME	Can create a paging file
SE_CREATE_PERMANENT_NAME	Can create a permanent object
SE_CREATE_TOKEN_NAME	Can create a primary token
SE_DEBUG_NAME	Enables process debugging
SE_INC_BASE_PRIORITY_NAME	Can change the priority of a process
SE_INCREASE_QUOTA_NAME	Can change a process's quota
SE_LOAD_DRIVER_NAME	Can load and unload device drivers
SE_LOCK_MEMORY_NAME	Can lock physical memory pages

SE_PROF_SINGLE_PROCESS_NAME	Can obtain profiling data
SE_REMOTE_SHUTDOWN_NAME	Can shut down a system over the network
SE_RESTORE_NAME	Can restore data
SE_SECURITY_NAME	Owner is the security operator Can view security logs, etc.
SE_SHUTDOWN_NAME	Can shut down the system.
SE_SYSTEM_ENVIRONMENT_NAME	Can modify configuration information in non-volatile RAM
SE_SYSTEM_PROFILE_NAME	Can profile the entire system
SE_SYSTEMTIME_NAME	Can modify the system time
SE_TAKE_OWNERSHIP_NAME	Can take ownership of an object
SE_TCB_NAME	Owner is part of the trusted computer base
SE_UNSOLICITED_INPUT_NAME	Can read unsolicited input from a terminal

You can see the privileges contained in your access token using the access token dump program in Listing 10.5. You acquire privileges through User Rights menu option in the User Manager. Generally rights are associated with groups, and by being a member of a group you acquire its privileges. The administrator can also assign specific rights to specific users.

In a program, you must enable a privilege before you can use it. For example, let's say that you dump your access token using the code in Listing 10.5, and you see that the SE_SHUTDOWN_NAME privilege is in your list of privileges. You would think that you should be able to write a one-liner program that reboots your machine using the following line:

```
success = ExitWindowsEx(EWX_REBOOT, 0);
```

When you run this line of code, however, it will fail. Look at the attributes associated with the SE_SHUTDOWN_NAME privilege in the output of the dump program. Privileges have three attribute bits:

SE_PRIVILEGE_ENABLED_BY_DEFAULT	(0x01)
SE_PRIVILEGE_ENABLED	(0x02)
SE_PRIVILEGE_USED_FOR_ACCESS	(0x80000000)

Right now, bit 1 (the SE_PRIVILEGE_ENABLED bit) is set to zero, indicating that the privilege is not enabled. You must first enable any privilege before you can use it. Certain privileges are enabled by default, a fact that you can also detect from the attributes of the privilege, but SE_SHUTDOWN_NAME does not happen to be one of them.

Listing 10.6 shows the proper way to enable a privilege before using it. When you run the program, it will reboot your machine. If you prefer to experiment with something more benign than rebooting, see the time changing code in Chapter 15 for another example. See Chapter 13 for more information on shutting down the system and logging off.

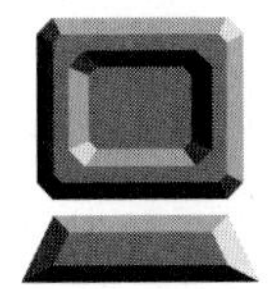

```
// sireboot.cpp

#include <windows.h>
#include <iostream.h>
#include <process.h>

void HandleError(char *s)
{
   cout << "Error in " << s << endl;
   cout << "Error code = " << GetLastError()
      << endl;
   exit(1);
}

BOOL EnablePrivilege(LPTSTR privilege)
{
   BOOL success;
   HANDLE token;
```

Listing 10.6
Enabling the SE_SHUTDOWN_NAME privilege allows you to reboot the system (Page 1 of 4)

```
    LUID luid;
    TOKEN_PRIVILEGES tokenPrivileges;

    // Get token for this process
    success = OpenProcessToken(GetCurrentProcess(),
       TOKEN_ADJUST_PRIVILEGES | TOKEN_QUERY,
       &token);
    if (!success)
    {
       HandleError("OpenProcessToken");
       return FALSE;
    }

    // Gets the value for a privilege
    success = LookupPrivilegeValue(0, privilege,
       &luid);
    if (!success)
    {
       HandleError("LookupPrivilegeValue");
       return FALSE;
    }

    // Enable the privilege
    tokenPrivileges.PrivilegeCount = 1;
    tokenPrivileges.Privileges[0].Luid = luid;
    tokenPrivileges.Privileges[0].Attributes =
       SE_PRIVILEGE_ENABLED;
    success = AdjustTokenPrivileges(token, FALSE,
       &tokenPrivileges, 0, 0, 0);
    // Always returns true, so check GetLastError
    if (GetLastError() != ERROR_SUCCESS)
    {
       HandleError("AdjustTokenPrivileges");
       return FALSE;
    }
```

Listing 10.6
Enabling the SE_SHUTDOWN_NAME privilege allows you to reboot the system (Page 2 of 4)

```
    return TRUE;
}

BOOL DisablePrivilege(LPTSTR privilege)
{
    BOOL success;
    HANDLE token;
    LUID luid;
    TOKEN_PRIVILEGES tokenPrivileges;

    // Get tokens for this process
    success = OpenProcessToken(GetCurrentProcess(),
        TOKEN_ADJUST_PRIVILEGES | TOKEN_QUERY,
        &token);
    if (!success)
    {
        HandleError("OpenProcessToken");
        return FALSE;
    }

    // Gets the value for a privilege
    success = LookupPrivilegeValue(0, privilege,
        &luid);
    if (!success)
    {
        HandleError("LookupPrivilegeValue");
        return FALSE;
    }

    // Disable the privilege
    tokenPrivileges.PrivilegeCount = 1;
    tokenPrivileges.Privileges[0].Luid = luid;
    // disable the privilege
    tokenPrivileges.Privileges[0].Attributes = 0;
    success = AdjustTokenPrivileges(token, FALSE,
```

Listing 10.6
Enabling the SE_SHUTDOWN_NAME privilege allows you to reboot the system
(Page 3 of 4)

```
            &tokenPrivileges, 0, 0, 0);
        // Always returns true, so...
        if (GetLastError() != ERROR_SUCCESS)
        {
            HandleError("AdjustTokenPrivileges");
            return FALSE;
        }
        return TRUE;
    }

    void main()
    {
        BOOL success;

        if (EnablePrivilege(SE_SHUTDOWN_NAME))
        {
            success = ExitWindowsEx(EWX_REBOOT, 0);
            if (success)
                cout << "Success. Shutting down shortly."
                    << endl;
            else
                HandleError("Shutting down");
        }
        DisablePrivilege(SE_SHUTDOWN_NAME);
    }
```

Listing 10.6
Enabling the SE_SHUTDOWN_NAME privilege allows you to reboot the system (Page 4 of 4)

The heart of Listing 10.6 is the **EnablePrivilege** function. Given a privilege, this function enables it. Note that it accepts one privilege name as an input parameter. This name must be specified as a string pointer as shown: If you look in the help file you will find that all privilege constants like SE_SHUTDOWN_NAME are defined as strings.

The goal of the **EnablePrivilege** function is to open the processes token and enable the privilege. It starts by calling **OpenProcessToken**.

OpenProcessToken	*Opens a process's access token so that it can be modified*

```
BOOL OpenProcessToken(
    HANDLE process,
    DWORD accessMask,
    PHANDLE tokenHandle)
```

process	A handle to the process to open
accessMask	The actions that need to be performed on the open token
tokenHandle	A pointer to the token returned by the function

Returns TRUE on success

GetCurrentProcess	*Returns a handle to the current process*

```
HANDLE GetCurrentProcess(VOID)
```

Returns a handle to the current process

The access mask passed to **OpenProcessToken** specifies what you plan to do with the access token once you have it open. You can specify any or all of the specific rights shown in Section 10.5.9 for access tokens. Here, the code requests TOKEN_QUERY so that it can get the current value of a privilege and TOKEN_ADJUST_PRIVILEGES so that it can modify a privilege. The **OpenProcessToken** function makes sure that you have the proper authority to perform the requested actions (by looking at security descriptor on the access token), and if you do it returns to you a handle to the token for the process. If you request an access right that you are not allowed to perform on the token, then the function fails. Alternatively, if you do not request the right and then later try to perform the action, the later call will fail.

The **EnablePrivilege** function in Listing 10.6 next tries to look up the LUID (Locally Unique Identifier) value of the requested privilege using a call to the **LookupPrivilegeValue** function.

LookupPrivilegeValue	*Retrieves a locally unique identifier for the privilege*
`BOOL LookupPrivilegeValue( LPCTSTR systemName, LPCTSTR privilege, PLUID pluid)`	
systemName	The name of the system. Pass 0 for the local system
privilege	The privilege to look up
pluid	A pointer that points to the location where the function should return the LUID
Returns TRUE on success	

Once it has the LUID value, the program uses it in a TOKEN_ PRIVILEGES structure to modify the privilege:

```
tokenPrivileges.PrivilegeCount = 1;
tokenPrivileges.Privileges[0].Luid = luid;
tokenPrivileges.Privileges[0].Attributes =
   SE_PRIVILEGE_ENABLED;
success = AdjustTokenPrivileges(token, FALSE,
   &tokenPrivileges, 0, 0, 0);
// Always returns true, so check GetLastError
```

A TOKEN_PRIVILEGES structure is defined in the `winnt.h` file to contain the following fields:

```
typedef struct _TOKEN_PRIVILEGES {
    DWORD PrivilegeCount;
    LUID_AND_ATTRIBUTES Privileges[ANYSIZE_ARRAY];
} TOKEN_PRIVILEGES;
```

The ANYSIZE_ARRAY constant is defined as 1, so as declared in this program you can only change one privilege at a time. When the system returns structures of this type however, or when you build your own structures of this type, then the array can contain more than one structure.

The LUID_AND_ATTRIBUTES type is also a structure and it is defined like this in `winnt.h`:

```
typedef struct LUID_AND_ATTRIBUTES {
    LUID  Luid;
    DWORD Attributes;
} LUID_AND_ATTRIBUTES;
```

The attributes in the LUID_AND_ATTRIBUTES structure are a bit mask that can contain any or all of the following values:

SE_PRIVILEGE_ENABLED_BY_DEFAULT
SE_PRIVILEGE_ENABLED
SE_PRIVILEGE_USED_FOR_ACCESS

In the code in Listing 10.6, the program places the LUID for the SE_SHUTDOWN_NAME privilege, as well as a request to enable it, into the **tokenPrivileges** variable and then passes the variable to the **AdjustTokenPrivileges** function to enable it.

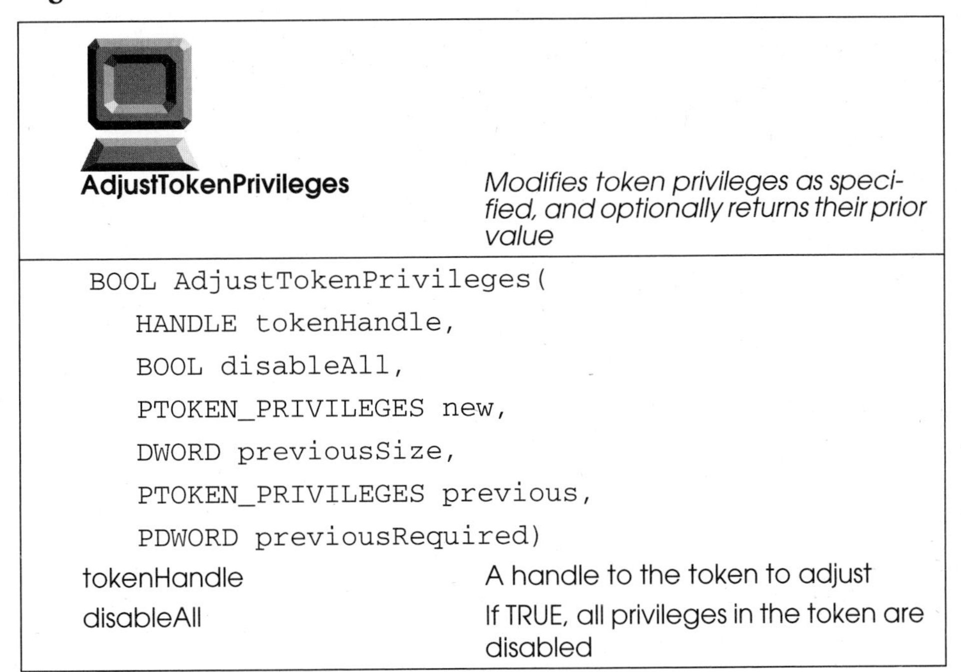

AdjustTokenPrivileges — *Modifies token privileges as specified, and optionally returns their prior value*

```
BOOL AdjustTokenPrivileges(
   HANDLE tokenHandle,
   BOOL disableAll,
   PTOKEN_PRIVILEGES new,
   DWORD previousSize,
   PTOKEN_PRIVILEGES previous,
   PDWORD previousRequired)
```

tokenHandle	A handle to the token to adjust
disableAll	If TRUE, all privileges in the token are disabled

new	Pointer to TOKEN_PRIVILEGES structure that contains the changes
previousSize	The size of the buffer in previous
previous	Points to a buffer. The function fills this buffer with the previous values of changed privileges
previousRequired	Can be used to find out how much space is needed for the previous buffer
Returns TRUE on success	

The code in Listing 10.6 does not request or need the previous value of the privilege so these values are 0 in the call to **AdjustTokenPrivileges**.

At the completion of the **EnablePrivilege** function in Listing 10.6, the requested privilege is enabled. In this case, the requested privilege is SE_SHUTDOWN_NAME, so the program can then proceed to reboot the system. See Chapter 13 for more information on rebooting.

The **DisablePrivilege** function in Listing 10.6 is somewhat superfluous, but shows that disabling privileges involves the exact same process with different attributes. In most cases you will simply enable a privilege in a process and leave it enabled.

You will need to use the principles described here whenever you want to perform any action that requires you to enable a privilege. These actions include such things as shutting down the system, setting the system time, taking ownership of an object, and so on.

10.8 Adding and Deleting ACEs

Listing 10.1 demonstrated how easy it is to create a new security descriptor for any object. Adding ACEs to a new security descriptor that you are creating from scratch is trivial. But what if you want to modify an existing security descriptor by adding or removing ACEs? While conceptually simple, performing additions and deletions to an existing security descriptor takes quite a bit of code because of the difference between *absolute* and *self-relative* security descriptors.

Listing 10.1 at the beginning of the chapter creates a security descriptor in absolute format. It creates a variable of type SECURITY_DESCRIPTOR:

```
SECURITY_DESCRIPTOR sd;
```

The current declaration for the SECURITY_DESCRIPTOR is shown below in this structure declaration copied from `winnt.h`:

```
typedef struct _SECURITY_DESCRIPTOR {
   BYTE  Revision;
   BYTE  Sbz1;
   SECURITY_DESCRIPTOR_CONTROL Control;
   PSID Owner;
   PSID Group;
   PACL Sacl;
   PACL Dacl;
   } SECURITY_DESCRIPTOR, *PISECURITY_DESCRIPTOR;
```

In actuality we are not supposed to look at this structure because it is supposed to be *opaque.* That is, you should only manipulate it using functions supplied in the API, rather than trying to manipulate it directly. Doing so guarantees that your code will work in the future as the security system matures. However, looking at the structure here doesn't hurt anything, and it allows you to see that a security descriptor is actually made up of five 32-bit values. The first value is a header containing the revision level, a reserved location named **Sbz1,** and a control value. The next four values are pointers to the four pieces of a security descriptor seen in Figure 10.2.

In Listing 10.1, the program creates the security descriptor by declaring areas of memory, filling them, and then pointing the different pointers in the security descriptor to those areas. The areas might also have been declared on the heap. This is called an *absolute* security descriptor and is pictured in Figure 10.7.

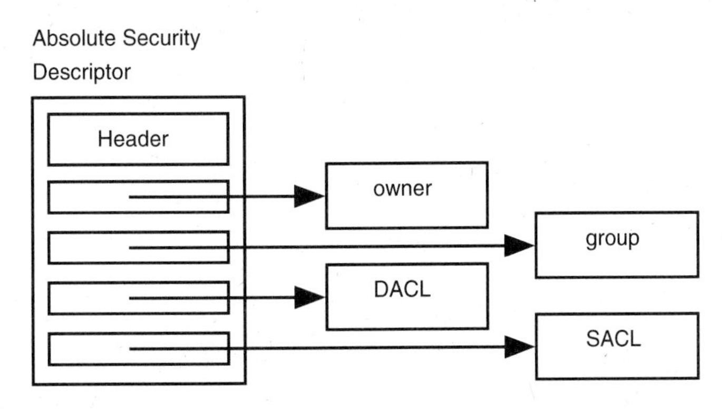

Figure 10.7
An absolute security descriptor points to its different elements.

A self-relative security descriptor, on the other hand, is self-contained. This is the sort of security descriptor you obtain when you ask the system to give you a copy of a security descriptor, as in the dump programs in Listings 10.4 and 10.5. The system creates a single block of memory that contains the five words of the security descriptor itself, along with all of the elements the four pointers reference. Figure 10.8 shows a self-relative security descriptor.

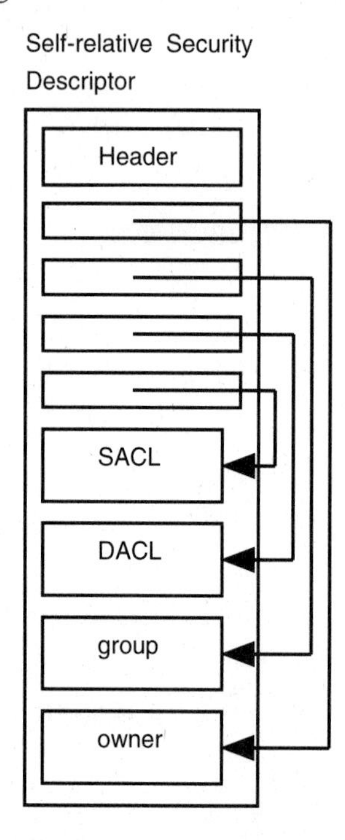

Figure 10.8
An self-relative security descriptor is self-contained.

Looking at Figure 10.8, you can begin to see the problem that arises when you try to change a security descriptor. You request from the system a copy of an existing security descriptor. It comes back, and it is in a self-relative format. If you try to add an ACE into the DACL, you have a problem because there is no room for the new ACE. What you end up having to do to add an ACE is turn the entire security descriptor into absolute format, increase the size of the DACL, and add the new ACE to it. You can then pass the absolute security descriptor back to the system to change the security descriptor.

Listing 10.7 demonstrates the process. When you run the program in Listing 10.7, it will obtain the security descriptor for the well-known

HKEY_CURRENT_USER key in the registry and add a new ACE to it. Before running Listing 10.7, run the Registry Editor (`regedt32.exe`) and examine the security permissions for the HKEY_CURRENT_USERS key. Run Listing 10.7, and then refresh the display to examine the descriptor again. You will find that it contains a new group called "Administrators" (or modify the code to add any other user or group). The registry is used in this example simply because all Windows NT machines have the registry editor and it contains a visual security editor. However, if you have an NTFS partition on your machine you can modify the code slightly to add a new ACE to a file's DACL instead. This same code will work on the security descriptor of any NT object.

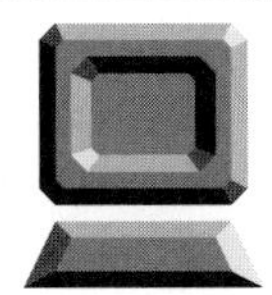

```
// addace.cpp

#include <windows.h>
#include <iostream.h>

VOID main(VOID)
{
  BOOL ret;
  LONG err;
  SECURITY_DESCRIPTOR *sdData;
  SECURITY_DESCRIPTOR absSD;
  PSID psid;
  PACL pacl;
  PACL pNewACL;
  DWORD newACLSize;
  BOOL byDef;
  BOOL haveDACL;
  DWORD sizeRqd;
  SID_NAME_USE sidType;
  DWORD sidSize;
```

Listing 10.7
Adding an ACE to an existing ACL (Page 1 of 8)

```
    UINT x;
    ACL_SIZE_INFORMATION aclSize;
    ACCESS_ALLOWED_ACE *pace;
    CHAR str[80];
    DWORD strSize;

    cout << "Adding \"Administrators\" "
      << "to HKEY_CURRENT_USER..."
      << endl;

    // ----- Get new group's SID -----

    // lookup SID from name
    sidSize=0;
    strSize=80;
    ret=LookupAccountName(NULL, "Administrators", NULL,
      &sidSize, str, &strSize, &sidType);

    if (sidSize)
    {
      // allocate memory for SID
      psid=(PSID) GlobalAlloc(GPTR, sidSize);
      // actually get SID
      strSize=80;
      ret=LookupAccountName(NULL, "Administrators",
        psid, &sidSize, str, &strSize, &sidType);
      if (!ret)
      {
        cerr << "Unable to get Administrators SID."
          << endl;
        return;
      }
    }
    else
    {
      cerr << "Administrators SID not available. "
```

Listing 10.7
Adding an ACE to an existing ACL (Page 2 of 8)

```
        << GetLastError()

        << endl;
      return;
    }

    // ----- Get a copy of the SD/DACL -----

    // find out how much mem is needed
    // to hold existing SD w/DACL
    sizeRqd=0;
    err=RegGetKeySecurity(HKEY_CURRENT_USER,
      DACL_SECURITY_INFORMATION,
      NULL, &sizeRqd);
    if (err != ERROR_INSUFFICIENT_BUFFER)
    {
      cerr << "Unable to get SD size."
        << endl;
      return;
    }

    // allocate that memory
    sdData=(SECURITY_DESCRIPTOR *)
      GlobalAlloc(GPTR, sizeRqd);
    if (sdData == NULL)
    {
      cerr << "Unable to allocate memory." << endl;
      return;
    }

    // actually get the SD info
    err=RegGetKeySecurity(HKEY_CURRENT_USER,
      DACL_SECURITY_INFORMATION,
      sdData, &sizeRqd);
    if (err != ERROR_SUCCESS)
    {
```

Listing 10.7
Adding an ACE to an existing ACL (Page 3 of 8)

```
    cerr << "Unable to get SD info." << endl;
    return;
  }

  // ----- Create a new absolute SD and DACL -----

  // initialize absolute SD
  ret=InitializeSecurityDescriptor(&absSD,
    SECURITY_DESCRIPTOR_REVISION);
  if (!ret)
  {
    cerr << "Unable to init new SD."
      << endl;
    return;
  }

  // get the DACL info
  ret=GetSecurityDescriptorDacl(sdData,
    &haveDACL, &pacl, &byDef);
  if (!ret)
  {
    cerr << "Unable to get DACL info." << endl;
    return;
  }

  if (!haveDACL)
  {
    // compute size of new DACL
    newACLSize= sizeof(ACCESS_ALLOWED_ACE) +
      GetLengthSid(psid) - sizeof(DWORD);
  }
  else
  {
    // get size info about existing DACL
    ret=GetAclInformation(pacl, &aclSize,
      sizeof(ACL_SIZE_INFORMATION),
```

Listing 10.7
Adding an ACE to an existing ACL (Page 4 of 8)

```
        AclSizeInformation);

      // compute size of new DACL
      newACLSize=aclSize.AclBytesInUse +
        sizeof(ACCESS_ALLOWED_ACE) +
        GetLengthSid(psid) -
        sizeof(DWORD);
    }

    // allocate memory
    pNewACL=(PACL) GlobalAlloc(GPTR, newACLSize);
    if (pNewACL == NULL)
    {
      cerr << "Unable to allocate memory." << endl;
      return;
    }

    // initialize the new DACL
    ret=InitializeAcl(pNewACL, newACLSize,
      ACL_REVISION);
    if (!ret)
    {
      cerr << "Unable to init new DACL."
        << endl;
      return;
    }

    // ----- Copy existing DACL into new DACL -----

    if (haveDACL)
    {
      // copy ACEs from existing DACL
      // to new DACL
      for (x=0; x<aclSize.AceCount; x++)
      {
        ret=GetAce(pacl, x, (LPVOID *) &pace);
```

Listing 10.7
Adding an ACE to an existing ACL (Page 5 of 8)

```
        if (!ret)
        {
          cerr << "Unable to get ACE."
            << endl;
          return;
        }

        ret=AddAce(pNewACL, ACL_REVISION, MAXDWORD,
          pace, pace->Header.AceSize);
        if (!ret)
        {
          cerr << "Unable to add ACE."
            << endl;
          return;
        }
      }
    }

    // ----- Add the new ACE to the new DACL -----

    // add access allowed ACE to new
    // DACL
    ret=AddAccessAllowedAce(pNewACL,
      ACL_REVISION, GENERIC_ALL, psid);
    if (!ret)
    {
      cerr << "Unable to add ACE."
        << endl;
      return;
    }

    // set the new DACL
    // in the absolute SD
    ret=SetSecurityDescriptorDacl(&absSD,
      TRUE, pNewACL, FALSE);
    if (!ret)
```

Listing 10.7
Adding an ACE to an existing ACL (Page 6 of 8)

```
    {
      cerr << "Unable to install DACL."
        << endl;
      return;
    }

    // check the new SD
    ret=IsValidSecurityDescriptor(&absSD);
    if (!ret)
    {
      cerr << "SD invalid."
        << endl;
      return;
    }

    // ----- Install the new DACL -----

    // install the updated SD
    err=RegSetKeySecurity(HKEY_CURRENT_USER,
      DACL_SECURITY_INFORMATION,
      &absSD);
    if (err != ERROR_SUCCESS)
    {
      cerr << "Unable to set registry key SD."
        << endl;
    }

    // ensure that SD has been updated
    RegCloseKey(HKEY_CURRENT_USER);

    // release memory
    if(GlobalFree(pNewACL))
    {
      cerr << "Unable to free memory." << endl;
      return;
    }
```

Listing 10.7
Adding an ACE to an existing ACL (Page 7 of 8)

```
        // release memory
        if(GlobalFree(psid))
        {
          cerr << "Unable to free memory." << endl;
          return;
        }

        // release memory
        if(GlobalFree(sdData))
        {
          cerr << "Unable to free memory." << endl;
          return;
        }

        cout << "Done." << endl;
    }
```

Listing 10.7
Adding an ACE to an existing ACL (Page 8 of 8)

The code in Listing 10.7 goes through six distinct phases in order to add a new ACE to an existing DACL:

1. Create a SID for the new group to be added to the DACL.
2. Get a copy of the existing DACL for the HKEY_CURRENT_USER key in the registry
3. Create a new absolute security descriptor and a new DACL big enough to hold the old DACL plus one new ACE
4. Copy the old DACL to the new one
5. Add the new ACE to the new DACL
6. Replace the old security descriptor's DACL for HKEY_CURRENT_USER with the new one

Phase 1 uses the **LookupAccountName** function to retrieve the SID for the group named “Administrators.” If your machine does not support this group, or if you want to use a different user or group, replace “Administrators” with any group you like.

LookupAccountName	*Returns a SID for the specified account*

```
BOOL LookupAccountName(
    LPCTSTR system,
    LPCTSTR accountName,
    PSID psid,
    LPDWORD sidBufferSize,
    LPTSTR domainName,
    LPDWORD domainNameLen,
    PSID_NAME_USE psnu)
```

system	Name of a remote system or 0 for local
accountName	The name of the account to look up
psid	A pointer to a buffer for the returned SID
sidBufferSize	The size of the psid buffer
domainName	A pointer to a buffer for the returned domain name
domainNameLen	Size of the domain name buffer
psnu	Returned enumerated type indicating the type of account

Returns TRUE on success

Phase 2 uses the **RegGetKeySecurity** function to obtain the existing DACL for the HKEY_CURRENT_USER key in the registry. It would be just as easy to use **GetFileSecurity** to obtain the DACL for a file. The function returns a self-relative security descriptor containing a copy of the key's DACL. As usual it goes through the two-step process of getting the buffer size required for the copy of the security descriptor, allocating the buffer, and then actually getting the copy of the security descriptor.

RegGetKeySecurity	*Gets the security descriptor for a registry key*

```
LONG RegGetKeySecurity(
   HKEY keyHandle,
   SECURITY_INFORMATION si,
   PSECURITY_DESCRIPTOR psd,
   LPDWORD secDescLen)
```

keyHandle	Handle to the registry key
si	Flags indicating the desired information from the security descriptor
psd	Pointer to the security descriptor buffer
secDescLen	The size of the buffer

Returns ERROR_SUCCESS on success

You can request any or all of the following pieces of the security descriptor in the **si** parameter:

OWNER_SECURITY_INFORMATION	object's owner
GROUP_SECURITY_INFORMATION	object's group
DACL_SECURITY_INFORMATION	object's DACL
SACL_SECURITY_INFORMATION	object's SACL

If you request all four together you receive a complete copy of the object's security descriptor. The data always comes back in self-relative format.

Phase 3 creates a new absolute-format security descriptor. It then looks at the existing DACL and calculates the size required for a new DACL that will hold the existing ACEs plus one new one. If the existing DACL is NULL then the size of the new DACL is the size of one access allowed ACE plus the size of the SID that the ACE will contain. The code subtracts the size of one DWORD because the ACE size by default contains one word for the SID, but that space is already accounted for when the code gets the SID's actual size

(SIDs are variably-sized objects). If the existing DACL is not NULL, then **GetAclInformation** returns the size of the existing DACL and this is added to the size of the new ACE and its SID.

GetAclInformation	*Returns information about the specified ACL*

`BOOL GetAclInformation(`
`PACL pacl,`
`LPVOID aclInfo,`
`DWORD aclInfoSize,`
`ACL_INFORMATION_CLASS aic)`	

pacl	A pointer to the ACL
aclInfo	Pointer to a buffer to hold the info
psd	The size of the buffer
aic	ACL_RVISION_INFORMATION or ACL_SIZE_INFORMATION
Returns TRUE on success	

Phase 4 copies the old DACL into the new DACL. Inside a **for** loop it gets each existing ACE using **GetAce** and then adds the ACE to the new DACL with **AddAce**. Phase 5 then adds the new ACE to the new DACL with **AddAccessAllowedAce**.

GetAce	*Gets the specified ACE from the specified ACL*

`BOOL GetAce(`
`PACL pacl,`
`DWORD aceIndex`
`LPVOID *ace)`	

pacl	Pointer to the ACL

aceIndex	The ACE to get
ace	Pointer to set with buffer address
Returns TRUE on success	

AddAce — *Gets the specified ACE from the specified ACL*

```
BOOL AddAce(
    PACL pacl,
    DWORD revision,
    DWORD index,
    LPVOID aceBuffer,
    DWORD aceBufferLen)
```

pacl	Pointer to the ACL
revision	Must be ACL_REVISION
index	Index pointing to insertion point. 0 for beginning, MAXDWORD for end, or location
aceBuffer	Buffer holding new ACE(s)
aceBufferLen	Size of aceBuffer
Returns TRUE on success	

Phase 6 completes the process by replacing the old DACL for HKEY_CURRENT_USERS with the new one using the **RegSetKeySecurity** function. The remainder of the program cleans up allocated memory.

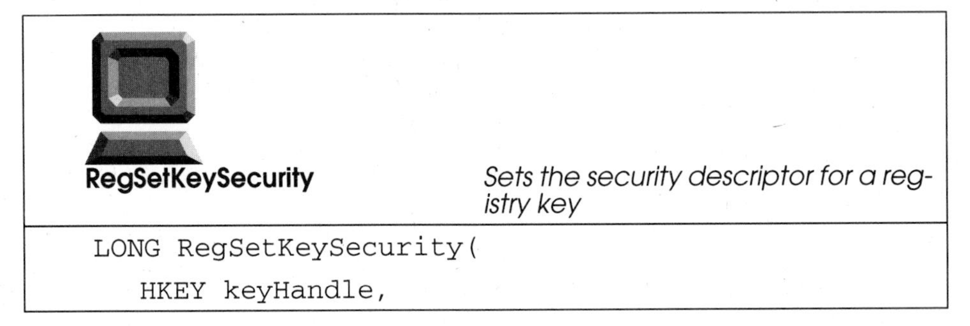

RegSetKeySecurity — *Sets the security descriptor for a registry key*

```
LONG RegSetKeySecurity(
    HKEY keyHandle,
```

```
    SECURITY_INFORMATION si,
    PSECURITY_DESCRIPTOR psd)
```

keyHandle	Handle to the registry key
si	Flags indicating the information being set
psd	Pointer to the security descriptor buffer
Returns ERROR_SUCCESS on success	

Removing an ACE from an existing security descriptor follows the same pattern, as shown in Listing 10.8. After you run Listing 10.7, you can run Listing 10.8 to remove the ACE that 10.7 added.

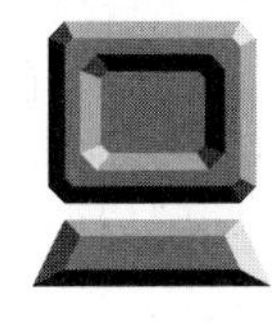

```
// remvace.cpp

#include <windows.h>
#include <iostream.h>

VOID main(VOID)
{
  BOOL ret;
  LONG err;
  SECURITY_DESCRIPTOR *sdData;
  SECURITY_DESCRIPTOR absSD;
  PSID psid;
  PACL pacl;
  BOOL byDef;
  BOOL haveDACL;
  DWORD sizeRqd;
  SID_NAME_USE sidType;
  DWORD sidSize;
```

Listing 10.8
Removing an ACE from an existing ACL (Page 1 of 7)

```
UINT x;
ACL_SIZE_INFORMATION aclSize;
ACCESS_ALLOWED_ACE *pace;
CHAR str[80];
DWORD strSize;

cout << "Removing \"Administrators\" "
  << "from HKEY_CURRENT_USER..."
  << endl;

// ----- Get SID of group to remove -----

// lookup SID from name
sidSize=0;
strSize=80;
ret=LookupAccountName(NULL, "Administrators", NULL,
  &sidSize, str, &strSize, &sidType);

if (sidSize)
{
  // allocate memory for SID
  psid=(PSID) GlobalAlloc(GPTR, sidSize);
  // actually get SID
  strSize=80;
  ret=LookupAccountName(NULL, "Administrators",
    psid, &sidSize, str, &strSize, &sidType);
  if (!ret)
  {
    cerr << "Unable to get Administrators SID."
      << endl;
    return;
  }
}
else
{
```

Listing 10.8
Removing an ACE from an existing ACL (Page 2 of 7)

```
    cerr << "Administrators SID not available."
      << endl;
    return;
  }

  // ----- Get the existing DACL -----

  // find out how much mem is needed
  // to hold existing SD w/DACL
  sizeRqd=0;
  err=RegGetKeySecurity(HKEY_CURRENT_USER,
    DACL_SECURITY_INFORMATION,
    NULL, &sizeRqd);
  if (err != ERROR_INSUFFICIENT_BUFFER)
  {
    cerr << "Unable to get SD size."
      << endl;
    return;
  }

  // allocate that memory
  sdData=(SECURITY_DESCRIPTOR *)
    GlobalAlloc(GPTR, sizeRqd);
  if (sdData == NULL)
  {
    cerr << "Unable to allocate memory." << endl;
    return;
  }

  // actually get the SD info
  err=RegGetKeySecurity(HKEY_CURRENT_USER,
    DACL_SECURITY_INFORMATION,
    sdData, &sizeRqd);
  if (err != ERROR_SUCCESS)
  {
```

Listing 10.8
Removing an ACE from an existing ACL (Page 3 of 7)

```
        cerr << "Unable to get SD info." << endl;
        return;
    }

    // ----- Create a new absolute SD -----

    // initialize absolute SD
    ret=InitializeSecurityDescriptor(&absSD,
        SECURITY_DESCRIPTOR_REVISION);
    if (!ret)
    {
        cerr << "Unable to init new SD."
            << endl;
        return;
    }

    // get the DACL info
    ret=GetSecurityDescriptorDacl(sdData,
        &haveDACL, &pacl, &byDef);
    if (!ret)
    {
        cerr << "Unable to get DACL info." << endl;
        return;
    }

    // ----- Search the DACL and delete ACE -----

    if (!haveDACL)
    {
        cout << "Security Descriptor DACL is NULL."
            << endl;
    }
    else
    {
        // get size info about existing DACL
```

Listing 10.8
Removing an ACE from an existing ACL (Page 4 of 7)

```
    ret=GetAclInformation(pacl, &aclSize,
      sizeof(ACL_SIZE_INFORMATION),
      AclSizeInformation);

    // remove Domain Users from DACL
    for (x=aclSize.AceCount; x>0; x--)
    {
      ret=GetAce(pacl, x - 1, (LPVOID *) &pace);
      if (!ret)
      {
        cerr << "Unable to get ACE."
          << endl;
        return;
      }

      ret=EqualSid(&pace->SidStart, psid);
      if (ret)
      {
        cout << "Deleting an ACE..."
          << endl;
        ret=DeleteAce(pacl, x - 1);
        if (!ret)
        {
          cerr << "Unable to delete ACE."
            << endl;
          return;
        }
      }
    }

  // ----- Add the DACL to absolute SD and install

    // set the new DACL
    // in the absolute SD
    ret=SetSecurityDescriptorDacl(&absSD,
```

Listing 10.8
Removing an ACE from an existing ACL (Page 5 of 7)

```
        TRUE, pacl, FALSE);
      if (!ret)
      {
        cerr << "Unable to install DACL."
          << endl;
        return;
      }

      // check the new SD
      ret=IsValidSecurityDescriptor(&absSD);
      if (!ret)
      {
        cerr << "SD invalid."
          << endl;
        return;
      }

      // install the updated SD
      err=RegSetKeySecurity(HKEY_CURRENT_USER,
        DACL_SECURITY_INFORMATION,
        &absSD);
      if (err != ERROR_SUCCESS)
      {
        cerr << "Unable to set registry key SD."
          << endl;
      }

      // ensure that SD has been updated
      RegCloseKey(HKEY_CURRENT_USER);
    }

    // release memory
    if(GlobalFree(psid))
    {
      cerr << "Unable to free memory." << endl;
```

Listing 10.8
Removing an ACE from an existing ACL (Page 6 of 7)

```
        return;
    }

    // release memory
    if(GlobalFree(sdData))
    {
        cerr << "Unable to free memory." << endl;
        return;
    }

    cout << "Done." << endl;
}
```

Listing 10.8
Removing an ACE from an existing ACL (Page 7 of 7)

To delete an ACE in an existing security descriptor, Listing 10.8 goes through six phases. Its first three phases mirror those of Listing 10.7:

1. Create a SID for the group to be deleted from the DACL
2. Get a copy of the existing DACL for the HKEY_CURRENT_USER key in the registry
3. Create a new absolute security descriptor
4. Scan the self-relative DACL for the ACE to delete and delete it if found
5. Install the modified DACL in the absolute security descriptor
6. Install the new DACL in HKEY_CURRENT_USER using the new absolute security descriptor

Phase 1 uses the **LookupAccountName** function to retrieve the SID for the group named “Administrators.” If you want to use a different user or group, replace “Administrators” with anything you like.

Phase 2 uses the **RegGetKeySecurity** function to obtain the existing DACL for the HKEY_CURRENT_USER key in the registry. It would be just as easy to use **GetFileSecurity** to obtain the DACL for a file. The function returns a self-relative security descriptor containing a copy of the key's DACL. As usual it goes through the two-step process of getting the buffer size required for the copy of the security descriptor, allocating the buffer, and then actually getting the copy of the security descriptor.

Phase 3 creates a new absolute-format security descriptor. Unlike Listing 10.7, it does not create a new DACL. Instead, Listing 10.8 will delete the ACE from the DACL returned in Phase 2.

Phase 4 uses **GetAclInformation** to get the number of ACEs in the DACL. It then uses a **for** loop to look at each ACE in the DACL until it finds one containing the SID it is looking for. The **EqualSid** function compares SIDs for equality. Once it finds an appropriate ACE, it deletes it with **DeleteAce**.

EqualSid	*Compares two SIDs*
`BOOL EqualSid( PSID psid1, PSID psid2)`	
psid1	The first SID
psid2	The second SID
Returns TRUE on success	

DeleteAce	*Deletes the specified ACE from the specified ACL*
`BOOL DeleteAce( PACL pacl, DWORD aceIndex)`	
pacl	Pointer to the ACL
aceIndex	The ACE to delete
Returns TRUE on success	

Phase 5 sets the newly modified DACL into the absolute security descriptor using the **SetSecurityDescriptorDacl** function. It then verifies the new security descriptor with **IsValidSecurityDescriptor** before installing it with **RegSetKeySecurity** in Phase 6.

SetSecurityDescriptorDacl	*Sets a DACL into an absolute security descriptor*

```
BOOL SetSecurityDescriptorDacl(
    PSECURITY_DESCRIPTOR psd,
    BOOL daclPresent,
    PACL pacl,
    BOOL daclDefaulted)
```

psd	Pointer to the security descriptor
daclPresent	Pass FALSE to create a NULL DACL
pacl	Pointer to the ACL
daclDefaulted	Pass TRUE if you got the DACL from somewhere else, or FALSE if you created or modified it yourself

Returns TRUE on success

IsValidSecurityDescriptor	*Checks a security descriptor for validity*

```
BOOL IsValidSecurityDescriptor(
    PSECURITY_DESCRIPTOR psd)
```

psd	Pointer to the security descriptor

Returns TRUE on success

You can apply the principles described above for adding and removing ACEs to any ACL in an NT system. The amount of code required is a bit bothersome, but the process is straightforward.

10.9 Impersonation

Sections 7.4 and 7.5 deal with named pipes. In all of the code samples in those sections, a named pipe server runs on one machine, and a named pipe client connects to the server and sends it messages. The client can run on the same machine as the server, or it can run on a different machine and connect over the network. You may recall that all through those sections you were warned that if you run the client on a different machine, *you should make sure that the logon ID and password used on the server and client machine are the same.* The reason for this admonition stems from the way that the security system handles default security descriptors.

The named pipe code in Chapter 7 creates all of its pipes with the following sort of call:

```
/* Create a named pipe for receiving messages */
ssnpPipe=CreateNamedPipe("\\\\.\\pipe\\ssnp",
  PIPE_ACCESS_INBOUND,
  PIPE_TYPE_MESSAGE | PIPE_WAIT,
  1, 0, 0, 150, 0);
```

The last parameter in the list is the security attributes parameter, and it is set to 0. This tells NT to create a *default security descriptor* for the new pipe. The default security descriptor contains a default DACL. If you go back to Section 10.6 and run the access token dumping program in Listing 10.5 you can see what your default DACL contains.

You will notice that your default DACL is specific to you. It allows only you or the NT system itself to access the object. This is fine for normal objects like processes, threads, and semaphores because you are the only one logged into the NT machine. However, when this default DACL is applied to the server end of a named pipe, it restricts the users who can connect to the pipe: Only you can connect. Therefore, when you try to connect from another machine, the account that you logon with must have the exact same name and password as the account on the server machine. If the network has a domain controller then this is guaranteed as long as you use the same account on both machines. If not, it's unlikely to work. See the book *Windows NT Administration: Single Systems to Heterogeneous Networks* for more information on domain controllers and networks.

If you want to create a server that *any* user can connect to, then you need to create a security descriptor with a NULL DACL. As discussed earlier, a NULL DACL is understood by the system to mean "any user can access this object." You would therefore use the following code to create a pipe that any user can access:

```
    InitializeSecurityDescriptor(&sd,
      SECURITY_DESCRIPTOR_REVISION);
    SetSecurityDescriptorDacl(&sd, TRUE, NULL,
      FALSE);
    sa.nLength= sizeof(SECURITY_ATTRIBUTES);
    sa.bInheritHandle = FALSE;
    sa.lpSecurityDescriptor = &sd;

    /* Create a named pipe for receiving messages */
    ssnpPipe=CreateNamedPipe("\\\\.\\pipe\\ssnp",
      PIPE_ACCESS_INBOUND,
      PIPE_TYPE_MESSAGE | PIPE_WAIT,
      1, 0, 0, 150, &sa);
```

Try this in Listing 10.3 to prove that it works correctly and that anyone can connect to the resulting pipe.

Letting anyone connect to a named pipe server creates a potential problem however. Let's say that the goal of the server is to let the user execute certain commands remotely. Let's say that one of those commands is a file delete command. Once the user connects, the user has the user ID *of the server process on the remote machine*. If the server is implemented as an NT service (see Chapter 9), then the server has SYSTEM privileges, and therefore so does the remote user. The remote user can therefore delete any file on the system.

What you would like instead is for the server to take on the identity of the client user while the user is connected. That way the client user can access only those files that are appropriate to him or her. NT provides a function that does this called **ImpersonateNamedPipeClient**, as demonstrated in Listing 10.9.

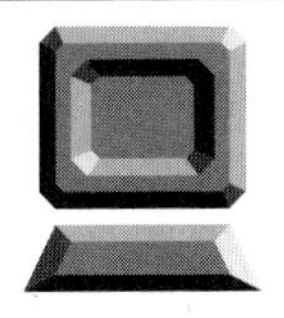

```
// imprecv.cpp

#include <windows.h>
```

Listing 10.9
Impersonating another user in a named pipe server (Page 1 of 4)

```
#include <iostream.h>

int main(void)
{
  char toDisptxt[80];
  HANDLE ssnpPipe;
  DWORD NumBytesRead;
  char buffer[80];
  DWORD bufferLen;
  SECURITY_ATTRIBUTES sa;
  SECURITY_DESCRIPTOR sd;

  InitializeSecurityDescriptor(&sd,
    SECURITY_DESCRIPTOR_REVISION);
  SetSecurityDescriptorDacl(&sd, TRUE, NULL,
    FALSE);
  sa.nLength= sizeof(SECURITY_ATTRIBUTES);
  sa.bInheritHandle = FALSE;
  sa.lpSecurityDescriptor = &sd;

  /* Create a named pipe for receiving messages */
  ssnpPipe=CreateNamedPipe("\\\\.\\pipe\\ssnp",
    PIPE_ACCESS_INBOUND,
    PIPE_TYPE_MESSAGE | PIPE_WAIT,
    1, 0, 0, 150, &sa);

  /* Check and see if the named pipe was created */
  if (ssnpPipe == INVALID_HANDLE_VALUE)
  {
    cerr << "ERROR: Unable to create a named pipe."
      << endl;
    return (1);
  }

  bufferLen = 80;
```

Listing 10.9
Impersonating another user in a named pipe server (Page 2 of 4)

```
GetUserName(buffer, &bufferLen);
cout << "Right now my user is: "
  << buffer
  << endl;
cout << "Waiting for connection..." << endl;

/* Allow a client to connect to the name pipe,
   terminate if unsuccessful */
if(!ConnectNamedPipe(ssnpPipe,
  (LPOVERLAPPED) NULL))
{
  cerr << "ERROR: Unable to connect a pipe "
    << GetLastError() << endl;
  CloseHandle(ssnpPipe);
  return (1);
}

cout << "Beginning impersonation...\n";

if (!ImpersonateNamedPipeClient(ssnpPipe))
{
  cerr << "ERROR: Cannot impersonate, "
    << GetLastError() << endl;
  CloseHandle(ssnpPipe);
  return(1);
}

bufferLen = 80;
GetUserName(buffer, &bufferLen);
cout << "Now my user is: "
  << buffer << endl;

/* Repeatedly check for messages until
   the program is terminated */
while(1)
{
```

Listing 10.9
Impersonating another user in a named pipe server (Page 3 of 4)

```
        /* Read the message and check to see if read
           was successful */
        if (!ReadFile(ssnpPipe, toDisptxt,
          sizeof(toDisptxt),
          &NumBytesRead, (LPOVERLAPPED) NULL))
        {
          cerr << "ERROR: Unable to read from pipe"
            << endl;
          CloseHandle(ssnpPipe);
          break;
        }

        /* Display the Message */
        cout << toDisptxt << endl;

      } /* while */

      cout << "Reverting back to original user.\n";
      RevertToSelf();

      bufferLen = 80;
      GetUserName(buffer, &bufferLen);
      cout << "Now my user is:  "
        << buffer
        << endl;
    }
```

Listing 10.9
Impersonating another user in a named pipe server (Page 4 of 4)

To test Listing 10.9, follow the same procedure used to test Listing 10.3. Compile and execute Listing 10.9 on one machine. It will display a message that indicates its current user ID. Logon to another machine with a different ID and use the code in Listing 7.7 to connect to the server. Listing 10.9 will recognize the connection, and then immediately copy the access token of the connected client into its thread. It will display its new identity. When you kill off the client, the server will revert back to its former identity using **RevertToSelf**. You should be able to connect to the server using any logon ID.

The call to **ImpersonateNamedPipeClient** causes the calling thread to take on the access token of the thread connected to the other end of the named pipe specified.

ImpersonateNamedPipeClient *Causes the calling thread to take on the access token of a connected client thread*

```
BOOL ImpersonateNamedPipeClient(
   HANDLE namedPipe)
```

namedPipe	The server end of a named pipe

Returns TRUE on success

The **RevertToSelf** function causes the calling thread to revert back to the access token of its parent process.

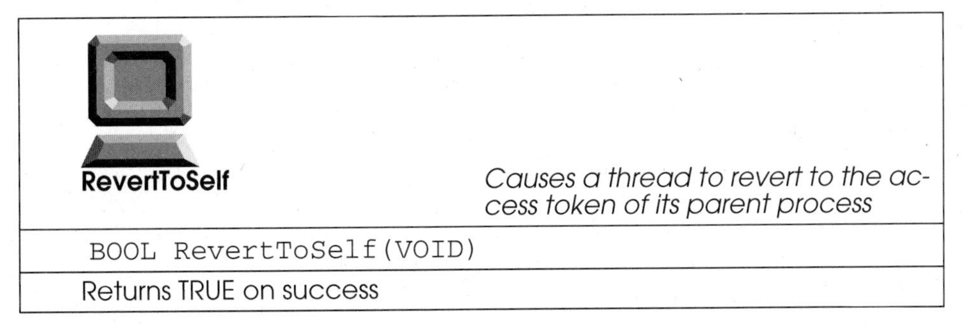

RevertToSelf *Causes a thread to revert to the access token of its parent process*

```
BOOL RevertToSelf(VOID)
```

Returns TRUE on success

In a multiple-client server like the ones shown in Section 7.5, each separate client thread can take on a different identity using the same technique. You can create extremely robust and secure servers using impersonation.

10.10 Conclusion

NT's security system is quite extensive. This chapter covers all of the basic concepts, and shows you the techniques you will need to handle the vast majority of common security situations. You can learn more by reading through the function descriptions in the security portion of the Win32 help file (start at Security Overview and branch out from there), and by creating simple experiments to test out the different concepts.

CONSOLES

11

There are many situations where an application does not require a full-blown graphical user interface. For example, most of the programs presented in this book are strictly text programs that produce text output in the command window. The terminal emulator presented in Chapter 12 is another example. The 32-bit API provides a facility called *consoles* that is useful in these situations.

Consoles are a convenience: They manage a two-dimensional array of characters for you and automatically handle input and display. They therefore make it very easy to create character-mode applications. If you write a text program that runs on the command line and uses **cin** and **cout**, you are using the API's console capabilities implicitly. In other situations you use them explicitly. In this chapter you will learn how to take advantage of both the "raw" and "cooked" console modes in your applications.

Compatibility Note: All of the code in this chapter works identically in Windows NT and Windows 95.

11.1 The Possibilities

The MS-DOS prompt window is built around a console, and in that form it is immediately recognizable. The console API provides a two-dimensional array of characters that scroll upward when the cursor hits the bottom of the window. The four most common ways to use a console are as follows:

1. If you want to create your own custom command interpreter to replace the MS-DOS prompt, you should use the console library.

2. If you want to add console input or output to a normal GUI or MFC program, you do that using consoles. For example, while debugging an MFC program, you might want to stream a set of coordinates out to a console as you are painting lines on a screen so that you can check the coordinates.
3. If you want to port a full-screen text program over to Windows, probably the easiest way to do it is through a console.
4. Any character-mode program where you need raw character-by-character access to the input stream is a good candidate for a console. If you run a program from the MS-DOS window as is, you can only access input a line at a time. The console commands let you switch over to a raw character-by-character mode. The terminal program demonstrated in Chapter 12 is a good example of this technique.

If you write any text-based program using either the stdio or iostream libraries and then run it in an MS-DOS window, you are using the console mode without even realizing it. You can use the console functions to add some interesting capabilities. For example, you can add color to the display and accept mouse input.

11.2 Raw versus Cooked Input

UNIX systems have long used the words *raw* and *cooked* to define the two different modes of character input. The same terminology applies to console input in the 32-bit API.

Cooked input is the normal input mode for console windows. It is what you get when you use **cout** and **cin,** or **printf** and **gets**, in a normal MS-DOS window. Cooked input is line-at-a-time input. The user types characters, but you do not receive any of the input until the user presses the Enter key. At that point, the entire line of characters gets placed into the input buffer and you can access them one at a time with **getc** or a line at a time with **gets**. The **getc** function, however, will not return anything *until* the user presses the return key.

Cooked-mode input is nice for most command-driven programs because all that the program cares about is a complete command line. Cooked-mode input also allows the input functions to handle the backspace key automatically. Since no input appears in the input buffer until the user hits return, the system can delete characters when the user hits the backspace key.

If you are trying to create a text editor, however, cooked-mode input is infuriating. In a text editor, you want to receive each character *as it is typed*, and cooked-mode input does not allow that. Raw input mode places each character into the input buffer when it is received, and lets you use it immediately in your code. In Windows, the raw input mode also gives you access to mouse input, so you can let the user use the mouse in a variety of ways. For example, you might use the mouse to let the user select areas of text. When retrieving characters in the raw input mode, you can either retrieve the characters by waiting for them with a normal **ReadFile** statement that retrieves one character, or you can use overlapped input that allows you to do other processing until a character arrives.

11.3 Simple Examples

To get a feel for the console's capabilities, let's start with two simple examples. The first one, shown in Listing 11.1, demonstrates the simplest possible use of a console in cooked mode. When you run the program, it will echo input line by line until you type the word "exit."

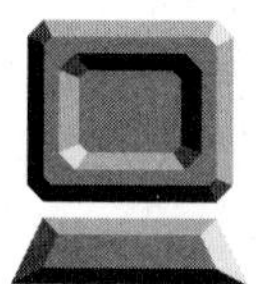

```
// cooked.cpp

#include <windows.h>
#include <iostream.h>
#include <string.h>

void ErrorHandler(char *s, DWORD err)
{
   cout << s << endl;
   cout << "Error number: " << err << endl;
   ExitProcess(err);
}
```

Listing 11.1
A simple console program (Page 1 of 2)

```
void ProcessIO(HANDLE consoleStdin,
   HANDLE consoleStdout)
{
   char buffer[1000];
   DWORD numRead, numWrite;

   do
   {
      ReadFile(consoleStdin, buffer,
         1000, &numRead, 0);
      buffer[numRead]='\0'; // will have CR/LF
      WriteFile(consoleStdout,
         buffer, strlen(buffer),
         &numWrite, 0);
   } while  (strncmp(buffer, "exit", 4) != 0);
}

VOID main(void)
{
   HANDLE consoleStdout, consoleStdin;

   // Get handles for standard in and out
   consoleStdin = GetStdHandle(STD_INPUT_HANDLE);
   consoleStdout = GetStdHandle(STD_OUTPUT_HANDLE);
   // they must be invalid if equal
   if (consoleStdin == consoleStdout)
      ErrorHandler("In GetStdHandle",
         GetLastError());

   // Process user I/O
   ProcessIO(consoleStdin, consoleStdout);
}
```

Listing 11.1
A simple console program (Page 2 of 2)

The program starts by retrieving the standard input and standard output handles for the process. Every process, even those using a graphical user interface, have standard input, output, and error handles that you can access using the **GetStdHandle** function.

GetStdHandle	*Retrieves a process's handle to stdin, stdout or stderr*
`HANDLE GetStdHandle( DWORD device)`	
device	Possible values: STD_INPUT_HANDLE, STD_OUTPUT_HANDLE, STD_ERROR_HANDLE
Returns a handle to the requested device or INVALID_HANDLE_VALUE	

Once you have the handles, you can read and write using the normal **ReadFile** and **WriteFile** commands seen in Chapter 2. Each time the user presses the return key, the **ReadFile** statement retrieves one line of input from the buffer.

If you run Listing 11.1 from a normal MS-DOS window, the program will make use of the existing window's input and output buffers. The program *inherits* the console of the process that spawned it, if that process has a console. If the originating process does not have a console—for example, if you launch the executable for Listing 11.1 from the File Manager—then a new console is created automatically. The system recognizes that it is a console mode program and creates the console it needs for its input and output.

It is also possible to detach from the originating process's console and create a new one, as demonstrated in Listing 11.2. This listing also shows how to detach from the console of the launching program and create a new console. If you run Listing 11.1 from an MS-DOS prompt it will use the MS-DOS window as its console. On the other hand, if you run Listing 11.2 from the same MS-DOS window, it will create its own, separate console window for its input and output.

```
// cooked2.cpp

#include <windows.h>
#include <iostream.h>
#include <string.h>

void ErrorHandler(char *s, DWORD err)
{
   cout << s << endl;
   cout << "Error number: " << err << endl;
   ExitProcess(err);
}

void ProcessIO(HANDLE consoleStdin,
   HANDLE consoleStdout)
{
   char buffer[1000];
   DWORD numRead, numWrite;

   do
   {
      ReadFile(consoleStdin, buffer,
         1000, &numRead, 0);
      buffer[numRead]='\0';
      WriteFile(consoleStdout, buffer,
         strlen(buffer), &numWrite, 0);
   } while  (strncmp(buffer, "exit", 4) != 0);
}

VOID main(void)
```

Listing 11.2
Creating a separate console (Page 1 of 2)

```
{
   HANDLE consoleStdout, consoleStdin;
   BOOL success;

   success = FreeConsole();
   if (!success)
      ErrorHandler("In FreeConsole",
         GetLastError());
   success = AllocConsole();
   if (!success)
      ErrorHandler("In AllocConsole",
         GetLastError());

   // Get handles for standard in and out
   consoleStdin = GetStdHandle(STD_INPUT_HANDLE);
   consoleStdout = GetStdHandle(STD_OUTPUT_HANDLE);
   // they must be invalid if equal
   if (consoleStdin == consoleStdout)
      ErrorHandler("In GetStdHandle",
         GetLastError());

   // Process user I/O
   ProcessIO(consoleStdin, consoleStdout);

   success = FreeConsole();
   if (!success)
      ErrorHandler("In FreeConsole",
         GetLastError());
}
```

Listing 11.2
Creating a separate console (Page 2 of 2)

The program in Listing 11.2 starts with a call to **FreeConsole**.

FreeConsole	*Detaches the process from its spawning console*
`BOOL FreeConsole(VOID)`	
Returns TRUE on success	

The call to **FreeConsole** in Listing 11.2 detaches the new process from the console it inherited when it started. If it starts from an MS-DOS prompt, the call to **FreeConsole** detaches it from the MS-DOS window and leaves the process "floating" for a moment with no way to communicate. If a process calls **FreeConsole** and no other process is using that console, the existing console closes.

The subsequent call to **AllocConsole** in Listing 11.2 creates a new console.

AllocConsole	*Creates a new console for the process calling the function*
`BOOL AllocConsole(VOID)`	
Returns TRUE on success	

Once it has created a console, Listing 11.2 gets the input and output handles for it and begins reading and writing.

You can use the **AllocConsole** function to allocate a console for your GUI applications as well. For example, if you create an application using MFC as described in the book *Visual C++: Developing Professional Applications in Windows 95 and NT using MFC* by Marshall Brain and Lance Lovette (ISBN 0-13-305145-5) then the program by default does not have a console. There are many situations where a console for such a program would be useful, however, especially during debugging. For example, you can stream pixel coordinates and other variables out to the console during the run and examine them while the program is on the screen. You can send this sort of output to a console using a normal **cout** statement. Listing 11.3 shows how to create a console inside an MFC program.

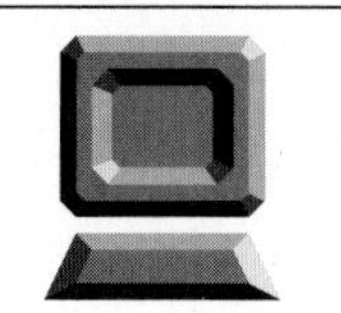

```
// button.cpp

#include <afxwin.h>
#include <iostream.h>

#define IDB_BUTTON 100

// Declare the handles for the console
HANDLE consoleStdout, consoleStdin;

// Declare the application class
class CButtonApp : public CWinApp
{
public:
   virtual BOOL InitInstance();
};

// Create an instance of the application class
CButtonApp ButtonApp;

// Declare the main window class
class CButtonWindow : public CFrameWnd
{
   CButton *button;
public:
   CButtonWindow();
   ~CButtonWindow();
   afx_msg void HandleButton();

   DECLARE_MESSAGE_MAP()
};
```

Listing 11.3
Allocating a console inside an MFC program (Page 1 of 3)

```
// The message handler function
void CButtonWindow::HandleButton()
{
   DWORD n;

   Beep(700,100);
   // Two different ways to write to the console
   WriteFile(consoleStdout, "hello\n", 6, &n, 0);
   cout << "test string" << endl;
}

// The message map
BEGIN_MESSAGE_MAP(CButtonWindow, CFrameWnd)
   ON_COMMAND(IDB_BUTTON, HandleButton)
END_MESSAGE_MAP()

// The InitInstance function is called once
// when the application first executes
BOOL CButtonApp::InitInstance()
{
   // Create an auxiliary console for cout to use.
   // As soon as this function returns you
   // can write to it.
   AllocConsole();

   // Get handles for standard in and out
   consoleStdin = GetStdHandle(STD_INPUT_HANDLE);
   consoleStdout = GetStdHandle(STD_OUTPUT_HANDLE);
   // they must be invalid if equal
   if (consoleStdin == consoleStdout)
      return FALSE;

   m_pMainWnd = new CButtonWindow();
   m_pMainWnd->ShowWindow(m_nCmdShow);
```

Listing 11.3
Allocating a console inside an MFC program (Page 2 of 3)

```
    m_pMainWnd->UpdateWindow();

    return TRUE;
}

// The constructor for the window class
CButtonWindow::CButtonWindow()
{
    CRect r;

    // Create the window itself
    Create(NULL,
        "CButton Tests",
        WS_OVERLAPPEDWINDOW,
        CRect(0,0,200,200));

    // Get the size of the client rectangle
    GetClientRect(&r);
    r.InflateRect(-20,-20);

    // Create a button
    button = new CButton();
    button->Create("Push me",
        WS_CHILD|WS_VISIBLE|BS_PUSHBUTTON,
        r,
        this,
        IDB_BUTTON);
}

// The destructor for the window class
CButtonWindow::~CButtonWindow()
{
    delete button;
    CFrameWnd::~CFrameWnd();
}
```

Listing 11.3
Allocating a console inside an MFC program (Page 3 of 3)

When you run the program shown in Listing 11.3, you will see a button as well as a new console associated with the program. When you click the button, output will appear in the console. As the program demonstrates, you can use either the **WriteFile** or the **cout** functions to write to the console. In the **InitInstance** function for the application, the calls to **AllocConsole** and **GetStdHandle** create and attach the console.

11.4 Raw Input

One of the nicest things about the examples in the previous section is the fact that they are so simple. In Listing 11.1, for example, the program allocates a console, gets its handles, and begins writing to it. The console automatically handles backspacing, scrolling, and so on.

There are many situations, however, where you would like more control over the input and output streams. For example, you may want to retrieve characters one at a time as the user enters them. To do this, you need to get raw input from the console. Alternatively, you can create a GUI program and retrieve characters in the normal event-driven manner from the event queue. Using raw input from consoles is generally easier because the console continues to manage the two-dimensional output array for you and this simplifies text output considerably.

Listing 11.4 demonstrates how to get one character at a time from the input stream using the raw input mode.

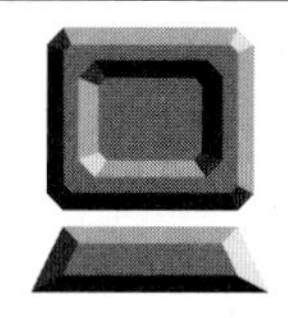

```
// raw.cpp

#include <windows.h>
#include <iostream.h>
```

Listing 11.4
Retrieving one character at a time from the input stream using the raw input mode
(Page 1 of 5)

```
void ErrorHandler(char *s, DWORD err)
{
   cout << s << endl;
   cout << "Error number: " << err << endl;
   ExitProcess(err);
}

void ScrollOneLine(HANDLE stdout)
{
   BOOL success;
   CONSOLE_SCREEN_BUFFER_INFO consoleInfo;
   SMALL_RECT scrollRect;
   CHAR_INFO consoleFill;
   COORD coord;

   // get current console size (may change)
   success = GetConsoleScreenBufferInfo(stdout,
      &consoleInfo);
   if (!success)
      ErrorHandler(
            "In GetConsoleScreenBufferInfo",
            GetLastError());

   // Define the rectangle to scroll
   scrollRect.Top = 0;
   scrollRect.Left = 0;
   scrollRect.Bottom = consoleInfo.dwSize.Y - 1;
   scrollRect.Right = consoleInfo.dwSize.X - 1;

   // Define destination of scrolled rectangle
   coord.X = 0;
   coord.Y = -1;

   // Define how to fill blank line
   consoleFill.Attributes =
```

Listing 11.4
Retrieving one character at a time from the input stream using the raw input mode (Page 2 of 5)

```
            consoleInfo.wAttributes;
        consoleFill.Char.AsciiChar = ' ';

        // Perform the scroll
        success = ScrollConsoleScreenBuffer(stdout,
         &scrollRect, 0,
            coord, &consoleFill);
        if (!success)
            ErrorHandler("In ScrollConsoleScreenBuffer",
                GetLastError());

    }

    VOID HandleCR(HANDLE stdout)
    {
        CONSOLE_SCREEN_BUFFER_INFO consoleInfo;
        BOOL success;

        success = GetConsoleScreenBufferInfo(stdout,
            &consoleInfo);
        if (!success)
            ErrorHandler("In GetConsoleScreenBufferInfo",
                GetLastError());

        // Move cursor to far left
        consoleInfo.dwCursorPosition.X = 0;

        // If the cursor is on the last line of
        // the console, then scroll the console,
        // else increment position
        if (consoleInfo.dwSize.Y - 1 ==
            consoleInfo.dwCursorPosition.Y)
            ScrollOneLine(stdout);
        else
            consoleInfo.dwCursorPosition.Y += 1;
```

Listing 11.4
Retrieving one character at a time from the input stream using the raw input mode
(Page 3 of 5)

```
   // Update the console
   success = SetConsoleCursorPosition(stdout,
      consoleInfo.dwCursorPosition);
   if (!success)
      ErrorHandler("In SetConsoleCursorPosition",
         GetLastError());
}

void ProcessIO(HANDLE stdin, HANDLE stdout)
{
   char buffer;
   DWORD numRead, numWrite;

   do
   {
      ReadFile(stdin, &buffer, 1, &numRead, NULL);
      if (buffer == '\r')
         HandleCR(stdout);
      else
         WriteFile(stdout, &buffer, 1,
                           &numWrite, NULL);
   } while  (buffer != 'X');
}

VOID main(void)
{
   DWORD oldMode, newMode;
   BOOL success;
   HANDLE stdout, stdin;

   // Get handles for standard in and out
   stdin = GetStdHandle(STD_INPUT_HANDLE);
   stdout = GetStdHandle(STD_OUTPUT_HANDLE);
   if (stdin == stdout) //they must be invalid
```

Listing 11.4
Retrieving one character at a time from the input stream using the raw input mode (Page 4 of 5)

```
            ErrorHandler("In GetStdHandle",
               GetLastError());

      // Get current console mode so can modify it
      success = GetConsoleMode(stdin, &oldMode);
      if (!success)
         ErrorHandler("In GetConsoleMode",
            GetLastError());
      newMode = oldMode & ~ENABLE_LINE_INPUT &
         ~ENABLE_ECHO_INPUT;
      success = SetConsoleMode(stdin, newMode);
       if (!success)
         ErrorHandler("In SetConsoleMode",
            GetLastError());

      // Process user I/O
      ProcessIO(stdin, stdout);

      // put the old mode back
      success = SetConsoleMode(stdin, oldMode);
      if (!success)
         ErrorHandler("In SetConsoleMode",
            GetLastError());
   }
```

Listing 11.4
Retrieving one character at a time from the input stream using the raw input mode (Page 5 of 5)

The program in Listing 11.4 starts by getting the handles for stdin and stdout. It then proceeds to put the console into raw input mode using the **GetConsoleMode** and **SetConsoleMode** functions.

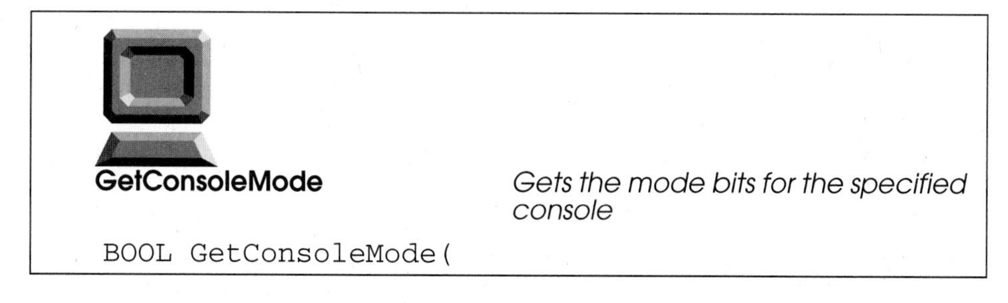

GetConsoleMode *Gets the mode bits for the specified console*

```
BOOL GetConsoleMode(
```

```
    HANDLE consoleHandle,
    LPDWORD mode)
```

consoleHandle	A handle to a console
mode	A pointer to a DWORD to hold the mode bits

Returns TRUE on success

SetConsoleMode *Sets the mode bits for the specified console*

```
BOOL SetConsoleMode(
    HANDLE consoleHandle,
    DWORD mode)
```

consoleHandle	A handle to a console
mode	A pointer to a DWORD holding the new mode bits

Returns TRUE on success

The call to **GetConsoleMode** gets the current mode of the console. This mode is then modified to remove the line input and echo capabilities, and sent back to the console using **SetConsoleMode**. The console understands the following mode bits for input:

ENABLE_LINE_INPUT	Input returned only after CR
ENABLE_ECHO_INPUT	Keystrokes are echoed to stdout
ENABLE_PROCESSED_INPUT	Ctrl-C, backspace, and line feeds are handled by console
ENABLE_WINDOW_INPUT	Window size changes are reported in the event queue
ENABLE_MOUSE_INPUT	Mouse motion is reported in the event queue

In Listing 11.4, the removal of the LINE_INPUT and ECHO_INPUT bits causes characters to be reported as they are typed rather than at the end of a line, and also does not echo them to the output.

Listing 11.4 enters a while loop in the **ProcessIO** function. The while loop reads each character and echoes it to the output until the user types an 'X'. The function must also detect and handle newline characters properly. When it sees a newline character, the program must move the cursor over to the left and down one line. In addition, if the cursor is at the bottom of the window, the program must scroll the console. In cooked mode all of this happens automatically, but in raw mode you have to handle it yourself.

The **GetConsoleScreenBufferInfo** function returns all of the information necessary to reposition the buffer during scrolling.

GetConsoleScreenBufferInfo	*Gets all screen buffer information for the console*

`BOOL GetConsoleScreenBufferInfo(`
`HANDLE consoleHandle,`
`PCONSOLE_SCREEN_BUFFER_INFO info)`	

consoleHandle	A handle to a console
info	A pointer to a record to contain the console information
Returns TRUE on success	

The **GetConsoleScreenBufferInfo** function returns a CONSOLE_SCREEN_BUFFER_INFO structure, which contains the following information:

```
typedef struct _CONSOLE_SCREEN_BUFFER_INFO {
    COORD      dwSize; // Size of the console
    COORD      dwCursorPosition;
    WORD       wAttributes; // Color attributes
    SMALL_RECT srWindow; // Area currently seen
    COORD      dwMaximumWindowSize;
} CONSOLE_SCREEN_BUFFER_INFO ;
```

Alternatively, the functions **GetConsoleCursorInfo** and **GetLargest-ConsoleWindowSize** return cursor and window size fields of this structure individually.

GetConsoleCursoInfo *Gets cursor information for the console*

```
BOOL GetConsoleCursorInfo(
   HANDLE consoleHandle,
   PCONSOLE_CURSOR_INFO cursorInfo)
```

consoleHandle	A handle to the console output
cursorInfo	A pointer to a record to contain the console cursor information

Returns TRUE on success

GetLargestConsoleWindowSize *Gets window size information for the console*

```
COORD GetLargestConsoleWindowSize(
   HANDLE consoleHandle)
```

consoleHandle	A handle to the console output

Returns a COORD structure holding width and height

```
typedef struct _COORD {
   SHORT X;
   SHORT Y;
} COORD;
```

The console consists of a fixed-size window on the screen, as well as a same-size or larger buffer area off-screen. If the buffer is larger than the window, the window will display scroll bars so that the user can move around and view the entire buffer.

The **dwSize** field contains the size of the buffer. The **dwCursorPosition** field indicates where the cursor is in the buffer. The **wAttributes** field indicates the foreground and background colors that will be applied to any character written to the buffer. See Section 11.6 for details on color. The **srWindow** field is a rectangle that defines what the current window is displaying from the screen buffer. The **dwMaximumWindowSize** field contains the maximum size of a console window that can appear on the screen given the screen's size.

Using this information, the code in Listing 11.4 moves the cursor to the far left and down one line, and then sets the new position into the buffer using the **SetConsoleCursorPosition** function.

SetConsoleCursorPosition	*Sets the cursor position in the screen buffer*

`BOOL GetConsoleScreenBufferInfo(`
`HANDLE consoleHandle,`
`COORD coord)`	

consoleHandle	A handle to a console
coord	The new cursor position
Returns TRUE on success	

If the cursor happens to be on the last line of the screen buffer, then the buffer must scroll. It does it in the **ScrollOneLine** function using the following code:

```
success = GetConsoleScreenBufferInfo(stdout,
   &consoleInfo);

// Define the rectangle to scroll
scrollRect.Top = 0;
scrollRect.Left = 0;
scrollRect.Bottom = consoleInfo.dwSize.Y - 1;
scrollRect.Right = consoleInfo.dwSize.X - 1;

// Define destination of scrolled rectangle
```

```
coord.X = 0;
coord.Y = -1;

// Define how to fill blank line
consoleFill.Attributes =
   consoleInfo.wAttributes;
consoleFill.Char.AsciiChar = ' ';

// Perform the scroll
success = ScrollConsoleScreenBuffer(stdout,
   &scrollRect, 0,
   coord, &consoleFill);
```

The code first gets the buffer information. Using that, it defines the rectangle to scroll. Here it picks the entire buffer, but you can choose smaller parts of it as well. It then defines the position the buffer should be scrolled to. Here the buffer is moved up one line. The top line of the buffer will be lost during this operation. You must also define how the console should fill the new blank line created at the bottom of the window during the scroll. Here the new line is filled with blanks, and the same colors as the rest of the buffer are used as the fill colors.

Having set up everything for the scroll operation, the code can actually scroll the window using the **ScrollConsoleScreenBuffer** function

ScrollConsoleScreenBuffer *Scrolls the console buffer as specified*

```
BOOL ScrollConsoleScreenBuffer(
   HANDLE consoleHandle,
   PSMALL_RECT sourceRect,
   PSMALL_RECT clipRect,
   COORD destination,
   PCHAR_INFO fillStruct)
```

consoleHandle	A handle to a console

sourceRect	The rectangle of characters to move
clipRect	Rectangle defining area affected
destination	The point where the upper left corner of the source rectangle should move to
fillStruct	The character and colors to use for filling
Returns TRUE on success	

As you can see, the **ScrollConsoleScreenBuffer** function has a great deal of flexibility in how it scrolls the buffer. If you are creating a complete vt-100 terminal emulator, for example, it would be very easy to emulate any possible rectangular movement code for the terminal using these built-in scrolling capabilities.

The scrolling code makes the program a bit longer, but as you can see the code is straightforward. Once you've typed the code in, you will use it the same way in every console program that you create.

Let's say that you want to use the raw input mode with the **WaitForSingleObject** function (see Section 6.4 for more information on **Wait** functions). For example, in Chapter 12 the terminal emulator program uses this capability. That program actually uses **WaitForMultipleObject** so that it can wait for either a character from the keyboard or a character from the modem. In order to use either of the **Wait** functions however, the **ProcessIO** function needs some modification, as shown in Listing 11.5.

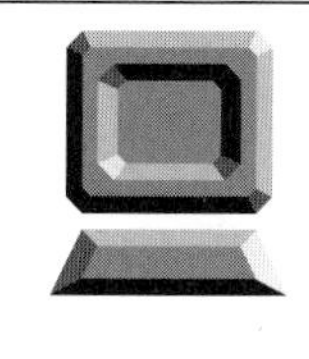

```
// raw2.cpp

void ProcessIO(HANDLE consoleStdin,
   HANDLE consoleStdout)
{
   char buffer;
```

Listing 11.5
Replace the **ProcessIO** function in Listing 11.4 with this new version (Page 1 of 3)

```
    DWORD numRead, numWrite;
    INPUT_RECORD inputEvent;
    DWORD s;
    char *t="waiting\n";

    do
    {
       // wait for the user to do something
       do
       {
          s = WaitForSingleObject(consoleStdin, 0);
       } while (s==WAIT_TIMEOUT);
       // look into the input queue
       PeekConsoleInput(consoleStdin, &inputEvent,
          1, &numRead);
       if (numRead>0)
       {
          // Check the event. If it is unworthy,
          // then discard the event. Otherwise read
          // it and handle it normally.
          if (inputEvent.EventType != KEY_EVENT ||
             inputEvent.Event.
             KeyEvent.bKeyDown==FALSE ||
             inputEvent.Event.KeyEvent.
             uChar.AsciiChar==0)
          {
             ReadConsoleInput(consoleStdin,
                &inputEvent, 1, &numRead);
          }
          else
          {
             ReadFile(consoleStdin, &buffer, 1,
                &numRead, NULL);
             if (buffer == '\r')
                HandleCR(consoleStdout);
```

Listing 11.5
Replace the **ProcessIO** function in Listing 11.4 with this new version (Page 2 of 3)

```
                else
                    WriteFile(consoleStdout, &buffer, 1,
                        &numWrite, NULL);
            }
        }
    } while  (buffer != 'X');
}
```

Listing 11.5
Replace the **ProcessIO** function in Listing 11.4 with this new version (Page 3 of 3)

Here is the problem that Listing 11.5 is trying to solve: The input buffer for the console actually receives very low-level events from the keyboard. For example, each time the user presses down a key, the console's input buffer gets an event. It gets another event when the user releases the key. The same holds true even for the Shift and Alt keys. If the user presses and releases the shift or alt keys, events appear in the input buffer. The **ReadFile** function has no problem with this. It simply waits until a real "the user has entered a valid keystroke" event arrives, and then it retrieves the key. The **WaitForSingleObject** function, however, releases its wait on *any* of these low-level events. So, for example, if the user presses down the shift key and then releases it, the **WaitForSingleObject** function will release, but the **ReadFile** function will hang up waiting for a real keystroke.

The code in Listing 11.5 shows how to solve this problem. Each time the **WaitForSingleObject** function returns, the code examines the event to see if it is interesting or not. It uses **PeekConsoleInput** to look at the event without removing it from the queue.

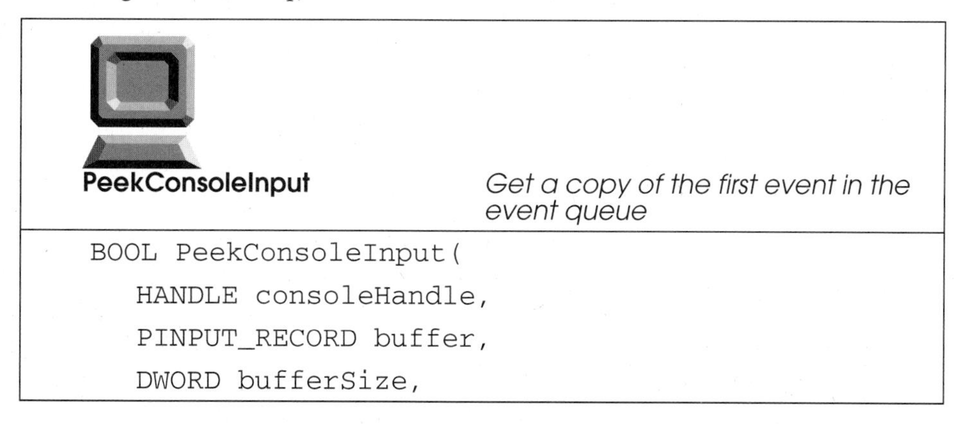

PeekConsoleInput *Get a copy of the first event in the event queue*

```
BOOL PeekConsoleInput(
    HANDLE consoleHandle,
    PINPUT_RECORD buffer,
    DWORD bufferSize,
```

LPDWORD numRead)	
consoleHandle	A handle to a console
buffer	Pointer to a buffer to hold the event(s)
bufferSize	Number of events buffer can hold
numRead	A pointer to a DWORD to hold the number of records read
Returns TRUE on success	

In Listing 11.5, the code is set up to copy one record from the input queue. It examines it with the following if statement:

```
if (inputEvent.EventType != KEY_EVENT ||
   inputEvent.Event.KeyEvent.bKeyDown==FALSE ||
   inputEvent.Event.KeyEvent.uChar.AsciiChar==0)
```

This statement checks the event to make sure that it contains a keystroke, that it is a "key up" event (the user is releasing the key rather than pressing it down), and that it contains a valid ASCII character (for example, a **KeyDown** event on the shift key alone will not return an ASCII character). If the event does not pass these three tests, the code discards it by making a call to **ReadConsoleInput**, which reads a low-level event from the console input queue. The code then loops back to the **Wait** function again to wait for the next event. Otherwise the code can call **ReadFile** because it knows the buffer contains an event that **ReadFile** will accept immediately.

ReadConsoleInput	*Reads a low-level event from the console's event queue*

`BOOL ReadConsoleInput(`
`HANDLE consoleHandle,`
`PINPUT_RECORD buffer,`
`DWORD bufferSize,`
`LPDWORD numRead)`	

consoleHandle	A handle to a console

buffer	Pointer to a buffer to hold the event(s)
bufferSize	Number of events buffer can hold
numRead	A pointer to a DWORD to hold the number of records read
Returns TRUE on success	

If you run the code in Listing 11.5 by replacing the **ProcessIO** function in Listing 11.4 with it, you will find that it works exactly the same way. However, the inner **do...while** loop in Listing 11.5 can run continuously because the program can accurately detect keystrokes. See Chapter 12 for an example of a practical use for this capability in a terminal emulator program.

11.5 Other Input Events

As demonstrated in Listing 11.5, the programmer can view a console input stream at two different levels. The **ReadFile** function accesses the input queue at a high level, returning one key at a time. There is also low-level access to the queue however, using the **PeekConsoleInput, ReadConsoleInput**, and **WriteConsoleInput** functions. Three types of events appear in the buffer:

- Keyboard events
- Mouse events
- Window re-size events

Listing 11.6 demonstrates how to access these low-level events.

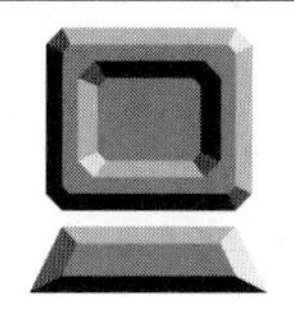

```
// events.cpp

#include <windows.h>
#include <iostream.h>

void ErrorHandler(char *s, DWORD err)
```

Listing 11.6
Accessing low-level input from a console (Page 1 of 4)

```
{
   cout << s << endl;
   cout << "Error number: " << err << endl;
   ExitProcess(err);
}

void ProcessIO(HANDLE consoleStdin,
   HANDLE consoleStdout)
{
   DWORD numRead, numWrite;
   int x=0;
   INPUT_RECORD inputRecord;
   char s[100];
   DWORD oldMode, newMode;

   GetConsoleMode(consoleStdin, &oldMode);
   newMode = oldMode | ENABLE_WINDOW_INPUT
      | ENABLE_MOUSE_INPUT;
   SetConsoleMode(consoleStdin, newMode);
   do
   {
      ReadConsoleInput(consoleStdin, &inputRecord,
         1, &numRead);
      switch (inputRecord.EventType)
      {
         case KEY_EVENT:
            strcpy(s, "keyboard event\n");
            break;
         case MOUSE_EVENT:
            strcpy(s, "mouse event\n");
            break;
         case WINDOW_BUFFER_SIZE_EVENT:
            strcpy(s, "resize event\n");
            break;
         default:
```

Listing 11.6
Accessing low-level input from a console (Page 2 of 4)

```
                strcpy(s, "other event\n");
                break;
          }
          WriteFile(consoleStdout, s, strlen(s),
             &numWrite, 0);
       } while  (x++ < 100);

       SetConsoleMode(consoleStdin, oldMode);

    }

    VOID main(void)
    {
       DWORD oldMode, newMode;
       BOOL success;
       HANDLE consoleStdout, consoleStdin;

       // Get handles for standard in and out
       consoleStdin = GetStdHandle(STD_INPUT_HANDLE);
       consoleStdout = GetStdHandle(STD_OUTPUT_HANDLE);
       if (consoleStdin == consoleStdout)
          ErrorHandler("In GetStdHandle",
             GetLastError());

       // Get current console mode so can modify it
       success = GetConsoleMode(consoleStdin,
          &oldMode);
       if (!success)
          ErrorHandler("In GetConsoleMode",
             GetLastError());
       newMode = oldMode & ~ENABLE_LINE_INPUT &
          ~ENABLE_ECHO_INPUT;
       success = SetConsoleMode(consoleStdin, newMode);
        if (!success)
          ErrorHandler("In SetConsoleMode",
```

Listing 11.6
Accessing low-level input from a console (Page 3 of 4)

```
                GetLastError());

        // Process user I/O
        ProcessIO(consoleStdin, consoleStdout);

        // put the old mode back
        success = SetConsoleMode(consoleStdin, oldMode);
        if (!success)
            ErrorHandler("In SetConsoleMode",
                GetLastError());
    }
```

Listing 11.6
Accessing low-level input from a console (Page 4 of 4)

When you run Listing 11.6, you will find that keyboard events, any mouse motion in the console, and resizing events all create output. The mouse and resizing events are enabled at the beginning of the **ProcessIO** function with a call to **SetConsoleMode**. The call to **ReadConsoleInput** reads each event as it arrives and the **switch** statement parses the events to display the appropriate strings. The **inputRecord** structure that **ReadConsoleInput** returns also contains all of the relevant information about each event.

SetConsoleMode	*Sets the mode bits for the specified console*

`BOOL SetConsoleMode(`
`    HANDLE consoleHandle,`
`    DWORD mode)`	

consoleHandle	A handle to a console
mode	A pointer to a DWORD holding the new mode bits
Returns TRUE on success	

The most common way to use the mouse would be to create a copy and paste facility for a command prompt window. For example, an XTerm window on an UNIX workstation lets you use the mouse to select an area of text and then later paste it into another or the same XTerm window. You could implement this capability using the mouse events shown here, along with the coloring capability shown in Section 11.6 and the **ReadConsole** and **WriteConsole** functions to access the output buffer.

Related functions of interest are **GetNumberOfConsoleInputEvents**, which tells you how many events are waiting in the queue, and **GetNumberOfConsoleMouseButtons**, which returns the number of buttons on the console's mouse.

GetNumberOfConsole InputEvents	*Returns the number of waiting input events*
`BOOL GetNumberOfConsoleInputEvents( HANDLE consoleInput, LPDWORD mumEvents)`	
consoleHandle	A handle to a console input
numEvents	The number of waiting events
Returns TRUE on success	

GetNumberOfConsole MouseButtons	*Returns the number of mouse buttons*
`BOOL GetNumberOfConsoleMouseButtons( LPDWORD numMouseButtons)`	
numMouseButtons	The number of mouse buttons
Returns TRUE on success	

As demonstrated in Listing 11.7, it is also possible to register a handler function to trap Ctrl-C, Ctrl-Break, Close, Logoff, and Shutdown events.

```
// handler.cpp

#include <windows.h>
#include <iostream.h>
#include <string.h>

void ErrorHandler(char *s, DWORD err)
{
   cout << s << endl;
   cout << "Error number: " << err << endl;
   ExitProcess(err);
}

void ProcessIO(HANDLE consoleStdin, HANDLE stdout)
{
   char buffer[1000];
   DWORD numRead, numWrite;

   do
   {
      ReadFile(consoleStdin, buffer, 1000,
         &numRead, 0);
      buffer[numRead]='\0'; // will have CR/LF
      WriteFile(stdout, buffer, strlen(buffer),
         &numWrite, 0);
   } while  (strncmp(buffer, "exit", 4) != 0);
}

BOOL HandlerFunc(DWORD ctrlChar)
{
```

Listing 11.7
Code that demonstrates a console control handler (Page 1 of 3)

```
    switch (ctrlChar)
    {
        case CTRL_C_EVENT:
            Beep(100, 100);
            return FALSE;
        case CTRL_CLOSE_EVENT:
            Beep(200, 200);
            return FALSE;
        case CTRL_BREAK_EVENT:
            Beep(300, 300);
            return FALSE;
        case CTRL_LOGOFF_EVENT:
            Beep(400, 400);
            return FALSE;
        case CTRL_SHUTDOWN_EVENT:
            Beep(500, 500);
            return FALSE;
        default:
            Beep(2000, 2000);
            return FALSE;
    }
}

VOID main(void)
{
    HANDLE consoleStdout, consoleStdin;
    BOOL success;

    // Get handles for standard in and out
    consoleStdin = GetStdHandle(STD_INPUT_HANDLE);
    consoleStdout = GetStdHandle(STD_OUTPUT_HANDLE);
    // they must be invalid if equal
    if (consoleStdin == consoleStdout)
        ErrorHandler("In GetStdHandle",
            GetLastError());
```

Listing 11.7
Code that demonstrates a console control handler (Page 2 of 3)

```
    success = SetConsoleCtrlHandler(
        (PHANDLER_ROUTINE)HandlerFunc, TRUE);
    if (!success)
        ErrorHandler("In SetConsoleCtrlHandler",
            GetLastError());

    // Process user I/O
    ProcessIO(consoleStdin, consoleStdout);
}
```

Listing 11.7
Code that demonstrates a console control handler (Page 3 of 3)

If you run the code in Listing 11.7 and then press Ctrl-C, it will beep before quitting because the handler function executes every time you press Ctrl-C. In the **HandlerFunc** function, you can also change the return value for CTRL_C_EVENT to TRUE, and the program will not quit in response to Ctrl-C. It will simply beep. When the return value is FALSE, the API passes the event to the next function in the handler chain. If it is TRUE it assumes this handler function has completed all necessary processing on the event.

The call to **SetConsoleCtrlHandler** in the main function causes the program to begin detecting the five control events.

SetConsoleCtrlHandler — *Enables the program to monitor control events*

```
BOOL SetConsoleCtrlHandler(
    PHANDLER_ROUTINE handlerRoutine,
    BOOL add)
```

handlerRoutine	A pointer to the handler function
add	TRUE if adding the handler or FALSE if removing it

Returns TRUE on success

The handler routine accepts a DWORD indicating the signal that the console has received, and can then switch off of the signal. The handler can return TRUE or FALSE.

In the case of Ctrl-C and Ctrl-Break, a TRUE value implies that the handler has handled the key and desires no further processing. In the case of the close, logoff and shutdown signals, the signals arrive during the closing operation so that you can do any necessary cleanup. Do not attempt to read or write from the console within the handler function because the console is already on its way down and may not respond properly.

11.6 Other Capabilities

Several other functions in the console API make it easy to implement advanced capabilities in your consoles. For example, consoles support the concept of an *active* buffer, and allow you to change the active buffer at any time. Listing 11.8 demonstrates the process.

```
// 2buff.cpp

#include <windows.h>
#include <iostream.h>
#include <string.h>

void ErrorHandler(char *s, DWORD err)
{
   cout << s << endl;
   cout << "Error number: " << err << endl;
   ExitProcess(err);
}

void ShowBuffers(HANDLE consoleStdin,
```

Listing 11.8
Switching between two buffers (Page 1 of 3)

```
      HANDLE consoleStdout, HANDLE newBuffer)
{
   char buffer[1000];
   DWORD numRead, numWrite;
   BOOL flag=TRUE;
   int x;

   for (x=0; x<10; x++)
   {
      WriteFile(consoleStdout, "Black\n", 6,
         &numWrite, 0);
      WriteFile(newBuffer, "White\n", 6, &numWrite,
         0);
   }
   do
   {
      ReadFile(consoleStdin, buffer, 1000,
         &numRead, 0);
      if (flag)
         SetConsoleActiveScreenBuffer(newBuffer);
      else
         SetConsoleActiveScreenBuffer(
            consoleStdout);
      flag = !flag;
      WriteFile(consoleStdout, buffer, numRead,
         &numWrite, 0);

   } while  (strncmp(buffer, "quit", 4) != 0);
}

VOID main(void)
{
   HANDLE consoleStdout, consoleStdin;
   HANDLE newBuffer;
```

Listing 11.8
Switching between two buffers (Page 2 of 3)

```
        // Get handles for standard in and out
        consoleStdin = GetStdHandle(STD_INPUT_HANDLE);
        consoleStdout = GetStdHandle(STD_OUTPUT_HANDLE);
        // they must be invalid if equal
        if (consoleStdin == consoleStdout)
           ErrorHandler("In GetStdHandle",
              GetLastError());

        // Create second buffer
        newBuffer = CreateConsoleScreenBuffer(
           GENERIC_READ | GENERIC_WRITE,
           0, 0, CONSOLE_TEXTMODE_BUFFER, 0);

        // Show the two different buffers
        ShowBuffers(consoleStdin, consoleStdout,
           newBuffer);
     }
```

Listing 11.8
Switching between two buffers (Page 3 of 3)

The code in Listing 11.8 starts by getting the input and output handles for the console. It then creates a new screen buffer using the **CreateConsole-ScreenBuffer** function.

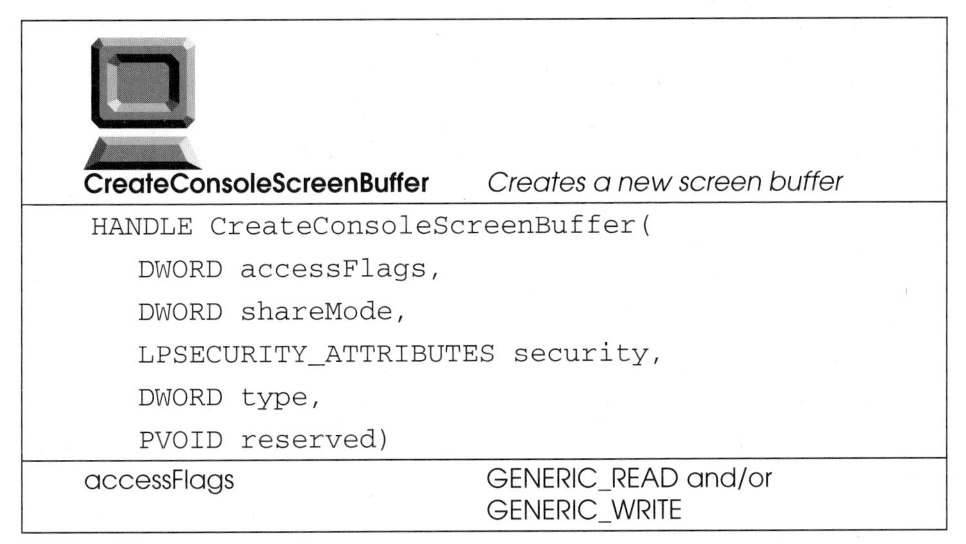

CreateConsoleScreenBuffer *Creates a new screen buffer*

```
HANDLE CreateConsoleScreenBuffer(
   DWORD accessFlags,
   DWORD shareMode,
   LPSECURITY_ATTRIBUTES security,
   DWORD type,
   PVOID reserved)
```

accessFlags	GENERIC_READ and/or GENERIC_WRITE

shareMode	FILE_SHARE_READ and/or FILE_SHARE_WRITE
security	Security attributes. See Chapter 10
type`	Must currently be CONSOLE_TEXTMODE_BUFFER
reserved	Reserved. Set to 0.
Returns a handle to the new buffer or INVALID_HANDLE_VALUE on error	

The new buffer initially has the same size as the existing console window. You can change it (or any console's buffer size) using the **SetConsoleScreen-BufferSize** function.

SetConsoleScreenBufferSize *Sets the specified buffer to a new size*

```
BOOL SetConsoleScreenBufferSize(
   HANDLE consoleHandle,
   COORD size)
```

consoleHandle	Handle to the console to change
size	The new console size
Returns TRUE on success	

Listing 11.8 simply uses the default size. It then calls the **ShowBuffers** function. This function demonstrates how to use two separate buffers. The function starts by placing 10 lines of information into the two buffers. Then each time the user presses the Enter key, the program sets the active buffer using the **SetConsoleActiveScreenBuffer** function.

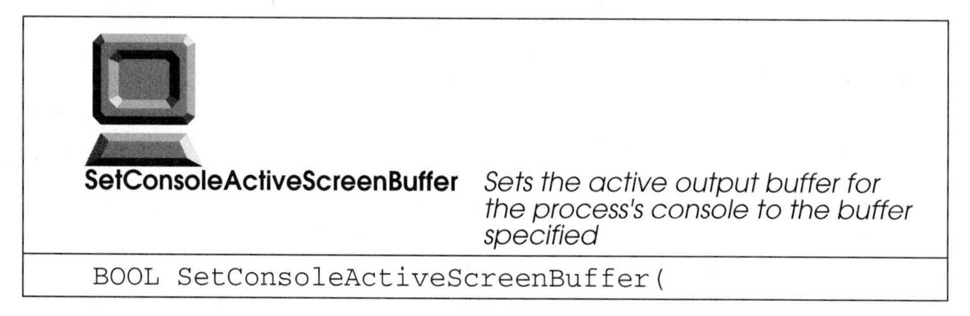

SetConsoleActiveScreenBuffer *Sets the active output buffer for the process's console to the buffer specified*

```
BOOL SetConsoleActiveScreenBuffer(
```

HANDLE consoleHandle)	
consoleHandle	Handle to the console
Returns TRUE on success	

Any process can have just one console window, and just one console input stream, but it can have many different output buffers. The **SetConsoleActiveScreenBuffer** function lets you choose among them. As soon as the function is called, the new buffer will appear and the scroll bars will change as necessary to accommodate the new buffer.

Another interesting capability involves coloring the output buffer, or placing characters directly into it. Listing 11.9 demonstrates coloring.

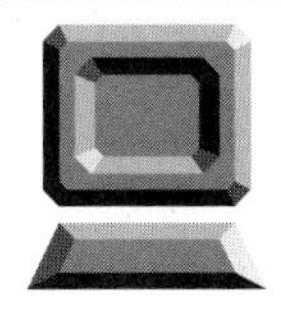

```
// color.cpp

#include <windows.h>
#include <iostream.h>

void ErrorHandler(char *s, DWORD err)
{
   cout << s << endl;
   cout << "Error number: " << err << endl;
   ExitProcess(err);
}

// Changes the colors of a range of cells.
// Make sure that the console you are
// using is not so big that the area
// colored is not off the screen.
void ChangeColors(HANDLE consoleStdin,
   HANDLE consoleStdout)
{
```

Listing 11.9
Changing the color of the output buffer (Page 1 of 2)

```
    COORD c;
    WORD color;
    DWORD numWrite;
    BOOL success;

    // Fill in the color of a range of 200 cells.
    color = BACKGROUND_RED | FOREGROUND_GREEN;
    c.X = 20;
    c.Y = 10;
    success = FillConsoleOutputAttribute(
        consoleStdout, color, 200, c, &numWrite);
    cout << numWrite << endl;
    if (!success)
        ErrorHandler("In FillConsoleOutputAttribute",
            GetLastError());
}

VOID main(void)
{
    HANDLE consoleStdout, consoleStdin;

    // Get handles for standard in and out
    consoleStdin = GetStdHandle(STD_INPUT_HANDLE);
    consoleStdout = GetStdHandle(STD_OUTPUT_HANDLE);
    if (consoleStdin == consoleStdout)
        ErrorHandler("In GetStdHandle",
            GetLastError());

    // Process user I/O
    ChangeColors(consoleStdin, consoleStdout);
}
```

Listing 11.9
Changing the color of the output buffer (Page 2 of 2)

Every cell in the output buffer has an X,Y coordinate, a character, and a color attribute byte. The code in Listing 11.9 simply modifies the attribute bytes of a set of 200 characters:

```
color = BACKGROUND_RED | FOREGROUND_GREEN;
c.X = 20;
c.Y = 10;
success = FillConsoleOutputAttribute(
   consoleStdout, color, 200, c, &numWrite);
```

The **FillConsoleOutputAttribute** function (and the nearly identical **WriteConsoleOutputAttribute** function) accepts a color byte, a starting position, and the number of characters to apply the color to. It changes their color attributes.

FillConsoleOutputAttribute — *Fills in the color attribute bytes of a range of character positions in the buffer*

```
BOOL FillConsoleOutputAttribute(
   HANDLE consoleHandle,
   WORD color,
   DWORD numberOfCells,
   COORD startingCoord,
   LPDWORD numWritten)
```

consoleHandle	Handle to the console
color	The new attribute byte
numberOfCells	Number of cells to change
startingCoord	The coordinates of the starting character
numWritten	Number of cells actually changed

Returns TRUE on success

The color byte can contain combinations of red, green, and blue or black for both the foreground and background colors. The **FillConsoleOutputAttribute** function fills runs of cells line by line starting at the indicated position.

The **SetConsoleTextAttribute** function sets the color attribute byte and applies it to all characters that subsequently appear in the text output buffer.

SetConsoleTextAttribute	*Sets the color attribute byte for all subsequent output*

```
BOOL SetConsoleTextAttribute(
   HANDLE consoleHandle,
   WORD attribute)
```

consoleHandle	Output console handle
attribute	The attribute byte
Returns TRUE on success	

Two other useful convenience functions are **GetConsoleTitle** and **SetConsoleTitle**, which get and set the verbiage in the title bar of the console's window.

SetConsoleTitle	*Sets the console's title*

```
BOOL SetConsoleTitle(
   LPTSTR title)
```

title	The new title
Returns TRUE on success	

GetConsoleTitle	*Gets the console's title*

```
DWORD GetConsoleTitle(
   LPTSTR buffer,
   DWORD numRead)
```

buffer	The buffer in which to place the title

numRead	The size of the buffer
Returns the number of characters copied to the buffer, or 0 on error	

11.7 Conclusion

You will find that you use consoles whenever you need to create programs that have pure text input and/or output and you do not want or need to create a full graphical application to handle it. You can also use consoles to provide a pure text output stream for an MFC program.

Chapter 12 contains a simple terminal program that uses the raw console input modes described in this chapter.

COMMUNICATIONS

12

The communications portion of the Win32 API handles both parallel and serial communications through the computer's I/O ports. It also handles an interface to the telnet portion of the TCP/IP package, which you install in the Network applet of the Control Panel. Using the Communications capabilities of Windows, you can talk to modems and other serial devices, printers and other parallel devices, and other computers acting as telnet servers on the network.

Compatibility Note: All of the code in this chapter works identically in Windows NT and Windows 95.

12.1 The Possibilities

One of the most common ways to use the communications capabilities of the 32-bit API is to communicate with a modem. For example, you might want to implement a bulletin board system, or create a terminal emulator:

- In a bulletin board system, the program implementing the system runs continuously. It places the modem in auto answer mode, and when a call comes in begins a BBS session. The BBS program uses the communications capabilities of Windows for all modem communications.
- In a terminal program, the modem connects with a remote computer system and transfers characters. Most terminal emulators recognize certain *escape sequences* that are interpreted as special terminal commands. For example, on a vt-100 terminal the escape character (ASCII 27) followed by "[;H" followed by another escape character followed by "[2J" means "clear screen." For a vt100 terminal emulator, the program will recognize perhaps 30 different sequences like this to provide full-screen editing capabilities.

Another way to use the communications capabilities of the 32-bit API is to talk with unsupported input and output devices, or devices that use their own human-readable protocols. For example, many high-end digitizing tables use serial lines to communicate pointer positions and keystrokes from the puck. You can create a system to read from such a table fairly easily using the API's communications facilities.

It is also very easy to communicate with telnet sockets on other computer systems using the `\\.\telnet` port. Once you open a connection to this port, you get a `telnet>` prompt and can begin any normal telnet interaction. This capability makes it extremely easy to communicate with other telnet machines on the network. Note that you must load the TCP/IP module in the Network applet of the Control Panel, and that you must start the telnet service, for this capability to work.

12.2 Understanding Serial Communications

In order to fully understand some of the serial communications code described below, it will be helpful to have a good mental image of what is happening when a computer system talks to a modem via an RS-232 communications line. All of the terminology used in RS-232 lingo normally refers to a connection between a terminal and a modem as shown in Figure 12.1. In a normal RS-232 cable, the lines pass straight through from corresponding pin to corresponding pin as shown in Figure 12.1. The following table shows the differences between 9-pin and 25-pin cables:

Signal	DB9 pin	DB25 pin
DCD	1	8
RX	2	3
TX	3	2
DTR	4	20
GND	5	7
DSR	6	6
RTS	7	4
CTS	8	5
RI	9	22

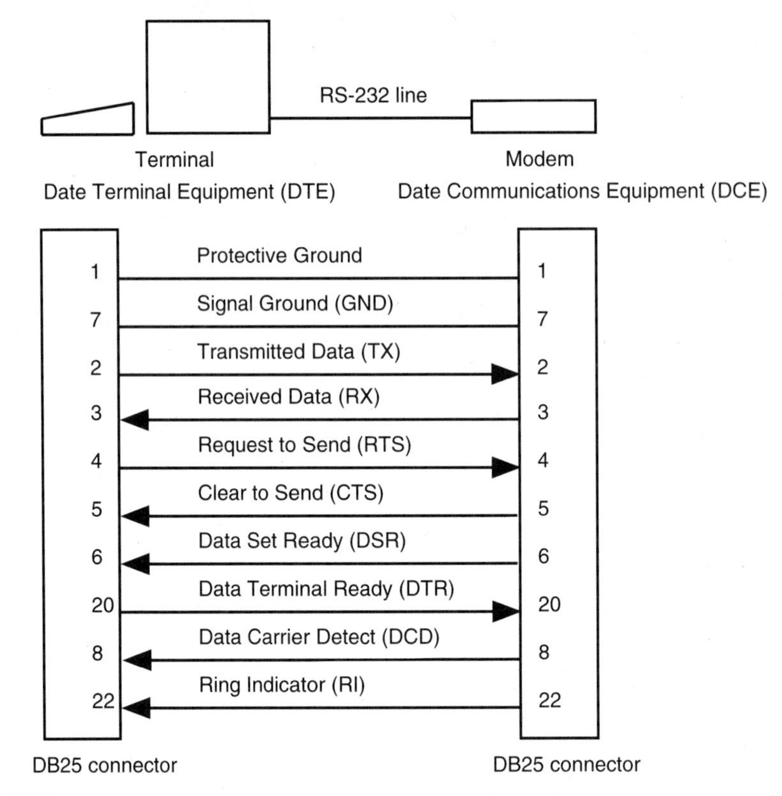

Figure 12.1
RS-232 Signaling conventions.

On a null-modem cable, the wiring is set up to transpose all appropriate signals, as shown in Figure 12.2. You use a null modem cable to connect two computers directly together without intervening modems, or to connect a computer to a printer. Because both the computer and the printer are considered to be DTE devices, you cannot connect them together directly.

In a typical communication session, the "terminal," which in this case is your computer, raises the DTR line to indicate that it is ready to begin a transmission. The modem will raise the DSR line when it is turned on to indicate that it is ready. Your computer will then raise the RTS line when it wants to transmit and the modem will respond on the CTS line. The computer then begins to transmit. When data is incoming, the modem raises the DCD line.

In the code that follows, you will notice the use of the **EscapeCommFunction** function to raise and lower the DTR line. You will also notice that

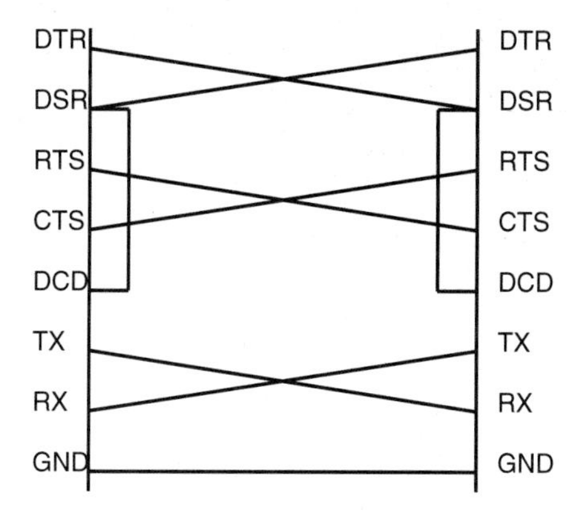

Figure 12.2
Proper null modem cable wiring. In some cases, RTS, CTS, and DCD are all wired together. In extreme cases, only the RX, TX and GND signals are used.

the DCB structure allows flow control to occur in three different ways. The two hardware techniques rely either on the DTR/DSR lines or the RTS/CTS lines. These techniques depend both on your modem supporting all appropriate signals, as well as your modem cable actually carrying all signals. If you have problems with hardware flow control, check your modem and cable first to make sure they are working as expected.

12.3 A Simple Communications Application

The easiest way to understand how the communications facilities of the 32-bit API work is to look at an extremely simple example of modem communications. While this first example does not accomplish anything particularly useful, it does demonstrate all of the steps that must be followed to create a successful connection.

Listing 12.1 contains a very simple communications program. To use it you will need a Hayes-compatible modem hooked to one of your serial communications ports. With a modem connected, Listing 12.1 sends the command "at" to the modem and receives back the modem's response, which is "ok." Any Hayes compatible modem understands the characters "at" to be an "attention" command and responds with "ok" to indicate that the modem is functioning properly.

```
// commtest.cpp

#include <windows.h>
#include <iostream.h>

void ErrorHandler(char *message, DWORD error)
{
   cout << message << endl;
   cout << "Error number = " << error << endl;
   ExitProcess(1);
}

void main()
{
   HANDLE comHandle;
   BOOL success;
   DCB dcb;
   char str[100];
   DWORD numWrite, numRead;
   COMMTIMEOUTS timeouts;

   // Open the comm port. Can open COM, LPT,
   // or \\\\.\\TELNET
   comHandle = CreateFile("COM2",
      GENERIC_READ|GENERIC_WRITE,
      0, 0, OPEN_EXISTING,
      FILE_ATTRIBUTE_NORMAL, 0);
   if (comHandle == INVALID_HANDLE_VALUE)
      ErrorHandler("In CreateFile",
         GetLastError());
```

Listing 12.1
A simple demonstration program (Page 1 of 3)

```
    // Get the current settings of the COMM port
    success = GetCommState(comHandle, &dcb);
    if (!success)
       ErrorHandler("In GetCommState",
          GetLastError());

    // Modify the baud rate, etc.
    dcb.BaudRate = 2400;
    dcb.ByteSize = 8;
    dcb.Parity = NOPARITY;
    dcb.StopBits = ONESTOPBIT;

    // Apply the new comm port settings
    success = SetCommState(comHandle, &dcb);
    if (!success)
       ErrorHandler("In SetCommState",
          GetLastError());

    // Change the ReadIntervalTimeout so that
    // ReadFile will return immediately. See
    // help file
    timeouts.ReadIntervalTimeout = MAXDWORD;
    timeouts.ReadTotalTimeoutMultiplier = 0;
    timeouts.ReadTotalTimeoutConstant = 0;
    timeouts.WriteTotalTimeoutMultiplier = 0;
    timeouts.WriteTotalTimeoutConstant = 0;
    SetCommTimeouts( comHandle, &timeouts );

    // Set the Data Terminal Ready line
    EscapeCommFunction(comHandle, SETDTR);

    // Send an "at" command to the modem
    // Be sure to use \r rather than \n
    strcpy(str, "at\r");
```

Listing 12.1
A simple demonstration program (Page 2 of 3)

```
      success = WriteFile(comHandle, str, strlen(str),
         &numWrite, 0);
      if (!success)
         ErrorHandler("In WriteFile", GetLastError());

      // Wait 2 seconds and then retrieve from the
      // modem
      Sleep(2000);
      success = ReadFile(comHandle, str,
         100, &numRead, 0);
      if (!success)
         ErrorHandler("In ReadFile", GetLastError());

      // Print the string received
      cout << numRead << endl;
      str[numRead]='\0';
      cout << str << endl;

      // Clear the DTR line
      EscapeCommFunction(comHandle, CLRDTR);

      CloseHandle(comHandle);
   }
```

Listing 12.1
A simple demonstration program (Page 3 of 3)

The code in Listing 12.1 starts by calling the **CreateFile** function to open a handle to the COM2 communication port. Change this port number as necessary for your machine. On a normal Windows workstation you are likely to have one or two serial communications lines labeled COM1 and COM2, along with one parallel port labeled LPT1.

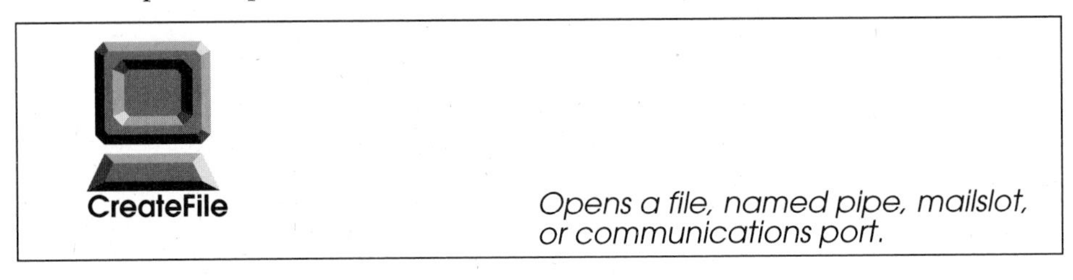

Opens a file, named pipe, mailslot, or communications port.

```
HANDLE CreateFile(
    LPCTSTR name,
    DWORD accessMode,
    DWORD shareMode,
    LPSECURITY_ATTRIBUTES securityAttributes,
    DWORD create,
    DWORD attributes,
    HANDLE templateFile)
```

name	Name of the file to open
accessMode	Read/Write mode
shareMode	The way the file should be shared
securityAttributes	Address of a security structure. See Chapter 10
create	The way the file should be created
attributes	Settings for normal file attribute bits
templateFile	File containing extended attributes

Returns a handle on success, or INVALID_HANDLE_VALUE

When you call **CreateFile** on any of these ports, the system checks to make sure that the port is not already in use by some other process, and if it is it returns the appropriate error code. If the port is available, you are granted exclusive access to it. The parameters and constants used in the call to **CreateFile** here are the same as those used when opening a file, as described in Chapter 2. The following parameters to **CreateFile** must be set as specified:

- Set the **accessMode** function to allow read and write access
- Set **shareMode** to 0 to indicate exclusive access
- Set the **create** parameter to OPEN_EXISTING, since the COM port already exists
- Set **attributes** to FILE_ATTRIBUTES_NORMAL
- Set **templateFile** to 0

Since COM2 is a serial communications port, the next step is to set communications parameters such a baud rate and parity. Each port retains whatever settings it had from its last use, so it is important to set all relevant parameters to new values to make sure that you are using known settings. The code first calls the **GetCommState** function to retrieve the existing settings.

GetCommState	*Retrieves the current state of the port*

`BOOL GetCommState(`
`   HANDLE commHandle,`
`   LPDCB dcb)`	

commHandle	Handle to a comm port
dcb	A pointer to a DCB structure
Returns TRUE on success	

The DCB structure returned by **GetCommState** contains 28 fields, and is best understood by carefully reading its description in the help file. The following brief summary of the DCB structure is copied from Microsoft's Win32 API help file:

```
typedef struct _DCB {
  DWORD DCBlength; // sizeof(DCB)
  DWORD BaudRate; // current baud rate
  DWORD fBinary: 1; // binary mode, no EOF check
  DWORD fParity: 1; // enable parity checking
  DWORD fOutxCtsFlow:1; // CTS output flow control
  DWORD fOutxDsrFlow:1; // DSR output flow control
  DWORD fDtrControl:2; // DTR flow control type
  DWORD fDsrSensitivity:1; // DSR sensitivity
  DWORD fTXContinueOnXoff:1; // XOFF continues Tx
  DWORD fOutX: 1; // XON/XOFF out flow control
  DWORD fInX: 1; // XON/XOFF in flow control
  DWORD fErrorChar: 1; // enable error replacement
  DWORD fNull: 1; // enable null stripping
  DWORD fRtsControl:2; // RTS flow control
  DWORD fAbortOnError:1; // abort rds/wrs on error
  DWORD fDummy2:17; // reserved
  WORD wReserved; // not currently used
  WORD XonLim; // transmit XON threshold
```

```
    WORD XoffLim;// transmit XOFF threshold
    BYTE ByteSize; // number of bits/byte, 4-8
    BYTE Parity; // 0-4=no,odd,even,mark,space
    BYTE StopBits; // 0,1,2 = 1, 1.5, 2
    char XonChar; // Tx and Rx XON character
    char XoffChar; // Tx and Rx XOFF character
    char ErrorChar; // error replacement character
    char EofChar; // end of input character
    char EvtChar; // received event character
} DCB;
```

In Listing 12.1, only the baud rate, the number of bits per character, the parity, and the number of stop bits are modified. The changes are then sent to the COM port using the **SetCommState** function.

SetCommState	*Sets the current state of the port*

`BOOL SetCommState(`
`    HANDLE commHandle,`
`    LPDCB dcb)`	

commHandle	Handle to a comm port
dcb	A pointer to a DCB structure
Returns TRUE on success	

It is also possible to set values into a DCB structure using the **BuildCommState** function. It accepts a string compatible with the string accepted by the `mode` command at the command line.

Listing 12.1 next sets timeout values. These values are again retained from use to use so it is important to set them if you have certain behavior that you are expecting. These values give you very subtle control over the timeout behavior of your program during reads and writes, and guarantee that your program does not stall in the event of communication problems. For example, a **ReadFile** operation told to return with 100 bytes will stall until it finds 100 bytes in the input buffer. If there is a communication error however, 100 bytes will never arrive and the program gets stuck. Using timeouts, you can instruct the program to return immediately from any **ReadFile** operation regardless of the number of bytes found, or to return after a specified number of milliseconds.

The **ReadIntervalTimeout** value controls timeouts on the interval between characters. For example, you might set it to 1000 to indicate that a **ReadFile** operation should return if two characters are spaced out by more than one second. If you set **ReadIntervalTimeout** to 0, no interval timeouts are used. If you set it to MAXDWORD as shown in the code, and if the other two read intervals are set to 0, then the system returns immediately from any **ReadFile** operation with whatever the input buffer contains.

The **ReadTotalTimeoutMultiplier** and **ReadTotalTimeoutConstant** values let you set a timeout based on the number of bytes specified in the **ReadFile** statement. If you ask to read 100 bytes, for example, the following equation determines the timeout value.

```
Total timeout value = 100 * ReadTotalTimeoutMultiplier +
          ReadTotalTimeoutConstant
```

After this specified number of milliseconds have elapsed, the **ReadFile** function returns regardless of how many bytes it has actually read. The same process is used for the Write multiplier and constant in an outgoing direction.

Listing 12.1 uses the timeout values to ensure that a call the **ReadFile** function returns immediately. Once the timeout structure has been set up, it is passed to the system with the **SetCommTimeouts** function.

SetCommTimeouts	*Sets the timeout values of the port*

`BOOL SetCommTimeouts(`
`HANDLE commHandle,`
`LPCOMMTIMEOUTS timeouts)`	

commHandle	Handle to a comm port
timeouts	A pointer to a COMMTIMEOUTS structure
Returns TRUE on success	

With all of these preliminaries taken care of, the program is ready to begin communicating with the modem. It sets the DTR line (see Section 12.2) to indicate that it is ready using the **EscapeCommFunction** function.

EscapeCommFunction *Performs a specified operation*

```
BOOL EscapeCommFunction(
   HANDLE commHandle,
   DWORD operation)
```

commHandle	Handle to a comm port
operation	The operation

Returns TRUE on success

The valid operations for **EscapeCommFunction** are listed below:

SETDTR	Turns on the DTR line
CLRDTR	Turns off the DTR line
SETRTS	Turns on the RTS line
CLRRTS	Turns off the RTS line
SETXON	Turns on XON flow control as though XON were received
SETXOFF	Turns off XON flow control as though XOFF were received
SETBREAK	Stops all transmission until CLRBREAK is received
CLRBREAK	Resumes transmission

The SETBREAK and CLRBREAK operations are also duplicated in the **SetCommBreak** and **ClearCommBreak** functions.

The code in Listing 12.1 uses the SETDTR operation to properly inform the modem that the "terminal" is ready and about to begin transmission. All of the other signals are handled automatically by the comm port and are not normally manipulated manually. A terminal emulator program will frequently contain a Break option which you can implement with SETBREAK or **SetCommBreak**.

Listing 12.1 next uses the normal **WriteFile** command (Chapter 2) to send the command "at" to the modem. A Hayes-compatible modem will respond to this command by echoing back the characters and then sending an "ok" response to indicate that it is alive. If the modem is working properly and if it has lights on its front panel, you should see the RX and TX lights glow as the "at" characters are received and echoed, and then half a second later see the TX light glow again when the OK is sent back.

WriteFile *Writes a block of bytes to a file*

```
BOOL WriteFile(
    HANDLE fileHandle,
    CONST VOID *buffer,
    DWORD bytesToWrite,
    LPDWORD bytesWritten,
    LPOVERLAPPED overlapped)
```

fileHandle	Handle to a file created by **CreateFile**
buffer	Data to write
bytesToWrite	The number of bytes to write
bytesWritten	The number of bytes actually written
overlapped	Overlapped structure. See Section 6.5.

Returns TRUE on success

The program in Listing 12.1 pauses two seconds to wait for the OK response, and then calls **ReadFile**. Because of the timeout settings, the read operation returns immediately and the output appears on the console. You should see "at" followed by a blank line and then "ok."

ReadFile *Reads bytes from the specified file*

```
BOOL ReadFile(
    HANDLE file,
    LPVOID buffer,
    DWORD requestedBytes,
    LPDWORD actualBytes,
    LPOVERLAPPED overlapped)
```

file	File handle created with **CreateFile**
buffer	Buffer to hold the read bytes
requestedBytes	The number of bytes desired
actualBytes	The number of bytes actually placed in the buffer
overlapped	Pointer to overlapped structure. See Section 6.5
Returns TRUE on success	

If you experience problems you should check for the following:

1. Make sure the modem is Hayes compatible. If it is not, look up the equivalent for the "at" command on your modem and use it instead
2. Make sure that the modem is on
3. Make sure that the cable is connected properly between computer and modem
4. Make sure the cable is connected to the proper comm port
5. Make sure that the cable has its wires set up properly. For example, if you connect the computer and modem but do not see the lights glow when the program runs, suspect the cable and try a different one. You may be using a null-modem cable instead of a normal cable.
6. Make sure you are sending a '\r' rather than a '\n' at the end of the "at" command.

12.4 Getting Communications Events

The communications functions provide a way to detect certain communications events, and these events can improve the responsiveness of your programs. We can improve on Listing 12.1 to some degree by using an *event character.*

The API is able to sense any of the following events:

EV_BREAK	Break was sent in the input
EV_CTS	The CTS line changed
EV_DSR	The DSR line changed
EV_ERR	An error was detected: CE_FRAME, CE_OVERRUN, and CE_RXPARITY are possible.
EV_RING	The modem sensed a ring
EV_RLSD	The DCD line changed
EV_RXCHAR	A character was received
EV_RXFLAG	The special event character (as indicated by the EvtChar field in the DCB) was received
EV_TXEMPTY	The last character of the last **WriteFile** operation was sent

The event most easy to trigger, at least when you have an external modem that is properly cabled, is the Data Set Ready (DSR) event. Each time you turn the modem on or off, the DSR line changes state. Another easy event to trigger is the EV_RING. Modems can detect when the phone rings. If in auto-answer mode, the modem picks up and tries to communicate with the caller. If not in auto-answer mode however, the modem will trigger EV_RING and you can detect it in your code. You might use this in a productivity manager application to count how many phone calls the user receives each day.

The EV_RXFLAG capability can be extremely useful if you want your code to be sensitive to a special character in the input stream. For example, you might want to make your code sensitive to the newline character. Once you know that a newline character is waiting in the input buffer, it is possible to read a line from the buffer and respond to it.

To demonstrate the EV_RXFLAG capability, add the following line to the code in Listing 12.1 in order to enable the communications event. Place this line with the other lines that set the DCB structure near the top of Listing 12.1 so that the program knows what the event character is:

```
// set the event character
dcb.EvtChar = '\n';
```

Here, the event character is set to the newline character. The following code, which you should use in place of the **Sleep** and **ReadFile** calls in Listing 12.1, then responds to the event character.

```
// Set the mask to wait for the event
// character. Note change to dcb above
SetCommMask(comHandle, EV_RXFLAG);

// Wait for the character, then read a line
WaitCommEvent(comHandle, &mask, 0);
success = ReadFile(comHandle, str, 100,
   &numRead, 0);
if (!success)
   ErrorHandler("In ReadFile", GetLastError());
str[numRead]='\0';
cout << str << "%" << endl;

// Wait for the character, then read a line
WaitCommEvent(comHandle, &mask, 0);
success = ReadFile(comHandle, str, 100,
   &numRead, 0);
if (!success)
   ErrorHandler("In ReadFile", GetLastError());
str[numRead]='\0';
cout << str << "%" << endl;
```

The code starts with a call to **SetCommMask**, which makes the program sensitive to the specified events.

SetCommMask	*Sets the event mask*
`BOOL SetCommMask( HANDLE commHandle, DWORD mask)`	
commHandle	Handle to a comm port
mask	One or more of the mask bits ored together
Returns TRUE on success	

Once you have set the mask, you wait for an event using the **WaitCommEvent** function.

WaitCommEvent	*Waits for an event specified by SetCommMask*
`BOOL WaitCommEvent( HANDLE commHandle, LPDWORD mask, LPOVERLAPPED overlap)`	
commHandle	Handle to a comm port
mask	pointer to a DWORD—will contain the event that released the wait
overlap	An overlapped structure (see Chapter 6)
Returns TRUE on success	

The **WaitCommEvent** function will efficiently wait for one of the specified events to occur. Once any of the events occurs, the function will return. You can detect which of the events occurred by looking at the **mask** value and anding it with the different EV_ constants. If an error is detected, you should call the **ClearCommError** function to clear the error. See Section 12.8 for details.

In the code shown above, the program is sensitive to the newline character. It calls the **ReadFile** function to read the input buffer, and then displays the line to the console. The settings in the timeout structure cause the call to **ReadFile** to return immediately with one line.

In the case shown above, the program happens to read a line correctly because of the delay the modem uses before it returns the "ok" response. In more general cases, however, there is nothing to prevent a character from arriving during the interval between the triggering of the event and the call to **ReadFile**. You may therefore want to structure your code so that it reads one character at a time up to the event character each time the event is triggered.

12.5 A Simple Bulletin Board System

A bulletin board system normally runs all of the time, and waits for users to call. With the modem in auto-answer mode, the modem will automatically connect with the user, and send back the string "CONNECT" to indicate that a session has started. The bulletin board system generally asks the user to log in, and then starts processing user commands.

The code in Listing 12.2 demonstrates the basic communications code for a BBS of this type. Normally you would place code like this in an NT service (see Chapter 9) so that it runs in the background all of the time. The program places the modem in auto answer mode and then waits, using a **ReadFile** call, for a character. Once it sees the word "CONNECT" in the input, it returns the string "You're in" to the user and then begins echoing the user's input. When the user types "X" the program quits.

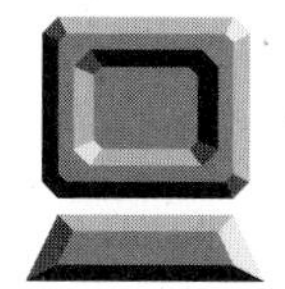

```
// bbs.cpp

#include <windows.h>
#include <iostream.h>

void ErrorHandler(char *message, DWORD error)
{
   cout << message << endl;
   cout << "Error number = " << error << endl;
   ExitProcess(1);
}

void main()
{
   HANDLE comHandle;
   BOOL success;
   char str[100];
```

Listing 12.2
The communications portion of a simple Bulletin Board system (Page 1 of 4)

```
    DCB dcb;
    char c;
    DWORD numWrite, numRead;
    COMMTIMEOUTS timeouts;
    char inputBuffer[1000];
    int inputBufferCntr = 0;
    BOOL connected = FALSE;

    // Open the comm port
    comHandle = CreateFile("COM2",
       GENERIC_READ|GENERIC_WRITE,
       0, 0, OPEN_EXISTING,
       FILE_ATTRIBUTE_NORMAL, 0);
    if (comHandle == INVALID_HANDLE_VALUE)
       ErrorHandler("In CreateFile",
          GetLastError());

    // Get the current COMM settings
    success = GetCommState(comHandle, &dcb);
    if (!success)
       ErrorHandler("In GetCommState",
          GetLastError());

    // Set the baud rate, etc.
    dcb.BaudRate = 2400;
    dcb.ByteSize = 8;
    dcb.Parity = NOPARITY;
    dcb.StopBits = ONESTOPBIT;

    // Save the COMM settings
    success = SetCommState(comHandle, &dcb);
    if (!success)
       ErrorHandler("In SetCommState",
          GetLastError());

    // Set the timeouts so ReadFile does
```

Listing 12.2
The communications portion of a simple Bulletin Board system (Page 2 of 4)

```
    // not return until it has data
    timeouts.ReadIntervalTimeout = 0;
    timeouts.ReadTotalTimeoutMultiplier = 0 ;
    timeouts.ReadTotalTimeoutConstant = 0 ;
    timeouts.WriteTotalTimeoutMultiplier = 0 ;
    timeouts.WriteTotalTimeoutConstant = 0 ;
    SetCommTimeouts( comHandle, &timeouts ) ;

    // Set the DTR line
    EscapeCommFunction(comHandle, SETDTR);

    // Set modem to auto answer mode
    strcpy(str, "atq0&d1s0=2\r");
    success = WriteFile(comHandle, str, strlen(str),
       &numWrite, 0);
    if (!success)
       ErrorHandler("In WriteFile", GetLastError());

    // Respond to incoming data
    do
    {
       // Get a character from the modem
       success = ReadFile(comHandle, &c, 1,
          &numRead, 0);
       if (!success)
          ErrorHandler("In ReadFile",
             GetLastError());

       // if its not alphanumeric, discard it
       if (!isalnum(c) && c != 10 && c != 13)
          continue;

       // if connected, echo it back
       if (connected)
       {
          success = WriteFile(comHandle, &c, 1,
```

Listing 12.2
The communications portion of a simple Bulletin Board system (Page 3 of 4)

```
            &numWrite, 0);
         if (!success)
            ErrorHandler("In WriteFile",
               GetLastError());
      }
      // if it's CR or LF, then check for
      // the word CONNECT. The word CONNECT
      // means that it is time to start
      // acting like a bulletin board
      else if (c == 10 || c == 13)
      {
         inputBuffer[inputBufferCntr]='\0';
         cout << inputBuffer << endl;
         if (strncmp(inputBuffer, "CONNECT", 7)==0)
         {
            connected = TRUE;
            strcpy(str, "You're in...\r\n");
            cout << "You're in..." << endl;
            success = WriteFile(comHandle, str,
               strlen(str), &numWrite, 0);
            if (!success)
               ErrorHandler("In WriteFile",
                  GetLastError());
         }
         inputBufferCntr = 0;
      }
      // otherwise add to buffer
      else
         inputBuffer[inputBufferCntr++] = c;
   } while (c != 'X'); // Once user types 'X', done

   // Clear the DTR line
   EscapeCommFunction(comHandle, CLRDTR);

   CloseHandle(comHandle);
}
```

Listing 12.2
The communications portion of a simple Bulletin Board system (Page 4 of 4)

The first part of Listing 12.2 looks just like Listing 12.1. It opens a connection with the COM port using **CreateFile** and sets up the DCB and timeout structures. Note that the read timeouts in Listing 12.2 are set so that **ReadFile** does not return until it detects data. Once the program has set up everything, it raises DTR and sends a string to the modem telling it to turn on its auto-answer mode.

The code now enters a loop in which it uses a **ReadFile** statement to wait for a character. If the word "CONNECT" has not yet been seen, it places each character in an input buffer that holds one line of characters. As soon as a return or line feed character (ASCII 10 and 13) appears in the input stream, the program recognizes it as an end-of-line indication and looks for the word "CONNECT" in the input buffer. Once it finds it, a session begins. The BBS sends back the string "You're in..." and then simply echoes the user's input. In a real BBS program you would want to ask the user to log in and then begin to interpret user commands.

The input buffer demonstrated here is one way to buffer lines. The technique described in the previous section using comm events and an event character is another way to do it. With either technique, you end up reading one character at a time from the input stream because you never know how many characters form a line in the input buffer.

In a BBS that handles multiple modems, threads can make the design of the program significantly easier. You can assign one thread to each COM port that you are managing. See Chapter 5 for details.

12.6 Flow Control

The 32-bit API supports three different types of flow control:

1. Xon/Xoff (software)
2. RTS/CTS (hardware)
3. DTR/DSR (hardware)

Flow control is used by the comm libraries at both the sending and receiving ends to prevent buffer overflow. When the comm system receives characters, it places them in an input buffer. If the system does not pull characters out of the buffer fast enough to match the rate at which they arrive, then the buffer will fill and eventually overflow. Flow control allows a receiver to send a signal back to the sender that tells it to stop sending characters because of an impending buffer overflow. When the buffer is again clear, the receiver can send another signal to the sender telling it to resume.

Xon/Xoff flow control uses special character value passed in the normal input stream as the signal. Ctrl-S (XOFF) is normally used to halt the flow, while Ctrl-Q (XON) resumes it. Because the characters appear in the normal data stream, they cannot be used while transmitting binary data.

The two hardware flow control methods use modem control lines to regulate the flow. These lines are discussed at the beginning of the chapter. These control methods both rely on the RS-232 cable and modem correctly supporting the designated lines. For flow control to work properly, the modems at both ends of the connection need to be using the same method.

You can use the **GetCommProperties** function to determine what types of flow control the current comm driver for the specified port supports. In the case of hardware flow control, this does not necessarily mean that the method will actually work (for example, if the cable is missing the necessary wires, the comm driver will not know about it), but it does indicate whether or not the driver knows how to support the specified protocol.

GetCommProperties	*Returns information about the driver for the specified port*

`BOOL GetCommProperties(`
`    HANDLE commHandle,`
`    LPCOMMPROP properties)`	

commHandle	Handle to a comm port
properties	A pointer to a properties structure
Returns TRUE on success	

The COMMPROP structure contains quite a bit of useful information about the comm device. The following summary is copied from the Microsoft API help file and will give you an idea of what is available. See the description in the help file for more information.

```
typedef struct _COMMPROP {
```

```
    WORD wPacketLength; // packet size, in bytes
    WORD wPacketVersion; // packet version
    DWORD dwServiceMask; // services implemented
    DWORD dwReserved1; // reserved
    DWORD dwMaxTxQueue; // max Tx bufsize, in bytes
    DWORD dwMaxRxQueue; // max Rx bufsize, in bytes
    DWORD dwMaxBaud; // max baud rate, in bps
    DWORD dwProvSubType; // specific provider type
    DWORD dwProvCapabilities; // caps supported
    DWORD dwSettableParams; // changable parameters
    DWORD dwSettableBaud; // allowable baud rates
    WORD wSettableData; // allowable byte sizes
    WORD wSettableStopParity; // stop bits/parity
    DWORD dwCurrentTxQueue; // Tx buffer size,bytes
    DWORD dwCurrentRxQueue; // Rx buffer size,bytes
    DWORD dwProvSpec1; // provider-specific data
    DWORD dwProvSpec2; // provider-specific data
    WCHAR wcProvChar[1]; // provider-specific data
} COMMPROP;
```

The **dwProvCapabilities** field tells you which of the different flow control capabilities are available.

You activate the flow control features using a DCB structure and the **SetCommState** function. To turn on Xon/Xoff flow control, set the following fields:

```
dcb.fInX = dcb.fOutX = TRUE;
dcb.XonLim = 50 ;
dcb.XoffLim = 200 ;
dcb.XonChar = 17;
dcb.XoffChar = 19;
```

These settings turn on XON/XOFF flow control for both sending and receiving, indicate that Ctrl-Q (ASCII 17) and Ctrl-S (ASCII 19) should be used as the XON and XOFF characters, and set the sizes where flow is stopped and resumed. The **fTXContinueOnXoff** field is also relevant.

To turn on RTS/CTS flow control, set the following fields:

```
dcb.fOutxCtsFlow = TRUE ;
dcb.fRtsControl = RTS_CONTROL_HANDSHAKE ;
```

To turn on DTR/DSR flow control, set the following fields:

```
dcb.fOutxDsrFlow = TRUE ;

dcb.fDtrControl = DTR_CONTROL_HANDSHAKE ;
```

12.7 A Simple TTY Terminal Program

Creating a complete terminal emulator program is not a trivial problem. While conceptually simple, there are a large number of details that make things difficult. For example, any real terminal emulator needs to understand the escape sequences of the one or more terminals it is emulating, and you generally end up building a small state machine to handle it. In order to demonstrate the communications portion of a terminal emulator, this section presents a very simple TTY-style terminal program that you can use to connect to a remote machine via either a modem or the TELNET facility.

One of the more interesting problems handled by this program is the "two input stream problem." In a terminal program, the user can hit a character on the keyboard at any time and this character must be sent to the modem immediately. At the same time, a character can appear in the modem's input buffer at any moment, and it needs to appear on the screen immediately so the user can see it. You cannot have the code accept a user keystroke and then wait for a modem keystroke, because the two input streams are completely independent of one another. Instead you have to wait for characters from either stream and respond to them immediately. This program uses NT's **WaitForMultipleObjects** function (see Chapter 6), along with overlapped I/O (see Chapter 6), to solve the problem. You could also use separate threads (see Chapter 5) to monitor the two input sources.

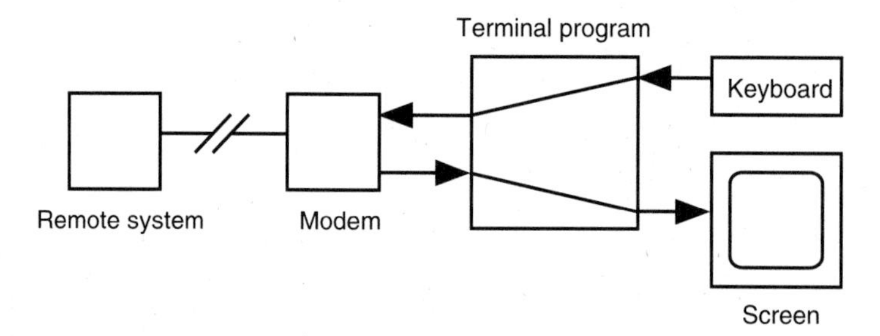

Figure 12.3
The terminal program must handle two input streams simultaneously and asynchronously.

Listing 12.3 contains the code for the terminal emulator program. It is currently set up to communicate with a modem on COM2. In this mode you should run the program and then type "atdt 555-5555" (use an appropriate phone number) to dial out to a BBS or remote computer system. If you want to try using the TELNET facility to connect to a telnet server such as a UNIX machine on the network, use "\\\\.\\TELNET" for the **portString** variable in the **main** function. *Make sure you have loaded the TCP/IP facility in the Network applet of the Control Panel, and also make sure you have started the Telnet service in the Services applet of the Control Panel or the TELNET port will not work.* You should immediately see a `telnet>` prompt and you can use it normally. Type "help" if you need help.

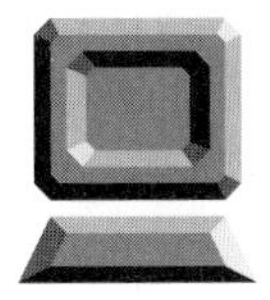

```
// term.cpp

#include <windows.h>
#include <iostream.h>
#include <stdio.h>
#include <string.h>

void ErrorHandler(char *s, DWORD err)
{
   cout << s << endl;
   cout << "Error number: " << err << endl;
   ExitProcess(err);
}

// Scrolls the console up one line
void ScrollOneLine(HANDLE consoleStdout)
{
   BOOL success;
```

Listing 12.3
A simple TTY terminal emulator (Page 1 of 9)

```
CONSOLE_SCREEN_BUFFER_INFO consoleInfo;
SMALL_RECT scrollRect;
CHAR_INFO consoleFill;
COORD coord;

// get current console size (may change)
success = GetConsoleScreenBufferInfo(
   consoleStdout, &consoleInfo);
if (!success)
   ErrorHandler("In GetConsoleScreenBufferInfo",
      GetLastError());

// Define the rectangle to scroll
scrollRect.Top = 0;
scrollRect.Left = 0;
scrollRect.Bottom = consoleInfo.dwSize.Y - 1;
scrollRect.Right = consoleInfo.dwSize.X - 1;

// Define destination of scrolled rectangle
coord.X = 0;
coord.Y = -1;

// Define how to fill blank line
consoleFill.Attributes =
   consoleInfo.wAttributes;
consoleFill.Char.AsciiChar = ' ';

// Perform the scroll
success =
   ScrollConsoleScreenBuffer(consoleStdout,
      &scrollRect, 0,
   coord, &consoleFill);
if (!success)
   ErrorHandler("In ScrollConsoleScreenBuffer",
      GetLastError());
```

Listing 12.3
A simple TTY terminal emulator (Page 2 of 9)

```
}

// Handles the newline character
VOID NewLine(HANDLE consoleStdout)
{
   CONSOLE_SCREEN_BUFFER_INFO consoleInfo;
   BOOL success;

   // Find out where cursor is
   success =
      GetConsoleScreenBufferInfo(consoleStdout,
         &consoleInfo);
   if (!success)
      ErrorHandler("In GetConsoleScreenBufferInfo",
         GetLastError());

   // Move cursor to far left
   consoleInfo.dwCursorPosition.X = 0;

   // If the cursor is on the last line
   // of the console, then scroll the console,
   // else increment position
   if (consoleInfo.dwSize.Y - 1 ==
      consoleInfo.dwCursorPosition.Y)
      ScrollOneLine(consoleStdout);
   else
      consoleInfo.dwCursorPosition.Y += 1;

   // Update the console
   success =
      SetConsoleCursorPosition(consoleStdout,
      consoleInfo.dwCursorPosition);
   if (!success)
      ErrorHandler("In SetConsoleCursorPosition",
```

Listing 12.3
A simple TTY terminal emulator (Page 3 of 9)

```
            GetLastError());
    }

    // Initializes the port
    HANDLE SetupCommPort(char *port)
    {
       HANDLE comHandle;
       BOOL success;
       DCB dcb;
       COMMTIMEOUTS timeouts;

       // Open the file
       comHandle = CreateFile(port,
          GENERIC_READ|GENERIC_WRITE,
          0, 0, OPEN_EXISTING,
          FILE_FLAG_OVERLAPPED, 0);
       if (comHandle == INVALID_HANDLE_VALUE)
          ErrorHandler("In CreateFile",
          GetLastError());

       // Set timeouts so ReadFile does not
       // return until data is available
       timeouts.ReadIntervalTimeout = 0 ;
       timeouts.ReadTotalTimeoutMultiplier = 0 ;
       timeouts.ReadTotalTimeoutConstant = 0 ;
       timeouts.WriteTotalTimeoutMultiplier = 0 ;
       timeouts.WriteTotalTimeoutConstant = 0 ;
       SetCommTimeouts( comHandle, &timeouts ) ;

       // Get current settings and change them
       success = GetCommState(comHandle, &dcb);
       if (!success)
          ErrorHandler("In GetCommState",
          GetLastError());
```

Listing 12.3
A simple TTY terminal emulator (Page 4 of 9)

```
    dcb.BaudRate = 2400;
    dcb.ByteSize = 8;
    dcb.Parity = NOPARITY;
    dcb.StopBits = ONESTOPBIT;

    success = SetCommState(comHandle, &dcb);
    if (!success)
       ErrorHandler("In SetCommState",
          GetLastError());

    EscapeCommFunction(comHandle, SETDTR);
    return comHandle;
 }

 void ProcessIO(HANDLE consoleStdin,
    HANDLE consoleStdout)
 {
    char readBuffer, writeBuffer;
    DWORD numRead, numWrite;
    INPUT_RECORD inputEvent;
    DWORD s;
    HANDLE comHandle, readEvent, writeEvent;
    HANDLE handles[2];
    OVERLAPPED overlappedRead, overlappedWrite;
    BOOL success;
    char *portString = "COM2";

    // Set up the comm port. Can setup COM, LPT
    // or \\\\.\\TELNET. If you do TELNET, make sure
    // you have the TCP/IP package loaded and
    // the telnet service started
    comHandle = SetupCommPort(portString);

    // Set up for overlapped reading and
    // writing on the port
```

Listing 12.3
A simple TTY terminal emulator (Page 5 of 9)

```
      overlappedRead.Offset =
         overlappedWrite.Offset = 0;
      overlappedRead.OffsetHigh =
         overlappedWrite.OffsetHigh = 0;
      readEvent = CreateEvent(0, TRUE, FALSE, 0);
      writeEvent = CreateEvent(0, FALSE, FALSE, 0);
      overlappedRead.hEvent = readEvent;
      overlappedWrite.hEvent = writeEvent;

      // Set up handles array
      // for WaitForMultipleObjects
      handles[0] = consoleStdin;
      handles[1] = readEvent;

      // Prime the pump by getting the read
      // process started
      success = ReadFile(comHandle, &readBuffer, 1,
         &numRead, &overlappedRead);
      do
      {
         // Wait for either a keystroke or a
         // modem character. Time out after
         // 1000 seconds
         s = WaitForMultipleObjects(2, handles,
            FALSE, 1000000);
         if (s==WAIT_TIMEOUT)
            break;
         // If it is a character from the
         // keyboard then...
         else if (s==WAIT_OBJECT_0)
         {
            // Get a copy of the character but
            // leave it in the queue
            PeekConsoleInput(handles[0], &inputEvent,
               1, &numRead);
```

Listing 12.3
A simple TTY terminal emulator (Page 6 of 9)

```
          if (numRead>0)
          {
             // If it is a mouse event, or a key up
             // event, or if it is not a valid
             // ASCII character (eg-a shift key),
             // then read and discard the keystroke.
             if (inputEvent.EventType !=
                KEY_EVENT ||
                inputEvent.Event.KeyEvent.bKeyDown
                == FALSE ||
                inputEvent.Event.KeyEvent.
                uChar.AsciiChar==0)
                ReadConsoleInput(handles[0],
                   &inputEvent, 1, &numRead);
             // Otherwise, read the keystroke
             // and send it to the comm port.
             else
             {
                ReadFile(handles[0], &writeBuffer,
                   1, &numWrite, 0);
                success = WriteFile(comHandle,
                   &writeBuffer, 1, &numWrite,
                   &overlappedWrite);
                GetOverlappedResult(comHandle,
                   &overlappedWrite, &numWrite,
                   TRUE);
                overlappedWrite.Offset += numWrite;
             }
          }
       }
       // If the character is coming in from
       // the comm port, then...
       else if (s==WAIT_OBJECT_0 + 1)
       {
          // Get the character and send it
```

Listing 12.3
A simple TTY terminal emulator (Page 7 of 9)

```
            // to the console
            success = GetOverlappedResult(comHandle,
               &overlappedRead, &numRead, TRUE);
            overlappedRead.Offset += numRead;
            WriteFile(consoleStdout, &readBuffer, 1,
               &numWrite, 0);
            ResetEvent(readEvent);
            // Wait for the next character
            // from the comm port
            ReadFile(comHandle, &readBuffer, 1,
               &numRead, &overlappedRead);
         }
      // Terminate when the user types an 'X'
      } while  (writeBuffer != 'X');

      // Close all handles
      CloseHandle(readEvent);
      CloseHandle(writeEvent);
      CloseHandle(comHandle);
   }

   VOID main(void)
   {
      DWORD oldMode, newMode;
      BOOL success;
      HANDLE consoleStdout, consoleStdin;

      // Get handles for standard in and out
      consoleStdin = GetStdHandle(STD_INPUT_HANDLE);
      consoleStdout = GetStdHandle(STD_OUTPUT_HANDLE);
      if (consoleStdin == consoleStdout)
         ErrorHandler("In GetStdHandle",
            GetLastError());

      // Get current console mode so can modify it
```

Listing 12.3
A simple TTY terminal emulator (Page 8 of 9)

```
        success = GetConsoleMode(consoleStdin,
           &oldMode);
        if (!success)
           ErrorHandler("In GetConsoleMode",
              GetLastError());
        newMode = oldMode & ~ENABLE_LINE_INPUT &
           ~ENABLE_ECHO_INPUT;
        success = SetConsoleMode(consoleStdin, newMode);
           if (!success)
           ErrorHandler("In SetConsoleMode",
              GetLastError());

        // Process user I/O
        ProcessIO(consoleStdin, consoleStdout);

        // put the old mode back
        success = SetConsoleMode(consoleStdin, oldMode);
        if (!success)
           ErrorHandler("In SetConsoleMode",
              GetLastError());
}
```

Listing 12.3
A simple TTY terminal emulator (Page 9 of 9)

The code in Listing 12.3 uses the console code from Listing 11.5 as its basis. The console is in raw mode so that the program can get each individual character typed by the user as it arrives and pass it to the modem.

The **SetupCommPort** function initializes the communications port using the same techniques seen in Listing 12.1. The timeouts are set so that the **ReadFile** function does not return until it has input.

The **ProcessIO** function handles all of the input and output for the two streams of data. It uses overlapped reads and writes (see Chapter 6) on the communications port, so the first part of the code creates the overlapped structures and events to make this possible. The event in the overlapped read structure is key to the success of this program: By starting an overlapped read operation on the comm port and then waiting on the overlapped event, the program can detect when the modem has a character in the input buffer ready for processing.

The program actually waits on two events all of the time, using the **WaitForMultipleObjects** function. The array contains the read event from the comm port, along with the input handle for the console. This input handle indicates when the user has typed a key. When **WaitForMultipleObjects** detects that either the modem or the console has a waiting character, it returns. The program then figures out which input source is ready, and processes the character. If the character arrives on the modem, it gets sent to the screen. If a character arrives from the keyboard, the program first peeks at the buffer to make sure that it contains a valid keystroke. If it does, the code sends the character to the modem.

12.8 Other Communications Functions

There are several other communications functions that you may find useful in special situations. The **PurgeComm** function, for example, purges the contents of the input or output buffer.

PurgeComm	*Clears input or output buffers*

`BOOL PurgeComm(`
`HANDLE commHandle,`
`DWORD action)`	

commHandle	Handle to a comm port
action	The action(s) to perform
Returns TRUE on success	

Four actions are possible, one at a time or in combination with one another:

PURGE_TXABORT	Terminate all write operations
PURGE_RXABORT	Terminate all read operations
PURGE_TXCLEAR	Clear output buffer
PURGE_RXCLEAR	Clear input buffer

The **FileFlushBuffers** function, on the other hand, flushes the output buffer to the receiver, subject to normal flow control constraints. This function will not return until the buffer is empty.

FlushFileBuffers	*Empties the output buffer*
`BOOL FlushFileBuffers(` `   HANDLE commHandle)`	
commHandle	Handle to a comm port
Returns TRUE on success	

The **SetupComm** function lets you change the size of the buffers.

SetupComm	*Sets buffer size*

`BOOL SetupComm(`
`   HANDLE commHandle,`
`   DWORD inputBufferSize,`
`   DWORD outputBufferSize)`	

commHandle	Handle to a comm port
inputBufferSize	The size of the input buffer
outputBufferSize	The size of the output buffer
Returns TRUE on success	

The **TransmitCommChar** function transmits the specified character immediately, ahead of any other characters in the output buffer. It is like placing the character at the very first location in the output buffer—it is still subject to flow control but will be sent next. It is useful for sending Ctrl-C characters to halt commands.

TransmitCommChar	*Transmits a character ahead of buffer contents*

`BOOL TransmitCommChar(`
`commHandle,`
`char c)`	

commHandle	Handle to a comm port
c	The character to transmit
Returns TRUE on success	

12.9 Conclusion

You will find that the communications portion of the API makes it easy to communicate with serial and parallel ports on your Windows workstation. At the same time, the communications API has all of the features necessary to control the many details that apply to modem communications.

The API, along with the telnet port, makes it extremely easy to communicate with other machines supporting telnet servers on a TCP/IP network. For example, if there is a UNIX machine on your network, the telnet port available in the communications API makes communications with it trivial.

SYSTEM INFORMATION

13

The system information functions let you gather information about the system you are currently using. For example, you can examine the number of processors in use on an NT machine and then use this information to dynamically decide on the number of threads to create in a multi-threaded application. The system information functions also include a pair functions that let you initiate a system shutdown, or to cancel that shutdown once it has begun.

Compatibility Note: All of the code in this chapter up to section 13.4 works identically in Windows NT and Windows 95. The code in Section 13.4 will not work in Windows 95.

13.1 The GetSystemInfo Function

The **GetSystemInfo** function returns information about the hardware of the system on which your program is running. This information is useful when you want to tune your application's behavior to the hardware that is available.

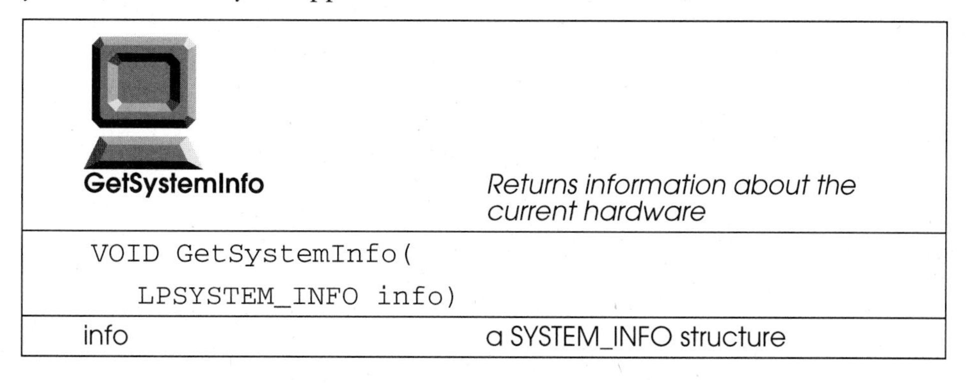

GetSystemInfo	*Returns information about the current hardware*

```
VOID GetSystemInfo(
    LPSYSTEM_INFO info)
```

info	a SYSTEM_INFO structure

Returns nothing

The function returns a SYSTEM_INFO structure that contains several pieces of immediately obvious information, along with others that are more obscure, as shown below:

```
typedef struct _SYSTEM_INFO {
    DWORD  dwOemId;
    DWORD  dwPageSize;
    LPVOID lpMinimumApplicationAddress;
    LPVOID lpMaximumApplicationAddress;
    DWORD  dwActiveProcessorMask;
    DWORD  dwNumberOfProcessors;
    DWORD  dwProcessorType;
    DWORD  dwAllocationGranularity;
    DWORD  dwReserved;
} SYSTEM_INFO;
```

Listing 13.1 demonstrates the use of this function and prints out all of the data it returns.

```
// sigsi.cpp

#include <windows.h>
#include <iostream.h>
#include <iomanip.h>

void main()
{
   SYSTEM_INFO si;

   GetSystemInfo(&si);
```

Listing 13.1
Code demonstrating the GetSystemInfo function (Page 1 of 2)

```
        cout << "OEM: " << si.dwOemId << endl;
        cout << "PageSize: " << si.dwPageSize << endl;
        cout << "Minimum app address: "
           << si.lpMinimumApplicationAddress << endl;
        cout << "Maximum app address: "
           << si.lpMaximumApplicationAddress << endl;
        cout << "Active processor mask: " << hex
           << si.dwActiveProcessorMask << endl;
        cout << "Number of processors: "
           << si.dwNumberOfProcessors << endl;
        cout << "Processor type: "
           << si.dwProcessorType << endl;
    }
```

Listing 13.1
Code demonstrating the GetSystemInfo function (Page 2 of 2)

Some of the more obvious pieces of information contained in the structure include the number of processors, the type of processor used (it returns a constant that you can match against predefined constants in the API's header file), and the OEM string. Other values indicate memory addressing boundaries and virtual memory parameters. See the description of the SYSTEM_INFO structure in the 32-bit API help file for more information on the individual fields.

13.2 Other System Information Functions

In addition to the **GetSystemInfo** function described in the previous section, there are a number of other information functions scattered throughout the API. Each of them is exercised in the code shown in Listing 13.2.

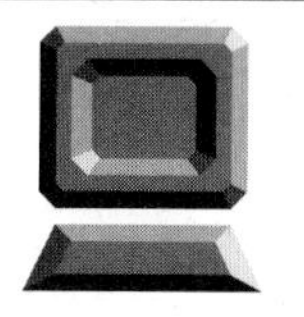

```
    // siinfo.cpp
```

Listing 13.2
Code demonstrating the GetComputerName, GetKeyboardType, GetSysColor, GetSystemDirectory, GetWindowsDirectory, GetSystemMetrics, GetVersion, and GetUserName functions (Page 1 of 3)

```
#include <windows.h>
#include <iostream.h>
#include <iomanip.h>


/////////
// needs user32.lib
/////////


void main()
{
   BOOL success;
   int result;
   char s[1000];
   int bufferSize = 1000;
   char computerName[MAX_COMPUTERNAME_LENGTH + 1];
   DWORD computerNameLen = MAX_COMPUTERNAME_LENGTH
      + 1;

   success = GetComputerName(computerName,
      &computerNameLen);
   if (success)
      cout << "Computer name: " << computerName
         << endl;

   cout << "Keyboard type: " << GetKeyboardType(0)
      << endl;
   cout << "Keyboard subtype: "
      << GetKeyboardType(1) << endl;
   cout << "Number of function keys: "
      << GetKeyboardType(2) << endl;
```

Listing 13.2
Code demonstrating the GetComputerName, GetKeyboardType, GetSysColor, GetSystemDirectory, GetWindowsDirectory, GetSystemMetrics, GetVersion, and GetUserName functions (Page 2 of 3)

```
        cout << "Border color: " << hex
           << GetSysColor(COLOR_ACTIVEBORDER) << endl;

        result = GetSystemDirectory(s, 1000);
        cout << "System directory: " << s << endl;

        result = GetWindowsDirectory(s, 1000);
        cout << "Windows directory: " << s << endl;

        cout << "Number of mouse buttons: "
           << GetSystemMetrics(SM_CMOUSEBUTTONS)
           << endl;

        DWORD version;
        version = GetVersion();
        if ((version & 0x80000000) == 0)
           cout << "This is NT \n";
        else
           cout << "This is not NT\n";
        cout << "Version number: "
           << (version & 0x000000FF) << endl;
        cout << "Revision number: "
           << ((version & 0x0000FF00) >> 8) << endl;

        char userName[100];
        DWORD userNameLen = 100;
        success = GetUserName(userName, &userNameLen);
        cout << "User name: " << userName << endl;
    }
```

Listing 13.2
Code demonstrating the GetComputerName, GetKeyboardType, GetSysColor, GetSystemDirectory, GetWindowsDirectory, GetSystemMetrics, GetVersion, and GetUserName functions (Page 3 of 3)

Each of the functions demonstrated in Listing 13.2 is straightforward. The **GetComputerName** function returns the network name of the current machine.

GetComputerName	*Returns the network name of the computer*
`BOOL GetComputerName( LPTSTR buffer, LPDWORD bufferLen)`	
buffer	Contains the network name of the computer upon return
bufferLen	The length of the name
Returns TRUE on success	

You pass into the function a buffer and the buffer's length. The function fills the buffer and returns the length of the name.

The **GetKeyboardType** function returns three different pieces of information depending on the integer constant passed in when you call the function.

GetKeyboardType	*Returns information about the keyboard*
`int GetKeyboardType( int info)`	
info	An integer constant that controls the information returned
Returns keyboard information	

When you pass a 0, 1, or 2 to **GetKeyboardType**, the function returns the keyboard type, subtype, and the number of function keys, respectively. The value returned is an integer that decodes to various pieces of information. See the help file for decoding information.

The **GetSysColor** function lets you determine the currently chosen color for all of the differentiated objects in the Windows user interface. These are the same objects you see in the Colors applet of the Control Panel when you create your own color schemes.

GetSysColor	*Returns color values for user interface objects*
`DWORD GetSysColor(` `   int index)`	
index	A constant indicating the object color desired.
Returns a 32-bit color word	

The API defines 21 different constant values that specify the pieces of the user interface for which colors are defined:

COLOR_ACTIVEBORDER
COLOR_ACTIVECAPTION
COLOR_APPWORKSPACE
COLOR_BACKGROUND
COLOR_BTNFACE
COLOR_BTNSHADOW
COLOR_BTNTEXT
COLOR_CAPTIONTEXT
COLOR_GRAYTEXT
COLOR_HIGHLIGHT
COLOR_HIGHLIGHTTEXT
COLOR_INACTIVEBORDER
COLOR_INACTIVECAPTION
COLOR_INACTIVECAPTIONTEXT
COLOR_MENU
COLOR_MENUTEXT
COLOR_SCROLLBAR
COLOR_SHADOW

COLOR_WINDOW
COLOR_WINDOWFRAME
COLOR_WINDOWTEXT

The function returns a DWORD value that indicates the RGB value for the color of the item requested. You can use the **SetSysColor** function to set colors.

SetSysColor — *Sets color values for user interface objects*

```
BOOL SetSysColors(
    int numElements,
    CONST INT *displayElements,
    CONST COLORREF *rgbValues)
```

numElements	The number of elements being set
displayElements	An array of constants indicating which elements to set
rgbValues	An array of RGB values, one for each element

Returns TRUE on success

The **GetSystemDirectory** and **GetWindowsDirectory** functions return the system and Windows directory for the machine. The location of these directories are useful in some installation programs, and also when looking for certain standard files and DLLs. Both functions accept a buffer and an integer indicating its maximum length. Both return the directory path in the buffer, and the length of the path in the integer value.

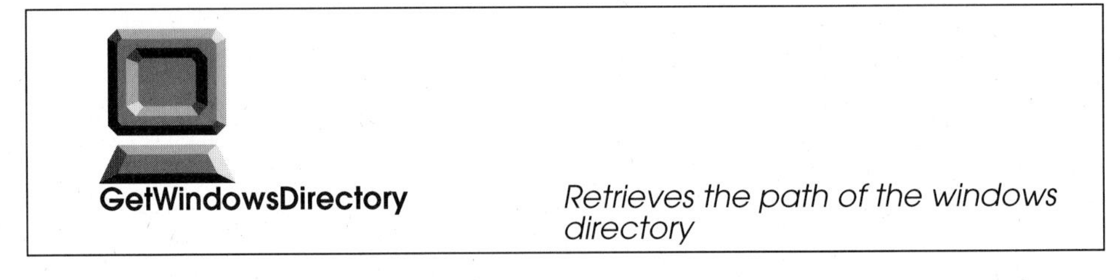
GetWindowsDirectory — *Retrieves the path of the windows directory*

GetSystemDirectory	*Retrieves the path of the system directory*
`UINT GetWindowsDirectory( LPTSTR buffer, UINT bufferLen)`	
buffer	Character buffer used to return the path
bufferLen	Length of the buffer
Returns the number of characters copied to the buffer. If the number is greater than bufferLen use a buffer of that size.	

The **GetSystemMetrics** function retrieves a wide variety of minutiae about the current machine. It can return information as obscure as the width and height of the cursor, or something as important as the number of buttons on the mouse. Forty different values are available from this function, as listed below:

SM_CXBORDER	Non-resizable window frame width
SM_CYBORDER	Non-resizable window frame height
SM_CYCAPTION	Window caption height
SM_CXCURSOR	Cursor width
SM_CYCURSOR	Cursor height
SM_CXDLGFRAME	Dialog window frame width
SM_CYDLGFRAME	Dialog window frame height
SM_CXDOUBLECLK	Double click rectangle width
SM_CYDOUBLECLK	Double click rectangle height
SM_CXFRAME	Resizable window frame width
SM_CYFRAME	Resizable window frame height
SM_CXFULLSCREEN	Full-screen client area width
SM_CYFULLSCREEN	Full-screen Client area height
SM_CYHSCROLL	Arrow height on HScrollbar
SM_CXICON	Icon width
SM_CYICON	Icon height
SM_CXICONSPACING	ProgMan icon tiling width

SM_CYICONSPACING	ProgMan icon tiling height
SM_CYKANJIWINDOW	Kanji window height
SM_CYMENU	Single-line menu bar height
SM_CXMIN	Window minimum width
SM_CYMIN	Window minimum height
SM_CXMINTRACK	Window minimum tracking width
SM_CYMINTRACK	Window minimum tracking height
SM_CMOUSEBUTTONS	Number of mouse buttons
SM_CXSCREEN	Screen width
SM_CYSCREEN	Screen height
SM_CXSIZE	Title bar bitmap width
SM_CYSIZE	Title bar bitmap height
SM_CXVSCROLL	Arrow width on VScrollbar
SM_CYVSCROLL	Arrow height on VScrollbar
SM_CXHTHUMB	Thumb width on HScrollbar
SM_CYVTHUMB	Thumb height on VScrollbar
SM_DBCSENABLED	Double-byte charset status
SM_DEBUG	Debug version
SM_MENUDROPALIGNMENT	Pop-up menu alignment
SM_MOUSEPRESENT	0 if no mouse installed
SM_PENWINDOWS	Handle to Pen Windows DLL
SM_SWAPBUTTON	0 if mouse buttons not swapped

See the help file for complete descriptions. You should look through the list at least once so that you know what is possible.

GetSystemMetrics	*Returns a wide variety of system information*
`int GetSystemMetrics(` `    int index)`	
index	A constant indicating the piece of information desired.
Returns the requested value	

The **GetVersion** function returns information about the operating system currently running on the system. Most significantly, it can tell you whether the operating system is Windows NT or not, and what the version number and revision number are.

GetVersion	*Returns NT status and version number*
`DWORD GetVersion(VOID)`	
Returns version and status encoded in a DWORD	

An encoding scheme is used to pack three pieces of data into the DWORD value returned by the function. The high-order bit, if it is 1, indicates that the system is running Windows NT. The low-order byte contains the version number, for example version 3. The byte above it indicates the revision number.

The final function demonstrated in Listing 13.2 is the **GetUserName** function. This function returns the login name of the user that owns the process. This function is useful whenever you need to know or display the current user ID.

GetUserName	*Returns the user name*

`BOOL GetUserName(`
`LPTSTR buffer,`
`LPDWORD bufferLen)`	

buffer	The buffer that will hold the returned name
bufferLen	The length of the buffer
Returns TRUE on success	

You pass in a character array and the length of the array. The function returns the name and the length of the name. If the function fails, it is because the buffer is too short.

To get information about the memory system, use the **GlobalMemory-Status** function. See Chapter 15.

13.3 Getting and Setting Environment Strings

Environment variables often contain information that is useful during the execution of a program. For example, you might want to retrieve the current path so that you can search it for a specific directory name. To retrieve environment variables, use the **ExpandEnvironmentString** function, as shown in Listing 13.3.

```
// siees.cpp

#include <windows.h>
#include <iostream.h>

void main()
{
   char s[1000];
   DWORD result;

   result = ExpandEnvironmentStrings("%path%",
      s, 1000);
   if (result == 0)
   {
      cout << "Error: " << GetLastError() << endl;
      return;
   }
   cout << s << endl;
}
```

Listing 13.3
Using the **ExpandEnvironmentString** function

The function accepts a string containing one or more environment variable names wrapped in "%" characters, just as you would reference the variable in a batch file. When the function returns, the buffer is filled with all of the values for the variables requested.

ExpandEnvironmentStrings — *Retrieves environment variable values*

```
DWORD ExpandEnvironmentStrings(
    LPCTSTR envVars,
    LPTSTR buffer,
    DWORD bufferLen)
```

envVars	String containing the environment values to expand.
buffer	The buffer that will hold the returned values.
bufferLen	The length of the buffer.

Returns the size of the returned string, or zero on error.

If an environment variable is not found, it is not expanded. It is copied into the buffer in its original form. Otherwise, the buffer contains the value of the requested environment variable. The DWORD value returned by the function will be zero if an error occurred during execution.

The **GetEnvironmentVariable** function is equivalent to the **ExpandEnvironmentStrings** function, but expands only one variable at a time.

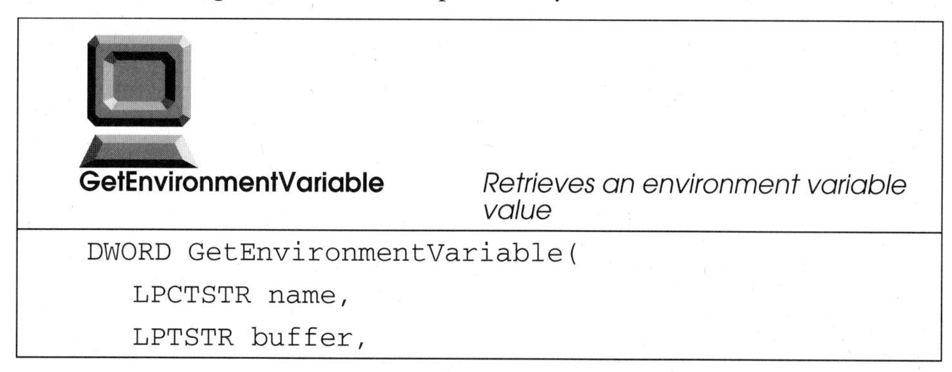

GetEnvironmentVariable — *Retrieves an environment variable value*

```
DWORD GetEnvironmentVariable(
    LPCTSTR name,
    LPTSTR buffer,
```

```
    DWORD bufferLen)
```

name	String containing the environment variable to get.
buffer	The buffer that will hold the returned value.
bufferLen	The length of the buffer.

Returns the size of the returned string, or zero on error.

It is also possible to set environment strings using the **SetEnvironment-Variable** function.

SetEnvironmentVariable	*creates or modifies an environment variable*

```
BOOL SetEnvironmentVariable(
    LPTSTR variableName,
    LPTSTR newValue)
```

variableName	The name of the variable to create or change
newValue	The new value for the variable

Returns TRUE on success, FALSE on failure and sets GetLastError.

Pass a new or existing variable name into the **variableName** parameter. Pass the new value into the **newValue** parameter. A NULL value for **newValue** will delete an existing variable.

13.4 Shutting Down the System

It is possible to log the current user off, reboot the system, or shut down the system, from within a program. There are many special situations where these capabilities prove useful. For example, you might want a program to run and then log off the current user when it is done. Then, by locking the screen, you can walk away from the machine and know that it will make itself available to other users upon completion of the program. Listing 13.4 demonstrates how to log off the current user.

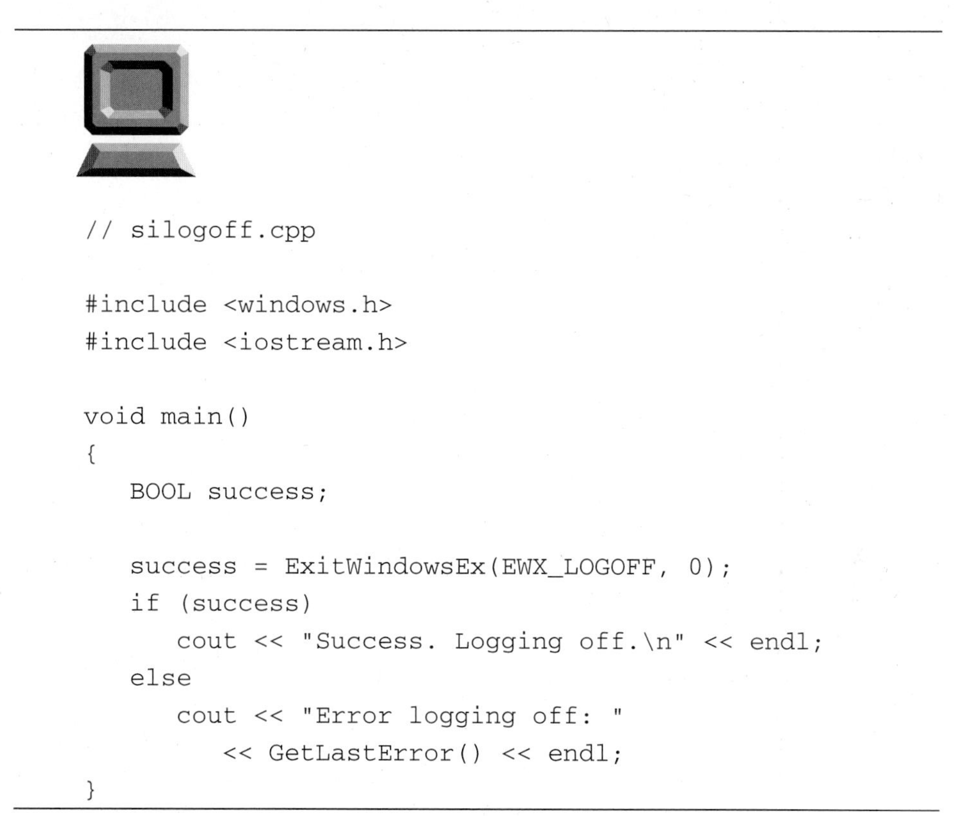

```
// silogoff.cpp

#include <windows.h>
#include <iostream.h>

void main()
{
   BOOL success;

   success = ExitWindowsEx(EWX_LOGOFF, 0);
   if (success)
      cout << "Success. Logging off.\n" << endl;
   else
      cout << "Error logging off: "
         << GetLastError() << endl;
}
```

Listing 13.4
Logging off the system

ExitWindowsEx	*Logs off or reboots the system*

`BOOL ExitWindowsEx(`
`   UINT options,`
`   DWORD reserved)`	

options	Tells the function what to do.
reserved	Ignored
Returns TRUE on success	

By passing different constants into **ExitWindowsEx**, you can cause it to shutdown and reboot the system as well. Listing 13.5 shows how to reboot the system.

```
// sireboot.cpp

#include <windows.h>
#include <iostream.h>
#include <process.h>

void HandleError(char *s)
{
   cout << "Error in " << s << endl;
   cout << "Error code = " << GetLastError()
      << endl;
   exit(1);
}

BOOL EnablePrivilege(LPTSTR privilege)
{
   BOOL success;
   HANDLE token;
   LUID luid;
   TOKEN_PRIVILEGES tokenPrivileges;

   // Get token for this process
   success = OpenProcessToken(GetCurrentProcess(),
      TOKEN_ADJUST_PRIVILEGES | TOKEN_QUERY,
      &token);
   if (!success)
   {
```

Listing 13.5
Rebooting the system (Page 1 of 4)

```
        HandleError("OpenProcessToken");
        return FALSE;
    }

    // Gets the value for a privilege
    success = LookupPrivilegeValue(0, privilege,
        &luid);
    if (!success)
    {
        HandleError("LookupPrivilegeValue");
        return FALSE;
    }

    // Enable the privilege
    tokenPrivileges.PrivilegeCount = 1;
    tokenPrivileges.Privileges[0].Luid = luid;
    tokenPrivileges.Privileges[0].Attributes =
        SE_PRIVILEGE_ENABLED;
    success = AdjustTokenPrivileges(token, FALSE,
        &tokenPrivileges, 0, 0, 0);
    // Always returns true, so check GetLastError
    if (GetLastError() != ERROR_SUCCESS)
    {
        HandleError("AdjustTokenPrivileges");
        return FALSE;
    }
    return TRUE;
}

BOOL DisablePrivilege(LPTSTR privilege)
{
    BOOL success;
    HANDLE token;
    LUID luid;
```

Listing 13.5
Rebooting the system (Page 2 of 4)

```
    TOKEN_PRIVILEGES tokenPrivileges;

    // Get tokens for this process
    success = OpenProcessToken(GetCurrentProcess(),
       TOKEN_ADJUST_PRIVILEGES | TOKEN_QUERY,
       &token);
    if (!success)
    {
       HandleError("OpenProcessToken");
       return FALSE;
    }

    // Gets the value for a privilege
    success = LookupPrivilegeValue(0, privilege,
       &luid);
    if (!success)
    {
       HandleError("LookupPrivilegeValue");
       return FALSE;
    }

    // Disable the privilege
    tokenPrivileges.PrivilegeCount = 1;
    tokenPrivileges.Privileges[0].Luid = luid;
    // disable the privilege
    tokenPrivileges.Privileges[0].Attributes = 0;
    success = AdjustTokenPrivileges(token, FALSE,
       &tokenPrivileges, 0, 0, 0);
    // Always returns true, so...
    if (GetLastError() != ERROR_SUCCESS)
    {
       HandleError("AdjustTokenPrivileges");
       return FALSE;
    }
```

Listing 13.5
Rebooting the system (Page 3 of 4)

```
        return TRUE;
    }

    void main()
    {
        BOOL success;

        if (EnablePrivilege(SE_SHUTDOWN_NAME))
        {
            success = ExitWindowsEx(EWX_REBOOT, 0);
            if (success)
                cout << "Success. Shutting down shortly."
                    << endl;
            else
                HandleError("Shutting down");
        }
        DisablePrivilege(SE_SHUTDOWN_NAME);
    }
```

Listing 13.5
Rebooting the system (Page 4 of 4)

To reboot the system, you must enable the shutdown privilege. The **EnablePrivilege** and **DisablePrivilege** functions handle the enabling and disabling of the SE_SHUTDOWN_NAME privilege required to reboot the system. See Section 10.7 for details. If the user running the code is able to gain the shutdown privilege, then the **ExitWindowsEx** function will succeed and the system will reboot. It is also possible to shut down the system rather than reboot it using the EWX_SHUTDOWN constant.

The **InitiateSystemShutdown** function performs a system shutdown as well, but uses an intermediate dialog that warns the current user of the impending loss of service. This function can also be revoked using the **AbortSystemShutdown** function. If you call the abort function before the shutdown timer has expired, then the shutdown operation will be canceled. Listings 13.6 and 13.7 demonstrate the use of these two functions. These are code fragments: Use them in place of the **main** function in Listing 13.5.

```
void main()
{
   BOOL success;

   if (EnablePrivilege(SE_SHUTDOWN_NAME))
   {
      success = InitiateSystemShutdown(0,
         "Shutting Down", 30, FALSE, FALSE);
      if (success)
         cout << "Success. Shutting down shortly."
            << endl;
      else
         HandleError("InitiateSystemShutdown");
   }
   DisablePrivilege(SE_SHUTDOWN_NAME);
}
```

Listing 13.6
Initiating a system shutdown. Replace the main function in Listing 13.5 with this code

```
void main()
{
   BOOL success;

   if (EnablePrivilege(SE_SHUTDOWN_NAME))
   {
```

Listing 13.7
Aborting a system shutdown. Replace the main function in Listing 13.5 with this code (Page 1 of 2)

```
            success = AbortSystemShutdown(0);
            if (success)
               cout << "Success. Shut down canceled."
                  << endl;
            else
               HandleError("AbortSystemShutdown");
         }
         DisablePrivilege(SE_SHUTDOWN_NAME);
      }
```

Listing 13.7
Aborting a system shutdown. Replace the main function in Listing 13.5 with this code (Page 2 of 2)

The **InitiateSystemShutdown** function accepts several parameters. The **machineName** parameter indicates the name of the machine to shutdown. If you want to shut down the current machine, pass a null string and enable the SE_SHUTDOWN_NAME privilege. If you want to shut down a remote machine, pass the network name of the machine into this parameter and enable the SE_REMOTE_SHUTDOWN_NAME privilege. See Section 10.7 for details on privileges.

InitiateSystemShutdown *Shuts down the system*

```
BOOL InitiateSystemShutdown(
   LPTSTR machineName,
   LPTSTR message,
   DWORD timer,
   BOOL forceAppsClosed,
   BOOL reboot)
```

machineName	The name of the machine to shut down.
message	The message to display to the user
timer	The length of time to display the message

forceAppsClosed	Causes system to force applications to close.
reboot	If true, system reboots after shutdown
Returns TRUE on success	

The **message** parameter contains the message that you want to display to the user warning of the impending shutdown. The **timer** parameter indicates the amount of time that the message will remain on the screen. If the timer value is zero, no message appears. The **forceAppsClosed** parameter causes any uncooperative applications to be forced closed so that the shutdown operation can proceed to completion. The **reboot** parameter causes the system to automatically reboot after the shutdown.

While the shutdown dialog is on the screen, it is possible to abort the shutdown using the **AbortSystemShutdown** function. This function accepts a machine name just as **InitiateSystemShutdown** does, and also requires that the appropriate privileges be obtained.

AbortSystemShutdown	*Aborts a system shutdown*
`BOOL AbortSystemShutdown(` `LPTSTR machineName)`	
machineName	The name of the machine to abort shutdown on.
Returns TRUE on success	

DYNAMIC LINK LIBRARIES

14

Dynamic Link Libraries, or DLLs, give your applications an extra level of modularity. They also make the operating system extensible to some extent. Many of Windows' operating system features are supplied in DLLs rather than being embedded in the system. You can extend the operating system yourself by creating your own DLLs.

In this chapter you will learn about the design and implementation of dynamic link libraries. You will also learn about the advantages and disadvantages of the two different ways to link DLL code to an application.

Compatibility Note: All of the code in this chapter works identically in Windows NT and Windows 95.

14.1 The Possibilities

Dynamic Link Libraries give you a way to break up an application into separate modules. An application designed using DLLs contains the normal EXE file, but the executable finds and links to one or more external binary object files at runtime. This architecture opens up several possibilities:

- Since the DLL is a separate and completely stand-alone entity, you can have one group of programmers independently develop a DLL while another group works on the application. The only connection needed between the two groups is a header file that defines the function prototypes for the DLL functions. If the DLL needs to change, you do not have to recompile the application. Just swap the old DLL file for a new one.

- You can extend the operating system by creating and publishing a DLL and a header file that describes it. Other programmers can use the DLL without having access to the source code. For example, the compressed file handling capabilities described in Chapter 2 come from their own DLL called LZ32.DLL.
- You can make certain portions of an application replaceable. For example, you might put language-dependent features of a program in a DLL so that you can swap DLLs to create multi-language distributions. Or you might put device-dependent features in a DLL so that you can ship different DLLs to different clients without changing the entire application.

DLLs are extremely easy to create. You will find yourself using them frequently to modularize your code once you understand them.

14.2 Overview

Figure 14.1 shows the difference between a normal executable and an executable that uses dynamic link libraries.

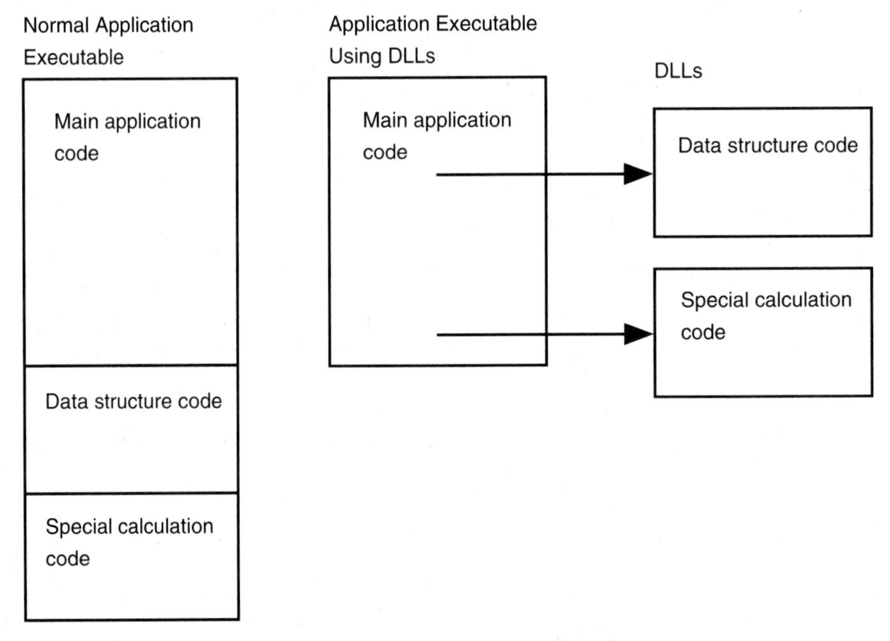

Figure 14.1
A normal executable compared to an executable that uses DLLs. The normal application contains all object code in its EXE. The DLL application links to the DLLs at runtime.

Any application that you write in Windows actually uses DLLs without your really being aware of it. For example, a normal MFC program of any size links to, among other things, KERNEL32.DLL, USER32.DLL, ADVAPI32.DLL, COMDLG32.DLL, GDI32.DLL, WINSPOOL.DLL, OLE32.DLL, SHELL32.DLL, and so on. As you can see, Windows uses DLLs quite extensively. You can find all of Windows' DLLs in the `system32` directory.

DLLs are popular because they have a number of important advantages:

1. You can change a DLL without recompiling applications. For example, suppose it was decided that NETAPI32.DLL contained a serious flaw. You could obtain and load a new DLL for it onto your machine and nothing else would have to change. The next time you run an application, the application would use the new DLL.
2. DLLs save a tremendous amount of disk space. For example, NETAPI32.DLL consumes 250K of disk space. However, it only consumes that disk space once. There might be 20 applications on your hard disk that use NETAPI32.DLL, and if it weren't for DLLs they would all have to contain their own personal copy of that object code at a cost of about five meg of disk space. When you consider that the `system32` directory contains over 150 DLL files used by potentially hundreds of applications, that is a lot of disk space being saved.
3. The same savings seen in disk space also apply to memory when an application is running. If two running applications use NETAPI32.DLL, only one copy of the DLL needs to exist in memory.
4. DLLs let you add capabilities to the operating system. For example, the email capability of Windows exists in MAPI.DLL. Any application (for example, Microsoft Word) that wants to include an email interface uses MAPI to do it. Anyone can develop and distribute their own DLLs.
5. As a programmer you might want to create a graphics library, an advanced matrix manipulation library, or a statistics library, and sell it. DLLs give you the ideal way to do that. You ship the DLL, along with a header file that describes the interface to the functions. You also supply a LIB file that lets new programs link to the DLL when they are compiled. Programmers can then use the DLL seamlessly just like they use any other DLL.

There really are not any disadvantages to using a DLL. There is no noticeable overhead involved in calling a DLL function as compared to calling an internal function.

A DLL typically contains a suite of related functions. For example, the MAPI.DLL file contains a set of functions that form the messaging API for Windows. If you place a statistical library in a DLL, then all of the functions have to do with statistics. The functions can be independent of one another, or they can work together sharing global variables for fast intercommunication. You can get a good feeling for DLL design by looking at DLL header files in the `mstools\h` or the `msvc\include` directory.

14.3 Creating a Simple DLL

DLLs share with RPCs (see Chapter 8) a certain amount of startup complexity. That is, the first time you see them it all seems complicated because there are several different and unfamiliar pieces needed to make the system work. The goal of this section is to show you how easy it is to compile and run the simplest possible DLL. The next section explains how the program and DLL work together.

The goal of the DLL presented in this section and the next is simple: The DLL contains one function called **MultiHonk** that accepts one integer parameter. The function beeps. If you pass it a 3 it beeps three times. It takes seven files to build the DLL and a test application for it, as shown in Listings 14.1 through 14.7.

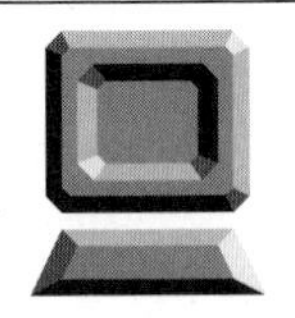

```
// snd.cpp

#include <windows.h>
```

Listing 14.1
The implementation of the MultiHonk function contained in the DLL (snd.cpp) (Page 1 of 2)

```
#include "snd.h"

void MultiHonk(DWORD iterations)
{
  UINT i;

  for (i=0; i<iterations; i++)
  {
    Beep(200, 50);
    Sleep(1000);
  }
}
```

Listing 14.1
The implementation of the MultiHonk function contained in the DLL (snd.cpp) (Page 2 of 2)

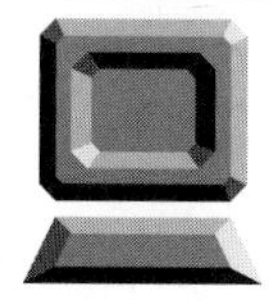

```
// snd.h

extern "C"
{
void MultiHonk(DWORD iterations);
}
```

Listing 14.2
The header file for the DLL (snd.h)

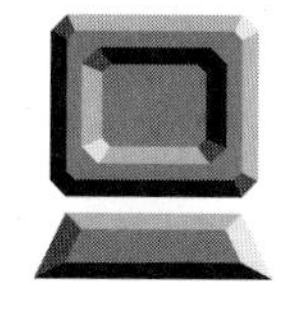

```
; snd.def
```

Listing 14.3
The def file for the DLL, identifying the name and exported function (snd.def) (Page 1 of 2)

```
LIBRARY snd

EXPORTS
   MultiHonk
```

Listing 14.3
The def file for the DLL, identifying the name and exported function (snd.def) (Page 2 of 2)

```
DLL=snd
NODEBUG=1

!include <ntwin32.mak>

$(DLL).dll: $(DLL).obj $(DLL).exp
   $(link) -dll $(ldebug) $(conlibs) \
     $(DLL).obj $(DLL).exp -out:$(DLL).dll

$(DLL).lib $(DLL).exp: $(DLL).def
   $(implib) -def:$(DLL).def \
     -machine:$(CPU) -out:$(DLL).lib

$(DLL).obj: $(DLL).cpp $(DLL).h
   $(cc) $(cflags) $(cdebug) \
     $(cvars) $(DLL).cpp
```

Listing 14.4
The makefile needed to compile Listings 14.1 through 14.3 and produce the snd.dll and snd.lib files required by an application that wants to use the DLL

```
// honker1.cpp

#include <windows.h>
#include <stdlib.h>
#include <iostream.h>

#include "sndlt.h"

VOID main(VOID)
{
  DWORD iterations;
  CHAR iterStr[100];

  cout << "Enter the number of beeps to produce: ";
  cin.getline(iterStr, 100);

  iterations=atoi(iterStr);

  // make the beeps
  MultiHonk(iterations);
}
```

Listing 14.5
A simple application that uses the DLL (honker1.cpp)

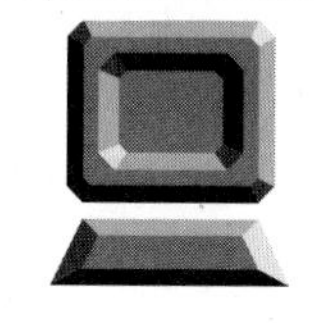

```
// sndlt.h
```

Listing 14.6
The header file that lets Listing 14.5 use the DLL (sndlt.h) (Page 1 of 2)

```
extern "C"
{
void MultiHonk(DWORD iterations);
}
```

Listing 14.6
The header file that lets Listing 14.5 use the DLL (sndlt.h) (Page 2 of 2)

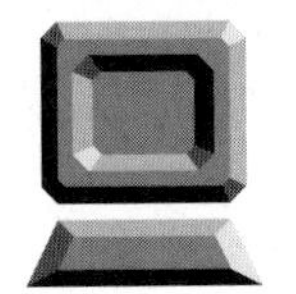

```
APP=honker1
NODEBUG=1

!include <ntwin32.mak>

$(APP).exe: $(APP).obj
   $(link) $(conlflags) $(ldebug) \
     $(conlibs) snd.lib $(APP).obj \
     -out:$(APP).exe

$(APP).obj: $(APP).cpp sndlt.h
   $(cc) $(cflags) $(cdebug) $(cvars) \
     $(APP).cpp
```

Listing 14.7
A makefile for the application

The DLL files consist of the code for the DLL function (Listing 14.1), the header file for the DLL (Listing 14.2), and a DEF file that describes to the library manager which functions this DLL is going to export to the applications that use it (Listing 14.3). DLLs do not necessarily export all of the functions that they contain. A DLL can contain internal "helper" functions that it does not make available to applications.

The makefile in Listing 14.4 (or the VC++ project file on the diskette) compiles and creates the DLL. It forms a normal OBJ file from `snd.cpp` using the normal compiler. The "library manager" ($(implib)) takes the DEF file an uses it to produce a LIB file and an EXP file. The normal linker uses the EXP file and the OBJ file to produce the DLL file.

Normally, you place Listings 14.1 through 14.4 in their own directory. Use nmake or VC++ to create the DLL. You can then put the DLL file either in the application's directory or somewhere in the PATH. You can copy the LIB file to the application's directory or to a standard LIB directory known to the compiler. The application also needs to be able to access `sndlt.h`, the header file that describes the DLL, either by copying it or placing it in a standard header directory that the compiler knows about. Note that right now `snd.h` and `sndlt.h` are the same, but they will generally differ, as described in later sections.

Listing 14.5 contains an application that uses the DLL. It includes the DLL's header file and then calls the DLL function like it would any other function. The makefile in Listing 14.7 compiles the application and links it to `snd.lib`. When you run the application, it will automatically look for the file `snd.dll` in the normal PATH and use it. If it cannot find `snd.dll`, the program will not execute.

Normally you would place Listings 14.5, 14.6, and 14.7 in their own application directory. For this simple experiment, it is probably easiest to then copy into that directory the files `snd.dll` and `snd.lib` from the DLL directory.

Figure 14.2 shows a diagram that explains the interrelationships between Listings 14.1 through 14.7.

When you run the application, it will look for the DLL file. If you hide `snd.dll` (either by moving, deleting, or renaming it), the program will fail and display a dialog advising you of the problem. If you copy `snd.dll` into the application's directory or your path so that the application can find it, then the application will ask you for a number and then it will call **MultiHonk** so it beeps that many times.

14.4 Understanding a Simple DLL

Looking at Listings 14.1 through 14.7, you can see that two of the files are completely normal. Listing 14.1 is the implementation of the DLL function, and it contains no surprises. Listing 14.5 contains the code for the application and it is normal as well.

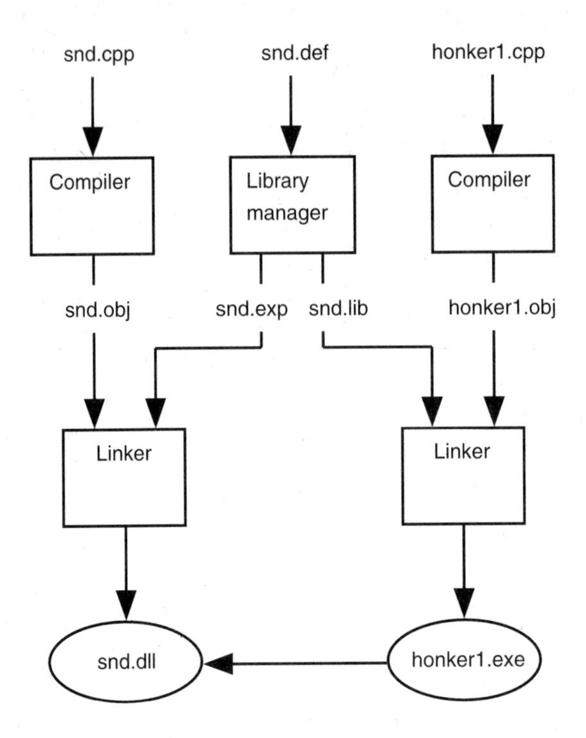

Figure 14.2
How Listings 14.1 through 14.7 work together to form a working DLL and application.

The header file in Listing 14.2 is easy to understand. It contains a prototype for **MultiHonk** that is standard. The prototype is wrapped in the `extern "C"` statement to tell the C++ compiler to turn off its name mangling. DLL files as shown here contain normal C functions.

The DEF file in Listing 14.3 is new. DLLs rely on the *Library Manager* to build the LIB file that the application needs in order to link to the DLL. The DEF file declares for the Library Manager the name of the library (snd) and the names of all of the functions that the DLL exports. The DLL file here exports one function named **MultiHonk**. Larger DLLs may export as many functions as they need. DLLs do not have to export all of the functions they contain. These unexported "helper" functions can be used by other functions in the DLL as usual. For each exported function in the DLL, create one line containing the function's name in the EXPORTS section of the DEF file.

The makefile in Listing 14.4 compiles Listing 14.1 normally to produce an OBJ file. Next the make file executes the Library Manager on the DEF file to produce an EXP file and a LIB file. The EXP file gets used by the linker when creating the actual DLL file. The LIB file gets used by the linker for any application that wants to link to the DLL.

The makefile in Listing 14.7 compiles Listing 14.5 to produce the application's OBJ file. The linker takes this OBJ along with the DLL's LIB file to create the application.

When you run the application, the operating system will hunt for any DLLs it needs. The OS looks in the application's load directory, the current directory, the winnt system32 directory, the winnt directory, and the PATH directories for DLLs. If it doesn't find a DLL it needs, the application displays a dialog box indicating the problem and terminates.

When you want to create a DLL of your own, take the following steps:

1. Create a header file that prototypes and describes all of the functions in the DLL. *Make sure* you wrap all functions in this header file with `extern "C"` as seen in Listing 14.2. If you are using *load-time* linking without an entry-point function as is done here, then you can use this same header file in the application. If you are using *run-time* linking then you need to create a different header file for the application. See Section 14.5 for details.
2. Create the implementations for the DLL functions in a CPP file. This file should include the header file from step 1.
3. Create a DEF file. It needs a LIBRARY line to name the library and an EXPORTS section. Place the name of every function in the header file, one per line, in the EXPORTS section.
4. Create a makefile modeled after Listing 14.4.

Place all four of these files in their own directory and use nmake or VC++ to create the DLL. Make the DLL and LIB files available to any applications that need to use the DLL either by copying the files to the application's source directories or by copying them to standard directories known to the compiler and linker.

To create an application that uses the DLL, all that you need to do is include the DLL's header file into the application and link the application to the LIB file for the DLL. When the application runs it will automatically load and use the DLL file.

14.5 Load-time versus Run-time Linking

The above example uses what is called *load-time linking* to connect the DLL to the application. In load-time linking, the operating system automatically loads the DLL for the application as soon as the application starts. If the OS cannot find the necessary DLL, the application cannot run. You access almost all DLLs using load-time linking because it is easy and transparent. The application programmer needs to put nothing in the application's code to use the DLL.

Run-time linking gives the application a little more control. In run-time linking, the application tells the operating system when to load the DLL. The operating system then tells the application whether the DLL is available. If it is not, the application can decide how to deal with the problem.

Probably the best-known example of the use of run-time linking is the way Microsoft Word loads MAPI.DLL. MAPI is the messaging API and allows Word to support email features. If MAPI.DLL is missing, Word simply advises the user of the problem with a dialog box, disables its email menu options, and continues. If Word were written so that it used load-time linking with MAPI.DLL, then the user would be unable to run Word on machines that did not have MAPI.DLL.

Listings 14.8 through 14.10 show how to write and compile an application so that it uses run-time linking. Listing 14.8 does the same thing that Listing 14.5 does, but contains the code to perform the run-time linking. *The DLL file and directory do not have to change in any way to use run-time linking.* The DLL itself does not care whether the application uses load-time or run-time linking. Once you create a DLL, any application can use load-time or run-time linking on it interchangeably.

```
// honker2.cpp
```

Listing 14.8
An simple application that uses the DLL with run-time linking (honker2.cpp). Compare with Listing 14.5 (Page 1 of 3)

```
#include <windows.h>
#include <stdlib.h>
#include <iostream.h>

#include "sndrt.h"

VOID main(VOID)
{
  DWORD iterations;
  CHAR iterStr[100];
  CHAR modName[MAX_PATH];
  HINSTANCE sndHandle;

  cout << "Enter the number of beeps to produce: ";
  cin.getline(iterStr, 100);

  iterations=atoi(iterStr);

  // map snd.dll into process
  sndHandle=LoadLibraryEx("snd", NULL,
    0);

  if (sndHandle == NULL)
  {
    cerr << "Sorry, unable to use DLL." << endl;
    return;
  }
  else
  {
    // load function name with address mapped from
    // snd.dll
    MultiHonk=(void (*)(DWORD))GetProcAddress(
      sndHandle, "MultiHonk");

    if (MultiHonk == NULL)
```

Listing 14.8
An simple application that uses the DLL with run-time linking (honker2.cpp). Compare with Listing 14.5 (Page 2 of 3)

```
        {
          cerr
            << "Sorry, MultiHonk function not in DLL."
            << endl;
          // release the DLL
          FreeLibrary(sndHandle);
          return;
        }
        else
        {
          GetModuleFileName(sndHandle, modName,
            MAX_PATH);
          cout << "Using DLL: " << modName
            << endl;

          // make the beeps
          MultiHonk(iterations);
          // release the DLL
          FreeLibrary(sndHandle);
        }
      }
    }
```

Listing 14.8
An simple application that uses the DLL with run-time linking (honker2.cpp). Compare with Listing 14.5 (Page 3 of 3)

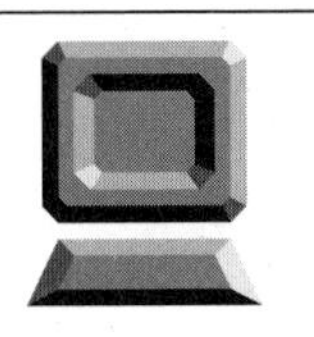

```
// sndrt.h

void (*MultiHonk)(DWORD iterations);
```

Listing 14.9
The header file needed for the application to use the DLL with run-time linking (sndrt.h)

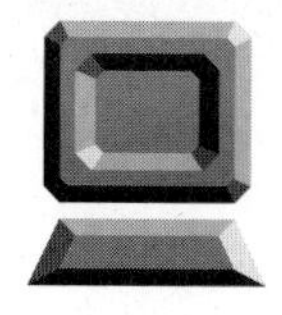

```
APP=honker2
NODEBUG=1

!include <ntwin32.mak>

$(APP).exe: $(APP).obj
   $(link) $(conlflags) $(ldebug) \
     $(conlibs) $(APP).obj -out:$(APP).exe

$(APP).obj: $(APP).cpp sndrt.h
   $(cc) $(cflags) $(cdebug) $(cvars) \
     $(APP).cpp
```

Listing 14.10
A makefile for the application using run-time linking

Listing 14.8 is somewhat longer than Listing 14.5 because an application that uses run-time linking must load the DLL itself. Listing 14.8 starts the process by calling the **LoadLibraryEx** function.

LoadLibraryEx	Loads the object code for a DLL and maps it into the application's address space

```
HINSTANCE LoadLibraryEx(
   LPCTSTR libraryFile,
   HANDLE file,
   DWORD flags)
```

libraryFile	The DLL to load. The function will automatically append ".dll"
file	Reserved. Must be NULL

flags	Indicates whether the entry point function should be called
Returns a handle to the DLL or 0 on error	

The **LoadLibraryEx** function loads the DLL. It accepts "snd" as the name of the DLL and appends ".dll" to it. It will search the directory that the application loaded from, the current directory, the winnt system32 and winnt directory, and all of the directories in the PATH in its attempt to find the DLL. If it cannot find the DLL file, it returns NULL. Listing 14.8 prints an error message and dies if the DLL is missing, but you will probably want to do something more elaborate in a production application.

The application's next step is to load the addresses of all of the functions needed in the DLL. Note that the header file in Listing 14.9 is very different from the header file in Listing 14.6. In Listing 14.9, the functions in the DLL are declared as pointers to functions. The application must then initialize these pointers before it can call any of the DLL's functions. There will be one pointer for each function in the DLL, and a line to initialize each pointer in the application. The **GetProcAddress** function returns the address of one function.

GetProcAddress	*Gets the address of one function from the DLL*
`FARPROC GetProcAddress( HMODULE module, LPCSTR funcName)`	
module	The handle to the DLL returned by **LoadLibraryEx**
funcName	The name of the function to look up
Returns the address of the function or 0 on error	

If the function does not exist in the DLL, then Listing 14.8 quits. Otherwise, the program calls **GetModuleFileName** simply to demonstrate it. The **GetModuleFileName** returns the name of the DLL file.

GetModuleFileName	*Gets the name of the DLL file*
`DWORD GetModuleFileName( HMODULE module, LPTSTR buffer, DWORD bufferLen)`	
module	The handle to the DLL returned by **LoadLibraryEx**
buffer	The buffer it will return the name in
bufferLen	The length of the buffer
Returns the length of the name in the buffer or 0 one error	

The call to **MultiHonk** in Listing 14.8 is anticlimactic. It looks just like a normal function call. The program then calls **FreeLibrary** to clean up and quits.

FreeLibrary	*Unmaps the DLL if nothing else is using it*
`BOOL FreeLibrary( HINSTANCE module)`	
module	The handle to the DLL returned by **LoadLibraryEx**
Returns TRUE on success	

As you can see, run-time linking is not particularly difficult. It simply requires you to load the DLL and map its functions manually rather than letting the operating system do it for you. Compiling the run-time linked version is identical to compiling the load-time linked version except that you do not have to link the code to the LIB file for the DLL.

You can run-time link to any existing or new DLL, because a DLL does not care whether it is load-time or run-time linked to the application. If you want to run-time link a DLL to one of your own applications, take the following steps:

1. Create a header file that declares each function in the DLL as a pointer to the function. You can normally look at the standard DLL header file and convert it to this form.
2. Modify the application so that it loads the DLL file manually and gets the address of each function in the DLL.
3. Free the DLL when it is no longer needed.

14.6 DLL Entry Points

A DLL can optionally contain a special function called the *entry point function*. This function is called automatically each time a new process loads or unloads the DLL and each time that an attached process creates or destroys a thread. Applications do not care whether or not a DLL contains an entry-point function. You do not have to modify either load-time or run-time linked applications to accommodate an entry point.

Entry-point functions exist primarily so that DLLs can properly initialize variables or data structures that are private to the processes or threads using the DLL. For example, if the DLL needs to maintain a separate copy of a certain data structure for each process that attaches, the entry point function is the place to perform the initialization. It is a bit like the constructor and destructor in a C++ class.

Listings 14.11 through 14.14 demonstrate the creation of an entry-point function.

```
// snd.cpp

#include <windows.h>

#include "snd.h"
```

Listing 14.11
The implementation of a DLL containing an entry-point function (snd.cpp)
(Page 1 of 3)

```
BOOL WINAPI SndEntryPoint(HINSTANCE dllHandle,
  DWORD reason, LPVOID situation)
{
  CHAR buf[80];

  switch(reason)
  {
    case DLL_PROCESS_ATTACH:
      if (situation)
        wsprintf(buf, "DLL statically loaded.");
      else
        wsprintf(buf, "DLL dynamically loaded.");
      break;

    case DLL_THREAD_ATTACH:
      wsprintf(buf, "New thread starting.");
      break;

    case DLL_PROCESS_DETACH:
      if (situation)
        wsprintf(buf, "DLL released by system.");
      else
        wsprintf(buf, "DLL released by program.");
      break;

    case DLL_THREAD_DETACH:
      wsprintf(buf, "Thread terminating.");
      break;

    default:
      return FALSE;
  }

  MessageBox(NULL, buf, "DLL Info",
    MB_OK | MB_ICONINFORMATION);
```

Listing 14.11
The implementation of a DLL containing an entry-point function (snd.cpp)
(Page 2 of 3)

```
    return TRUE;
  }

  void MultiHonk(DWORD iterations)
  {
    UINT i;

    for (i=0; i<iterations; i++)
    {
      Beep(200, 50);
      Sleep(1000);
    }
  }
```

Listing 14.11
The implementation of a DLL containing an entry-point function (snd.cpp)
(Page 3 of 3)

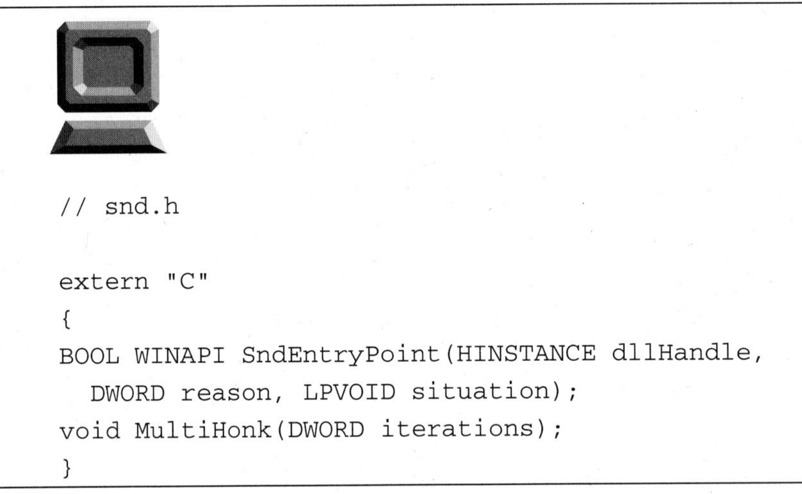

```
// snd.h

extern "C"
{
BOOL WINAPI SndEntryPoint(HINSTANCE dllHandle,
  DWORD reason, LPVOID situation);
void MultiHonk(DWORD iterations);
}
```

Listing 14.12
The header file for the DLL in Listing 14.11 (snd.h)

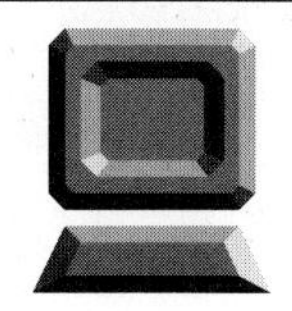

```
LIBRARY snd

EXPORTS
   MultiHonk
```

Listing 14.13
The DEF file for the DLL in Listing 14.11 (snd.def)

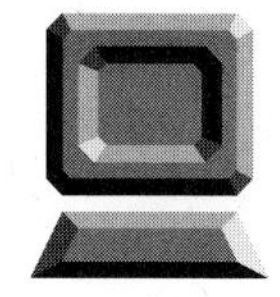

```
DLL=snd
ENTRY=SndEntryPoint
NODEBUG=1

!include <ntwin32.mak>

$(DLL).dll: $(DLL).obj $(DLL).exp
   $(link) -dll -entry:$(ENTRY)$(DLLENTRY) \
     $(ldebug) $(guilibs) $(DLL).obj \
     $(DLL).exp -out:$(DLL).dll

$(DLL).lib $(DLL).exp: $(DLL).def
   $(implib) -def:$(DLL).def \
     -machine:$(CPU) -out:$(DLL).lib

$(DLL).obj: $(DLL).cpp $(DLL).h
   $(cc) $(cflags) $(cdebug) $(cvars) \
     $(DLL).cpp
```

Listing 14.14
The makefile to create a DLL containing an entry point

If you create a new directory and compile the DLL file in Listings 14.11 through 14.14, you can use the file `snd.dll` with either `honker1.exe` or `honker2.exe`. You do not even have to recompile these applications. When you run them however, you will find that the DLLs display message boxes when the processes attach and detach the DLL to show that the entry point function is working. If you modify the applications so that they create and destroy threads, you will find that dialogs also appear when threads come and go.

Listing 14.11 contains the new function **SndEntryPoint**. This function can have any name, but it must follow the parameter prototype and internal structure shown in the example.

DLLEntryPoint	*Standard prototype for a DLL entry point function*

`BOOL WINAPI DllEntryPoint(`
`HINSTANCE module,`
`DWORD reason`
`LPVOID situation)`	

module	A handle to the DLL module
reason	enumerated type indicating why the function was called (process attachment, thread creation, etc.)
situation	Specifies whether the DLL was run-time (dynamically) or load-time (statically) loaded
You can return TRUE or FALSE through the function. If you return FALSE then the process attached to the DLL is told that the DLL failed	

The entry-point function in Listing 14.11 takes a standard approach and switches off of the **reason** parameter. It handles all four possible reasons:

DLL_PROCESS_ATTACH

DLL_THREAD_ATTACH

DLL_PROCESS_DETACH

DLL_THREAD_DETACH

In Listing 14.11, the code uses the **reason** and **situation** values to form a message that appears in a message box. In a real application you can do anything you like.

The value that the entry point function returns controls how the application calling the DLL responds. If you return FALSE, a load-time linked application will die. A run-time linked application will believe that the DLL loading failed, just as it would if the DLL file did not exist.

Note that the header file for the DLL in Listing 14.12 contains a prototype for the DLL function. The DLL header file that the application uses should not contain this function. Use the same header files seen in Listing 14.6 and 14.9 for the application. Also note that the makefile for the DLL has to declare the name of the entry-point function for the linker (see the diskette).

14.7 Memory Models

The simple DLL above uses no variables at all, either local or global. That makes the DLL simple and easy to understand, but it is not very realistic. A typical DLL needs to use memory. Local variables inside of functions are easy, because they work as expected. You have to think a little bit and plan carefully before you use global static or dynamic variables in a DLL however, because variables inside of DLLs work in slightly unexpected ways.

Let's say that you want to create a DLL that implements a stack data structure. The stack is to be created dynamically on the heap. This *sounds* simple, but DLLs allow you to create at least four different memory models for your simple stack DLL, as shown in Figure 14.3.

The implementation for the first configuration, where many processes can have zero or more stacks that are private to the process, is standard and the most easily created. Listings 14.15 through 14.18 show the files needed to implement this sort of stack DLL.

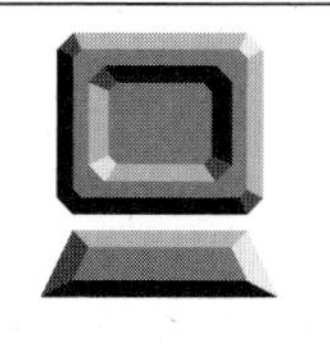

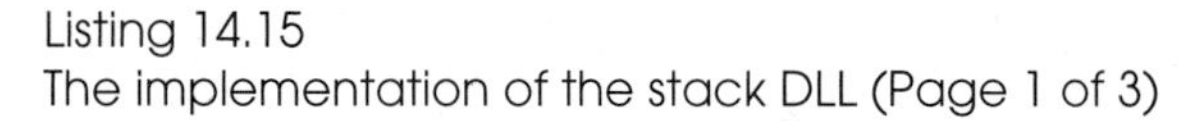

```
// stack.cpp
```

Listing 14.15
The implementation of the stack DLL (Page 1 of 3)

```
#include <windows.h>
#include "stack.h"

void init(stack *top)
{
  *top=0;
}

void push(stack *top, int value)
{
  stacknode *temp;

  temp = (stacknode *) GlobalAlloc(GPTR,
    sizeof stacknode);
  temp->data = value;
  temp->next = *top;
  *top = temp;
}

int pop(stack *top)
{
  stacknode *temp;
  int value;

  if (*top == 0)
    return 0;
  temp = *top;
  value = (*top)->data;
  *top = (*top)->next;
  delete temp;
  return value;
}

void destroy(stack *top)
{
```

Listing 14.15
The implementation of the stack DLL (Page 2 of 3)

```
    while (*top != 0);
      pop(top);
}
```

Listing 14.15
The implementation of the stack DLL (Page 3 of 3)

```
// stack.h

typedef struct _stacknode
{
   int data;
   struct _stacknode *next;
} stacknode, *stack;

extern "C"
{
   void init(stack *s);
   void push(stack *s, int i);
   int pop (stack *s);
   void destroy(stack *s);
}
```

Listing 14.16
The header file for the stack DLL

```
LIBRARY stack
```

Listing 14.17
The DEF file for the stack DLL (Page 1 of 2)

```
EXPORTS
   init
   push
   pop
   destroy
```

Listing 14.17
The DEF file for the stack DLL (Page 2 of 2)

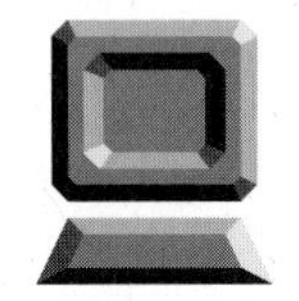

```
DLL=stack
NODEBUG=1

!include <ntwin32.mak>

$(DLL).dll: $(DLL).obj $(DLL).exp
   $(link) -dll $(ldebug) $(conlibs) \
     $(DLL).obj $(DLL).exp -out:$(DLL).dll

$(DLL).lib $(DLL).exp: $(DLL).def
   $(implib) -def:$(DLL).def \
     -machine:$(CPU) -out:$(DLL).lib

$(DLL).obj: $(DLL).cpp $(DLL).h
   $(cc) $(cflags) $(cdebug) \
     $(cvars) $(DLL).cpp
```

Listing 14.18
The makefile for the stack DLL

Given this structure for the DLL, each process can declare one or more stacks and call the **push** and **pop** functions as needed. Each process must call **init** before using the stack and **destroy** to clean up. The **push** and **pop** functions will allocate and deallocate memory on the heap. Any memory allocated by **GlobalAlloc** (see Chapter 15) will belong to the process that called **push**, so all of the stacks are completely independent and isolated.

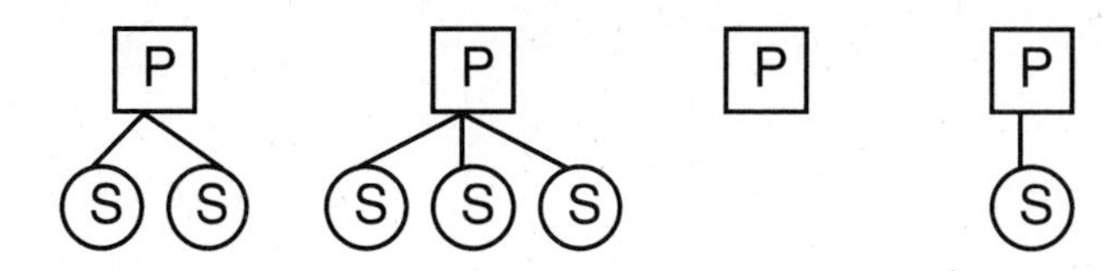

1. Each process using the DLL can create zero or more stacks for its own, private use

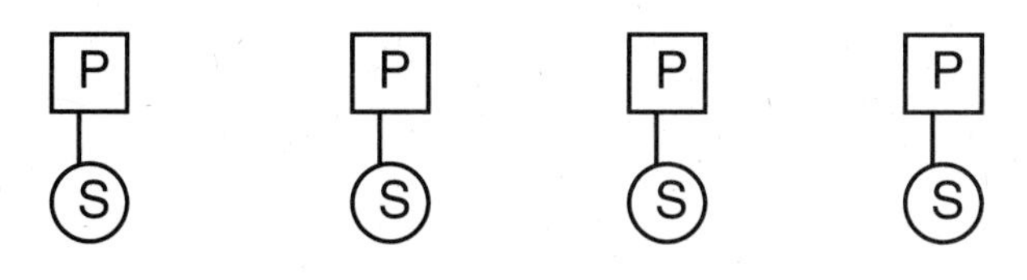

2. Each process automatically receives one private stack when it attaches to the DLL.

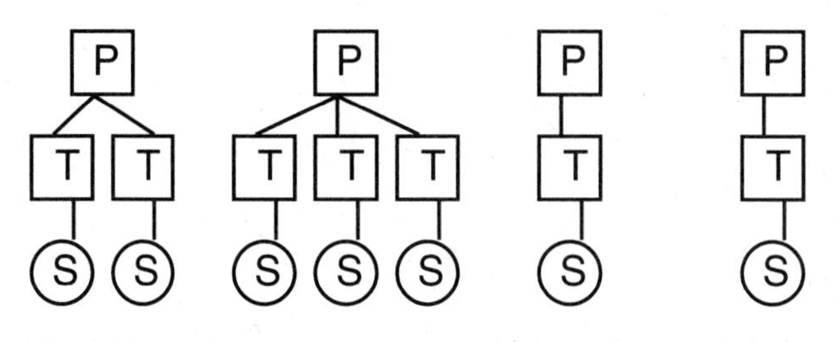

3. Each thread of each process automatically receives one private stack.

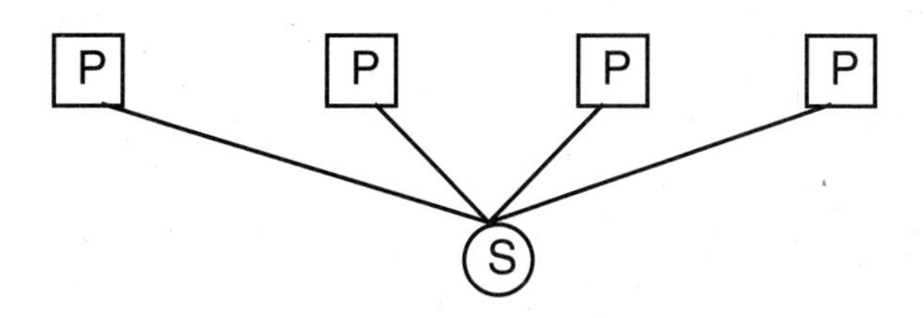

4. All processes share one global stack owned by the DLL.

Figure 14.3
Four possible memory configurations for stacks implemented in a DLL.

If you want the DLL to manage just one stack for each process that attaches to it, as shown in part 2 of Figure 14.3, then you should create a single global variable in the DLL itself. The DLL will create a new instance of that global variable for each process that attaches. Then you can use explicit **init** and **destroy** functions as shown previously, or you can use the entry point function in the DLL to do the initialization and destruction when the processes attach and detach. See Section 14.6 for information on entry-point functions. It would also be possible to create an array or linked list of stack pointers in the DLL to give each process multiple stacks.

If you want to give each thread its own stack, then you can use the thread-local-storage feature described in Chapter 5. When the process attaches, you let the entry point function create a new TLS location for it, and then whenever the process creates a new thread you let the DLL_THREAD_ATTACH case of the entry-point function initialize the stack and place a pointer to it in the TLS location for the thread.

Creating the last structure shown in Figure 14.3 is not easy if you want to use dynamic memory. Whenever you call **GlobalAlloc** in the DLL, the memory allocated is owned by the process that called the DLL. This is troublesome for a global stack because the different threads cannot point into each other's address spaces. The only possible solution is to create shared memory with a File Mapping (see Chapter 2), and then use that shared memory for the stack nodes. Unfortunately, shared memory is treated as an array of elements, so you will have to implement your own memory allocation functions *and* embed synchronization mechanisms (see Chapter 6) in them and the stack code to prevent the different processes from stepping on each other.

If you want to create normal global variables that are shared by all processes, and if you are willing to forget about sharing dynamic variables, then that is easy. Add the following to your DEF file:

```
SECTIONS
    .bss READ WRITE SHARED ; unitialized globals
    .data READ WRITE SHARED ; initialized globals
```

The first line handles uninitialized globals and makes them shared among all processes. The second line does the same for initialized globals.

14.8 Conclusion

DLLs give you an extremely effective modularization tool that has no significant disadvantages. You will find yourself using them frequently once you get used to them.

If you want your DLL to be able to emulate the **GetLastError** behavior of API calls, see Section 15.6. See also exception handling in Section 15.5.

MISCELLANEOUS

15

This chapter describes six other system services that are important to any application developer working in Windows:

1. The registry
2. The event log
3. Memory management
4. Time
5. The Error handler
6. Structured Exception handling

All of these topics are small, straightforward, and easy to understand.

Compatibility Note: All of the code in this chapter, with the exception of Section 15.2, works identically in Windows NT and Windows 95. Section 15.2 will not work in Windows 95.

15.1 Registry

The registry is a single, well-organized location that stores *all* system, application, and user configuration information. If you are a former Windows 3.1 programmer, then you are familiar with INI files. All of that information is now in the registry. If you are a UNIX programmer you are familiar with the use of "dot files" to store application and user information, along with a variety of different text files to store system information. In Windows, all of this information is centralized in the registry.

Normally a user or administrator does not manipulate the registry directly, although this sort of manipulation is possible using the Registry Editor. Instead, applications either act as editors for certain sections of the registry, or use the registry as a storage area for configuration information they need to save from run to run. For example, the User Manager is nothing but a large editor for the user information section in the registry.

The registry will initially seem confusing because it already contains thousands of entries, most of which have cryptic names. The overall structure is easy to understand, however: The registry works just like a directory tree. A directory *tree* consists of *directories* which can contain other directories or *files*. Files have a name and their contents. A registry tree is called a *hive*. It contains *keys*. Keys can hold other keys or *values*. Values emulate variables more than they do files: they have a name and contain data of some specific type. See Figure 15.1. You reference specific keys and values using paths that look just like file paths, using the "\" character as a separator.

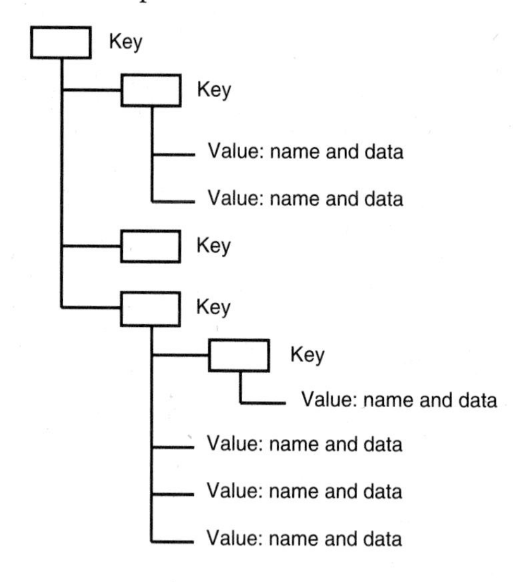

Figure 15.1
Registry hives mirror the structure of directory trees exactly.

You can view the registry directly using the Registry Editor (`regedt 32.exe` in NT, `regedit.exe` in Windows 95). You will see a display that looks remarkably similar to that of the File Manager, right down to many of the menus and options. The Registry Editor always lets you view four main hives (think of them like you do drives in the File Manager):

- HKEY_CURRENT_USER: Profile information for the current user, such as Program Manager groups and screen colors
- HKEY_USERS: Profile information for all users with accounts on this machine
- HKEY_LOCAL_MACHINE: Information about this machine and its applications
- HKEY_CLASSES_ROOT: Information used by the File Manager and OLE to open applications. For example, this section associates different file extensions with applications.

The registry overview in the Win32 help file contains a good description of what these hives contain, and what the main sections inside of them do. The file `regentry.hlp` in the Resource Kit contains detailed explanations of common registry keys and values.

When you are creating an application, there are typically only three things that it will need to do with the registry:

1. Add keys and values to the registry
2. Modify values
3. Read values previously stored

Some keys and values that the application creates will be static. For example, when you install an application you will typically have the installation program create a key in the registry for the application itself. This key is static in that it never changes. Under this key will go other application keys and values. The installation program will typically create static values like the version number, installation date, owner's name, and so on inside the application key. All of this information normally goes in HKEY_LOCAL_MACHINE.

Other values that the application places in the registry will change frequently. For example, you might store the current workspace configuration in the registry each time a user quits the application. To do this properly, you will create appropriate keys and values in each user's hive, typically by working through the HKEY_CURRENT_USER hive.

You can store just about anything you like anywhere you like in the registry. However, you *should* store any permanent application information in the

HKEY_LOCAL_MACHINE\Software key. Any user-specific configuration information for the application should appear in the HKEY_CURRENT_USER\Software key. Create a new key for your application. Or even better, create a new key containing your company's name and then create different application keys inside of it like Microsoft does. Then build whatever structure you like within that key.

Depending on what you listen to, a value can have five (as far as the Registry Editor is concerned) or 10 (as far as the **RegSetValueEx** API function is concerned) different types. The Registry Editor will let you create the following five types through its Add Value option:

REG_BINARY	Binary data
REG_DWORD	32-bit value
REG_EXPAND_SZ	Environment variable references such as %PATH%
REG_MULTI_SZ	Null-terminated string array like argv
REG_SZ	Null-terminated string

The **RegSetValueEx** function allows the following ten types:

REG_BINARY	Binary data
REG_DWORD	32-bit value
REG_DWORD_LITTLE_ENDIAN	DWORD MSB last, same as DWORD
REG_DWORD_BIG_ENDIAN	DWORD MSB first
REG_EXPAND_SZ	Environment variable references such as %PATH%
REG_LINK	A Unicode symbolic link
REG_MULTI_SZ	Null-terminated string array like argv
REG_NONE	Undefined
REG_RESOURCE_LIST	Resource list for a device-driver
REG_SZ	Null-terminated string

You should reserve the registry for short values. Anything big (large chunks of text, bitmaps, etc.) should be stored in a separate file. Use the registry to store the name of those files.

Listing 15.1 shows how to create a new key in the registry. Start up the Registry Editor (`regedt32.exe` in NT, `regedit.exe` in Windows 95) and look in the "HKEY_CURRENT_USER\Software" key. Compile and run Listing 15.1, and refresh the registry display if the editor is not in auto-refresh mode. You will see that it contains a new key named "Interface Technologies."

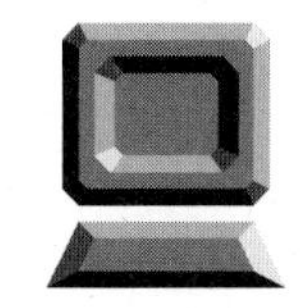

```
// addkey.cpp

#include <windows.h>
#include <iostream.h>

VOID main(VOID)
{
  LONG ret;
  HKEY keyHandle;
  DWORD disposition;

  // add a key for the new vendor
  ret=RegCreateKeyEx(HKEY_CURRENT_USER,
    "Software\\Interface Technologies",
    0, NULL, REG_OPTION_VOLATILE,
    KEY_ALL_ACCESS, NULL, &keyHandle,
    &disposition);
  if (ret != ERROR_SUCCESS)
  {
    cerr << "Unable to create key"
      << endl;
```

Listing 15.1
Adding a key to the registry (Page 1 of 2)

```
        return;
      }

      switch (disposition)
      {
        case REG_CREATED_NEW_KEY:
          cout << "New key added to registry."
            << endl;
          break;

        case REG_OPENED_EXISTING_KEY:
          cout << "Existing key opened."
            << endl;
          break;

        default:
          cout << "Key disposition unknown."
            << endl;
      }

      // close the new key
      ret=RegCloseKey(keyHandle);
      if (ret != ERROR_SUCCESS)
      {
        cerr << "Unable to close new key"
          << endl;
        return;
      }
    }
```

Listing 15.1
Adding a key to the registry (Page 2 of 2)

Listing 15.1 starts by calling the **RegCreateKeyEx** function to create a new key.

RegCreateKeyEx *Creates or opens a key in the registry*

```
LONG RegCreateKeyEx(
    HKEY keyHandle,
    LPCTSTR keyName,
    DWORD reserved,
    LPTSTR className,
    DWORD options,
    REGSAM sam,
    LPSECURITY_ATTRIBUTES security,
    PHKEY resultHandle,
    LPDWORD disposition)
```

Parameter	Description
keyHandle	Handle to an open key or one of the four HKEYs
keyName	The key to create
reserved	Reserved. Pass 0.
className	The class of the key. Any string
options	Specify REG_OPTION_VOLATILE or REG_OPTION_NON_VOLATILE
sam	Access mask. See Section 10.5.10 for values
security	Security descriptor for the key. See Chapter 10
resultHandle	Handle to the new or opened key
disposition	Returns REG_CREATED_NEW_KEY or REG_OPENED_EXISTING_KEY

Returns ERROR_SUCCESS on success

The call to **RegCreateKeyEx** in Listing 15.1 creates the key "HKEY_CURRENT_USER\Software\Interface Technologies," or opens a handle to it if it already exists. The code creates it as a volatile key, which means that the next time you reboot your machine the key will disappear (a great way to test things). If you want to create a permanent key then create it as non-volatile. The call to **RegCreateKeyEx** also specifies KEY_ALL_ACCESS. If you as a user do not have sufficient privilege in Windows NT to create keys on your machine, the call will fail here. See Chapter 10 for details on security. When the function finishes it returns a handle to the new or existing key, along with a disposition flag that tells you whether the key is new or old.

Having created the key, the program closes the handle and quits.

RegCloseKey	*Closes a key handle*
`LONG RegCloseKey(` `   HKEY keyHandle)`	
keyHandle	Handle to an open key
Returns ERROR_SUCCESS on success	

Listing 15.2 shows how to add a value to a key. Any key can hold values and other keys, just like any directory can hold files and other directories. When you run Listing 15.2 and refresh the Registry Editor, you will find that the Registry contains a new key called "HKEY_CURRENT_USER\Software\Interface Technologies\Sample Application," and inside of it is a value named "sampval" of type REG_SZ (a string) with the value "This is a sample string value." You change a value simply by setting it again.

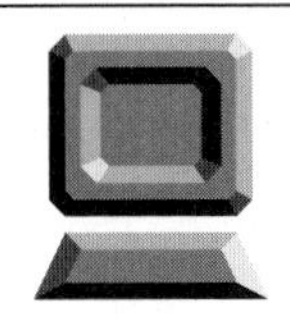

```
// addvalue.cpp
```

Listing 15.2
Adding a value to the registry (Page 1 of 3)

```
#include <windows.h>
#include <iostream.h>
#include <string.h>

VOID main(VOID)
{
  LONG ret;
  HKEY keyHandle1, keyHandle2;
  DWORD disposition;

  // add or open a key for the vendor
  ret=RegCreateKeyEx(HKEY_CURRENT_USER,
    "Software\\Interface Technologies",
    0, NULL, REG_OPTION_VOLATILE,
    KEY_ALL_ACCESS, NULL, &keyHandle1,
    &disposition);
  if (ret != ERROR_SUCCESS)
  {
    cerr << "Unable to create key 1"
      << endl;
    return;
  }

  // add or open a key for the app
  ret=RegCreateKeyEx(keyHandle1,
    "Sample Application",
    0, NULL, REG_OPTION_VOLATILE,
    KEY_ALL_ACCESS, NULL, &keyHandle2,
    &disposition);
  if (ret != ERROR_SUCCESS)
  {
    cerr << "Unable to create key 1"
      << endl;
    return;
  }
```

Listing 15.2
Adding a value to the registry (Page 2 of 3)

```
    // Add a new value to the registry
    char *val = "This is a sample string value";
    ret=RegSetValueEx(keyHandle2, "sampval",
      0, REG_SZ, (CONST BYTE *) val,
      strlen(val)+1);

    // close the keys
    ret=RegCloseKey(keyHandle1);
    ret=RegCloseKey(keyHandle2);
}
```

Listing 15.2
Adding a value to the registry (Page 3 of 3)

Listing 15.2 starts like Listing 15.1. It calls **RegCreateKeyEx** to create or open keys (You can use **RegOpenKeyEx** to open a key if you know it exists or want to test for existence). It then calls **RegSetValueEx** to set the value. If the value does not exist, the function creates it. If it does it changes it.

RegSetValueEx *Sets a value*

```
LONG RegSetValueEx(
   HKEY hkey,
   LPCTSTR valueName,
   DWORD reserved,
   DWORD type,
   CONST BYTE * data,
   DWORD dataLen)
```

keyHandle	Handle to an open key
valueName	The name of the value
reserved	Reserved. Pass 0
type	The type of the value
data	The data for the value

dataLen	The length of the data. Be sure to include the null character in strings
Returns ERROR_SUCCESS on success	

In Listing 15.2 the code creates a value of type REG_SZ with a string value.

You can read values from the registry using the **RegQueryValueEx** function.

RegQueryValueEx	*Gets a value*
`LONG RegQueryValueEx( HKEY keyHandle, LPTSTR valueName, LPDWORD lpdwReserved, LPDWORD type, LPBYTE data, LPDWORD lpcbData)`	
keyHandle	Handle to an open key
valueName	The name of the value to query
reserved	Reserved. Pass 0
type	Returned type of the value. Pass address
data	Returned data for the value. Pass array or buffer address
dataLen	Size of the buffer. Pass address.
Returns ERROR_SUCCESS on success	

The **RegQueryValueEx** function returns the value and its length along with its type.

Like a directory tree, there are certain cases where it is useful to traverse the registry tree. For example, you might want to hunt through the registry for a particular value. Listing 15.3 demonstrates the process. It enumerates all the Program Manager's groups stored in the registry under the current user's profile. First it enumerates the subkeys of the "HKEY_CURRENT_USER\Control Panel" key, and then it enumerates the values of the "HKEY_CURRENT_USER\Control Panel\Desktop" key.

```
// showgrps.cpp

#include <windows.h>
#include <iostream.h>

VOID main(VOID)
{
  LONG ret;
  HKEY keyHandle;
  CHAR subKeyName[80];
  DWORD subKeyNameSize;
  CHAR valueName[80];
  DWORD valueNameSize;
  BYTE value[80];
  DWORD valueSize;
  DWORD n;
  FILETIME lastUpdate;

  // open the key to enumerate
  ret=RegOpenKeyEx(HKEY_CURRENT_USER,
    "Control Panel", 0,
    KEY_ENUMERATE_SUB_KEYS,
    &keyHandle);
  if (ret != ERROR_SUCCESS)
  {
    cerr << "Unable to open subkey"
      << endl;
```

Listing 15.3
A program that traverses a portion of the registry tree and dumps the values it finds there (Page 1 of 4)

```
    return;
  }

  cout << "As subkeys:" << endl << endl;

  // show all the subkeys
  n=0;
  do
  {
    subKeyNameSize=80;
    ret=RegEnumKeyEx(keyHandle, n,
      subKeyName, &subKeyNameSize,
      NULL, NULL, NULL, &lastUpdate);
    if (ret == ERROR_SUCCESS)
    {
      cout << subKeyName << endl;
      n++;
    }
  } while (ret == ERROR_SUCCESS);

  cout << endl << "There are " << n
    << " groups listed." << endl << endl;

  // close the key
  ret=RegCloseKey(keyHandle);
  if (ret != ERROR_SUCCESS)
  {
    cerr << "Unable to close subkey"
      << endl;
    return;
  }

  // open the key to enumerate
  ret=RegOpenKeyEx(HKEY_CURRENT_USER,
    "Control Panel\\Desktop",
```

Listing 15.3
A program that traverses a portion of the registry tree and dumps the values it finds there (Page 2 of 4)

```
      0, KEY_QUERY_VALUE,
      &keyHandle);
    if (ret != ERROR_SUCCESS)
    {
      cerr << "Unable to open subkey"
        << endl;
      return;
    }

    cout << "As values:" << endl << endl;

    // show all the values
    n=0;
    do
    {
      valueNameSize=80;
      valueSize=80;
      ret=RegEnumValue(keyHandle, n,
        valueName, &valueNameSize,
        NULL, NULL, value, &valueSize);
      if (ret == ERROR_SUCCESS)
      {
        cout << valueName << " is "
          << value << endl;
        n++;
      }
    } while (ret == ERROR_SUCCESS);

    cout << endl << "There are " << n
      << " groups listed." << endl;

    // close the key
    ret=RegCloseKey(keyHandle);
    if (ret != ERROR_SUCCESS)
    {
```

Listing 15.3
A program that traverses a portion of the registry tree and dumps the values it finds there (Page 3 of 4)

```
        cerr << "Unable to close subkey"
          << endl;
        return;
      }
    }
```

Listing 15.3
A program that traverses a portion of the registry tree and dumps the values it finds there (Page 4 of 4)

Typical output from Listing 15.3 looks like this:

```
As subkeys:

Cache
Color Schemes
Colors
Current
Cursors
Custom Colors
Desktop
International
IOProcs
Keyboard
MMCPL
Mouse
Patterns
Screen Saver.3DFlyingObj
Screen Saver.3DPipes
Screen Saver.Bezier
Screen Saver.Marquee
Screen Saver.Mystify
Screen Saver.Stars
Sound
Sounds

There are 21 groups listed.

As values:

CoolSwitch is 1
CursorBlinkRate is 530
BorderWidth is 3
```

```
ScreenSaveTimeOut is 900
ScreenSaveActive is 1
SCRNSAVE.EXE is SSSTARS.SCR
ScreenSaverIsSecure is 1
Pattern is (None)
Wallpaper is (None)
TileWallpaper is 0
GridGranularity is 0
IconSpacing is 75
IconTitleWrap is 1
IconTitleFaceName is MS Sans Serif
IconTitleSize is 9
IconTitleStyle is 0
DragFullWindows is 0

There are 17 groups listed.
```

If you look in these particular portions of the registry with the Registry Editor, you will see that the key names and values are the same as the values produced by Listing 15.3.

Listing 15.3 uses the **RegEnumKeyEx** and **RegEnumValueEx** functions to enumerate keys and values.

RegEnumKeyEx *Enumerates keys*

```
LONG RegEnumKeyEx(
    HKEY keyHandle,
    DWORD subkeyNum,
    LPTSTR buffer,
    LPDWORD bufferLen,
    LPDWORD reserved,
    LPTSTR class,
    LPDWORD classLen,
    PFILETIME lastWrite)
```

keyHandle	Handle to an open key
subkeyNum	Index of the key to get

buffer	Buffer for returned key name
bufferLen	Size of the buffer. Pass address
reserved	Reserved. Pass 0
class	Returned data for the class. Pass array or buffer address
classLen	Size of the buffer. Pass address
lastWrite	Time of last write to the key
Returns ERROR_SUCCESS on success	

RegEnumKeyEx accepts an open key handle. It treats all of the keys inside as a numbered list starting at index 0. The function returns the information about the specified key, or it returns an appropriate error code. Listing 15.3 prints the name of each key found to stdout.

RegEnumValue *Enumerates values in a key*

```
LONG RegEnumValue(
    HKEY keyHandle,
    DWORD valueNum,
    LPTSTR buffer,
    LPDWORD bufferLen,
    LPDWORD reserved,
    LPDWORD type,
    LPBYTE data,
    LPDWORD dataLen)
```

keyHandle	Handle to an open key
valueNum	Index of the value to get
buffer	Buffer for returned value name
bufferLen	Size of the buffer. Pass address
reserved	Reserved. Pass 0
type	Returned type of the value. Pass address
data	Returned data for the value. Pass array or buffer address

dataLen	Size of the buffer. Pass address
Returns ERROR_SUCCESS on success	

RegEnumValue follows the same pattern as **RegEnumKeyEx**, getting each value one by one based on an index. The program prints out each value it finds.

You can use the functions described in this section to create keys and read and write values within your own applications. Other registry functions allow you to save and restore entire hives, and this would be useful when designing your own backup programs.

15.2 The Event Log

Compatibility Note: The code in this section does not work in Windows 95 at the time of publicxation due to unimplemented functions.

The event log centrally records error, warning, and information messages from the operating system, the security system, and applications. When you are developing your own software you will want to use the event log to record certain types of error and warning information.

You do not to throw all application errors into the event log. For example, if the user enters an invalid file name, you want to display the appropriate error message to the user. However, if the application tries to allocate memory and cannot, you should advise the user and also insert a message in the event log. The administrator needs to know about this problem so that the machine's physical or virtual memory space can be increased if necessary. Place into the event log information that the administrator of the system needs to see to fix system problems. Here are some examples of valid events to place in the event log:

1. Resource problems: lack of memory, network errors and timeouts, disk errors, problems connecting on the network, communication port problems, and so on
2. Missing or corrupted registry keys (may indicate that the program was installed incorrectly or illegally, or that something corrupted the registry)
3. Missing or disabled services
4. Startup problems due to missing files, DLLs, and so on

You might also have the installation program insert a message to indicate successful installation, so the administrator knows when new applications get loaded by users.

When creating a service (see Chapter 9) you will want to use the event log to record all error messages. The event log is really the only output channel that a service has available, and the administrator is the only one who can fix any problems that arise.

Run the Event Viewer now to get a good mental image of what a typical event contains. Look in the Event Viewer's "application section." Each event in the event list has a date, time, source, category, event number, user, and computer. If you double click on a specific event, you will find that this information is echoed, and the event also contains an English description and possibly some supplemental data.

The Event Viewer uses a very interesting string handling technique so that it can manage multiple display languages easily. When you add a message to the event log, you supply integer values for both the event itself and the category of the event. The event log then maps these values into a string table that you create with a message compiler (`mc.exe`). The string table is attached to either the application's EXE, or more commonly to one of its DLLs, as a resource.

In order for the event viewer to handle your application's event records correctly and completely, you need to place several entries into the registry. In the absence of these registry entries, the best that the event viewer can do is display the integer error codes. If the registry entries are in place, and if you use the message compiler to set up event message strings, then your events will display proper error messages in the viewer. Listing 15.4 sets up the registry entries for you.

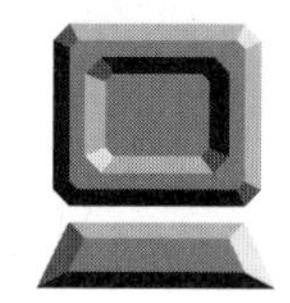

```
// instsrc.cpp

#include <windows.h>
#include <iostream.h>
```

Listing 15.4
Code that sets up the proper registry values for an application that wants to write to the Event Viewer. Typically this functionality goes in an installation program (Page 1 of 5)

```
#include <stdlib.h>

VOID ShowUsage(VOID)
{
  cout << "Install an Event Logging Source"
    << endl;
  cout << "Usage: instsrc <sourcename> "
    << "<msg&ctgy file> "
    << "<category count>" << endl << endl;
  cout
    << "sourcename    = name that application uses"
    << endl
    << "                to report events"
    << endl;
  cout
    << "msg&ctgy file= complete pathname to file"
    << endl
    << "                which has the message table"
    << endl
    << "                for event and category ID's"
    << endl;
  cout
    << "catgy count   = number of categories used"
    << endl << "                to classify events"
    << endl
    << endl;
  cout
    << "Example: instsrc TTT C:\\ttt\\ttt.dll 2"
    << endl;
}

VOID main(int argc, char *argv[])
{
  LONG ret;
```

Listing 15.4
Code that sets up the proper registry values for an application that wants to write to the Event Viewer. Typically this functionality goes in an installation program
(Page 2 of 5)

```
    HKEY keyHandle;
    DWORD eventTypes;
    CHAR strBuf[80];
    DWORD disposition;
    DWORD categoryCount;

    if (argc != 4)
    {
      ShowUsage();
      return;
    }

    // build the path for the new key
    strcpy(strBuf, "SYSTEM\\CurrentControlSet\\");
    strcat(strBuf,
      "Services\\EventLog\\Application\\");
    strcat(strBuf, argv[1]);

    // add a key for the new source
    ret=RegCreateKeyEx(HKEY_LOCAL_MACHINE,
      strBuf, 0, NULL, REG_OPTION_NON_VOLATILE,
      KEY_SET_VALUE, NULL, &keyHandle, &disposition);
    if (ret != ERROR_SUCCESS)
    {
      cerr << "Unable to create key: "
        << argv[1] << endl
        << "Check and make sure you"
        << " are a member of Administrators."
        << endl;
      return;
    }

    if (disposition == REG_OPENED_EXISTING_KEY)
    {
```

Listing 15.4
Code that sets up the proper registry values for an application that wants to write to the Event Viewer. Typically this functionality goes in an installation program
(Page 3 of 5)

```
    cout << "Updating existing source information."
      << endl;
  }

  // add the EventMessageFile value to key
  ret=RegSetValueEx(keyHandle, "EventMessageFile",
    0, REG_EXPAND_SZ, (LPBYTE) argv[2],
    strlen(argv[2]) + 1);
  if (ret != ERROR_SUCCESS)
  {
    cerr << "Unable to add value to key"
      << endl;
    return;
  }

  // specify the event types supported
  eventTypes=EVENTLOG_ERROR_TYPE |
    EVENTLOG_WARNING_TYPE |
    EVENTLOG_INFORMATION_TYPE;

  // add the TypesSupported value to key
  ret=RegSetValueEx(keyHandle, "TypesSupported",
        0, REG_DWORD, (LPBYTE) &eventTypes,
        sizeof(DWORD));
  if (ret != ERROR_SUCCESS)
  {
    cerr << "Unable to add value to key"
      << endl;
    return;
  }

  categoryCount=(DWORD) atoi(argv[3]);

  if (categoryCount)
```

Listing 15.4
Code that sets up the proper registry values for an application that wants to write to the Event Viewer. Typically this functionality goes in an installation program
(Page 4 of 5)

```
    {
      // add the CategoryCount value to key
      ret=RegSetValueEx(keyHandle, "CategoryCount",
            0, REG_DWORD, (LPBYTE) &categoryCount,
            sizeof(DWORD));
      if (ret != ERROR_SUCCESS)
      {
        cerr << "Unable to add value to key"
          << endl;
        return;
      }

      // add the CategoryMessageFile value to key
      ret=RegSetValueEx(keyHandle,
        "CategoryMessageFile",
        0, REG_EXPAND_SZ, (LPBYTE) argv[2],
        strlen(argv[2]) + 1);
      if (ret != ERROR_SUCCESS)
      {
        cerr << "Unable to add value to key"
          << endl;
        return;
      }
    }

    // close the key
    RegCloseKey(keyHandle);
  }
```

Listing 15.4
Code that sets up the proper registry values for an application that wants to write to the Event Viewer. Typically this functionality goes in an installation program (Page 5 of 5)

You need to run Listing 15.4 only once for an application. Typically you would place code like this in the installation program. When you run Listing 15.4 you should pass it the name that the application will use to report events (see below), the full path to the file that contains the message table (normally an EXE or DLL file), and the total number of different categories used by your application. Listing 15.4 creates a registry key for the application in the "HKEY_LOCAL_MACHINE\SYSTEM\CurrentControlSet\Services\EventLog\Application""HKEY_LOCAL_MACHINE\SYSTEM\CurrentControlSet\Services\EventLog\" portion of the registry. It then adds four values: EventMessageFile, TypesSupported, CategoryMessageFile, and CategoryCount. If you look in that same section you will find the same sorts of values for other applications already on the machine.

Listing 15.5 contains a typical application that places events in the event log. It creates two different types of events. The first one is very simple, while the second one uses substitution strings and has supplemental data. Listing 15.6 contains the message file for the message compiler, and Listing 15.7 contains a makefile that will create the application and link the message file to it.

```
// logevent.cpp

#include <windows.h>
#include <iostream.h>

#include "msgs.h"

VOID main(VOID)
{
  BOOL ret;
  LPCSTR mergeStrs[] = {"LOGEVENT.EXE"};
  HANDLE logHandle;

  // get a handle to log events with
  logHandle=RegisterEventSource(NULL,
    "LogEvent");
  if (logHandle == NULL)
```

Listing 15.5
A typical application that records events in the event log (logevent.cpp) (Page 1 of 2)

```
        {
          cerr << "Unable to get log handle"
            << endl;
          return;
        }

        cout << "Reporting event #1." << endl;

        ret=ReportEvent(logHandle,
          EVENTLOG_INFORMATION_TYPE,
          CAT_ONE, MSG_ONE, NULL, 0, 0,
          NULL, NULL);
        if (!ret)
        {
          cerr << "Unable to log an event"
            << endl;
          return;
        }

        cout << "Reporting event #2." << endl;

        ret=ReportEvent(logHandle,
          EVENTLOG_WARNING_TYPE,
          CAT_TWO, MSG_TWO, NULL, 1,
          sizeof(HANDLE), mergeStrs,
          &logHandle);
        if (!ret)
        {
          cerr << "Unable to log an event"
            << endl;
          return;
        }

        DeregisterEventSource(logHandle);
      }
```

Listing 15.5
A typical application that records events in the event log (logevent.cpp) (Page 2 of 2)

```
MessageIdTypedef=WORD

MessageId=0x1
SymbolicName=CAT_ONE
Language=English
Category #1
.

MessageId=
SymbolicName=CAT_TWO
Language=English
Category #2
.

MessageIdTypedef=DWORD

MessageId=0x100
Severity=Informational
Facility=Application
SymbolicName=MSG_ONE
Language=English
This is message #1.
.

MessageId=
Severity=Warning
Facility=Application
SymbolicName=MSG_TWO
Language=English
Application %1 is about to exit.
(The event data is the log handle which
is about to be closed.)
.
```

Listing 15.6
The message file for the application in Listing 15.5 (msgs.mc)

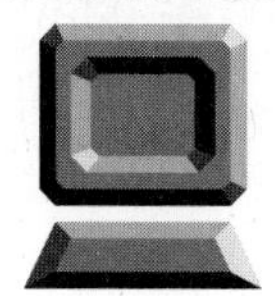

```
APP=logevent
MSGS=msgs
NODEBUG=1

!include <ntwin32.mak>

$(APP).exe: $(APP).obj $(MSGS).res
   $(link) $(conlflags) $(ldebug) \
     $(conlibs) $(APP).obj $(MSGS).res \
     advapi32.lib -out:$(APP).exe

$(APP).obj: $(APP).cpp $(MSGS).h
   $(cc) $(cflags) $(cdebug) $(cvars) \
     $(APP).cpp

$(MSGS).rc $(MSGS).h: $(MSGS).mc
   mc $(MSGS).mc

$(MSGS).rbj: $(MSGS).rc
   $(rc) $(rcvars) $(MSGS).rc
```

Listing 15.7
The makefile that compiles the application and its message file and links the messages to the EXE (makefile)

If you place Listings 15.5 through 15.7 in a directory of their own and run the makefile, it will produce an EXE named `logevent.exe`. This EXE file also contains the message file.

Now run Listing 15.4 to create the proper entries in the registry for this program. A typical run might look like this:

```
instsrc LogEvent c:\xxx\yyy\logevent.exe 2
```

Supply the proper path to your executable in place of `xxx\yyy`.

The message file in Listing 15.6 contains two parts. The first part maps category numbers to category names. The second part maps event numbers to event descriptions. The first line of each part is a header that identifies the type of the message IDs. Category IDs are always of type WORD, while message IDs are always of type DWORD.

A category description in the message file is straightforward, as duplicated below from Listing 15.6:

```
MessageId=
SymbolicName=CAT_TWO
Language=English
Category #2
.
```

The first line identifies the category ID number. This is the integer value that maps an ID to a string. If left blank, it tells the system to increment from the previous value, or you can specify a specific value. The second line is the symbolic name for the category ID number. The third line identifies the language. With a bit of extra work (see the help file for the message compiler) you can create strings for a variety of other languages as well. The fourth line is the category name associated with the ID. This is the string that will appear in the category field of the event viewer.

An event description in the message file follows the same format:

```
MessageId=
Severity=Warning
Facility=Application
SymbolicName=MSG_TWO
Language=English
Application %1 is about to exit.
(The event data is the log handle which
is about to be closed.)
.
```

The message ID is an integer value. If left blank, it tells the system to increment from the previous value, or you can specify a specific value. The next line indicates the severity of the event. This value controls the icon that appears next to the event in the viewer. There are three possibilities:

1. Informational
2. Warning
3. Error

The next value identifies the facility. There are two possibilities:

1. Application
2. System (for services)

Then, as with categories, you specify the symbolic name (used in Listing 15.5), the language, and the actual string. The string can contain language-independent substitution strings by marking them with "%1," "%2," and so on in the string.

The message compiler takes all of this information and produces a resource file for the message table that the linker attaches to the EXE.

The code in Listing 15.5 actually produces events in the event viewer. If you run the EXE you will see two new events appear for each execution. The code starts this process by connecting to the event log with the **RegisterEventSource** function.

RegisterEventSource	*Connects an application to the event log*

```
HANDLE RegisterEventSource(
    LPCTSTR server,
    LPCTSTR source)
```

server	Name of machine on network or 0 for local machine
source	Points to the subkey in the registry containing the event log information

Returns a handle to the event log or 0 on error

You pass **RegisterEventSource** the same string you passed as the first parameter to Listing 15.4.

Listing 15.5 then creates two new events in the log using two calls to the **ReportEvent** function.

ReportEvent *Records an event in the event log*

```
BOOL ReportEvent(
   HANDLE eventSource,
   WORD eventType,
   WORD category,
   DWORD event,
   PSID userSid,
   WORD numStrings,
   DWORD dataSize,
   LPCTSTR *stringArray,
   LPVOID data)
```

Parameter	Description
eventSource	Handle from **RegisterEventSource**
eventType	Type of event
category	A symbolic name for a category from the message file
event	A symbolic name for the event from the message file
userSid	A SID for the user, or NULL if irrelevant
numStrings	The number of substitution strings being passed in stringArray
dataSize	The number of bytes in the supplemental data block
stringArray	An argv style pointer to array of pointers to strings
data	A pointer to a block of supplemental data

Returns TRUE on success

Listing 15.5 creates two events in the log. The first is very simple, while the second one uses substitution strings and supplemental data. Substitution strings are language-independent strings, such as file names, that get substituted into the message string automatically. If there is more than one you create an array of pointers to string, like an argv array, and pass **ReportError** a pointer to that array. Supplemental data can contain anything you like, but it will always be displayed in binary. You pass in the address of the buffer holding the data. Here the value of the **logHandle** variable is passed.

When you are done reporting events to the event log, deregister as shown using the **DeregisterEventSource** function.

DeregisterEventSource	*Disconnects an application from the event log*
`BOOL DeregisterEventSource(` `   HANDLE eventLog)`	
eventLog	Handle to the event log from **RegisterEventSource**
Returns TRUE on success	

15.3 Time

The 32-bit API contains a number of functions for getting and setting times on a Windows system. Listing 15.8 demonstrates all of the different time-retrieval functions.

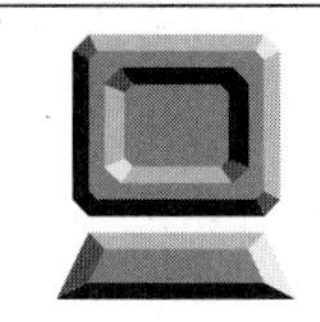

```
// timeshow.cpp

#include <windows.h>
#include <iostream.h>
```

Listing 15.8
The time-retrieval functions (Page 1 of 5)

```
VOID DumpTimeStruct(LPSYSTEMTIME st)
{
  cout << "Year          : "
    << st->wYear << endl;
  cout << "Month         : "
    << st->wMonth << endl;
  cout << "Day of Week : "
    << st->wDayOfWeek << endl;
  cout << "Day           : "
    << st->wDay << endl;
  cout << "Hour          : "
    << st->wHour << endl;
  cout << "Minute        : "
    << st->wMinute << endl;
  cout << "Second        : "
    << st->wSecond << endl;
  cout << "Milliseconds: "
    << st->wMilliseconds << endl;
}

VOID main(VOID)
{
  SYSTEMTIME st;
  HANDLE file;
  FILETIME ft;
  DWORD ret;
  TIME_ZONE_INFORMATION tzi;
  CHAR name[32];

  cout << "Tick Count is: "
    << GetTickCount() << endl << endl;

  // get UTC time
  GetSystemTime(&st);
```

Listing 15.8
The time-retrieval functions (Page 2 of 5)

```
    cout << "Current time (UTC):"
      << endl;
    DumpTimeStruct(&st);

    // get local time
    GetLocalTime(&st);

    cout << endl << "Current time (local):"
      << endl;
    DumpTimeStruct(&st);

    // get a file handle
    file=CreateFile("C:\\AUTOEXEC.BAT",
      GENERIC_READ, 0, NULL, OPEN_EXISTING,
      FILE_ATTRIBUTE_NORMAL, NULL);

    // get last write time
    GetFileTime(file, NULL, NULL, &ft);

    // close file handle
    CloseHandle(file);

    // convert file time to system time
    // structure
    FileTimeToSystemTime(&ft, &st);

    cout << endl
      << "Last write time (UTC) of AUTOEXEC.BAT:"
      << endl;
    DumpTimeStruct(&st);

    // get time zone info
    ret=GetTimeZoneInformation(&tzi);

    // report time zone
```

Listing 15.8
The time-retrieval functions (Page 3 of 5)

```
    switch(ret)
    {
      case TIME_ZONE_ID_UNKNOWN:
        cout << endl << "Time zone not known."
          << endl;
        break;

      case TIME_ZONE_ID_STANDARD:
        cout << endl
          << "It is currently Standard Time."
          << endl;
        break;

      case TIME_ZONE_ID_DAYLIGHT:
        cout << endl
          << "It is currently Daylight Savings Time."
          << endl;
        break;

      default:
        cerr << "Unable to get time zone "
          << "information." << endl;
        return;
    }

    // report info from time zone
    // structure
    cout << endl << "Time Zone Information:"
      << endl;
    cout << "Bias: " << tzi.Bias
      << endl << endl;
    cout << "Standard Time Data" << endl
      << "-----" << endl;
    WideCharToMultiByte(CP_ACP, NULL,
      tzi.StandardName, -1, name, 32,
```

Listing 15.8
The time-retrieval functions (Page 4 of 5)

```
        NULL, NULL);
    cout << "Standard Name: " << name
      << endl;
    cout << "Transition Date/Time:" << endl;
    DumpTimeStruct(&tzi.StandardDate);
    cout << "Standard Bias: "
      << tzi.StandardBias << endl;
    cout << "-----" << endl << endl;
    cout << "Daylight Savings Time Data" << endl
      << "-----" << endl;
    WideCharToMultiByte(CP_ACP, NULL,
      tzi.DaylightName, -1, name, 32,
      NULL, NULL);
    cout << "Daylight Name: " << name
      << endl;
    cout << "Transition Date/Time:" << endl;
    DumpTimeStruct(&tzi.DaylightDate);
    cout << "Daylight Bias: "
      << tzi.DaylightBias << endl;
    cout << "-----" << endl;
}
```

Listing 15.8
The time-retrieval functions (Page 5 of 5)

Listing 15.8 starts by printing out the value of the **GetTickCount** function. This function indicates how long the system has been running, in milliseconds. After about 50 days, the count cycles back to zero because of the limits of a 32-bit integer. We have used this function at several points in this book to generate a random value. It is also useful for testing elapsed times.

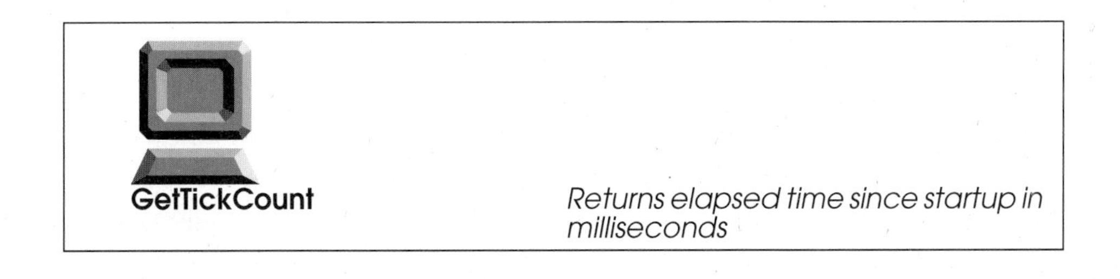

DWORD GetTickCount(VOID)
Returns the time

Listing 15.8 next dumps both the system time and the local time using **GetSystemTime** and **GetLocalTime**. These functions both return a structure of time information that the **DumpTimeStructure** function prints.

GetSystemTime	*Returns the system time and date in UTC*
GetLocalTime	*Returns the local time and date*
`VOID GetSystemTime( LPSYSTEMTIME time)`	
time	A pointer to a SYSTEMTIME structure
Returns nothing	

System time is GMT (or UCT), while local time is adjusted for the time zone that you have set in the Time and Date applet of the Control Panel. Both return a structure that looks like this (from the winnt.h header file):

```
typedef struct _SYSTEMTIME {
    WORD wYear;
    WORD wMonth;
    WORD wDayOfWeek;
    WORD wDay;
    WORD wHour;
    WORD wMinute;
    WORD wSecond;
    WORD wMilliseconds;
} SYSTEMTIME;
```

The **GetFileTime** function accepts a file handle and retrieves its file times from the disk (see also Section 2.4.1). It returns the creation time, the last access time, and the last write time. The FAT file system records only the last write time, but other file systems hold all three. Listing 15.8 uses the **FileTime-ToSystemTime** function to convert the file time to system time.

GetFileTime — *Returns the times for a file from the file system*

```
BOOL GetFileTime(
    HANDLE fileHandle,
    LPFILETIME creation,
    LPFILETIME lastAccess,
    LPFILETIME lastWrite)
```

fileHandle	Handle to a file
creation	Time of file creation
lastAccess	Time of last access
lastWrite	Time of last write

Returns TRUE on success

FileTimeToSystemTime — *Converts a file time to system time*

```
BOOL FileTimeToSystemTime(
    CONST FILETIME * fileTime,
    LPSYSTEMTIME systemTime)
```

fileTime	A file time value
systemTime	A system time structure

Returns TRUE on success

The **GetTimeZoneInformation** function returns information about the time zone used on the current machine.

GetTimeZoneInformation	*Returns information about the current time zone*
`DWORD GetTimeZoneInformation( LPTIME_ZONE_INFORMATION tzi)`	
tzi	Pointer to a time zone information structure
Returns daylight savings time flag or 0xffffffff on error	

The time zone information structure tells you about the current time zone, as shown here copied from winnt.h:

```
typedef struct _TIME_ZONE_INFORMATION {
    LONG       Bias;
    WCHAR      StandardName[ 32 ];
    SYSTEMTIME StandardDate;
    LONG       StandardBias;
    WCHAR      DaylightName[ 32 ];
    SYSTEMTIME DaylightDate;
    LONG       DaylightBias;
} TIME_ZONE_INFORMATION;
```

The return value tells you about the daylight savings time status, as shown in the code.

Listing 15.9 demonstrates how to set the system time and date.

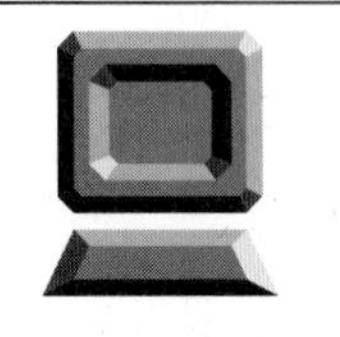

```
// settime.cpp
```

Listing 15.9
Setting the system time (Page 1 of 5)

```
#include <windows.h>
#include <iostream.h>

BOOL AdjustPrivilege(LPCTSTR privilege,
  DWORD attribute)
{
  BOOL ret;
  HANDLE procToken;
  LUID luid;
  TOKEN_PRIVILEGES tp;

  // get a handle to the access token used
  // by this process
  ret=OpenProcessToken(GetCurrentProcess(),
    TOKEN_ADJUST_PRIVILEGES, &procToken);
  if (!ret)
    return(FALSE);

  // get LUID for privilege
  ret=LookupPrivilegeValue(NULL, privilege,
    &luid);
  if (!ret)
  {
    CloseHandle(procToken);
    return(FALSE);
  }

  // fill in token privileges struct
  tp.PrivilegeCount=1;
  tp.Privileges[0].Luid=luid;
  tp.Privileges[0].Attributes=attribute;

  // attempt to enable privilege
  AdjustTokenPrivileges(procToken, FALSE, &tp,
```

Listing 15.9
Setting the system time (Page 2 of 5)

```
      NULL, NULL, NULL);

    if (GetLastError() != ERROR_SUCCESS)
      ret=FALSE;
    else
      ret=TRUE;

    CloseHandle(procToken);

    return(ret);
  }

  VOID DumpTimeStruct(LPSYSTEMTIME st)
  {
    cout << "Year         : "
      << st->wYear << endl;
    cout << "Month        : "
      << st->wMonth << endl;
    cout << "Day of Week : "
      << st->wDayOfWeek << endl;
    cout << "Day          : "
      << st->wDay << endl;
    cout << "Hour         : "
      << st->wHour << endl;
    cout << "Minute       : "
      << st->wMinute << endl;
    cout << "Second       : "
      << st->wSecond << endl;
    cout << "Milliseconds: "
      << st->wMilliseconds << endl;
  }

  VOID main(VOID)
  {
    SYSTEMTIME st;
```

Listing 15.9
Setting the system time (Page 3 of 5)

```
    // get local time
    GetLocalTime(&st);

    cout << endl << "Current time (local):"
      << endl;
    DumpTimeStruct(&st);

    st.wYear++;

    // enable set system time privilege (delete in win95)
    if (!AdjustPrivilege(SE_SYSTEMTIME_NAME,
      SE_PRIVILEGE_ENABLED))
    {
      cerr << "Must have set system time "
        << "privilege." << endl;
      return;
    }

    // set new time
    SetLocalTime(&st);

    // get local time
    GetLocalTime(&st);

    cout << endl << "New current time (local):"
      << endl;
    DumpTimeStruct(&st);

    st.wYear--;

    // reset time
    SetLocalTime(&st);

    // get local time
    GetLocalTime(&st);
```

Listing 15.9
Setting the system time (Page 4 of 5)

```
    cout << endl << "Current time (local):"
      << endl;
    DumpTimeStruct(&st);

    // disable set system time privilege (delete in win95)
    AdjustPrivilege(SE_SYSTEMTIME_NAME, 0);
}
```

Listing 15.9
Setting the system time (Page 5 of 5)

In order to set the system time in Windows NT, you must have the SE_SYSTEM-TIME_NAME privilege, and you must enable that privilege (see Chapter 10). In Windows 95 anyone can set the time and you can delete the call to **AdjustPrivilege** from the code. The code in Listing 15.9 gets the system time, enables the privilege, increments the year simply to demonstrate a change, sets the time using the **SetLocalTime** function, gets the new time, dumps this time to show that it is in fact different, and then sets it back to its original value. If you want to set the time it is generally easiest to start with an already-filled SYSTEMTIME structure and modify it, although you can create one from scratch as well.

SetLocalTime	*Sets the system time*
`BOOL SetLocalTime(` `   CONST SYSTEMTIME * time)`	
time	Pointer to a SYSTEMTIME structure
Returns TRUE on success	

15.4 Memory

The 32-bit API contains its own memory allocation and deallocation functions. Normally you will use functions like **new** or **malloc** to allocate memory inside an application, but there are cases where you must use the API calls. Probably the best example of a place where you must use the API allocation functions is inside a DLL, where a call to **new** fails.

The API contains two identical sets of memory allocation functions. One starts with **Local** (e.g. **LocalAlloc**), while the other starts with **Global** (e.g. **GlobalAlloc**). In older versions of Windows the two sets had different uses, but in Windows they are identical and completely interchangeable.

Use the **GlobalAlloc** and **GlobalFree** functions to allocate or deallocate a block of memory from the heap.

GlobalAlloc — *Allocates memory from the heap*

```
HGLOBAL GlobalAlloc(
   UINT flags,
   DWORD numBytes)
```

flags	Allocation flags
numBytes	Number of bytes to allocate

Returns a pointer or handle to the block allocated, or 0 on error

GlobalFree — *Frees a block of memory*

```
HGLOBAL GlobalFree(
   HGLOBAL memHandle)
```

memHandle	The block to free

Returns 0 on success or the handle on error

The **GlobalAlloc** function accepts a number of flags that control the behavior of the function or its resulting block of memory, as listed below. Many of these flags are carried over for compatibility reasons from earlier versions of

Windows and are meaningless in Windows. The normal flag to use for standard allocations is GPTR:

GMEM_FIXED	The memory block resides at a fixed location in memory
GMEM_MOVEABLE	Meaningless in NT and 95
GPTR	Combines GMEM_FIXED and GMEM_ZEROINIT. The standard flag to use when allocating memory
GHND	Meaningless in NT and 95
GMEM_DDESHARE	Meaningless in NT, but should be specified if the memory is being used for DDE
GMEM_DISCARDABLE	Allocates a discardable block of memory. Ignored by some implementations
GMEM_LOWER	Meaningless in NT and 95
GMEM_NOCOMPACT	Must satisfy the memory request without compacting or discarding memory
GMEM_NODISCARD	Must satisfy the memory request without compacting or discarding memory
GMEM_NOT_BANKED	Meaningless in NT and 95
GMEM_NOTIFY	Meaningless in NT and 95
GMEM_SHARE	Same as GMEM_DDESHARE
GMEM_ZEROINIT	All bytes in block are initially set to zero. This takes time, so you can speed up an application by not zeroing the block

A typical memory allocation looks like this in a program, here from Listing 14.15 in the DLL chapter:

```
stacknode *temp;
temp = (stacknode *) GlobalAlloc(GPTR,
  sizeof stacknode);
```

With the exception of the flag parameter, this call looks identical to a normal **malloc** call. The HGLOBAL type returned by **GlobalAlloc** acts just like a pointer once you cast it and assign the value to a pointer.

Note that because this code uses the GPTR flag, it returns zeroed memory. If you do not require initialized memory, then use GMEM_FIXED instead and save a little CPU time. For example, Listing 15.10 allocates memory using the GPTR flag. On my machine it takes the code about 12 seconds to execute. By changing the flag to GMEM_FIXED the run time drops to 10 seconds.

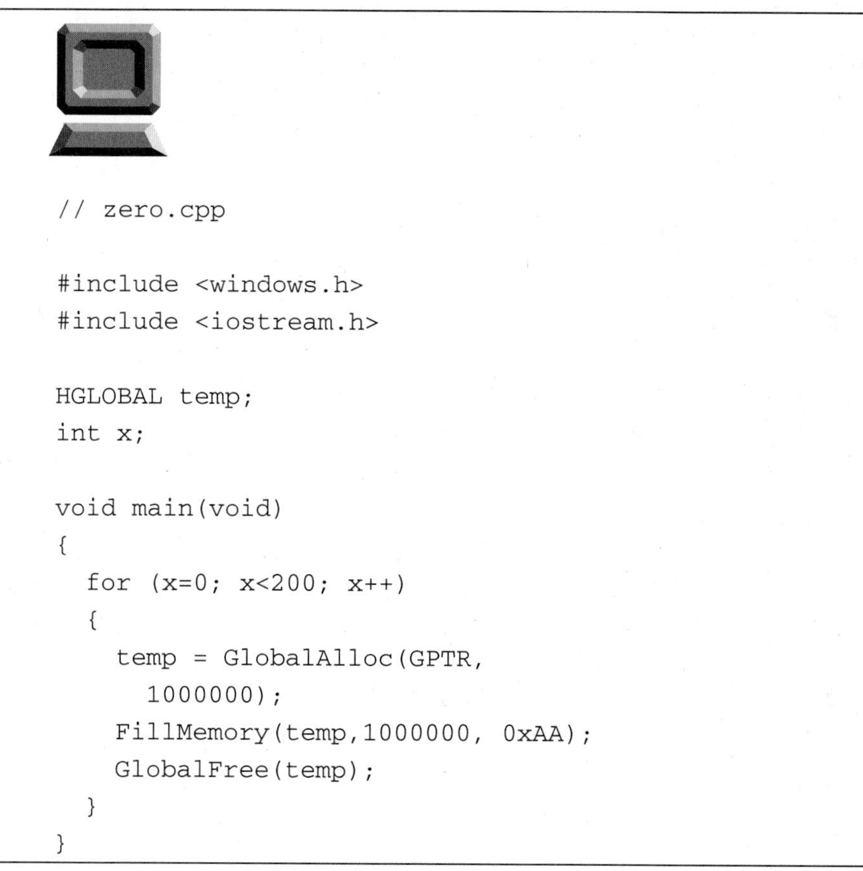

```
// zero.cpp

#include <windows.h>
#include <iostream.h>

HGLOBAL temp;
int x;

void main(void)
{
  for (x=0; x<200; x++)
  {
    temp = GlobalAlloc(GPTR,
      1000000);
    FillMemory(temp,1000000, 0xAA);
    GlobalFree(temp);
  }
}
```

Listing 15.10
A simple memory allocation program that allocates a 1 million-byte block 200 times

When the system allocates a block of memory it often rounds the size of the block up. There are times when it is useful to know the actual block size (you can legally access all of the allocated bytes), or to get the size of an unknown block for which you have just received a pointer. Use **GlobalSize** to get a block's size.

GlobalSize	*Returns the actual size of a block given its handle*
`DWORD GlobalSize(` `   HGLOBAL address)`	
address	The address of the block
Returns the size or 0 on error	

In other cases, you may receive a handle and want to check it to make sure that you are able to access the memory that the handle points to before you actually use it. In the 32-bit API four different functions check memory pointers:

IsBadCodePtr	Checks a function pointer for read access
IsBadReadPtr	Checks a pointer for read access
IsBadWritePtr	Checks a pointer for write access
IsBadStringPtr	Checks a string pointer for read access

IsBadCodePtr	*Checks a function address to see if the thread can call it*
`BOOL IsBadCodePtr(` `   FARPROC address)`	
address	The address to check
Returns FALSE if memory address is accessible	

IsBadReadPtr

Checks a range of bytes to see if the thread can read them

```
BOOL IsBadReadPtr(
    CONST BYTE *address
    UINT numBytes)
```

address	The address to check
numBytes	The number of bytes in the block

Returns FALSE if all memory is accessible

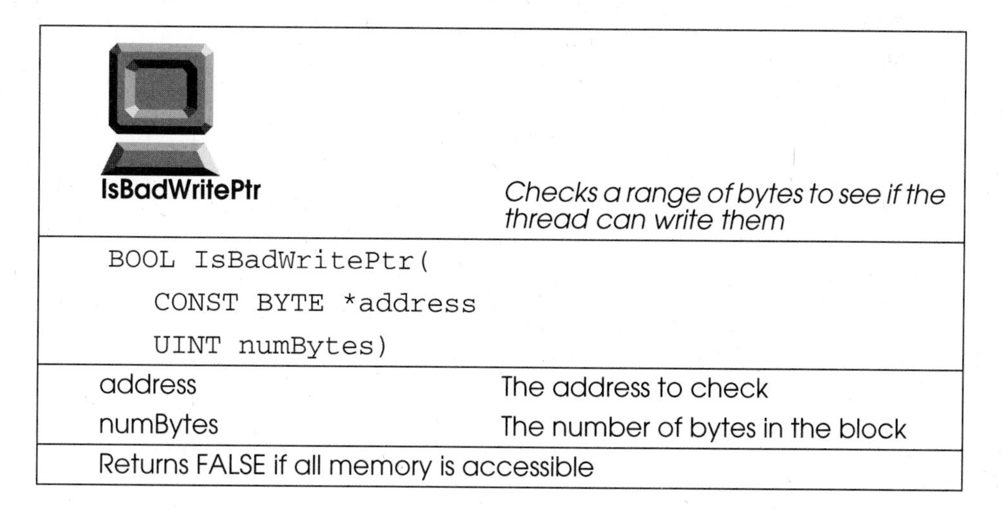

IsBadWritePtr

Checks a range of bytes to see if the thread can write them

```
BOOL IsBadWritePtr(
    CONST BYTE *address
    UINT numBytes)
```

address	The address to check
numBytes	The number of bytes in the block

Returns FALSE if all memory is accessible

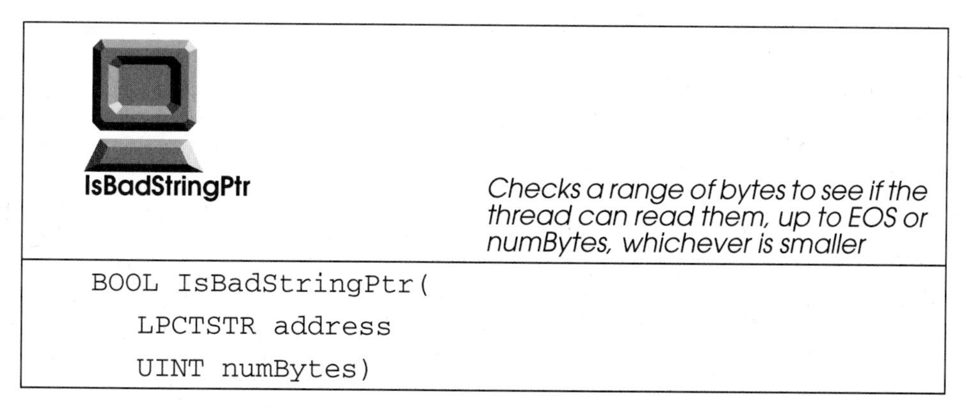

IsBadStringPtr

Checks a range of bytes to see if the thread can read them, up to EOS or numBytes, whichever is smaller

```
BOOL IsBadStringPtr(
    LPCTSTR address
    UINT numBytes)
```

address	The address to check
numBytes	The number of bytes in the block
Returns FALSE if all memory is accessible	

In all likelihood you do not want to be checking all of your pointers for validity each time you use them. Structured exception handling (Section 15.5) is a better way to handle memory exceptions.

The API provides the **GlobalMemoryStatus** function to get the status of the memory system.

GlobalMemoryStatus *Returns status information about the memory system*

```
VOID GlobalMemoryStatus(
   LPMEMORYSTATUS status)
```

status	A pointer to a status record
Returns nothing	

The **GlobalMemoryStatus** function returns a structure of type MEMORYSTATUS, as shown below from the winnt.h file:

```
typedef struct _MEMORYSTATUS {
    DWORD dwLength;
    DWORD dwMemoryLoad;
    DWORD dwTotalPhys;
    DWORD dwAvailPhys;
    DWORD dwTotalPageFile;
    DWORD dwAvailPageFile;
    DWORD dwTotalVirtual;
    DWORD dwAvailVirtual;
} MEMORYSTATUS, *LPMEMORYSTATUS;
```

To use **GlobalMemoryStatus**, declare a structure of type MEMORYSTATUS. Initialize its **dwLength** field to **sizeof(MEMORYSTATUS)**. Pass the address of the structure to **GlobalMemoryStatus**. When the function returns, the **dwMemoryLoad** field contains the percentage of memory currently in use.

The last two fields tell you how much total memory space is available in the machine's virtual address space, and how much is in current use.

The API provides four functions for copying and filling blocks of memory:

CopyMemory	Copies the contents of one block to another provided that the blocks do not overlap
MoveMemory	Copies the contents of one block to another if they do overlap
FillMemory	Fills a block with the byte specified
ZeroMemory	Fills a block with zeros

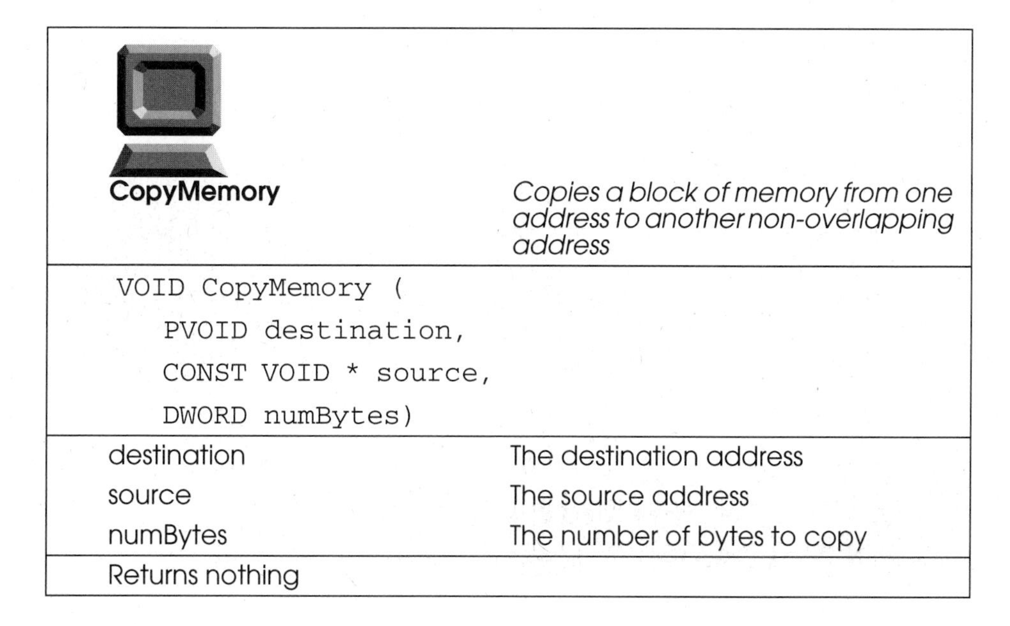

CopyMemory — *Copies a block of memory from one address to another non-overlapping address*

```
VOID CopyMemory (
   PVOID destination,
   CONST VOID * source,
   DWORD numBytes)
```

destination	The destination address
source	The source address
numBytes	The number of bytes to copy

Returns nothing

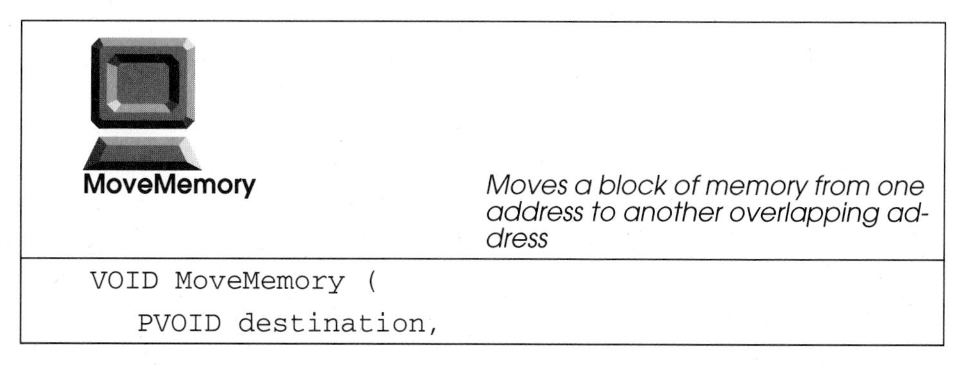

MoveMemory — *Moves a block of memory from one address to another overlapping address*

```
VOID MoveMemory (
   PVOID destination,
```

```
    CONST VOID * source,
    DWORD numBytes)
```

destination	The destination address
source	The source address
numBytes	The number of bytes to move

Returns nothing

FillMemory	*Fills a block of memory with the specified value*

```
VOID FillMemory (
    PVOID destination,
    DWORD numBytes,
    BYTE fill)
```

destination	The destination address
numBytes	The number of bytes to copy
fill	The value to fill with

Returns nothing

ZeroMemory	*Fills a block of memory with zero*

```
VOID ZeroMemory (
    PVOID destination,
    DWORD numBytes)
```

destination	The destination address
numBytes	The number of bytes to zero

Returns nothing

The API includes a facility to create a private heap and allocate memory from it. The new heap is private to the process that created it. To use this facility, you can call the **HeapCreate** function and specify the maximum size for the private heap. Windows will allocate all of that memory at once and make it available. You then access it using **HeapAlloc** and **HeapFree** to allocate and free memory on this private heap. You use **HeapAlloc** in the same way you use **GlobalAlloc**.

There are several ways to use private heaps. For example, you might want to give different threads in an application their own private heaps if you expect memory fragmentation to be especially bad when their allocations are mixed. Or, if you know a critical application will need 150 Meg of memory and you do not want it to start unless you *know* that much space is available, you can allocate the entire 150 meg in a private heap at startup. Your application is then guaranteed to have all of the memory it needs throughout its run.

15.5 Structured Exception Handling

Compatibility Note: Visual C++ provides a better exception handling mechanism that is described in the book "Visual C++: Developing Professional Applications in Windows 95 and NT using MFC" by Marshall Brain and Lance Lovette.

You will use structured exception handling (SEH) in your programs in two different ways. First, SEH is Windows' communication channel when hardware and software exceptions occur. A typical exception is an invalid memory access via a pointer. SEH is also useful because you can raise exceptions in your own code and catch and use them just like system exceptions. Both techniques are demonstrated in this section.

Let's say that you create and run a program that offends the computer. For example, you set a pointer **p** to NULL and then say:

```
*p=5;
```

When you execute this program, it will die with an application error. What is really happening is that the system generated an exception. Because you did not handle it, the system invoked the default exception handler, which terminates the application.

To instead trap an exception and handle it within your program, you can use structured exception handling as demonstrated in Listing 15.11.

```
// catch.cpp

#include <windows.h>
#include <iostream.h>

VOID main(VOID)
{
  CHAR *ptr;

  // point the pointer to an
  // invalid address
  ptr=NULL;

  __try
  {
    // attempt to assign a value
    // to the location pointed
    // to by the pointer
    *ptr=5;
  }
  __except(EXCEPTION_EXECUTE_HANDLER)
  {
    // report the exception type
    cerr << "Caught exception code: 0x"
      << hex << GetExceptionCode()
      << endl;
  }
}
```

Listing 15.11
A simple example of exception handling

Listing 15.11 contains two new key words: **try** and **except**, both of which use braces to wrap blocks of code. The **try** key word tells the compiler to monitor any of the code in the try block for exceptions. The block following **try** is called a *guarded body of code*. The **except** keyword marks a block of code that the system will execute if an exception occurs. This is called the *exception handler*. The block of code in the **try** block should be sequential. It should not contain any **break**, **continue**, **goto**, or **return** statements, because these are treated and handled like exceptions.

Listing 15.11 contains an invalid instruction, in this case an invalid memory access. When the system executes that instruction, it traps the invalid access. If you execute the code in a normal program, the program simply dies and either the *abnormal termination* dialog appears or Dr. Watson pops up. But in Listing 15.11, the program instead executes the code following the **except** keyword.

Immediately following **except** is a set of parentheses that contain the *filter expression*, which is generally either a constant value as shown here or a function call that returns a constant value. Following the filter expression is the exception handler, a block of code that the system executes if the filter expression indicates EXCEPTON_EXECUTE_HANDLER. Other valid values for the filter expression to indicate are EXCEPTION_CONTINUE_EXECUTION (the code in the try block should continue as though nothing happened) and EXCEPTION_CONTINUE_SEARCH (the system tries to find another exception handler on the stack).

Listing 15.11 presents an extremely simple example. The filter expression for the **except** block indicates that the handler code should always execute, so the handler runs and prints an error to stderr. Part of the output contains the exception code, returned by the **GetExceptionCode** function.

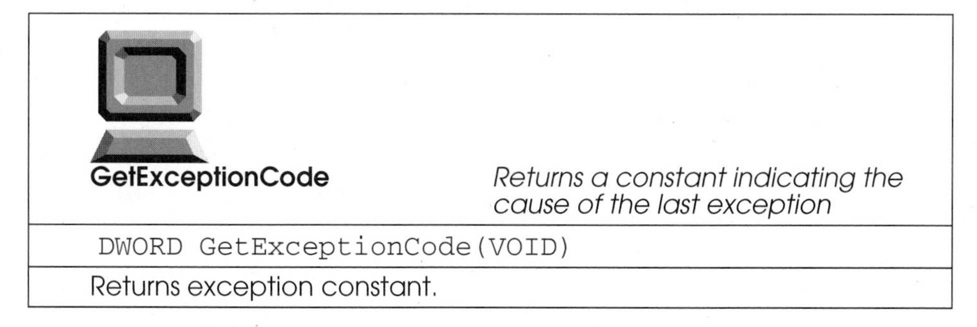

GetExceptionCode — *Returns a constant indicating the cause of the last exception*

```
DWORD GetExceptionCode(VOID)
```

Returns exception constant.

The constant returned by **GetExceptionCode** is an integer value that matches one of the following constants:

EXCEPTION_ACCESS_VIOLATION	Cannot access the address specified
EXCEPTION_BREAKPOINT	Breakpoint found
EXCEPTION_DATATYPE_MISALIGNMENT	System tried to read data not on the proper word boundary for the hardware
EXCEPTION_SINGLE_STEP	One instruction executed in single-step mode
EXCEPTION_ARRAY_BOUNDS_EXCEEDED	If the hardware supports array bounds checking, then this exception indicates that the bounds were exceeded
EXCEPTION_FLT_DENORMAL_OPERAND	Floating point value too small
EXCEPTION_FLT_DIVIDE_BY_ZERO	Divide by zero error
EXCEPTION_FLT_INEXACT_RESULT	Value cannot be represented exactly (e.g. - 10/3)
EXCEPTION_FLT_INVALID_OPERATION	Other floating point exceptions
EXCEPTION_FLT_OVERFLOW	Floating point overflow
EXCEPTION_FLT_STACK_CHECK	Stack overflow or underflow during floating point operation
EXCEPTION_FLT_UNDERFLOW	Floating point underflow
EXCEPTION_INT_DIVIDE_BY_ZERO	Integer divide by zero
EXCEPTION_INT_OVERFLOW	Integer overflow
EXCEPTION_PRIV_INSTRUCTION	Privileged instruction executed in user mode

STATUS_ NONCONTINUABLE_ EXCEPTION	The thread tried to continue execution but the exception cannot be continued

Not all hardware will generate all of these codes. Following execution of the handler function the code drops out the bottom of the handler and continues from that point.

If the filter expression indicates EXCEPTION_CONTINUE_ EXECUTION, then the code in the **try** block continues from the point of the exception as though nothing had happened. Certain exceptions cannot continue however, and in that case a STATUS_NONCONTINUABLE_EXCEPTION exception immediately gets raised to indicate that continuation is impossible.

If the filter expression indicates EXECEPTION_CONTINUE_SEARCH, then the system searches for another exception handler. Here it is helpful to understand the implementation of the exception handling system. When you put a **try** keyword in your code, an *exception frame* is placed on the stack. The frame is removed at the bottom of the guarded block of code. This is identical to the system's treatment of a local variable on the stack: when you declare the variable it is placed on the stack and it is removed from the stack when the bottom of that variable's block is reached.

When an exception occurs, the system scans the stack from the top (in the stack sense of the word top) looking for an exception frame. The frame tells it where to find the **except** statement. The system finds the first one and tries the **except** block. **Try-except** statements can be nested. One inner **try-except** pair might handle a certain exception, but it may want to pass certain more generic exceptions up to a **try-except** pair that it is nested within. When the system sees EXECEPTION_CONTINUE_SEARCH in a filter expression, it returns to the stack and continues searching for the next exception frame. Eventually it will get to the system exception frame at the very bottom of the stack. In this case the system exception handler—the default mechanism used normally by programs—executes and terminates the application.

Normally you place a function call in the filter expression. This function decides what action the code wishes to take in response to particular exception codes and returns the appropriate constant value. In simple cases like the one shown in Listing 15.11, however, the exception handler foregoes the function call and uses a constant instead.

There is a second way to handle exceptions using a **try-finally** pair. The **finally** block is similar to an **except** block, except that it *always* executes at the end of the try block regardless of whether or not an exception occurs. Since it always executes, it does not have a filter expression. Instead, you can use the **AbnormalTermination** function inside the **finally** block to decide whether an exception was generated or not.

AbnormalTermination	Indicates whether the try block generated an exception or not inside a **finally** block
`BOOL AbnormalTermination(VOID)`	
Returns TRUE on an exception	

Listing 15.12 demonstrates the **try-finally** pair. It first uses the **finally** block without generating an exception, and then uses it during an exception.

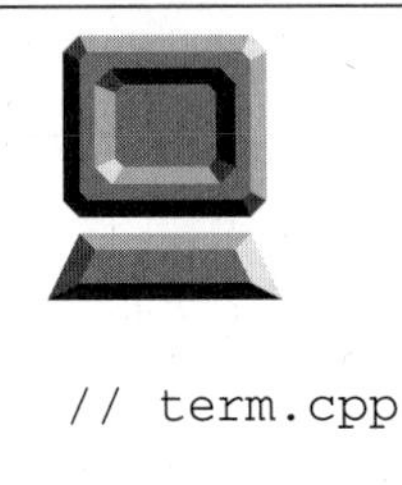

```
// term.cpp

#include <windows.h>
#include <iostream.h>

VOID main(VOID)
{
  CHAR *ptr;

  // point the pointer to an
  // invalid address
```

Listing 15.12
Demonstration of the try-finally pair (Page 1 of 3)

```
    ptr=NULL;

    __try
    {
      cout << "No problems." << endl;
    }
    __finally
    {
      if (AbnormalTermination())
        cerr << "Cleaning up after exception."
          << endl;
      else
        cout << "Cleaning up after normal"
          << " execution." << endl;

      // clean up
    }

    __try
    {
      cout << endl << "Make problems." << endl;
      // attempt to assign a value
      // to the location pointed
      // to by the pointer
      *ptr=5;
    }
    __finally
    {
      if (AbnormalTermination())
        cerr << "Cleaning up after exception."
          << endl;
      else
        cout << "Cleaning up after normal"
          << " execution." << endl;
```

Listing 15.12
Demonstration of the try-finally pair (Page 2 of 3)

```
            // clean up
        }
    }
```

Listing 15.12
Demonstration of the try-finally pair (Page 3 of 3)

The try-finally construct allows the programmer to gracefully clean up regardless of the success of the operation in the try block. This is especially useful when dealing with synchronization mechanisms (see Chapter 6) that must be released to allow other threads to continue.

Although hardware exceptions are right now the most common way to use Windows' exception handling mechanism, it is also possible for you to design and use your own exceptions. Probably the best current example of this process can be found in the RPC system (see Chapter 8). The RPC facility uses exceptions as an alternate signaling mechanism to indicate RPC system problems. For example, if you create a **CalcPixel** function as demonstrated in Section 8.2, the return value and parameters for the function are defined by you. There is no way for the RPC system to signal its own errors, such as failed network connections or server communication problems. Therefore it uses the exception mechanism to signal its problems.

Listing 15.13 demonstrates the process of creating and raising your own exceptions. It also shows how to override the system's default exception handler.

```
// softexpt.cpp

#include <windows.h>
#include <iostream.h>

#define TYPE_1 0x1   // an ignored exception
#define TYPE_2 0x2   // a handled exception
```

Listing 15.13
User-defined exception handling (Page 1 of 5)

```
#define TYPE_3 0x3  // an unhandled exception

VOID MakeException(DWORD type)
{
  switch(type)
  {
    // recoverable exeception
    case TYPE_1:
      RaiseException(TYPE_1, 0, NULL,
        NULL);
      break;

    // exception which must be handled
    case TYPE_2:
      RaiseException(TYPE_2,
        EXCEPTION_NONCONTINUABLE, NULL,
        NULL);
      break;

    // just generate an exception
    case TYPE_3:
      RaiseException(TYPE_3, 0, NULL,
        NULL);
      break;
  }
}

DWORD Filter(EXCEPTION_POINTERS *ep)
{
  cerr << "Dumping some exception info:" << endl;
  cerr << "Code : 0x" << hex
    << ep->ExceptionRecord->ExceptionCode << endl;
  cerr << "Flags: 0x" << hex
    << ep->ExceptionRecord->ExceptionFlags << endl;
  cerr << "Addr : " << hex
    << ep->ExceptionRecord->ExceptionAddress
```

Listing 15.13
User-defined exception handling (Page 2 of 5)

```
        << endl;
      // arguments from RaiseException can also
      // be retrieved from "ep"

      // decide what to do based on type
      switch(ep->ExceptionRecord->ExceptionCode)
      {
        case TYPE_1:
          cerr << "Allow execution to continue."
            << endl;
          return(EXCEPTION_CONTINUE_EXECUTION);
          break;

        case TYPE_2:
          cerr << "Execute exception handler block."
            << endl;
          return(EXCEPTION_EXECUTE_HANDLER);
          break;

        case TYPE_3:
          cerr
            << "Pass exception to debugger or system."
            << endl;
          return(EXCEPTION_CONTINUE_SEARCH);
          break;

        default:
          return(EXCEPTION_EXECUTE_HANDLER);
      }
    }

    VOID TryExcept(DWORD type)
    {
      __try
      {
        MakeException(type);
```

Listing 15.13
User-defined exception handling (Page 3 of 5)

```
    }
    __except(Filter(GetExceptionInformation()))
    {
      // report the exception type
      cerr << "Caught exception code: 0x"
        << hex << GetExceptionCode()
        << endl;
    }
  }

  // User defined exception filter which
  // gets dispatched whenever user code
  // does not handle an exception
  LONG TopLevelExceptionFilter
    (EXCEPTION_POINTERS *ep)
  {
    // exception information can be used
    // from "ep" if needed

    cerr << "Exception filtered by user "
      << "defined \"Unhandled Exception "
      << "Filter\"." << endl;
    Beep(300, 100);
    MessageBox(NULL, "Managing Exception",
      "Programmer Defined Filter",
      MB_OK | MB_ICONINFORMATION);

    // allow exception handler to execute which
    // causes program termination
    return(EXCEPTION_EXECUTE_HANDLER);
    // use care when returning
    // EXCEPTION_CONTINUE_EXECUTION
    // because an infinite loop of
    // exceptions may occur
  }
```

Listing 15.13
User-defined exception handling (Page 4 of 5)

```
VOID main(VOID)
{
  cout << "Generate an exception which "
    << "can be ignored."
    << endl;
  TryExcept(TYPE_1);

  cout << endl
    << "Generate an exception which "
    << "can be handled."
    << endl;
  TryExcept(TYPE_2);

  // Replace system exception filter
  // with a custom filter
  SetUnhandledExceptionFilter(
    (LPTOP_LEVEL_EXCEPTION_FILTER)
    TopLevelExceptionFilter);

  // generate an exception which
  // gets passed out to the newly
  // defined custom filter
  cout << endl
    << "Generate an exception which "
    << "is not handled."
    << endl;
  TryExcept(TYPE_3);
}
```

Listing 15.13
User-defined exception handling (Page 5 of 5)

For the sake of example, Listing 15.13 generates, or *raises*, three different exceptions (TYPE_1, TYPE_2, and TYPE_3) which are ignored, handled, or not handled, respectively. The main function demonstrates the first two, and then calls the **SetUnhandledExceptionFilter** function to replace the system exception handler with a custom exception handler before generating an unhandled exception.

SetUnhandledExceptionFilter — *Replaces the system's exception handler with a custom handler*

```
LPTOP_LEVEL_EXCEPTION_FILTER
   SetUnhandledExceptionFilter(
      LPTOP_LEVEL_EXCEPTION_FILTER filter)
```

filter	The custom filter function

Returns address of prior filter

When the code wants to generate an exception, it calls the **RaiseException** function. This function accepts an exception code along with supplemental exception data if desired.

RaiseException — *Generates a user-defined exception*

```
VOID RaiseException(
   DWORD exceptionCode,
   DWORD exceptionFlags,
   DWORD numArguments,
   CONST DWORD * arguments)
```

exceptionCode	The user-defined exception code
exceptionFlags	Specify EXCEPTION_NONCONTINUABLE if this exception cannot be continued, 0 otherwise
numArguments	The number of DWORD words of supplemental data
arguments	Pointer to a buffer holding supplemental data of DWORDs

Returns nothing

When a function calls **RaiseException**, it stops execution while the system searches for an exception handler. That is, a piece of code called the function that is raising the exception, and that piece of code may or may not have an exception handler in place to handle the function's new exception. The system searches to see if a handler is in place. If not, the search will eventually arrive at the system exception handler, which terminates the application. However, if it does find an exception handler frame on the stack it executes it. That frame, may handle the exception, or it may allow the function to continue execution.

Exceptions are useful for trapping system errors and terminating the application gracefully. When you are developing your own libraries, you will find that custom exceptions give you an extra channel of communication and therefore can be very useful in special situations.

15.6 Error Handling

The **GetLastError** and **Beep** functions have been used throughout this book. There are several other error handling functions however, and you will find them useful for special situations or when trying to polish an application or DLL.

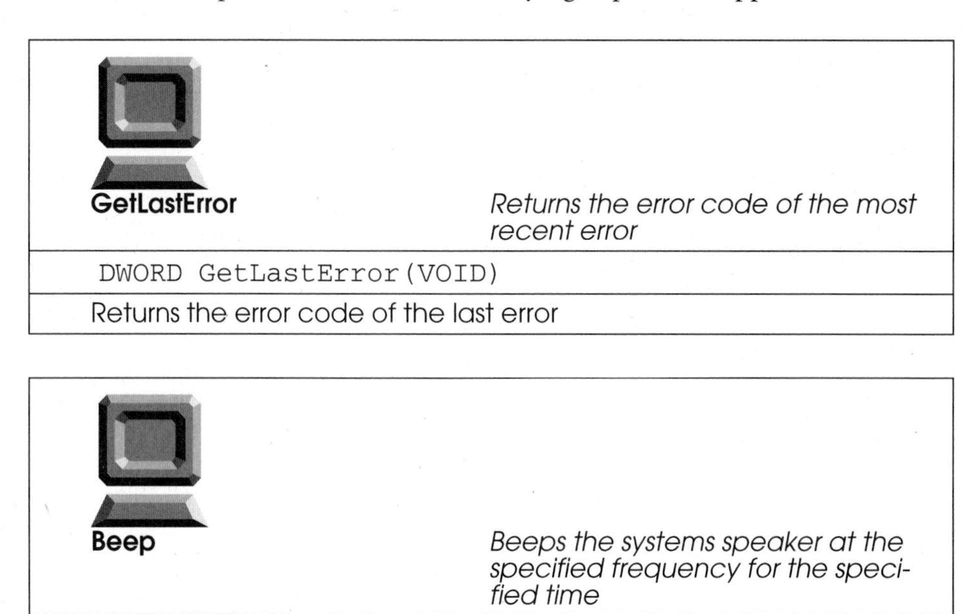

GetLastError — *Returns the error code of the most recent error*

```
DWORD GetLastError(VOID)
```

Returns the error code of the last error

Beep — *Beeps the systems speaker at the specified frequency for the specified time*

```
BOOL Beep(
    DWORD freq,
    DWORD duration)
```

freq	Frequency of the sound
duration	Time in milliseconds for beep
Returns TRUE on success	

For example, in certain cases you want a window that does not currently have focus to be able to get the user's attention. If it beeps it confuses the user because the user does not know where the beep is coming from. However, if the application beeps *and* flashes its title bar or icon, then the user knows which window needs attention. The **FlashWindow** function flashes the title bar for you.

FlashWindow	*Flashes a window's title bar or icon*

`BOOL FlashWindow(`
`HWND window,`
`BOOL status)`	

window	Handle of window to flash
status	Whether the title bar should appear enabled or not
Returns TRUE on success	

A simple beep generated by **Beep** is fairly mundane in a world of multimedia. There are two ways for you to improve the sound output of your applications. **MessageBeep** lets you play one of the five system-defined error sounds. The user chooses these sounds in the Sound applet of the Control Panel:

MB_ICONASTERISK

MB_ICONEXCLAMATION

MB_ICONHAND

MB_ICONQUESTION

MB_OK

The **PlaySound** function lets you play any WAV file, either on disk or in a resource file. You can pass this function several different flags:

SND_ALIAS	The file name actually specifies an entry in the sounds section of the registry

SND_ASYNC	Play the sound in the background and return immediately
SND_FILENAME	The file name specifies the name of a valid WAV file
SND_NODEFAULT	Do not use default sound if alias not found
SND_NOWAIT	Fail immediately if no WAV device is present
SND_RESOURCE	The file name specifies the name of a resource inside the module specified
SND_SYNC	Play the sound and do not return until it is done

MessageBeep *Plays one of the system sounds*

```
BOOL MessageBeep(
   UINT type)
```

type	The type of sound to produce

Returns TRUE on success

PlaySound *Plays a WAV file*

```
BOOL PlaySound(
   LPCTSTR fileName,
   HANDLE module,
   DWORD soundFlags)
```

fileName	The name of the file or resource to play
module	If fileName contains a resource name, a handle to the module containing the resource

soundFlags	Flags controlling the behavior of the function
Returns TRUE on success	

The **SetErrorMode** function determines how the application behaves when it receives a system error. The function accepts one of three values:

SEM_FAILCRITICALERRORS	Critical errors are returned to the application rather than being handled by Windows
SEM_NOGPFAULTERRORBOX	Use only if creating a debugger
SEM_NOOPENFILEERRORBOX	If the system cannot find a file, it returns the error to the application rather than displaying a system error message.

SetErrorMode	*Determines the application's behavior on system errors*
`UINT SetErrorMode(` `   UINT errorMode)`	
errorMode	The new error mode
Returns previous mode	

Finally, especially when you are creating your own DLLs, you will want to emulate the **GetLastError** behavior of the API functions in your own functions. The **SetLastError** and **SetLastErrorEx** functions let you set a thread's last error value. Any call to **GetLastError** will return this value until the value is set by some other function. Inside your DLL you can advise the caller of errors by calling this function and then passing back an error indicator.

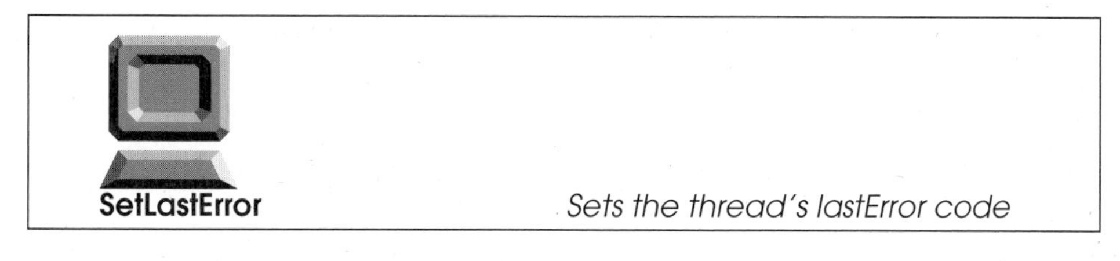

SetLastError	*Sets the thread's lastError code*

```
VOID SetLastError(
   DWORD error)
```

error	The last error
Returns nothing	

SetLastErrorEx — *Sets the thread's lastError code, along with debugger information*

```
VOID SetLastErrorEx(
DWORD error
DWORD type)
```

error	The last error
type	Type information for the debugger
Returns nothing	

A

COMPILING THE CODE IN THIS BOOK

This book contains hundreds of code listings. You will find that these listings break down into four different categories:

1. Pure console programs that read and write text data (you can compile these either with the SDK or Visual C++)
2. GUI programs using the 32-bit API (you can compile these either with the SDK or Visual C++)
3. GUI programs using MFC (you must compile these using Visual C++)
4. Other programs: DLL code, RPC code, and others (you can compile these either with the SDK or Visual C++)

This appendix contains information on compiling the first three types of code using the Win32 SDK or Visual C++. The fourth type of code is covered when the code appears. For example, the RPC chapter contains makefiles for compiling RPC programs. You compile these programs using the same techniques that you use to compile the first three categories of code.

The supplied diskette contains appropriately adjusted makefiles for the code in each directory, and also contains Visual C++ makefiles. This saves you the trouble of creating your own. ***In addition, README files in each directory on the diskette contain important compilation instructions that you will find extremely helpful.*** This appendix is intended to act as an introduction to compilation.

If you have compilation problems, be sure to contact the information server described in Appendix B to obtain free updates.

A.1 Compiling with the Win32 SDK

The code in Listing A.1 represents a typical console program named `textsamp.cpp`. The makefile in Listing A.2 will compile it under the SDK. Note that the makefile's first line reads "APP=textsamp." Change the name in this line to compile different programs.

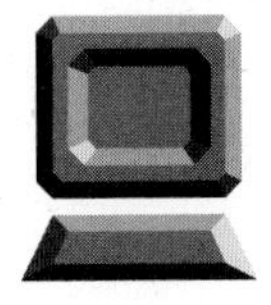

```
// textsamp.cpp

#include <windows.h>
#include <iostream.h>

void main(void)
{
  int x;

  for (x=0; x<10; x++)
  {
    cout << "Hello" << endl;
    Beep(100, 50);
    Sleep(250);
  }
}
```

Listing A.1
A simple console program (textsamp.cpp)

```
APP=textsamp
NODEBUG=1

!include <ntwin32.mak>

$(APP).exe: $(APP).obj
   $(link) $(conlflags) $(ldebug) \
     $(conlibsmt) $(APP).obj -out:$(APP).exe

$(APP).obj: $(APP).cpp
   $(cc) $(cflags) $(cdebug) \
     $(cvarsmt) $(APP).cpp
```

Listing A.2
A makefile for Listing A.1 (textsamp.cpp). Run `mstools\setenv.bat` before trying to compile, and then type "nmake" to compile. Change the first line to compile a different file

Before you can compile Listing A.1 with the makefile in Listing A.2, you often must set some environment variables. The easiest way to do this is to run the file `setenv.bat` in the `mstools` directory. You might also consider looking at which variables are set by setenv, and then setting them permanently in your account using the System applet in the Control Panel. Once the environment variables are set, create a new directory, place Listings A.1 and A.2 in it, and then type "nmake" to compile the code.

Note that in many cases you will have to add extra libraries to the link line of the makefile. The library `advapi32.lib` is especially popular. If your program will not link, expect missing libraries. For example, to add the advanced API library to the makefile, change the link line in the makefile so that it looks like this:

```
$(APP).exe: $(APP).obj
   $(link) $(conlflags) $(ldebug) advapi32.lib \
```

```
        $(conlibsmt) $(APP).obj -out:$(APP).exe
```

Certain programs in Chapters 3 and 4 also want to link to `mpr.lib`. The `mstools\lib` directory contains all of the normal system libraries: Use qgrep in the lib directory with the "-l" option to find libraries.

Also note that the makefile uses "convarsmt" and "conlibsmt." These are multi-threaded versions of the libraries, and they guarantee that multi-threaded code will work correctly.

To compile GUI applications created using the 32-bit API (as opposed to MFC programs, which are described below), use the makefile shown in Listing A.4. Listing A.3 contains `winsamp.cpp`, which represents a typical GUI application with a **WinMain** main function. It simply displays a message box and quits. The "ranmon" programs in Chapter 7 need this makefile.

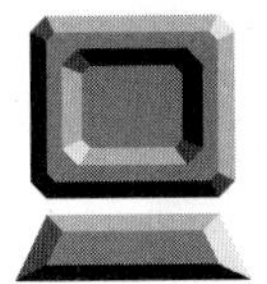

```
// winsamp.cpp

#include <windows.h>
#include <iostream.h>

int WINAPI WinMain(HANDLE ghInstance,
  HANDLE hPrevInstance, LPSTR lpCmdLine,
  int nCmdShow)
{
  Beep (100, 100);
  MessageBox(NULL, "Sample message",
    "Winsamp", MB_OK | MB_ICONHAND);
  return 0;
}
```

Listing A.3
A typical Windows GUI program (winsamp.cpp)

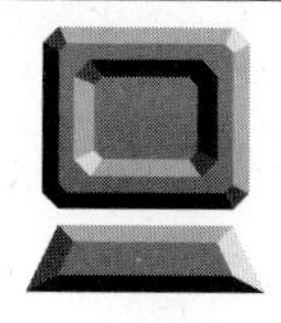

```
APP=winsamp
NODEBUG=1

!include <ntwin32.mak>

$(APP).exe: $(APP).obj
   $(link) $(guilflags) $(ldebug) \
     $(guilibsmt) $(APP).obj -out:$(APP).exe

$(APP).obj: $(APP).cpp
   $(cc) $(cflags) $(cdebug) \
     $(cvarsmt) $(APP).cpp
```

Listing A.4
A makefile for Listing A.3

As with the console program, create a new directory. Place in it Listing A.3 with the file name "winsamp.cpp" and Listing A.4 with the file name "makefile." Type "nmake" to compile the code.

This book contains a number of MFC (Microsoft Foundations Class library) programs. These programs require that you use Visual C++ to compile them. Listing A.5 represents a typical MFC program

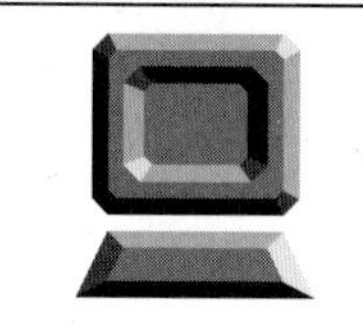

```
// mfcsamp.cpp

#include <afxwin.h>
```

Listing A.5
A typical MFC program (mfcsamp.cpp) (Page 1 of 4)

```
#define IDB_BUTTON 100

// Declare the application class
class CButtonApp : public CWinApp
{
public:
   virtual BOOL InitInstance();
};

// Create an instance of the application class
CButtonApp ButtonApp;

// Declare the main window class
class CButtonWindow : public CFrameWnd
{
   CButton *button;
public:
   CButtonWindow();
   ~CButtonWindow();
   afx_msg void HandleButton();

   DECLARE_MESSAGE_MAP()
};

// The message handler function
void CButtonWindow::HandleButton()
{
   Beep(700,500);
}

// The message map
BEGIN_MESSAGE_MAP(CButtonWindow, CFrameWnd)
   ON_COMMAND(IDB_BUTTON, HandleButton)
END_MESSAGE_MAP()
```

Listing A.5
A typical MFC program (mfcsamp.cpp) (Page 2 of 4)

```
// The InitInstance function is called once
// when the application first executes
BOOL CButtonApp::InitInstance()
{
   m_pMainWnd = new CButtonWindow();
   m_pMainWnd->ShowWindow(m_nCmdShow);
   m_pMainWnd->UpdateWindow();
   return TRUE;
}

// The constructor for the window class
CButtonWindow::CButtonWindow()
{
   CRect r;

   // Create the window itself
   Create(NULL,
      "CButton Tests",
      WS_OVERLAPPEDWINDOW,
      CRect(0,0,200,200));

   // Get the size of the client rectangle
   GetClientRect(&r);
   r.InflateRect(-20,-20);

   // Create a button
   button = new CButton();
   button->Create("Push me",
      WS_CHILD|WS_VISIBLE|BS_PUSHBUTTON,
      r,
      this,
      IDB_BUTTON);
}

// The destructor for the window class
```

Listing A.5
A typical MFC program (mfcsamp.cpp) (Page 3 of 4)

```
CButtonWindow::~CButtonWindow()
{
   delete button;
   CFrameWnd::~CFrameWnd();
}
```

Listing A.5
A typical MFC program (mfcsamp.cpp) (Page 4 of 4)

To compile the code, create a new directory. Copy Listing A.5 into a file named "mfcsamp.cpp." Create a new project file and add the MFC code file to the project as described in Section A.2. Many of the larger MFC programs in this book also use an RC file to handle their menus. Simply add an RC file to the project and it will be compiled automatically.

See Chapter 6 of *Visual C++: Developing Professional Applications in Windows 95 and NT using MFC* by Marshall Brain and Lance Lovette (ISBN 0-13-305145-5) for more information on MFC application development.

A.2 Compiling with Visual C++

You can compile the code in this book using Visual C++ either by creating new project files, by loading Visual C++ project files from the diskette, or by loading the makefiles supplied on the diskette as external makefiles. The latter option is required for several of the applications in this book.

To compile a program using a project file supplied on the diskette (they end with a ".mak" extension), simply load the project file by double-clicking on it and Build the project.

To load a normal MAKEFILE into Visual C++, perform the following steps. Listing A.1 in the previous section represents a simple console program. Listing A.2 is its normal makefile. You can either type these two files in or copy them from the diskette that came with the book. To compile this code under Visual C++:

1. Start Visual C++.
2. Since Visual C++ remembers any previously open project and its files, go into the **File** menu and choose the **Close** option as many times as you are allowed. This clears out the old project and its files.

3. Select the **Open** option in the **File** menu. In this dialog, change to the directory that contains the code contained in Listings A.1 and A.2. Type "makefile." into the **File Name** field (or choose "All Files" from the **File Type** list and double-click on "makefile").
4. The code should compile without error using the **Build** option in the **Project** menu. Run it with the **Execute** option in the **Project** menu.

Follow the same steps for the other example files seen in Section A.1.

To compile multiple files in the same directory, close the current project using the **Close** option in the **File** menu. Change the APP or FILENAME value in the makefile. Load the modified makefile using the **Open** option in the **File** menu.

You should be able to compile all of the code presented in this book using Visual C++, with the possible exception of the RPC code in Chapter 8. Visual C++ version 2.x does not contain the MIDL compiler, so there is no way to compile the IDL files. The SDK contains the MIDL compiler however (midl.exe), and if you borrow it and place it in the VC++ BIN directory you can compile RPC code without problems. Also copy WINNT.MAK to the VC++ INCLUDE directory, and consider also borrowing the SDK's RPC.HLP file as a reference.

CONTACTING THE AUTHOR

B

Windows NT and Windows 95, like all operating systems, will change over time. We want to keep your copy of the book current by providing you with correction and update pages via FTP and the World Wide Web. If you find errors in the book, or if you have any questions, comments, or suggestions for improving the book, we would like to hear from you. Your comments will help us improve later editions, and we'll post your corrections so other readers can take advantage of them.

You can contact the author either by U.S. mail or by electronic mail. Electronic mail is preferred. The U.S. mail address is:

Interface Technologies
P.O. Box 841
Zebulon, NC 27597

To send suggestions, comments, or corrections via electronic mail, address e-mail to:

comments@iftech.com

To ask a question, send e-mail to:

questions@iftech.com

To request a list of the available update and correction pages, as well as free supplements, send e-mail to:

info@iftech.com

In the last case, the message can contain anything or nothing at all. The mail system will send an automated reply with a list of topics and further instructions.

These e-mail addresses are on the Internet and will suffice on mail systems connected directly to the Internet. If you are using CompuServe, you can add the prefix "INTERNET:" to the address to get your message onto the Internet. For example:

```
INTERNET:comments@iftech.com
```

Other mail services such as MCImail, as well as many PC bulletin boards, also offer Internet access. See the documentation for your specific system for details.

About Interface Technologies

Interface Technologies, Inc. has distinguished itself as a premier supplier of programmer training and software development services in a variety of computing environments. These services are supplied with the specific goal of helping the client to increase programmer productivity by improving software design, documentation and development processes.

Technical classes offered by Interface Technologies give programmers the skills they need to rapidly master new, advanced programming environments. These skills are necessary in any company that wants to create leading-edge applications. ITI's classes feature extensive, hands-on exercises, expert instruction, and an intensive pace that builds confidence and self-assurance. Programmers leave the class ready to begin creating their own applications immediately. All ITI classes are delivered at the client's site, an approach that saves both time and money for the client and ensures that programmers are available to handle any emergencies that may arise during the course of training.

As authors of Prentice Hall's huge Visual C++ book, Prentice Hall's bridge series on Windows NT, Digital Press's "Motif Programming: The Essentials and More," and numerous other books and articles, ITI's areas of specialty include object oriented design and C++ programming, Windows 95 and Windows NT application development, and GUI design and implementation using MFC and Motif. ITI also offers consulting services such as project management and auditing, human factors and design analysis, software testing and verification, and network design and administration. Our clients include a number of large firms in the financial district of New York City, several large telecommunications companies, numerous manufacturing and consumer products companies, and a variety of smaller firms, all dedicated to the creation of modern, reliable systems using either in-house programming staff or outside resources.

If you would like more information on ITI's courses and how they can help increase programmer productivity, please call 1-800-224-4965 today, or find us on the web at http://www.iftech.com.

ERROR CODES

C

Whenever you use the **GetLastError** function, you get error codes that do not have any meaning. The table below reveals the first ten:

```
The operation completed successfully.
ERROR_SUCCESS                          0

Incorrect function.
ERROR_INVALID_FUNCTION                 1

The system cannot find the file specified.
ERROR_FILE_NOT_FOUND                   2

The system cannot find the path specified.
ERROR_PATH_NOT_FOUND                   3

The system cannot open the file.
ERROR_TOO_MANY_OPEN_FILES              4

Access is denied.
ERROR_ACCESS_DENIED                    5
```

```
The handle is invalid.
ERROR_INVALID_HANDLE                6

The storage control blocks were destroyed.
ERROR_ARENA_TRASHED                 7

Not enough storage is available to process this command.
ERROR_NOT_ENOUGH_MEMORY             8

The storage control block address is invalid.
ERROR_INVALID_BLOCK                 9

The environment is incorrect.
ERROR_BAD_ENVIRONMENT               10
```

To get a complete listing of the several thousand error codes available, look in the WINERROR.H file in the include directory of Visual C++ or the SDK. This file has a complete listing of all codes along with one line descriptions like the ones shown above.

INDEX

Numerics

64-bit file system 35
64-bit math 94

A

AbnormalTermination
  definition 824
AbortSystemShutdown 737
  definition 740
accept 361
  definition 361
access control entries, see also ACEs 546
access control list, see also ACL 546
access mask 547, 580, 607
access rights 561
access token 544, 585
access tokens, examining existing 573
access, mutual exclusion 218
ACE 554, 612
  access allowed 546
  access denied 546
  audit access 546
  deleting 631
ACE header 547
AddAccessAllowedAce 623
  definition 554
AddAce 623
  definition 624
AddConnection 109
AdjustTokenPrivileges 610
  definition 609
alertable wait 267
AllocConsole
  definition 647
api32.hlp 17
application errors 786
archive attribute 38
array access 77
asynchronous I/O 258
AttachThreadInput 149
attention command 685
attribute bits 38
attributes
  files 38
auditing 542
authentication 325
author, contacting xvi
autoexec.bat 465
automatic binding 393

B

baud rate 691
Beep 832
  definition 832
beginthread 324, 371
bind 348
  definition 349
binding, manual 403
bInheritHandle 201
bits per character 691
blocking behavior 276
bounded buffer problem 230
broadcast connections 286
bugs in the 32-bit API 18
bulletin board system 467, 682, 699
bulletin boards 283
bytes per sector 93

C

C++ xii
C2 certified security 23
CAD/CAM program 164

CallNamedPipe 317
cell directory service 392, 402
change function handle 257
change handles 272
change notification 272
ChangeServiceConfig 513
Chat program, multi-user 283, 308
cin xii
ClearCommBreak 693
ClearCommError 698
client/server systems 286, 317
  TCP/IP 363
clients, intercommunicating 325
CloseHandle 29, 297
  definition 32
closesocket
  definition 350
clusters 93
code
  compiling 9, 837, 846
  guarded body 821
code, selling 743
color 678
COLOR_
  constants 725
colors 725
comments xvi, 846
COMMPROP structure 704
communications 682
  bulletin board system 682
  client/server 339
  escape sequences 682
  examples 685
  flushing buffers 717
  I/O ports 682
  interprocess 202
  modems 682
  overview 683
  parallel devices 682
  possibilities 682
  problems 695
  purging buffers 716
  serial 683
  serial devices 682
  TCP/IP 682
  telnet 682
  telnet servers 682
  terminal program 682
  vt100 682
communications program 685
Compatibility Notes 24, 86, 115, 139, 204, 258, 282, 307, 325, 373, 390, 401, 402, 466, 540, 640, 682, 719, 741, 769, 786, 819
compiler optimizations 150
completion routines 267
compress command 69
Compuserve 847
compute servers 373
compute-bound program 171
conference server 308
configuration information 510, 769
connections 283
  accepting 338
  adding 108
  broadcast 339
  canceling 108
  deleting 108
  point-to-point 339
  UDP 340
ConnectNamedPipe 317, 324
  definition 316
console 715
  possibilities 640
console input 257
console programs 9, 837
consoles 640
  color 678
  cooked input 641
  examples 642
  inheriting 644
  low-level events 663, 668
  overview 641
  raw input 641, 651
  reading low-level events 664
  scrolling 657
constants 55, 56, 58
containers 98
contents xiv
ControlService 486, 519
  definition 496, 518
cooked input 641
cooperative multi-tasking 141
CopyFile 45
CopyMemory 817
  definition 817
correction pages 846
corrections 846
cout xii
CP/M 85
CPUs, multiple 142, 171
CREATE_ 56
CREATE_NEW 54
CREATE_SUSPENDED 191

CreateConsoleScreenBuffer 566
definition 675
CreateDirectory 116, 564
definition 117
CreateDirectoryEx 564
CreateEvent 262, 572
definition 237
CreateFile 29, 59, 201, 270, 297, 317, 551, 563, 599, 688
definition 31, 54, 688
CreateFileMapping 568
definition 79
CreateMailslot 290, 566
definition 294
CreateMutex 572
definition 220
CreateNamedPipe 565
definition 314
CreateProcess 566
definition 196
CreateSemaphore 573
definition 227
CreateService
definition 491
CreateThread 148, 567
definition 148
Creation time 33
critical sections 211, 212
Ctrl-Break 669
Ctrl-C 669
Ctrl-Q 705
Ctrl-S 705
CTS line 684

D

DACL 552
Daemons 465
data types 394
DCD line 684
deadlocks 241
DEF file 750
Definition
AbortSystemShutdown 740
accept 361
AddAccessAllowedAce 554
AddAce 624
AdjustTokenPrivileges 609
AllocConsole 647
Beep 832
bind 349
ChangeServiceConfig 513
CloseHandle 32
closesocket 350
ConnectNamedPipe 316
ControlService 496, 518
CopyMemory 817
CreateConsoleScreen Buffer 675
CreateDirectory 117
CreateEvent 237
CreateFile 31, 54, 688
CreateFileMapping 79
CreateMailslot 294
CreateMutex 220
CreateNamedPipe 314
CreateProcess 196
CreateSemaphore 227
CreateService 491
CreateThread 148
definition 45
DeleteAce 632
DeleteFile 48
DeleteService 497
DeregisterEventSource 799
DLLEntryPoint 762
EnterCriticalSection 213
EnumServicesStatus 524
EqualSid 632
EscapeCommFunction 693
ExitThread 192
ExitWindowsEx 733
ExpandEnvironment Strings 731
FileIoCompletion Routine 271
FileTimeToSystem Time 805
FillConsoleOutput Attribute 679
FillMemory 818
FindCloseChange Notification 275
FindFirstChange Notification 274
FindNextChange Notification 275
FlashWindow 833
FlushFileBuffers 717
FlushViewOfFile 83
FreeConsole 647
FreeLibrary 757
GetAce 585, 623
GetAclInformation 584, 623
GetCommProperties 704
GetCommState 690
GetComputerName 724

Definition *(continued)*
- GetConsoleCursoInfo 658
- GetConsoleMode 655
- GetConsoleScreen BufferInfo 657
- GetConsoleTitle 680
- GetCurrentProcess 607
- GetCurrentThread 193
- GetCurrentThreadId 193
- GetDiskFreeSpace 93
- GetDriveType 91
- GetEnvironment Variable 731
- GetExceptionCode 821, 824
- GetExpandedName 76
- GetFileAttributes 38
- GetFileInformationBy Handle 40
- GetFileSize 36
- GetFileTime 33, 805
- GetFullPathName 43
- gethostbyname 372
- GetKernelObject Security 581
- GetKeyboardType 724
- GetLargestConsole WindowSize 658
- GetLastError 12, 832
- GetLocalTime 804
- GetLogicalDrives 96
- GetLogicalDrive Strings 96
- GetMailslotInfo 296
- GetModuleFileName 757
- GetNumberOfConsole InputEvents 669
- GetNumberOfConsole MouseButtons 669
- GetOverlappedResult 262
- GetProcAddress 756
- GetSecurityDescriptor Dacl 584
- GetSecurityDescriptor Group 583
- GetSecurityDescriptor Owner 582
- GetStdHandle 644
- GetSysColor 725
- GetSystemDirectory 726, 727
- GetSystemInfo 719
- GetSystemMetrics 728
- GetSystemTime 804
- GetTempFileName 50
- GetTempPath 49
- GetThreadPriority 187
- GetTickCount 803
- GetTimeZone Information 806
- GetUserName 729
- GetVersion 729
- GetVolume Information 88
- GlobalAlloc 811
- GlobalFree 811
- GlobalMemoryStatus 816
- GlobalSize 814
- Handler 485
- htonl 347
- htons 348
- InitializeAcl 552
- InitializeCritical Section 212
- InitializeSecurity Descriptor 551
- InitiateSystem Shutdown 739
- InterlockedDecrement 241
- InterlockedExchange 241
- InterlockedIncrement 240
- IsBadCodePtr 814
- IsBadReadPtr 815
- IsBadStringPtr 815
- IsBadWritePtr 815
- IsValidSecurity Descriptor 633, 639
- listen 361
- LoadLibraryEx 755
- LockFile 60
- LockFileEx 61
- LockServiceDatabase 517
- LookupAccountName 553, 621
- LookupAccountSid 582
- LookupPrivilegeValue 608
- LZClose 71
- LZCopy 74
- LZOpenFile 70
- LZRead 71
- LZSeek 70
- MapViewOfFile 80
- MessageBeep 834
- MoveFileEx 47
- MoveMemory 817
- OpenEvent 238

OpenProcessToken 607
OpenSCManager 490
OpenSemaphore 228
OpenService 12, 495
PeekConsoleInput 663
PlaySound 834
PulseEvent 240
PurgeComm 716
QueryServiceConfig 510
QueryServiceStatus 496
RaiseException 831
ReadConsoleInput 664
ReadFile 32, 694
ReadFileEx 270
recvfrom 349
RegCloseKey 776
RegCreateKeyEx 775
RegEnumKeyEx 784, 785
RegGetKeySecurity 622
RegisterEventSource 797
RegisterServiceCtrlHandler 484
RegQueryValueEx 779
RegSetKeySecurity 624
RegSetValueEx 778
ReleaseMutex 223
ReleaseSemaphore 229
RemoveDirectory 11
ReportEvent 798
ResetEvent 239
ResumeThread 192
RpcBindingFree 414
RpcBindingFromStringBinding 413
RpcNsBindingExport 400
RpcServerInqBindings 399
RpcServerListen 400
RpcServerRegisterIf 399
RpcServerUseAllProtseqsIf 398
RpcStringBindingCompose 412
RpcStringFree 414
ScrollConsoleScreenBuffer 660
send 351
ServiceMain 484
SetCommMask 697
SetCommState 691
SetCommTimeouts 692
SetConsoleActiveScreenBuffer 676
SetConsoleCtrlHandler 672
SetConsoleCursorPosition 659
SetConsoleMode 656, 668
SetConsoleScreenBufferSize 676
SetConsoleTextAttribute 680
SetConsoleTitle 680
SetEnvironmentVariable 732
SetErrorMode 835
SetEvent 239
SetFileAttributes 39
SetFilePointer 57
SetLastError 835
SetLastErrorEx 836
SetLocalTime 810
SetSecurityDescriptorDacl 555, 633
setsockopt 351
SetSysColor 726
SetThreadPriority 187
SetUnhandledExceptionFilter 831
SetupComm 717
SetVolumeLabel 97
Sleep 149
SleepEx 271
socket 348
StartService 519
StartServiceCtrlDispatcher 481
TlsAlloc 185
TlsFree 185
TlsGetValue 186
TlsSetValue 186
TransmitCommChar 718
UnlockFile 61
UnlockFileEx 62
UnlockServiceDatabase 518
UnmapViewOfFile 80
WaitCommEvent 698
WaitForMultipleObjects 157, 256
WaitForSingleObject 152, 256
WNetAddConnection2 110
WNetCancelConnection2 110
WNetEnumResources 105

Definition *(continued)*
 WNetGetConnection 112
 WNetGetLastError 108
 WNetGetUser 113
 WNetOpenEnum 104
 WriteFile 54, 694
 WSACleanup 350
 WSASStartup 346
 ZeroMemory 818
DELETE constants 562
DeleteAce
 definition 632
DeleteCriticalSection 212
DeleteFile
 definition 48
DeleteService
 definition 497
DeregisterEventSource
 definition 799
design, RPCs 376
dining philosophers problem 242
directories
 creating 116
 deleting 116
 Windows 726
DisablePrivilege 610, 737
discretionary access control list 545
diskette, included with book xiii
disks 25
DLL_ constants 762
DLLEntryPoint
 definition 762
DLLs
 code 741
 entry point function 758
 examples 744
 loading 755
 memory models 763
 overview 742
 possibilities 741
documentation 17
domain controllers 297
domain name, fully qualified 337
domains 98, 297
dot files 769
Dr. Watson 821
drive letter 96
drive letters 85
drive strings 94
DRIVE_
 constants 91
drives
 enumerating 98
 maximum size 91
 mounting 85
 type 89
DSR line 684
DTE devices 684
DTR line 684, 693
DuplicateHandle 193
Dynamic Link Libraries, see also DLLs 741

E

e-mail 846
ENABLE_
 constants 656
EnablePrivilege 606, 610, 737
EnterCriticalSection
 definition 213
EnumDependentServices 525
EnumerateResources 104
EnumServicesStatus
 definition 524
environment strings 143, 730
environment variables 730
EqualSid
 definition 632
error codes 13, 849
error handling 11, 819, 832
escape sequences 682
EscapeCommFunction 684
 definition 693
EV_
 constants 696
event 257
event character 695, 696
event log 786
 application errors 786
 Event Viewer 787
 message compiler 787
 recording events 792
 registry keys 792
 string table 787
 supplemental data 799
event logging 484
Event Viewer 787
events 211, 235
 automatic 235
 keyboard 668
 manual 235
 mouse 668
 resizing 668
events, recording 792
except 821
exception handler 821
exception handling mechanisms 434
EXCEPTION_
 constants 822

exceptions 462, 819
exceptions, RPC 434, 826
ExitThread
  definition 192
ExitWindowsEx 734
  definition 733
expand command 70
ExpandEnvironmentString 730
ExpandEnvironmentStrings
  definition 731
EXPORTS 750
external makefiles 844

F

facility 797
file handles 71
file mapping 76, 203
FILE_ 58
  constants 547
FILE_ATTRIBUTE_ 56
  constants 38
FILE_NOTIFY_
  constants 274
FILE_SHARE_ 56
FILE_SHARE_READ 59
FileIoCompletionRoutine
  definition 271
files 49, 76
  all information 40
  attributes 38
  compressed 68
  copying 45
  deleting 45
  information 33
  locking 59
  moving 45
  operations 45
  overview 25
  paths 43
  performance 73
  positions 58
  reading 26, 27, 52
  seeking 57
  size 35
  temporary 57
  times 33
  writing 26, 52
FILETIME 35
FileTimeToSystemTime 805
  definition 805
FillConsoleOutputAttribute
  definition 679
FillMemory 817
  definition 818
filter expression 821
finally 824
FindCloseChangeNotification
  definition 275
FindFirstChangeNotification
  definition 274
FindNextChangeNotification 275
  definition 275
finger 283, 354
first_is 396
FlashWindow
  definition 833
flow control 703
FlushFileBuffers
  definition 717
FlushViewOfFile
  definition 83
forceAppsClosed 740
fread 26
free clusters 93
FreeConsole
  definition 647
FreeLibrary
  definition 757
FS_
  constants 89
ftp 354
fwrite 26

G

games, multi-player 283
GENERIC_ 55
  constants 548
GENERIC_READ 554
GENERIC_WRITE 54
GetAce
  definition 585, 623
GetAclInformation 632
  definition 584, 623
GetCommProperties
  definition 704
GetCommState
  definition 690
GetComputerName 297
  definition 724
GetConsoleCursoInfo
  definition 658
GetConsoleMode
  definition 655
GetConsoleScreenBufferInfo
  definition 657
GetConsoleTitle
  definition 680
GetCurrentProcess
  definition 607
GetCurrentThread 192
  definition 193
GetCurrentThreadId
  definition 193

GetDiskFreeSpace 91
 definition 93
GetDriveType 89
 definition 91
GetEnvironmentVariable
 definition 731
GetExceptionCode
 definition 821
GetExitCodeThread 170
GetExpandedName 75
 definition 76
GetFileAttributes 38
 definition 38
GetFileInformationBy
 Handle 40
 definition 40
GetFileSecurity 563, 564,
 631
GetFileSize 35
 definition 36
GetFileTime 33, 804
 definition 33, 805
GetFullPathName 43
 definition 43
gethostbyname 371
 definition 372
GetKernelObjectSecurity
 566
 definition 581
GetKeyboardType
 definition 724
GetLargestConsoleWindow
 Size
 definition 658
GetLastError 12, 832, 849
 definition 12, 832
getline xii
GetLocalTime
 definition 804
GetLogicalDrives
 definition 96
GetLogicalDriveStrings
 definition 96
GetMailslotInfo 295
 definition 296
GetModuleFileName 756
 definition 757
GetNumberOfConsole
 InputEvents
 definition 669
GetNumberOfConsole
 MouseButtons
 definition 669
GetOverlappedResult 259,
 262
 definition 262
GetProcAddress
 definition 756
GetSecurityDescriptor
 Dacl 584
GetSecurityDescriptor
 Group
 definition 583
GetSecurityDescriptor
 Owner 582
 definition 582
GetStartupInfo 195
GetStdHandle
 definition 644
GetSysColor
 definition 725
GetSystemDirectory
 definition 726, 727
GetSystemInfo 178
 definition 719
GetSystemMetrics 727
 definition 728
GetSystemTime
 definition 804
GetTempFileName
 definition 50
GetTempPath
 definition 49
GetThreadPriority
 definition 187
GetTickCount
 definition 803
GetTimeZoneInformation
 definition 806
GetTokenInformation 601
GetUserName
 definition 729
GetVersion
 definition 729
GetVolumeInformation 86
 definition 88
global variables 143
GlobalAlloc
 definition 811
GlobalFree
 definition 811
GlobalMemoryStatus
 definition 816
GlobalSize
 definition 814
GMT 804
goal, of book 17
GUI applications 158, 276
GUI programs 9, 837

H

handle 13
handle table 201
handle, string-binding 412
Handler
 definition 485
handles 255
 context 451, 461
 explicit handles 464
 implicit 402

inheriting 198
signaled 257
unsignaled 257
handles, explicit 445
handles, files 71
heap 143
HeapAlloc 819
HeapFree 819
help file 17
hidden attribute 38
hives 771
HKEY_
hives 771
HKEY_CURRENT_USER 771
htonl 347
definition 347
htons 347
definition 348
http://www.iftech.com 848

I

I/O ports 682
IDL compiler 397
IDL file 390, 396, 444
IDL files 380
ImpersonateNamedPipeClient 635
definition 639
in 396
index xiii
information
files 33
volume 86
INI files 769
InitializeAcl
definition 552
InitializeCriticalSection
definition 212
InitializeSecurityDescriptor 551
definition 551
InitiateSystemShutdown 737
definition 739
Interface Technologies 846
interlocked operations 240
InterlockedDecrement 240
definition 241
InterlockedExchange 240
definition 241
InterlockedIncrement 240
definition 240
Internet 847
Interprocess Communication 202
IP address 337, 352
IP packets 339
IsBadCodePtr 814
definition 814
IsBadReadPtr 814
definition 815
IsBadStringPtr 814
definition 815
IsBadWritePtr 814
definition 815
IsValidSecurityDescriptor 632
definition 633
ITI 848

K

kernel object 13
keys 770
creating 773

L

largeint 36
Last Access time 33
Last Write time 33
last_is 396
LeaveCriticalSection 212
Leigh Ann Brain xvi
length_is 396
letters
drives 85
LIB file 750
Library Manager 750
listen
definition 361
listening 338
LoadLibraryEx
definition 755
load-time linking 751, 752
localhost 411
LockFile
definition 60
LOCKFILE_
constants 65
LockFileEx 60
definition 61
locks 542
LockServiceDatabase
definition 517
logical drives 94
Logoff 669
logon announcement 498
logon announcement service 508
LookupAccountName 620, 631
definition 553, 621
LookupAccountSid 601
definition 582
LookupPrivilegeValue
definition 608
low-level event 663, 664
LUID_AND_ATTRIBUTES 609
LZClose 70
definition 71

LZCopy
    definition 74
LZOpenFile 70
    definition 70
LZRead 70
    definition 71
LZSeek 70
    definition 70

M

mailslot servers 289
mailslots 203, 498
    message length 295
    names 295
    naming 297, 307
    networks 287, 288
    timeout value 295, 297
Mandelbrot program
    performance 171
Mandelbrot set 158, 377, 435
Mandelbrot sets 419
manual binding 392
mapping programs 164
MapViewOfFile
    definition 80
max_is 396
maximum file name 89
MB_
    constants 833
MCImail 847
memory
    allocation 810
    checking memory
        printers 814
    size 813
    status 816
memory models 763
message compiler 787
message map 280
message mode 317
message, custom 280
message, maximum length 295
MessageBeep
    definition 834
metrics 727
MFC xii, 276, 837
MFC program 841
Microsoft Foundation Class library, see also MFC 158
MIDL 397
Mike Meehan xvi
min_is 396
modems 682
Motif Programming 847
MOVEFILE_
    constants 47
MoveFileEx 46
    definition 47
MoveMemory 817
    definition 817
MS-DOS 84
multi-tasking
    preemptive multi-
        tasking 141
multi-threading 141, 445
mutex 257
mutexes 211, 218
    abandoned 223

N

name server 391, 401
named pipe server 314
named pipes 202, 307, 375
    buffering 315
    client/server systems 317
    connection security 635
    connections 309
    direction 315
    impersonation 633
    intercommunicating
        clients 325
    naming 315
    networks 288
    security 310, 558
named pipes, guaranteed delivery 308
names
    mailslots 295
NETRESOURCE 106
network
    possibilities 282
network communications 282
network impersonation 633
network name 724
network protocols 390
network segments 339
networks 98
    broadcast connections 284, 286
    client/server
        connections 284
    client/server systems 286
    communicating 287
    copying files 287
    direct connections 283
    mailslots 287, 288
    named pipes 288, 307
    naming 285
    overview 285
    point-to-point
        connection 286
    RPCs 287
    TCP connections 354
    TCP/IP connections 336

O

object 13
objects 255
OnExit 180
OnIdle 164
on-line index xiii
Open Software Foundation (OSF) 389
OpenEvent
    definition 238
OpenMutex 221
OpenProcessToken 568, 606
    definition 607
OpenSCManager 570
    definition 490
OpenSemaphore
    definition 228
OpenService 570
    definition 12, 495
OpenThreadToken 568
optimizations, compiler 150
out 396, 453
OVERLAPPED 261
overlapped I/O 59, 258, 315, 335, 715
overview
    files 25
    processes 143
    threads 142
owner 545

P

parallel devices 682
parameter options 395
parity 691
passwords 542
paths
    files 43
PC bulletin boards 847
PeekConsoleInput
    definition 663
pending connections 361
performance
    files 73
    performance 76
    RISC machine 142
Performance Meter 444
physical drives 85
pkzip 69
PlaySound 833
    definition 834
point-to-point connection 286
port 338
port number 362
possibilities 25, 86, 116
    network 282
    processes and threads 139
preemptive environment 209
preemptive multi-tasking 210
primary domain 297
primary group 545
printers
    enumerating 98
priority class 198
PRIORITY_CLASS
    constants 187
private heap 818
privileges 544, 601
    enabling 810
process 257
processes 139, 193, 204
    overview 143
processes, background 465
project files 844
protocol family 347
protocol, RPCs 412
pseudohandle 192
ptr 396
PulseEvent
    definition 240
PURGE_
    constants 716
PurgeComm
    definition 716

Q

QueryServiceConfig
    definition 510
QueryServiceStatus
    definition 496
questions xvi, 1, 846
questions, RPCs 461
queuing 211
quirks 84

R

race condition 250
RaiseException
    definition 831
Ranmon 299
raw input 641
raw mode 715
read only attribute 38
READ_
    constants 562
ReadConsoleInput 664
    definition 664
readers/writers problem 251
ReadFile 26, 29, 53, 73, 261, 290, 317, 336, 642, 644, 663
    definition 32, 694
ReadFileEx 267
    definition 270
ready queues 189
rebooting 610

recvfrom
  definition 349
redundant data 69
ref 396, 454
REG_
  constants 772
RegCloseKey
  definition 776
RegCreateKeyEx 569
  definition 775
RegEnumKeyEx
  definition 784, 785
RegEnumValue 786
RegGetKeySecurity 631
  definition 622
RegisterEventSource
  definition 797
RegisterServiceCtrlHandler 469, 482
  definition 484
registry 401, 556, 769
  adding keys 791
  adding values 776
  creating keys 773
  enumerating keys and values 784
  keys 770
  values 770
Registry Editor 770
registry keys 556
  event log 792
RegOpenKeyEx 778
RegQueryValueEx
  definition 779
RegSaveKey 569
RegSetKeySecurity 632
  definition 624
RegSetValueEx
  definition 778
ReleaseMutex 245
  definition 223
ReleaseSemaphore
  definition 229
remote name 111
remote procedure calls, see also RPCs 373
RemoveDirectory
  definition 11
ReportEvent
  definition 798
ResetEvent
  definition 239
Resource Kit 771
RESOURCE_
  constants 106
RESOURCEDISPLAYTYPE_
  constants 107
RESOURCETYPE_
  constants 107
RESOURCEUSAGE_
  constants 106
ResumeThread 149, 191
  definition 192
RevertToSelf 638
RISC machine
  performance 142
router 339
routing 325
RPC client 375, 392
RPC exceptions 826
RPC name server 390
RPC server 375, 525
RPC servers, shutting down 462
RpcBindingFree
  definition 414
RpcBindingFromStringBinding
  definition 413
RpcExceptionCode 462
RpcMgmtStopServerListening 462, 539
RpcNsBindingExport
  definition 400
RpcNsBindingImportBegin, RpcNsBindingImportNext 462
RpcNsBindingImportDone 462
RPCs 318, 467
  automatic binding 393
  common questions 461
  context handles 451
  data types 394
  design issues 376
  examples 380
  exceptions 434, 462
  explicit manual binding 445
  IDL compiler 397
  IDL files 380, 390, 396
  implicit handles 402
  Mandelbrot sets 419
  manual binding 392, 403
  MIDL 397
  name server 391, 401
  network protocols 390
  networks 287
  overview 375
  parameter options 396
  passing arrays 444
  passing pointers 454
  performance 374, 377, 435
  possibilities 373
  RpcServerUseAllProtseqs 463

RpcServerUseAll
ProtseqsIf 463
rundown function 453
string-binding handle
412
termination 539
RpcServerInqBindings
definition 399
RpcServerListen 461, 538
definition 400
RpcServerRegisterIf 399
definition 399
RpcServerUnregisterIf 462
RpcServerUseAllProtseqs
463
RpcServerUseAllProtseqsIf
461, 463
definition 398
RpcStringBindingCompose
definition 412
RpcStringFree
definition 414
RS-232 signaling
conventions 684
RTS line 693
Run and Notify MONitor
system, see also Ranmon
299
rundown function 453
run-time linking 751, 752
rwho command 340

S

scheduler 188
SCM 469
ScrollConsoleScreenBuffer
definition 660
SDK 11, 837
SE_
constants 602
SE_GR OUP_
constants 599
SE_PRIVILEGE_
constants 599, 609
sectors 26, 93
per cluster 93
securable objects 561
security 540
access rights 561
access token 544
adding and deleting
ACEs 610
auditing 542
deleting ACEs 631
dumping access tokens
585
dumping security
descriptors 574
enabling privileges 602
examples 549
files 549
impersonation 633
locks 542
named pipes 310, 558
overview 541
passwords 542
possibilities 540
privileges 544, 601
registry 556
registry keys 556
user rights 544
vocabulary 544
vocabulary summary
548
security descriptor 545, 552
absolute 611
default 634
discretionary access
control list 545
owner 545
primary group 545
self-relative 612
system access control
list 545
security descriptors
examining 581
self-relative 610
security identifier 554
Security Identifier, see also
SID 547
SECURITY_
DESCRIPTOR 610
SECURITY_
INFORMATION
constants 622
SEM_
constants 835
semaphores 211, 225, 258
sendto
definition 351
serial devices 682
serial number
volume 89
Service Control Manager
468
Service Entry Table 504
Service_
constants 486
SERVICE_TABLE_
ENTRY 480
ServiceMain 469, 482, 503
definition 484
services 465
beep example 470, 506
configuration
information 510
control constant 518
controlling 518
database 517
displaying dialogs 498

services *(continued)*
- enumerating 521, 524
- error codes 486
- initialization 487, 507
- installation 467
- installing and removing 488
- logon announcement service 508
- multiple 503
- overview 467
- pausing 485, 487
- possibilities 466
- problems 507
- resuming 487
- RPC server 525
- starting 483
- StartServiceCtrlDispatcher 482
- Startup Parameters 468
- stopping 485, 487, 495

Services applet 488
SetCommBreak 693
SetCommMask
- definition 697

SetCommState 705
- definition 691

SetCommTimeouts
- definition 692

SetConsoleActiveScreenBuffer
- definition 676

SetConsoleCtrlHandler
- definition 672

SetConsoleCursorPosition
- definition 659

SetConsoleMode 655
- definition 656, 668

SetConsoleScreenBufferSize
- definition 676

SetConsoleTextAttribute
- definition 680

SetConsoleTitle
- definition 680

SetEnvironmentVariable
- definition 732

SetErrorMode
- definition 835

SetEvent
- definition 239

SetFileAttributes 39
- definition 39

SetFilePointer 57
- definition 57

SetFilePosition 73
SetFileSecurity 563, 564
SetKernelObjectSecurity 566
SetLastError
- definition 835

SetLastErrorEx
- definition 836

SetLocalTime
- definition 810

SetSecurityDescriptorDacl 632
- definition 555, 633

setsockopt
- definition 351

SetSysColor
- definition 726

SetThreadPriority 187, 188
- definition 187

SetUnhandledExceptionFilter
- definition 831

SetupComm
- definition 717

SetUpCommPort 265
SetVolumeLabel 96
- definition 97

share mode 59
shared devices 98
shared global resources 209
shut down 732
Shutdown 669
shutdown privilege 737
SID 554, 582
SidType
- constants 554

single-tasking 141
size
- files 35

size_is 396
Sleep 189
- definition 149

SleepEx 267
- definition 271

SM_
- constants 727

SND_
- constants 833

SOCKADDR_IN structure 347
socket 337, 348
- definition 348

sound 834
source code xiii
space
- free 91

special character 696
STANDARD_
- constants 547, 562

start command 194
StartService
- definition 519

StartServiceCrtl Dispatcher 469, 480
definition 481
Startup group 465
startup information 195
Startup Parameters, services 468
starvation 241
status board application 288
stdio.h 26
stop bits 691
string 396
string table 787
stripe sets 85
structured exception handling, see also SEH 819
suggestions 846
sumup_ServerIfHandle 399
supplemental data 799
supplements 846
suspended threads 189
SuspendThread 191
synchronization 204
bugs 241
synchronization mechanisms 143, 211
synchronization methods 503
SYNCHRONIZE
constants 562
system access control list 545
system attribute 38
system exception frame 823
system information 719
functions 719
system metrics 727
system services 10
system, shutdown 732
SYSTEM_INFO 720

T

talk 354
TCP
client/server system 363
TCP connections 354
TCP packets 339
TCP/IP 682
connections, accepting 338
domain name, fully qualified 337
IP address 337
listening 338
point-to-point connections 339
port 338
socket 337
UDP connections 340
TCP/IP, overview 336
telnet 354, 682
TELNET facility 706
telnet servers 682
temporary 49
terminal emulator program 706
terminal program 682
termination, abnormal 821
terminology 9
Thread Local Storage 181
THREAD_PRIORITY_
constants 188
threads 139, 204, 258, 280
multiple 180
mutual exclusion 210
overview 142
priorities 186
serialized 210
simple 143
suspended 189, 191
synchronization 204
three-dimensional rendering programs 164
time
files 33
time slice 141, 189
time zone 804
timeout value 295, 297
timeout values 691
TlsAlloc 181
definition 185
TlsFree 181
definition 185
TlsGetValue 181
definition 186
TlsSetValue 181
definition 186
TOKEN_PRIVILEGES 608
TransmitCommChar 717
definition 718
TRUNCATE_EXISTING 56
try 821
TSR (Terminate and Stay Resident) 465

U

U.S. mail address 846
unique 396
UNIX 26, 84, 465, 540, 707, 769
UnlockFile 61
UnlockFileEx 62
UnlockServiceDatabase
definition 518
UnmapViewOfFile 80
update pages 846
user names 112
user rights 544
ut 651

V

values 770
values, adding 776
version
  operating system 729
version changes xvi
Visual C++ 11, 837, 844, 846
vocabulary 544
volatile key 776
volatile modifier 150
volume
  information 86
  serial number 89
volume label
  setting 96
volume name 89
volume sets 85
volumes 85
vt100 682

W

wait functions 255
WAIT_TIMEOUT 152
WaitCommEvent 698
WaitForMultipleObjects 247, 255, 267, 706
  definition 157, 256
WaitForMultipleObjectsEx 267
WaitForSingleObject 170, 222, 229, 245, 255, 661, 663
  definition 152, 256
WaitForSingleObjectEx 267
waiting, efficient 211, 297
WAV file 833
web 848
Windows directories 726
Windows 3.1 21, 84
Windows 9 20
Windows NT 20
Windows Sockets API 337
WINERROR.H 850
WINLOGON 586
WNet functions 98
WNetAddConnection2 98, 109, 110
WNetCancelConnection2 110
WNetEnumResources 98, 105
WNetGetConnection 111
  definition 112
WNetGetLastError
  definition 108
WNetGetUser 112
  definition 113
WNetOpenEnum 98, 104
  definition 104
World Wide Web 848
WRITE_ constants 562
WriteConsoleOutputAttribute 679
WriteFile 26, 53, 290, 297, 336, 644, 651
  definition 54, 694
WriteFileEx 267
WSACleanup 349
  definition 350
WSAStartup 346

X

XOFF 704
XON 704
XON flow control 693

Z

ZeroMemory 817